엑스포지멘터리

시편 III

Psalms

엑스포지멘터리 시편 Ⅲ

초판 1쇄 발행 2019년 10월 20일
3쇄 발행 2025년 3월 27일

지은이 송병현

펴낸곳 도서출판 이엠
등록번호 제25100-2015-000063
주소 서울시 강서구 공항대로 222, 1014호
전화 070-8832-4671
E-mail empublisher@gmail.com

내용 및 세미나 문의 스타선교회: 02-520-0877 / EMail: starofkorea@gmail.com / www.star123.kr

ISBN 979-11-86880-66-1 93230

※ 가격은 표지 뒷면에 있습니다.

「이 도서의 국립중앙도서관 출판시 도서목록(CIP)은 서지정보유통지원시스템 홈페이지(http://seoji.nl.go.kr)와 국가자료공동목록시스템(http://www.nl.go.kr/kolisnet)에서 이용하실 수 있습니다. (CIP제어번호:CIP2015000753)」

엑스포지멘터리

시편 III

Psalms

| 송병현 지음 |

EXPOSItory comMENTARY

한국 교회를 위한 하나의 희망

저의 서재에는 성경 본문 연구에 관한 많은 책이 있습니다. 그중에는 주석서들도 있고 강해서들도 있습니다. 그러나 그중에 송병현 교수가 시도한 이런 책은 없습니다. 엑스포지멘터리, 듣기만 해도 가슴이 뛰는 책입니다. 설교자와 진지한 성경 학도 모두에게 꿈의 책이 아닐 수 없습니다. 이런 책이 좀 더 일찍 나올 수 있었다면 한국 교회가 어떠했을까를 생각해 봅니다. 저는 이 책을 꼼꼼히 읽어 보면서 가슴 깊은 곳에서 큰 자긍심을 느꼈습니다.

이 책은 지금까지 복음주의 교회가 쌓아 온 모든 학문적 업적을 망라하고 있을 뿐만 아니라 한국 교회 강단이 목말라하는 모든 실용적 갈망에 해답을 던져 줍니다. 이 책에서는 실제로 활용할 수 있는 충실한 신학적 정보가 일목요연하게 제시됩니다. 그러면서도 또한 위트와 감탄을 자아내는 감동적인 적용들도 제공됩니다. 얼마나 큰 축복이며 얼마나 신나는 일이며 얼마나 큰 은총인지요. 저의 사역에 좀 더 일찍 이런 학문적 효과를 활용하지 못한 것이 아쉽기만 합니다. 진실로 한국 교회의 내일을 위해 너무나 소중한 기여라고 생각합니다.

일찍이 한국 교회 1세대를 위해 박윤선 목사님과 이상근 목사님의 기여가 컸습니다. 그러나 이제 한국 교회는 새 시대의 리더십을 열어야 하는 교차로에 서 있습니다. 저는 송병현 교수가 이런 시점을 위해 준비된 선물이라고 생각합니다. 진지한 강해 설교를 시도하고자 하는 모든 이와 진지한 성경 강의를 준비하고자 하는 모든 성경공부 지도자에게 어떤 대가를 지불하고서라도 우선 이 책을 소장하고 성경을 연구하는 책상 가까운 곳에 두라고 권면하고 싶습니다. 앞으로 계속 출판될 책들이 참으로 기다려집니다.

한국 교회는 다행스럽게 말씀과 더불어 그 기초를 놓을 수 있었습니다. 이제는 그 말씀으로 어떻게 미래의 집을 지을 것인가를 고민하고 있습니다. 이 〈엑스포지멘터리 시리즈〉는 분명한 하나의 해답, 하나의 희망입니다. 이 책과 함께 성숙의 길을 걸어갈 한국 교회의 미래가 벌써 성급하게 기다려집니다. 더 나아가 한국 교회 역사의 성과물 중의 하나인 이 책이 다른 열방에도 나누어졌으면 합니다. 이제 우리는 복음에 빚진 자로서 열방을 학문적으로도 섬겨야 하기 때문입니다. 이 책을 한국 교회에 허락하신 우리 주님께 감사와 찬양을 드립니다.

이동원 | 지구촌교회 원로목사

총체적 변화를 가져다줄 영적 선물

교회사를 돌이켜볼 때, 교회가 위기에 처해 있었다면 결국 강단에서 하나님의 말씀이 제대로 선포되지 못한 데서 그 근본 원인을 찾을 수 있습니다. 영적 분별력이 있는 사람이라면 모두 이에 대해 동의할 것입니다. 사회가 아무리 암울할지라도 강단에서 선포되는 말씀이 살아 있는 한, 교회는 교회로서의 기능이 약화되지 않고 오히려 사회를 선도하고 국민들의 가슴에 희망을 안겨 주었습니다. 백 년 전 영적 부흥이 일어났던 한국의 초대교회가 그 좋은 예입니다. 이러한 영적 부흥은 살아 있는 하나님의 말씀이 강단에서 영적 권위를 가지고 "하나님께서 이렇게 말씀하셨다"고 선포되었을 때 나타났던 현상입니다.

오늘날에는 날이 갈수록 강단에서 선포되는 말씀이 약화되거나 축소되고 있습니다. 이런 상황 속에서 출간되는 송병현 교수의 〈엑스포지멘터리 시리즈〉는 한국 교회와 전 세계에 흩어진 7백만 한인 디아스포라에게 주는 커다란 영적 선물이 아닐 수 없습니다. 이 시리즈는 하나님의 말씀을 쉽게 이해할 수 있도록 풀이한 것으로, 목회자와 선교사는 물론이고 평신도들의 경건생활과 사역에도 큰 도움이 될 것입니다. 무엇보다도 저는 이 시리즈가 강단에서 원 저자이신 성령님의 의도대로 하나님 나라 복음이 선포되게 하여 믿는 이들에게 총체적 변화(total transformation)를 다시 경험할 수 있는 계기를 마련해 주리라 확신합니다.

송병현 교수는 지금까지 구약학계에서 토의된 학설 중 본문을 석의하는 데 불필요한 내용들은 걸러내는 한편, 철저하게 원 저자가 전하고자 하는 메시지를 현대인들이 가장 잘 이해할 수 있도록 전하고자 부단히 애를 썼습니다. 이 시리즈를 이용하는 모든 이에게 저자의 이런 수고와 노력에 걸맞은 하나님의 축복과 기쁨과 능력이 함께하실 것을 기대하면서 이 시리즈를 적극 추천합니다.

이태웅 | GMTC 초대 원장, 글로벌리더십포커스 원장

주석과 강해의 적절한 조화를 이뤄낸 시리즈

한국 교회는 성경 전체를 속독하는 '성경통독' 운동과 매일 짧은 본문을 읽는 '말씀 묵상'(QT) 운동이 세계 어느 나라 교회보다 활성화되어 있습니다. 얼마나 감사한 일인지 모릅니다. 그러나 상대적으로 책별 성경연구는 심각하게 결핍되어 있는 것이 사실입니다. 때때로 교회 지도자들 중에도 성경해석의 기본이 제대로 갖춰져 있지 않아 성경 저자가 말하려는 의도와 상관없이 본문을 인용해서 자신이 하고 싶은 말을 하는 분들이 적지 않음을 보고 충격을 받은 일도 있습니다. 앞으로 한국 교회가 풀어야 할 과제가 '진정한 말씀의 회복'이라면 이를 위해 가장 중요한 것은 바른 말씀의 세계로 인도해 줄 좋은 주석서와 강해서를 만나는 일일 것입니다.

좋은 주석서는 지금까지 축적된 다른 성경학자들의 연구 결과가 잘 정돈되어 있을 뿐 아니라 저자의 새로운 영적·신학적 통찰이 번뜩이는 책이어야 합니다. 또한 좋은 강해서는 자기 견해를 독자들에게 강요하는(impose) 책이 아니라, 철저한 본문 석의 과정을 거친 후에 추출되는 신학적·사회과학적 연구가 배어 있는 책이어야 할 것이며, 글의 표현이 현학적이지 않은, 독자들에게 친절한 저술이어야 할 것입니다.

그러나 솔직히 말씀드리면, 저는 서점에서 한국인 저자의 주석서나 강해서를 만나면 한참을 망설이다가 내려놓게 됩니다. 또 주석서를 시리즈로 사는 것은 어리석은 행동이라는 말을 신학교 교수들에게 들은 뒤로 여간해서 시리즈로 책을 사지 않습니다. 이는 아마도 풍성한 말씀의 보고(寶庫) 가운데로 이끌어 주는 만족스러운 주석서를 아직까지 발견하지 못했기 때문일 것입니다. 그러나 제가 처음으로 시리즈로 산 한국인 저자의 책이 있는데, 바로 송병현 교수의 〈엑스포지멘터리 시리즈〉입니다.

송병현 교수의 〈엑스포지멘터리 시리즈〉야말로 제가 가졌던 좋은 주석서와 강해서에 대한 모든 염원을 실현해 내고 있습니다. 이 주석서는 분명 한국 교회 목회자들과 평신도 성경 교사들의 고민을 해결해 줄 하나님의 값진 선물입니다. 지금까지 없었던, 주석서와 강해서의 적절한 조화를 이뤄낸 신개념의 해설주석이라는 점도 매우 신선하게 다가옵니다. 또한 쉽고 친절한 글이면서도 우물 깊은 곳에서 퍼올린 생수와 같은 깊이가 느껴집니다. 이 같은 주석 시리즈가 한국에서 나왔다는 사실에 저는 감격하지 않을 수 없습니다. 이 땅에서 말씀으로 세상에 도전하고자 하는 모든 목회자와 평신도에게 이 주석 시리즈를 적극 추천합니다.

이승장 | 예수마을교회 목사, 성서한국 공동대표

시리즈 서문

"너는 오십세까지는 좋은 선생이 되려고 노력하고, 그 이후에는 좋은 저자가 되려고 노력해라." 내가 시카고 근교에 위치한 트리니티 신학교(Trinity Evangelical Divinity School) 박사과정을 시작할 즘에 지금은 고인이 되신 스승 맥코미스키(Thomas E. McComiskey)와 아처(Gleason L. Archer) 두 교수님께서 주신 조언이었다. 너무 일찍 책을 쓰면 훗날 아쉬움이 많이 남는다며 하신 말씀이었다. 박사학위를 마치고 1997년에 한국에 들어와 신대원에서 가르치기 시작하면서 나는 이 조언을 마음에 새겼다. 사실 이 조언과 상관없이 내가 당시에 당장 책을 출판한다는 일은 불가능한 일이었다. 중학교를 다니던 70년대 중반에 캐나다로 이민을 갔다가 20여 년 만에 귀국하여 우리말로 강의하는 일 자체가 당시 나에게는 매우 큰 도전이었으며, 책을 출판하는 일은 사치로 느껴졌기 때문이다.

세월이 지나 어느덧 나는 선생님들이 말씀하신 오십을 눈앞에 두었다. 1997년에 귀국한 후 지난 10여 년 동안 나는 구약 전체에 대한 강의안을 만드는 일을 목표로 삼았다. 내 자신에게 동기를 부여하기 위하여 내가 몸담고 있는 신대원 학생들에게 학기마다 새로운 구약 강해

과목을 개설해 주었다. 감사한 것은 지혜문헌을 제외한 구약 모든 책의 본문관찰을 중심으로 한 강의안을 13년 만에 완성할 수 있었다는 점이다. 앞으로 수년에 거쳐 이 강의안들을 대폭 수정하여 매년 2-3권씩을 책으로 출판하려 한다. 지혜문헌은 잠시 미루어두었다. 시편 1권(1-41편)에 대하여 강의안을 만든 적이 있었는데, 본문관찰과 주해는 얼마든지 할 수 있었지만, 무언가 아쉬움이 남았다. 삶의 연륜이 가미되지 않은 데서 비롯된 부족함이었다. 그래서 나는 지혜문헌에 대한 주석은 육십을 바라볼 때쯤 집필하기로 작정했다. 삶을 조금 더 경험한 후로 미루어 놓은 것이다. 아마도 이 시리즈가 완성될 때쯤이면, 자연스럽게 지혜문헌에 대한 책들을 출판할 때가 되지 않을까 싶다.

이 시리즈는 설교를 하고 성경공부를 인도해야 하는 중견목회자들과 평신도 지도자들을 마음에 두고 집필한 책들이다. 나는 이 시리즈의 성향을 exposimentary("해설주석")이라고 부르고 싶다. Exposimentary라는 단어는 내가 만들어낸 용어이다. 해설/설명을 뜻하는 expository라는 단어와 주석을 뜻하는 commentary를 합성하였다. 대체적으로 expository는 본문과 별 연관성이 없는 주제와 묵상으로 치우치기 쉽고, commentary는 필요이상으로 논쟁적이고 기술적일 수 있다는 한계를 의식해서 이러한 상황을 의도적으로 피하고 가르치는 사역에 조금이나마 실용적이고 도움이 되는 교재를 만들기 위하여 만들어낸 개념이다. 나는 본문의 다양한 요소와 이슈들에 대하여 정확하게 석의하면서도 전후 문맥과 책 전체의 문형(文形; literary shape)을 최대한 고려하여 텍스트의 의미를 설명하고 우리의 삶과 연결하려고 노력했다. 또한 히브리어 사용은 최소화했다.

이 시리즈를 내 놓으면서 감사할 사람이 참 많다. 먼저, 지난 25년 동안 나의 인생의 동반자가 되어 아낌없는 후원과 격려를 해주었던 아내 임우민에게 감사한다. 아내를 생각할 때마다 참으로 현숙한 여인을(cf. 잠31:10-31) 배필로 주신 하나님께 감사할 뿐이다. 아빠의 사역을 기도와 격려로 도와준 지혜, 은혜, 한빛에게도 고마운 마음을 표한다. 평생 기도와 후원을 아끼지 않은 친가와 처가 친척들에게도 감사하다는 말을 전하고 싶다. 항상 옆에서 돕고 격려해준 평생친구 장병환·윤인옥, 박선철·송주연 부부들에게도 고마움을 표하는 바이며, 시카고 유학시절에 큰 힘이 되어주셨던 이선구 장로님·최화자 권사님 부부에게도 이 자리를 빌려 평생 빚진 마음을 표하고 싶다. 우리 가족이 20여 년 만에 귀국하여 정착할 수 있도록 배려를 아끼지 않으신 백석학원 설립자 장종현 목사님에게도 감사하는 바다. 우리 부부의 영원한 담임 목자이신 이동원 목사님에게도 고마움을 표하고 싶다.

2009년 겨울 방배동에서

감사의 글

스타선교회의 사역에 물심양면으로 헌신하여 오늘도 하나님의 말씀이 온 세상에 선포되는 일에 기쁜 마음으로 동참하시는 백영걸, 정진성, 장병환, 임우민, 정채훈, 송은혜, 강숙희 이사님들께 감사의 마음을 전하고 싶습니다. 이사님들의 헌신이 있기에 세상은 조금 더 살맛나는 곳이 되고 있습니다.

2019년 아카시아 향기가 진동하는 방배동에서

일러두기

엑스포지멘터리(exposimentary)는 '해설/설명'을 뜻하는 엑스포지토리(expository)라는 단어와 '주석'을 뜻하는 코멘터리(commentary)를 합성한 단어다. 본문의 뜻과 저자의 의도와는 별 연관성이 없는 주제와 묵상으로 치우치기 쉬운 엑스포지토리(expository)의 한계와 필요이상으로 논쟁적이고 기술적일 수 있는 코멘터리(commentary)의 한계를 극복하여 목회현장에서 가르치고 선포하는 사역에 실질적으로 도움이 되도록 하는 새로운 장르다. 본문의 다양한 요소와 이슈들에 대하여 정확하게 석의하면서도 전후 문맥과 책 전체의 문형(文形; literary shape)을 최대한 고려하여 텍스트의 의미를 설명하고 성도의 삶과 연결하려고 노력하는 설명서다. 엑스포지멘터리는 다음과 같은 원칙을 바탕으로 인용한 정보를 표기한다.

1. 참고문헌을 모두 표기하지 않고 선별된 참고문헌으로 대신한다.
2. 출처를 표기할 때 각주(foot note) 처리는 하지 않는다.
3. 출처 표기는 괄호 안에 하되 페이지는 밝히지 않는다.
4. 여러 학자들이 동일하게 해석할 때 모든 학자들을 표기하지 않고

일부만 표기한다.

5. 한 출처를 인용하여 설명할 때, 설명이 길어지더라도 각 문장마다 출처를 표기하지 않는다.

주석은 목적과 주 대상에 따라 인용하는 정보 출처와 참고문헌 표기가 매우 탄력적으로 제시되는 장르다. 참고문헌이 없이 출판되는 주석들도 있고, 각주가 전혀 없이 출판되는 주석들도 있다. 또한 각주와 참고문헌이 없이 출판되는 주석들도 있다. 엑스포지멘터리 시리즈는 이 같은 장르의 탄력적인 성향을 고려하여 제작된 주석이다.

선별된 약어표

개역	개역성경
개정	개역성경개정판
공동	공동번역
새번역	표준새번역 개정판
현대	현대인의 성경
아가페	아가페 쉬운성경
BHK	Biblica Hebraica Kittel
BHS	Biblica Hebraica Stuttgartensia
ESV	English Standard Version
CSB	Nashville: Broadman & Holman, Christian Standard Bible
KJV	King James Version
LXX	칠십인역(Septuaginta)
MT	마소라 사본
NAB	New American Bible
NAS	New American Standard Bible
NEB	New English Bible

NIV	New International Version
NRS	New Revised Standard Bible
TNK	Jewish Publication Society Tanakh
TNIV	Today's New International Version
AAR	American Academy of Religion
AB	Anchor Bible
ABD	The Anchor Bible Dictionary
ABRL	Anchor Bible Reference Library
ACCS	Ancient Christian Commentary on Scripture
AJSL	American Journal of Semitic Languages and Literature
ANET	J. B. Pritchard, ed., The Ancient Near Eastern Texts Relating to the Old Testament. 3rd. ed. Princeton: Princeton University Press, 1969.
ANETS	Ancient Near Eastern Texts and Studies
AOTC	Abingdon Old Testament Commentary
ASORDS	American Schools of Oriental Research Dissertation Series
BA	Biblical Archaeologist
BAR	Biblical Archaeology Review
BASOR	Bulletin of the American Schools of Oriental Research
BBR	Bulletin for Biblical Research
BCBC	Believers Church Bible Commentary
BDB	F. Brown, S. R. Driver & C. A. Briggs, A Hebrew and English Lexicon of the Old Testament. Oxford: Clarendon Press, 1907.
BETL	Bibliotheca Ephemeridum Theoloicarum Lovaniensium
BibOr	Biblia et Orientalia
BibSac	Bibliotheca Sacra

BibInt	Biblical Interpretation
BJRL	Bulletin of the John Rylands Library
BJS	Brown Judaic Studies
BLS	Bible and Literature Series
BN	Biblische Notizen
BO	Berit Olam: Studies in Hebrew Narrative & Poetry
BR	Bible Review
BRS	The Biblical Relevancy Series
BSC	Bible Student Commentary
BT	The Bible Today
BTCB	Brazos Theological Commentary on the Bible
BV	Biblical Viewpoint
BZAW	Beihefte zur Zeitschrift für die alttestamentliche Wissenschaft
CAD	Chicago Assyrian Dictionary
CBC	Cambridge Bible Commentary
CBSC	Cambridge Bible for Schools and Colleges
CBQ	Catholic Biblical Quarterly
CBQMS	Catholic Biblical Quarterly Monograph Series
CB	Communicator's Bible
CHANE	Culture and History of the Ancient Near East
DSB	Daily Study Bible
EBC	Expositor's Bible Commentary
ECC	Eerdmans Critical Commentary
EncJud	Encyclopedia Judaica
EvJ	Evangelical Journal
EvQ	Evangelical Quarterly
ET	Expository Times

ETL	Ephemerides Theologicae Lovanienses
FOTL	Forms of Old Testament Literature
GCA	Gratz College Annual of Jewish Studies
GKC	E. Kautszch and A. E. Cowley, Gesenius' Hebrew Grammar. Second English edition. Oxford: Clarendon Press, 1910.
GTJ	Grace Theological Journal
HALOT	L. Koehler and W. Baumgartner, The Hebrew and Aramaic Lexicon of the Old Testament. Trans. by M. E. J. Richardson. Leiden: E. J. Brill, 1994–2000.
HBT	Horizon in Biblical Theology
HSM	Harvard Semitic Monographs
HOTC	Holman Old Testament Commentary
HUCA	Hebrew Union College Annual
IB	Interpreter's Bible
ICC	International Critical Commentary
IDB	Interpreter's Dictionary of the Bible
ISBE	G. W. Bromiley (ed.), The International Standard Bible Encyclopedia. 4 vols. Grand Rapids: 1979–88.
ITC	International Theological Commentary
J–M	P. Joüon–T. Muraoka, A Grammar of Biblical Hebrew. Part One: Orthography and Phonetics. Part Two: Morphology. Part Three: Syntax. Subsidia Biblica 14/I–II. Rome: Editrice Pontificio Istituto Biblico, 1991.
JAAR	Journal of the American Academy of Religion
JANES	Journal of Ancient Near Eastern Society
JNES	Journal of Near Eastern Studies

JBL	Journal of Biblical Literature
JBQ	Jewish Bible Quarterly
JJS	Journal of Jewish Studies
JSJ	Journal for the Study of Judaism
JNES	Journal of Near Eastern Studies
JSOT	Journal for the Study of the Old Testament
JSOTSup	Journal for the Study of the Old Testament Supplement Series
JPSTC	JPS Torah Commentary
LCBI	Literary Currents in Biblical Interpretation
MHUC	Monographs of the Hebrew Union College
MJT	Midwestern Journal of Theology
MOT	Mastering the Old Testament
MSG	Mercer Student Guide
NAC	New American Commentary
NCB	New Century Bible Commentary
NCBC	New Collegeville Bible Commentary
NEAEHL	E. Stern (ed.), The New Encyclopedia of Archaeological Excavations in the Holy Land. 4 vols. Jerusalem: Israel Exploration Society & Carta, 1993.
NIB	New Interpreter's Bible
NIBC	New International Biblical Commentary
NICOT	New International Commentary on the Old Testament
NIDOTTE	W. A. Van Gemeren, ed., The New International Dictionary of Old Testament Theology and Exegesis. Grand Rapids: Zondervan, 1996.
NIVAC	New International Version Application Commentary

OBC	Oxford Bible Commentary
Or	Orientalia
OTA	Old Testament Abstracts
OTE	Old Testament Essays
OTG	Old Testament Guides
OTL	Old Testament Library
OTM	Old Testament Message
OTS	Oudtestamentische Studiën
OTWSA	Ou−Testamentiese Werkgemeenskap in Suid−Afrika
PBC	People's Bible Commentary
PEQ	Palestine Exploration Quarterly
PSB	Princeton Seminary Bulletin
RevExp	Review and Expositor
RTR	Reformed Theological Review
SBJT	Southern Baptist Journal of Theology
SBLDS	Society of Biblical Literature Dissertation Series
SBLMS	Society of Biblical Literature Monograph Series
SBLSymS	Society of Biblical Literature Symposium Series
SHBC	Smyth & Helwys Bible Commentary
SJOT	Scandinavian Journal of the Old Testament
SJT	Scottish Journal of Theology
SSN	Studia Semitica Neerlandica
TBC	Torch Bible Commentary
TynBul	Tyndale Bulletin
TD	Theology Digest
TDOT	G. J. Botterweck and H. Ringgren (eds.), Theological Dictionary of the Old Testament. Vol. I−. Grand Rapids:

	Eerdmans, 1974–.
TGUOS	Transactions of the Glasgow University Oriental Society
THAT	Theologisches Handwörterbuch zum Alten Testament. 2 vols. Munich: Chr. Kaiser, 1971–1976.
TJ	Trinity Journal
TOTC	Tyndale Old Testament Commentaries
TS	Theological Studies
TWAT	Theologisches Wörterbuch zum Alten Testament. Stuttgart: W. Kohlhammer, 1970–.
TWBC	The Westminster Bible Companion
TWOT	R. L. Harris, G. L. Archer, Jr., and B. K. Waltke (eds.), Theological Wordbook of the Old Testament, 2 vols. Chicago: Moody, 1980.
TZ	Theologische Zeitschrift
UBT	Understanding Biblical Themes
VT	Vetus Testament
VTSup	Vetus Testament Supplement Series
W–O	B. K. Waltke and M. O'Connor, An Introduction to Biblical Hebrew Syntax. Winona Lake: Eisenbrauns, 1990.
WBC	Word Biblical Commentary
WBCom	Westminster Bible Companion
WCS	Welwyn Commentary Series
WEC	Wycliffe Exegetical Commentary
WTJ	The Westminster Theological Journal
ZAW	Zeitschrift für die alttestamentliche Wissenschaft

차례

선별된 참고문헌

(Select Bibliography)

Albright, W. F. "A Catalogue of Early Hebrew Lyric Poems." HUCA 22 (1950/51): 1–39.

Alden, R. L. *Psalms*, 3 vols. Chicago: Moody Press, 1974–76.

_____. "Chiastic Psalms (II): a study in the mechanics of Semitic poetry in Psalms 51–100." JETS 19.3 (Summer, 1976): 191–200.

_____. "Chiastic Psalms(III): a study in the mechanics of Semitic poetry in Psalms 101–150." JETS 21.3 (Sept. 1978): 199–210.

Alexander, T. D. "The Psalms and the After Life." IBS 9 (Jan. 1987): 2–17.

Allen, L. C. *Psalms 100-150*. rev. ed. WBC. Nashville: Thomas Nelson Publishers, 2002.

_____. "Faith on Trial: an Analysis of Psalm 139." Vox Evangelica 10 (1977): 5–23.

Allen, R. B. *When the Song is New: Understanding the Kingdom in the Psalms*. Nashville: Thomas Nelson Publishers, 1983.

Aloisi, J. "Who is David's Lord? Another Look at Psalm 110:1." DBSJ

10 (Fall 2005): 103–23.

Alter, R. *The Book of Psalms: A Translation with Commentary*. New York: W. W. Norton & Company, 2009.

Althann, R. "The Psalms of Vengeance against Their Ancient Near Eastern Background." JNSL 18 (1992): 1–11.

Anderson, A. A. *Psalms*, 2 vols. NCB. Grand Rapids: Eerdmans, 1972.

_____. "Index of Psalms According to Type." Pp. 239–42 in *Out of the Depths: The Psalms Speak for Us Today*. 3rd. ed. Ed. by Anderson, B. W.; S. Bishop. Louisville, KY: Westminster John Knox Press, 2000.

Anderson, B. W.; S. Bishop. *Out of the Depths: The Psalms Speak for Us Today*. 3rd. ed. Louisville, KY: Westminster John Knox Press, 2000.

Anderson, G. W. "Enemies and Evildoers in the Book of Psalms." BJRL 48 (1965–66): 18–29.

Anderson, R. D. "The Division and Order of the Psalms." WTJ 56.2 (Fall 1994): 219–241.

Auffret, P. "Note on the Literary Structure of Psalm 134." JSOT 45 (1989): 87–89.

Arnold, B. T.; B. E. Beyer, eds. *Readings from the Ancient Near East*. Grand Rapids: Baker, 2002.

Avishur, Y. *Studies in Hebrew and Ugaritic Psalms*. Jerusalem: Magnes Press, 1994.

Ballard, W. H. *The Divine Warrior Motif in the Psalms*. Richland Hills, Tex.: D & F Scott Publishing, 1999.

Ballard, H. W., W. D. Tucker, eds. *Introduction to Wisdom Literature and the Psalms*. Festschrift for Marvin E. Tate. Macon, GA.: Mercer

University Press, 2000.

Bar–Efrat, S. "Love of Zion: A Literary Interpretation of Psalm 137." Pp. 3–11 in *Tehillah le Moshe: Biblical and Judaic Studies in Honor of Moshe Greenberg*. Ed. by M. Cogan et al. Winona Lake, IN: Eisenbrauns, 1997.

Barker, D. G. "The Lord Watches Over You: A Pilgrimage Reading of Psalms 121." BibSac 152 (April–June 1995): 163–81.

_____. "The Waters of the Earth: An Exegetical Study of Psalm 104:1–9." GTJ 7.1 (Spring 1986): 57–80.

Barré, M. "Psalm 116: Its Structure and Its Enigmas." JBL 109 (1990): 61–78.

Barry, C. D. "Is Psalm 110 a Messianic Psalm?" BibSac 157: 626 (2000): 160–73.

Barton, S. C., ed. *Where Shall Wisdom Be Found? Wisdom in the Bible, the Church and the Contemporary World*. Edinburgh: T & T Clark, 1999.

Bateman, H. W. "Psalm 110:1 and the New Testament." BibSac 149 (Oct. 1992): 483–53.

Batto, B. F. "The Sleeping God: an Ancient Near Eastern Motif of Divine Sovereignty." Bib 68 (1987): 153–77.

Bautch, R. J. *Developments in Genre between Post-Exilic Penitential Psalms and the Psalms of Communal Lament*. Atlanta: SBL Press, 2003.

Beckwith, R. T. "The Early History of the Psalter." TynBul 46.1 (1995): 1–27.

Bee, E. "The Textual Analysis of Psalm 132." JSOT 6 (1978): 68–70.

Becking, B. "Does Exile Equal Suffering: A Fresh Look at Psalm 137." Pp. 183–202 in *Exile and Suffering*. Ed. by B. Becking and D. J.

Human. Leiden: E. J. Brill, 2009.

Bellinger, W. H. *Psalms. Reading and Studying the Book of Praises*. Peabody, Mass.: Hendrickson, 1990.

_____. *Psalms: A Guide to Studying the Psalter*. 2nd ed. Grand Rapids: Baker Publishing House, 2012.

_____. "Poetry and Theology: Psalm 133." Pp. 3–14 in *The Psalter as Witness, Poetry, Theology and Genre*. Ed. by W. D. Tucker, W. H. Bellinger. Waco, TX: Baylor University Press, 2017.

Berlin, A. "On the Interpretation of Psalm 133." Pp. 141–47 in *Directions in Biblical Hebrew Poetry*. Ed. by E. R. Follis. Sheffield: Sheffield Academic Press, 1988.

_____. "Psalms and the Literature of Exile." Pp. 65–86 in *The Book of Psalms: Composition and Reception*. Ed. by P. W. Flint et al. Leiden: E. J. Brill, 2005.

_____. "The Rhetoric of Psalm 145." Pp. 17–22 in *Biblical and Related Studies Presented to Samuel Iwry*. Ed. by A. Kort, S. Morschauer. Winnona Lake, IN: Eisenbrauns: 1985.

Berry, G. R. "The Titles of the Psalms." JBL 33.3 (1914): 198–200.

Beyerlin, W. *Werden und Wesen des 107. Psalms*. BZAW. Berlin: de Gruyter, 1975.

Boguslawski, S. O. "The Psalms: Prophetic Polemics against Sacrifice." IBS 5.1 (1983): 14–41.

Bonhoeffer, D. *Psalms: The Prayer Book of the Bible*. Trans. by J. H. Burtness. Minneapolis, MN: Augsberg Press, 1974.

Booij, T. H. "Psalm Cxxxix: Text, Syntax, Meaning." VT 55:1 (2005): 1–19.

_____. "Psalm CI 2—When Wilt Thou Come to Me?" VT 38 (1988):

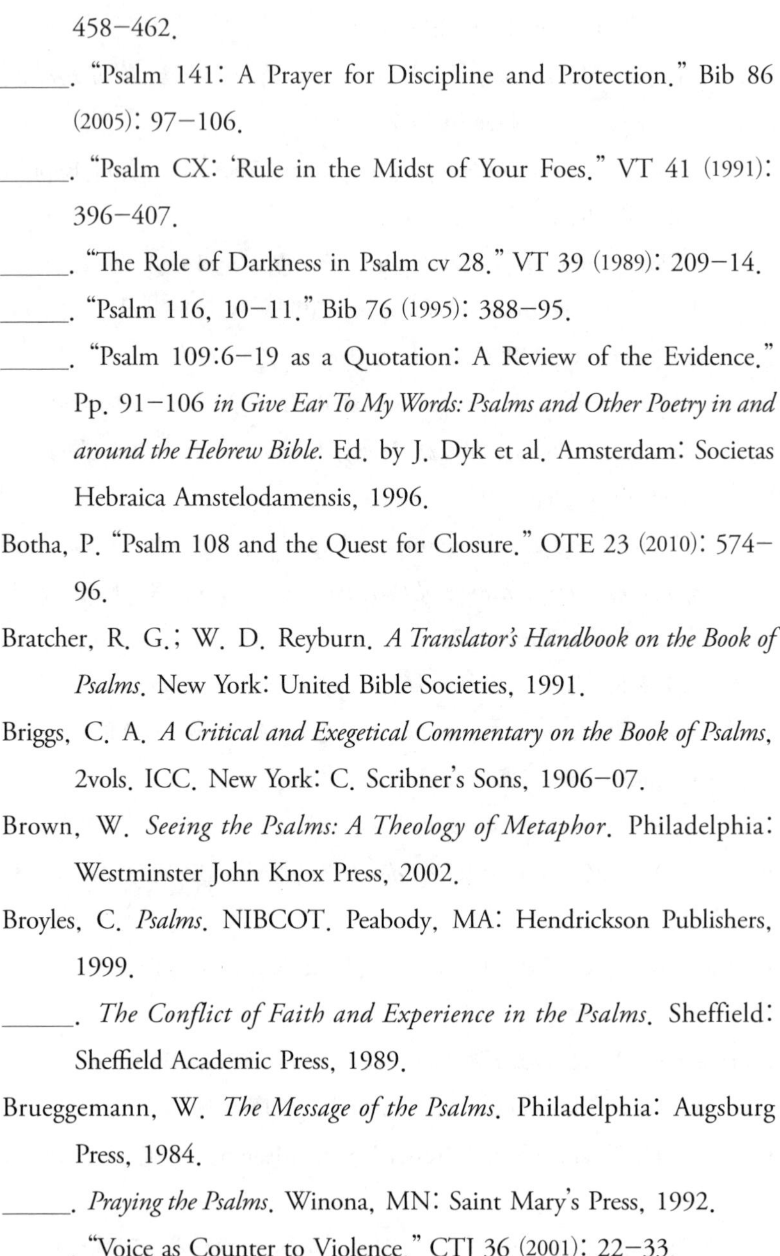

458–462.

_____. "Psalm 141: A Prayer for Discipline and Protection." Bib 86 (2005): 97–106.

_____. "Psalm CX: 'Rule in the Midst of Your Foes." VT 41 (1991): 396–407.

_____. "The Role of Darkness in Psalm cv 28." VT 39 (1989): 209–14.

_____. "Psalm 116, 10–11." Bib 76 (1995): 388–95.

_____. "Psalm 109:6–19 as a Quotation: A Review of the Evidence." Pp. 91–106 *in Give Ear To My Words: Psalms and Other Poetry in and around the Hebrew Bible.* Ed. by J. Dyk et al. Amsterdam: Societas Hebraica Amstelodamensis, 1996.

Botha, P. "Psalm 108 and the Quest for Closure." OTE 23 (2010): 574–96.

Bratcher, R. G.; W. D. Reyburn. *A Translator's Handbook on the Book of Psalms*. New York: United Bible Societies, 1991.

Briggs, C. A. *A Critical and Exegetical Commentary on the Book of Psalms*, 2vols. ICC. New York: C. Scribner's Sons, 1906–07.

Brown, W. *Seeing the Psalms: A Theology of Metaphor*. Philadelphia: Westminster John Knox Press, 2002.

Broyles, C. *Psalms*. NIBCOT. Peabody, MA: Hendrickson Publishers, 1999.

_____. *The Conflict of Faith and Experience in the Psalms*. Sheffield: Sheffield Academic Press, 1989.

Brueggemann, W. *The Message of the Psalms*. Philadelphia: Augsburg Press, 1984.

_____. *Praying the Psalms*. Winona, MN: Saint Mary's Press, 1992.

_____. "Voice as Counter to Violence." CTJ 36 (2001): 22–33.

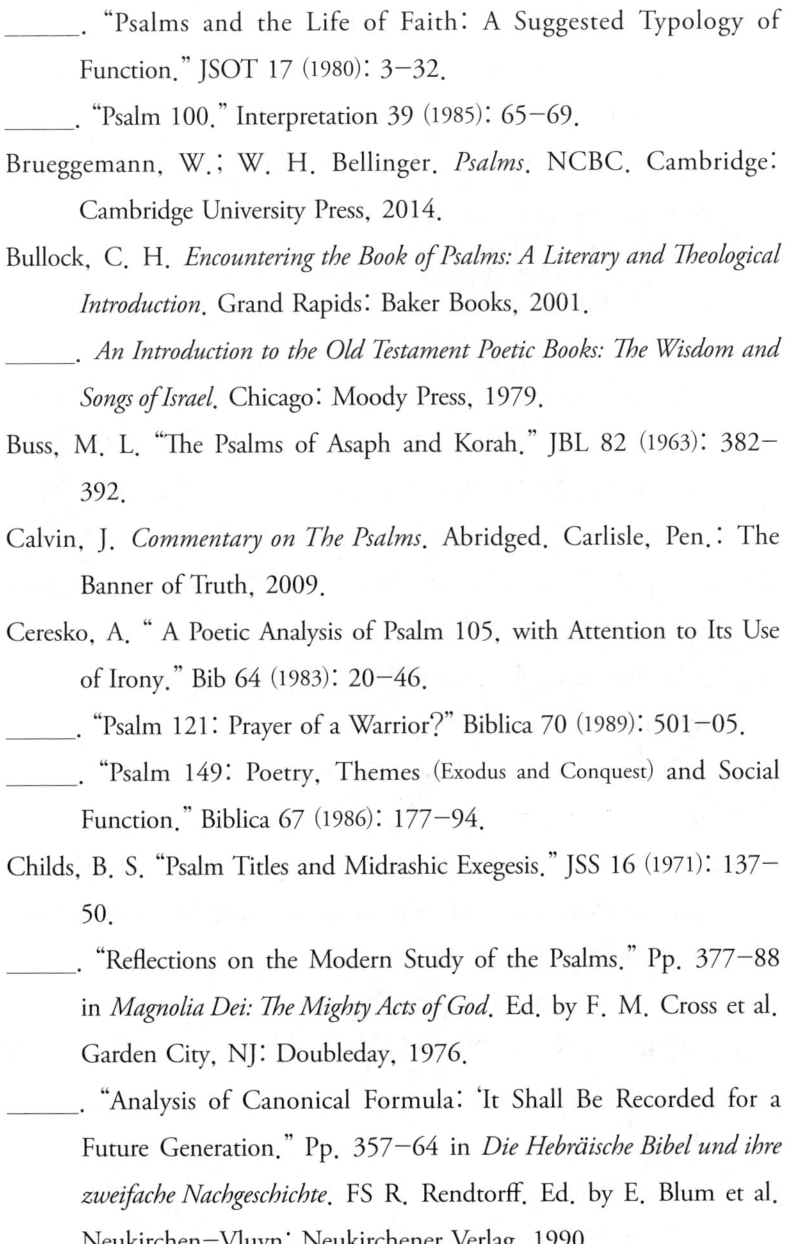

______. "Psalms and the Life of Faith: A Suggested Typology of Function." JSOT 17 (1980): 3–32.

______. "Psalm 100." Interpretation 39 (1985): 65–69.

Brueggemann, W.; W. H. Bellinger. *Psalms*. NCBC. Cambridge: Cambridge University Press, 2014.

Bullock, C. H. *Encountering the Book of Psalms: A Literary and Theological Introduction*. Grand Rapids: Baker Books, 2001.

______. *An Introduction to the Old Testament Poetic Books: The Wisdom and Songs of Israel*. Chicago: Moody Press, 1979.

Buss, M. L. "The Psalms of Asaph and Korah." JBL 82 (1963): 382–392.

Calvin, J. *Commentary on The Psalms*. Abridged. Carlisle, Pen.: The Banner of Truth, 2009.

Ceresko, A. " A Poetic Analysis of Psalm 105, with Attention to Its Use of Irony." Bib 64 (1983): 20–46.

______. "Psalm 121: Prayer of a Warrior?" Biblica 70 (1989): 501–05.

______. "Psalm 149: Poetry, Themes (Exodus and Conquest) and Social Function." Biblica 67 (1986): 177–94.

Childs, B. S. "Psalm Titles and Midrashic Exegesis." JSS 16 (1971): 137–50.

______. "Reflections on the Modern Study of the Psalms." Pp. 377–88 in *Magnolia Dei: The Mighty Acts of God*. Ed. by F. M. Cross et al. Garden City, NJ: Doubleday, 1976.

______. "Analysis of Canonical Formula: 'It Shall Be Recorded for a Future Generation." Pp. 357–64 in *Die Hebräische Bibel und ihre zweifache Nachgeschichte*. FS R. Rendtorff. Ed. by E. Blum et al. Neukirchen–Vluyn: Neukirchener Verlag, 1990.

_____. *Memory and Tradition in Israel*. London: SCM Press, 1962.

Christensen, D. L. "The Book of Psalms Within the Canonical Process in Ancient Israel." JETS 39.3 (Sept. 1996): 421–32.

_____. *Transformation of the War Oracle in Old Testament Prophecy: Studies in the Oracles Against the Nations*. Missoula, Montana: Scholars Press, 1975.

Clifford, R. J. *Psalms*, 2 vols. AOTC. Nashville, TN: Abingdon Press, 2002–03.

_____. "Creation in the Psalms." Pp. 57–69 in *Creation in the Biblical Traditions*. Ed. by R. J. Clifford and J. J. Collins. CBQMS. Washington, DC: Catholic Biblical Association of America, 1992.

_____. "Style and Purpose in Psalm 105." Bib 60 (1979): 420–27.

Clines, D. J. A. "Psalm Research Since 1955: II. The Literary Genres." TynBul. 20 (1969): 105–125.

_____. "Psalm Research Since 1955: I. The Psalms and the Cult." TynBul. 18 (1967): 103–26.

Collins, T. "Decoding the Psalms: A Structural Approach to the Psalter." JSOT 37 (1987): 41–60.

Cooper, A. M. "The Life and Time of King David according to the Book of Psalms. Pp. 117–31 in *The Poet and the Historian: Essays in Literary and Historical Biblical Criticism*. Chico, CA: Scholars, 1983.

Coote, R. B. "Psalm 139." Pp. 33–38 in *The Bible and the Politics of Exegesis*. FS N. K. Gottwald. Ed. by D. Jobling et al. Cleveland: Pilgrim, 1991.

Craigie, P. C. "The Comparison of Hebrew Poetry: Psalm 104 in the Light of Egyptian and Ugaritic Poetry." Semitics 4 (1974): 10–21.

_____. "Psalm 113." Interpretation 39 (1985): 70–74.

Creach, J. *Yahweh as Refuge and the Editing of the Hebrew Psalter*. Sheffield Academic Press, 1996.

Creager, H. L. "A Note on Psalm 109." JNES 6 (1947): 121–23.

Crenshaw, J. L. *The Psalms: An Introduction*. Grand Rapids: Wm. B. Eerdmans Publishers, 2001.

_____. "Wisdom Psalms?" CR 8 (2000): 9–17.

_____, ed. *Theodicy in the Old Testament*. Philadelphia: Fortress Press, 1983.

Croft, S. J. L. "The Antagonists in the Psalms." Pp. 15–48 in *The Identity of the Individual in the Psalms*. JSOTSup. Sheffield: Sheffield Academic Press, 1987.

_____. *The Identity of the Individual in the Psalms*. JSOTSup. Sheffield: Sheffield Academic Press, 1987.

Cross, F. M. *Canaanite Myth and Hebrew Epic*. Cambridge, MA: Harvard University Press, 1973.

Crossan, J. D. *The Birth of Christianity: Discovering what Happened in the Years after the Execution of Jesus*. San Francisco: Harper, 1998.

Crow, L. *The Song of Ascents (Psalms 120-134): Their Place in Israelite History and Religion*. Chico, CA: Scholars Press, 1996.

Crumpacker, M. M. "Formal analysis and the Psalms." JETS 24.1 (March 1981): 11–21.

Culley, R. C. *Oral Formulaic Language in the Biblical Psalms*. Toronto: University of Toronto Press, 1967.

_____. "Psalm 102, A Complaint with a Difference." Semeia 62 (1993): 19–35.

Curtis, E. M. "Ancient Psalms and Modern Worship." BibSac 153 (1997):

285–96.

Dahood, M. Psalms. 3 vols. AB. Garden City, NY: Doubleday, 1966–70.

Davidson, R. *The Vitality and Richness of Worship: A Commentary on the Book of Psalms*. Grand Rapids: Wm. B. Eerdmans Publishers, 1998.

Davies, G. H. "Psalm 95." ZAW 85 (1973): 183–95.

Day, J. *Crying for Justice*. Grand Rapids: Kregel Publications, 2005.

_____. *Psalms*. OTG. Sheffield: Sheffield Academic Press, 1992.

_____. *God's Conflict with the Dragon and the Sea: Echoes of Canaanite Myth in the Old Testament*. Cambridge: Cambridge University Press, 1985.

_____. "The Imprecatory Psalms and Christian Ethics." BibSac 159(April–June 2002): 166–86.

deClaissé–Walford, N. *Reading from the Beginning*. Macon, GA: Mercer University Press, 1997.

_____. *Psalms*. Edinburgh: T & T Clark, 2003.

deClaissé–Walford, N.; R. A. Jacobson, B. L. Tanner. *The Book of Psalms*. NICOT. Grand Rapids: Wm. B. Eerdmans Publishers, 2014.

Delitzsch, F. *Biblical Commentary on the Psalms*. Trans. by D. Eaton. London: Hodder and Stoughton, 1902.

Dell, K. J. "'I Will Solve My Riddle to the Music of the Lyre' (Psalm XLIX 4[5]): A Cultic Setting for Wisdom Psalms?" VT 54.4 (2004): 445–58.

Denton, R. C. "Exposition of an Old Testament Passage." JBR 15 (1947): 158–61.

Dillon, R. J. "The Psalms of the Suffering Just." Worship 61 (1987): 430–40.

Dion, P. E. "YHWH as Storm–god and Sun–god: The Double Legacy of Egypt and Canaan as Reflected in Psalm 104." ZAW 103 (1991): 43–71.

Dorsey, D. A. *The Literary Structure of the Old Testament. A Commentary on Genesis-Malachi*. Grand Rapids: Baker Publishing House, 1999.

Dray, S. P. "Psalm 130. Out of the Depth." Evangel 14:3 (1996): 66–67.

_____. "Embattling Faith in the Spiritual Night: An Exposition of Psalm 61." Evangel 18.1 (Spring 2000): 2–4.

Duhm, B. *Die Psalmen*. Tüginen: J. C. B. Mohr, 1922.

Durham, J. I. "The King as 'Messiah' in the Psalms." RE 81 (1984): 425–35.

Eaton, J. H. *Psalms*. TBC. London: SCM Press, 1967.

_____. *Kingship and the Psalms*. London: H. R. Allenson Publishers, 1976.

Ebeling, G. *Word of Faith*. Philadelphia: Minneapolis, MN: Fortress Press, Press, 1963.

Emerton, J. A. "How Does the LORD Regard the Deaths of His Saints in Psalm cxvi 15?" JTS 34 (1983): 146–56.

Enns, P. E. "Creation and Re–Creation: Psalm 95 and Its Interpretation in Hebrew 3:1–4:13." WTJ 55.2 (1993): 255–280.

Feininger, B. "A Decade of German Psalm–Criticism." JSOT 20 (1981): 91–103.

Firth, D. G. *Surrendering Retribution in the Psalms: Responses to Violence in the Individual Complaints*. Carlisle: Paternoster Press, 2005.

Fishbane, M. A. *Biblical Interpretation in Ancient Israel*. Oxford: Oxford University Press, 1985.

Flint, P. W. "The Book of Psalms in the Light of the Dead Sea Scrolls." VT 48.4 (1998): 453–72.

Flint, P.; P. Miller, eds. *The Book of Psalms: Composition and Reception*. Leiden: E. J. Brill, 2005.

Fløysvik, I. *When God Becomes My Enemy*. St. Louis, MO: Concordia Publishing House, 1997.

Fokkelman, J. *The Psalms in Form: The Hebrew Psalter in Its Poetic Shape*. Leiden: Deo Publishing, 2002.

Freedman, D. N. *Psalm 119: The Exaltation of Torah*. San Diego: Eisenbrauns, 1999.

_____. "Psalm 113 and the Song of Hannah." Pp. 243–61 in *Pottery, Poetry, and Prophecy, Studies in Early Hebrew Poetry*. Winnona Lake: Eisenbrauns, 1980.

Fretheim, T. E. "Psalm 132: A Form Critical Study." JBL 86 (1967): 289–300.

Frost, S. B. "The Christian Interpretation of the Psalms." Canadian Journal of Theology 5 (1959): 25–34.

_____. "Psalm 118: An Exposition." CJT 7 (1961): 155–66.

Futato, M. *Transformed by Praise*. Phillipsburg, NJ: P & R Publishing Company, 2002.

Geller, S. A. "The Language of Imagery in Psalm 114." Pp. 179–94 in *FS W. L. Moran*. Ed. by T. Abusch et al. Atlanta: Scholars Press, 1990.

Gerleman, G. "Psalm cx." VT 31 (1981): 1–19.

Gerstenberger, E. S. *Psalms, vol. 1*. FOTL. Grand Rapids: Eerdmans,

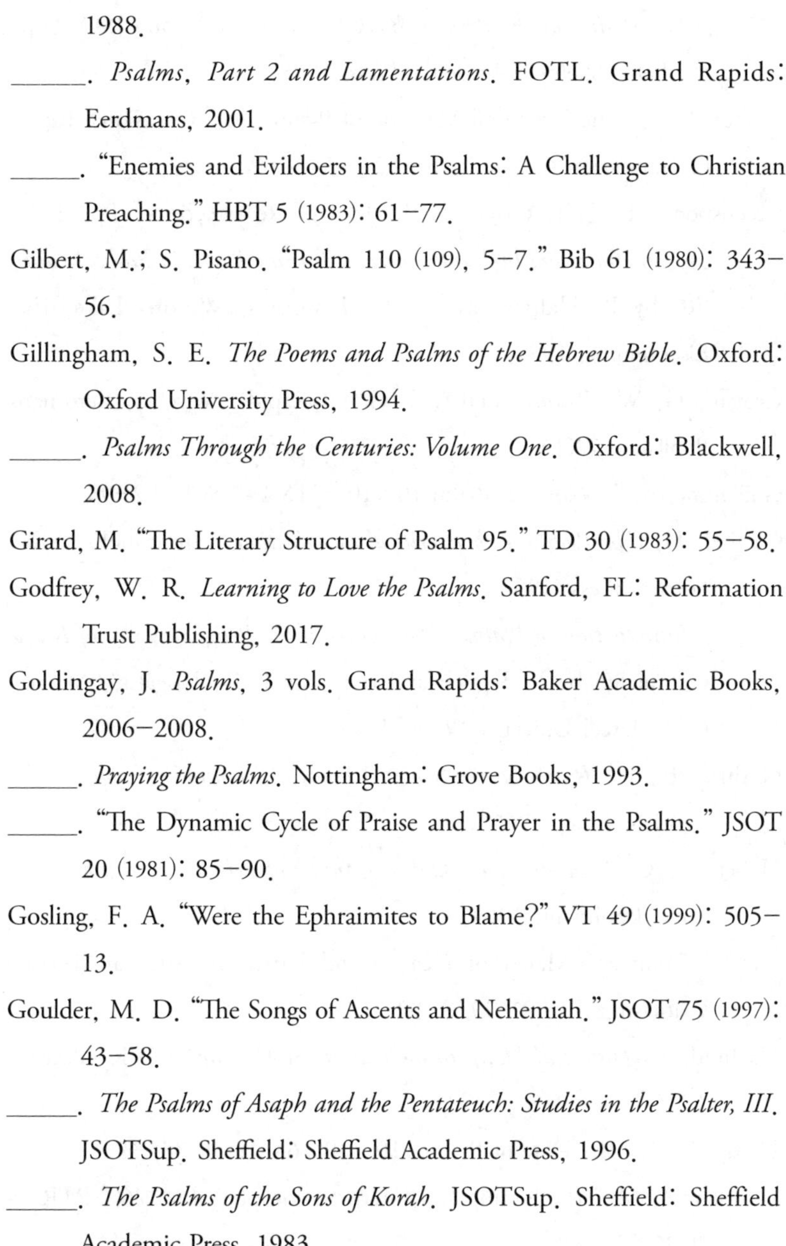

1988.

______. *Psalms, Part 2 and Lamentations*. FOTL. Grand Rapids: Eerdmans, 2001.

______. "Enemies and Evildoers in the Psalms: A Challenge to Christian Preaching." HBT 5 (1983): 61–77.

Gilbert, M.; S. Pisano. "Psalm 110 (109), 5–7." Bib 61 (1980): 343–56.

Gillingham, S. E. *The Poems and Psalms of the Hebrew Bible*. Oxford: Oxford University Press, 1994.

______. *Psalms Through the Centuries: Volume One*. Oxford: Blackwell, 2008.

Girard, M. "The Literary Structure of Psalm 95." TD 30 (1983): 55–58.

Godfrey, W. R. *Learning to Love the Psalms*. Sanford, FL: Reformation Trust Publishing, 2017.

Goldingay, J. *Psalms*, 3 vols. Grand Rapids: Baker Academic Books, 2006–2008.

______. *Praying the Psalms*. Nottingham: Grove Books, 1993.

______. "The Dynamic Cycle of Praise and Prayer in the Psalms." JSOT 20 (1981): 85–90.

Gosling, F. A. "Were the Ephraimites to Blame?" VT 49 (1999): 505–13.

Goulder, M. D. "The Songs of Ascents and Nehemiah." JSOT 75 (1997): 43–58.

______. *The Psalms of Asaph and the Pentateuch: Studies in the Psalter, III*. JSOTSup. Sheffield: Sheffield Academic Press, 1996.

______. *The Psalms of the Sons of Korah*. JSOTSup. Sheffield: Sheffield Academic Press, 1983.

______. *The Psalms of the Return: Book V, Psalms 107-150*. JSOTSup. Sheffield: Sheffield Academic Press, 1998.

Graber, P. L. "The Structural Meaning of Psalm 113." Occasional Papers in Translation 4 (1990): 340–52.

Greenspoon, L. "The Origin of the Idea of Resurrection." Pp. 247–322 in *Traditions in Transformation: Turning Points in Biblical Faith*. Ed. by B. Halpern and J. D. Levenson. Winona Lake, IN: Eisenbrauns, 1981.

Grogan, G. W. *Psalms*. THOTC. Grand Rapids: Wm. B. Eerdmans Publishers, 2008.

Guillaume, A. "A Note on Psalm 109:10." JTS 14 (1963): 92–93.

Gunkel, H. *The Psalms: a form-critical introduction*. Minneapolis, MN: Fortress Press, 1967.

______. *Introduction to Psalms: The Genres of the Religious Lyric of Israel*. Completed by J. Begrich and trans. by J. D. Nogalski. Macon, GA: Mercer University Press, 1998.

Guthrie, H. H. *Israel's Sacred Songs: A Study of Dominant Themes*. New York: Seabury, 1966.

Habel, N. C. *Yahweh versus Baal: A Conflict of Religious Cultures*. New York: Bookman, 1964.

______. "Yahweh, Maker of Heaven and Earth: A Study in Textual Criticism." JBL 91 (1972): 321–37.

Haglund, E. *Historical Motifs in the Psalms*. Stockholm: CWK Gleerup, 1984.

Hardy, E. R. "The Date of Psalm 110." JBL 64 (1945): 385–90.

Harman, A. M. "The Setting and Interpretation of Psalm 126." RTR 44 (1985): 74–80.

Harmon, A. M. "Aspects of Paul's Use of the Psalms." WTJ 32 (1969): 1–23.

Harrisville, R. A. "Paul and the Psalms." Word and World 5 (1985): 168–79.

Hay, D. M. *Glory at the Right Hand: Psalm 110 in Early Christianity*. Nashville: Abingdon Press, 1973.

Hayes, E. "The Unity of the Egyptian Hallel: Psalms 113–18." BBR 9 (1999): 145–56.

Herbert, A. S. "Our Present Understanding of the Psalms." The London Quarterly & Holborn Review (January 1965): 25–29.

Hilber, J. W. Cultic Prophecy in the Psalms. Berlin: de Gruyter, 2005.

Hiller, D. H. "A Study of Psalm 148." CBQ 40 (1978): 323–34.

Hillers, D. R. "Ritual Procession of the Ark and Ps 132." CBQ 30 (1968): 48–55.

Holladay, W. L. *The Psalms through Three Thousand Years: Prayerbook of a Cloud of Witnesses*. Minneapolis, MN: Fortress Press, 1993.

Holm–Nielsen, S. "The Exodus Traditions in Psalm 105." ASTI 11 (1977–78): 22–30.

Holman, J. "Analysis of the Text of Ps. 139." BZ 14 (1970): 37–71, 198–227.

_____. "A Semiotic Analysis of Psalm cxxxviii(LXX)." OtSt 26 (1990): 84–100.

Holst, S. "Psalmists in Cramped and Open Spaces: A Cognitive Perspective on the Theology of Psalms." SJOT 28 (2014): 266–279.

Hossfeld, F.–L.; E. Zenger. *Psalms*, 3 vols. Hermeneia. Minneapolis, MN: Fortress Press, 2006–11.

Houk, C. B. "Psalm 132." JSOT 6 (1978): 41–48.

Houston, W. "David, Asaph and the Mighty Works of God: Theme and Genre in the Psalm Collections. JSOT 68 (1995): 93–111.

Howard, D. M. *The Structure of Psalms 93-100*. Winona Lake, IN: Eisenbrauns, 1997.

_____. "Psalm 94 among the Kingship–of–Yhwh Psalms." CBQ 61 (1999): 667–85.

Human, D. J. "Psalm 136: A Liturgy with Reference to Creation and History." Pp. 73–88 in Psalms and Liturgy. Ed. by D. J. Human and C. J. A. Vos. JSOTSup. London: T & T Clark, 2004.

Hurvitz, A. "Wisdom Vocabulary in the Hebrew Psalter: A Contribution to the Study of 'Wisdom Psalms.'" VT 38 (1988): 41–51.

_____. "The History of a Legal Formula." VT 32 (1982): 257–67.

Hutton, R. R. "Cush the Benjamite and Psalm Midrash." HAR 10 (1986): 123–37.

Huweiler, E. F. "Patterns and Problems of Psalm 132." Pp. 199–215 in *The Listening Heart*. FS for R. E. Murphy. Ed. by K. G. Hoglund et al. JSOTSup. Sheffield: Sheffield Academic Press, 1987.

Hyde, C. "The Remembrance of the Exodus in the Psalms." Worship 62 (1988): 404–14.

Jaki, S. L. *Praying the Psalms, A Commentary*. Grand Rapids: Wm. B. Eerdmans Publishers, 2001.

Janowski, B. *Arguing with God: A Theological Anthropology of the Psalms*. Trans. by Armin Siedlecki. Lousville: Westminster John Knox Press, 2003.

Jarick, J. "The Four Corners of Psalm 107." CBQ 59 (1997): 270–87.

Jensen, J. E. "Is Psalm 110 Canaanite?" JBL 73 (1954): 152–56.

Johnson, A. R. *The Cultic Prophet and Israel's Psalmody*. Wales: University of Wales Press, 1979.

Kaiser, W. C. "The Promise Theme and the Theology of Rest." BibSac 130 (1973): 135–150.

Kässmann, M. "Covenant, Praise and Justice in Creation." Pp. 28–51 in *Eschatology*. D. G. Hallman. Maryknoll, NY: Orbis, 1994.

Keel, O. *The Symbolism of the Biblical World: Ancient Near Eastern Iconography and the Book of Psalms*. New York: Seabury, 1978.

Keet, C. C. *A Study of the Psalms of Ascents. A Critical and Exegetical Commentary Upon Psalms CXX to CXXXIV*. Greenwood: Attic, 1969.

Kellermann, U. "Psalm 137." ZAW 90 (1978): 43–58.

Kenik, H. A. "Code of Conduct for a King." JBL 95 (1976): 391–403.

Kidner, D. *Psalms,* 2 vols. TOTC. Downers Grove, IL: InterVarsity Press, 1973–75.

Kimelman, R. "Psalm 145: Theme, Structure, and Impact." JBL 133 (1994): 37–58.

Kirkpatrick, A. F. *The Book of Psalms*. Cambridge: Cambridge University Press, 1898.

Kissane, E. J. "The Interpretation of Psalm 110." ITQ 21 (1954): 103–14.

______. *The Book of Psalms*. 2 vols. Dublin: Browne & Nolan, 1953, 1954.

Kistemaker, S. *The Psalms Citations in the Epistle of the Hebrews*. Amsterdam, 1961.

Kitchen, K. A. *Ancient Orient and Old Testament*. London: InterVarsity Press, 1975.

Kitz, A. M. "Effective Simile and Effective Act: Psalm 109, Numbers 5, and KUB 26." CBQ 69 (2007): 550–56.

Knight, G. A. F. *Psalms*, 2 vols. DSB. 1982–83.

Knight, L. C. "I Will Show Him My Salvation: The Experience of Anxiety in Meaning of Psalm 91." RQ 43.4 (2001): 280–92.

Korpel, M. C. A., C. de Moor. "Fundamentals of Ugaritic and Hebrew Poetry." UF 18 (1986): 173–212.

Kraus, H–J. *Psalms*, 2 vols. Trans. by H. C. Oswald. Minneapolis, MN: Augusburg Press, 1988–89.

_____. *The Theology of the Psalms*. Trans. by K. Crim. Minneapolis: Augsberg, 1986.

Krawelitzski, J. "God the Almighty? Observations in Psalms." VT 64 (2014): 434–44.

Kselman, J. S. "Psalm 101: Royal Confession and Divine Oracle." JSOT 33 (1985): 45–62.

_____. "Psalm 146 in Its Context." CBQ 50 (1988): 586–99.

Kugel, J. L. "The Canonical Wisdom Psalms of Ancient Israel—Their Rhetorical, Thematic, and Formal Dimensions." Pp. 186–223 in *Rhetorical Criticism: Essays in Honor of James Muilenburg*. Ed. by J. J. Jackson and M. Kessler. Pittsburgh: Pickwick, 1974.

Kuntz, J. K. "Engaging the Psalms: Gains and Trends in Recent Research." CR 2 (1994): 77–106.

_____. "The Retribution Motif in Psalmic Wisdom." ZAW 89 (1977): 223–33.

Laato, A. "Psalm 132 and the Development of the Jerusalemite/Israelite Royal Ideology." CBQ 54 (1992): 49–66.

Leslie, E. A. Psalms: Translated and Interpreted in the Light of Hebrew

Worship. Nashville: Abingdon Press, 1949.

Leupold, H. C. *Exposition of the Psalms*. Grand Rapids: Baker, 1902.

Levenson, J. D. "A Technical Meaning for *n'm* in the Hebrew Bible." VT 35 (1985): 61–7.

_____. "The Sources of Torah." Pp. 559–74 in *Ancient Israel Religion*. Ed. by P. D. Miller et al. Philadelphia: Fortress Press, 1987.

Levine, H. J. *Sing Unto God a New Song: A Contemporary Reading of the Psalms*. Bloomington, IN: University Press, 1995.

Lewis, C. S. *Reflections on the Psalms*. San Diego: Harcourt Brace Jovanovich, 1959.

Limburg, J. *Psalms*. WBCom Louisville, KY: Westminster John Knox Press, 2000.

_____. *Psalms for Sojourners*. Minneapolis, MN: Fortress Press, 2002.

_____. "Psalm 121: A Psalm for Sojourners." Word & World 5 (1985): 180–87.

Lindars, B. "The Structure of Psalm CXLV." VT 29 (1989): 23–30.

Linton, O. "Interpretation of the Psalms in Early Church." Studia Patristica 4 (1961): 143–56.

Loewenstamm, S. E. "The Number of the Plagues in Psalm 105." Bib 52 (1971): 34–38.

Longman, T. *How to Read the Psalms*. Downers Grove, IL: InterVarsity Press, 1988.

_____. "Psalm 98: a Divine Warrior Victory Song." JETS 27.3 (Sept. 1984): 267–74.

Luke, K. "The Setting of Psalm 115." ITQ 34 (1967): 347–57.

Maloney, L. "A Portrait of the Righteous Person." RQ 45.3 (2003): 151–64.

Mandolfo, C. *God in the Dock: Dialogic Tension in the Psalms of Lament*. JSOTSup. New York: Sheffield Academic Press, 2002.

Massouh, S. "Psalm 95." TJ 4 (1983): 84–88.

Mathys, H. P. "Psalm CL." VT 50 (2000): 329–344.

Mays, J. L. *Psalms*. Interpretation. Louisville: Westminster John Knox Press, 1994.

______. "Past, Present, and Prospect in Psalm Study." Pp. 147–56 in *Old Testament Interpretation: Past, Present, and Future: Essays in Honor of Gene M. Tucker*. Ed. by J. L. Mays et al. Nashville, TN: Abingdon Press, 1995.

______. "The David of the Psalms." Interpretation 40 (1986): 143–55.

McCann, J. C. "The Book of Psalms." Pp. 639–1280 in *New Interpreter's Bible*, vol. 4. Nashville, TN: Abingdon Press, 1995.

______. *A Theological Introduction to the Book of Psalms: The Psalms as Torah*. Nashville, TN: Abingdon Press, 1993.

McCann, J. C., ed. *The Shape and Shaping of the Psalter*. Sheffield: Sheffield Academic Press, 1993.

McCarthy, D. J. "Creation Motifs in Ancient Hebrew Poetry." CBQ 29 (1967): 393–406.

McConville, J. G. "Statement of Assurance in Psalms of Lament." IBS 8.2 (1986): 64–75.

McFall, L. "The Evidence For a Logical Arrangement of the Psalter." WTJ 62.2 (2000): 223–56.

McKay, J. W. "Psalms of Vigil." ZAW 91 (1979): 229–47.

McKeating, H. "Divine Forgiveness in the Psalms." SJT 18 (1965): 69–83.

McKelvey, M. G. *Moses, David and the High Kingship of Yahweh: A*

Canonical Study of Book IV of the Psalter. Piscataway, NJ: Gorgias Press, 2014.

Mejia, J. "Some Observations on Psalm 107." BTB 5 (1975): 56–66.

Millard, M. *Die Komposition des Psalters. Ein formgeschichtlicher Ansatz: Die Komposition des Psalters*. Tübingen: Mohr Siebeck, 1994.

Miller, P. D. *Interpreting the Psalms*. Minneapolis, MN: Fortress Press, 1986.

_____. "The Poetry of Creation: Psalm 104." Pp. 178–92 in The Way of the Lord. FAT 29. Tübingen: Mohr Siebeck, 2004.

_____. "Psalm 127—The House That Yahweh Builds." JSOT 22 (1982): 119–32.

Mitchell, D. *The Message of the Psalter. An Eschatological Programme in the Book of Psalms.* Sheffield: Sheffield Academic Press, 1997.

Morgenstern, J. "The Cultic Setting of the Enthronement Psalms." HUCA 35 (1964): 1–42.

_____. "Psalm 121." JBL 58 (1939): 311–23.

Mowinkel, S. *Psalms in Israel's Worship*. 2 vols. Trans. by D. R. Ap-Thomas. Nashville, TN: Abingdon Press, 1962.

Mullen, E. T. *The Assembly of the Gods: The Divine Council in Canaanite and Early Hebrew Literature*. Chico: Scholars Press, 1980.

Murphy, R. E. *The Gift of the Psalms*. Peabody, Mass.: Hendrickson, 2000.

_____. "A Consideration of the Classification, 'Wisdom Psalms.'" Pp. 156–67 in *Congress Volume: Bonn 1962*. VTSup. Leiden: E. J. Brill, 1963.

Nasuti, H. P. "Historical Narrative and Identity in the Psalms." HBT 23.2 (2001): 132–53.

_____. *Tradition History and the Psalms of Asap*. Missoula: Scholars Press, 1988.

_____. "'Who is Like the Lord our God?' Relating Theology and Ethics in Psalm 113." Pp. 27–45 in *The Psalter as Witness: Poetry, Theology, Genre*. Ed by W. D. Tucker and W. H. Ellinger. Waco, TX: Baylor University Press, 2017.

Nel, P. J. "Psalm 110 and the Melchizedek Tradition." JNSL 22 (1996): 1–14.

Nelson, R. D. "Between Text and Sermon. Psalm 114." Int 63 (2009): 172–74.

Nogalski, J. D. "Reading David in the Psalter: A Study in Liturgical Hermeneutics." HBT 23.2 (2001): 168–91.

Obenhaus, S. R. "The Creation Faith of the Psalmists." TJ 21.2 (2000): 131–42.

Oesterley, W. O. E. *The Psalms*. London: The Society for Promoting Christian Knowledge, 1955.

Ofosu, A. "BATACH in the Book of the Psalms." IBS 15.1 (1993): 23–38.

Ogden, G. S. "Prophetic Oracles Against Foreign Nations and Psalms of Communal Lament: The Relationship of Psalm 137 to Jeremiah 49:7–22 and Obadiah." JSOT 24 (1982): 88–97.

Ollenburger, B. C. *Zion, the City of the Great King. A Theological Symbol of the Jerusalem Cult*. Sheffield: Sheffield Academic Press, 1987.

Osgood, H. "Dashing The Little Ones Against The Rock." PTR 1.1 (1903): 23–37.

Parsons, G. W. "Guidelines for Understanding and Proclaiming the Psalms." BibSac 147 (1990): 169–187.

Patton, C. L. "Psalm 132: A Methodological Inquiry." CBQ 57.4 (1995): 643–54.

Paul, M. J. "The Order of Melchizedek [Ps 110:4 and Heb 7:3]." WTJ 49 (1987): 195–211.

Perdue, L. G. "'Yahweh Is King over All the Earth': An Exegesis of Psalm 47." RQ 17.2 (1974): 85–98.

Perowne, J. J. S. *The Book of Psalms: A New Translation with Introductions and Notes Explanatory and Critical*. George Bell and Sons, 1878.

Peters, J. B. *The Psalms as Liturgies*. New York: Macmillan, 1922.

Pfeiffer, C. F. "Lothan (Gen 36:20) and Leviathan (Psalm 104:26)." EQ 32.4 (1960): 208–11.

Pollock, P. H. "Psalm 121." JBL 59 (1940): 411–12.

Porter, J. R. "The Interpretation of 2 Samuel vi and Psalm cxxxii." JTS 5 (1954): 161–73.

Prinsloo, W. S. "Psalm 149: Praise Yahweh with Tambourine and Two-edged Sword." ZAW 109 (1997): 395–407.

Rasmussen, M. D. *Conceptualizing Distress in the Psalms: A Form-Critical and Cognitive Semantic Study of* צרר *Word Group*. Piscataway, NJ: Gorgias Press, 2018.

Reynolds, C. B. "Psalm 125." Interpretation 48 (1994): 272–75.

Reynolds, K. A. *Torah as Teacher: The Exemplary Torah Student in Psalm 119*. VTSup. 137 (Leiden: Leiden: E. J. Brill, , 2010).

Ridderbos, H. N. *Die Psalmen*, 2 vols. Berlin: de Gruyter, 1972.

Riding, C. B. "Psalm 95 1–7c as a Large Chiasm." ZAW 88(1976): 418.

Ringgren, H. "Behold Your King Comes." VT 24 (1974): 207–11.

Roberts, J. J. M. "God's Imperial Reign According to the Psalter." HBT 23.2 (2001): 211–21.

_____. "The Davidic Origin of the Zion Tradition." JBL 92 (1973): 329–44.

_____. "The Enthronement of YHWH and David: The Abiding Theological Significance of the Kingship Language of the Psalms." CBQ 64 (2002): 675–86.

Robinson, B. P. "Form and Meaning in Psalm 131." Bib 79 (1998): 180–97.

Rogerson, J. W.; J. W. MacKay. *Psalms 51-100*. CBC. New York: Cambridge University Press, 1977.

Ross, A. P. *A Commentary on the Psalms*. 3 vols. Kregel Exegetical Library. Grand Rapids: Kregel Publishing, 2011–16.

Rowley, H. H. "Melchizedek and Zadok." Pp. 461–72 in *Festschrift to Alfred Bertholet zum 80 Geburtstag*. Ed. by O. Eissfeldt et al. Tübingen: Mohr, 1950.

Sabourin, L. *The Psalms, Their Origin and Meaning*. New Edition. New York: Alba House, 1974.

Sakenfeld, K. D. *The Meaning of Hesed in the Hebrew Bible: A New Inquiry*. Eugene, OR: Wipf & Stock Publishers, 2002.

Sanders, J. A. *The Dead Sea Psalms Scroll*. Ithaca, NY: Cornell University Press, 1967.

Sarna, N. M. *Songs of the Heart*. New York: Schocken, 1993.

_____. "The Psalm for the Sabbath Day (Ps 92)." JBL 81 (1962): 155–68.

Sawyer, J. F. A. "An Analysis of the Context and Meaning of the Psalm–Headings." Pp. 26–38 in *Transactions of the Glasgow University Oriental Society* 22 (1967–68).

Scaioloa, D. "The End of the Psalter" Pp. 701–10 in *The Composition of the Book of Psalms*. Ed. by E. Zenger. Leuven: Peeters, 2010.

Schaeffer, K. *Psalms*. BO. Collegeville, MN: Liturgical Press, 2001.

Schmutzer, A. J. "Psalm 91, Refuge, Protection and their Use in the New Testament." Pp. 85–108 in *The Psalms, Language for All Seasons of the Soul*. Ed. by A. J. Schmutzer, D. Howard. Chicago: Moody Press, 2013.

Schreiner, S. "Psalm 110." VT 27 (1977): 216–22.

Seybold, K. *Introducing the Psalms*. Trans. by G. Dunphy. Edinburgh: T & T Clark, 1990.

Sheppard, G. T. "Theology and the Book of Psalms." Interpretation 46.2 (1992): 143–155.

Sherwood, S. K. "Psalm 112." CBQ 51 (1989): 50–64.

Shoemaker, H. S. "Psalm 131." RevExp 85 (1988): 89–94.

Slomovik, F. "Toward an Understanding of the Formation of the Historical Titles in the Book of the Psalms." ZAW 91 (1979): 350–81.

Slotki, I. W. "Omnipresence, Condescension, and Omniscience in Psalm 113:5–6." JTS 32 (1931): 367–70.

Smick, E. B. "Mythopoetic Language in the Psalms." WTJ 44 (1982): 88–98.

Smith, M. S. *Psalms: The Divine Journey*. Mahwah, NJ: Paulist Press, 1987.

Snaith, N. H. "Selah." VT 2 (1952): 43–56.

______. *The Seven Psalms*. London: Epworth Press, 1964.

Soll, W. *Psalm 119: Matrix, Form, and Setting*. CBQMS. Washington, DC: Catholic Biblical Association, 1991.

Stevens, M. E. "Psalm 105." Interpretation 57(2003): 187–89.

Surburg, R. F. "Observations and Reflections on Giant Psalm." CTQ 42 (1982): 8–20.

Tate, M. E. *Psalms 51-100*. WBC. Waco, TX: Word, 1991.

Terrien, S. ECC. Grand Rapids: Wm. B. Eerdmans Publishers, 2002.

Tesh, S. E., W. D. Zorn. *Psalms*, 2 vols. The College Press NIV Commentary. Joplin, Mon.: College Press Publishing Company, 1999–2004.

Thirtle, J. W. *The Titles of the Psalms; Their Nature and Meaning Explained*. 2nd ed. New York: Henry Frowde, 1905.

Thomas, M. E. "Psalm 1 and 112 as a paradigm for the comparison of wisdom motifs in the Psalms." JETS 29.1 (March 1986): 15–24.

Tickle, P. *The Divine Hours: Prayers for Autumn and Wintertime*. New York: Doubleday, 2000.

Tidball, D. "Song of the Crucified One: The Psalms and the Crucifixion." SBJT 11.2 (Summer 2007): 48–61.

Torrance, T. F. "The First of the Hallel Psalms." EQ 27.1 (1955): 36–41.

_____. "The Last of the Hallel Psalms." EQ 28.2 (1956): 101–08.

Towns, E. L. *The Ultimate Guide to the Names of God: Three Bestsellers in One Volume*. Elgin, IL: Regal Books, 2014.

Travers, M. *Encountering God in the Psalms*. Grand Rapids: Kregel Publishing, 2003.

Tsevat, M. *A Study of the Language of Biblical Psalms*. JBLMS. Philadelphia: Society of Biblical Literature, 1955.

Tucker, W. D. "Revisiting the Plagues in Psalm cv." VT 55.3 (2005): 401–12.

_____. "A Poly–semiotic Approach to the Poor in the Psalms." PRSt 31 (2004): 425–39.

______. *Constructing and Deconstructing Power in Psalms 107-150*. Atlanta: Scholars Press, 2014.

Tucker, W. D., J. A. Grant. *Psalms, vol.2*. NIVAC. Grand Rapids: Zondervan, 2018.

Urbrock, W. J. "The Earth Song in Psalms 90–92." Pp. 65–83 in *Earth Story in Wisdom Tradition*. Ed. by N. C. Habel., S. Wurst. Sheffield: Sheffield Academic Press, 2001.

Van der Meer, W. "Psalm 110." Pp. 207–34 in *The Structural Analysis of Biblical and Canaanite Poetry*. JSOTSup. Ed. by W. van der Meer and J. C. deClaissé–Walford et al. Moor. Sheffield: Sheffield Academic Press, 1988.

Van der Toorn, K. "Ordeal Procedures in the Psalms and the Passover Meal." VT 38 (1988): 427–45.

Van der Wal, A. J. O. "The Structure of Psalm cxxix." VT 28 (1988): 364–67.

VanGemeren, W. "Psalms." Pp. 1–880 in *Expositor's Bible Commentary*, vol. 5. Grand Rapids: Zondervan, 1991.

Vawter, B. "Post–exilic Prayer and Hope." CBQ 37 (1975): 460–70.

Von Rad, G. *Old Testament Theology*, 2 vols. San Francisco: Harper & Row, 1965.

______. *Wisdom in Israel*. New York: Bloomsbury Publishing, 1993.

Vos, J. G. "The Ethical Problem of the Imprecating Psalms." WTJ 4 (1992): 123–38.

Waltke, B. K. "A Canonical Process Approach to the Psalms. Pp. 3–18 in *Tradition and Testament: Essays in Honor of Charles Lee Feinberg*. Ed. by J. S. Feinberg and P. D. Finberg. Chicago: Moody Press, 1981.

Walton, J. H. "Psalms: A Cantata about the Davidic Covenant." JETS 34.1 (March 1991): 21–31.

Ward, M. J. "Psalm 109: David's Poem of Vengeance." AUSS 18.2 (1980): 163–68.

Watson, W. G. E. "Reversed Rootplay in Ps 145." Bib 62 (1981): 101–102.

Watts, J. D. W. "Yahweh Malak Psalms." TZ 21 (1965): 341–48.

Weir, J. E. "The Perfect Way." EvQ 53 (1981): 54–59.

Weiser, A. *Psalms*. OTL. Louisville, KY: Westminster John Knox Press, 1962.

Wesselschmidt, Q. F., ed. *Psalms 51-150*. Ancient Christian Commentary on Scripture, VIII. Downersgrove, IL: InterVarsity Press, 2007.

Westermann, C. *The Psalms: Structure, Content and Message*. Philadelphia: Augsburg Press, 1980.

_____. *The Living Psalms*. Grand Rapids: Wm. B. Eerdmans Publishers, 1989.

_____. *The Praise of God in the Psalms*. Trans. by K. Crim. Richmond: John Knox Press, 1965.

Whybray, N. *Reading the Psalms as a Book*. JSOTSup. Sheffield: Sheffield Academic Press, 1996.

_____. "Psalm 119." Pp. 31–43 in *Wisdom, You Are My Sister*. Ed. by M. L. Barré. CBQMS. Washington: Catholic Biblical Association, 1997.

Wilcock, M. *The Message of Psalms*, 2 vols. BST. Downers Grove, IL.: InterVarsity Press, 2001.

Williams, D. M. *Psalms,* 2 vols. CC. Waco, TX: Word, 2000.

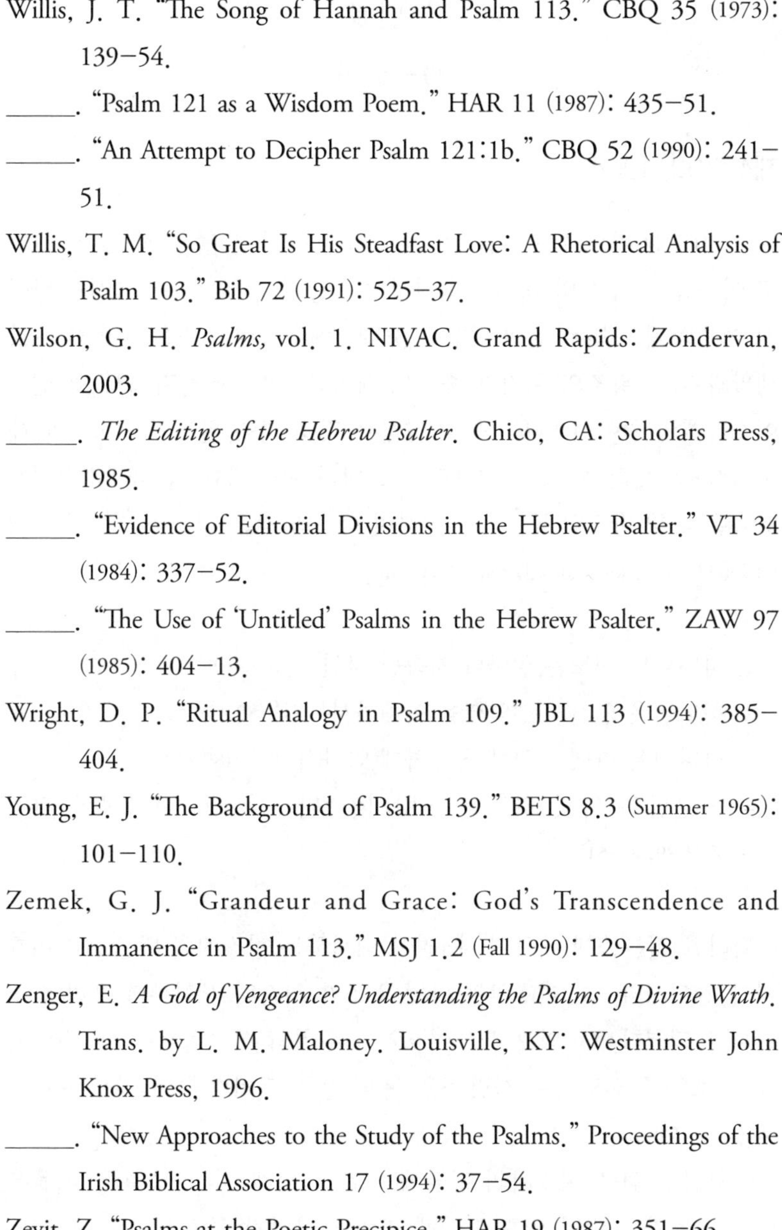

Willis, J. T. "The Song of Hannah and Psalm 113." CBQ 35 (1973): 139–54.

_____. "Psalm 121 as a Wisdom Poem." HAR 11 (1987): 435–51.

_____. "An Attempt to Decipher Psalm 121:1b." CBQ 52 (1990): 241–51.

Willis, T. M. "So Great Is His Steadfast Love: A Rhetorical Analysis of Psalm 103." Bib 72 (1991): 525–37.

Wilson, G. H. *Psalms,* vol. 1. NIVAC. Grand Rapids: Zondervan, 2003.

_____. *The Editing of the Hebrew Psalter.* Chico, CA: Scholars Press, 1985.

_____. "Evidence of Editorial Divisions in the Hebrew Psalter." VT 34 (1984): 337–52.

_____. "The Use of 'Untitled' Psalms in the Hebrew Psalter." ZAW 97 (1985): 404–13.

Wright, D. P. "Ritual Analogy in Psalm 109." JBL 113 (1994): 385–404.

Young, E. J. "The Background of Psalm 139." BETS 8.3 (Summer 1965): 101–110.

Zemek, G. J. "Grandeur and Grace: God's Transcendence and Immanence in Psalm 113." MSJ 1.2 (Fall 1990): 129–48.

Zenger, E. *A God of Vengeance? Understanding the Psalms of Divine Wrath.* Trans. by L. M. Maloney. Louisville, KY: Westminster John Knox Press, 1996.

_____. "New Approaches to the Study of the Psalms." Proceedings of the Irish Biblical Association 17 (1994): 37–54.

Zevit, Z. "Psalms at the Poetic Precipice." HAR 19 (1987): 351–66.

시편Ⅲ

90–150편

제4권(90–106편)

시편 90–106편으로 구성된 제4권은 시편 다섯 권 중 가장 짧다. 그리고 이 모음집 구성의 대부분이 찬양시로 중심 주제는 이스라엘의 왕이신 여호와께 드리는 찬양이다. 제3권은 예루살렘 함락과 바빌론 포로 생활과 다윗 왕조의 위기가 중심 주제이다. 이러한 상황에서 제4권이 이스라엘의 왕이신 여호와를 찬양하는 것은 다윗 왕조의 지속성에 대해 답하는 듯하다. 보다 구체적으로 말하자면 제3권을 마무리하면서 89편은 다윗 왕조의 몰락을 슬퍼하며 다음과 같은 질문들을 던졌던 것이다(cf. deClaissé–Walford et al., McCann).

1. 하나님의 진노는 얼마나 지속될 것인가?(89:46)
2. 하나님은 인간의 연약함을 이해하시는가?(89:47–48)
3. 하나님은 다윗 언약에 성실하게 임하시는가?(89:49)
4. 하나님은 다윗 왕조를 몰락시킨 원수들에게 보복하실 것인가?(89:50–51)

이러한 질문들에 대하여 제4권이 제시하는 간접적인 답은 "(1) 여호와가 왕이시다. (2) 여호와는 다윗 왕조가 시작되기 전부터 우리의 피난처가 되셨다. (3) 앞으로도 여호와는 우리의 피난처가 되실 것이다. (4) 여호와를 신뢰하는 사람들은 복을 받을 것이다." 이다(cf. Howard, Nogalski, Wilson).

이처럼 초점을 여호와의 왕권에 맞추기 위해 제4권에 속한 시들은 다윗 왕조가 누렸던 영광에 대해 거의 언급하지 않고, 주로 하나님의 창조 능력과 선조들에게 베푸신 선하심을 기념한다. 이스라엘은 처음부터 죄의 성향이 매우 짙은 민족이었지만 하나님은 그들을 버리지 않으셨다(시 95, 106편). 그러므로 다윗 왕조가 죄로 인해 몰락했다 해서 하나님이 이 백성을 버린 것은 아니다. 이 시들은 독자들에게 더 이상 다윗 왕조에 관심을 집중하지 말고, 오직 하나님께 관심을 집중할 것을 권면한다. 하나님만이 주의 백성이 의지할만한 분이시기 때문이다.

제4권은 다섯 권의 책들 중 본문이 가장 불완전한 책이다. 학자들은 실제로 칠십인역(LXX)이 때로는 마소라 사본과 상당히 다른 내용을 반영하고 있다고 생각한다(cf. Goldingay, Tate). 쿰란 공동체에서 발견된 시편 사본들도 1-3권은 별 차이가 없지만, 4-5권은 어느 정도의 차이가 나타난다(cf. Hossfeld-Zenger, Wilson).

제90편

하나님의 사람 모세의 기도

I. 장르/양식: 회중 탄식시(cf. 12편)

궁켈(Gunkel)이 신뢰시와 회중 탄식시 두 개의 독립적인 시로 구성된 것이라고 한 이후 많은 학자들이 그의 주장을 따랐다. 그러나 최근에 와서 대부분 주석가들은 한 편의 통일성을 지닌 시로 간주한다(Kraus). 하나의 시로 취급해도 흐름과 주제의 변화에 있어서 별 어려움이 없기 때문이다(cf. McCann).

이 시는 전쟁에 나가는 군인들이 부른 노래(War Oracle)라는 주장이 있고(Christensen), 전도서의 지성과 신학에서 비롯된 시라며 지혜시로 해석하는 이들도 있다(von Rad). 그러나 대부분 주석가들은 이 노래가 어느 정도는 지혜시의 성향을 지닌 것은 사실이지만, 공동체 탄식시로 구분되어야 한다고 한다(cf. Ross).

제4권에 속한 시편에서 모세의 이름이 종종 등장한다 하여 이 모음집을 '모세의 책'(Moses-book)이라고 하기도 하는데(Tate), 표제에서 모세를 언급하는 것은 이 시가 유일하다. 또한 13절은 출애굽기 32:12에 기록된 모세의 기도를 반영하고 있다(Freedman, cf. Tate). 이러한 상황을 고려하여 모세가 이 시를 저작했다고 생각하는 학자들이 있다(Delitzsch,

Jaki, cf. Anderson). 그러나 대부분 학자들은 모세의 저작권을 인정하지 않는다(Goldingay, Kirkpatrick, Hossfeld-Zenger, Tucker & Grant, von Rad). 주전 9세기에 저작되었다는 견해가 있고(Dahood), 주전 586년에 있었던 예루살렘 멸망 직후에 저작되었다는 주장도 있다(Terrien). 많은 주석가들은 포로기 혹은 그 이후를 지목한다(Broyles, Brueggemann & Bellinger, Goldingay, Grogan, Kirkpatrick, Tate, Tucker & Grant, Vawter). 이 시편의 내용이 상당히 오래 지속된 하나님의 진노가 이제는 끝나기를 바라고 있기 때문이다(Clifford, deClaissé-Walford et al.).

이 시가 포로기 시대에 저작된 것이라면 왜 모세를 언급하는 것일까? 아마도 포로기 공동체가 자신들을 위해 모세가 기도한다면 이렇게 말할 것으로 생각했기 때문일 것이다(Goldingay, Sheppard, Urbrock). 제4권을 시작하는 이 시편이 모세 시대의 일을 떠올리게 하고, 제4권을 마무리하는 106편이 광야 시대에 이스라엘이 저지른 죄들에 대해 고백하며 모세를 언급하는 것은(106:32) 분명한 메시지를 형성하고 있다.

여호와 하나님은 출애굽 때 시내 산에서 이스라엘의 왕이 되셨고, 다윗 왕조는 하나님이 이스라엘을 통치하시는 방법이었다. 이러한 상황에서 제3권은 다윗 왕조의 몰락을 슬퍼했다. 다윗 왕조의 몰락은 하나님의 이스라엘 통치가 끝난 것을 의미하는가 하는 신학적 딜레마를 만들었다(Brueggemann & Bellinger). 이러한 상황에서 제4권 편집자들은 하나님이 이스라엘의 왕이 되신 일을 지켜보았던 모세와 그의 시대에 있었던 일을 제4권의 시작과 끝에서 언급함으로써 다윗 왕조는 몰락했지만, 왕이신 하나님의 이스라엘 통치는 계속되고 있음을 암시한다. 다윗 왕조의 몰락이 언제까지 지속될 것이냐는 시편 89:46의 질문이 90:13에서는 주님이 언제까지 자기 백성에게서 떠나 계실 것이냐는 질문으로 바뀌는 것도 이러한 정황을 배경으로 한다(Schaefer). 시내 산 언약은 포로기 시대를 살아가는 사람들에게도 유효하다는 것이다.

표제는 모세를 '하나님의 사람'(אִישׁ־הָאֱלֹהִים)이라고 하는데, 구약에서

이 호칭은 선지자들에게 주로 사용된다. 모세도 이 타이틀로 불린 적이 있으며(신 33:1), 표제가 그를 하나님의 사람이라고 하는 것은 두 가지 메시지를 담고 있는 듯하다(Tucker & Grant). 첫째, 다윗 왕조의 왕들은 이 기준에 미치지 못한, 곧 하나님의 사람들이 아니었기 때문에 왕조가 몰락했다는 것이다. 둘째, 다윗 왕조와 상관없이 여호와는 자기 백성, 곧 하나님의 사람들을 통치하심으로 이 시편을 읽는 모든 사람은 하나님의 사람들이 될 수 있도록 노력해야 한다는 것이다. 영국의 성공회는 기도모음집에서 이 시편이 삶의 허무함을 노래하고 있다고 하여 장례식에서 사용하도록 권장한다(Goldingay).

II. 구조

대체적으로 학자들은 이 시를 1-2절, 3-6절, 7-12절, 13-17절 네 파트로 구분한다. 이러한 구분을 기준으로 더 자세하게 섹션화하면 다음과 같은 구조도 가능하다(VanGemeren, 매우 자세한 구조분석은 Alden을 참조하라). 이 주석에서도 다음 구조를 바탕으로 본문을 주해해 나가고자 한다.

A. 여호와가 하나님이시다!(90:1-2)
  B. 하나님의 백성 지배(90:3-6)
    C. 하나님의 진노(90:7-10)
    C'. 하나님의 진노에 대한 올바른 반응(90:11-12)
  B'. 하나님의 자비를 위한 기도(90:13-16)
A'. 여호와가 우리의 하나님이시기를!(90:17)

III. 주해

기자는 우리의 삶의 덧없음과 하나님의 영원하심을 대조하면서 주님의 은총을 구한다. 하나님이 그들의 죄로 인해 계속 진노하시면 그들에게는 어떠한 소망도 없기 때문이다. 그러므로 그는 하나님이 속히 그들의 삶을 기쁨과 즐거움으로 채워 주시기를 기도한다.

1. 여호와가 하나님이시다!(90:1–2)

1 주여
주는 대대에 우리의 거처가 되셨나이다
2 산이 생기기 전,
땅과 세계도 주께서 조성하시기 전
곧 영원부터 영원까지 주는 하나님이시니이다

기자는 하나님이 영원하신 주님이심을 선언하며 노래를 시작한다. 기자가 하나님을 '나의 주여'(אֲדֹנָי)(1절)로 부르는 것은 시편에서 이곳이 유일하다(Goldingay). 그가 하나님을 '나의 주인'이라고 부르는 것은 주인이 종의 말에 귀를 기울이듯이, 하나님이 자신의 기도에 귀를 기울여 달라는 의미다. 이는 노래를 시작하고 마무리하는 성호로 사용되었다(cf. 17절).

주님은 '대대로'(בְּדֹר וָדֹר) 계신 분이며(1절), '영원부터 영원까지'(עַד־עוֹלָם מֵעוֹלָם)(2절) 존재하시는 분이다. 또한 주님은 대대로 우리의 거처가 되셨다(1절). '거처'(מָעוֹן)는 피난처, 혹은 은신처를 의미한다(cf. 시 91:9). 모세도 하나님은 백성들의 '거처/피난처'가 되신다고 한적이 있다(신 33:27). 모세가 이렇게 말했을 때에는 이스라엘이 아직 '거처'를 얻지 못한(가나안에 입성하지 못한) 때이다. 그러므로 그는 주의 백성에게 오직 하나님만이 그들의 '거처'가 되심을 선포했다. 우리의 삶에서도 마찬가지다. 죄 많은 이 세상 어디에도 우리의 거처는 없다. 오직 하나님의 품이 우리가 오늘도 향해 가고 있는 '거처'일 뿐이다. 하나님만이 환난으로부터 우리를 보호하시고 숨기시며, 참 안식을 주시어 평안히 쉬게 하신다. 하나님이 우리의 은신처라는 것은 영적인 의미를 지녔기 때문에 예루살렘 성전이 있고 없고는 상관없다(Terrien). 주님은 이런 일을 '대대로', '영원부터 영원까지' 하시는 분이다.

백성의 거처가 되신 하나님은 세상이 시작되기 전부터 계셨다(2절). 산이 생기고 땅과 세계가 창조되기 전부터 하나님은 창조주이시다(2절). 기자가 사용하고 있는 이미지는 출산(birth)이다. 하나님이 산을 출산하시는지, 세상이 산을 출산하는지 확실하지는 않지만(cf. Goldingay, Keel, Kraus, McCann, Miller, VanGemeren), 둘의 차이가 별로 중요하지는 않다. 설령 세상이 산을 출산한다 할지라도, 그 세상을 창조하신 이는 하나님이시기 때문이다.

'땅'(אֶרֶץ)은 세상이 세워진 터전을, '세계'(תֵּבֵל)는 땅 위에 심어지고 세워진 모든 것을 의미한다(cf. HALOT). 세상과 그 안에 있는 모든 것이 하나님이 창조하신 걸작품이라는 뜻이다. 인간이 경험할 수 있는 것들 중 가장 영원한 것은 세상인데, 그 세상을 창조하신 하나님은 더욱더 영원하신 분이다. "주는 하나님이시다"(2c절)는 하나님은 자신이 창조하신 세상을 다스리는 왕이시며, 또한 창조된 세상과는 전적으로 다르심(otherness)을 강조한다(VanGemeren). 제3권은 다윗 왕조의 몰락을 슬퍼했는데, 편집자들이 제4권을 시작하면서 하나님은 이스라엘에 인간 왕이 있기 전부터 그들을 보호하신 왕이라고 하는 것은 그들이 다윗 왕조와 상관없이 하나님의 지속적인 보호를 받을 것임을 암시한다(Tucker & Grant, cf. Creach).

2. 하나님의 백성 지배(90:3-6)

3 주께서 사람을 티끌로 돌아가게 하시고
말씀하시기를 너희 인생들은 돌아가라 하셨사오니

[4] 주의 목전에는 천 년이 지나간 어제 같으며
밤의 한 순간 같을 뿐임이니이다
[5] 주께서 그들을 홍수처럼 쓸어가시나이다
그들은 잠깐 자는 것 같으며
아침에 돋는 풀 같으니이다
[6] 풀은 아침에 꽃이 피어 자라다가
저녁에는 시들어 마르나이다

앞 섹션에서 영원하신 하나님을 묵상한 기자는 인간의 덧없음을 생각해 본다. 영원하신 하나님과 비교할 때 인간은 티끌에 불과하다(3절). 이러한 비교는 삶의 허무함을 노래하는 전도서처럼 지혜문헌에 속하는 듯하다(Hossfeld–Zenger, Kraus, von Rad). 그러나 이 말씀은 잠시 후 하나님께 화를 멈추어 달라는 간구로 이어지기 때문에 원론적으로 인생의 허무함을 논하는 지혜문헌이 아니다. 그들에게 임한 하나님의 노를 멈추어 달라는 호소이다(Clifford, deClaissé–Walford et al.).

주님은 사람을 티끌로 돌아가게 하신다. '돌아가다'(שׁוּב)가 회개하라는 의미로 자주 사용된다 하여 본문에서도 하나님이 회개를 권면하시는 것이라고 해석하는 학자들이 있지만(Alter, cf. Ross), 문맥에 가장 잘 어울리는 해석은 단순히 생명이 다 되었으니 죽음(스올)으로 내려가라는 뜻이다(Eaton, Kirkpatrick).

'티끌'(דַּכָּא)은 무거운 무게에 짓눌려 바스러진 가루를 뜻한다(HALOT). 그러므로 삶의 무게에 짓눌려 '가루가 된' 사람의 죽음을 이렇게 묘사하는 듯하다(McCann). '티끌'(דַּכָּא)은 창세기 3:19에서는 '흙'(עָפָר)을 말하지만, 본문에서는 죄 지은 아담에게 죽을 것이라며 하신 말씀인 "너는 흙이니 흙으로 돌아갈 것이니라"를 연상케 한다(cf. Anderson). 인간은 흙으로 지어졌으며, 잠시 살다가 하나님이 명령하시면 곧 흙으로 돌아가야 하는 존재이다. 저자는 짧은 우리의 인생을 주관하시는 분은 하나님이심을 고백한다.

사람의 삶이 참으로 덧없다고 한 기자는 이와 대조적인 하나님의 영원하심을 묵상한다(4절). 주님께는 천 년이 지나간 어제 같으며 밤의 한순간 같을 뿐이라고 한다. 인류 역사상 가장 오래 산 사람은 므두셀라이며 그는 969세에 죽었다(창 5:27). 그도 천 년을 넘기지 못한 것이다. 그러므로 사람에게 천 년은 참으로 긴 세월이다. 반면에 영원하신 하나님께는 하루와 같다.

'밤의 한순간'(אַשְׁמוּרָה)은 보초병들이 불침번을 서는 일을 뜻한다(cf. HALOT). 보통 3시간(McCann) 혹은 4시간 정도의 시간을 의미한다(Ross, cf. 애 2:19). 하나님은 영원히 존재하시는 분이므로 인간인 우리는 감당할 수 없이 긴 세월이 주님에게는 한순간에 지나지 않을 정도로 짧은 시간이라는 의미이다.

영원하신 하나님은 사람들을 홍수처럼 쓸어 가신다(5a절). 요동치는 시간의 강물 앞에 인간은 한 방울의 물에 지나지 않는다. 그러므로 인간은 잠깐 자는 것 같으며, 아침에 돋는 풀과 같다(5b-c). 기자가 사용하고 있는 이미지는 건조한 가나안 지역에서 돋아난 풀이 며칠 사이에 누렇게 뜨고 마르는 일이다(VanGemeren). 이러한 이미지를 배경으로 기자는 우리의 삶은 아침에 돋은 풀이 꽃이 피어 자라다가 저녁에는 시들어 마르는 것처럼 된다고 한다(6절, cf. 사 40:6-7). 잠시 이 땅에 살다가 순식간에 죽음으로 영면하는 우리의 삶의 덧없음을 표현하는 비유이다(cf. 단 12:2): "주님께서 생명을 거두어 가시면, 인생은 한순간의 꿈일 뿐, 아침에 돋아난 한 포기 풀과 같이 사라져 갑니다"(새번역). 기자는 여러 비유가 순식간에 변하는 것처럼 우리의 삶도 불안하고 급변한다는 사실을 암시한다(Kidner). 앞 섹션이 묘사하는 하나님의 영원하심과 이 섹션이 묘사하는 인간의 덧없음이 매우 강한 대조를 이루고 있다.

3. 하나님의 진노(90:7-10)

[7] 우리는 주의 노에 소멸되며
주의 분내심에 놀라나이다
[8] 주께서 우리의 죄악을 주의 앞에 놓으시며
우리의 은밀한 죄를 주의 얼굴 빛 가운데에 두셨사오니
[9] 우리의 모든 날이 주의 분노 중에 지나가며
우리의 평생이 순식간에 다하였나이다
[10] 우리의 연수가 칠십이요 강건하면 팔십이라도
그 연수의 자랑은 수고와 슬픔뿐이요
신속히 가니 우리가 날아가나이다

기자는 앞 섹션에서 인생의 짧고 허무함을 노래했다. 이 섹션에서는 하나님의 심판을 받은 사람은 그나마 더 짧은 삶을 마감할 수밖에 없다고 탄식한다. 일부 주석가들은 7-8절을 '죄의 삯은 사망'(롬 6:23)이라는 신약 말씀의 구약 버전이라고 한다(Hossfeld-Zenger). 하나님의 노하심과 분내심은 지속적이고 끊이지 않는 인간의 죄와 반역에 대한 주님의 의로운 반응이다(Schaeffer). 그러나 하나님의 의로운 반응은 무능하고 연약한 인간을 소멸시킬 수밖에 없으며, 소스라치게 놀라게 할 수밖에 없다(7절). 다행인 것은 하나님이 용서하신 자들에게는 이렇게 반응하지 않으실 것이라는 사실이다. 하나님의 노하심과 분내심은 모든 사람이 아니라, 용서하지 않으신 자들에 대한 반응이다(Calvin, Tucker & Grant). 하나님의 노와 화가 죄지은 인간과 그들을 심판하시는 하나님을 구분하는 분명한 선이 되고 있다(VanGemeren).

그러므로 우리는 하나님이 화를 내시지 않는 삶을 살아야 한다. 만일 하나님이 우리에게 화를 내시면 우리의 삶은 고난과 역경의 연속이 되기 때문이다. 하나님이 화를 내시지 않게 하려면 죄를 짓지 않아야 한다. 안타깝게도 사람이 죄를 짓지 않고 살기는 쉽지 않다. 게다가 우리가 짓는 심각한 죄뿐만 아니라, 가장 은밀한 것까지 모두 하나님 앞에 드러난다(8절). 그러므로 세상에서 하나님 앞에 당당하게 설 수 있는 의인은 없다(롬 3:10). 오직 그리스도의 보혈을 통해 의인으로 칭함을 받은 사람들이 있을 뿐이다. 하나님의 자비를 구하는 것이 하나님의 화를 피하는 유일한 방법이다(cf. Anderson).

결국 죄를 지은 우리의 모든 날은 주님의 분노 중에 순식간에 지나가며 우리의 한평생은 한숨처럼 스러진다(9절). 하나님은 우리의 모든 죄를 벌하시며 가장 은밀한 죄까지 심판하시니 주님의 심판을 피할 수 있는 사람은 하나도 없다. 모두 다 죄로 인해 단명한다는 것이다. 설령 사람이 오래 산다 해도 70-80세를 넘기가 힘들다(10절). 성경에서 70년은 포로 생활과 연관하여 고난과 속박을 상징한다(렘 25:11-12; 슥 1:12). 그러므로 본문에서도 70년은 이스라엘의 포로 생활(Clifford), 혹은 우리의 삶이 수고와 슬픔으로 가득 차 있다는 의미를 지니고 있다(Goldingay, cf. 전 1:3; 욥 5:7). 짧은 삶이니 고통이 없거나, 슬픔과 수고로 가득한 날들이니 길기라도 한다면 조금 나을 텐데, 우리의 삶은 신속하게 사라진다. 마치 날아가는 새처럼 말이다. 기자는 인생의 허무함을 예술적으로 표현하고 있다.

4. 하나님의 진노에 대한 올바른 반응(90:11-12)

11 누가 주의 노여움의 능력을 알며
누가 주의 진노의 두려움을 알리이까
12 우리에게 우리 날 계수함을 가르치사
지혜로운 마음을 얻게 하소서

하나님의 노여움이 사람의 수명을 얼마나 단축하는지 아는 사람은 없다(11a절). 또한 사람의 수명을 단축하는 주님의 진노가 얼마나 두려운지 아는 사람은 없다(11b절). 그러므로 기자는 하나님께 지혜로운 마음을 달라고 기도한다. 우리의 사는 날이 얼마나 되는지를 헤아리는 지혜가 아니라 하나님의 진노가 얼마나 지속될 것인가를 알 만한 지혜이다(Clifford). 하나님의 진노에 대해 인간은 이러한 지혜를 구하는 기도로 반응해야 한다(Kirkpatrick). 만일 하나님의 진노가 얼마나 지속될 것인가를 알게 되면 주님의 진노가 언젠가는 끝날 것이라는 소망이 생긴다(deClaissé-Walford et al.).

사람이 어떻게 하면 제명을 다 살 수 있을까? 기자는 하나님의 노여움이 사람의 짧은 생애를 더 짧게 만든다고 탄식한다. 그러므로 그가 오래 살기 위해 구함은 다름 아닌 하나님의 심판이 언제까지 지속될 것인가에 대한 분별력이며, 다시는 죄를 짓지 않는 지혜로운 마음이다(12절). 그러므로 기자가 지혜로운 마음을 구하는 12절은 이 시편에서 가장 긍정적인 말씀이다(cf. McCann). 사람이 죄를 짓지 않으면 하나님의 노여움이 그에게 임하지 않을 것이고, 하나님의 진노가 임하지 않으면 그는 그에게 주어진 생을 다 살 수 있을 것이기 때문이다. 그가 구하는 '지혜로운 마음'(לְבַב חָכְמָה)은 여호와의 주인 되심을 의식하여 죄의 지배 아래 있는 것을 거부하는 마음이다(cf. Anderson, Brueggemann).

이 '지혜로운 마음'은 자연히 생기는 것이 아니다. 먼저 인간의 한계를 깨달아야 한다(Eaton, cf. 12a절). 그리고 나서 "우리를 가르쳐 주십시오"라며 기도할 때 생긴다. '가르쳐 주십시오'(12절)는 이 시편 전체가 어우러져 구성하는 핵심 메시지이다(Alter, cf. Tate). 기자는 하나님께 계수함(셈)을 가르쳐 달라고 하는 것이 아니라, 삶을 변화시키는 신학을 가르쳐 달라고 하고 있다(Wilcock). 우리가 하나님의 가르치심에 따라 죄를 짓지 않으면 하나님의 진노가 우리에게 임하지 않을 뿐만 아니라, 하나님이 우리로 인해 기뻐하실 것이다.

5. 하나님의 자비를 위한 기도(90:13-16)

13 여호와여
돌아오소서
언제까지니이까
주의 종들을 불쌍히 여기소서
14 아침에 주의 인자하심이 우리를 만족하게 하사
우리를 일생 동안 즐겁고 기쁘게 하소서
15 우리를 괴롭게 하신 날수대로와
우리가 화를 당한 연수대로 우리를 기쁘게 하소서
16 주께서 행하신 일을 주의 종들에게 나타내시며
주의 영광을 그들의 자손에게 나타내소서

기자는 주님이 그들에게 돌아오시기를 간구한다(13절). 그것은 그가 하나님을 심판하시는 분으로 이해하고, 자신들의 고통이 심판하시는 하나님의 진노하심에서 비롯되었다고 생각하기 때문이다. 주님께 돌아오시라고 하는 것은 생명을 거두어 가시라는 뜻으로 해석될 수도 있지만(Goldingay, 3절), 14-15절의 말씀을 감안하면 도와 달라는 간구로 보는 것이 합당하다. 또한 이것은 하나님이 언약을 맺어 자기 백성 삼으신 그들이 죄를 지었다 할지라도 망하도록 방관하시는 것은 도저히 있을 수 없는 일이라는 원망의 표현이기도 하다(Clifford). 이스라엘은 과거에 이집트와 광야에서 큰 위기를 맞았을 때에도 주님께 돌아오시라고 호소한 적이 있다(Grogan).

그들이 그들을 치신 분을 피하려고 하는 것이 아니라 오히려 그들 중에 임재해 주실 것을 요청하는 기도가 인상적이다. 그는 주님이 자신들의 죄로 인해 그들을 떠나셨다고 생각한다. 그러므로 주님이 다시 그들에게 돌아오실 때 비로소 그들의 죄 문제가 해결된 것으로 생각할 것이다. 저자는 하나님이 돌아오실 때 그들이 당면하고 있는 어려움과 문제들이 해결될 것을 확신한다. 하나님이 그들에게 돌아오시는 것은 곧 주님이 그들을 불쌍히 여기셨다는 증거가 되기 때문이다.

하나님이 그들에게 돌아오시면 그들의 슬픈 삶이 기쁨으로 변할 것이다. 주님이 그들을 만족하게 하시고 기쁘게 하실 것이기 때문이다(14절). 하나님이 그들에게 만족을 주시는 날, 그들은 자신들이 하나님께 용서와 자비를 구하며 그들에게 돌아오시도록 호소한 모든 노력이 헛되지 않았음을 깨닫게 될 것이다(Kidner).

아침마다 주의 인자하심은 그들을 만족하게 할 것이며, 평생 그들을 기쁘게 해 주실 것이다(14절). 그들이 바라는 것은 단 한 가지 하나님의 '인자하심'(חֶסֶד)이며, 매일 아침 하나님의 인자하심을 피부로 느끼는 그들은 '음식을 배불리 먹은 사람처럼 만족할 것'(שׂבע)이다. 하나님의 인자하심으로 만족한 그들은 일생 동안 '즐겁게 소리치고'(רנן) 주님의 자비로우심을 '기뻐할'(שׂמח) 것이다. 탈굼(Tg.)은 '에덴 동산의 기쁨과 즐거움'이라는 말로 해석한다(Goldingay).

저자는 주님이 진노하시어 그들을 괴롭게 한 날수대로, 그들이 화를 당한 연수대로 하나님이 그들을 기쁘게 하실 것을 기도한다(15절). 그가 '연수대로'(שְׁנוֹת)라며 복수를 사용하는 것으로 보아 최소한 몇 년에 달하는 상당한 기간 동안 주님의 징계로 인해 고통을 당하고 있음을 암시한다. 이제는 주님이 그들에게 노하시는 일을 멈추고 자비와 은혜로 대해 주시기를 기도하고 있다.

그는 하나님이 행하시는 일을 자신들의 눈으로 직접 보기를 원한다(16절). '일'(פֹּעַל)은 업적(accomplishment)을 뜻한다(cf. HALOT). 기자는 하나님이 그들에게 자비를 베풀어 행복하게 하시는 것을 주님의 '일'이라고 한다. 하나님이 하시는 일은 대체적으로 주의 백성에게 복된 일이며 그들을 행복하게 하시는 일이기 때문이다. 저자는 이같이 선한 하나님의 일이 자손 대대로 주의 백성에게 임하기를 기도하며 이 섹션을 마무리한다.

6. 여호와가 우리의 하나님이시기를!(90:17)

[17] 주 우리 하나님의 은총을 우리에게 내리게 하사
우리의 손이 행한 일을 우리에게 견고하게 하소서
우리의 손이 행한 일을 견고하게 하소서

기자는 16절에서 하나님의 일을 주의 백성에게 베푸시는 선한 업적으로 정의했다. 이제 그는 자신들이 서로에게 하나님처럼 선한 일을 하고자 하는 바람으로 기도를 마무리한다. 물론 그들은 하나님의 업적에 비교할 만한 일을 할 수는 없다. 이점을 강조하기 위하여 하나님의 '일'(פֹּעַל)과 자신들의 손이 행하는 '일'(מַעֲשֶׂה)을 묘사하며 서로 다른 단어를 사용한다. 하나님은 참으로 위대한 업적으로 평가되는 일을 하시지만, 그들이 하는 일은 작고 단순한 노동이다.

중요한 것은 그들도 하나님을 닮아 선한 일을 하고자 한다는 것이다. 그러므로 그는 하나님이 그들이 하고자 하는 일을 축복하시기를 원하며 그들이 하는 일을 견고하게 해 달라고 기도한다. '견고하다'(כון)는 '지속되다'는 의미를 지녔으며 이때까지 기자가 언급했던 모든 덧없음(순식간, 날아감, 마르는 풀 등)에 대한 매우 강력한 반전이다(Alter). 비록 우리의 생은 매우 짧지만, 우리가 행하는 선한 일은 오랫동안 기억되고 남을 것이다. 하나님이 우리가 하고자 하는 선한 일들을 축복하시고 사용하셔서 이 땅에서 주님의 뜻을 이루어 나가실 것이기 때문이다.

제91편

I. 장르/양식: 신뢰시(cf. 62편)

시편 90-92편은 매끄러운 흐름을 지닌 노래들이다. 이들 중 90편은 포로로 끌려간 사람들의 호소를 반영하고 있고, 91편은 그들의 호소에 응답하는 역할을 한다(Brueggemann & Bellinger, Kirkpatrick). 하나님의 응답을 확신하는 신뢰시인 것이다(Grogan, Sheppard). 그러므로 학자들은 보편적으로 이 시편이 포로기 시대에 저작된 것이라고 생각한다(Kirkpatrick, Schmutzer, Tate).

그러나 이 시편이 사용된 정황과 역사적 상황에 대해 구체적인 정보를 제공하지 않기 때문에 위 견해 외에도 다양한 추측이 있다. 이 시편을 성전으로 도피한 사람의 노래라 하기도 하고(Briggs, cf. 3-4절), 심각한 질병에서 회복된 사람의 노래로(cf. 5-7절) 더 나아가 레위기 14장이 정의한 정결 예식을 치를 때 부른 노래라고 하는 이도 있다(Levine). 또한 예배자가 성전에 입장할 때 입구에서 부른 노래(cf. Ross), 혹은 순례자들이 절기 때 예루살렘을 향해 가면서 부른 노래(Broyles), 혹은 왕이 전쟁으로 나갈 때 부른 노래(cf. Ross, Terrien), 혹은 새로이 여호와를 믿게 된 회심자의 노래라는 견해도 있다.

이처럼 다양한 견해가 제시되는 것은 91편이 사용하는 언어가 구체적이지 않아서 빚어진 일이다. 그러므로 이 노래는 매우 다양한 상황에서 불리고 적용될 수 있었던 노래임을 암시한다. 칠십인역(LXX)은 표제에 '찬양, 다윗의 노래'(αἶνος ᾠδῆς τῷ Δαυιδ)라는 말을 더하지만, 마소라 사본은 아무런 표제 없이 우리에게 전수되었다.

II. 구조

대부분 학자들은 이 시를 기자의 신앙 고백 혹은 많은 축복을 약속하며 선한 길을 택하라는 권면인 1-13절과 하나님의 말씀/신탁인 14-16절 두 파트로 구분한다(McCann, VanGemeren, cf. Hossfeld-Zenger). 본 주석에서는 이러한 구분을 존중하되, 본문 주해를 위해 1-13절을 세분화하여 다음과 같은 구조를 바탕으로 텍스트를 해석해 나가고자 한다.

A. 하나님이 보호하심(91:1-2)
  B. 원수들에게서 보호하심(91:3-8)
  B'. 천사들을 통해 보호하심(91:9-13)
A'. 하나님이 보호하심(91:14-16)

III. 주해

내용에 있어서 이 시편은 46편과 상당히 비슷하다(Weiser). 또한 90편의 내용과 깊은 연관성을 지녔다(cf. Tucker & Grant). 기자는 출애굽과 연관된 언어 외에도 여러 가지 이미지들을 사용하여 독자들에게 그들이 당면한 어려운 현실에서 눈을 들어 영원한 안식을 주시는 하나님을 바라보며 살 것을 권면한다.

하나님은 우리를 모든 재앙과 고난에서 보호하는 것을 기뻐하시는 분이다. 필요할 경우 천사들을 명령하여 우리의 길을 지키기도 하신다. 그러므로 기자는 우리의 삶에서 고난과 어려움이 닥쳐올 때, 보호를 기대하며 피난처이신 하나님께 피하라고 권면한다.

1. 하나님이 보호하심(91:1-2)

1 지존자의 은밀한 곳에 거주하며
전능자의 그늘 아래에 사는 자여,
2 나는 여호와를 향하여 말하기를
그는 나의 피난처요
나의 요새요
내가 의뢰하는 하나님이라 하리니

기자가 2절에 기록된 "그는 나의 피난처요… 하나님이라"는 말씀을 누가 해야 한다고 하는지가 확실하지 않다(cf. Alter, Hossfeld-Zenger). 흐름을 볼 때 하나님의 보호 아래 있는 자가 여호와를 향해 말하는 것이 가장 자연스럽지만, 마소라 사본은 2절에서 기자인지, 보호 아래 있는 자인지가 확실하지 않은 일인칭 '나'를 사용하고 있기 때문이다. 그래서 번역본들도 둘로 나눠져 있다: (1) "지존자의… 그늘 아래에 사는 자는 여호와를 향하여 말하기를…"(NAS, NRS, RSV, LXX, cf. 아가페, 현대인, 공동), (2) "지존자의… 그늘 아래에 사는 자여, 나는 여호와를 향하여 말하기를…"(개역개정, 새번역, NIV, ESV, TNK).

문맥을 고려하면 하나님의 보호 아래 있는 자가 하는 말이 맞다: "지존자의 은밀한 곳에… 그늘 아래에 사는 자는 여호와를 향하여 말하기를…"(cf. deClaissé-Walford et al., Schaefer, Tate). 이처럼 특정한 개인과 상관없는 3인칭 단수('누구든')로 노래를 시작하는 것이 지혜시의 특징이다(cf. 시 1편). 또한 합리적인 선택을 하라는 권면이기도 하다. 저자는 누구든 하나님을 의존하여 사는 사람은 이렇게 고백하도록 유도하고 있다.

기자가 1절에서 사용하는 '은밀한 곳'(סֵתֶר)과 '그늘'(צֵל)은 어미 새가 날개 아래에 새끼 새들을 두고 보호하는 이미지를 구성한다(Terrien, VanGemeren, cf. 3절). 고대 근동에서 어미 새가 새끼들을 보호하는 이미지는 왕이 백성들을 보살피는 이미지로 널리 사용되었다(Luke). 세상 왕들도 자기 백성을 어미 새가 새끼들을 보호하는 것처럼 하는데, 하물며 하나님은 얼마나 더 확실하게 자기 백성을 보호하시겠는가!

성경에서 '지존자'(עֶלְיוֹן)(1절)는 주님의 절대성을 강조하는 표현으로, 하나님이 다른 신들과 비교할 수 없음을 서술하기 위해 자주 사용된다. '전능자'(שַׁדַּי)는 하나님의 무한한 능력을 강조하는 성호다. 기자는 여호와가 세상 사람들이 신으로 믿는 것들과 완전히 다르다고 말하며 차별화(otherness)를 강조하기 위해 이 두 성호를 사용한다. 지존자이자 전능자이신 여호와는 자기 백성을 원수들의 눈에 띄지 않게 은밀한 곳에 숨기시고, 그들의 모든 공격에서 보호하신다. 그러므로 일부 주석가들은 이 시편이 위기에 처한 사람이 성전으로 도피하며 부른 노래라고 하지만, 굳이 그렇게 해석할 필요는 없다. 우리가 기도하고 찬양하며 예배를 드리는 일 자체가 하나님의 은밀한 곳에 숨어 세상의 모든 공격에서 보호받기를 원하는 것으로 해석될 수 있기 때문이다(cf. Terrien).

한 가지 인상적인 것은 이 시편이 그다지 긴 노래는 아닌데, 다양한 하나님의 성호를 골고루 사용하고 있다는 점이다: '지존자'(עֶלְיוֹן), '전능자'(שַׁדַּי), '여호와'(יהוה), '하나님'(אֱלוֹהַּ). 이 외에도 하나님을 '피난처'(מַחְסֶה)라고 하고 '요새'(מְצוּדָה)라고 하기도 한다. 기자는 이처럼 다양한 언어로 하나님의 능력과 속성을 묘사함으로써 하나님은 전지전능한 분이시고 하나님께 피하는 사람은 참으로 복이 있기에 주님을 의지해야 한다고 권면한다.

하나님의 보호를 받는 사람이 주님의 인자하심에 감격하여 여호와를 향해 "주는 나의 피난처요, 나의 요새요, 내가 의뢰하는 하나님"(2절, cf. 시 18:1–2)이라고 찬송함은 당연하다. 기자가 2절에서 하나님에 대해 세 가지로 말하고 있는 것들 중 '피난처'(מַחְסֶה)와 '요새'(מְצוּדָה)는 1절에서 '지존자'(עֶלְיוֹן)가 하시는 일과 같다. 지존자이신 하나님은 자신에게 피하는 자를 은밀한 곳에 숨기시고 피난처와 요새가 되어 주신다. 원수들의 공격으로 인해 절대 해를 당하지 않게 하실 것이다. 항상 주변 국가들의 군사적 위협에 시달렸던 고대 근동 정서에서 하나님이 완벽한 피난처와 요새가 되어 주심은 참으로 대단한 축복이다(Goldingay).

세 가지 중 마지막인 '내가 의뢰하는 하나님'(אֱלֹהַי אֶבְטַח־בּוֹ)은 1절의 '전능자'(שַׁדַּי)와 연관이 있는 표현이다. 여호와는 전능하신 하나님이시기 때문에 그를 의뢰하는 자들은 모두 만족할 것이다. 그러므로 여호와를 의뢰하는 사람은 복이 있다. 주님이 그를 보호하시고 인도하실 것이기 때문이다.

2. 원수들에게서 보호하심(91:3–8)

3 이는 그가 너를 새 사냥꾼의 올무에서와
심한 전염병에서 건지실 것임이로다
4 그가 너를 그의 깃으로 덮으시리니
네가 그의 날개 아래에 피하리로다
그의 진실함은 방패와 손방패가 되시나니
5 너는 밤에 찾아오는 공포와
낮에 날아드는 화살과
6 어두울 때 퍼지는 전염병과
밝을 때 닥쳐오는 재앙을 두려워하지 아니하리로다
7 천 명이 네 왼쪽에서,

만 명이 네 오른쪽에서 엎드러지나
이 재앙이 네게 가까이 하지 못하리로다
8 오직 너는 똑똑히 보리니
악인들의 보응을 네가 보리로다

기자는 1-2절에서 하나님은 자기 백성을 철통같이 보호하신다고 했는데, 우리는 주님께 어떤 보호를 기대할 수 있는가? 그는 하나님을 지목하는 3인칭 대명사(הוּא, 3절)를 강조형으로 사용하여 하나님이 반드시 자기 백성을 보호하실 것을 확신한다. 그는 네 가지 이미지를 활용하여 철두철미하게 보호하시는 하나님을 묘사한다. 하나님은 온갖 위험에서 우리를 보호하신다는 뜻이다(Broyles, cf. Grogan).

첫째, 하나님은 원수들이 우리를 잡으려고 놓은 올무에서 우리를 건지실 것이다(3a절). 사냥꾼이 올무를 놓는 것은 꼭 새를 잡겠다는 의지의 표현이다. 그러므로 이 비유는 하나님이 의도적이고 악의적인 원수들의 공격에서 자신에게 피하는 자들을 구원하시겠다는 선언이다.

둘째, 하나님은 심판 전염병에서 우리를 건지실 것이다(3b절). '심한 전염병'(דֶּבֶר הַוּוֹת)의 문자적인 의미는 '파괴의 가시'다(cf. HALOT). 그래서 칠십인역(LXX)은 이 문구를 병으로 제한하지 않고 우리를 괴롭게 하는 '모든 문제로부터'(ἀπὸ λόγου ταραχώδους)로 번역한다. 그러나 '사냥꾼의 올무'에 우리가 일상에서 당면할 수 있는 모든 문제를 포함하고 있기 때문에 질병으로 해석하는 것이 바람직하다. 하나님은 사람들이 줄 수 있는 온갖 환난과 질병으로 인한 고난에서 자기 백성을 지키시는 분이다.

셋째, 하나님은 온갖 고난과 악에서 구하신 우리를 보호하신다(4a-b절). 앞선 두 이미지는 하나님이 곤경에 처한 주의 백성을 구원하시는(빼내시는) 상황을 묘사한 것에 반해, 이 이미지는 구원하신 자들을 어떻게 보호하고 보존하시는가에 관한 것이다. 일부 학자들은 주님의 날개가 법궤의 뚜껑인 시은좌(施恩座, mercy seat)를 형성하고 있는 천사들의 날개라 하지만(cf. Kraus), 어미 새가 새끼 새를 보호하는 것이 이 말씀의 배경이 되고 있다(cf. 1절). 하나님은 원수들의 손에서 구원하신 이들을 마치 어미 새가 자기 날개 아래 새끼 새들을 지키듯 보호하실 것이다. 새 이미지가 계속되고 있다. 우리는 사냥꾼들이 잡으려는 연약한 새와 같은데, 하나님은 우리를 보호하시는 '어미 새'가 되어 우리를 품으신다. 그러므로 전능자의 날개 아래 머무는 사람은 복이 있다(cf. 룻 2:12; 시 17:8; 36:7; 57:1). 원수들의 온갖 공격에서 보호를 받을 것이기 때문이다.

넷째, 하나님은 우리의 방패와 손방패가 되시어 자연재해와 적들의 모든 공격에서 우리를 보호하실 것이다(4c-7절). '방패'(צִנָּה)는 온 몸을 가리는 큰 방패이다. '손방패'(סֹחֵרָה)는 30-40cm에 달하는 작은 방패를 의미하기도 하지만(ESV, NRS, RSV), 갑옷을 뜻할 수도 있고(새번역, 아가페, 공동), 심지어는 성벽을 뜻할 수도 있다(NIV). 중요한 것은 모두 방어하는 기구라는 사실이다. 하나님은 가장 든든한 방어막이 되시어 적들의 공격과 자연재해에서 우리를 철저하게 보호하신다.

하나님이 우리를 보호하시는 범위는 어느 정도인가? 하나님은 자연재해뿐만 아니라 적들의 심리적인 압박과 물리적인 공격에서 우리를 보호하신다(5절). 그러므로 우리는 밤이면 원수들이 조성하는 어떠한 심리적인 압박 혹은 '공포감'(מִפַּחַד)을 두려워할 필요가 없다. 하나님이 우리에게 평안한 마음을 주시어 보호하실 것이기 때문이다. 낮에 날아드는 적들의 화살을 두려워할 필요가 없다. 방패가 되시는 하나님이 우리를 적들의 공격에서 철저하게 보호하실 것이기 때문이다. 이처럼 하나님은 밤낮으로 우리를 보호하신다.

또한 하나님은 우리를 온갖 질병과 재앙에서 보호하신다(6절). 이번에도 기자는 어두움과 빛(밤과 낮) 이미지를 사용하여 말을 이어가고 있다. 어두울 때 퍼지는 전염병과 밝을 때 닥쳐오는 재앙에서도 우리를 보호하신다. 그러므로 우리는 모든 질병과 자연재해를 두려워할 필요가 없다.

하나님이 우리와 함께하시며 보호하시기 때문에 아무리 무서운 병이 우리를 위협해도 염려할 필요가 없다(7절). 일부 주석가들은 이 말씀이 치열한 전쟁터 이미지를 사용하고 있다고 하지만(Terrien), 문맥은 혹독한 전염병이 돌고 있는 상황을 의미한다. 설령 우리 옆에서 백 명이, 혹은 천 명이 전염병으로 쓰러진다 해도 염려할 필요가 없다. 하나님이 우리를 그 질병에서 보호하실 것이기 때문이다. 치료하시는 하나님, 곧 '여호와 라파'(יְהוָה רָפָא)의 의미를 떠올리게 하는 말씀이다.

하나님은 우리를 공격해오는 원수들도 응징하실 것이다(8절). 원수들은 자연재해 등을 통해 우연히 벌을 받는 것이 아니라, 하나님이 그들을 직접 응징하신다. 그것도 우리가 보는 앞에서! 그들이 벌을 받는 동안, 하나님은 우리를 위하여 잔칫상도 차려 주실 것이다(cf. 시 23:5). 그러므로 그들은 다시는 우리를 공격해 오지 못할 뿐만 아니라 하나님이 우리를 지키는 분이심을 깨닫고 더 이상 우리를 괴롭히지 않을 것이다.

3. 천사들을 통해 보호하심(91:9-13)

9 네가 말하기를
여호와는 나의 피난처시라 하고
지존자를 너의 거처로 삼았으므로
10 화가 네게 미치지 못하며
재앙이 네 장막에 가까이 오지 못하리니
11 그가 너를 위하여 그의 천사들을 명령하사
네 모든 길에서 너를 지키게 하심이라
12 그들이 그들의 손으로 너를 붙들어
발이 돌에 부딪히지 아니하게 하리로다

[13] 네가 사자와 독사를 밟으며
젊은 사자와 뱀을 발로 누르리로다

9절은 정확하게 번역하기가 쉽지 않다(cf. NIV, ESV, TNK). 그러나 의미는 분명하다(Tucker & Grant). 누구든 여호와를 자기 피난처라 하고 지존자를 거처로 삼은 사람들은 화를 당하지 않을 것이라는 뜻이다. 기자는 이미 '지존자'(עֶלְיוֹן)를 1절에서, '피난처'(מַחְסֶה)를 2절에서 하나님의 호칭으로 사용한적이 있다. 지존자는 하나님이 다른 신들과 전혀 다르다는 것(otherness)을 강조하는 성호이다. 우리의 피난처가 되시는 주님은 때와 장소를 초월하여 세상의 모든 고통과 환난에서 우리를 보호하시므로 곤경에 빠진 성도들이 피하곤 했던 성전보다 더 위대하시다(Schaefer).

그러므로 주님께 피하는 사람들에게는 화가 미치지 못하며, 재앙이 그들의 삶의 터전을 덮치지 못한다(10절). 10절의 이 두 부정사(미치지 못하며, 오지 못하리니)는 11절에서 두 긍정사(천사들을 명령하사, 지키게 하심이라)와 쌍을 이룬다(VanGemeren). 하나님의 보호에는 악이 우리를 해하지 못하도록 하는 방어도 있지만, 우리를 위해 일부러 하시는 것도 있다는 뜻이다.

하나님은 천사들을 보내 우리를 지키도록 하신다(11절). 하나님이 보내신 천사들은 우리가 가는 모든 길에서 우리를 어떠한 해도 당하지 않도록 철저하고 완벽하게 지킨다. 기자가 사용하는 이미지는 천사들이 우리를 그들의 손 위에 올려 놓고 보호하는 모습이다. 천사들이 우리를 그들의 손에 올려 놓고 보호하니, 우리의 발이 돌에 부딪힐 일이 없다(12절).

천사의 보호 아래 우리는 발을 상할 일이 없을 뿐만 아니라, 예전에 우리를 괴롭혔던 것들을 오히려 짓밟게 될 것이다(13절). 사자와 독사는 우리가 접하는 모든 위험과 위기를 상징한다(Anderson). 예전에는 사자와 독사를 두려워하고 피하며 도망 다녔다. 그러나 이것들을 오히려 밟아줄 때가 오고 있다. '밟고'(דרך), '누르는'(רמס) 것은 군사적인 승리를 상징한다(Hossfeld-Zenger). 우리를 괴롭게 하는 모든 사람들에게 보복할 날이 오고 있다는 뜻이다. 그날이 오면 우리는 생존자가 아니라 승자가 될 것이다(Kidner). 우리가 원수들을 짓밟을 날을 소망할 수 있는 것도 하나님이 우리에게 베풀어 주시는 은혜이다.

4. 하나님이 보호하심(91:14-16)

14 하나님이 이르시되
그가 나를 사랑한 즉 내가 그를 건지리라
그가 내 이름을 안즉 내가 그를 높이리라
15 그가 내게 간구하리니 내가 그에게 응답하리라
그들이 환난 당할 때에 내가 그와 함께 하여
그를 건지고 영화롭게 하리라
16 내가 그를 장수하게 함으로 그를 만족하게 하며
나의 구원을 그에게 보이리라 하시도다

이때까지 기자는 자신의 바람과 기도를 통해 하나님이 자기 백성을 철저하게 보호하시는 분이라고 선언했다. 이 섹션은 하나님이 백성을 보호하심에 대해 직접 하신 말씀을 회고하는 것으로 마무리한다. 하나님이 우리에게 마지막 말씀을 하시는 것은 우리의 소망과 확신의 근거가 된다(Brueggemann, Mays). 더 넓은 의미에서 시편 88편에서 시작된 하나님의 침묵이 드디어 이 섹션을 통해 마무리되고 있다(deClaissé-Walford et al.). 그렇기 때문에 이 말씀은 여러 면에서 가장 위대한 부분이라 할 수 있다(Gerstenberger).

하나님은 앞 섹션에서 보호를 구하며 기도한 백성들에게 응답하실 뿐만 아니라, 그들이 구하지 않은 것까지 복으로 주실 것을 약속하신다. 본문은 하나님이 간구하는 자기 백성에게 내리시는 축복을 다섯 가지로 언급한다.

첫째, 하나님은 기도하며 도움을 구하는 자기 백성을 원수들과 온갖 환난에서 건지실 것이다(14b절). 하나님이 그들을 건지시는 이유는 분명하다. 그들이 하나님을 사랑하기 때문이다. '사랑하다'(חשׁק)는 간절히 찾고 바란다는 뜻이다(VanGemeren, cf. HALOT, 신 7:7-8). 하나님은 주님을 사모하고 간절히 바라는 자기 백성을 반드시 돌보신다.

둘째, 하나님은 위기에서 구원한 백성을 존귀하게 여기시어 그들을 높이신다(14c절). 원수들의 손이 미치지 못하도록, 또한 온 세상으로 하여금 주님이 자기 백성을 어떻게 대하시는가를 보도록 하기 위해 그들을 높이신다. 그들을 미워하고 괴롭게 하던 원수들은 참으로 닭 쫓던 개가 지붕 쳐다보는 격이 될 것이다. 하나님이 자기 백성에게 이런 은혜를 베푸시는 것은 그들이 하나님의 이름을 알기 때문이다. 백성들이 주님의 이름을 존귀하게 여기는 것처럼, 하나님도 그들을 존귀하게 대하신다.

셋째, 하나님은 자기 백성의 기도에 응답하신다(15a절). 하나님은 무엇이든 자기 자녀가 구하는 것을 주신다. 그렇다고 해서 주님의 자녀가 마음대로 구하지는 않을 것이다. 주님의 자녀는 하나님이 응답하기를 기뻐하시는 것들을 사모하고 구하기 때문이다.

넷째, 하나님은 자기 백성이 환난을 당할 때 그들과 함께 하셔서, 그들을 건지시고 영화롭게 하실 것이다(15b-c절). 이는 성도들이 환난에서 면제되리라고 말하는 것은 아니다. 이 땅에 살면서 성도들도 때로는 세상 사람들처럼 환난을 당할 것이다. 그러나 그들은 세상 사람들과 분명히 다르다. 세상 사람들은 어떠한 소망도 없이 환난을 당하지만, 주의 백성은 그렇지 않다. 하나님의 개입과 구원을 소망할 수 있기 때문이다. 주님은 그들의 기대를 저버리지 않으실 것이다. 뿐만 아니라 하나님은 구원한 그들을 영화롭게 하신다. 세상 사람들의 부러움을 사게 하신다는 뜻이다.

다섯째, 하나님은 그들이 이 땅에서 장수할 수 있도록 하셔서 그들을 만족하게 하신다(16절). 기자는 바로 앞 시편에서 하나님께 주의 백성을 만족시켜 주시고 즐거워할 수 있도록 해 달라고 기도했는데(90:14-15), 드디어 하나님이 그들을 만족시키고 즐거워할 수 있도록 해 주신다. 하나님은 자기 백성의 기도를 하나도 놓치지 않으시고 모두 들어주셨다.

기자는 이 섹션에서 이때까지 그가 언급한 다섯 가지가 모두 합하여 '하나님이 구원을 자기 백성에게 보이시는 것'이라며 노래를 마무리 한다(16b절). 한 주석가는 '보다'(ראה)를 '만족하게 하다'로 번역해야 한다고 한다(Anderson). 이렇게 번역하면 16절을 구성하는 두 행이 좋은 평행을 이룬다. 그러나 이 동사가 이런 의미로 사용되는 예가 없으므로 '보다'를 유지하는 것이 바람직하다. 하나님의 구원은 참으로 자상하고 세세하여 주의 백성의 필요를 모두 채우는 놀라운 은혜이다. 주님은 오늘도 이 같은 구원을 우리에게 베푸신다.

제92편

안식일 찬송시

I. 장르/양식: 개인 찬양시(cf. 11편)

개인 찬양시인 이 노래의 내용은 감사시(thanksgiving psalm)(Brueggemann & Bellinger, Westermann)와 찬양을 통해 하나님의 의로운 다스림을 고백하는 지혜시(wisdom psalm)의 성격도 지녔다(Goldingay). 또한 시편의 배경이 되고 있는 상황이 거의 비슷하고, 도달하는 결론이 비슷하기 때문에 73편과 같이 읽어야 한다는 주장도 있다(Tucker & Grant).

저작한 사람이 왕 혹은 높은 관료였을 가능성이 있다 하여(cf. Goldingay, Tate) 히스기야 왕 혹은 요시야 왕 시대(주전 8-7세기)에 저작된 것이라는 추측이 있다(Terrien). 포로기 혹은 그 이후 시대에 저작된 것이라는 주장도 있다(Anderson). 그러나 대부분 학자들은 저작 시기와 정황에 대해 이렇다 할 언급을 하지 않는다. 노래가 정황을 논하는 일에 필요한 구체적인 정보를 제공하고 있지 않기 때문이다.

표제는 안식일을 언급하는데, 시편들 중 안식일과 연관된 표제를 지닌 것은 이 노래가 유일하다. 칠십인역(LXX)은 이 시편 외에도 24, 48, 81, 82, 93, 94편에 안식일 찬송시라는 표제를 붙인다(cf. Broyles, Tate). 또한 칠십인역은 다윗이 지은 시라는 말도 더하고 있다. 그러나 이 시편의 내용은 안식일과 별 관계는 없어 보인다(cf. deClaissé-Walford et al.). 그럼에도 불구하고 표제가 안식일을 언급하는 것은 이 시편이 한때는 안식일 예배에 사용되었을 가능성을 암시한다. 한 주석가는 이 시편이 장막절을 시작하는 안식일에 사용된 것이라고 한다(Wilcock). 실제로 랍비 문헌에는 이 노래가 안식일에 매일 드리는 제물을 드린 후에 불렸다는 기록이 남아 있다(McCann, Sarna).

편집자들이 이 시편에 안식일과 연관된 표제를 준 것은 이 시가 영원하고 종말론적인 안식을 노래한다고 생각했기 때문이라는 추측이 있다(Hossfeld-Zenger). 혹은 장차 오실 메시아를 기대하며 안식일에 부른 노래이기 때문이라는 견해도 있다(Terrien). 장차 오실 주님이 안식일의 주인이심은 맞지만(마 12:8), 이 노래가 메시아와 직접적인 연관이 있어 보이지는 않는다.

II. 구조

이 시편이 90, 91편과 유기적인 관계를 유지하고 있다고 주장하는 한 주석가는 다음과 같이 이 세 편의 구조를 제시했다(VanGemeren). 흥미로운 관찰이며 충분히 가능해 보인다.

A. 찬양(90:1-2)
  B. 탄식(90:3-17)
    C. 지혜시(91:1-13)
    C. 신탁(91:14-16)
A. 찬양(92:1-3)
  B. 감사(92:4-15)

주석가들은 92편에 대해 교차대구법적 구조를 제시하지만, 세부적으로는 다양한 각기 다른 구조를 제시한다(cf. Alden, Terrien, VanGemeren).

데이빗슨(Davidson)은 이 시편을 다음과 같이 분석한다. 이러한 구조를 바탕으로 테이트(Tate)는 이 시의 정점은 8절이라고 한다.

A. 1–3절
B. 4–6절
C. 7절
D. 8절
C′. 9절
B′. 10–11절
A′. 12–15절

일부 학자들은 이 노래를 1–5절, 6–11절, 12–15절 세 파트로 구분하지만(Tucker & Grant), 대부분 학자들은 찬양(1–3절)과 찬양 이유(4–15절) 두 파트로 구분한다(Gerstenberger, Hossfeld–Zenger, Tate, VanGemeren). 이 주석에서는 다음과 같은 구조를 바탕으로 본문을 주해해 나가고자 한다.

A. 성실하신 여호와를 찬양(92:1–3)
B. 주님이 악인들을 벌하심(92:4–7)
C. 영광 받으실 여호와(92:8)
B′. 주님이 악인들을 벌하심(92:9–11)
A′. 의로우신 여호와를 찬양(92:12–15)

III. 주해

이 땅에서 의롭게 살려고 노력하는 사람들이 가장 허탈해하는 것들 중 하나는 악인들의 번성이다. 기자는 때가 되면 하나님이 반드시 악인들을 망하게 하실 것이라며 의인들에게 낙심하지 말 것을 권면한다. 또한 그날이 되면 하나님은 분명 의인들을 번성케 하실 것이다. 주님은 세상을 다스리시는 의로운 통치자이기 때문이다.

1. 성실하신 여호와를 찬양(92:1-3)

[1] 지존자여
십현금과 비파와 수금으로 여호와께 감사하며
[2] 주의 이름을 찬양하고
아침마다 주의 인자하심을 알리며
[3] 밤마다 주의 성실하심을 베풂이 좋으니이다

이 섹션의 절(節) 순서가 상당히 혼란스럽다. 마소라 사본, 영어 번역본들, 한국어 번역본들이 각기 다르다. 마소라 사본을 따르자면 개역개정의 1절은 4절이며, 개역개정의 2절은 마소라 사본에서는 3절이다. 개역개정의 3절은 마소라 사본의 3절에 포함되어 있다. 영어 번역본들도 제 각각이다. 이 주석에서는 개역개정의 순서에 따라 본문을 살펴보고자 한다.

기자는 여호와가 다른 신들과는 질적으로 다르다는 사실을 강조하는 성호인 '지존자'(עֶלְיוֹן)(cf. 시 91:1)를 부르며 노래를 시작한다. 그는 주님이 그에게 베풀어 주신 은혜를 생각하며 세 가지를 하는 것이 좋다고 생각한다. 이 정황에서 '좋다'(טוֹב)는 즐겁고 기쁘다는 뜻이다. 저자는 무슨 일을 기쁘고 즐겁다고 하는가?

첫째, 그는 하나님께 감사하기를 원한다(1b절). 그가 하고자 하는 일이 세 가지인 것처럼 십현금과 비파와 수금 세 가지 악기를 동원하여 하나님께 감사를 드리고자 한다. 이 악기들은 성전에서 레위 사람들로 구성된 찬양대가 주님을 찬양하며 사용하던 것들이다(VanGemeren, cf. Hossfeld-Zenger). 기자는 자신이 이 노래를 성전에서 부르고 있음을 암시한다(cf. 13절). 하나님의 은혜를 경험한 사람으로서 주님께 감사하는 것은 기쁘고 즐거운 일이다.

둘째, 그는 주님의 이름을 찬양하고자 한다(2a절). 하나님이 베푸신 큰 은혜를 기념하고자 하는 기자는 주님의 이름을 찬양할 것이다. 이름은 그 이름을 지닌 이의 인격과 존재를 모두 상징하기 때문에 주님의 이름을 찬양하는 것은 주님의 모든 것(전인적인 것)에 경의를 표하며 기뻐하는 일이다. 하나님이 하신 일과 하나님의 성호는 서로 떼어 놓을 수 없는 관계이다(Hossfeld-Zenger).

셋째, 그는 하루 종일 주님의 인자하심과 성실하심을 온 세상에 알리고자 한다(2b-3절). 개역개정의 번역이 다소 애매하지만, 본문의 의미는 확실하다. 기자는 아침이면 주의 인자하심을 묵상하며 사람들에게 알리고, 밤이면 주의 성실하심을 기념하며 사람들에게 알리기를 즐거워한다(cf. 새번역, 아가페, 현대인, 공동, NIV, NAS). 아침과 밤이 언급되는 것은 이 노래가 성전에서 아침과 저녁마다 드린 제물과 연관되어 있음을 의미할 수 있다(Broyles).

'인자하심'(חֶסֶד)은 하나님이 자기 백성을 대하시는 자세(많은 은혜를 베푸심), '성실하심'(אֱמוּנָה)은 이 자세의 지속성(꾸준하심)을 강조한다(cf. HALOT). 이스라엘은 출애굽 이후로 하나님의 인자하심과 성실하심을 꾸준히 경험하며 살아왔다(Tucker & Grant, cf. 출 34:6). 하나님은 자기 백성에게 큰 은혜를 끊임없이 베푸신다. 우리는 주님의 은혜가 끊임없는 것처럼 우리가 경험한 하나님의 은혜를 끊임없이 기념하며 다른 이들에게 알려야 한다.

2. 주님이 악인들을 벌하심(92:4-7)

4 여호와여
주께서 행하신 일로 나를 기쁘게 하셨으니
주의 손이 행하신 일로 말미암아 내가 높이 외치리이다

5 여호와여
주께서 행하신 일이 어찌 그리 크신지요
주의 생각이 매우 깊으시니이다
6 어리석은 자도 알지 못하며
무지한 자도 이를 깨닫지 못하나이다
7 악인들은 풀 같이 자라고
악을 행하는 자들은 다 흥왕할지라도
영원히 멸망하리이다

기자는 앞 섹션에서 하나님이 베푸신 은혜를 기념하며 찬양하겠다고 했지만, 구체적으로 하나님이 하신 일이 무엇인지에 관해서는 말하지 않았다. 이 섹션에서는 하나님이 하신 일의 한 예가 흥왕하던 악인들이 멸망하도록 하신 일이라 한다(7절). 그들은 '풀 같이' 왕성하게 자라지만, 하나님은 그들을 '바람에 흩날리는 겨'처럼 취급하실 것이다(시 1:4).

저자는 하나님이 하신 일로 인해 그를 기쁘게 하셨다며 이 섹션을 시작한다(4b절). 성경에서 주께서 행하신 '일'(פֹּעַל)은 백성을 구원하신 위대한 사역을 의미한다(McCann, cf. 신 32:4; 시 44:1; 90:16; 95:2). 주의 손이 행하신 '일들'(מַעֲשִׂים)은 주님의 구원과 창조 사역을 뜻한다(cf. 수 24:31; 삿 2:7, 10; 시 8:3; 19:1; 33:4; 103:22). 그러므로 이 두 개념은 하나님의 구원과 창조 사역을 가장 포괄적으로 묘사한다(deClaissé-Walford et al.). 이 노래의 표제가 안식일과 연관된 것은 아마도 이런 이유에서 일 것이다. 안식일은 우리를 구원하신 창조주 하나님을 기념하는 날이기 때문이다.

일부 번역본들은 기자가 하나님이 하신 일을 보고 기뻐하는 것으로 번역했지만(새번역, 아가페, 현대인, 공동), 마소라 사본이 표현하고자 하는 의미는 하나님이 그를 기쁘게 하셨다는 뜻이다(개역개정, NIV,

ESV, NRS, TNK). 하나님이 행하신 일을 통해 그를 만족시키셨다(cf. 시 90:14-16). 그러므로 감격한 기자는 주님의 손이 이루신 일에 대해 목소리를 높여 외치기를 원한다(4c절). 본문에서 '외치다'(רנן)는 앞으로도 계속 그렇게 할 것이라는 반복적인 의미를 함축하고 있다(Goldingay).

기자는 생각할수록 하나님이 하신 일의 놀라움에 감탄한다(5절). 그러므로 그는 이런 일을 행하신 주님은 참으로 생각이 깊으신 분이라며 찬양한다. 그가 경험한 하나님의 놀라우신 일이 무엇인지 우리는 알 수 없다. 아마도 그는 하나님이 하시는 모든 일이 놀랍다며 이렇게 말하는 듯하다.

세상 모든 사람이 하나님이 행하신 놀라운 일을 보고 깨닫고 감탄하는 것은 아니다. 어떤 사람들은 주님이 하시는 일에 대하여 전혀 알지도, 깨닫지도 못한다(6절). 그들은 전능자께서 모든 악을 멸하실 것을 의식하지 못한다는 뜻이다(Anderson). 기자는 이런 사람을 어리석은 자, 무지한 자라고 한다. 오직 지혜와 분별력이 있는 사람들만이 주님이 하시는 일을 보고 깨달을 수 있다. 그렇다면 이는 지혜로운 사람은 하나님과 그의 사역을 깨닫고 인정하는 사람이며, 어리석은 사람은 하나님을 알지 못하고 그의 사역을 깨닫지 못하는 사람이라고 정의하는 것으로 이해할 수 있다. 하나님을 알고 모르고가 지혜로운 사람과 어리석은 자의 차이가 되는 것이다. 그러므로 우리는 주님이 하시는 일을 보고 깨달을 수 있도록 항상 기도해야 한다.

하나님이 자기 백성을 기쁘게 하고 그들을 만족시키기 위해 하신 일들 중에는 번성하는 악인들을 멸망하게 하신 일이 포함되어 있다(7절). 근동의 여름 햇볕은 얼마나 강한지 아침에 싹튼 식물을 낮에 말리고 태우기도 한다(Goldingay). 본문에서 악인들이 망하기 전에 비교되는 이미지는 한동안 왕성하게 자라는 식물이다. 그들이 풀같이 왕성하게 자라고 흥왕할지라도 순식간에, 영원히 멸망할 것이다. '흥왕하다'(צוץ)는 꽃처럼 피어난다는 뜻이다(HALOT).

악인들이 당장은 성공하고 번성하는 듯하고, 때로는 하나님의 심판과 개입이 더디거나 없는 것 같지만, 하나님은 반드시 그들을 영원히 멸망시키신다(cf. Eaton). 그러므로 악인들이 번성하는 것은 곧 하나님의 심판을 재촉한다(Broyles). 이렇게 하여 하나님은 주님이 다스리시는 세상에서 정의와 공의를 행하셔서 주의 백성들이 이 땅에서 의롭게 살 이유를 재차 확인시켜 주신다.

3. 영광 받으실 여호와(92:8)

8 여호와여
주는 영원토록 지존하시니이다

악인들이 멸망하도록 하는 분은 여호와이시며, 주님은 영원토록 지존하신 분이다. '영원토록 지존하다'(מָרוֹם לְעֹלָם)는 영원히 높임을 받으신다는 뜻이다. 하나님이 자기 백성을 위해 하시는 일은 주님이 얼마나 높고 위대하신가를 잘 보여준다. 그러므로 주님은 영원히 영광을 받기에 합당하시다.

4. 주님이 악인들을 벌하심(92:9-11)

9 여호와여
주의 원수들은 패망하리이다
정녕 주의 원수들은 패망하리니
죄악을 행하는 자들은 다 흩어지리이다
10 그러나 주께서 내 뿔을 들소의 뿔 같이 높이셨으며
내게 신선한 기름을 부으셨나이다

[11] 내 원수들이 보응 받는 것을 내 눈으로 보며
일어나 나를 치는 행악자들이 보응 받는 것을 내 귀로 들었도다

7절은 하나님이 악인들을 멸망시키실 것이라고 선언했는데, 이 섹션은 하나님이 왜 그들을 벌하시는지를 밝힌다. 악인들은 주의 백성을 괴롭히는 적들일 뿐만 아니라 하나님의 원수들이기도 하다(9d절). 그러므로 하나님은 반드시 주님의 원수가 된 자들을 벌하여 망하도록 하실 것이다(9절). 기자는 이러한 사실을 확신하며 원수들이 망할 것을 세 차례나 강조한다: "패망하리이다… 패망하리니… 흩어지리이다."

여호와께서는 원수들은 멸하시지만, 자기 백성들은 높이신다(10절). 이러한 사실을 강조하기 위해 '그러나 당신은'(וְאַתָּה)이 강조형으로 사용되고 있다. 주님은 그들을 들소의 뿔 같이 높이시며 신선한 기름을 부으신다. '들소'로 번역된 단어(רְאֵם)의 의미가 정확하지는 않다(cf. HALOT). 분명히 지금은 멸종했지만 뿔이 있는 짐승들 중 가장 큰 짐승으로서 들소 중 한 종류였을 것이다(Eaton). 이 들소는 강인함의 상징일 뿐만 아니라 뿔을 가장 높이 치켜드는 짐승이다. 하나님이 자기 백성의 뿔(능력)을 참으로 높이셔서 공격해 오는 원수들을 얼마든지 물리칠 수 있도록 하실 것을 의미한다(Hossfeld-Zenger, Kirkpatrick). '신선한 기름'(שֶׁמֶן רַעֲנָן)은 올리브유를 뜻하며(cf. 시 52:8), 사람에게 기름을 부으시는 것은 그들을 매우 존귀하게 여겨 따로 구분하신다는 의미이다(Shaefer, cf. 시 23:5; 104:15). 하나님은 혹독한 세상에서 지칠 대로 지친 자기 백성에게 힘을 주시고 그들의 영혼을 소생시키기 위해 그들의 삶에 개입하신다(Goldingay).

자기 백성을 존귀하게 하신 하나님은 그들이 보는 앞에서 백성들의 원수들을 벌하신다(11절). 하나님과 악은 함께 존재할 수 없기 때문이다(VanGemeren). 백성들은 그들의 원수들이 주님께 벌을 받는 것을 직접 볼 것이며, 그들이 벌을 받아 괴로워하는 소리를 직접 들을 것이다.

때로는 우리가 악이 성행하는 것을 보지만, 우리가 최종적으로 듣게 될 것은 심판을 받은 악의 신음 소리다.

우리는 악들이 번성할수록 그들의 심판의 날도 가까이 오고 있다는 사실을 깨달아야 한다(cf. Schaefer). 그날이 되면 주님은 백성들이 보는 앞에서 그들의 원수들을 벌하여 그들을 위로하고자 하신다. 그날이 되면 주의 백성들과 그들을 괴롭히는 악인들은 대조되는 운명을 맞이할 것이다.

5. 의로우신 여호와를 찬양(92:12-15)

12 의인은 종려나무 같이 번성하며
레바논의 백향목 같이 성장하리로다
13 이는 여호와의 집에 심겼음이여
우리 하나님의 뜰 안에서 번성하리로다
14 그는 늙어도 여전히 결실하며
진액이 풍족하고 빛이 청청하니
15 여호와의 정직하심과
나의 바위 되심과
그에게는 불의가 없음이 선포되리로다

하나님이 악인들을 심판하여 멸하시고 나면 의인들이 번성하는 시대가 열릴 것이다. 기자는 의인들이 잘 될 것을 강조하기 위해 12-13절에서 '번성하다'(פרח)를 두 차례 언급하고 시편 1편을 연상케 하는 이미지들을 사용한다. 그는 앞에서 악인들의 번성을 식물이 자라는 것으로 묘사했다(7절). 저자는 이 섹션에서 의인의 번성도 왕성하게 자라는 식물로 표현한다. 그러나 분명한 차이가 있다. 악인들은 풀과 꽃처럼 잠시 자라다가 한순간에 뽑혀 사라지는 연약한 식물이지만(7절), 의인들은 종려나무와 백향목이다(12절).

종려나무와 백향목은 잡초와 꽃보다 훨씬 더디게 자라는 식물들이다. 그러나 시간이 지나면 잡초나 꽃은 한 해를 견디지 못하고 시들지만, 종려나무와 백향목은 해를 거듭하며 크고 높이 자라는 아름드리 나무들이다. 레바논의 백향목은 삼천 년을 넘게 살면서 종자를 퍼뜨리는 솔방울을 생산하는 것으로 알려져 있다(Hossfeld-Zenger). 그러므로 이 나무들은 힘과 장수와 선망(羨望)의 상징이었다(사 2:13; 65:22; 호 14:5-6; 슥 11:2). 악인들은 잠시 번성하다가 순식간에 사라지지만, 의인들은 오랫동안 지속되는 차원이 다른 번성을 누릴 것이라는 뜻이다.

종려나무와 백향목이 이처럼 번성할 수 있는 것은 이 나무들이 여호와의 집에 심겼기 때문이다(13절, cf. 렘 17:7-8; 시 1:3). 성전은 상징적으로 에덴 동산을 연상케 하는 정원이기도 했다(Hossfeld-Zenger, cf. Brueggemann & Bellinger). 그러므로 주님의 성전에 심어진 모든 것은 하나님의 끊임없는 보살핌을 받으며 자란다. 주의 백성은 항상 주님의 보호 아래 있다는 뜻이다. 그러므로 그들은 하나님의 뜰 안에서 왕성하게 번성할 것이다. 하나님의 보호를 받으며 번성하는 의인들은 늙어도 여전히 왕성한 삶을 살고 많은 열매를 맺을 것이며, 생기로 충만하여 빛을 발할 것이다(14절).

자기 자녀들이 평생 번성할 수 있도록 보호하시고 배려하시는 하나님은 찬양을 받기에 합당한 분이시다. 그러므로 기자는 여호와의 정직하심과 주님이 의지할 바위가 되심과 그에게는 불의가 없으심을 온 세상에 선포하며 살 것을 다짐한다(15절). '선포하다'(נגד)가 2절에서는 '알리다'로 번역되었다. 하나님의 인자하심을 아침마다 온 세상에 알리겠다며 노래를 시작한 기자가 주님의 정직하심과 바위 되심과 불의가 없으심을 온 세상에 알리겠다며 마무리한다.

여호와의 '정직하심'(יָשָׁר)은 일정한 기준에 따라 사람들의 행위를 판단하시는 곧으심을 강조한다(cf. HALOT). 하나님이 악인들을 벌하고 의인들에게 복을 주시는 원리는 모든 사람에게 예외 없이 적용된다는 뜻이다. 하나님이 바위가 되셨다는 것은 주님이 환난(악인들의 공격) 중에 그를 보호하셨음을 상징한다. 기자는 세상을 공평하게 심판하시고, 자기 백성을 적들의 공격에서 보호하시는 하나님에게 '불의'(עַוְלָה)가 없음을 온 세상에 알릴 것이다. 하나님은 모든 악함과 악의와 부정에서 자유하신 분이라는 뜻이다(cf. HALOT). 그러므로 하나님은 우리가 참으로 믿고 의지할 만한 분이시다.

제93편

I. 장르/양식: 회중 찬양시(cf. 29편)

이 노래에는 95편에서처럼 찬양하라는 직접적인 권면은 없지만, 찬양시가 확실하다(Brueggemann & Bellinger, cf. Goldingay). 더 나아가 이 시편은 왕이신 여호와의 세상 통치를 기념하는 모음집(93–100편, 일부 학자들은 94편은 예외로 취급함, cf. McCann)을 시작하는 노래이다(Hossfeld–Zenger, VanGemeren). 거의 모든 학자들은 모빙클(Mowinckel)이 처음으로 이 노래들을 '즉위시'(enthronement psalms)라고 부른 이후 이 장르로 간주한다(deClaissé–Walford et al.).

이 노래들이 어떤 정황에서 어떤 의미로 사용되었는가에 대해서는 아직도 논란이 있다. 모빙클(Mowinckel)은 즉위시들이 가을이면 신년 축제에서 하나님이 왕으로 (재)취임하는 일을 기념하며 사용되었다고 했다. 이러한 주장에 따라 그와 그를 따르는 학자들은 이 노래를 시작하는 히브리어 문구(יְהוָה מָלָךְ)를 "여호와가 왕이 되셨다"(has become king)로 번역했다. 하나님이 가을이면 이스라엘의 왕으로 취임하셨다는 것을 강조하기 위해서였다.

모빙클이 이렇게 주장한 근거는 가나안과 바빌론 종교였다. 주변 국가들의 종교에서 이런 예식이 있었으니 당연히 이스라엘도 이런 예식을 했을 것이라는 주장이다. 그러나 이스라엘에 실제로 이런 예식이 있었는가에 대해 대부분 학자들은 의문을 제기한다(Kitchen, cf. Tate). 이스라엘이 이런 예식을 정기적으로 행한 것을 뒷받침할 만한 어떠한 증거도 없기 때문이다. 심지어는 즉위시의 타당성을 인정하는 사람들도 이런 예식은 없었던 것으로 결론을 내린다(cf. deClaissé-Walford et al., Hossfeld-Zenger, McCann, Ollenburger).

그러므로 오늘날에는 대부분의 학자들이 논쟁의 핵심에 서 있는 히브리어 문구(יְהוָה מָלָךְ)를 "여호와가 왕이시다/다스리신다"("has always been king" 혹은 "Yahweh reigns")라는 말로 번역을 한다(cf. Kraus). 모빙클이 주장하는 것처럼 하나님은 매년 신년 축제에서 왕으로 취임하시는 것이 아니라, 영원히 이스라엘의 왕이셨다는 점을 강조하는 번역이다. 게다가 이 표현이 하나님의 영원한 왕권을 강조하는 것은(cf. Anderson), 시편 제3권이 제기한 위기에 매우 중요하고 적절한 반응이라 할 수 있다(McCann).

모빙클의 주장에 동의하지는 않지만, 이 노래가 절기 때 사용된 것이 맞다고 생각하는 이들은 대안을 제시한다. 크라우스(Kraus)는 여호와의 왕 되심이 아니라, 시온이 하나님의 임재가 임하는 곳으로 선택받은 것과 그곳에서 다윗 계열 왕이 통치하는 것을 기념하는 예식에서 사용되었다고 한다. 바이저(Weiser)는 언약 갱신 예식에서 사용된 노래라고 한다.

이 시편의 저작 연대에 대하여 추측하는 것은 거의 불가능한 일이라는 것이 대부분 사람들의 결론이다(cf. Ross, VanGemeren). 내용을 살펴보면 이렇다 할 단서가 없기 때문이다. 그럼에도 불구하고 이 노래가 주전 12-10세기에 저작된 것이라 하기도 하고(Howard), 내용의 일부가 가나안 신화와 연관되었다며 주전 10세기에 저작된 것이라는 견해도 있다(Dahood). 정확한 저작 시기를 알 수는 없지만, 여호와께서 세상을 다스리신다는 이 노래는 바빌론 포로 생활이 끝날 무렵 매우 특별한 의미를 지니고 불렸을 것이다(Brueggemann & Bellinger, McCann, Ross). 하나님이 세상을 통치하시기 때문에 바빌론에 끌려와 있는 그들에게 드디어 자유를 주어 조국으로 돌아갈 수 있게 하셨다는 생각에서이다.

마소라 사본에 의하면 이 시편에는 표제가 없다. 그러나 칠십인역(LXX)은 표제에 이 노래가 다윗에 의해 저작되었으며, 이스라엘이 아직 자신들의 땅에 거할 때 안식일 바로 전날에 부르던 노래라는 정보를 제공한다. 이러한 정보가 얼마나 역사적으로 타당성을 지니고 있는지는 알 수 없으며, 언제 삽입되었는지에 대해서도 알려진 바가 없다.

II. 구조

총 다섯 절로 구성된 이 짧은 시편은 다음과 같이 세 섹션으로 구분하여 본문을 주해해 나가고자 한다.

A. 하나님이 왕—창조주이심(93:1-2)
B. 하나님이 무질서를 다스리심(93:3-4)
C. 하나님의 굳건한 통치(93:5)

III. 주해

하나님이 세상을 다스리신다는 사실은 이 노래뿐 아니라 93-100편 모음집의 핵심이며(cf. 93:1; 96:10; 97:1; 99:1) 요약이다(Wilson, Mays). 또한 제3권에서 백성들이 제기한 위기에 대한 하나님의 반응이다(McCann). 여호와께서 아직도 세상을 다스리시기에 기대하는 마음으로 주님이 행하실 일을 기다리라는 뜻이다. 그렇다면 하나님은 무엇을 다스리시는가? 하나님은 세상과 창조하신 세상의 질서를 위협하는 무질서의 상징인 물을 다스리시며, 이스라엘을 다스리신다.

1. 하나님이 왕—창조주이심(93:1-2)

> 1 여호와께서 다스리시니
> 스스로 권위를 입으셨도다
> 여호와께서 능력의 옷을 입으시며
> 띠를 띠셨으므로
> 세계도 견고히 서서 흔들리지 아니하는도다
> 2 주의 보좌는 예로부터 견고히 섰으며
> 주는 영원부터 계셨나이다

기자는 "여호와께서 다스리신다"(יְהוָה מָלָךְ)라는 선언으로 이 노래를 시작한다(1a절). 이 문장은 "여호와께서 왕이시다"로 번역 될 수도 있으며(현대인, NAS, NRS, TNK), 하나님의 절대적이고 아름다운 통치를 강조한다(Kitchen). 구문론적으로 '여호와'가 강조형으로 사용되면서 세상을 다스리는 이는 다른 신들이 아니라 여호와이심을 확실히 한다(VanGemeren). 그러므로 이 문장에는 감탄 기호 '!'가 추가되어야 한다(Kidner).

이미 언급한 것처럼 여호와가 왕이 되신 시점에 대하여 아직도 학자들 사이에 어느 정도의 논쟁이 계속되고 있다. 모빙클(Mowinckel) 등은 가나안과 바빌론 종교를 근거로 매년 가을에 있었던 신년 축제 때 여호와께서 왕으로 취임 혹은 재취임하셨다고 했다(cf. Hossfeld-Zenger, Tate). 그러나 이렇게 간주하기에는 증거가 부족하다는 것이 대부분 학자들의 생각이다(cf. Goldingay, Hossfeld-Zenger, Tucker & Grant, Ross). 그러므로 그들은 여호와의 통치는 세상이 창조되기 전부터 시작되어 영원히 지속되는 것으로 이해한다. 하나님의 다스림에는 시작도 끝도 없으며, 영원하다는 것이다.

왕이신 여호와께서는 온 세상을 다스리는 분에게 걸맞은 의복을 입으셨다(1b-d절). 이 말씀은 하나님이 하시는 모든 일과 연관된 영광을 묘사하는 시적인 표현이다(VanGemeren). 기자는 주님이 입으신 복장에 대해 세 가지를 지적한다.

첫째, 권위를 입으셨다(1b절). '권위'(גֵּאוּת)는 '걸출함/빛남'(illustriousness)을 의미한다(cf. HALOT). 하나님이 온 세상을 다스리는 절대권자에게 어울리는 복장을 입으셨다는 뜻이다. 기자가 이처럼 올바른 의복을 강조하는 것은 고대 근동에서 의복이 입고 있는 사람의 신분을 상징했기 때문이다(cf. Anderson). 그러므로 옷은 곧 입은 사람의 능력을 과시하는 것으로 이해할 수 있다(Broyles).

둘째, 능력의 옷을 입으셨다(1c절). 1절에서 '입으셨다'(לָבֵשׁ)가 두 차례 연거푸 반복되어(לָבֵשׁ לָבֵשׁ) 번역에 어려움을 더한다. 번역본들은 두 번째 동사를 "주님이 입으셨다"라는 독립적인 의미를 지닌 문장으로 번역하거나(ESV, NAS, NRS, RSV, TNK), 개역개정처럼 '입으셨다'를 두 차례 반복하면서 권위/능력 혹은 띠를 입으신 것과 연결하여 번역한다(공동, 아가페, NIV). 어느 쪽으로 해석하든 간에 하나님이 온 세상을 다스리는 왕에 걸맞는 의복을 갖춰 입으셨다는 뜻이다.

셋째, 하나님은 띠도 띠셨다(1d절). 띠는 허리를 동여매는 것으로 의복의 가장 마지막 구성 요소(piece)다. 이는 의복 착용을 완성하는 패션 아이템이면서 동시에 신분을 나타내는 역할도 담당한다. 또한 착용자가 편안하게 움직일 수 있도록 돕는 실용성도 가지고 있다. 성경에서 띠는 전쟁에 임하는 자의 준비된 모습을 묘사하기 위해 사용되기도 한다(Anderson, Hossfeld-Zenger, McCann). 하나님은 신적인 전사로서 보좌에 앉아 계셨던 것이다(cf. Longman).

권위와 능력의 옷을 입으신 하나님이 세상을 다스리시니 세상은 흔들림 없이 견고하고 평안하다(1e절). 하나님은 영원히 왕이셨지만, 그 왕권은 창조된 세상을 통해 표현되었다. 그러므로 하나님의 왕권과 창조된 세상은 떼어놓을 수 없는 관계를 유지하고 있다(Mays). 또한 하나님을 대적하거나 주님의 통치를 방해할 만한 자는 없다. 세상 모든 권세가 하나님의 통치에 복종한다. 그러므로 주님이 다스리시는 세상이 흔들림 없이 견고하다는 것은 곧 하나님의 통치가 견고하다는 뜻이다.

하나님의 절대적인 왕권은 태초부터 시작된 일이다(2절). 이는 여호와께서 세상을 자신의 계획과 의지에 따라 통치하기에 적합하도록 창조하셨다는 사실을 암시한다. 고대 근동 신화들이 세상은 신들의 갈등과 우연으로 창조되었다고 주장하는 것과 강력한 대조를 이룬다.

왕이신 하나님이 앉으시는 보좌는 예로부터 견고하게 세워져 있었고, 주님은 영원에서부터 계셨다. '예로부터'(מֵאָז)와 '영원부터'(מֵעוֹלָם)는 사람이 도저히 가늠할 수 없는 아득한 옛날을 뜻한다. 하나님은 우리가 의식할 수 있는 가장 오래된 때보다도 더 일찍부터 세상을 다스리는 왕이셨다.

2. 하나님이 무질서를 다스리심(93:3-4)

3 여호와여
큰 물이 소리를 높였고
큰 물이 그 소리를 높였으니
큰 물이 그 물결을 높이나이다
4 높이 계신 여호와의 능력은
많은 물 소리와 바다의 큰 파도보다 크니이다

개역개정이 세 차례나 '큰 물'(3절)로 번역한 히브리어 단어(נְהָרוֹת)의 기본적인 의미는 '강들'이다. 강들이 모이면 바다가 되고 홍수가 될 수 있기 때문에 번역본들에 따라 이 말을 '강들'(새번역, 공동, LXX, cf. HALOT) 혹은 '바다'(아가페, 현대인, NIV, TNK, cf. Dahood) 혹은 '홍수'(ESV, NAS, RSV, CSB)로 번역하기도 한다. 고대 근동 신화에서 강은 세상의 질서와 경계를 위협하는 무질서의 괴물로 자주 등장한다(cf. ANET) 구약에서는 바닷물이 경계선을 무너뜨리려고 하는 것처럼 종종 열방이 이스라엘의 경계선을 무너뜨리려는 물로 묘사된다(Anderson, Kirkpatrick, cf. 사 8:7; 17:12). 본문도 이러한 이미지를 배경으로 하고 있다(cf. Day, Habel). 그러므로 저자가 3절에서 세 차례나 큰 물이 소리를 높이고 물결을 높였다고 하는 것은 무질서가 창조주께 반역하여 여호와께서 세상에 세우신 질서와 경계선들을 위협했다는 뜻이다(cf. Eaton, Habel).

그러나 무질서가 아무리 물결을 높여도 주님이 정해 두신 경계선을 위협할 수 없으며 높이 계신 하나님께도 닿을 수 없다(4절). 무질서는 결코 하나님께 위협이 되지 못한다. 오히려 높이 계신 하나님의 능력은 많은 물(무질서)이 내는 소리와 파도보다 훨씬 더 크다. 하나님이 무질서를 통제하시고 다스리신다는 뜻이다. 하나님은 세상에 존재하는 모든 권세와 세력을 지배하신다(Anderson).

3. 하나님의 굳건한 법도(93:5)

5 여호와여
주의 증거들이 매우 확실하고
거룩함이 주의 집에 합당하니
여호와는 영원무궁하시리이다

온 우주의 통치자이신 하나님이 이스라엘과 특별한 관계를 맺으셨다. 하나님이 관계를 맺으신 증표로 그들에게 증거들과 주님의 집을 주셨다. '증거'(עֵדוּת)는 문서를 뜻한다(HALOT). 시편 119편은 이를 율법의 의미로 13차례나 사용한다(VanGemeren). 이와 동일하게 여기서도 하나님이 이스라엘에게 시내 산에서 주신 율법을 뜻하는 것으로 이해할 수 있다(cf. Broyles). 이스라엘은 세상 모든 민족들 중 유일하게 하나님의 율법을 받는 특권을 누린 민족이었다.

하나님은 그들 중에 자기 집(בֵּיתְךָ)도 주셨다. 주님의 집은 '즐겁고 거룩한'(נַאֲוָה־קֹדֶשׁ) 곳이다. 주님의 집은 세상 모든 집과 '구별되는'(קֹדֶשׁ) 집이었으며, 주의 백성들에게 '기쁨을 주는'(נאה) 집이었다. 하나님은 참으로 자신과 잘 어울리는 집에 머무셨다. "여호와는 영원무궁하시리이다"라는 히브리어 문장(יְהוָה לְאֹרֶךְ יָמִים)을 문자적으로 번역한 것이지만(cf. 공동) 의미가 정확하지가 않다. 그래서 많은 번역본들이 여호와의 집이 영원한 것으로 번역한다(새번역, 아가페, 현대인, NIV, NRS, TNK). 본문의 의미를 더 정확하게 표현하는 번역이다. 신약에서 하나님의 백성 통치는 예수 그리스도를 통해 영원히 지속된다. 이 시편이 하나님의 영원한 통치를 선언한다고 해서 한때는 '종말론적 여호와 시'(eschatological Yahwistic psalm)로 불리기도 했다(Deitzsch, cf. Kidner).

제94편

I. 장르/양식: 회중 탄식시(cf. 12편)

모빙클(Mowinckel)이 이 시편을 회중 탄식시로 구분한 이후 대부분 학자들은 그의 주장을 따른다. 그러나 이 노래는 최소한 세 가지 장르를 반영하고 있다: 회중 탄식시(1-7절), 지혜시(8-15절), 개인 탄식시(16-23절). 더 나아가 지혜시 섹션은(8-15절)은 어리석은 사람들에게 하는 말(8-11절)과 의인들에게 하는 말(12-15절)로 구분된다.

이 시편의 내용이 이렇다 보니 하나님의 왕권을 찬양하는 시들로 구성된 93-100편에서 예외로 취급되기도 한다(cf. McCann). 반면에 한 주석가는 이 시를 "참 아름다워라 주님의 세계는"이라는 가사말로 시작하는 찬송에 비교한다. 이 세상이 때로는 악이 성행하는 곳 같지만, 하나님이 아직도 통치하는 세상이기 때문에 아름답다는 것이다(Mays). 그러므로 "여호와께서 다스리신다"(יְהוָה מָלָךְ)는 말은 나오지 않지만, 같은 테마를 이어가고 있다.

이러한 차원에서 이 노래도 93-100편으로 구성된 찬양시 모음집의 자연스러운 일원이라며 일부 학자들은 이 시편을 감사시(psalm of thanksgiving)(Dahood) 혹은 언젠가는 하나님이 악인들을 심판하실 것을 확신하는 신뢰시(psalm of trust)(Brueggemann & Bellinger, deClaissé-Walford et al.)라고 하기도 한다. 의인에게 복을 내리고, 악인을 벌하는 것은 왕이 하는 일이기 때문에 이 시를 즉위시(enthronement psalm)라고 하기도 한다(cf. deClaissé-Walford et al.).

이 시는 주변 시편들과 잘 어울린다는 것이 많은 학자들의 결론이다. 92편의 주제인 악인들의 성행과 93편의 주제인 여호와의 왕권을 하나로 묶는 역할을 하기 때문이다(Tucker & Grant, cf. Ross). 비록 이 시편이 탄식시로 구분되기는 하지만 찬양 모음집인 93-100편에서 발견되는 것은, 찬양시 모음집인 제4권(90-106편)을 탄식시 모음집인 제3권(73-89편)과 더 가깝게 연결하기 위해서다(Wilson, cf. Howard).

이 시편의 저작 연대를 추측하기란 쉽지 않다. 시가 언급하고 있는 악인들의 성행과 의인들의 고통은 이스라엘 역사에서 언제든 있어 왔기 때문이다. 한 미드라쉬는 이 노래가 유태인들이 바빌론 사람들에 의해 불타는 성전을 바라보며 부른 노래라고 한다(Ross, cf. Terrien). 또한 이 시편의 저작 시기를 매우 오래전으로 보는 견해가 있다(Dahood). 이 시편은 원래 미래를 묘사하는 미완료형을 과거의 일을 회고하는 데 사용하고 있는 특성을 지녔는데, 이를 매우 오래된 문법에 따른 것으로 이해하여 저작 시기를 매우 오래전으로 보았던 것이다(Dahood).

학자에 따라 이 시편은 주전 9세기(Howard), 혹은 예루살렘이 함락되었던 주전 587년(Terrien), 혹은 아직 성전이 건재할 때에 악인들의 멸망을 바라며 종교적인 축제 때 부른 것으로(Weiser), 혹은 포로기 이후에 저작되어 사용된 것으로(Grogan, Wilcock) 이해하기도 한다. 이와는 달리 시대적 범위를 넓혀 이사야와 미가 선지자 시대(주전 8세기)부터 페르시아 시대(주전 5세기)까지로 폭넓게 보는 학자도 있다(Anderson). 이처럼 다양한 견해가 제시되는 것은 이 시가 정확히 언제 저작되고 어떤 상황에서 불린 것인지에 대해 별로 알려진 바가 없다는 뜻이기도 하다.

칠십인역(LXX)은 표제에서 이 노래가 주의 4일째(수요일)에 불린 노래라고 한다. 아마도 옛적에 유태인들이 이 노래를 수요일이면 종종 불렀던 점을 회고하고 있는 듯하다.

II. 구조

이 노래는 회중 탄식시(1-7절)와 어리석은 사람들에게 주는 경고(8-11절), 의인들을 위한 권면(12-15절), 개인 탄식시(16-23절)로 구성되었으며, 중심은 의인들에 대한 권면인 12-15절이다(Howard, Tate). 이 주석에서는 다음과 같은 구조를 바탕으로 본문을 주해해 나가고자 한다(cf. Tate, VanGemeren).

A. 복수하시는 하나님(94:1-2)
  B. 악인들의 괴롭힘(94:3-7)
    C. 어리석은 자들을 위한 경고(94:8-11)
    C'. 의인들을 위한 권면(94:12-15)
  B'. 악인들에게서 보호하심(94:16-19)
A'. 악을 벌하시는 하나님(94:20-23)

III. 주해

이 시편은 왕이신 하나님이 악인들을 벌하시고 의인들을 축복하시기를 간절히 바란다. 왕이 하는 일 중 하나가 자신이 통치하는 나라에서 공의와 정의를 실현하는 것이기 때문이다. 그러므로 여호와가 왕이신 나라에서 의인들은 하나님의 축복을 기대할 수 있고, 악인들은 징벌을 피할 수 없다.

1. 복수하시는 하나님(94:1-2)

[1] 여호와여
복수하시는 하나님이여
복수하시는 하나님이여
빛을 비추어 주소서
[2] 세계를 심판하시는 주여
일어나사 교만한 자들에게 마땅한 벌을 주소서

노래를 시작하면서 기자는 하나님의 성호를 세 차례 반복하여 부르는데, 맨 먼저 이스라엘과 언약을 맺으신 하나님 '여호와'를 부르고, 이후 두 차례는 '복수하시는 하나님'(אֵל־נְקָמוֹת)을 부른다(cf. 신 32:35, 41, 43; 33:2; 시 58:10; 79:10; 렘 51:6; 겔 25:12, 14, 17). 마치 여호와께서 주의 백성과 언약을 맺으셨기 때문에 그들을 위해 꼭 원수들에게 복수하실 것이라는 기대감을 조성하고 있다.

저자는 복수하시는 하나님이 빛을 비추시기를 간절히 바란다(1절, cf. 신 33:2; 시 50:2; 80:1). 그는 하나님의 현현을 바라고 있으며(McCann, VanGemeren), 빛이 온 세상을 비추듯 하나님의 심판이 온 세상에 임하여 벌을 받을 자들에게는 벌을 내리시라는 뜻이다. 만일 하나님이 그들을 벌하지 않으시면 세상의 기초가 흔들린다(Kugel). 그러므로 하나님은 세상을 심판하시는 분이다(2a절). 세상에서 행해지는 불의에 분노한 기자는 하나님이 직접 찾아오셔서 잘못된 일들을 바로잡기를 간절히 바라고 있다(Alter, Broyles). 그가 하나님께 벌하시라고 간구하는 악인들은 다름 아닌 '교만한 자들'(גֵּאִים)이다. 하나님이 가장 싫어하는 악이 교만이다(cf. 시 10:2; 31:18, 23; 36:11; 잠 29:23; 사 2:12). 하나님을 의지하여 살지 않고 오히려 자신들이 신처럼 살려고 하기 때문이다.

기자는 하나님을 의지하지 않는 교만한 자들에게 마땅한 벌을 내리시기를 기도한다. '마땅한'(גְּמוּל)은 '적절한/상응하는'을 뜻한다(HALOT). 성경은 종종 의인들은 그들에게 적절한 상을 받을 것이라며 이 단어를 사용한다(cf. 시 13:6). 세상의 모든 죄가 '마땅한 벌'(상응하는 벌)을 받는다는 것은 선행에 포상이 있는 것처럼 모든 악행도 각각 어떤 응징을 받게 될 것임을 암시한다(VanGemeren, cf. 시 28:4; 애 3:64). 교만한 자들이 받을 만한 마땅한 벌은 죽음 외에는 없다.

2. 악인들의 괴롭힘(94:3-7)

3 여호와여
악인이 언제까지,
악인이 언제까지 개가를 부르리이까
4 그들이 마구 지껄이며
오만하게 떠들며
죄악을 행하는 자들이 다 자만하나이다
5 여호와여
그들이 주의 백성을 짓밟으며
주의 소유를 곤고하게 하며
6 과부와 나그네를 죽이며
고아들을 살해하며
7 말하기를 여호와가 보지 못하며
야곱의 하나님이 알아차리지 못하리라 하나이다

기자는 세상에서 악인들이 성행하는 것은 도대체 이해가 되지 않는 일이라며 '악인들이 언제까지?'(עַד־מָתַי רְשָׁעִים)라는 말을 두 차례 반복한다(3절). 의로우신 여호와께서 다스리는 세상에서 악인들이 승리하여(승승장구하여) 개가를 부름은 절대 있을 수 없다는 것이 그의 논리이다

(cf. Goldingay). ‘개가를 부르다’(עלז)는 ‘승리에 도취하여 노래를 부르다’ 라는 뜻이다(HALOT).

의로우신 하나님이 다스리시는 현실에서 악인들은 자신들의 승승장구에 대해 마구 지껄이며 오만하게 떠들어 댄다(4절). 악인들의 죄는 제일 먼저 그들의 교만한 화법에서 드러난다. 일부 번역본들은 4절도 수사학적인 질문으로 표현한다(NAS, TNK, KJV). 이는 상당수의 학자들에게 지지를 받는다(Dahood, Broyles, Kirkpatrick). 질문형으로 해석할 경우 의로우신 하나님이 다스리시는 세상에서 믿기 어려운 일이 벌어지고 있으니 속히 오셔서 상황을 바로잡으시라는 염원으로 이해할 수 있다.

죄악을 행하는 자들이 모두 자만하다. ‘그들이 자만하다’(יִתְאַמְּרוּ)는 상당히 특이한 형태의 동사로서 ‘자신들을 반복적으로 자랑하다’는 의미를 갖고 있다(Goldingay). 그들은 자신들이 행한 온갖 악에 대해 수치심을 느끼는 것이 아니라, 오히려 자랑스럽게 생각하여 자랑질을 하고 있다는 뜻이다.

악인들이 자랑스럽게 생각하는 악한 일은 어떤 것들인가? 다름 아닌 여호와의 백성에게 해를 끼치는 일이다. 그들의 죄는 입으로 오만방자하게 떠들어 대는 것에 그치지 않고, 악한 행동으로도 드러난다. 기자는 악인들의 만행을 네 동사로 묘사하고 있다(5-6절): ‘짓밟다(יְדַכְּאוּ)… 곤고하게 하다(יְעַנּוּ)… 죽이다(יַהֲרֹגוּ)… 살해하다(יְרַצֵּחוּ)’ 그들은 주의 백성을 모두 없애기로 작정하고 온갖 나쁜 짓을 하고 있다.

그들이 주의 백성을 괴롭히는 것은 하나님의 재산권을 침해하는 행위이기도 하다. 주의 백성은 하나님의 소유이기 때문이다(5c절). ‘소유’(נַחֲלָה)는 소유자와 결코 떼어놓을 수 없는 유산을 뜻한다(HALOT, cf. 신 4:20; 시 28:9). 주의 백성은 여호와께서 결코 소유권을 포기할 수 없는 주님의 가족이자 소유이다(deClaissé-Walford et al.). 그러므로 재산권을 침해당한 하나님은 절대로 침묵하지 않으실 것이다.

악인들의 폭력성은 가장 연약한 자들을 가만히 두지 않는다(6절). 그들은 보호를 받아야 할 사회적 약자들의 3대 상징인 과부들과 나그네들과 고아들을 죽인다. 하나님은 이 약자들이 강자들의 희생양이 되는 것을 막기 위해 그들을 보호하는 아버지를 자청하셨다(cf. 출 22:21-22; 신 10:18; 24:19; 시 10:14; 말 3:5). 이러한 사실을 무시한 악인들은 약자들을 죽이고 살해한다. 그들은 약자들을 상대로 다투며, 의도적으로 살인을 하기도 한다. 기자는 신체적인 살인뿐 아니라 인격적인 살인도 염두에 두고 있다(Anderson).

이 악인들은 참으로 비겁한 자들이다. 아무런 저항도 할 수 없는 사람을 상대로 무자비하게 폭력을 행사하는 것은 비겁한 자들이나 하는 짓이기 때문이다. 약자들의 아버지이신 하나님은 '자녀들'이 살해당하는 모습을 지켜보고 있지만은 않으실 것이다. 분명히 그들을 벌하실 것이다(cf. 1절).

악인들이 무자비한 무력을 행사하면서도 후환을 두려워하지 않음은 하나님이 그들의 소행을 모를 것이라고 생각하기 때문이다(7절). 그들은 하나님이 그들의 만행을 보지 못하고 알아차리지도 못한다고 확신한다. 이와 같은 확신은 그들이 하나님을 우상으로 취급하기 때문이다. 구약은 하나님과 우상의 가장 기본적인 차이를 듣고 보는 것에 두었다. 하나님은 우리의 작은 신음소리도 들으시고 아주 세세한 것들도 보시지만, 우상들은 전혀 듣지도 보지도 못한다. 따라서 그들이 이스라엘의 하나님이 보지 못한다고 확신하는 것은 하나님을 세상에 널려 있는 여러 우상들 중 하나로 보았기 때문이라고 할 수 있다. 그들의 착각은 하나님에 대한 무지함에서 비롯되었던 것이다.

3. 어리석은 자들을 위한 경고(94:8-11)

8 백성 중의 어리석은 자들아
너희는 생각하라

무지한 자들아
너희가 언제나 지혜로울까
9 귀를 지으신 이가 듣지 아니하시랴
눈을 만드신 이가 보지 아니하시랴
10 뭇 백성을 징벌하시는 이
곧 지식으로 사람을 교훈하시는 이가
징벌하지 아니하시랴
11 여호와께서는 사람의 생각이 허무함을 아시느니라

기자는 자신들이 저지르는 만행을 하나님이 절대 알지 못하신다고 확신하는 악인들을 '어리석은 자들', '무지한 자들'이라고 한다(8절). 이 둘은 서로 비슷한 말로 사용된다. '어리석은 자들'(בֹּעֲרִים)은 짐승들처럼 사리 판단을 잘 하지 못하는 사람들을(cf. 시 92:6), '무지한 자들'(כְּסִילִים)은 지혜가 부족한 미련한 사람들을 뜻한다(NIDOTTE, cf. 시 49:10; 92:6). 기자는 하나님과 사람들을 속이는 것을 지혜라고 생각하여 후환을 두려워하지 않고 온갖 악한 짓을 하는 악인들을 안타깝다고 생각한다. 그러므로 그는 그들을 정죄하기 보다는 "너희가 언제나 지혜로울까?"라며 탄식한다(8d절).

어리석고 무지한 이들의 문제는 올바른 교육을 통한 지식의 습득으로 해결될 수 있다. 악인이 악을 버림은 올바른 지식을 접할 때만이 가능하다. 그러므로 12절은 주의 법으로 교훈을 받는 자가 복이 있다고 한다(cf. 10절). 어리석고 무지한 악인들이 깨달아야 할 지식과 습득해야 할 진리는 어떤 것들인가?

기자는 9-10절에서 수사학적인 질문들을 사용해 그들이 깨달아야 할 것들을 지적한다.

첫째, 하나님은 사람이 하는 모든 말을 들으시는 분이다(9a절). 사람이 들을 수 있는 귀를 지니게 된 것은 하나님이 들을 수 있는 귀를 만들어 주셨기 때문이다. 귀가 듣는 일을 하도록 디자인하신 하나님이 하물며 사람들의 말을 듣지 않으시겠냐는 논리다. 주님은 사람들이 하는 모든 말을 들으시되 자기 백성의 가장 작은 신음소리도 들으신다.

둘째, 하나님은 사람이 하는 모든 일을 지켜보시는 분이다(9b절). 사람의 귀를 만드신 것처럼 하나님은 그들의 눈도 만드셨다. 사람의 눈을 보도록 디자인하신 분이 세상에서 일어나는 모든 일을 관찰하고 계신다. 심지어는 가장 어둡고 숨겨진 곳에서 일어나는 일도 모두 지켜보신다.

어리석은 자들의 생각이 모자란다는 사실이 확연히 드러나는 순간이다. 사람이 보고 듣도록 창조하신 분이 정작 자신은 듣지 못하고 보지 못하시겠는가!(Broyles). 또한 듣는 것과 보는 것은 하나님과 우상들의 가장 기본적인 차이이기도 하다. 우상들은 보지 못하고 듣지 못한다. 반면에 이스라엘의 하나님 여호와는 세상에서 일어나는 모든 일을 보고 들으신다.

셋째, 하나님은 세상 모든 백성을 징벌하시는 분이다(10절). 하나님은 백성들을 심판하실 때 무작정, 맹목적으로 하지 않으신다. 주님은 자신의 귀와 눈으로 듣고 본 것에 따라 사람들을 심판하신다(cf. 9절). 하나님의 징벌은 사람들의 언행에 대한 하나님의 대응이다.

하나님은 사람들의 언행을 평가하실 때 어떤 기준으로 하시는가? 주님은 이미 사람들에게 주신 지식에 따라 그들을 판단하신다(10b절). 하나님이 이 지식으로 사람을 교훈하시는 것으로 보아 '지식'(דַּעַת)은 하나님이 사람들에게 가르쳐 주신 올바른 삶이다. 사람들에게 의로운 삶에 대해 가르치신 하나님은 정작 그들이 그 기준에 따라 살았는지를 판단하신다.

여호와께서 옳은 삶에 대해 사람들에게 먼저 가르치시고 이후 그들이 그 가르침에 따라 살았는지를 판결하시는 것은 사람의 생각이 허무하다는 것을 아시기 때문이다(11절). 전도서를 생각나게 하는 말씀이다

(cf. 전 1:12-18). '허무함'(הֶבֶל)은 전도서에서 '헛됨'으로 번역되며 삶의 부질없음을 나타내는 뜻으로 자주 사용된다(cf. 시 39:5; 78:33; 전 1:1). 사람의 생각은 아무것도 아니라는 뜻이다(Weiser). 하나님은 사람의 생각이 곧지 못하고 자주 흔들리기 때문에 먼저 그들을 가르치시고 이후 그들이 그렇게 살았는지에 대해 심판하신다.

4. 의인들을 위한 권면(94:12-15)

12 여호와여
주로부터 징벌을 받으며
주의 법으로 교훈하심을 받는 자가 복이 있나니
13 이런 사람에게는 환난의 날을 피하게 하사
악인을 위하여 구덩이를 팔 때까지 평안을 주시리이다
14 여호와께서는 자기 백성을 버리지 아니하시며
자기의 소유를 외면하지 아니하시리로다
15 심판이 의로 돌아가리니
마음이 정직한 자가 다 따르리로다

하나님의 가르침을 받고 그 기준에 따라 징벌을 받는 사람은 복이 있다(12절). 어떻게 살든 간에 하나님의 제재를 받지 않는 자들은 하나님이 포기하셨거나 버리셨다는 뜻이다. 반면에 하나님이 가르치시고 징벌하시는 것은 그를 사랑하여 포기하거나 버리지 않으셨기 때문이다. 그러므로 기자는 하나님의 징벌을 받는 사람은 복이 있다고 한다. '복이 있다'(אַשְׁרֵי)는 1편을 연상케 하는 표현이다(cf. Hossfeld-Zenger). 주님이 법으로 가르치시고 교훈하시는 사람은 복이 있다.

또한 하나님의 교훈과 징벌은 환난 날을 피하게 하는 효과를 발휘한다(13절). 주님이 심판하시는 날이 되면 악인들은 헤어나올 수 없는 심판의 구덩이에 빠져들게 된다. 반면에 하나님이 평소에 징벌하면서 양육하신 사람들은 벌을 받을 일이 없다. 그러므로 그들은 하나님이 악인들을 잡으려고 구덩이를 파실 때에도 평안하다.

하나님은 어떤 사람들을 택하여 양육하고 징벌하여 환난 날을 피하게 하시는가? 여호와께서 자기 백성이라고 정하신 사람들이며, 자기 소유로 택하신 사람들이다(14절). 하나님은 그들의 왕이며 그들은 하나님의 백성이다. 또한 그들은 하나님과 떼어놓을 수 없는 '소유물/유산'(נַחֲלָה)이다(cf. 5절). 그러므로 하나님이 그들을 버리시는 것은 왕이 자기 백성을 버리는 것과 같으며, 사람이 자기 유산을 스스로 포기하는 것과 같다. 하나님은 절대 그들을 버리지 않으실 것이다.

하나님이 행하시는 심판은 분명 의로 돌아갈 것이다(15a절). 정의가 하나님의 심판과 함께할 것이라는 뜻이다(Kraus, cf. 새번역, 아가페, NIV, ESV, NAS, NRS). 그러므로 마음이 정직한 사람은 하나님의 심판에 모두 수긍하고 그대로 받아들일 것이다(15b절). 주님의 심판이 얼마나 의롭고 공평한지 그 누구도 불평하지 않을 것이라는 뜻이다.

5. 악인들에게서 보호하심(94:16-19)

16 누가 나를 위하여 일어나서 행악자들을 치며
누가 나를 위하여 일어나서 악행하는 자들을 칠까
17 여호와께서 내게 도움이 되지 아니하셨더면
내 영혼이 벌써 침묵 속에 잠겼으리로다
18 여호와여
나의 발이 미끄러진다고 말할 때에
주의 인자하심이 나를 붙드셨사오며
19 내 속에 근심이 많을 때에
주의 위안이 내 영혼을 즐겁게 하시나이다

이 시편을 시작하면서 1-7절에서는 온 공동체가 악인이 성행하는 것을 탄식했는데 이제 노래를 마무리 하면서 16-23절에서는 기자가 개인적으로 탄식한다. 기자는 자신이 악인들에게 참으로 억울한 일을 당하고 있다고 생각한다. 그러나 그들에게 대항할 힘은 없다. 그를 괴롭히는 이들이 매우 강하기 때문이다. 그러므로 그는 누군가가 나서서 그를 대신해 악인들을 응징하기를 바란다(16절). 기자의 이 같은 바람은 온 세상에서 자기보다 강한 자들에게 억울하게 당하는 모든 사람의 바람이기도 하다.

기자는 여호와께서 그를 대신해서 원수들을 벌하셨을 뿐만 아니라 그를 구원하셨던 일을 떠올린다. 그러므로 그는 하나님이 그를 돕지 않으셨다면 그는 이미 침묵 속에 잠겼을 것이라고 한다(17절). '침묵'(דּוּמָה)은 죽음을 상징한다(cf. 시 115:17). 그는 하나님이 돕지 않으셨다면, 자신은 이미 죽었을 것이라고 하는 것이다.

기자의 발이 미끄러질 때 하나님의 인자하심(חַסְדְּךָ)이 그를 붙드셨다(18절). 그의 마음에 근심이 많을 때에 주님의 위안이 그를 즐겁게 했다(19절). '위안'(תַּנְחוּם)은 어머니가 자식을 위로하는 이미지를 배경으로 한다(cf. HALOT, NIDOTTE). 하나님이 그와 함께 하시면서 철두철미하게 보호하셨을 뿐만 아니라, 그에게 평안을 주셨다는 뜻이다. 하나님의 이 같은 보호를 받으면 그 누구든 사망의 음침한 골짜기를 지날지라도 해를 두려워할 필요가 없다.

6. 악을 벌하시는 하나님(94:20-23)

20 율례를 빙자하고
재난을 꾸미는 악한 재판장이
어찌 주와 어울리리이까
21 그들이 모여 의인의 영혼을 치려하며

무죄한 자를 정죄하여 피를 흘리려 하나
22 여호와는 나의 요새이시요
나의 하나님은 내가 피할 반석이시라
23 그들의 죄악을 그들에게로 되돌리시며
그들의 악으로 말미암아 그들을 끊으시리니
여호와 우리 하나님이 그들을 끊으시리로다

하나님은 세상을 다스리실 때에 직접 하시지 않고 인간 지도자들을 세워 통치하신다. 그러므로 이상적인 상황은 인간 지도자들이 하나님의 말씀에 따라 세상을 다스리는 것이다. 문제는 하나님이 그들을 세우셨다는 사실을 거부하고 무시하는 악한 지도자들이 많이 있다는 것이다. 그들은 하나님의 말씀을 대신할 악한 율례를 세우고 백성들에게 강요하기도 한다. 20절은 번역하기가 어렵지만 의미를 이해하는 것은 그다지 어렵지 않다(cf. McCann, Tate), '율례'(חֹק)(20절)는 '율법', '법전'을 뜻한다(cf. HALOT).

거룩하신 하나님과 세상의 악한 지배자들은 어떤 관계를 유지하고 있는가? 전혀 상관없다는 것이 기자의 결론이다: "악한 재판장이 주님과 사귈 수 있습니까? 율례를 빌미로 재난을 만드는 자가 주님과 어울릴 수 있습니까?"(새번역). 이 수사학적인 질문들은 강력한 '아니요'(No)를 요구한다. 하나님은 타당한 이유 없이 사람들을 괴롭게 하는 지도자들과 함께하시지 않는다.

하나님은 이상한 법을 만들어 의인의 영혼을 치고 무죄한 사람을 정죄하여 피를 흘리도록 하는 지도자들의 계획이 이루어지지 않도록 하신다(cf. 21절). 그들의 법 집행은 백성들을 돕는 것이 아니라 그들에게 재난을 안겨주는 일이기 때문이다(Hossfeld-Zenger, cf. 20절). 의인들을 사랑하시는 주님은 이런 일을 묵인하지 않으신다.

그렇다면 주님은 악한 지도자들의 계획을 어떻게 방해하시는가? 하나님이 직접 나서서 의인들을 보호하신다. 주님은 그들의 요새가 되시며 피할 반석이 되셔서 악인들(악한 재판장들)의 판결이 그들을 해하지 못하도록 하신다(22절). 결국 의인들을 해하려던 악인들의 계획이 실패하게 된다.

뿐만 아니라 하나님은 악인들에게 그들의 죄악을 되돌리셔서 그들을 끊으신다(23a-b절). 그들이 의인들을 잡으려고 판 함정에 스스로 빠지게 하신다는 뜻이다. 이러한 사실을 확신하며 기자는 한 번 더 주께서 그들을 끊으실 것이라고 선언하고 노래를 마무리한다(23c절). 정의로 세상을 다스리시는 하나님은 자기 영토에서 악이 성행하는 것을 오래 지켜보지는 않으실 것이다.

제95편

I. 장르/양식: 회중 찬양시(cf. 29편)

일부 학자들은 전형적인 찬양시로 구성된 1-7c절과 선지자적인 신탁인 7d-11절을 두 개의 독립적인 노래로 구분하기도 한다(cf. Anderson, Davies, Goldingay, Mowinckel). 더 나아가 첫 번째 섹션은 세 개의 서로 다른 형식의 예배로의 부름(1, 2, 6절)이 있으며, 이러한 현상은 서로 다른 정황에서 사용된 양식들이 편집을 통해 하나가 된 것이라는 주장도 있다(cf. Hossfeld-Zenger, McCann). 그러나 두 장르가 같은 시에서 사용되는 것은 81편에서도 발견되는 현상이라며 구조와 사용된 단어 분석을 통해 통일성을 지닌 한 편의 시라고 결론짓는 주장도 만만치 않다(Girard, Howard, Massouh, Riding).

이 노래가 하나님의 왕 되심을 유일한 주제로 삼고 있지는 않지만, '크신 왕'(3절)과 하나님이 왕이심을 찬양하는 섹션(93-100편)에 포함되어 있으므로 즉위시(enthronement psalm)로 구분해야 한다는 주장이 있다(McCann, cf. deClaissé-Walford et al.). 더 나아가 이 시편과 100편은 즉위시로 구성된 96-99편을 감싸는 역할을 하고 있다(Tate, cf. Goldingay). 그러나 신탁(7-11절)이 포함되어 있기 때문에 이 시편은 선지자적 권면

(prophetic exhortation) 혹은 하나님의 신적 심판(divine judgment)으로 취급되어야 한다는 주장도 있다.

이 시편이 언제 저작되었으며, 어떤 정황에서 사용되었는가에 대해서는 알려진 것보다 알려지지 않은 것이 더 많다. 그럼에도 불구하고 학자들은 다양한 추측을 내놓았다. 이스라엘이 가을이면 드렸던 신년 예배에서 여호와의 왕 되심을 찬양하며 사용된 것이라는 주장이 있다(Mowinckel). 장막절에서 사용된 것이라는 학자도 있다(Grogan). 요시야가 종교개혁을 단행했던 주전 622년경에 저작되고 처음 사용되었다가 포로기 이후에는 성전 회복을 기대하며 사용된 것이라는 추측이 있다(Terrien). 이 노래가 이른 포로 시대에 저작된 것이라는 주장이 있는가 하면(Tate), 시편의 내용이 말라기 2장과 이사야 57-59장과 비슷하다 하여 늦은 포로기를 주장하는 학자들도 있다. 그러나 이 시가 광야 전승을 인용하고 있는 것은 아모스 선지자나 이사야 선지자보다 이른 시기에 저작된 것임을 암시한다는 추측도 있다(Mowinckel).

어떤 학자는 즉위시의 내용이 완전하게 성취될 종말을 노래하고 있음을 들어 이 시편을 종말론적인 해석으로 제안하기도 한다(Kaiser). 어찌 되었든 이 시편은 여호와의 위대하심을 확인할 필요가 있을 때면 언제나 불렀던 노래임은 확실하다(Ross). 이 시편의 저작 연대와 처음 불린 구체적인 정황을 알 수는 없지만, 오늘날이라도 주님의 위대하심을 확인하고 싶을 때 묵상할 만한 노래이다.

마소라 사본은 표제를 반영하고 있지 않다. 반면에 칠십인역(LXX)은 표제에 '다윗의 찬양시'(αἶνος ᾠδῆς τῷ Δαυιδ)라는 말을 더한다. 다윗과 같은 믿음을 지닌 사람이 부를 만한 노래라 해서 이런 표제를 더한 것으로 생각된다.

II. 구조

이미 언급한 것처럼 많은 학자들이 이 노래를 1–7c절과 7d–11절 두 섹션으로 구분한다. 데이비스(Davies)는 첫 섹션을 1–5절과 6–7c절 두 파트로 구분하여 첫 파트인 1–5절은 성전 문 밖에서 행했던 예배 부름(1–2절)과 이 예배 부름에 대한 찬양대의 반응(3–5절)을 반영하고 있다고 한다. 또한 두 번째 파트인 7d–11절은 밖에 있던 사람들이 성전 안으로 들어오자 다시 한번 예배 부름(6절)이 있었고, 이 예배 부름에 대한 찬양대의 반응(7a–c절)을 반영하고 있는 것이라 한다. 이러한 점을 감안하여 이 주석에서는 다음과 같은 구조로 본문을 주해해 나가고자 한다(cf. Davies, McCann, VanGemeren).

A. 예배 부름(95:1–2)

B. 창조주—왕이신 여호와 찬양(95:3–5)

A′. 예배 부름(95:6)

B′. 언약을 맺으신 여호와 찬양(95:7a–c)

C. 선지자적 신탁(95:7d–11)

III. 주해

기자는 창조주이시자 세상을 통치하시는 여호와를 찬양할 것을 권면한다. 주의 백성이 창조주이시자 세상을 다스리시는 여호와께 드릴 수 있는 올바른 반응은 적극적이고 긍정적인 예배이기 때문이다. 이어 그는 출애굽 세대가 광야에서 하나님께 반역한 일을 교훈 삼아 같은 죄를 반복하지 않도록 권한다. 과거는 우리에게 자신을 돌아보는 거울이 되어야 한다는 뜻이다.

1. 예배 부름(95:1-2)

[1] 오라
우리가 여호와께 노래하며
우리의 구원의 반석을 향하여 즐거이 외치자
[2] 우리가 감사함으로 그 앞에 나아가며
시를 지어 즐거이 그를 노래하자

기자는 하나님께 예배를 드리기 위해 모인 공동체에게 주님을 찬양하고 경배할 것을 네 가지로 권면한다.

첫째, 여호와께 노래하자(1b절). '노래하다'(רנן)는 본문이 사용하고 있는 피엘(piel) 형태에서는 기뻐서 어쩔 줄 모르는 감정을 묘사한다(HALOT, cf. 시 96:12; 98:4, 8). 주체할 수 없는 감격으로 하나님께 찬양의 노래를 드리자는 호소이다.

둘째, 구원의 반석을 향하여 즐거이 외치자(1c절). 즐거이 외치는 것은 하나님의 주권에 대한 우리의 올바른 반응이다(cf. 시 47:1; 66:1; 81:1; 98:4, 6). '구원의 반석'(צוּר יִשְׁעֵנוּ)은 하나님을 '신적 용사'(Divine Warrior)로 묘사할 때 사용되는 표현이다(VanGemeren, cf. 신 32:4, 15, 18; 시 18:2, 31, 46; 98:2). '즐거이 외치다'(רוע)는 군인들이 전쟁에서 적군을 향해 돌격할 때 외치는 함성 소리다(cf. NIDOTTE). 우리를 온갖 위험에서 보호하시고 구원하시는 용사이신 주님을 향해 세상에서 가장 큰 소리로 기쁨의 함성을 지르라는 권면이다.

하나님께 즐거이 외치며 노래하라는 것은 곧 시끄러운 예배를 드리라는 의미다(Goldingay). 백성인 우리는 왕이신 하나님을 경배하는데 목소리를 아끼지 말아야 한다(Anderson). 마치 축제에 흥분한 사람들처럼 소리를 질러야 한다(cf. Hossfeld-Zenger). 지나치게 조용하게만 예배를 드리는 것에 익숙해져 있는 일부 교회들에게는 좋은 권면이다.

하나님은 우리의 우레와 같은 찬양을 듣기에 합당하신 분이다. 주님은 우리의 구원의 반석이 되시기 때문이다. 어떤 상황인지 정확히 알 수는 없지만, 여호와께 예배를 드리기 위해 모인 공동체는 큰 위기에서 주님의 구원을 경험한 것이 확실하다(cf. Schaefer). 그러므로 주님의 은혜로 구원을 입은 백성이 가장 큰 소리로 주님을 경배함은 당연하다고 할 수 있다.

셋째, 감사함으로 주님 앞에 나아가자(2a절). '감사함'(תּוֹדָה)은 감사 제물을 의미할 수도 있다(cf. HALOT). 그러나 본문에서는 단순히 마음의 표현으로 보는 것이 바람직하다(McCann, cf. 시 50:14, 23; 100:3). 경배와 찬양이 감사함을 동반하지 않는다면 경배하는 사람도, 경배를 받으시는 이도 별로 기쁘지 않다. 기쁨이 함께하지 않는 찬양은 위선에 불과하다. 그러므로 찬양에는 필수적으로 감사가 동반되어야 한다. 감사가 있는 찬양은 예배자와 하나님께 감동을 안겨준다.

넷째, 시를 지어 즐거이 주님을 노래하자(2d절). '시를 지어'(בִּזְמִרוֹת)의 더 정확한 의미는 '노래들을 통해/시들로'이다. 하나님을 경배하고 찬양할 때 마음에서 우러나는 절제되지 않은 말로 하는 것도 좋지만, 시와 노래처럼 절제된 말을 통해 하는 것도 좋다. 사람이 시(노래)를 지으려면 깊은 묵상이 필요하고 자신의 생각을 논리 정연하게 연출할 줄 알아야 하기 때문이다. 그러므로 이 말씀은 하나님이 우리를 위해 하신 일을 되돌아보며 마음속 깊은 곳에서 우러나는 찬양과 경배로 주님을 예배하자는 권면이다. 기자는 이 세상에서 사람이 드릴 수 있는 가장 감격적인 경배와 찬양을 주님께 드리고자 한다.

2. 창조주—왕이신 여호와 찬양(95:3-5)

3 여호와는 크신 하나님이시요
모든 신들보다 크신 왕이시기 때문이로다

[4] 땅의 깊은 곳이 그의 손 안에 있으며
산들의 높은 곳도 그의 것이로다
[5] 바다도 그의 것이라
그가 만드셨고 육지도 그의 손이 지으셨도다

기자는 앞 섹션(1-2절)에서 하나님을 목청 높여 찬양하자고 했다. 이 섹션에서는 우리가 하나님을 찬양하기에 합당한 이유들을 나열한다. 일부 학자들에 의하면 앞 섹션은 예배를 인도하는 사람이 성전에 들어서기 전에 바깥에서 선포한 말씀이며, 이 섹션은 아직도 성전 바깥에서 있는 찬양대의 예배 부름에 대한 답례이다(cf. Davies).

기자는 우리가 하나님을 찬양할 내용을 세 가지로 정리한다.

첫째, 우리는 하나님이 세상 그 누구와 비교할 수 없이 크고 위대하신 분임을 찬양해야 한다(3절). 저자는 여호와가 참으로 '크신 하나님'(אֵל גָּדוֹל)이시며 모든 신들보다 '크신 왕'(מֶלֶךְ גָּדוֹל)이시라며 '큰'(גָּדוֹל)을 두 차례 사용한다. 이것은 하나님이 세상 어떤 존재와도 비교 불가라는 사실을 강조한다. 하나님이 얼마나 크신지 사람들은 세상 어디서든 주님을 경험할 수 있으며, 모든 신들보다 크신 왕이기 때문에 하나님은 신들과 인간들을 모두 다스리신다. 저자가 하나님이 모든 신들보다 크신 왕이라고 하는 것은 그들의 존재를 인정하기 때문이 아니다. 사람이 상상할 수 있는 위대한 존재들보다 더 크신 분이라는 점을 강조할 뿐이다.

둘째, 우리는 여호와가 세상의 가장 깊은 곳에서 가장 높은 곳까지 모두 소유하신 분임을 찬양해야 한다(4절). 우리가 눈으로 볼 수 있는 가장 높은 산들의 '꼭지들'(תוֹעֲפוֹת)뿐만 아니라 도저히 가늠할 수 없는 세상의 가장 '깊은 곳들'(מֶחְקָר)까지 모두 주님의 손 안에 있다. 이것들이 모두 '주님의 손 안에'(בְּיָדוֹ) 있다는 것은 세상의 가장 깊은 곳과 가장 높은 곳 사이에 있는 모든 것도 하나님의 통제(다스림) 아래 있다는 뜻이다(cf. Weiser). 이 둘 사이에 있는 우리도 하나님의 다스림 아래 있으므로 우리를 다스리시는 하나님을 찬양하는 것은 지극히 당연한 일이다.

셋째, 우리는 여호와는 바다와 육지를 창조하신 창조주임을 찬양해야 한다(5절). 기자는 4절에서 하나님이 온 세상을 소유하신 분이라는 점을 강조했다면, 이번에는 하나님이 세상에 있는 모든 것을 창조하신 분임을 강조한다. 세상을 다스리시는 하나님의 왕권은 창조에 바탕을 두고 있다(Tucker & Grant, VanGemeren, cf. 시 24:1; 89:11). 사람들이 사는 육지(יַבֶּשֶׁת)뿐만 아니라, 그들이 가장 두려워했던 바다(הַיָּם)도 창조하셨다. 창조주 하나님이신 여호와는 바다와 육지에 사는 모든 생명을 창조하셨으며, 주님께 지음을 받은 사람들이 그들을 창조하신 분을 찬양하는 것은 당연한 일이다.

3. 예배 부름(95:6)

[6] 오라
우리가 굽혀 경배하며
우리를 지으신 여호와 앞에 무릎을 꿇자

이 시편이 성전에 들어오기 전에 밖에 모여 있는 사람들이 부르기 시작한 것이라고 하는 학자들은 이 구절을 두 번째 예배 부름이라고 하며 밖에 있던 사람들이 성전 안으로 들어와 진행하는 것이라고 한다(cf. Davies). 예배를 인도하는 이가 회중이 경건한 마음으로 예배를 드리도록 외치는 부분이다.

기자는 예배에 있어서 우리가 갖추어야 할 가장 기본적인 자세를 강조한다. 그는 하나님 앞에서 우리가 취해야 하는 자세는 백성이 자기 왕 앞에서 취하는 자세가 되어야 한다고 한다(McCann, cf. 삼상 24:8; 삼하

14:4, 22; 왕상 1:31). 마치 백성이 왕 앞에서 자신을 낮추듯, 왕이신 하나님 앞에서 자세를 낮출 것을 두 차례 권면한다. '굽혀 경배하다'(חוה)는 엎드린 자세를 묘사하는 표현으로(HALOT), 사람이 취할 수 있는 가장 낮은 자세를 가리킨다. 옛적 이스라엘 사람들은 완전히 엎드린 상태에서 찬양하며 기도하곤 하였다. '무릎을 꿇다'(ברך)도 낮은 자세뿐만 아니라 완전히 복종한다는 의미를 지녔다.

저자는 우리가 하나님 앞에서 이처럼 최대한 낮은 자세를 취해야 하는 이유도 알려준다. 여호와는 우리를 지으신 창조주이기 때문이다. 세상 만물을 창조하신 여호와는 모든 피조물의 경배를 받을 권리가 있으시다. 특히 자기 자신이 창조주의 놀라운 걸작품이라고 생각하는 사람들은 더욱더 주님을 찬양할 이유가 있다.

4. 언약을 맺으신 여호와 찬양(95:7a-c)

7 그는 우리의 하나님이시요
우리는 그가 기르시는 백성이며
그의 손이 돌보시는 양이기 때문이라

이 부분은 인도자가 성전 안에서 외친 예배 부름에 찬양대가 반응한 것이다(Davies). 우리가 창조주 하나님 앞에서 온전히 엎드려 예배를 드려야 한다는 권면에 전적으로 동의하는 내용으로 구성되어 있다. 우리는 두 가지 이유에서 하나님을 경배해야 한다.

첫째, 여호와는 우리의 하나님이시기 때문이다. 주님은 우리를 창조하신 분일 뿐만 아니라 우리를 다스리시는 왕이시다. 그러므로 백성이 왕을 찬양하는 것은 당연한 일이다.

둘째, 여호와는 우리의 목자이시기 때문이다. 고대 근동에서는 왕을 흔히 목자로, 백성을 그가 인도하는 양으로 표현했다(렘 23:1-4; 겔

34:1-10). 우리의 왕이신 창조주는 우리를 창조하시고 나서 방치하지 않으셨다. 우리를 철두철미하게 보살피신다. 마치 목자가 양떼를 정성껏 보살피듯 우리를 양육하신다(cf. 시 23편). 그러므로 기자는 우리가 하나님이 기르시는 백성이며, 돌보시는 양이라고 한다(cf. 시 79:13; 100:3; 요 10:11-14). 주님은 목자가 되어 우리를 인도하시며, 우리의 모든 필요를 채우시는 분이다. 우리는 목자이신 주님이 베푸시는 은혜를 즐기면서, 우리 또한 하나님께 언약적 충성을 다해야 한다는 사실을 항상 기억해야 한다(Anderson).

5. 선지자적 신탁(95:7d-11)

7d 너희가 오늘 그의 음성을 듣거든
8 너희는 므리바에서와 같이
또 광야의 맛사에서 지냈던 날과 같이
너희 마음을 완악하게 하지 말지어다
9 그 때에 너희 조상들이
내가 행한 일을 보고서도
나를 시험하고 조사하였도다
10 내가 사십 년 동안
그 세대로 말미암아 근심하여 이르기를
그들은 마음이 미혹된 백성이라
내 길을 알지 못한다 하였도다
11 그러므로 내가 노하여 맹세하기를
그들은 내 안식에 들어오지 못하리라 하였도다

이 섹션은 선지자적 선포(신탁)이다(Grogan). 아마도 예배를 인도하는 사람이 회중에게 선포했을 것으로 생각된다(Davies). 내용은 이 순간 예배를 드리려고 주님 앞에 모인 사람들이 과거에 그들의 조상들이 저지른 죄를 교훈 삼아 같은 불순종을 반복하지 않도록 하라는 것이다. 우리는 과거가 현재의 거울이 되도록 해야 한다.

하나님은 예전에 그들의 조상들에게 말씀하셨던 것처럼 지금도 말씀하신다(7d절). 주님이 지금도 말씀하신다는 점을 강조하기 위해 기자는 이 말씀을 인용하면서 '오늘'(הַיּוֹם)을 부각시킨다(cf. 히 3:7). '오늘'은 아직도 주님께 순종할 기회가 열려 있는 이 순간이다(Kirkpatrick). 하나님은 예전에 그들의 조상이 광야에서 반역한 일을 회상하시며 매우 안타까워하신다(Hossfeld-Zenger). 이 순간 주님 앞에 서 있는 공동체도 하나님의 말씀을 거역하면 안 된다. 만일 그들이 반역하면 하나님은 다시 한번 매우 안타까워하실 것이기 때문이다.

하나님은 이스라엘의 광야 여정에서 구체적으로 두 사건을 회고하신다(8절). 바로 므리바와 맛사에서 있었던 일이다(cf. 출 17장; 민 20장). '므리바'(מְרִיבָה)는 '다툼'이라는 의미를, '맛사'(מַסָּה)는 '시험'이라는 의미를 가지고 있다(VanGemeren). 이 사건들은 광야 생활 초기와 말기에 있었던 일로서 이스라엘이 한 순간 하나님을 시험한 것이 아니라, 꾸준히 시험한 것을 강조한다(Grogan).

이스라엘은 이 두 곳에서 하나님께 반역했다(cf. 출 17:1-7; 민 14:3; 20:1-13; 21:5; 27:14; 신 6:16; 9:22; 32:51; 33:8; 시 81:7). 또한 이 두 장소는 당시 하나님을 의심하고 시험하려는 믿음이 없는 이스라엘을 상징하기도 한다(cf. 시 78:18, 41, 56; 히 3:7-11). 그들은 계속 "하나님이 죽이시려고 우리를 이집트에서 이끌어 내셨는가?"라는 질문을 하며 하나님을 의심하고 시험했다. 생각해보면 이스라엘의 이러한 행위는 도대체 이해가 되지 않는다. 그들은 이집트에 있을 때부터 수많은 기적과 은혜를 경험하며 이곳에 도착했기 때문이다.

그들의 반역은 자신들이 경험한 바를 반역하는 행위이기도 하다. 그들이 하나님의 은혜와 기적을 경험하고도 반역한 것은 그들의 마음이 완악했기 때문이다(cf. 8c절). '완악하다'(קשה)는 마음이 굳어 있었다는 뜻이다(cf. HALOT). 그들은 어떠한 놀라운 일로도 감동 받지 않는 무디어진 마음을 지녔기 때문에 온갖 은혜를 경험하고도 깨닫지 못했던 것이다. 그러므로 하나님은 그 앞에 서 있는 그들의 후손들에게 마음가짐을 바로 하라고 말씀하신다(8c절). 만일 그들이 조상들처럼 굳은 마음을 가지면, 그들도 조상들처럼 하나님이 행하신 온갖 기적을 보고서도 주님을 시험할 것이기 때문이다(9절). 사람이 하나님을 처음 만나면 당연히 시험할 수도, 조사할 수도 있다. 그러나 조상들은 그 이상이었다. 그들은 하나님이 이집트 사람들에게 열 재앙을 행하시는 동안 온갖 기적들을 경험했다. 하나님은 그들을 위해 홍해도 가르시고, 아무것도 없는 시내 산 밑에서 1년 동안 먹이시고 입히셨다. 그러므로 그들은 하나님을 시험해서는 안 되었다. 하나님을 시험하는 것은 불신의 표현이기 때문이다.

하나님은 어떻게 해서든 그들의 조상들이 불신을 떨쳐 버리기를 바라셨다. 그래서 이후로 광야 생활 40년 동안 온갖 기적과 은혜를 베푸셨지만, 그들은 변하지 않았다(10절). 그들의 마음이 미혹되었던 것이다. 여기서 '미혹되다'(תעה)는 자기 마음대로 생각하거나 스스로 방황하는 것을 의미한다(cf. NIDOTTE). 그들은 자신들이 원하는 길을 갈지언정 하나님의 길은 알지 못한다고 잡아뗐다. 하나님과 주님이 그들에게 베푸신 은혜를 인정하지 않았던 것이다.

결국 하나님의 은혜는 그들의 마음의 병을 치료할 수 없었다. 그들이 앓았던 마음의 병은 선한 것을 보고도 전혀 감동을 받지 못하는 냉담(apathy)이었을 것이다. 그러므로 하나님은 40년 내내 그들로 인해 근심하셨다(10절). '근심하다'(קוט)는 역겹게 느낀다는 뜻이다(Kidner, cf. HALOT). 그러므로 하나님은 그들에게 노하셔서 그들이 결코 주님의 안식에 들어오지 못한다고 맹세하셨다(11절). 하나님은 그들을 용서하지 않으신 것이다. 이 사실은 용서가 너무나도 쉽게 선포되는 오늘날의 기독교인들에게 경종을 울린다(deClaissé-Walford et al.).

주님이 베풀어 주시는 은혜를 은혜로 받고, 주님과 맺은 언약을 실천하는 사람만이 하나님의 영원한 안식에 들어갈 수 있다(cf. Anderson). 감사하지 않는 사람은 하나님이 받지 않으실 것이다. 하나님이 지난날을 회고하시는 이유는 주님 앞에 서 있는 현세대가 그들의 죄를 반복하지 않도록 하기 위해서이다.

제96편

I. 장르/양식: 회중 찬양시(cf. 29편)

하나님은 온 세상의 찬양과 경배를 받기에 합당하신 분임을 노래하는 이 시편은 서술적 찬양시(descriptive praise psalm)이다(Grogan, Westermann). 시의 전반적인 내용은 여느 찬양시처럼 매우 긍정적이고 밝지만, 마지막 절이 여호와께서 세상을 심판하러 오실 것을 선언하고 있기 때문에 종종 심판하러 오실 여호와를 찬양하는 시로 간주되기도 한다(Briggs, Ringgren). 이 노래는 97-99편과 매우 유사한 언어를 사용하고 있다 하여 96-99편은 같은 저자에 의해 저작된 시라고 하는 이들도 있다(VanGemeren).

모빙클(Mowinckel)은 이 노래가 해마다 행해졌던 여호와의 즉위식에서 사용된 즉위시(enthronement psalm)라고 했다(cf. Brueggemann & Bellinger). 그러나 대부분 학자들은 이 시가 즉위시라는 것에 대해 부정적이다. 역대기상 16장은 다윗이 법궤를 예루살렘으로 모셔온 일과 연관하여 시편 세 개를 편집하여 사용하는데, 여기에 이 시가 포함되어 있다.

이 시편의 주제들이 이사야서 후반부와 상당히 비슷하다는 것이 학

자들의 결론이다: 우상 숭배 비난(사 40:18-31; 41:21-24; 44:6-8), 하나님의 창조 사역(사 40:22; 42:5; 44:24; 45:12), 하나님의 구원에 대한 자연의 반응(사 49:13; 55:12)과 열방의 반응(사 45:20; 49:7; 56:3-8; 60:9-12, 14, 16; 66:18). 그러므로 이사야서 후반부가 포로기 시대 혹은 이후에 저작된 것이라고 주장하는 사람들은 이 시편도 이때 저작된 것이라고 한다(Kraus, Tate, Terrien). 저작 시대를 포로기 이후 시대라고 하지 않으면서 이사야 40-66장과 이 시편은 같은 신학적 시대와 정황에서 저작된 것이라는 주장도 있다(Anderson, cf. McCann).

많은 학자들이 이 시편의 저작 시기로 포로기 혹은 그 이후를 지목하지만, 포로기 전인 왕정 시대에 저작된 것이라 하는 학자들도 있다(Howard). 이 노래가 다윗이 법궤를 예루살렘으로 모셔올 때 부른 것이라면(cf. 대상 16장), 일찍 저작되었을 가능성은 더욱더 높아진다. 칠십인역(LXX)은 표제에 "귀향 후 성전이 완성되었을 때. 다윗의 노래"라는 말을 더하는데, 이 노래가 사용된 정황을 말하고 있는 것뿐이기에 저작 시기를 가늠하는 일에는 별로 도움이 되지 않는다.

II. 구조

이 시편의 구조를 논할 때 가장 논쟁이 되는 것은 10절을 어떻게 간주할 것이냐 이다. 일부 학자들은 앞 섹션에 포함하고, 다른 사람들은 뒤 섹션에 포함하기도 하고, 아예 독립적으로 취급하는 이들도 있다(cf. Clifford, Gerstenberger, Hossfeld-Zenger, Tate). 이 주석에서는 새번역처럼 10절을 뒤 섹션에 포함하여 다음과 같은 구조를 바탕으로 본문을 주해해 나가고자 한다.

A. 찬양 권면(96:1-3)

  B. 거룩하신 창조주 여호와(96:4-6)

A'. 찬양 권면(96:7-9)

B′. 심판하시는 왕 여호와(96:10-13)

III. 주해

세상 그 누구와 비교할 수 없는 이스라엘의 하나님 여호와이시다. 주님은 온 세상을 창조하신 분이다. 주님은 세상을 다스리시는 왕이다. 또한 주님은 세상을 심판하시는 심판자이다. 그러므로 주님은 세상 신들과 비교 불가한 거룩하신 분이다. 이 위대하신 하나님이 세상을 심판하러 오신다.

1. 찬양 권면(96:1-3)

[1] 새 노래로 여호와께 노래하라
온 땅이여 여호와께 노래할지어다
[2] 여호와께 노래하여
그의 이름을 송축하며
그의 구원을 날마다 전파할지어다
[3] 그의 영광을 백성들 가운데에,
그의 기이한 행적을 만민 가운데에 선포할지어다

기자는 '새 노래'로 여호와께 찬양을 드리라는 권면으로 노래를 시작한다(1a절, cf 시 13:6; 27:6; 33:3; 104:33; 144:9; 149:1). 이 시편의 내용을 살펴보면 이스라엘이 새 노래로 부를 만한 새로운 내용은 없다(Alter). 새로움은 '온 세상'이 여호와를 찬양하는 것으로 제한되어 있다(Broyles). 일상적으로 '새 노래'의 주제는 전쟁에서 승리하신 여호와를 기념하는 것인데(cf. Longman), 이 노래는 전쟁과 상관없어 보인다.

우리가 경험하는 하나님의 신실하심은 매일 새롭기 때문에 우리는 매일 하나님께 새 노래를 부를 수 있다(Anderson). 또한 미래에 대한 기대와 소망도 새로운 노래의 주제이다(Gerstenberger). 현실이 어떻든 우리가 주님과 함께하는 미래를 꿈꿀 수 있는 한, 우리는 항상 새로운 노래를 부를 수 있다.

이 시편을 95편과 연계하여 해석한다면, 이스라엘의 조상들이 광야에서 주님께 부르던 노래와 다른 노래로 부르라는 뜻이 된다(cf. McCann, Tucker & Grant). 예전에는 불순종과 불만이 그들의 노래 주제였다면, 이제는 순종과 경배를 주제로 삼아 노래를 부르라는 것이다. 그러므로 새로움은 새로운 내용이라기보다는 새로운 마음 자세에 초점이 맞추어져 있다(cf. Brueggemann).

여호와는 자기 백성들의 경배뿐 아니라 온 땅의 찬양을 받기에도 합당하신 분이므로 본문은 세 차례나 주님을 찬양할 것을 주문한다: "노래하라… 노래할지어다… 노래하라"(1-2a절). 주님이 온 세상을 창조하신 분이기 때문이다. 그러므로 기자는 온 세상도 주의 백성들처럼 여호와께 노래할 것을 주문한다(1b절).

그렇다면 세상은 주님께 어떤 노래를 부를 것인가? 기자는 크게 세 가지를 제안한다.

첫째, 주님의 이름을 송축하라(2b절). '송축하다'(ברך)는 '복을 빌어 주다, 무릎을 꿇다'는 뜻이다(HALOT). 무릎을 꿇는 것은 하나님을 경배하기 위해 무릎을 꿇고 낮은 자세를 취한다는 의미이다(McCann, cf. 시 95:6). 복을 빌어준다는 것은 사람이 하나님께 할 수 있는 일이 아니다. 그러므로 주님의 이름이 참으로 복되다는 것을 세상 사람들에게 지속적으로 알려야 한다.

둘째, 날마다 여호와의 구원을 전파하라(2c절). '전파하다'(בשר)는 '새로운 소식을 전한다'는 의미이다(HALOT). 이 히브리어 단어가 헬라어로 번역이 되면서 '복음/좋은 소식'이라는 단어가 탄생했다(Mays). 우리는 뉴스를 전하듯 매일 주님의 구원을 전해야 한다. 우리가 경험하고 누린 주님의 은혜와 구원에 대해서 매일 주변 사람들에게 증거해야 한다.

셋째, 하나님의 영광, 곧 주님의 기이한 행적을 백성들에게 선포하라(3절). 이 말씀에서 '영광'(כָּבוֹד)과 '기이한 행적들'(נִפְלָאוֹת)은 평행을 이룬다. 하나님의 영광을 온 세상에 선포하는 것은 곧 사람들에게 주님이 행하신 기이한 행적들(기적들)에 대해 알리는 것이다(cf. Tucker & Grant). '선포하다'(ספר)는 '기록하다, 회고하다'는 뜻이다. 아마도 이 노래를 처음으로 부른 공동체는 최근에 하나님의 놀라운 은혜를 경험했을 것이다(Briggs). 우리는 우리가 경험한 하나님의 구원과 은혜를 그대로 알리면 된다.

2. 거룩하신 창조주 여호와(96:4-6)

4 여호와는 위대하시니 지극히 찬양할 것이요
모든 신들보다 경외할 것임이여
5 만국의 모든 신들은 우상들이지만
여호와께서는 하늘을 지으셨음이로다
6 존귀와 위엄이 그의 앞에 있으며
능력과 아름다움이 그의 성소에 있도다

이 섹션의 핵심은 하나님의 다르심(otherness) 혹은 거룩하심(차별되심)이다. 기자는 여호와는 참으로 위대하시므로 지극히 찬양하라고 한다(4a절). '위대하다'(גָּדוֹל)는 매우 크다는 의미로 종종 하나님의 왕권과 연관되어 등장한다(cf. 시 48:1; 145:3). 하나님은 참으로 크신 왕이므로 주님의 크심에 걸맞는 찬양, 곧 '지극한 찬양'(מְהֻלָּל מְאֹד)을 드리라 한다. '지극한'(מְאֹד)은 참으로 힘과 능력이 있다는 것을 의미한다(HALOT). 여호와는 참으로 위대하신 분이기에 우리가 가장 힘있는 찬양을 드리기에 합당하다.

여호와는 다른 신들과 비교될 수 없는 분이시다. 당연하다. 다른 신들은 모두 돌과 나무덩어리로 구성된 우상들에 불과하기 때문이다. 그러므로 우리는 모든 신들보다 여호와를 경외해야 한다(4b절). '경외하다'(ירא)는 '두려워하다'는 뜻이다. 경건한 삶을 위해서라도 우리 모두에게는 하나님을 두려워하는 마음이 필요하다. 하나님이 어떤 분이신가를 알고 나면 주님을 경외하는 일은 그다지 어렵지 않다.

기자는 5절에서 우리가 왜 여호와만을 경외해야 하는가를 말한다. 세상의 모든 신들은 우상들에 불과하지만, 여호와는 하늘을 지으신 창조주이기 때문이다. 우상들은 돌과 나무덩어리에 불과하다. 그러므로 그들은 보지도 못하고, 듣지도 못하고, 말하지도 못한다. 이 말씀은 우상 숭배의 어리석음에 대한 매우 강력한 논증(polemic)이다(Hossfeld-Zenger).

반면에 여호와는 들으시고, 보시고, 말씀하신다. 우상 숭배자들이 아무리 자신들의 신들도 보고 들을 뿐만 아니라 행할 능력이 있다고 주장해도 그것은 거짓이다. 오직 보고, 듣고, 행하는 신은 여호와 한 분뿐이시다. 하나님이 우리의 귀와 눈과 입을 창조하셨기 때문이다. 또한 하나님은 온 세상을 덮고 있는 하늘도 지으셨다.

그러므로 창조주의 존귀와 위엄이 주님과 있다(6a절). '존귀'(הוֹד)는 왕에게서 풍겨 나오는 권위를, '위엄'(הָדָר)은 왕에 걸맞은 품위를 뜻한다(cf. NIDOTTE). 그러므로 이 말씀은 왕이신 하나님을 노래한다. 또한 능력과 아름다움이 주님의 성소에 있다(6b절). '능력'(עֹז)은 '힘'을, '아름다움'(תִּפְאֶרֶת)은 '영광, 광채'를 의미한다(HALOT). 하나님이 머무시는 거룩한 처소인 성소가 주님의 영광으로 인해 빛을 발한다. '존귀—위엄—능력—아름다움'은 우리가 하나님을 찬양할 이유에 대해 매우 아름다운 원형(circularity)으로 표현한다(Hossfeld-Zenger).

3. 찬양 권면(96:7-9)

[7] 만국의 족속들아
영광과 권능을 여호와께 돌릴지어다
여호와께 돌릴지어다
[8] 여호와의 이름에 합당한 영광을 그에게 돌릴지어다
예물을 들고 그의 궁정에 들어갈지어다
[9] 아름답고 거룩한 것으로 여호와께 예배할지어다
온 땅이여 그 앞에서 떨지어다

창조주이시며 세상 모든 신들과 비교할 수 없이 거룩하신 여호와는 온 세상을 다스리는 왕이기도 하다. 그러므로 주님을 찬양하는 일은 이스라엘의 몫일 뿐만 아니라 온 세상 민족들의 의무이자 특권이다. 기자는 이러한 논리에서 세상 모든 민족들에게 영광과 권능을 '여호와께 드리라/돌리라'(הָבוּ לַיהוָה)는 명령을 세 차례 반복한다(7-8a절). 성경에서 '돌리라'(הָבוּ)는 명령은 항상 행동을 요구한다(deClaissé-Walford et al., cf. 창 11:3, 4, 7; 출 1:10). 오직 하나님만이 세상 모든 사람들의 찬양과 경배를 받기에 합당하신 분이므로 여호와의 이름에 합당한 영광을 지체하지 말고 주님께 곧바로 돌리라고 한다. '영광'(כָּבוֹד)은 3절에서 이미 사용된 단어이며, '권능'(עֹז)은 6절에서 '능력'으로 번역된 단어이다. 하나님의 영광과 권능은 우리가 찬양과 경배를 통해 주님의 이름을 드높일 때 온 세상을 가득 채운다.

기자는 하나님을 예배하러 궁정(성전 뜰)으로 나갈 때, 예물을 들고 갈 것을 권면한다(8b절). '예물'(מִנְחָה)은 하나님께 존경과 감사를 담아 드리는 선물이며, 오직 하나님을 의지하여 그 은혜로 살아가는 사람들의 고백이다. 성경은 상한 심령이 주께 드릴 수 있는 최고의 제물이라고 한다(시 51:17). 상한 심령을 가진 사람은 결코 주님 앞에 교만할 수 없

고, 모든 것이 주님의 은혜라며 주님께 모든 영광을 돌리기 때문이다.

우리는 세상에서 가장 아름답고 영광스러운 찬양과 경배로 여호와를 예배해야 한다(9a절). 주님은 찬양과 경배를 받기에 합당하시며, 우리가 주님을 경배할 때 온 세상이 주님 앞에서 두려워 떨 것이기 때문이다. '떨다'(חיל)는 산모가 고통으로 인해 몸을 비틀며 떠는 모습이다(HALOT). 주님의 백성은 주님께 경의를 표하지만, 세상은 주님 앞에서 심히 두려워하고 떨 것이다.

4. 심판하시는 왕 여호와(96:10-13)

10 모든 나라 가운데서 이르기를
여호와께서 다스리시니
세계가 굳게 서고 흔들리지 않으리라
그가 만민을 공평하게 심판하시리라 할지로다
11 하늘은 기뻐하고
땅은 즐거워하며
바다와 거기에 충만한 것이 외치고
12 밭과 그 가운데에 있는 모든 것은 즐거워할지로다
그 때 숲의 모든 나무들이 여호와 앞에서 즐거이 노래하리니
13 그가 임하시되 땅을 심판하러 임하실 것임이라
그가 의로 세계를 심판하시며
그의 진실하심으로 백성을 심판하시리로다

기자는 주님의 백성들에게 세상에 사는 모든 이방인들(גּוֹיִם) 중에 "여호와가 다스리신다"(혹은 "여호와가 왕이시다")(יְהוָה מָלָךְ)라고 선포할 것을 권면한다(10a-b절). 모빙클(Mowinckel)은 이 문장을 "여호와가 (예배가 진행되는 도중) 왕이 되셨다"(YHWH has just [in this liturgical action] become

King)로 해석할 것을 제안했지만, 그다지 설득력이 있는 것은 아니다. 하나님은 태초부터 영원히 왕이시기 때문이다.

10절은 이 시편의 절정일 뿐만 아니라 구약 전체의 핵심 메시지이다(Brueggemann & Bellinger). 여호와는 이스라엘을 다스리실 뿐만 아니라 온 세상을 다스리시는 왕이다(cf. 사 2:2-4; 미 4:1-4). 여호와께서 세상을 다스리신다는 선포는 세상에 사는 모든 사람에게 하나님이 그들의 왕이심을 인정하는 반응을 요구한다(Tucker & Grant).

여호와께서 다스리시는 세상은 굳게 서서 결코 흔들리지 않을 것이다(10c절). 한때는 이 말씀이 지구가 영원히 자전하는 것을 뜻하는 것으로 해석되었다고 한다(cf. Kidner). 그러나 그런 의미는 본문에서 발견할 수 없다. 주님의 세상 통치는 영원할 것이라는 말씀이다.

여호와의 세상 통치는 심판으로 표현된다(10d, 13절). 하나님은 세상 만민을 공평과 의와 진실로 심판하실 것이라고 하는데, 심판은 왕의 고유 권한이다. 그러므로 주님이 세상을 다스리는 왕이라는 사실은 민족들을 심판하심으로 드러낼 것이다. '공평'(מֵישָׁרִים)은 이미 알리고 세운 기준에 따라 평가한다는 뜻이다(cf. Hossfeld-Zenger). '의'(צֶדֶק)는 옳음을, '진실'(אֱמוּנָה)은 성실을 뜻한다(13절). 하나님의 심판은 '심지 않은 것을 거두는' 심판이 아니다. 모든 사람은 창조주가 원하시는 기준과 원칙을 어느 정도 알고 있다. 사도 바울은 이것을 양심이라고 한다(롬 2:15).

기자는 여호와의 심판을 기뻐하는 것들을 일곱 가지로 나열한다(11-12절): '하늘, 땅, 바다, 바다에 있는 것, 밭, 밭에 있는 것, 숲의 모든 나무들.' 숫자 7이 사용되는 것은 하나님이 창조하신 세상의 완벽함을 강조한다(Shaefer). 또한 자연 만물이 하나님의 심판을 기뻐한다는 의미이다.

자연이 왜 이렇게 기뻐하는 것일까? 하나님은 세상을 참으로 아름답게 창조하셨는데(cf. 창 1장), 자연은 인간들 때문에 여러 차례 심판을 받고 파괴되었다(cf. 창 3, 4, 6-9장). 그러므로 신약은 자연 만물이 주님의 재림을 학수고대하고 있다고 한다(cf. 롬 8:18-22). 주님이 세상을 심판하시는 날, 주의 백성들만 회복되는 것이 아니라, 자연도 회복될 것이기 때문이다. 하나님의 세상 통치는 항상 종말론적인 면을 지니고 있다(McCann).

제97편

I. 장르/양식: 회중 찬양시(cf. 29편)

이 시편은 여호와의 왕 되심을 기념하는 서술적 찬양시(descriptive praise psalm)(Grogan, Westermann) 혹은 즉위시(enthronement psalm)로 분류된다(cf. deClaissé-Walford et al., Ross). 구체적인 정황은 알 수 없지만, 특정한 예배 때 사용되었을 것이다(Ross).

내용면에서 이 시편은 구약의 여러 텍스트를 연상케 하는데(VanGemeren), 한 주석가는 96편과 97편을 쌍둥이 시편들이라고 한다(Tate). 이 노래는 시편 제3권이 제기한 신학적 위기에 대한 답이며, 종말론적으로 읽혀야 한다(McCann).

이 시편과 96편과 제2이사야서(40-55장)는 매우 유사하다 하여 저작 시기를 늦은 포로기 시대 혹은 그 이후 제2성전이 완성된 다음에 불린 노래라는 견해가 있다(Terrien). 그러나 대부분 학자들은 저작 시기와 정황에 대해 침묵한다. 본문에서 구체적인 증거를 포착할 수 없기 때문이다.

II. 구조

이 시편의 구조를 논할 때 가장 논쟁이 되는 이슈는 6절이 앞 섹션(1-5절)과 혹은 뒤 섹션(7-9절)과 함께 취급되느냐이다. 학자들 사이에는 첫 섹션이 5절에서 끝나며 6절은 새로운 섹션을 시작한다는 견해(deClaissé-Walford et al., Gerstenberger, Goldingay, Hossfeld-Zenger, McCann)와, 첫 섹션이 5절이 아니라 6절에서 끝이 난다는 견해가 있다(Kraus, Terrien, Tucker & Grant, VanGemeren). 새번역은 6절을 앞·뒤 섹션과 연관되지 않은 독립적인 섹션으로 취급한다. 이 주석에서는 6절을 하나님의 현현(1-5절)에 대한 세상의 반응으로 간주하여 다음과 같은 구조를 바탕으로 본문을 주해해 나가고자 한다.

A. 여호와의 현현(97:1-5)

B. 현현에 대한 올바른 반응(97:6-9)

A′. 여호와의 보호(97:10-12)

III. 주해

이 노래도 시편집의 핵심 메시지, 곧 "여호와께서 다스리신다"를 선언한다. 여호와는 주의 백성뿐 아니라 온 세상의 경배와 찬양을 받기에 합당하시다. 온 세상을 창조하시고 다스리시는 하나님은 자기 백성을 영원히 버리지 않으실 것이며 곧 구원하실 것이다. 구원의 은혜가 주의 백성이 아닌 그들의 하나님 여호와에게서 시작될 것임을 선언한다.

1. 여호와의 현현(97:1-5)

[1] 여호와께서 다스리시나니
땅은 즐거워하며

허다한 섬은 기뻐할지어다

2 구름과 흑암이 그를 둘렀고

공의와 정의가 그의 보좌의 기초로다

3 불이 그의 앞에서 나와

사방의 대적들을 불사르시는도다

4 그의 번개가 세계를 비추니

땅이 보고 떨었도다

5 산들이 여호와의 앞

곧 온 땅의 주 앞에서

밀랍 같이 녹았도다

하나님 통치와 현현의 기본적인 성향이 여기서는 매우 긍정적으로 묘사되어 있다.

첫째, 여호와의 통치는 세상을 즐겁게 한다(1절, cf. 시 93:1; 96:10; 99:1). "여호와께서 다스리신다"/"여호와가 왕이시다"가 가장 많은 학자들의 지지를 받지만(cf. Alter, Tucker & Grant), 아직도 상당수가 "여호와가 왕이 되셨다/여호와가 통치를 시작하셨다"로 해석한다(Eaton, Goldingay, Tucker & Grant, Weiser). 이 사람들은 여호와의 왕위 취임식에서 이 노래가 사용되었다고 생각하기 때문이다.

하나님은 보좌에 앉아 계심으로 세상을 다스리시는 것이 아니라 현현을 통해 매우 역동적으로 다스리신다(Broyles). 그러므로 하나님의 통치를 받는 땅과 허다한 섬들이 기뻐한다. '허다한 섬들'(אִיִּים רַבִּים)은 멀리 떨어져 있는 섬들을 뜻한다(Goldingay). 그러므로 땅과 허다한 섬들은 온 세상을 상징한다. 왕이신 여호와의 통치는 이스라엘에 제한되어 있지 않고, 범우주적인 통치임을 분명히 하고 있다(McCann). 온 세상이 주님의 통치를 기뻐하고 즐거워한다.

둘째, 하나님이 앉아 계시는 보좌는 사람이 도저히 감당할 수 없는 찬란한 광채를 발한다. 그러므로 구름과 흑암이 그를 둘렀다(2a절). 흑암과 구름은 하나님의 현현의 상징이다(VanGemeren, cf. 신 4:11, 22; 시 18:9-11; 욜 2:2; 습 1:15). '흑암'(עֲרָפֶל)은 매우 진한 어두움이며 '구름'(עָנָן)보다 가리는 능력이 훨씬 더 뛰어나다(cf. HALOT). 하나님은 얼마나 강력한 광채를 발하시는지 사람들은 절대 직접 볼 수 없다. 성경에서 빛은 생명의 근원이자 구원의 상징이다. 여호와의 통치는 세상에 생명을 주고 온 세상을 구원한다.

셋째, 하나님은 공의와 정의로 세상을 다스리신다(2b절). 공의와 정의가 주님이 앉아 계신 보좌의 기초라고 하는데, '공의'(צֶדֶק)는 옳고 그름에 대한 기준을, '정의'(מִשְׁפָּט)는 법의 공평한 적용을 강조하며 주님의 통치의 가장 중요한 두 가지 원리이다. 하나님은 모든 사람이 동의할 기준에 따라 공평하게 세상을 다스리신다. 공의와 정의는 여호와의 통치에 반영되어 있기 때문에 세상에서 행해지는 모든 악은 하나님의 통치를 위협하는 행위이다(cf. McCann).

넷째, 하나님은 악인들을 심판하신다(3절). 2절은 하나님이 공의와 정의로 세상을 다스리신다고 했다. 이제 3절은 하나님의 공평하고 의로운 통치를 위반 혹은 위협하는 사람들에 관한 것이다. 그들을 사르는 불이 '하나님 앞에서'(לְפָנָיו) 나온다. 본문은 하나님이 이 땅에 임하시는 날 세상의 모든 악인들이 하나님의 심판을 받을 것을 선언한다. 심판을 받는 '주님의 대적들'(צָרָיו)은 누구인가? 하나님의 통치 원칙을 거부한 사람들이다. 성경은 주의 백성의 원수들이 곧 주님의 원수들이라고 한다.

다섯째, 왕이신 하나님의 위엄이 온 세상을 두렵게 한다(4-5절). 번개를 주관하시는 주님이 세계를 비추시니 땅이 떨고(cf. 시 77:16; 합 3:10), 산들이 밀랍이 녹듯이 녹아 내린다(cf. 미 1:4; 나 1:5). 창조주 하나님의 위엄이 얼마나 대단한지 세상에서 가장 높은 산들도 밀랍이 녹듯이 녹아 내린다.

2. 현현에 대한 올바른 반응(97:6-9)

[6] 하늘이 그의 의를 선포하니
모든 백성이 그의 영광을 보았도다
[7] 조각한 신상을 섬기며
허무한 것으로 자랑하는 자는
다 수치를 당할 것이라
너희 신들아 여호와께 경배할지어다
[8] 여호와여
시온이 주의 심판을 듣고 기뻐하며
유다의 딸들이 즐거워하였나이다
[9] 여호와여
주는 온 땅 위에 지존하시고
모든 신들보다 위에 계시니이다

창조주요 통치자이신 여호와의 현현은 온 세상을 하나님의 의와 영광으로 가득 차게 했다. 기자는 이러한 상황을 하늘이 주님의 의를 선포하고 모든 백성이 여호와의 영광을 본 것이라고 한다(6절). 하나님의 임재가 온 세상에 가득하다는 뜻이다. 주님의 영광이 세상을 가득 채우니 제일 먼저 우상 숭배자들이 수치를 당한다(7절). 7절은 이 노래의 중심이자 핵심 메시지다(Grogan).

그들은 이때까지 조각한 신상과 허무한 것을 신들이라고 숭배해왔다. 그러나 하나님의 영광이 온 세상을 채우는 날, 그들은 신들이라고 숭배한 것들이 모두 거짓이라는 사실을 깨닫게 될 것이다. 그들은 돌과 나무 동상들이 실제로 존재하는 신들을 표현하는 것이라고 생각했다. 그러나 사실 그것들은 돌덩어리와 나무덩어리에 지나지 않는다. 돌덩어리와 나무덩어리가 상징하거나 표현하는 실제 신들은 없으므로, 그들은 신들이라고 숭배하는 것들이 인간들의 어리석고 가증스러운 상상력의 결과라는 사실을 깨닫게 될 것이다(cf. von Rad). 그러므로 그들은 허무맹랑한 것들을 신으로 숭배한 자신들을 부끄럽게 생각하게 될 것이다. 여호와 하나님은 얼마나 위대하신지, 설령 세상에 신들이 있다 해도 그 신들은 모두 하나님을 경배해야 한다(7d절). 사고와 논리를 지닌 인간은 더욱더 여호와를 예배해야 한다.

여호와께서 열방을 심판하셨다는 소식이 시온과 유다에 들리자, 유다의 딸들이 즐거워한다(8절). '유다의 딸들'은 유다의 마을들을 의미한다(Grogan). 소식을 듣고 온 땅이 기뻐한다는 뜻이다. 당연하다. 그동안 주의 백성인 이스라엘을 참으로 괴롭게 한 자들이 열방인데, 그들이 여호와의 심판을 받았으니 이스라엘을 상징하는 시온과 유다의 온 땅이 기뻐한다. 열방이 심판을 받아 망함으로써 주의 백성의 회복이 더 가까워졌기 때문이다.

여호와께서 열방은 심판하시고, 자기 백성은 기쁘게 하심으로써 모든 신들보다 위에 계시는 지존자임을 온 세상에 드러내셨다(9절). 당시 사람들은 세상 모든 민족은 각자 수호신이 있다고 생각했다. 여호와는 이스라엘의 수호신으로 간주되었다. 이러한 상황에서 이스라엘의 신이신 여호와께서 신들과 그들이 보호하는 민족들을 심판하셨으니, 여호와가 지존자이심이 온 천하에 드러난 것이다. '지존자'(עֶלְיוֹן)와 '위에 있다'(נַעֲלֵיתָ)는 같은 어원에서 비롯된 단어들이다. 여호와는 이 세상뿐만 아니라 신들이 거주하는 하늘에서도 비교할 자가 없는, 차원/클래스(class)가 완전히 다른 분이심을 뜻한다(cf. Tucker & Grant). 물론 이 말이 신들의 존재를 인정하는 것은 아니다. 단지 고대 근동 사람들의 세계관에 따른 언어를 사용한 것뿐이다. 여호와 외에 신은 없다.

3. 여호와의 보호(97:10-12)

10 여호와를 사랑하는 너희여
악을 미워하라
그가 그의 성도의 영혼을 보전하사
악인의 손에서 건지시느니라
11 의인을 위하여 빛을 뿌리고
마음이 정직한 자를 위하여 기쁨을 뿌리시는도다
12 의인이여
너희는 여호와로 말미암아 기뻐하며
그의 거룩한 이름에 감사할지어다

이 섹션은 여호와가 지존자이심을 믿는 사람들이 어떤 마음으로 살아야 하는지를 제안한다. 10절의 문법이 다소 매끈하지 않은 부분이 있지만(cf. Hossfeld-Zenger, McCann), 의미는 명확하다.

첫째, 주님의 자녀들은 악을 미워해야 한다(10a-b절). '여호와를 사랑하는 것'과 '악을 미워하는 것' 두 가지가 대조된다. '사랑하다'(אהב)는 감정적인 언어이다(cf. NIDOTTE). 하나님을 사랑한다는 것은 주님을 생각하면 너무 좋아 흥분이 된다는 뜻이다. 마치 사랑에 빠진 사람이 연인을 생각할 때 느끼는 감정처럼 말이다. '미워하다'(שנא)는 원수처럼 생각한다는 의미이다(cf. NIDOTTE). 그러므로 하나님을 열정적으로 사랑하는 것은 곧 악을 원수처럼 생각하여 가까이하지 않는 것을 뜻한다.

둘째, 주님의 자녀들은 하나님의 끊임없는 구원과 보호를 기대할 수 있다(10c-d절). 주님이 우리의 영혼을 보전하신다고 하는데, '보전하다'(שמר)는 보초병이 철두철미하게 감시하는 상황을 묘사한다. 하나님은 해를 당하지 않도록 우리의 삶을 철저하게 지키신다. 우리가 악인들의 공격을 받아 곤경에 빠지면 주님은 우리를 그들의 손에서 건져 내신다. 그러므로 우리는 다윗과 같이 “사망의 음침한 골짜기를 지날지라도 해를 두려워하지 않을 것이다”라고 고백할 수 있다(시 23:4).

셋째, 주님의 자녀들은 하나님이 뿌려 주시는 빛과 기쁨을 누리며 살 수 있다(11절). 11절의 문법도 매끈하지는 않다(cf. Kraus). 그러나 의미는 확실하다. 여호와께서는 의인들을 악인들의 손에서 건지실 뿐만 아니라(10절), 그들의 삶을 빛과 기쁨으로 채우신다. 성경에서 빛은 생명을 상징한다. 주님은 온갖 죄악과 죽음으로 가득한 이 세상에서 의롭고 정직하게 살려고 노력하는 주의 백성들에게 생명이 되어 주시고 기쁨을 주신다.

넷째, 주님의 자녀들은 여호와 한 분만을 기뻐하며 살 수 있다(12절). 이것이 하나님이 내려 주시는 온갖 축복의 목적이다. 주님이 우리를 보호하시고, 생명도 주시며, 기쁨도 주시는 이유는 이 모든 선한 것들이 주님께로부터 온 것이라는 사실을 깨닫게 하시기 위해서이다. 그러므로 이 진리를 깨닫는 사람은 그가 누리는 축복이 아니라, 그 축복을 주시는 주님만을 사모하고 기뻐한다. 주님 외에는 모든 것이 부수적인 것들이기 때문이다. 또한 오직 주님만으로 기뻐하는 사람은 어떠한 상황에 처하더라도 주님께 감사한다.

제98편

시

I. 장르/양식: 회중 찬양시(cf. 29편)

이 노래와 시편 96편은 내용이 매우 유사하여 종종 같은 저자의 작품으로 간주되기도 한다(VanGemeren, Westermann). 이 두 시편의 가장 기본적인 차이는 이 시편이 열방이나 그들의 우상들을 언급하지 않는다는 것이다. 그들은 이미 사라졌고 오직 여호와만이 중심 무대를 차지하고 있기 때문이다(Grogan). 이 두 시편이 비슷한 것은 저자가 같아서가 아니라, 주제가 같고 사용하는 단어들이 비슷해서 일 것이다(Anderson, deClaissé-Walford et al.).

이 시편은 '시'(מִזְמוֹר)라는 매우 간략한 표제를 지녔다. 그럼에도 불구하고 93-100편 중 유일하게 표제를 지닌 시이다. 그러므로 학자들은 편집자들이 98-99편을 이 모음집에 포함시키기 위해 표제가 짧은 휴지(休止, caesura) 역할을 하도록 하기 위해 삽입한 것으로 생각한다(Hossfeld-Zenger).

이 노래는 언제 저작되고 어느 상황에서 사용된 노래일까? 여호와의 왕 되심을 기념하는 축제에서 불린 것이라고 하는 이들이 있다(Brueggemann & Bellinger). 다른 학자들은 여호와께서 이스라엘 군대를 이끌고 성전(聖戰)에서 승리한 후에 돌아오면서 개선가(凱旋歌)로 부른 노래라고 한다(Longman).

제2성전이 재건된 포로기 이후 시대에 저작된 노래라고 하는 이들도 있다(Terrien). 그러나 이 시가 역사적 정황으로 간주될 만한 정보를 제공하고 있지 않기 때문에(cf. Goldingay), 구체적인 상황은 알 수 없다. 단지 주의 백성이 하나님의 놀라운 은혜를 경험하고 난 후에 불렀던 노래인 것은 확실하다. 이 노래에서는 이스라엘이 여러 전쟁에서 경험했던 승리가 마치 한 사건처럼 묶여 종말론적인 의미를 지니고 있다(Weiser, cf. Tate, VanGemeren).

II. 구조

일부 학자들은 이 시를 두 파트로 구분하지만(Kraus, Tate), 대부분 주석가들은 세 파트로 구분한다(deClaissé-Walford et al., Gerstenberger, Hossfeld-Zenger, Terrien, VanGemeren). 이 주석에서도 다음과 같이 세 파트로 구분하여 본문을 주해하고자 한다.

A. 이미 구원을 이루신 하나님을 찬양(98:1-3)
    B. 목소리와 악기로 하나님을 찬양(98:4-6)
A'. 장차 오실 하나님을 찬양(98:7-9)

III. 주해

하나님의 놀라운 구원을 경험한 공동체는 하나님께 감사할 뿐만 아니라, 자신들이 경험한 구원을 하나님이 미래에 하실 일을 조금이나마 맛볼 수 있는 계기로 삼았다. 하나님이 그들의 삶에서 이루신 일이 미래에 대한 증표가 된 것이다. 하나님의 놀라운 기적을 경험한 공동체는 오로지 찬양으로 하나님을 경배한다.

1. 이미 구원을 이루신 하나님을 찬양(98:1-3)

1 새 노래로 여호와께 찬송하라
그는 기이한 일을 행하사
그의 오른손과 거룩한 팔로 자기를 위하여
구원을 베푸셨음이로다
2 여호와께서 그의 구원을 알게 하시며
그의 공의를 뭇 나라의 목전에서
명백히 나타내셨도다
3 그가 이스라엘의 집에 베푸신 인자와 성실을 기억하셨으므로
땅 끝까지 이르는 모든 것이
우리 하나님의 구원을 보았도다

기자는 온 공동체가 새로운 노래로 여호와를 찬송하라는 권면으로 이 시편을 시작한다(1a절). '새 노래'(שִׁיר חָדָשׁ)는 전에는 불린 적이 없는 새로운 노래를 의미할 수도 있지만(cf. HALOT), 이미 존재하는 노래라 할지라도 새로운 각오와 마음 자세로 부르라는 뜻으로 해석될 수 있다(cf. Tucker & Grant). 본문이 묘사하고 있는 이미지는 전쟁에서 승리하고 돌아오는 용장을 백성들이 목청을 높여 찬양하는 것이다(Longman, VanGemeren, cf. 시 33:3; 40:3; 96:1; 144:9). 전쟁에서 승리하심을 통해 하나님이 참으로 특별한 은혜를 베푸셨으니, 주님의 은혜에 걸맞게 온 마음을 다해 주님을 찬양하라는 뜻이다.

저자가 주님이 구체적으로 어느 전쟁에서 승리하시고, 어떤 상황에서 주의 백성에게 구원을 베푸셨는가에 대해 언급하지 않는 것은 과거에 이루신 모든 구원 사역을 생각하도록 하기 위한 의도로 볼 수 있다(VanGemeren). 하나님이 승리를 통해 자기 백성에게 베푸신 은혜는 참으로 '기이한 일'(נִפְלָאוֹת)이다(1b절, cf. 시 106:7). 기이한 일은 이적과 기

적으로 하나님이 하시는 일이다. 하나님은 사람들이 사용하는 방법이 아니라, 아주 다른 '기이한 일'을 행하셔서 자기 백성에게 구원을 베푸셨다(1d절).

주님은 이 기이한 일을 오른손과 팔로 이루셨다(1c절, cf. 출 15:11-12; 사 52:10). 하나님의 손과 팔은 힘과 능력과 특별한 신분을 상징한다(Goldingay, cf. 사 51:9-11). 하나님은 자기 백성에게 구원을 베풀기 위해 온갖 능력으로 마음껏 역사하셨다. 이러한 상황에 가장 잘 어울리는 하나님의 구원은 아마도 바로와 이집트를 상대로 승리하신 후 이루신 출애굽 사건일 것이다(Brueggemann & Bellinger, Goldingay, cf. 출 15장). 또한 하나님은 이 놀라운 일을 그의 백성뿐만 아니라, 자신을 위해서도 하셨다(1c절). 여호와가 이스라엘의 하나님이라는 명성에 걸맞은 사역을 하셨다는 뜻이다.

또한 이 말씀은 앞으로 주의 백성이 당면할 모든 역경에도 하나님 여호와께서 개입하셔서 구원하실 것임을 암시한다. 심지어는 바빌론에서도 그들을 구원하셔서 새로운 출애굽을 이루실 것을 기대할 수 있다(Goldingay, Kraus, Leupold, McCann). 하나님은 자기 백성을 끝까지 보호하시고 구원하시기 때문이다.

하나님은 온 세상이 그가 백성을 구원하신 역사를 알기 원하신다(2절). 하나님이 자기 백성을 구원하신 일을 온 세상이 인정하는 것이 이스라엘의 구속 역사의 정점이기 때문이다(Weiser). 또한 열방은 이 일을 통해 전사이신 여호와가 자기 백성과 맺으신 '언약에 대한 충성'(חֶסֶד)(3절)을 이행하기 위해 온갖 기적과 이적으로 구원하시는 성실하신 신이라는 사실을 알아야 한다. 또한 그들은 이런 위대하신 하나님의 백성이 된 이스라엘도 특별하다는 것을 깨달아야 한다. 기자는 하나님이 백성을 구원하신 일을 '공의'(צְדָקָה)라고 하는데, 본문에서는 억울한 일을 당하거나 곤경에 처한 사람을 방치하지 않고 바로 잡는 것을 뜻한다(Kidner, cf. 새번역, 아가페, RSV).

이 말씀은 하나님이 자기 백성을 구원하시는 목적 중에는 온 세상이 주님과 주의 백성에 대해 알게 하기 위한 목적도 포함되었음을 의미한다. 그러므로 하나님의 구원을 경험한 우리도 항상 세상 사람들에게 하나님의 놀라우신 능력과 사랑에 대해 증거해야 한다.

하나님이 자기 백성에게 구원을 베푸신 것은 그들에게 인자와 성실을 베푸시는 일을 기억하셨기 때문이다(3a절). '기억, 인자, 성실, 이스라엘'은 모두 여호와께서 이스라엘과 맺으신 언약과 연관된 단어들이다(Tucker & Grant). 또한 구약에서 하나님의 기억하심은 항상 사람들을 위한 은혜와 구원으로 이어진다(cf. 창 6-9장; 삼상 1장). 하나님이 자기 백성에게 인자와 성실을 베푸신 일은 주님이 백성 삼으신 사람들만이 아는 사적인 일이 아니라, 온 세상이 보고 인정하는 사실이다(3b-c절). 온 세상은 하나님의 구원 사역에 대해 알아야 한다. 구원을 입은 우리는 그들에게 알리고 가르칠 책임이 있다.

2. 목소리와 악기로 하나님을 찬양(98:4-6)

4 온 땅이여
여호와께 즐거이 소리칠지어다
소리 내어 즐겁게 노래하며
찬송할지어다
5 수금으로 여호와를 노래하라
수금과 음성으로 노래할지어다
6 나팔과 호각 소리로
왕이신 여호와 앞에 즐겁게 소리칠지어다

전사이신 여호와께서 전쟁에서 승리하여 자기 백성에게 구원을 베푸셨다는 사실을 온 땅이 알게 되면 어떠한 반응을 보여야 할까? 저자는 즐겁게 소리치며 주님을 찬송하라고 한다(4절). 신적인 전사(divine warrior)이신 여호와께서 전쟁을 하시면 온 자연이 꺾이고, 마르고, 시들해진다(cf. 사 24:4-13). 그러나 여호와께서 승리하시면 자연은 생기와 왕성함을 얻어 하나님을 찬양하게 된다(Greenspoon). 본문에서도 이러한 현상이 묘사되고 있다(Tucker & Grant).

또한 목소리로만 찬양할 것이 아니라 온갖 악기를 동원해서 주님을 찬양하라고 한다(5-6절). 사람의 목소리만이 찬양에 동원할 수 있는 것은 아니다. 세상에 존재하는 모든 악기들을 동원해서 주님을 찬양함이 바람직하다. 기자는 이러한 사실을 강조하기 위해 '수금, 나팔, 호각'의 3(=만수)가지 악기를 언급한다. 자기 백성을 구원하신 하나님은 세상에 있는 모든 악기를 통해 찬양 받을 자격을 충분히 소유하셨기 때문이다. 사실 말이 악기이지 이 세 가지 중 '나팔'(חֲצֹצְרָה)과 '호각'(שׁוֹפָר)은 악기라기보다는 신호 도구였으며, 큰 소리가 필요한 전쟁터에서 주로 사용되었다. 악기로서의 감미로움이나 다듬어진 소리는 찾아볼 수 없다.

이러한 사실이 우리에게 주는 교훈은 분명하다. 찬양은 소수에게만 주어진 특권이 아니라, 모든 사람에게 주어진 권리이자 축복이다. 또한 세상에서 가장 거친 소리를 내는 도구라도 하나님을 찬양하는 데 사용될 수 있다. 아직도 일부 교회에서는 경건을 빌미로 드럼과 기타 등을 찬양에서 배제한다. 별로 바람직한 결정은 아니다.

3. 장차 오실 하나님을 찬양(98:7-9)

7 바다와 거기 충만한 것과
세계와 그 중에 거주하는 자는 다 외칠지어다
8 여호와 앞에서 큰 물은 박수할지어다
산악이 함께 즐겁게 노래할지어다

9 그가 땅을 심판하러 임하실 것임이로다
그가 의로 세계를 판단하시며
공평으로 그의 백성을 심판하시리로다

온 땅에게 여호와를 찬양할 것을 권한(cf. 4절) 기자가 범위를 더 넓히고 있다. 바다와 그 안에 있는 모든 생명(식물과 동물)과 사람뿐만 아니라 세상 중에 거하는 모든 생명체들이 주님께 외칠 것을 권유한다(Briggs). 바다가 외치는 것처럼 땅도 외치라는 권면을 받는데, 땅을 대표하는 것은 큰 물과 산악이다(8절). 개역개정이 '큰 물'로 번역한 히브리어 단어(נְהָרוֹת)의 의미는 '강들'이다(시 93:3, cf. 새번역, 아가페, NIV, NAS, TNK). 강들이 모이면 큰 물(홍수, cf. NRS)이 된다 하여 이렇게 번역한 것으로 보이지만, 바로 다음 행에 등장하는 '산들'(הָרִים)이 이 단어와 쌍을 이루고 있다는 점을 생각할 때 '강들'이 더 정확한 번역이다. 또한 '큰 물'은 하나님의 창조 사역을 위협하는 '원시적인 물'(primeval water)로 오해될 수 있기 때문에 피하는 것이 좋다(cf. Anderson, McCann, Terrien). 하나님은 바다와 그 안에 있는 모든 것뿐만 아니라, 육지에 있는 산들과 강들의 찬양을 받기에 합당하신 분이다.

하나님께 지음을 받은 피조물들은 전쟁에서 승리하시고 이스라엘의 왕이 되신 하나님을 찬양해야 한다(Longman). 또한 여호와는 장차 세상을 심판하러 오는 심판주이시다(9절). 고대 근동에서는 왕이 곧 최종 재판관이었다. 그러므로 이스라엘의 왕이신 하나님은 그들의 재판관이기도 하시다. 그러나 본문에서 주님은 장차 이스라엘뿐만 아니라 온 세상을 심판하러 오신다. 여호와는 이스라엘의 왕이실 뿐만 아니라 온 세상의 왕이시기 때문이다. 하나님의 권세는 종말에 주님이 이 땅에 임하실 때뿐만 아니라 성도들의 예배를 통해서도 온 천하에 드러난다(Kidner).

기자는 하나님이 과거에 자기 백성을 구원하신 일이 언젠가는 온 세상을 심판하실 근거가 될 것이라며 과거에 이루신 구원을 종말론적으로 승화시키고 있다(Schaefer, cf. Oesterley). 그러나 세상이 하나님의 심판에 대해 두려워할 필요는 없다. 주님의 판단은 의로우시며 공의로우시기 때문이다. 주님은 심지 않은 것을 거두시는 분이 아니다. 사람들에게 의롭게 살 수 있는 기회를 충분히 주셨다. 그러므로 여호와의 심판은 공평하다.

제99편

I. 장르/양식: 회중 찬양시(cf. 29편)

이 시편은 여호와의 왕 되심을 노래하는 즉위시(enthronement psalm)이며 93-100편에 달하는 즉위시 모음집의 결론이라 할 수 있다(Brueggemann & Bellinger, McCann, VanGemeren). 즉위시들은 제4권(90-106편)의 중심을 형성하면서 제3권(73-89편)이 묘사하고 있는 이스라엘의 어려움(바빌론으로 끌려가 사는 것)에 대한 적절한 반응이다. 편집자들은 이 즉위시들을 통해 두 가지를 선포한다. 첫째, 이스라엘이 바빌론으로 끌려가게 된 것은 그들의 하나님 여호와의 무능함으로 인해 비롯된 일이 아니라, 창조주께서 허락하신 일이다. 둘째, 여호와께서는 이스라엘에게 옛 것보다 더 좋은 새로운 출애굽을 이루셔서 그들을 바빌론에서 돌아오게 하실 것이며, 그들을 다시 자기 백성으로 삼으실 것이다. 이처럼 즉위시들은 제3권이 제시한 문제에 대해 적절하게 답하고 있기 때문에 현 위치를 차지하고 있는 것이다.

여호와의 왕 되심을 선언하는 즉위시가 주류를 이루는 제4권의 시작에서 시편 90편은 표제에서 시내 산 언약을 통해 하나님이 이스라엘의 왕이 되심을 선포했던 모세의 이름을 언급하였다. 그리고 즉위시들의 절정인 99편에서 시내 산 언약과 깊은 연관이 있는 모세를(6절, cf. 출 15:1-18) 다시금 언급한다. 모세는 시편 제4권에서 여섯 차례(시 99:6; 103:7; 105:26; 106:16, 23, 32) 언급될 정도로 중요하다. 그러므로 한 주석가는 제4권(90-106편)을 '모세의 책'이라고 부른다(Tate). 또한 아론도 언급한다(시 99:6; 105:26; 106:16).

이처럼 모세와 아론을 언급하여 출애굽 사건과 시내 산 일을 회상하게 하는 것은 오직 여호와만이 이스라엘의 왕이시라는 점을 강조하는 듯하다. 또한 이 시편이 이스라엘이 인간 왕을 세우는 일을 반대했던 선지자 사무엘(6절)을 언급하는 것도 우연은 아니다(cf. McCann). 포로가 되어 바빌론으로 끌려간 이스라엘의 소망은 오직 여호와 하나님이 그들의 왕이라는 사실에 있다. 기자는 제사장직의 상징인 아론을 6절에서 언급함으로써 하나님은 기도를 들으시고 용서하는 분이시라는 제사장적인 요소와 연결시킨다(Creach, Tucker & Grant).

이 시편은 언제쯤 저작되었을까? 학자들의 견해는 다양하다. 포로기 이전인 왕정 시대에 저작되었다는 주장도 있고(Anderson, Kraus), 바빌론 포로기 혹은 포로기 이후인 페르시아 시대를 저작 연대로 제안하는 이들도 있다(Terrien). 그러나 포로기 이후 시대를 저작 시기로 지목하는 사람들도 이 시의 일부는 포로기 이전에서 유래했을 것으로 추정한다. 결국 설득력 있는 결론은 존재하지 않는다는 뜻이다(Goldingay, cf. Gerstenberger).

이 노래가 어떤 정황에서 사용되었는지에 대해서도 학자들은 대부분 침묵한다. 여호와의 왕 되심이 중요한 주제였던 장막절(Feast of Tabernacle)에 사용되었을 것이라는 추측에서 언약 갱신 예식과 연관성이 있어 보인다는 추론까지 있다(cf. Ross). 어떤 정황에서 처음 사용되었건 간에 관점은 여호와의 왕권이 굳건하게 세워지는 종말을 염두에 두고 저작되었음을 알 수 있다.

II. 구조

이 시는 거의 같은 내용이 5절과 9에서 반복된다. 그렇다 보니 1-5절과 6-9절 두 부분으로 구분할 것을 제안하는 사람들이 있다(cf. Gerstenberger, Hossfeld-Zenger, VanGemeren). 그러나 후렴구처럼 반복되는 것은 5절과 9절 전체가 아니라 3절과 5절과 9절을 마무리하는 "주님은 거룩하시다"(קָדוֹשׁ הוּא)라는 문장이다(McCann, Ross, Tucker & Grant). 또한 이 문장이 세 차례 반복되는 것은 이사야 6:3에서 스랍들이 하나님을 향해 "거룩하다, 거룩하다, 거룩하다"(קָדוֹשׁ קָדוֹשׁ קָדוֹשׁ)라고 외친 일을 연상케 한다(Delitzsch, cf. Terrien). 그러므로 세 차례 반복되는 "주님은 거룩하시다"는 여호와 하나님의 완벽하신 성품과 선하심을 강조한다(Tucker & Grant). 이 주석에서는 다음과 같은 구조를 바탕으로 본문을 주해해 나가고자 한다.

A. 시온에 임하신 여호와(99:1-3)
B. 공의와 정의를 행하시는 여호와(99:4-5)
C. 기도에 응답하시고 용서하시는 여호와(99:6-9)

III. 주해

일부 학자들이 주장하는 것처럼 이 노래가 바빌론 포로 시절에 자주 사용된 노래라면 참으로 의미 있는 메시지의 선포라 할 수 있다. 주의 백성이 바빌론으로 오게 된 것은 여호와의 무능으로 빚어진 일이 아니라, 여호와께서 그들에게 내리신 징벌의 결과라고 하기 때문이다(cf. 8절). 하나님은 그들을 용서하실 뿐 아니라 분명 회복시키실 것이다. 하나님이 그들을 다시 자기 백성으로 삼으시는 날, 온 세상은 하나가 되어 하나님을 경배하게 될 것이다. 그러므로 이 노래는 종말론적인 관점에서 이스라엘뿐 아니라, 온 세상의 왕이신 여호와 하나님을 찬양한다.

1. 시온에 임하신 여호와(99:1-3)

1 여호와께서 다스리시니
만민이 떨 것이요
여호와께서 그룹 사이에 좌정하시니
땅이 흔들릴 것이로다
2 시온에 계시는 여호와는 위대하시고
모든 민족보다 높으시도다
3 주의 크고 두려운 이름을 찬송할지니
그는 거룩하심이로다

기자는 이 섹션에서 여호와 하나님의 지위에 대해 네 가지로 노래한다.

첫째, 여호와는 온 세상을 다스리시는 분이다(1a-b절, cf. 시 93:1; 96:10; 97:1). '다스린다'는 것은 공의와 정의로 통치하고 판단하는 것을 전제한다. 그러므로 세상 만민이 그들의 왕이신 여호와 앞에서 두려워 떤다(1, 3절). 하나님은 의인은 격려하시지만, 죄인은 심판하신다. 또한 세상 모든 사람은 죄인이다. 그러므로 세상 사람들은 하나님의 통치권을 두려워할 수밖에 없다(cf. Tucker & Grant).

둘째, 여호와는 천사들의 찬양과 경배를 받기에 합당하신 분이다(1c-d절). 하나님이 그룹 사이에 있는 보좌에 앉으셨다는(cf. 삼상 4:4; 삼하 6:2) 이미지는 법궤의 뚜껑인 시은좌에서 비롯된 것이지만(cf. 레 16:13; 시 80:1), 주님이 하늘에 있는(세상에서 가장 높은) 왕의 자리에 앉으셨다는 뜻이다(VanGemeren). '그룹'은 하나님의 초월성(이 세상의 모든 것과 질적으로 다름)을 강조하는 존재들이기 때문이다(cf. 삼상 4:4). 이 말씀의 가장 기본적인 의미는 세상을 통치하고 다스리신다는 뜻이지만, 주님의 보좌를 천사들이 받들고 있다는 사실도 중요하다. 하나님은 얼마나 위대하신지 사람뿐 아니라, 천사들의 섬김을 받기에 합당하신 분이라는 점을 강조하기 때문이다.

셋째, 여호와는 시온에서 세상을 다스리신다(2절). 하나님은 온 세상이 감당하기에도 부족한 위대하신 분이다. 이처럼 위대하신 분이 보잘것없는 시온에 거하신다! 그러므로 하나님의 시온에 임하심은 단지 주의 백성들에게만 영향을 미치는 것이 아니라, 온 세상에 영향을 미치는 매우 위대한 사건이다(Tucker & Grant). 하나님이 결정만 하시면 언제든 세상에서 가장 크고 위대한 민족의 섬김을 받으실 수 있다. 그러나 하나님은 연약한 이스라엘을 택하셔서 낮은 자들의 하나님이 되셨다. 그러므로 하나님이 시온에 거하시는 것은 상당히 충격적이라 할 수 있다(McCann). 비록 주의 백성이 연약하고 힘이 없지만, 여호와는 가장 위대하시고 세상 모든 민족보다 높으시다. 이스라엘의 비천한 모습이 하나님의 위대하심을 가리지는 못한다.

넷째, 여호와는 거룩하신 하나님이다(3절). '거룩'(קָדוֹשׁ)은 다르고 차별된다는 뜻이다. 여호와 하나님은 세상의 가장 위대한 민족을 자기 백성으로 삼으셔서 그들의 찬양을 받기에 합당하시지만, 가장 연약한 자들을 택하여 낮은 자들의 하나님이 되셨으니, 주님은 참으로 거룩하시다. 온 세상은 경외를 자아내는 이 낮은 자들의 하나님의 이름을 찬송해야 한다.

2. 공의와 정의를 행하시는 여호와(99:4-5)

4 능력 있는 왕은 정의를 사랑하느니라
주께서 공의를 견고하게 세우시고
주께서 야곱에게 정의와 공의를 행하시나이다
5 너희는 여호와 우리 하나님을 높여
그의 발등상 앞에서 경배할지어다

그는 거룩하시도다

개역개정은 4절이 언급하고 있는 '능력 있는 왕'을 인간 왕으로 해석할 수 있는 여지를 두고 번역했지만(cf. 아가페, NAS, TNK), 이 왕은 분명 하나님이시다(cf. 새번역, NIV, ESV, NRS, CSB). 이 섹션은 1절에서 시작된 하나님에 대한 찬양을 이어가고 있다. 찬양의 주제는 하나님의 공의롭고 정의로우심이다. 하나님은 힘도 있으시고 도덕성도 지니신 분이다(Grogan).

'정의'(מִשְׁפָּט)는 법정 판결과 연관되며, '공의'(צְדָקָה)는 옳고 그름과 연관된다. 이 두 가지는 본문에서처럼 자주 쌍으로 등장하여 하나님의 기본적인 성품을 표현한다. 세상의 왕들은 능력을 자랑하지만, 그들보다 더 큰 능력을 갖추신 여호와는 자신의 능력을 뽐내지 않고 공의와 정의를 사랑하는 것을 자랑하신다(cf. Tucker & Grant).

여호와 하나님은 정의를 사랑하시며, 공의를 견고하게 세우시는 분이다(cf. 시 9:7-8; 72:1-2; 96:13; 97:2). 하나님은 세상에 공의와 정의가 세워지도록 노력하시는 분이 아니라, 공의와 정의로 세상을 다스리시는 분이다(McCann). 이 두 가지를 통치 기준으로 삼아 세상을 다스리신다는 뜻이다(cf. 암 5:7-13, 21-24; 미 3:1-12). 주님은 특히 이스라엘을 다스리실 때 공의와 정의로 하셨다(4c절). 바빌론으로 끌려와 이 노래를 부르는 이들에게 이 말씀은 매우 특별한 의미를 지녔다. 그들이 바빌론으로 끌려온 것은 여호와께서 공의와 정의를 행하신 결과임을 인정해야 하기 때문이다. 하나님 스스로 죄 지은 백성을 내치신 것이다.

이러한 사실을 깨달은 사람들은 누가 권하지 않아도 스스로 의로우신 하나님을 찬양하게 될 것이다. 공의와 정의를 실현하기 위해 심지어 자기 백성까지 내치는 신은 세상에 없다. 하나님은 자기 백성을 편애하여 그들이 어떤 죄를 짓든 간에 상관하지 않는 분이 아니시기 때문이다.

그러므로 기자는 세상 사람들에게 주님의 발등상 앞에 엎드려 주님의 거룩하심을 경배하라고 한다. 성전에 있는 법궤는 하나님의 세상 통치와 임재의 상징이었기 때문에(Ross), 법궤는 주님의 '발등상'이 되었다(deClaissé-Walford et al., cf. 시 132:7-8; 대상 28:2). 성경은 성전(사 60:13)과 예루살렘(애 2:1)도 하나님의 발등상이라고 한다.

3. 기도에 응답하시고 용서하시는 여호와(99:6-9)

6 그의 제사장들 중에는 모세와 아론이 있고
그의 이름을 부르는 자들 중에는 사무엘이 있도다
그들이 여호와께 간구하매 응답하셨도다
7 여호와께서 구름 기둥 가운데서 그들에게 말씀하시니
그들은 그가 그들에게 주신 증거와 율례를 지켰도다
8 여호와 우리 하나님이여
주께서는 그들에게 응답하셨고
그들의 행한 대로 갚기는 하셨으나
그들을 용서하신 하나님이시니이다
9 너희는 여호와 우리 하나님을 높이고
그 성산에서 예배할지어다
여호와 우리 하나님은 거룩하심이로다

여호와는 이스라엘을 구원하시고 온 세상을 공의와 정의로 다스리시는 위대한 왕이시다. 또한 주님은 백성들의 기도를 들으시는 자상한 분이시다. 모세는 하나님이 이스라엘에게 율법을 주실 때 사용한 대리인(agent)일뿐만 아니라, 형 아론과 함께 이스라엘 종교에서 제사장직을 상징했다(6절). 모세와 아론과 사무엘이 한꺼번에 언급되는 것은 이들이 공의와 정의를 주의 백성들에게 실현한 모형(prototype)이기 때문이라고 하는 학자도 있지만(Kraus), 이 섹션의 메시지가 중보기도에 맞춰져 있음을 감안하면 설득력이 부족하다.

한 주석가는 모세가 제사장이 아니었다는 점을 근거로 '제사장'(כֹּהֵן)을 '종/섬기는 자'로 해석할 것을 제안하지만, 그럴 필요는 없다. 모세는 제사장권과 왕권과 선지자권이 함께 임하는 메시아의 모형이었기 때문이다. 모세도 제사장 역할을 한 것이다. 또한 이 말씀이 제사장들의 기도를 통한 중보역할을 강조하기 때문에 모세가 제사장으로 불리는 것은 별 문제가 없다(Tucker & Grant, cf. Goldingay).

자신은 평생 이스라엘을 위한 기도를 멈추는 죄를 범하지 않겠다고 했던 사무엘은 주님께 부르짖는 사람들의 상징이었다(6절, cf. 삼상 12:23). 하나님은 그들의 기도에 응답하셨다(6c, 8a-b절, cf. 출 14:15; 17:11-12; 삼상 7:5; 12:16-18). 이 말씀은 하나님이 자기 종들의 기도를 들으시는 너그럽고 자비로운 분이시며 앞으로도 계속 주의 백성들의 기도를 들으실 것을 암시한다.

여호와께서는 구름 기둥 가운데서 그들에게 말씀하셨다(7절). 만일 '그들'이 아론과 모세와 사무엘 세 사람을 두고 하는 말이라면, 이 말씀은 이 세 사람과 하나님의 특별한 관계를 상징하는 것으로 볼 수 있다(Delitzsch, cf. Goldingay). 이 세 사람은 다른 사람들이 누리지 못한 특권(매우 가까운 곳에서 구름 기둥을 통해 말씀하신 하나님을 경험함)을 누린 사람들이라는 뜻이다. 그러나 바로 다음 행이 언급하는 증거와 율례는 이 세 사람뿐 아니라 이스라엘 모두가 지켰다. 그러므로 '그들'을 온 이스라엘로 해석하는 것이 바람직하다.

하나님은 자기 백성들에게 증거와 율례를 주셨다(7절). 출애굽 때 이스라엘에게 율법을 주신 일을 상기시키는 표현이다. '증거'(עֵדוּת)와 '율례'(חֹק)는 율법을 칭하는 전문적인 용어다. 저자는 이스라엘이 하나님의 백성이 되어 받은 율법을 지키려고 노력했고, 어느 정도는 성공했다고 한다(7b절, cf. McCann). 그러나 우리가 알다시피 율법은 하나의 시스템이기 때문에 대부분의 율법을 잘 지킨다고 해도 한두 가지라도 지키지 못하면 율법을 범하게 된다.

그러므로 하나님은 전반적으로 그들이 율법을 준수한 만큼 그들의 기도에 응답하셨지만(Tucker & Grant), 그들이 율법을 범한 부분에 대해서는 그들이 행한 대로 갚으셨다(8c절). 그들에게 벌을 내리셨다는 것이다. 그럼에도 불구하고 다행인 점은 하나님이 벌하신 그들을 용서하셨다는 사실이다(8d절). 그러므로 이 말씀은 인간의 죄에도 불구하고 율법의 구원 능력과 치유 능력을 강조한다(Hossfeld-Zenger). 그렇다면 하나님이 그들을 징계하신 것은 그들이 미워서가 아니라 죄의 값을 치르게 하기 위해서이며, 죄 문제가 해결되면 다시 그들을 사랑하기 위함임을 알 수 있다.

이러한 사실을 깨달으면 심지어 징계를 받은 사람이라도 주님께 감사할 수 있고, 용서받은 사람은 주님을 찬양할 수 있게 된다. 그러므로 기자는 온 세상 사람들에게 이처럼 위대하시고 거룩하신 여호와를 높이고 찬양할 것을 권면한다(9절, cf. Kirkpatrick). 경배와 찬양은 하나님의 통치에 승복하는 행위이며, 하나님의 거룩하신 임재에 대한 적절한 반응이다(VanGemeren).

기자는 주님이 계신 거룩한 산 시온(cf. 2절)을 찾아가 그곳에서 주님을 예배하라고 한다. 온 세상의 왕이신 하나님의 보좌가 시온에 있기 때문이다(cf. 1절). 그러므로 이 말씀은 언젠가는 온 세상이 시온으로 몰려가 여호와께 엎드려 경배할 날을 꿈꾸고 있다.

제100편
감사의 시

I. 장르/양식: 회중 찬양시(cf. 29편)

이 시편은 하나님의 왕 되심을 찬양하는 즉위시 모음집(96-99편) 바로 다음에 등장하면서 95편과 쌍이 되어 이 모음집(96-99편)을 감싸며(Tate) 결론 역할을 하는 듯하다(Ross). 이러한 정황은 이 시도 모음집의 공통적인 양식인 즉위시로 취급되기를 바라는 편집자들의 의도를 반영한 듯하다(McCann, Tate, VanGemeren).

전통적으로 이 노래는 회당과 기독교 예배에서 매우 중요한 역할을 담당했으며 가장 자주 사용된 시편 중 하나였다(Goldingay). 한 주석가는 이 시편을 개혁주의 신앙의 '깃발 찬송'(banner hymn)이라고 하기도 한다(McCann, cf. Grogan). 또한 창세기 1-2장을 근거해서는 모든 인류가 하나님을 누리기 위해 창조되었다는 웨스트민스터 신앙고백 소요리 문답의 첫 번째 질문에 대한 답을 도출하기 어렵지만, 이 시편은 그 정답을 가능케 한다는 주장도 있다(Goldingay).

그러나 모든 학자들이 이 시편의 가치를 인정하는 것은 아니다. 궁켈(Gunkel)은 이 노래가 성전에서 성가대가 사라진 지 오래된 시점에 저작되었으며, 저자가 이미 다른 시편들에서 사용된 문구들을 모아 조합하여 지루하고 따분한 노래를 만든 것이라며 혹평했다. 그러나 대부분 학자들은 궁켈과 견해를 달리한다. 한 주석가는 이 노래를 '참 예배를 위한 제작품'(genuine worship composition)이라고 한다(Gerstenberger).

이 시가 성전이 존재하는 것을 전제하는 것을 감안하여 저작 시기를 왕정 시대로 보는 주석가들이 있다(Ross, cf. Anderson). 그러나 이 성전이 솔로몬 성전인지 혹은 귀향민들이 세운 성전인지 확실하지는 않다. 귀향민들이 주전 520-16년에 재건한 성전이라고 생각하는 사람들은 포로기 이후 시대(페르시아 시대)를 저작 시기로 본다(Terrien).

이 노래가 사용된 정황에 대해 학자들은 대체적으로 순례자들이 성전 입성을 사모하며 불렀거나 예배를 드리러 성전에 모인 공동체가 성전에 들어서면서 일종의 '입례송'으로 부른 노래라고 한다(Gunkel). 이 시편이 즉위시라는 점을 근거로 신년예배 때 여호와의 왕 되심을 기념하며 불린 것이라는 주장도 있지만, 거의 모든 주석가들은 한 예배를 특정하지는 않는다(cf. deClaissé-Walford et al.). 노래의 보편적인 내용을 감안할 때, 여러 절기 때 불릴 만한 노래이다(VanGemeren).

II. 구조

일곱 개의 권면과 두 가지 이유로 구성된 이 시편의 구조는 쉽게 파악할 수 있다. 이 주석에서는 다음과 같은 구조를 바탕으로 본문을 주해해 나갈 것이다.

A. 네 개의 찬양 권면(100:1-3a)
　B. 권면에 대한 첫 번째 이유(100:3b-e)
A′. 세 개의 찬양 권면(100:4)
　B′. 권면에 대한 두 번째 이유(100:5)

III. 주해

이 시편은 우리가 하나님을 찬양해야 하는 이유를 정확하게 가르쳐 준다. 주님은 우리의 창조주이시며 왕이시고 목자이시기 때문이다(3절). 또한 하나님은 선하시고 우리를 사랑하시는 분이며 영원히 의지할 수 있는 성실하신 분이기에 우리의 찬양을 받기에 합당하시다. 이 짧은 시편은 성경에서 만수(滿數)인 7개의 복수형 명령문들을 중심으로 구성되어 있다: "부르라, 섬기라, 나아가라, 알지어다, 들어가라, 감사하라, 송축하라"(deClaissé-Walford et al.).

1. 네 개의 찬양 권면(100:1-3a)

1 온 땅이여
여호와께 즐거운 찬송을 부를지어다
2 기쁨으로 여호와를 섬기며
노래하면서 그의 앞에 나아갈지어다
3a 여호와가 우리 하나님이신 줄 너희는 알지어다

기자는 온 세상(땅)에게 여호와를 찬양하라는 권면으로 노래를 시작한다(1절, cf. 시 95:1-2). 여호와는 얼마나 위대하고 놀라운 분이신지 이스라엘만 홀로 주님을 찬양하기에는 너무나도 아쉽다. 그러므로 그는 세상 모든 사람들에게 여호와를 찬양하라고 한다. 범우주적인 하나님은 범우주적인 찬양을 받기에 합당하신 분이기 때문에 주님을 찬양하는 공동체가 '온 세상'보다 조금이라도 작으면 옳지 않다(McCann). 또한 찬양은 우리의 충성이 누구를 향하고 있는가를 확인할 수 있는 가장 좋은 방법이다(Brueggemann).

물론 현 세상에는 여호와가 누구이신지, 왜 그를 찬양해야 하는지를 모르는 사람들이 많다. 그러므로 이 말씀은 언젠가는 온 세상이 주님을 경배하게 될 것이라는 이 노래의 종말론적인 관점을 반영하고 있다. 우리도 같은 꿈을 꾸었으면 좋겠다. 언젠가는 세상 모든 사람이 그들의 창조주이신 여호와 앞에 무릎을 꿇고 경배하는 꿈을 꾸자.

이 섹션을 구성하고 있는 네 개의 권면 중 세 개는 온 세상이 여호와를 찬송할 것을 권하고 있으며, 나머지 하나는 여호와가 누구이신가를 인정하는 일을 권하고 있다.

첫 번째 권면은 여호와께 즐거운 찬송을 부르라는 것이다(1b절). 개역개정이 "즐거이 찬송을 부르다"로 번역한 히브리어 동사(רוע)의 기본적인 의미는 전쟁터에서 군인이 진군하면서 적들에게 위압감을 주기 위해 소리치는 모습이다(HALOT). 목청껏, 사람이 낼 수 있는 최고의 큰 소리로 주님께 외치라는 의미이다.

두 번째 권면은 기쁨으로 여호와를 섬기라는 것이다(2a절). '섬기다'(עבד)는 종들이 주인에게 시중을 드는 모습이다(HALOT). 예배와 섬김은 동전의 양면성이며, 떼어 놓을 수 없는 관계를 형성한다(cf. 수 24장). 시편에서는 인간이든 신들이든 간에 상관없이 왕을 섬기는 일을 묘사하는 데 사용된다(Mays, cf. 시 2:11; 18:43; 22:30; 72:11; 97:7). 여호와가 어떤 분이신지를 알고 나면 서로 하나님을 섬기려 할 것이며, 하나님은 자신이 종들로 선택한 소수에게만 섬길 수 있는 특권을 주신다. 그러므로 하나님의 선택을 받은 사람들은 자신의 삶을 오직 하나님을 섬기는 일에 맞추고 기쁨으로 예배하게 된다(McCann).

세 번째 권면은 노래하면서 주님 앞에 나아가는 것이다(2b절). 이 권면이 충격적이고 파격적인 것은 주의 백성이 아니라 온 세상에게 주님께 나오라고 하기 때문이다(Goldingay). '노래하면서'(בִּשְׂמְחָה)는 사람이 기쁨으로 흥분된 모습을 나타낸다. 피조물인 사람이 이러한 기쁨을 누릴 수 있는 유일한 방법은 창조주 하나님과 하모니를 이루며 사는 것이다(VanGemeren). 이 세 가지 권면을 하나로 묶는 주제는 넘치는 기쁨이다.

사람이 하나님을 예배할 때에는 기쁨과 즐거움이 넘치는 마음으로 경배해야 함을 암시한다. 우리가 매주 함께 드리는 예배도 이러했으면 좋겠다.

네 번째 권면은 여호와가 누구이신가를 깨달으라는 것이다(3a절). 이는 여호와를 찬양할 것을 명하는 앞선 세 권면과 차이를 가진다. 이 말씀은 이 시편의 구조적인 중심일 뿐만 아니라, 신학적인 심장이기도 하다(Tucker & Grant, cf. deClaissé-Walford et al., Hossfeld-Zenger). 또한 구약 종교의 가장 기본적인 교리라고도 할 수 있다(Terrien). 하나님을 올바르게 아는 것이 얼마나 중요한지를 강조하기 위해 기자는 먼저 권고하는 차원에서 명령문으로 '알지어다'로 말하고(Gerstenberger), 문장 구조에서도 강조되는 위치에 '알다'(ידע)를 두었다. 하나님이 어떤 분이신가를 알고 나서야 비로소 마음속 깊은 곳에서 우러나오는 참된 경배를 드릴 수 있다. '하나님을 안다'는 것은 자신의 삶을 하나님께 온전히 드려 하나님을 섬긴다는 뜻이다(Tucker & Grant). 하나님을 잘 알지 못하고 드리는 찬양은 내용이 비어 있는 꽹과리 소리일 뿐이다. 진정한 예배와 경배는 하나님을 아는 참 지식에서 시작된다.

그가 이처럼 강조하는 하나님에 대한 지식은 어떤 것인가? 여호와가 우리의 하나님이라는 사실이다. 이러한 선언은 평범해 보이지만, 실상은 많은 것을 함축하고 있다(cf. 3b, 5절). 또한 하나님을 아는 지식은 사람이 스스로 터득할 수 있는 것이 아니다. 하나님이 주셔야 가질 수 있는 지식이다. 동사 '알다'(ידע)는 인격적인 관계 형성을 전제하기 때문이다.

2. 권면에 대한 첫 번째 이유(100:3b-e)

3b 그는 우리를 지으신 이요
우리는 그의 것이니

그의 백성이요
그의 기르시는 양이로다

저자는 "하나님을 알지어다" 라며 독자들을 권면했는데(3a절), 그는 정작 우리가 하나님에 대해 어떤 지식을 얻기를 바라는가? 우리는 하나님과 우리의 관계에 대해 네 가지를 알고 인정해야 한다.

첫째, 하나님은 우리를 지으신 분이다(3a절). '짓다'(עשה)는 '만들다, 창조하다'라는 뜻을 가지고 있다(HALOT). 이는 하나님이 우리를 창조하셨다는 의미와 함께 오늘날 우리가 누구인가는 하나님의 빚어가심의 결과라는 의미가 함축되어 있다(cf. McCann). 창조주 하나님은 이 순간에도 우리를 만들어가신다.

둘째, 하나님의 지음 받은 우리는 하나님의 것(소유)이라는 사실을 알아야 한다(3c절). 이 히브리어 문구를 문자적으로 번역하면 '그가 자신을 위해 우리를 지으셨다'(הוּא־עָשָׂנוּ וְלוֹ)가 된다. 하나님이 우리를 지으셨기 때문에 우리가 하나님의 소유가 된 것이 아니라, 하나님이 처음부터 자신을 위해 우리를 지으셨다는 뜻이다. 우리는 하나님을 위하는 목적으로 창조된 것이다.

셋째, 우리는 하나님의 백성이다(3d절). 앞 구절은 하나님이 자신을 위해 우리를 창조하셨다고 했는데, 과연 어디에 쓰시려고 우리를 만드신 것일까? 본문은 하나님이 자기 백성 삼으시려고 우리를 창조하셨다고 한다. 하나님이 우리를 백성 삼으셨다는 것은 하나님이 우리를 다스리시는 왕이 되셨다는 뜻이다. 그러므로 하나님의 다스림을 받는 이들은 피조물들 중에서 가장 영광스러운 특권을 누린다. 창조주께서 친히 그들의 왕이 되셨기 때문이다.

넷째, 우리는 여호와께서 기르시는 양이다(3e절). "그의 기르시는 양이로다"(צֹאן מַרְעִיתוֹ)는 히브리어 숙어이며 우리는 목자이신 하나님이 일꾼 등 다른 사람에게 맡겨 키우게 하는 양이 아니라, 직접 기르시는 양이라는 의미를 지녔다(Clifford). 고대 근동에서는 왕과 백성의 관계를 종종 목자와 양떼로 표현했다. 이 말씀도 이러한 이미지를 배경으로 하고 있다. 양은 먼 곳을 보지 못하는 매우 근시적인 안목을 지닌 짐승이다. 이런 짐승에게 목자의 인도는 삶과 죽음을 좌우할 수 있다. 하나님은 우리의 선한 목자가 되셔서 우리를 생명의 길로 인도하시는 분이다. 그러므로 이 목자의 인도하심을 거부하는 양은 매우 어리석으며 온갖 위험에 노출될 수 있다. 반면에 하나님을 목자로 섬기는 사람들은 주님의 양으로서 누리는 특권이 많다(cf. 시 23편; 눅 15:3-6; 요 10:1-18). 여호와는 이스라엘뿐만 아니라 온 세상 모든 민족의 목자이시다(McCann).

3. 세 개의 찬양 권면(100:4)

[4] 감사함으로 그의 문에 들어가며
찬송함으로 그의 궁정에 들어가서 그에게 감사하며
그의 이름을 송축할지어다

노래를 시작하며 네 차례(1-2절) 하나님을 찬송할 것을 권면한 기자가 이 섹션에서는 세 차례 더 하나님을 찬양할 것을 권한다. 하나님을 찬양하라는 것에서는 1-2절과 맥을 같이 하지만, 1-2절이 기쁨을 강조한 것에 반해 이 섹션은 감사함을 강조한다. 하나님이 우리의 왕이 되심을 생각하면 당연히 감사가 나올 것이다.

첫째, 우리는 감사한 마음으로 주님의 문에 들어가야 한다(4a절). 바로 앞에서 하나님과 주의 백성을 목자와 양떼로 묘사했기 때문에 이 문은 양들이 보호받기 위해 들어가는 우리의 문일 수 있다. 그러나 다음 구절이 궁정(성전 뜰, cf. 현대인)을 언급하는 것으로 보아 성전 문에 들어서는 모습으로 해석하는 것이 바람직하다. 주님을 예배하기 위해 주님의 처소를 찾을 때에 기쁨(cf. 1–2절) 만큼이나 중요한 것이 주께서 우리의 삶에 하신 일에 대한 감사의 마음이다.

둘째, 우리는 성전 문을 지나 성전 뜰에서 주님을 찬양하고 감사해야 한다(4b절). 성전 뜰은 예배가 진행되는 곳이다. 하나님을 예배할 때 감사와 찬송이 중심을 이루게 하라는 권면이다.

셋째, 우리는 하나님의 이름을 송축하는 예배를 드려야 한다(4c절). 하나님의 이름을 송축한다(ברך)는 것은 하나님을 축복한다는 의미를 지녔는데, 축복은 강자가 약자에게 내려 주는 것이다. 그러므로 이 말씀은 하나님의 구원하시는 은혜를 경험한 사람이 감사한 마음으로 하나님께 반응하는 것을 의미한다(Eaton). 예배를 통해 하나님의 이름을 드높이라는 뜻이다. 자기 백성을 축복하시는 하나님은 우리의 가장 열렬하고 진솔한 찬양을 받기에 합당하신 분이다.

4. 권면에 대한 두 번째 이유(100:5)

5 여호와는 선하시니
그의 인자하심이 영원하고
그의 성실하심이 대대에 이르리로다

앞 섹션(4절)에서 세 차례 감사한 마음으로 주님을 경배하라고 했던 기자는 우리가 마음을 다해 주님을 찬양하고 감사해야 하는 이유를 말한다. 그는 하나님의 거룩하신 성품들 중 세 가지를 강조하며 하나님은 찬양 받기에 합당하신 분이라고 한다. 주님의 이 성품들은 우리의 삶을 행복하고 가치 있게 한다(Tate).

첫째, 여호와는 선하시다(5a절, cf. 시 106:1; 107:1; 136:1). 고대 근동의 신들은 인간들을 선하게 대하지 않았다. 그들은 항상 인간들을 괴롭히고 이용하려 들었다(cf. ANET). 이러한 정서에서 '여호와는 선하시다'는 것은 매우 파격적인 선언이다(cf. Tucker & Grant). '선하다'(טוֹב)는 하나님의 가장 기본적인 속성이며, 우리가 하나님에게 좋은 일을 기대할 수 있는 근거가 된다(cf. 창 1장). 선하신 하나님은 항상 선한 것들을 자기 백성에게 주시는 분이다.

둘째, 하나님은 영원히 인자하신 분이다(5b절). 여기서 사용된 히브리어 문구(לְעוֹלָם חַסְדּוֹ)의 문자적 의미는 '그의 인자(헤세드)는 영원에 이른다'는 뜻이다. 기자가 하나님의 선하심(좋으심)을 이미 언급했으니, 이곳에서 '인자'(חֶסֶד)는 언약적 충성으로 이해되어야 한다(cf. Schaefer, Sakenfeld). 하나님은 누구와 언약을 맺으시면 그 언약을 영원히 존중하신다는 뜻이다. 하나님은 사람하고 달라서 한번 언약을 맺으시면 절대 먼저 잊으시거나 파괴하시는 일이 없다.

셋째, 하나님은 성실하심이 대대에 이르시는 분이다(5c절). '성실'(אֱמוּנָה)은 꾸준함을 강조하는 단어로써 하나님이 어떤 일을 결정하시면 끝까지 책임을 다하시며 그 일을 꾸준히 해 나가신다는 의미를 지녔다. 하나님의 성실하심은 우리가 하나님의 말씀과 약속을 믿을 수 있는 근거가 된다. 하나님의 이 세 가지 속성은 여호와께서 이스라엘과 세우신 언약의 성향을 정의하는 개념들이다(cf. 출 34:6-7). 기자는 이 세 가지 속성을 지니신 하나님께 감사하며 찬양하는 것을 우리가 해야 할 당연한 일이라고 한다.

제101편

다윗의 시

I. 장르/양식: 개인 찬양시(cf. 11편)

한 학자는 개인 찬양시인 이 시편은 평민들이 여호와를 섬기는 성도는 이렇게 살아야 한다며 자신들의 기도를 담아 부른 노래라고 한다(Gerstenberger). 이 시편이 이상적인 하나님 백성의 삶을 묘사하고 있다는 것이다. 그러나 대부분 학자들은 이 시가 왕이 종종 부른 왕족시(royal psalm)이거나(Brueggemann & Bellinger, Goldingay, VanGemeren), 새 왕이 취임할 때 자신이 섬기는 하나님과 다스리는 백성에게 충성을 선언하기 위해 사용한 일종의 선서였다고 한다(Grogan, Mays, McCann, Ross).

이 시가 선언문이 아니라 기도문에 더 가깝다고 하여 왕 등 지도자가 선서를 할 때 사용한 것이 아니라 불만과 불평을 표현하고 있는 왕족시라고 하는 이들도 있다(Allen). 이 시의 일부(2a, 3-5, 7절)는 원래 한 왕족시를 구성하고 있는 조각들이었는데, 훗날 저자가 기도시로 바꾼 것이라고 하는 학자도 있다(Seybold). 더 나아가 이 시편이 왕이 부른 노래가 아니라, 사사나 장로 등 자신이 사는 집과 성과 땅에 대해 권리와 책임을 가진 지도층에 속한 사람이 부른 노래로 풀이하는 관점도 있다(deClaissé-Walford et al.). 저자가 이 세 가지(집, 성, 땅)가 그의 권세 아래 있다는 것을 전제하기 때문이다.

이 시편이 왕의 취임식과 연관이 있다고 생각한 영국 성공회의 일반 기도서(Book of Common Prayer)는 이 노래를 매년 영국 왕이 즉위한 날을 기념하는 예식에서 사용하라고 권고한다(Goldingay). 그러나 이 시편과 잠언 1-9장은 깊이 연관된다 하여(cf. Kenik) 지혜시라고 하는 학자들도 있다(Weir). 장르와 정황에 대하여도 이처럼 다양한 견해가 존재하는 것을 감안하면 이 시편은 정확한 해석이 어려워 학자들을 당혹하게 하는 수수께끼 같은 시편이라는 평가가 실감난다(McCann).

시편 표제에 다윗의 이름이 등장하는 것은 86편 이후 처음 있는 일이며, 90편으로 시작된 제4권에서도 처음 있는 일이다. 제4권에서 표제에 다윗의 이름이 등장하는 노래는 이 시편과 103편이 유일하다. 이 노래는 언제쯤 누가 저작한 것일까? 포로기 이후를 저작 시기로 보는 사람들도 있지만(cf. Tucker & Grant), 대부분 왕정 시대로 본다. 왕정 시대에 저작된 것으로 보는 학자들(Ross, Terrien) 중에는 다윗을 저자로 간주하는 이들도 있다(cf. Allen, Hossfeld-Zenger). 다윗이 자기보다 더 나은 이상적인 왕이 올 것을 기대하며 저작한 노래라는 것이다. 반면에 왕정 시대에 저작되었지만, 다윗 시대에 저작된 것이 아니라고 하는 이들 중에는 구체적으로 주전 620년경, 곧 요시야 시대를 지목하는 이들도 있다(Anderson). 요시야가 본문이 묘사하고 있는 왕의 모습과 가장 비슷하다고 생각해서이다.

대부분 학자들이 결론짓는 것처럼 이 시는 왕족시가 분명한데, 그렇다면 어떤 정황에서 사용된 것일까? 이미 언급한 것처럼 새 왕의 취임과 연관되어 사용된 것으로 보는 것이 가장 유력하다(Mays, McCann, Ross, Terrien). 또한 가을이면 드리는 신년 예배에서 사용한 것이라는 추측이 있다(Mowinckel). 매년 왕의 취임을 기념하며 사용된 것이라는 뜻이다. 이 시편이 주의 백성을 다스리는 인간 왕의 취임식과 연관되어 사용된 것은 거의 확실하지만, 시의 종말론적인 관점도 의식하며 해석해야 한다. 이 시는 장차 오실 이상적인 왕 혹은 메시아를 기대하는 노래이기 때문이다(cf. Ross, Terrien).

II. 구조

이 노래의 구조를 논할 때 "언제까지 내게 임하시겠나이까?"(2절)라는 질문의 역할이 분석을 매우 어렵게 한다. 그럼에도 불구하고 이 질문은 이 시편의 핵심이다(McCann, Terrien). 학자들은 이 시편이 여러 단어와 문구들을 반복적으로 사용하고 있음을 의식하여 시의 일부에서 교차대구법적 구조를 포착한다(cf. Allen, Kselman, McCann, VanGemeren). 다음은 크셀맨(Kselman)이 제시하는 구조이다. 히브리어와 영어의 순서가 우리말과 달라서 영어를 직접표기하고 괄호 안에 개역개정의 번역을 삽입했다.

A. 3a절 "before my eyes"(내 눈 앞에)
  B. 3a절 "*speech* of worthlessness"(비천한 것)
    C. 3b절 "those *doing* crooked things"(배교자들의 행위)
      D. 5b절 "haughtiness of *eyes*"(눈이 높음)
      D′. 6a절 "my *eyes* (are upon)"(내 눈이 [살펴])
    C′. 7a절 "those *doing* deceit"(거짓을 행하는 자)
  B′. 7b절 "those *speaking* lies"(거짓말 하는 자)
A′. 7b절 "before my eyes"(내 목전에)

이 주석에서는 이 시편을 왕이 취임하면서 하나님을 잘 섬기고 백성을 공의와 정의로 잘 다스릴 것을 선서하면서 사용한 시로 간주하고자 한다. 이러한 이해를 근거로 다음과 같은 구조를 바탕으로 본문을 주해해 나가고자 한다.

A. 의인의 삶을 다짐함(101:1-2b)

B. 악과 악인들을 멀리할 것을 다짐함(101:2c-5)
A′. 의인들을 가까이할 것을 다짐함(101:6)
B′. 악인들을 벌할 것을 다짐함(101:7-8)

III. 주해

신적인 왕이신 하나님은 자기 백성을 다스리실 때 직접 하지 않으시고 세우신 인간 왕 등을 통해서 통치하신다. 메시아이신 예수님은 하나님의 이 같은 통치 방식의 결정체라 할 수 있다. 이 시편은 왕이신 하나님의 권위를 위임받은 사람이 어떻게 주의 백성을 다스려야 하는가에 관한 것이다. 한때 유럽에서 이 시편은 하나님이 세우신 왕 혹은 메시아의 노래로 간주되어 '왕자의 노래'(the prince's psalm)라고 불리기도 했다(VanGemeren).

1. 의인의 삶을 다짐함(101:1-2b)

[1] 내가 인자와 정의를 노래하겠나이다
여호와여 내가 주께 찬양하리이다
[2a] 내가 완전한 길을 주목하오리니
주께서 언제까지 내게 임하시겠나이까

기자는 왕으로 취임하며 하나님이 그에게 맡겨 주신 주의 백성을 어떻게 다스릴 것인가를 다짐해 본다(Kirpatrick). 비록 이 노래가 왕 같은 지도자의 노래이기는 하지만, 모든 주의 백성이 주님 안에서 살아가는 삶의 가이드라인으로 삼을 만하다(cf. Gerstenberger). 왕은 제일 먼저 인자와 정의를 노래하겠다고 다짐한다(1a절). 왕이 정의와 인자를 베풀겠다고 하는 것은 여호와가 이런 분이시며, 그를 대신해서 백성을 통치하는 인간 왕의 당연한 반응이기 때문이다(Allen).

'인자'(חֶסֶד)는 자비와 긍휼을, '정의'(מִשְׁפָּט)는 공정한 판결을 의미한다. 이 두 가지는 하나님이 언약을 맺고 이스라엘을 다스리시는 일과 연관이 있으며(cf. Broyles, Tucker & Grant), 하나님이 세상을 통치하시는 방식이기도 하다(cf. 출 34:6-7; 호 12:6; 미 6:8; 마 23:23). 또한 인간 왕이 이 둘을 동시에 적용해야 하나님이 기뻐하시는 재판을 할 수 있다. 이러한 이유로 비록 이 시가 "하나님이 왕이시다"라는 주제를 중점적으로 노래하고 있는 93-100편과 따로 분류되지만, 같은 메시지의 맥을 이어가고 있는 것으로 간주되기도 한다(McKelvey).

어떤 판결이든 정의만 강조한다면 재판에 회부된 사람들을 매우 힘들고 억울하게 할 수 있다. 반면에 인자만 강조하면 원칙과 기준이 잘 지켜지지 않는 판결이 나올 수 있다. 이 둘이 어우러질 때 범법자들이라 할지라도 법의 원칙과 정신에 따라 예외와 '눈물'이 인정된다. 그러므로 통치자가 이 두 원리를 병행하여 다스리는 것은 매우 중요하다. 또한 이 두 원리는 하나님이 우리를 대하실 때 적용하시는 자비로운 기준이다. 왕은 인자와 정의로 하나님이 맡겨 주신 백성을 다스려 하나님이 기뻐하시는 통치를 하겠다며 하나님 닮기를 소망한다.

왕은 항상 주님을 찬양할 것을 다짐한다(2a절). 그는 그와 하나님의 관계가 끊어지면 하나님의 권위를 위임받아 하나님이 기뻐하시는 방식대로 통치하고자 하는 그의 열정이 물거품이 될 것을 잘 알고 있다. 그러므로 그는 무슨 일이 있어도 항상 하나님과의 관계를 유지할 것을 다짐한다. 하나님과 관계를 유지하는 가장 좋은 방법은 무엇인가? 끊임없이 여호와를 찬양하는 일이다. 찬양은 하나님과 우리를 하나로 묶는 힘을 지녔기 때문이다.

이어 왕은 항상 완전한 길을 배우며 살 것을 다짐한다(2a절). 개역개정이 '주목하다'로 번역한 단어(שׂכל)는 '관심을 쏟다' 혹은 '배우다, 깨닫다'는 뜻을 지녔으며(Goldingay, cf. 새번역, NAS, NRS, TNK), 지혜 사상에서 온 개념이다(VanGemeren, cf. 잠 19:16; 사 41:20). '완전한 길'(דֶּרֶךְ תָּמִים)은 삶에 흠이 없다는 뜻이며(cf. 시 18:23; 78:72; 왕상 9:4), 하나님이 기뻐하시는 삶의 방식이다. 또한 '길'은 평생 이 길을 걸을 것을 전제한다(deClaissé-Walford et al.). 왕은 하나님의 통치 방식에 따라 백성을 다스릴 뿐만 아니라, 주님이 인정하시는 삶의 방식을 배워 실천하며 평생 살아가겠다고 다짐한다. 왕은 어떻게 해서든 주님을 닮아가겠다며 몸부림치고 있다.

그렇다면 그는 무엇을 통해 이 '완전한 길'에 대해 배울 수 있는가? 구약은 하나님의 율법이 사람에게 '길'(דֶּרֶךְ)을 제시한다고 한다. 그러므로 그는 하나님의 말씀을 배우고 깨달아 주님이 기뻐하시는 '완전한 길'을 걸을 수 있다(cf. 신 17:18-20). 그는 율법을 주야로 배우겠다고 다짐하고 있는 것이다(cf. 신 17:17-20). 왕은 하나님의 율법(Torah)이 잘 실현되도록 하는 역할을 자청하고 있다(Kraus, cf. deClaissé-Walford et al.).

개역개정이 "주께서 언제까지 내게 임하시겠나이까?"로 번역한 2b절의 의미와 역할을 이해하기는 쉽지 않다(Booij, cf. Allen, Hossfeld-Zenger, McCann). 이 문장을 문자적으로 번역하면 "당신은 언제나 저에게 오시렵니까?"이다. 이러한 질문은 하나님의 도움을 갈망하며 애가나 탄식시에 나올 만한 것인데, 이 노래는 새 왕이 취임하는 즐거운 분위기에서 불린 노래이다(cf. Longman, VanGemeren). 그래서 일부 번역본들은 "내가 이것(앞에서 다짐한 좋은 통치)을 언제나 이룰 수 있을까?"(When shall I attain it? cf. NRS, TNK)라고 해석하고 표기했다. 왕이 다짐한 것들이 결코 쉽지 않다는 것을 알기에 자신에게 이런 질문을 하고 있다는 것이다.

그러나 히브리어 문장(מָתַי תָּבוֹא אֵלָי)의 문자적 의미인 "당신(주님)은 언제나 저에게 오시렵니까?"도 이 문맥에서 충분한 의미를 지닐 수 있다. 왕은 이때까지 자신은 하나님이 세상을 통치하는 원칙에 따라 자기 백성을 다스릴 것을 다짐했고(1a절), 하나님과 그의 관계가 단절되는 일이 없도록 끊임없이 하나님을 찬양하겠다는 각오를 밝혔다(1b절).

또한 율법을 공부하고 배워서 하나님이 기뻐하시는 '완전한 길'을 걷겠다고 했다(2a절). 이 모든 것은 그의 의지일 뿐이다. 하나님이 그와 함께하시지 않으면 그는 다짐한 것들 중 아무것도 이룰 수 없다. 그러므로 온 마음을 다해 하나님을 사모하는 왕은 이 질문을 통해 주님이 그와 함께 동행해 주시기를 바란다. 자신이 주님의 함께하심을 이처럼 사모하고 있으니 속히 그를 찾아오시라고 염원한다. 왕은 하나님이 그에게 오셔서 도와주셔야 그가 꿈꾸고 있는 거룩한 통치가 가능하다는 것을 잘 알고 있다.

2. 악과 악인들을 멀리할 것을 다짐함(101:2c-5)

2c 내가 완전한 마음으로 내 집안에서 행하리이다
3 나는 비천한 것을 내 눈앞에 두지 아니할 것이요
배교자들의 행위를 내가 미워하오리니
나는 그 어느 것도 붙들지 아니하리이다
4 사악한 마음이 내게서 떠날 것이니
악한 일을 내가 알지 아니하리로다
5 자기의 이웃을 은근히 헐뜯는 자를 내가 멸할 것이요
눈이 높고 마음이 교만한 자를 내가 용납하지 아니하리로다

왕은 율법을 배우고 익혀 하나님이 인정하시는 '완전한 길'을 걷겠다고 다짐했다(2a절). 그는 왜 완전한 길을 배우려고 하는가? 그가 '완전한 길'을 알게 되면 그의 마음도 완전해질 것이기 때문이다(2c절). '완전한 마음'에서 '완전한'(תֹּם)은 '완전한 길'에서의 '완전한/흠 없는'(תָּמִים)과 같은 의미를 지녔고, 같은 어원에서 비롯된 단어들이다. 하나님의 말씀인 율법을 통해 깨우칠 수 있는 '완전한 길'(דֶּרֶךְ)이 왕의 삶을 주관할 '완전한 마음'(לֵבָב)으로 이어지고 있다. 하나님의 말씀은 배울수록 회개하고, 배울수록 삶이 경건해진다. 그렇다고 해서 완전한 마음이 죄를 전혀 짓지 않는 것을 의미하지는 않는다(Tucker & Grant). 살아 있는 한 사람은 죄를 지으며 살아간다. 그러므로 이 말씀은 왕이 죄를 최대한 짓지 않으면서 살아가겠다는 의지의 표현으로 이해할 수 있다.

기자는 결단을 표현하는 여러 개의 동사를 통해 완전한 마음(율법을 통해 얻은 하나님을 경외하는 마음)으로 모든 유형의 악을 멀리할 것을 다짐한다: "행하리라… 두지 않을 것이다… 미워할 것이다… 붙들지 않을 것이다… 떠날 것이다… (알지) 아니하리로다… 멸할 것이다… (용납하지) 아니하리로다."

왕은 무엇보다도 자기 집안을 경건과 거룩으로 다스릴 것이다(2c절). 하나님의 인자와 정의가 실현되는 집안이 되게 하겠다는 뜻이다(cf. 1절). 고대 근동의 모든 문화권에서 왕궁은 철저하게 베일에 가려진 비밀스러운 공간으로서 일반인들은 그 안에서 어떤 일이 일어나는 지를 알 수 없었다(Kirkpatrick). 그런데 이 왕은 백성을 주님의 인자와 정의로 다스리기 전에 먼저 자기 집안을 같은 방식으로 다스리겠다고 한다. 필요하다면 언제든 자신의 사적인 공간인 왕궁을 공개하겠다는 각오이다(cf. Tucker & Grant). 왕이 백성들을 다스리는 원리로 자기 집안을 다스리겠다고 하는 것은 참으로 지혜로운 결정이다. 왕이 롤모델링(role-modeling)으로 다스릴 때 백성들은 쉽게 설득되기 때문이다.

집안에서 인자와 정의를 실현한 왕은 하나님의 정의로 악과 악인들을 벌할 것을 다짐한다(3-5절). 그는 개인적으로 악을 멀리하는 것으로 만족할 수 없어서 악을 적극적으로 응징하고자 한다. 그러므로 왕은 이 섹션에서 다섯 가지 악을 근절하겠다며 자신이 다스리는 나라에서 악의 모든 유형을 근절하겠다는 의지를 표현한다.

첫째, 왕은 비천한 것을 자기 눈 앞에 두지 않을 것이다(3a절). '비천한 것'(דְּבַר־בְּלִיָּעַל)은 무용지물이나 사악한 것을 뜻한다(HALOT). 우상들을 일컫는 말이다. 하나님의 권위를 위임받아 주의 백성을 다스리는 왕이 절대 우상을 숭배하지 않겠다고 다짐하는 것은 당연한 일이다. 이슈는 이러한 각오가 과연 얼마나 지속될 것인가 이다.

둘째, 왕은 배교자들의 행위를 미워할 것이다(3b절). '배교자들의 행위'(עֲשֹׂה־סֵטִים)는 하나님을 배신한 자들이 하는 짓으로(NIDOTTE), 그들이 저지르는 죄를 뜻한다. 왕은 악인들의 죄를 미워할 것이며 그들이 하는 일이라면 그 어느 것 하나도 붙들지 않을 것이다(3c절). 하나님을 배신한 자들과 상종하지 않겠다는 다짐이다.

셋째, 왕은 사악한 마음을 떨칠 것이다(4a절). '사악한 마음'(לֵבָב עִקֵּשׁ)은 비뚤어지거나 진실이 없는 마음을 의미한다(HALOT). 그는 오직 진실하고 바른 마음으로 백성들을 다스릴 것을 다짐한다. 왕에게서 사악한 마음이 사라지면 악한 일도 함께 사라진다(4b절). '악한 일'(רָע)은 모든 유형의 악을 묘사하는 가장 기본적이고 포괄적인 단어이다. 왕은 악이라면 어떠한 유형도 가까이하지 않겠다는 각오를 다지고 있다. 그리하여 그는 악을 '알지 않겠다'(לֹא אֵדָע)고 한다.

넷째, 왕은 이웃을 헐뜯는 자를 멸할 것이다(5a절). '헐뜯다'(לשן)는 중상모략을 하거나 거짓 증언을 한다는 뜻이다(cf. 출 23:7; 레 19:15-18). '은근히'(בַסֵּתֶר)의 더 정확한 번역은 '숨어서/몰래'이다(cf. 새번역, 아가페, NIV, NAS). 악인들은 이런 짓을 숨어서 하지만 왕이 그들을 벌할 때는 그들의 만행이 온 천하에 드러날 것이다.

다섯째, 왕은 교만한 자들을 용납하지 않을 것이다(5b절). 고대 근동에서 가장 교만한 자들은 왕들이었다(Clifford, Tucker & Grant). 그러므로 왕인 저자는 세상의 왕들과 다르게 살겠다고 다짐하고 있다. 그는 '눈이 높고 마음이 교만한 자'를 결코 용납할 수 없다고 한다. '눈이 높다'(גְּבַהּ־עֵינַיִם)는 것은 다른 사람들을 무시한다는 뜻이다. '마음이 교만하다'(רְחַב לֵבָב)를 문자적으로 번역하면 '마음이 넓다'는 뜻이다(HALOT). 삶에 어떠한 가치관이나 기준이 없어 하나님의 말씀처럼 절대적인 것을 인정하지 않는다는 뜻이다(cf. McCann). 이 시편에서는 '완전한 마음'(2c절)과 대조를 이루고 있다(Brueggemann, Goldingay). 성경은 교만을 가장 심각한 죄악이라고 한다. 교만은 창조주 하나님을 의지하지 않는 것에서 시작되며 모든 죄의 근원이 되기 때문이다. 그러므로 교만한 사람은 주의 참 백성이 될 수 없다. 왕은 하나님을 경외하지 않는 교만한 자들을 용납하지 않을 것이다.

겉모습으로는 '눈이 높고 교만한' 사람을 가늠하기가 쉽지 않다. 교만은 사람의 눈에 보이지 않는 마음의 문제이기 때문이다. 그러므로 왕은 은밀한 곳에서 죄를 짓는 사람을 멸하고(5a절), 교만한 자를 용납하지 않을 것을 다짐하며 자신이 다스리는 나라에서는 공중 장소에서 드러나는 범죄 행위뿐 아니라 은밀한 곳에서 마음으로 짓는 죄까지 제재하겠다고 다짐하고 있다(cf. VanGemeren).

3. 의인들을 가까이할 것을 다짐함(101:6)

6 내 눈이 이 땅의 충성된 자를 살펴 나와 함께 살게 하리니
완전한 길에 행하는 자가 나를 따르리로다

왕은 이 구절에서 시편 1편이 한 것처럼 악인들을 제제할 부정적인 일들(3-5절)을 먼저 언급한 다음에 의인들을 격려할 긍정적인 일을 말한다. 한 학자는 6-8절은 왕이 스스로 다짐하는 말이 아니라, 하나님이 그의 질문(2절)에 대해 선지자를 통해 답을 하는 것이라고 한다(Kselman). 충분한 설득력이 있는 주장이며, 왕의 '속히 오소서'라며 기도한 것에 대한 하나님의 답이라는 장점을 지닌 해석이다. 그러나 왕의 스피치가 계속되고 있는 것으로 해석해도 별 문제는 없다. 왕이 하나님의 말씀과 기준에 따라 자기 백성들을 대할 것을 다짐하고 있기 때문이다.

왕이 악인들은 멀리하고 벌하기까지 하지만, 의인들은 가까이할 것이다. 그는 의인들을 찾을 것이며, 찾으면 곁에 두고 함께 살 것을 다짐한다. 왕이 찾는 의인은 ‘이 땅의 충성된 자들’(נֶאֶמְנֵי־אֶרֶץ)이다. 충성된 자들은 믿고 의지할 만한 사람들을 뜻한다(HALOT). 또한 왕이 가까이 할 ‘이 땅의 충성된 자들’은 그가 멸할 ‘이 땅의 모든 악인들’(כָּל־רִשְׁעֵי־אָרֶץ)과 강력한 대조를 이룬다. 그는 한 부류와는 서로 의지하며 살지만, 한 부류는 모두 사라질 때까지 응징을 이어갈 것이라고 한다. 그렇다면 왕이 믿고 의지할 만한 사람은 어떤 사람인가? 바로 다음 행은 ‘완전한 길’에 행하는 자라고 한다.

기자는 2절에서 이미 ‘완전할 길’(בְּדֶרֶךְ תָּמִים)은 율법에서 비롯된 삶의 지침이라고 했다. 그러므로 왕이 가까이할 충성된 자들은 그들의 왕처럼 율법이 제시하는 삶의 방식에 따라 살아가는 사람들이다. 왕의 선택을 받은 그들은 왕과 함께 살면서 왕을 따를 것이다. ‘따르다’(שׁרת)의 더 정확한 번역은 ‘섬기다’이다(새번역, 아가페, NIV, NAS, NRS, TNK). 의인들은 왕을 매우 가까운 곳에서 섬기는 특권을 누리게 될 것이다. 왕이 그들을 인정했기 때문이다.

4. 악인들을 벌할 것을 다짐함(101:7-8)

7 거짓을 행하는 자는 내 집안에 거주하지 못하며
거짓말하는 자는 내 목전에 서지 못하리로다
8 아침마다 내가 이 땅의 모든 악인을 멸하리니
악을 행하는 자는 여호와의 성에서 다 끊어지리로다

왕은 신실한 사람들은 옆에 둘 것이지만(6절), 거짓된 자들은 상종하지 않겠다고 다짐한다. 그는 거짓을 행하는 자들이 그와 함께 살지 못하게 할 것이다(7a절). 또한 거짓을 말하는 사람들을 왕 앞에 서지 못하게 할 것이다(7b절). 왕이 이 악인들의 삶을 인정하지 않을 뿐만 아니라 그들이 잘 되는 것을 결코 용납하지 않을 것이란 뜻이다.

뿐만 아니라 왕은 자기가 다스리는 땅에서 모든 악인이 멸망할 때까지 아침마다 그들을 벌할 것이다(8a절). 아침은 왕이 여러 소송을 듣고 판결을 내리는 시간이다(Grogan). 그는 매일 아침마다 공의와 정의를 실현하는 판결을 내리겠다고 다짐한다. 악인을 멸하는 것은 하나님이 하시는 역할이다. 그러므로 이 말씀과 시편 18:40은 이러한 원리에서 예외라 할 수 있다(Hossfeld-Zenger). 인간 왕이 하나님이 하실 일을 하고 있기 때문이다.

왕이 벌할 악인들은 어떤 사람인가? 그들은 바로 '악을 행하는 자들'(כָּל־פֹּעֲלֵי אָוֶן)이다(8b절). 왕으로서 자기가 다스리는 나라에서 일어나는 모든 악행에 대해 분명히 책임을 묻겠다는 의지의 표현이다. 이렇게 해서 그가 다스리는 여호와의 성인 예루살렘에서 악인들이 모두 사라지게 할 것이다. 왜 예루살렘인가? 예루살렘에서 일어나는 일이 온 나라에 영향을 미치기 때문이다(Anderson). 악인들은 의로운 왕이 다스리는 세상에서 설 자리가 없다. 이 노래를 부르는 왕은 자신이 다스리는 나라에서 공의와 정의를 완전하게 실현하겠다고 다짐하지만 현실은 그렇지 않을 것이다. 그러므로 이 시편은 메시아를 통해 최종적으로 실현될 것이다(Kidner).

제102편

고난 당한 자가 마음이 상하여 그의 근심을 여호와 앞에 토로하는 기도

I. 장르/양식: 개인 탄식시(cf. 3편)

전통적으로 교회는 이 시편을 7개의 참회시(penitential psalm, cf. 시 6, 32, 38, 51, 102, 130, 143편) 중 하나로 사용해 왔다. 이 시편들은 내용이 회개에 초점이 맞춰져 있거나, 교회가 이러한 용도로 사용했기 때문에 참회시로 분류되었으며, 102편은 후자의 경우이다(deClaissé-Walford et al., VanGemeren). 유태인들의 구두 토라(oral Torah) 전승에 관한 문헌인 미쉬나(Mishnah)는 유태인들이 이 시편을 금식할 때 사용한 것이라 기록하고 있다(Taanith 2:3).

대체적으로 시편의 표제들은 시의 내용과 잘 어울리지 않는데, 이 시편의 표제는 노래 내용과 참으로 잘 어울린다(Tucker & Grant, McCann). 시편 편집자(들)가 독자들에게 이 시를 사용할 적절한 정황을 제공하고 있는 것이다(Grogan). 이 시는 곤경에 처한 사람이 하나님께 도움을 청하는 모범적인 기도 사례로 간주되기도 하지만(Brueggemann & Bellinger), 국가가 당면한 정치적 위기에 대한 개인적인 기도와 탄식으로 취급되기도 한다(Tucker & Grant). 또한 한 왕의 탄식시이며 가을 축제 때 사용된 것이라는 추측도 있다(Eaton, Mowinckel).

이 시편을 해석하는 일에 있어서 난제로 꼽히는 것은 같은 시에 단수와 복수가 함께 존재한다는 점이다. 이러한 상황이 양식비평가들에게는 매우 어려운 문제가 되었으며, 결과적으로 매우 다양한 추측과 해석을 낳기도 했다(cf. Allen, McCann, Ross). 그럼에도 불구하고 이 시가 통일성을 지닌 한편의 시라는 사실은 확실하다(Mays). 이 노래는 개인적인 탄식에서 공동체의 간구와 염려로 발전한다(Culley).

저작 연대에 대한 학자들의 견해도 매우 다양하다. 왕정 시대에 저작된 개인 탄식시라고 하는 이도 있지만(Weiser), 12-22절을 탄식시의 일부로 보기에는 메시지가 지나치게 소망적이다. 그러므로 한 학자는 왕정 시대에 저작된 탄식시였지만 포로기를 지나며 미래에 관한 약속(12-22절)이 첨부된 것이라고 한다(Childs). 일부 학자들은 12-22절을 '선지자적 찬양'(prophetic hymn)이라고 부르며, 포로기 때 죄인들과 함께 끌려가 좌절하고 절망하는 의인들의 마음에 희망의 불을 지피기 위해 삽입된 것이라 한다(Broyles, Kraus).

대부분 학자들은 바빌론 포로기 혹은 그 이후에 저작되었으며, 주전 586년에 있었던 예루살렘의 비극적인 운명을 배경으로 기자 자신이 타국에서 경험하고 있는 고통에 대해 기도하고 회복을 소망하기 위해 저작한 것이라고 한다(Anderson, McCann, Terrien, VanGemeren). 이 시편의 표제가 바빌론의 기도문들의 표제와 상당히 비슷하다는 주장이 있는가 하면(Gerstenberger), 그다지 비슷하지 않다고 하는 이들도 있다(Tucker & Grant). 저작 시기를 가장 늦게 보는 사람들은 주전 2세기 마카비(Maccabee) 시대에 안티오쿠스 에피파네(Antiochus Epiphanes)의 만행으로 인해 파괴되고 오염된 하나님의 도성을 슬퍼하기 위해 저작된 것이라 한다(Briggs).

II. 구조

이 시는 대체적으로 1-11절과 12-22절과 23-28절 세 파트로 구분하거나, 중앙 섹션(12-22절)은 그대로 두고 앞(1-11절)과 뒤(23-28절)를 각각 두 파트로 구분하여 다섯 섹션으로 구분하기도 한다(deClaissé-Walford et al., Tucker & Grant, McCann, VanGemeren). 이 주석에서도 이 노래를 다음과 같이 다섯 섹션으로 구분하여 주해해 나가고자 한다.

A. 시작 기도(102:1-2)
  B. 탄식(102:3-11)
    C. 확신(102:12-22)
  B'. 탄식(102:23-24)
A'. 마무리 확신(102:25-28)

III. 주해

죄로 인한 징계와 고통으로 괴로워하는 노래이다(cf. 20, 23-24절). 그렇다 보니 탄식과 애가가 시의 전반적인 분위기를 조성한다. 그러나 한 중앙에 소망이 등장한다. 이 소망은 하나님이 시온(성전)에서 온 세상의 왕 되심에 근거하고 있다. 기자의 유일한 소망은 공동체에 임한 하나님의 임재다.

1. 시작 기도(102:1-2)

[1] 여호와여
내 기도를 들으시고
나의 부르짖음을 주께 상달하게 하소서
[2] 나의 괴로운 날에 주의 얼굴을 내게서 숨기지 마소서

주의 귀를 내게 기울이사
내가 부르짖는 날에 속히 내게 응답하소서

심한 고통 속에서 기자는 주님을 향해 울부짖는다. 하지만 그에게는 하나님이 그의 기도를 들으실 것이라는 확신이 없다. 그러하기에 그는 "내 부르짖음이 주님께 이르게 해 주십시오"(1c절, 새번역)라고 호소하며 노래를 시작한다. 1-2절을 구성하고 있는 문장과 문구들은 모두 다윗과 연관된 시편들에서 인용하여 저작된 것이다(Kissane).

여호와는 분명 우리의 기도를 들으시는 분이지만, 종종 우리의 영적 상태에 따라 기도를 들어주지 않으실지도 모른다는 불안감이 엄습할 수 있다. 다행인 것은 우리의 불안감이 하나님이 우리의 기도에 항상 귀를 기울이신다는 사실을 바꿀 수 없다는 점이다. 그러므로 불안하여 기도하기 어려울 때가 하나님이 우리의 기도를 들어주실 가장 좋은 때이다.

저자는 자신이 참으로 괴로운 때를 지나고 있다고 호소한다. 그가 사용하는 단어들과 문구들은 모세가 간구할 때 사용한 것들로 그의 시대에는 이미 정형화된 표현이 되었다(Briggs, McCann, Tucker & Grant, cf. "내 기도"=39:12; 65:2, "나의 부르짖음"= 18:6, "주의 얼굴을 내게서 숨기지 마소서"=13:1; 27:9; 69:17, "나의 괴로운 날에"=59:16, "주의 귀를 기울이소서"=31:2; 71:2; 88:2, "내가 부르짖을 때"=56:9, "속히 내게 응답하소서"=69:17). 그는 당시 믿음 공동체가 흔히 사용하던 용어로 주님께 기도하고 있었던 것이다. 그렇다면 기자는 그가 생각한 만큼 모든 것에서 소외된 삶을 살고 있지 않다고 볼 수 있다(Kidner). 다만 그는 같은 기도 용어를 사용하는 공동체를 따라 기도했던 것이다.

'나의 괴로운 날'(יוֹם צַר לִי)은 처한 상황이 매우 나빠 아무것도 할 수 없어 무기력하게 느껴지는 때를 의미한다(cf. HALOT). 이런 날 가장 두려운 것은 하나님이 우리를 버리셨다는 생각이다. 그러므로 기자는 자신이 처한 어려움에 상관없이 하나님이 아직도 곁에 계시다는 사실을 확인하고 싶어한다. 또한 성경에서 하나님이 사람에게 얼굴을 보이시는 것은 곧 구원과 은혜를 베푸심으로 이해한다(cf. 민 6:25). 그러므로 기자는 하나님께 얼굴을 숨기지 마시라고 호소한다(2a절). 그는 하나님이 기도에 귀를 기울여 주시기만 한다면 그가 처한 문제는 해결된 것이나 다를 바 없다는 믿음으로 하나님께 부르짖고 있다. 가장 절박할 때가 가장 간절한 기도를 드리게 한다.

2. 탄식(102:3–11)

3 내 날이 연기 같이 소멸하며
내 뼈가 숯 같이 탔음이니이다
4 내가 음식 먹기도 잊었으므로
내 마음이 풀 같이 시들고 말라 버렸사오며
5 나의 탄식 소리로 말미암아
나의 살이 뼈에 붙었나이다
6 나는 광야의 올빼미 같고
황폐한 곳의 부엉이 같이 되었사오며
7 내가 밤을 새우니
지붕 위의 외로운 참새 같으니이다
8 내 원수들이 종일 나를 비방하며
내게 대항하여 미칠 듯이 날뛰는 자들이 나를 가리켜 맹세하나이다
9 나는 재를 양식 같이 먹으며
나는 눈물 섞인 물을 마셨나이다
10 주의 분노와 진노로 말미암음이라
주께서 나를 들어서 던지셨나이다
11 내 날이 기울어지는 그림자 같고

내가 풀의 시들어짐 같으니이다

자신의 기도에 귀를 기울여 달라고 하나님께 호소한 기자는 자신이 처한 어려운 상황에 대해 회고한다. 그는 욥처럼 고통을 당하고 있다(Grogan). 그의 간곡한 호소는 그의 삶의 덧없음에 근거를 두고 있다(Kraus). 그래서 그는 자신의 삶을 연기(3절, cf. 호 13:3; 시 37:20), 타는 숯(3절, cf. 시 6:2; 31:10; 애 1:13), 시든 풀(4, 11절, cf. 시 90:5-6; 사 40:6-8), 석양의 그림자(11절, cf. 욥 8:9; 14:2)로 묘사한다. 모두 다 그의 삶의 허무함을 묘사하는 표현이다(cf. 시 90:5-11; 사 40:6-8).

저자는 혹독한 육체적 고통에 시달리고 있으며(Mays, Shaefer, Tucker & Grant), 수명이 단축되고 있다는 느낌을 떨칠 수가 없다. 그는 온 몸이 불에 타는 듯한 고통을 느낀다(3b절). 그러므로 그는 뼈가 숯같이 탔다며 이 일로 인해 자신의 날이 연기같이 소멸하고 있다고 탄식한다(3a절). '연기'(עָשָׁן)는 눈에 보일 뿐 무게나 실체가 없다가 순식간에 사라지는 것에 불과하다. 고통으로 인해 생명이 단축될 뿐만 아니라 순식간에 사라질 위협을 느끼고 있다는 뜻이다.

온 몸이 불에 타는 듯한 고통 속에 있으니, 음식을 제대로 먹을 수가 없다(4a절, cf. 욥 19:20). 그러므로 그의 몸은 날이 갈수록 수척해지고 생기를 잃고 말라가는 풀과 같다(4b절). 그가 유일하게 할 수 있는 일은 신음 속에서 하나님께 탄식 소리를 내는 것뿐이다(5a절). 음식을 삼킬 수 없어 그의 살가죽은 뼈에 붙었다(5b절, cf. 욥 19:20).

기자는 음식을 삼키지 못해 점점 야윌 뿐만 아니라, 잠도 잘 수 없다(6-7절). 그는 자신을 광야의 올빼미, 황폐한 곳의 부엉이, 외로운 참새에 비교한다. 올빼미와 부엉이는 밤에 활동하는 야행성 새들이다. 게다가 이 새들은 부정한 맹금류들이다. 그러므로 저자는 자신을 밤을 헤매는 부정한 새들에 비유하면서 자신의 처량함을 한탄한다. 그는 밤이면 잠을 이룰 수 없으며, 부정해서 하나님께 나아갈 수도 없는 새들처럼 처량한 신세가 되었던 것이다.

결국 그는 뜬눈으로 밤을 새우기 일쑤이며 그런 자신을 '외로운 참새'에 비교한다. 개역개정이 '참새'로 번역한 단어(צִפּוֹר)는 특정한 새가 아니라 단순히 날개를 가진 일반적인 새를 뜻한다(cf. HALOT). 이 말씀이 강조하고자 하는 바는 외로움이다. 밤새 잠을 이룰 수 없어 뜬눈으로 밤을 지새운 기자는 자신을 지붕 위에서 홀로 날을 맞이하는 처량하고 외로운 새에 비교한다. 또한 이 새들이 있는 장소도 상징성을 지닌 듯하다. 광야와 황폐한 곳과 지붕은 하나님의 품에서 멀리 떨어져 있음을 상징한다(deClaissé-Walford et al.). 그는 성전에서 멀리 떨어진 곳에 거하는 부정한 새처럼 하나님께 나아갈 수 없다.

기자는 병든 몸과 잠을 이루지 못하는 밤들로 인해 너무나도 고통스럽다. 그런데 '그의 상처에 소금을 뿌리는 자들'이 있다. 그는 이들을 '원수들'(אֹיֵב)이라고 하는데, 곧 그를 비방하고 대항하는 자들이다(8절). '비방하다'(חרף)는 비아냥거리는 말투로 화나게 만드는 것을 뜻한다(HALOT). 원수들이 저자에게 직접 위협을 가하지는 않는다. 그들의 비방은 하나님이 그를 치고 계시다는 것을 상기시키는 것뿐이다(Kirkpatrick). 고대 근동에서는 사람이 질병을 앓게 되는 것은 신들이 그를 징계했기 때문이라고 생각했다. 이러한 정서에서 원수들은 아마도 고통 속에서 신음하는 그에게 "너의 하나님은 어디에 있느냐?"며 조롱한 것으로 생각된다(VanGemeren, cf. 시 22:7-8; 42:3, 10).

'대항하다'(הלל)는 '조롱한다'는 의미를 지녔다(HALOT, cf. NRS, ESV, TNK). 이 사람들은 어떠한 정당한 이유 없이 단지 그가 아파서 쇠약해진 몰골을 보고 함께 아파하기는커녕 오히려 그를 조롱하는 일에 신바람이 났다. 게다가 그들은 그의 이름을 저주로 사용한다(cf. 새번역, 아가페, 현대인, 창 12:3; 사 65:15). 정당한 이유 없이 이런 짓을 하는 사람은 절대 친구가 아니다. 그러므로 기자는 그들을 원수들이라고 부른다.

저자는 매우 어려운 시간을 보내고 있다. 하나님께 버림받았다는 생각을 떨칠 수 없고, 사람들의 비방과 저주를 견뎌내야 했다. 그는 자신의 딱한 처지를 '재를 양식으로 먹고, 눈물 섞인 물을 마시는 일'에 비교한다(9절). '재'(אֵפֶר)와 '눈물'(בְּכִי)은 슬픔의 상징이다. 사람이 매우 슬픈 일을 당하면 재를 뒤집어쓰고 눈물을 흘린다. 기자는 자신의 처량한 신세를 재를 먹는 것과 눈물 섞인 물을 마시는 것으로 표현한다. 그는 예전에 음식을 먹듯 재를 먹고 있다며 탄식한다(Allen). 개역개정이 '물'로 번역한 단어(שִׁקּוּי)는 '음료수/마실 것'(cf. NIDOTTE)이라는 뜻을 지니고 있지만 본문에서는 물을 의미한다. 슬픔에서 헤어나지 못하는 사람이 생명을 유지하기 위해 겨우 마시는 것이 물 외에 다른 것은 될 수가 없기 때문이다.

'재를 먹고, 눈물을 마시는 일'보다 기자를 더 고통스럽게 하는 것은 하나님이 그를 버리셨다는 생각이다. 그는 하나님이 그에게 진노하셨기 때문에 그를 들어서 내던지셨다는 생각에서 벗어날 수가 없다(10절). 그는 자신의 죄를 떠올리며, 하나님이 그를 징계하신다고 생각한다(VanGemeren).

'들어서 던지다'(נְשָׂאתַנִי וַתַּשְׁלִיכֵנִי)(10절)는 혐오스러운 것을 내팽개치는 듯한 매우 강력한 표현이다. 만일 하나님이 그를 버리셨다면, 그에게는 어떠한 소망도 없다. 그러므로 그는 자신의 삶을 기울어지는 그림자 같다고 한다(11a절). '기울어지는 그림자 같다'(יָמַי כְּצֵל נָטוּי)는 것은 석양의 그림자처럼 곧 수명이 다할 것이라는 뜻이다(cf. 공동, 아가페, 현대인, NIV, ESV, NRS). 또한 그는 자신은 '풀의 시들어짐 같다'며 한탄한다(11b절). 건강을 잃어 날이 갈수록 몸이 수축해지고 생기를 잃어간다는 뜻이다. 기자는 자신의 삶은 어떠한 소망도 없다며 절망하고 있다. 하나님이 그를 버리셨다는 생각이 그를 깊은 영적 수렁에 빠지게 한 것이다.

3. 확신(102:12–22)

[12] 여호와여
주는 영원히 계시고
주에 대한 기억은 대대에 이르리이다
[13] 주께서 일어나사
시온을 긍휼히 여기시리니
지금은 그에게 은혜를 베푸실 때라
정한 기한이 다가옴이니이다
[14] 주의 종들이 시온의 돌들을 즐거워하며
그의 티끌도 은혜를 받나이다
[15] 이에 뭇 나라가 여호와의 이름을 경외하며
이 땅의 모든 왕들이 주의 영광을 경외하리니
[16] 여호와께서 시온을 건설하시고
그의 영광 중에 나타나셨음이라
[17] 여호와께서 빈궁한 자의 기도를 돌아보시며
그들의 기도를 멸시하지 아니하셨도다
[18] 이 일이 장래 세대를 위하여 기록되리니
창조함을 받을 백성이 여호와를 찬양하리로다
[19] 여호와께서 그의 높은 성소에서 굽어보시며
하늘에서 땅을 살펴보셨으니
[20] 이는 갇힌 자의 탄식을 들으시며
죽이기로 정한 자를 해방하사
[21] 여호와의 이름을 시온에서,
그 영예를 예루살렘에서 선포하게 하려 하심이라
[22] 그 때에 민족들과 나라들이 함께 모여
여호와를 섬기리로다

기자가 아무리 자신과 삶을 둘러보아도 소망할 만한 것이라고는 하나도 찾을 수 없다. 그러므로 그는 자신에게 맞춰진 시선을 잠시 주님께 돌려본다. 주님이 어떤 분이시고 어떤 일을 하시는가를 묵상해보니 새로운 힘과 소망이 생긴다! 그는 하나님에 대해 다음과 같이 묵상하며 노래를 이어간다.

첫째, 여호와는 영원히 계시고, 대대로 기억되시는 분이다(12절). 앞에서 기자는 자신은 곧 죽을 것이고, 그가 죽으면 그의 기억도 순식간에 사라질 것을 깨달았다(cf. 3, 11절). 반면에 하나님은 영원하신 분이다. 그와 하나님의 이 같은 대조적인 면모를 강조하기 위해 기자는 대조형 접속사(וְ)를 사용해 12절을 시작한다: "인간의 나약함이 하나님의 영원하심을 만나고 있다"(Schaefer, cf. Culley, Goldingay). '여호와는 영원히 계신다'(אַתָּה יְהוָה לְעוֹלָם)는 왕이신 하나님이 영원히 다스리신다는 뜻이다(cf. 새번역, 공동, 아가페, 현대인, NIV, ESV, NS, NRS). 하나님의 통치에는 끝이 없으므로 주님은 영원히 기억될 것이다.

둘째, 지금은 영원한 왕이신 하나님이 시온에 은혜를 베푸실 때이다(13절). 시온은 이스라엘과 하나님 사이에 맺어진 언약에 연관된 모든 것의 상징이며, 또한 종말론적으로는 하나님의 통치의 상징이기도 하다(VanGemeren). '긍휼히 여기다'(רחם)는 모성애를 바탕으로 한 단어이다(NIDOTTE). '은혜를 베풀다'(חנן)는 베풀지 않아도 되는 선처를 베푼다는 뜻이다(cf. HALOT). 이 두 단어는 출애굽한 이스라엘이 광야에서 금송아지를 만들었을 때, 모세가 하나님의 진노를 진정시키기 위해 눈물로 드린 기도에서 사용된 것들이다(출 34:6). 기자는 자신의 소망을 옛적 출애굽 사건에 근거하고 있는 것이다(McCann).

두 단어는 사람이 상상할 수 있는 가장 끈끈하고 애틋한 사랑을 뜻한다. 하나님은 백성들의 신앙의 구심점이 되는 시온을 사랑하기를 이같이 하신다. 또한 하나님이 아끼시는 시온에 은혜를 베풀 시간이 임했다! 지금은 하나님의 은혜를 기대할 만한 때(עֵת)이다. 주님께서 그들에게 은혜를 베푸시기로 '정한 기한'(מוֹעֵד)이 되었기 때문이다. 이 시편이 포로기 이후에 저작된 것이라 주장하는 사람들은 이 말씀을 여호와께서 성전을 재건하실 때가 이른 것으로 해석한다(cf. Calvin, McCann, VanGemeren). 가능한 해석이지만, 곤경에 처한 성도들이 하나님의 처소를 바라보며 언제든 드릴 수 있는 기도이기도 하다(Clifford, deClaissé-Walford et al.).

셋째, 하나님이 시온에 은혜를 베푸시면 주의 종들은 기뻐하고, 세상은 하나님을 두려워할 것이다(14-16절). 하나님이 시온에 은혜를 베푸신다는 것은 하나님이 그곳에 임하셨음을 전제한다. 그러므로 하나님을 사모하는 사람들이 모두 기뻐하며 즐거워한다. 심지어는 시온의 돌들과 먼지까지 그들을 기쁘게 한다. 하나님이 그곳에 임하셨기 때문이다.

하나님이 직접 임하셔서 시온을 건설하시고 영광을 나타내셨다는 소식이 온 세상에 퍼지자(16절), 온 열방과 왕들이 하나님을 경외한다(15절). '경외하다'(ירא)는 두려워한다는 의미를 지녔다. 열방이 여호와는 자신들의 신들과 다르다는 사실을 깨닫고 여호와를 두려워한다. 그들의 신들은 숭배자들의 '단물을 빨아먹고' 내팽개치는데, 여호와는 자기 백성이 어떠한 상황에 처해 있든 상관하지 않으시고, 심지어는 절망적인 상황에 처했다 할지라도(cf. 1-11절) 끝까지 그들과 함께 하시며 은혜를 베푸시기 때문이다. 열방이 아직 하나님을 경배하고 찬양하는 단계에 온 것은 아니지만, 상황이 상당히 고무적이다. 여호와를 경외하는 것이 구원에 이르게 하는 참 지식의 시작이기 때문이다. 잠시 후, 22절에 가서 열방이 구원에 이르는 경배를 여호와께 드린다.

넷째, 하나님은 빈궁한 자의 기도를 들으신다(17절). 하나님은 분명 우리의 경배와 찬양을 받기에 합당하신 분이지만, 사람들에게 이런 것을 요구하기 위해 시온에 임하신 것이 아니다. 그들을 사랑하고 섬기기 위해 오셨다. 하나님이 시온에 임하신 것은 가장 연약한 자들의 기도를 들어 주시기 위해서이다. 하나님이 죄인인 우리의 기도를 멸시하지 않으시고 들어 주시기 위해 우리를 찾아오신다는 사실이 참으로 감동적이다.

다섯째, 하나님의 은혜는 기록되어 두루두루 찬양되기에 합당하다(18절). 하나님의 은혜를 경험한 사람들은 장래 세대들을 위해 그 은혜를 기록으로 남기는 것이 좋다. 훗날 세대들이 우리가 경험한 하나님의 은혜를 기념하고 묵상하며 하나님을 찬양하게 하기 위함이다. 현재와 미래가 불안하고 불확실할 때, 과거에 베풀어 주신 은혜를 묵상하는 일처럼 효과적인 처방은 없다. 그러므로 기자는 하나님의 은혜를 경험한 사람들에게 기록을 남기라고 권면한다.

여섯째, 하나님은 자기 백성들을 살리기 위해 하늘에서 내려오셨다(19-20절). 기자는 여호와께서 시온에 임하신 것은 하늘에서 이 땅을 굽어살피셨기 때문이라고 한다(19절). 세상에서 어떤 일이 벌어지고 있는지 살펴보신 결과라는 것이다. 주님이 이 땅을 살피시면서 무엇을 목격하셨는가? 갇힌 자의 탄식을 들으셨고, 사형 선고를 받은 사람들의 통곡 소리를 들으셨다(20절). 갇힌 자와 사형 선고를 받은 사람 모두 절망적인 상황에서 억압당하는 자들을 뜻한다(VanGemeren). 출애굽 때 이집트에 갇혀 있던 이스라엘 사람들을 연상케 한다(Tucker & Grant, cf. 출 3:7-10). 하나님은 그들을 속박과 죽음에서 해방시키고 소망을 주기 위해 오셨다. 죽을 사람들을 살리기 위해 오신 것이다.

일곱째, 하나님이 죽을 자들을 살리시는 것은 은혜를 경험한 그들이 주님을 찬양하도록 하기 위해서다(21-22절). 하나님의 선하심을 경험한 사람들은 주님의 놀라운 이름을 시온과 예루살렘에서, 곧 세상의 중심에서 선포해야 한다. 경험한 일을 사적인 은혜로 취급하지 말고 그가 속한 온 공동체, 더 나아가 온 세상이 함께 나누고 기뻐하는 기회로 삼으라는 권면이다.

우리가 경험한 주님의 은혜를 온 세상과 나누는 이유는 분명하다.

우리의 간증을 들은 세상 사람들이 하나님을 섬기도록 하기 위해서다(22절). 22절은 온 열방이 은혜를 경험한 성도들의 간증을 들으려고 예루살렘에 모여 있는 모습을 묘사한다(cf. NIV, ESV, NRS, TNK). 열방이 그들의 간증을 듣게 하기 위해 하나님이 이미 그들을 시온에 모아 두신 모습이다. 열방은 간증을 듣고 나서 여호와를 섬길 것을 결단한다(Hossfeld-Zenger, cf. 사 2장, 미 4장). 드디어 구원에 이르는 믿음을 갖게 된 것이다. 그들이 이러한 믿음을 갖게 된 것에는 성도들의 간증이 중요한 역할을 했다.

4. 탄식(102:23-24)

23 그가 내 힘을 중도에 쇠약하게 하시며
내 날을 짧게 하셨도다
24 나의 말이
하나님이여
나의 중년에 나를 데려가지 마옵소서
주의 연대는 대대에 무궁하나이다

잠시 하나님 임재의 환상의 나래를 펼치고 그 소망으로 기뻐하던 기자는 자신의 암울한 현실로 돌아왔다. 그는 여전히 아프고 생명에 위협을 느낀다. 그는 자신에게 일어난 일 모두가 하나님이 하신 것이라고 생각하여(cf. 10절), 하나님이 자신의 힘을 꺾으시고 수명을 단축시키셨다고 탄식한다. 물론 사실이 아니다. 그러나 특별한 이유도 모른 채 혹독한 육체적 고통을 당하는 주의 백성은 이렇게 생각할 수 있다.

그는 하나님께 자기를 죽게 내버려두지 말라고 기도한다(24절). "병을 주시는 이도 하나님이시고, 그 병을 낫게 하시는 분도 하나님이시다"라는 애가의 모순이 그대로 드러나고 있다(Tucker & Grant). 개역개정이 '나의 중년'으로 번역한 문구(בַּחֲצִי)의 더 정확한 의미는 '나의 중간에'(in the midst)이다(cf. HALOT, NIV, ESV, NAS TNK). 이는 중년을 지나고 있는 사람이 아닌, 나이에 상관없이 한참 삶을 살고 있는 사람이 자신의 삶이 이 순간 끊기는 일이 없도록 간구하는 기도이다.

그는 자신의 짧은 생애를 하나님의 영원하심에 대조한다(24d절). 영원히 존재하시는 하나님(cf. 12절)에 비하면 설령 자신의 삶이 중간에 끊기지 않고 끝까지 살아진다 하더라도 하나님의 영원하심에 비하면 턱없이 짧다는 사실을 상기시킨다. 이와 같은 비교는 그나마 중간에 그의 삶이 끊기는 일은 없도록 호소하기 위한 것으로 이해할 수 있다.

5. 마무리 확신(102:25-28)

25 주께서 옛적에 땅의 기초를 놓으셨사오며
하늘도 주의 손으로 지으신 바니이다
26 천지는 없어지려니와
주는 영존하시겠고
그것들은 다 옷 같이 낡으리니
의복 같이 바꾸시면 바뀌려니와
27 주는 한결같으시고
주의 연대는 무궁하리이다
28 주의 종들의 자손은 항상 안전히 거주하고
그의 후손은 주 앞에 굳게 서리이다 하였도다

영원하신 하나님(cf. 12, 24절)은 사람이 보기에는 영원히 존재하는 듯한 세상의 기초를 놓으시고, 바다를 창조하신 분이다(25절, cf. 창 1장). 여호와의 무한한 힘과 조정 능력과 창조 능력을 강조하는 말씀이다(Tucker & Grant). 그러나 우리 눈에는 영원한 듯한 세상도 하나님처럼 영원하지 않다. 때가 되면 세상은 옷이 낡아 없어지듯 없어질 것이다. 그러나 하나님은 영원히 계신다(26절). 하나님은 사람이 낡아 못쓰게 된 옷을 새 옷으로 바꾸는 것처럼 낡은 세상을 새로운 세상으로 바꾸실 수 있다. 기자는 여호와 하나님은 마음만 먹으시면 언제든 천지를 창조하시고 재창조하실 수 있는 분임을 고백한다.

세상은 언제든 바뀔 수 있지만, 하나님은 바뀌지 않고 한결같으시며 영원히 사신다(27절). 저자는 하나님의 불변성에 기대를 건다. 주님은 옛적에 자기 백성을 보호하시고 축복하실 것을 약속하셨다. 그러므로 하나님은 이 약속을 지키기 위해서라도 종들의 자손이 항상 안전하게 살게 해 주실 것이며, 그들의 후손이 주님 앞에서 끊기는 일이 없도록 하실 것이다(28절). 하나님은 한번 약속하시면 변하지 않으시고 한결같이 그 약속을 지키시는 분이기 때문이다. 포로기를 이 시편의 저작 시기로 보는 사람들은 기자가 언젠가는 그의 후손들이 예루살렘 성전에서 다시 하나님을 찬양할 날이 올 것을 소망하며 이 노래를 부르고 있다고 한다(Broyles).

고통스러운 현실을 당면한 기자가 절망으로 시작했던 기도가 아무것도 바뀌지 않은 상황에서 확신과 믿음으로 끝나는 것이 인상적이다. 우리가 아무리 힘들고 어려운 상황에 처한다 할지라도 우리의 기도와 소망의 근거를 하나님께 두면 우리도 이렇게 기도할 수 있다. 우리는 어떠한 상황에 처하더라도 항상 미래를 소망할 수 있다(Tucker & Grant, cf. Allen).

제103편

다윗의 시

I. 장르/양식: 회중 찬양시(cf. 29편)

이 시편은 하나님의 사역을 통해 언약 백성과 온 세상에 내려 주시는 자비를 묵상하는 노래이다. 대체적으로 이 시는 개인 찬양시로 간주되지만(Allen, Grogan, Ross, VanGemeren, cf. 1-2절), 1인칭 복수(we)형으로 진행되는 10-14절을 감안하면 그 부분은 회중 찬양시로 취급될 수도 있다. 또한 찬양시와 감사시를 합해 놓은 것이라는 해석도 있다(Brueggemann & Bellinger). 아마도 기자가 하나님이 하시는 일에 대해 묵상하면서 개인적으로 시작한 찬양이 점차 주변 사람들뿐만 아니라 온 우주가 하나님의 자비로우심을 찬양해야 한다는 확신으로 이어지기 때문에 이러한 변화를 갖게 된 것으로 생각된다.

기자는 1-5절에서는 자신을 두고 '나'(I)와 '당신'(you)이라고 하고, 6-9절에서는 이스라엘의 과거를 두고 '그들'(they)이라고 언급한다. 이어 10-14절에서는 이스라엘의 과거와 현재를 두고 '우리'(we)라고 표현하고, 15-18절에서는 온 인류를 언급한다. 마지막으로 19-22절에서는 우주와 세상에게 하나님을 찬양할 것을 권면한다(Allen). 찬양의 주체가 단지 일인칭 단수와 복수에 제한되지 않는다. 그러므로 이 시편에서 단수(I)와 복수(we)의 차이는 별 의미가 없으며 동일하게 취급될 수 있다(Gerstenberger). 또한 천사들까지 하나님을 찬양하도록 하는 권면 대상의 범위(scope)는 시편 모음집에서 가장 넓은 것 중 하나이다(deClaissé-Walford et al.).

저자는 개인적으로 경험한 일에 대해 묵상하며 감사하다가 찬양으로 이어 가고 있다(Mowinckel). 그는 어떤 일을 경험한 것일까? 일부 학자들은 3-5절을 바탕으로 이 시편은 기자가 심각한 질병에서 회복된 다음에 부른 노래라고 한다(Kraus, Terrien). 또한 이 병자는 자신이 심하게 아팠던 일을 곤경에 처한 이스라엘의 경험으로 승화시키고 있다고 생각하는 이도 있다(Terrien). 이 노래의 내용은 간증시(testimony psalm)와 찬양시(praise psalm)의 중간쯤에 위치한다(Goldingay).

그러나 기자는 어떤 특정한 상황(병에서 회복된 일)에서 하나님을 찬양하는 것이 아니라, 주님의 전반적인 사역(3-6절)과 성품(6-19절)을 중심으로 노래하고 있다(cf. McCann). 그러므로 이 노래가 병에서 회복된 사람이 부른 노래라고 단정하기에는 다소 어려움이 있다(cf. Allen, deClaissé-Walford et al.).

이 시편과 104편은 매우 밀접한 관계가 있다는 것이 대부분 학자들의 결론이다(cf. Brueggemann & Bellinger, Goldingay, Kirkpatrick, VanGemeren). 각 시편의 시작과 끝이 같고(103:1, 22; 104:1, 35), 내용도 상당 부분 103편을 더 발전시키기 때문이다. 심지어는 이 두 시편이 같은 저자에 의하여 집필된 것이라는 견해도 있다(Kirkpatrick). 특히 103:19-22을 104편이 더 확대해 노래하는 성향이 짙다.

이 노래는 예배에서 사용되었기 때문에 개인적인 면모와 공동체적인 면모를 담고 있다(cf. McCann). 일부 학자들은 이 노래가 이스라엘의 축제/절기에 사용되었을 것이라 한다. 구체적으로 가을 축제를 지목하는 이들도 있다(Eaton). 그러나 입증할 만한 증거가 부족하니 사용 용도에 대한 논의는 추측으로 남겨두는 것이 좋다.

중세기 랍비 킴히(Kimchi)는 시편의 언어가 포로기를 배경으로 하고 있다고 주장했다(cf. Goldingay). 또한 이 노래가 출애굽기 32-34장의 내용을 반영하고 있지만, 아람어적인 성향과 이사야 40-66장과의 언어적 연관성은 포로기 이후 시대에 저작된 것임을 암시한다는 학자들도 있다(Goldingay). 반면에 이 시편은 왕정 시대에 저작된 것이며, 예레미야와 이사야가 이 시편의 고유 표현을 인용한 것이라며 영향력의 방향을 이사야—예레미야에서 이 노래가 아니라, 이 노래에서 이사야—예레미야로 보는 학자들도 있다(Kidner).

II. 구조

"내 영혼아, 여호와를 송축하라"(בָּרֲכִי נַפְשִׁי אֶת־יְהוָה)는 문장이 이 시편을 시작하고, 마무리하며 전체를 감싸고 있다(1, 22절). 하나님을 찬양하라는 1-2절과 20-22절에는 '축복하다/송축하다'(ברך)가 6차례 등장하면서 이러한 기능을 더 강화 시킨다. 나머지 부분(3-19절)은 여호와의 '자비'(חֶסֶד)에 대한 묵상이다(deClaissé-Walford et al.).

기자는 하나님의 완전하심을 노래하는 일에 심혈을 기울인다. 그는 하나님의 완전하신 성품을 총체적으로 강조하기 위해 '모든'(כל)을 여러 차례 반복하여 노래에 통일성을 더한다(1-3, 6, 19, 21-22절). 또한 이 노래가 알파벳 시(acrostic poem)는 아니지만, 히브리어 알파벳 숫자인 22절로 구성되어 이 같은 총체성과 통일성을 증강시킨다(McCann, Schaefer).

이 주석은 '여호와의 헤세드'를 이 시편의 핵심으로 삼아 다음과 같은 구조를 바탕으로 본문을 주해해 나가고자 한다(cf. deClaissé-Walford et al., McCann, deClaissé-Walford et al.).

A. 찬양 부름(103:1-2)

B. 개인에게 내리시는 헤세드(103:3-9)

B'. 공동체에게 내리시는 헤세드(103:10-16)

B″. 온 세상에 내리시는 헤세드(103:17-19)
A′. 찬양 부름(103:20-22)

III. 주해

이 노래는 시편들 중에서 하나님의 사역과 성품에 대해 매우 확실하고 명확하게 묘사하고 있다. 여러 면에서 출애굽기 34:6-7에 기록된 말씀에 대한 깊은 묵상으로 여겨지기도 한다. 기자는 각 개인으로부터 온 세상에 이르기까지 세상 모든 사람이 하나님의 헤세드를 경험하며 살고 있으므로 세상에 있는 모든 천사와 사람들에게 찬양을 받기에 합당하신 분이라고 한다. 하나님이 얼마나 위대하신 분으로 묘사가 되어 있는지 이 시편을 묵상하다 보면 하나님을 찬양하고 싶어서 저절로 무릎을 꿇게 된다(Tucker & Grant).

1. 찬양 부름(103:1-2)

1 내 영혼아
여호와를 송축하라
내 속에 있는 것들아
다 그의 거룩한 이름을 송축하라
2 내 영혼아 여호와를 송축하며
그의 모든 은택을 잊지 말지어다

기자는 하나님을 세 차례나 송축하라는 권면으로 노래를 시작한다. 권면의 대상은 이스라엘이나 다른 사람이 아니라, 저자 자신이다. 그는 다른 사람에게 찬양을 권면하기 전에 먼저 자기 영혼에게 주님을 찬양할 것을 권면하고 있다. 찬양은 인도하는 사람 안에서 시작될 때 가장 힘있고 감동적인 찬양이 되기 때문이다.

'송축하다'(ברך)는 '축복하다'는 의미를 지녔다. 그러나 하나님은 사람을 축복하셔도 사람은 하나님을 축복할 수 없기 때문에(cf. Tucker & Grant) 개역개정은 '송축하다'(새번역은 '찬송하다'로 번역함)로 번역한다. 하나님께 이 단어가 적용될 때는 '감사한 마음으로 따뜻하게 찬양할 것'을 요구한다(Eaton). 그러나 이 말씀에서는 '무릎을 꿇고 경의를 표하라'는 의미로 해석되는 것이 바람직하다(McCann, cf. 시 16:7; 26:12; 34:1; 63:4).

이 두 절은 하나님을 송축하라는 권면을 세 차례 하고 있지만, 실제 히브리어 텍스트에는 두 차례(1절과 2절에 각각 한 차례) 등장한다. 1절을 구성하고 있는 두 문구가 한 동사를 공유하고 있기 때문에 이렇게 해석해야 한다. 시편의 끝 부분(20-22절)에도 하나님을 송축하라는 권면이 세 차례 등장하며 시작 부분과 쌍을 이루고 있다.

그는 무엇보다도 마음속 깊은 곳에서 우러나오는 찬송으로 주님을 경배하고자 한다. 그러므로 그는 '자기 영혼'(נַפְשִׁי)이 여호와를 경배할 것을 두 차례 반복적으로 권면한다(1a, 2a절). 또한 그의 몸을 구성하고 있는 모든 장기들, 즉 '내 속에 있는 모든 것들'(כָּל־קְרָבַי)에게 하나님을 경배할 것을 주문한다(1c절). 그는 마음(영혼)과 몸을 다해 온전히 주님을 찬송하고자 한다.

저자는 자기의 몸과 마음에게 하나님의 거룩한 이름을 찬양하고, 주님의 모든 은택을 잊지 말라고 명령한다. 하나님의 '거룩한 이름'(קָדְשׁוֹ שֵׁם)은 주님의 속성을 요약하는 표현으로서(McCann), 주님은 본질적으로 완벽하고 존귀하며(VanGemeren), 다른 신들의 것과 비교할 수 없이 거룩(특별함, 차별화됨)하다는 의미를 지녔다. 하나님이 어떤 분이신지가 그의 이름에 요약되어 있는 것이다(Hossfeld-Zenger).

'은택'(גְּמוּל)은 여호와께서 주님을 섬기는 사람들에게 허락하시는 온갖 '혜택/이득'(benefit)이다(HALOT). 하나님을 믿는다는 이유로 주님이 내려 주시는 축복을 의미하는 것이다. 그는 하나님이 그에게 주신 온갖 '혜택'(은혜)을 두고두고 기념하며 살 것을 다짐한다. 잊는다는 의미는 자연스럽게 잊혀짐이 아닌 알면서도 무시하려 하는 행위를 가리킨다(Anderson). 그러므로 잊음은 곧 찬양의 반대말이 될 수 있다(VanGemeren).

2. 개인에게 내리시는 헤세드(103:3–9)

3 그가 네 모든 죄악을 사하시며
네 모든 병을 고치시며
4 네 생명을 파멸에서 속량하시고
인자와 긍휼로 관을 씌우시며
5 좋은 것으로 네 소원을 만족하게 하사
네 청춘을 독수리 같이 새롭게 하시는도다
6 여호와께서 공의로운 일을 행하시며
억압 당하는 모든 자를 위하여 심판하시는도다
7 그의 행위를 모세에게,
그의 행사를 이스라엘 자손에게 알리셨도다
8 여호와는 긍휼이 많으시고 은혜로우시며
노하기를 더디 하시고 인자하심이 풍부하시도다
9 자주 경책하지 아니하시며
노를 영원히 품지 아니하시리로다

하나님을 믿으면 어떤 '혜택/이득'을 누릴 수 있는가? 기자는 주로 분사(participle)를 사용하여 하나님을 찬양한다: "용서하시고… 치료하시고… 속량하시고… 관을 씌우시고… 만족하게 하시는 분"(3–5절). 하나님이 하시는 이 일들은 그가 직접 경험한 은혜를 포함할 수 있지만, 하나님이 항상 행하시는 일상적인 주님의 사역이다. 또한 기자는 2인칭 단수 '너'(you)를 사용하여 하나님이 자기 백성에게 행하시는 일을 나열한다(cf. deClaissé-Walford et al.). 그러므로 '너'(you)를 '우리'(we)로 대입해도 전혀 문제가 없다(cf. Gerstenberger). 그는 하나님이 우리를 위해 하시는 일 여덟 가지를 나열한 후, 하나님의 성품 여섯 가지를 언급한다.

첫째, 하나님은 우리의 죄악을 용서하신다(3a절). 하나님을 믿는 사람들이 누리는 가장 기본적이고 중요한 혜택이다(McKeating, Tucker & Grant). 죄 사함 한 가지 만으로도 우리는 영원히 주님을 찬양할 수 있다. 강조점은 '너의 모든 죄악'(כָּל־עֲוֹנֵכִי)에 있다. '죄악'(עָוֹן)은 죄와 죄의 결과를 총체적으로 일컫는 말이다(VanGemeren, cf. 시 32:1; 51:2; 90:8). 하나님이 용서하실 수 없는 죄는 없으며, 주님은 우리의 모든 죄 문제를 해결하는 것을 기뻐하시는 분이다(Willis). 죄가 우리를 하나님께 나아갈 수 없게 하기 때문이다. 그러므로 죄 문제가 해결되면 우리는 언제든 주님의 은혜의 보좌로 나아갈 수 있다.

둘째, 하나님은 우리의 병을 고치신다(3b절, cf. 출 15:26; 신 32:39; 사 57:18-19; 렘 30:17). '고치다/치료하다'(רפא)는 일상적으로 육체적인 병에 관계되어 사용되지만, 본문에서는 영적인 병이나 극복하기 어려운 힘든 상황과 관계된 것으로 볼 수도 있다(VanGemeren). 그러나 바로 앞 행에서 '영적인 병'이라 할 수 있는 죄를 이미 언급했으므로 이 행에서는 육체적인 병으로 해석하는 것이 바람직하다(cf. Tucker & Grant). 육체적인 질병이 때로는 사람이 하나님께 나아가는 동기가 될 수 있기 때문에 하나님은 항상 우리의 질병을 곧바로 치료하시지는 않는다(Kidner).

하나님은 우리의 죄를 사하시고 나면 우리의 질병도 치료하기를 기뻐하신다. 순서는 분명하다. 우리는 영적인 병인 죄를 먼저 용서받고 난 후에 육체적인 병을 치료해 주심을 기대해야 한다. 죄 사함이 육체적인 병 나음보다 더 중요하기 때문이다. 예수님도 병이 낫고자 찾아온 중풍 병자의 죄를 사하시면서 육체적인 병보다 죄를 용서받음이 더 어렵다고 하셨다(마 9:1-8). 이 말씀의 강조점도 '너의 모든 병'(תַּחֲלֻאָיְכִי־

כֹּל)에 있다. 이는 여호와께서 우리가 앓는 모든 병을 하나도 빠짐없이 치료하실 수 있음을 의미한다.

셋째, 하나님은 생명을 위협하는 위기에서 우리를 구원하신다(4a절). 기자가 사용하는 이미지는 스스로는 절대 헤어 나오지 못하는 구덩이에 빠진 사람의 절박한 상황이다(cf. 공동, NIV, ESV, NRS, NAS). 하나님이 꺼내 주지 않으시면 도저히 죽음을 피할 길이 없다. 기자는 구원하시는 하나님을 '속량자'(גֹּאֵל)라고 부르는데, '기업을 무를 자'라는 뜻을 지녔다(cf. 출 6:6; 15:13; 시 74:2; 77:15; 사 43:1; 51:10). 하나님이 곤경에 처한 사람을 마치 자기 가족/친척을 구하시듯 기꺼이 구원하신다는 의미다.

넷째, 하나님은 구원한 우리를 존귀하게 하신다(4b절). 주님은 생명을 위협하는 구덩이에서 우리를 건져내시고 우리의 머리에 관을 씌우신다. 우리와 하나님의 관계는 '인자'(חֶסֶד)와 '긍휼'(רַחֲמִים)에 근거한 것이며(Mays), 하나님은 인자와 긍휼로 만든 관을 우리에게 씌우신다. 이는 왕이 취임식에서 왕관을 쓰고 백성들 앞에 모습을 드러내는 상황이다(Anderson). 하나님이 인자와 긍휼로 우리를 존귀하게 하셨으며, 앞으로도 인자와 긍휼로 우리를 보호하시고 인도하실 것을 모든 사람이 보는 앞에서 다짐하시는 행위다. 또한 면류관을 씌우시는 것은 구덩이에서 죽음을 맞이하던 비천한 우리를 존귀하게 세우셨다는 증표이기도 하다.

다섯째, 하나님은 좋은 것으로 우리의 소원을 이루어 주시는 분이다(5a절). '만족하다'(שׂבע)는 사람이 실컷 먹어 더 이상 바랄 것이 없는 상황을 묘사하는 단어이다(HALOT, cf. 출 16:8, 12; 사 58:11; 렘 32:40; 33:9, 11; 시 23:6). 하나님은 무엇으로 우리가 원하는 바 이상으로 채우시는가? '선한 것'(טוֹב)이다. 하나님은 항상 우리에게 좋은 것으로 주시고 나쁜 것은 주지 않으신다.

여섯째, 하나님은 우리의 젊음을 새롭게 하시는 분이다(5b절). 독수리가 매일 새로운 힘을 공급받지 못하면 자유로이 하늘을 날 수 없는 것처럼(cf. 사 40:31), 우리도 하나님이 새 힘을 허락하지 않으시면 삶을 의욕적으로 살 수 없다. 하나님은 우리에게 힘과 살아갈 의지를 공급하셔서 매일 창공을 나는 독수리처럼 되게 하신다.

일곱째, 하나님은 공의로운 재판을 하시는 분이다(6절, cf. 시 9:7-8; 89:14; 96:13; 97:2; 98:9). 이때까지 언급된 여섯 가지가 각 개인의 삶에 적용되는 하나님의 사역이었다면, 지금부터는 우리가 속한 공동체에 관한 것들이다. 하나님은 자기 백성들로 구성된 공동체에서 공의와 정의가 실현되는 것을 기뻐하신다. 그러므로 주님은 항상 공의로운 일을 행하시며 억압당하는 자들을 위해 심판하신다. '공의로운 일'(צְדָקָה)은 법의 기준이 공평하게 적용되도록 하여 잘못된 것을 바로잡는 일이다(cf. Alter, VanGemeren). 편파적인 판결로 억울하게 당하는 사람이 없도록 하신다. '억압당하는 자들'(עֲשׁוּקִים)은 짓눌리고 착취당하는 사람들을 의미한다(HALOT). 하나님은 공동체 안에서 필요 이상의 폭력과 억압으로 억울하게 짓밟히는 사람들이 없는가를 살피셔서 재판하신다. 만일 억울하게 당하는 사람들이 있다면 그들에게 자유를 주실 것이다.

여덟째, 하나님은 우리가 주님의 사역에 대해 알기를 원하신다(7절). 옛적에는 모세에게 '자신의 길들'(דְּרָכָיו), 곧 하나님이 어떻게 역사하시고 은혜를 베푸셨는가를 알게 하셨다. 이후 이스라엘에게 '자신의 행사들/하신 일들'(עֲלִילוֹתָיו)을 꾸준히 알려주셨다. 주의 백성들은 하나님이 그들을 위해 행하신 일들을 두루두루 기념하며 감사해야 한다. 또한 하나님이 과거에 하신 일을 묵상하는 것은 주의 백성들에게 오늘을 살 수 있는 힘과 원동력이 된다.

하나님이 하시는 일 여덟 가지를 나열한 기자는 이어 하나님의 성품 여섯 가지를 언급한다(8-9절): '긍휼하심, 은혜로우심, 노하기를 더디하심, 인자가 많으심, 자주 경책하지 않으심, 노를 영원히 품지 않으심.' 이 말씀은 아론이 금송아지를 만들어 하나님을 분노케 한 일이 있었던 바로 다음에 모세가 하나님께 눈물로 기도하던 대목과 매우 유사하다(출 34:6-7). 앞에서 모세를 언급한 기자가(7절) 모세의 가르침을 회상하고 있는 것이다.

첫째, 하나님은 긍휼하시다(רַחוּם). 이는 어머니의 자궁(womb)과 연관된 단어이다. 어머니의 아이를 향한 모성적인 사랑과 관심을 뜻한다.

둘째, 하나님은 은혜로우시다(חַנּוּן). 아무런 전제 조건 없이, 심지어는 받을 자격이 전혀 없는 사람들에게까지 베푸는 일방적인 배려를 뜻한다(cf. 출 33:12, 16-17). 학자들은 하나님의 시기가 은혜를 베푸시는 근거가 되기도 한다고 주장한다.

셋째, 하나님은 노하기를 더디하신다(אֶרֶךְ אַפַּיִם). 이 문구를 문자적으로 해석하면 '긴 코를 가지다'라는 뜻이다. 히브리 사람들은 사람이 화가 나면 코에서 열이 나는 것으로 이해했다. 그러므로 코가 길면 그만큼 열을 식힐 수 있는 공간이 많아서 화를 더디 낸다고 생각했다(Brueggemann).

넷째, 하나님은 인자가 많으신 분이다(רַב־חָסֶד). 인자(חֶסֶד)는 근본적으로 언약/계약을 충실하게 이행한다는 뜻을 바탕으로 하고 있다. 그러므로 하나님이 인자가 많은 분이라는 사실은 이스라엘과의 언약을 충실하게 지키며 이행하실 것을 암시한다. 뿐만 아니라 필요에 따라서 이스라엘의 많은 과오도 용서하고 용납하여 언약관계를 유지하시겠다는 의지의 표현이다.

다섯째, 하나님은 자주 경책하지 않으시는 분이다(לֹא־לָנֶצַח יָרִיב). 이 표현은 하나님은 그 누구와도 오랫동안 다투지 않으신다는 뜻이다(cf. HALOT). 하나님이 때로는 우리의 죄를 질책하시지만, 잠시 하시는 일이지 오래 지속하지는 않으신다(cf. 사 3:12; 57:16; 렘 2:9; 미 6:2). 만일 하나님의 책망이 오랜 시간 동안 지속된다면 세상에는 살아남을 사람이 없다. 그러므로 우리가 하나님의 징계를 받는다 해도 절망할 필요가 없는 것은 그 심판이 우리를 회복시키기 위함이며 우리가 회개하면 곧 멈출 것이라는 소망이 있기 때문이다.

여섯째, 하나님은 노를 영원히 품지 않으시는 분이다(לֹא לְעוֹלָם יִטּוֹר). 하나님은 누구를 용서하시면 용서받은 죄로 인해 더 이상 그를 질타하지 않으신다. 그 순간부터 하나님은 그의 과거를 과거로 묻어 두신다. 세상 말로 하나님은 '뒤끝'이 없으신 분이다.

3. 공동체에게 내리시는 헤세드(103:10–16)

10 우리의 죄를 따라 우리를 처벌하지는 아니하시며
우리의 죄악을 따라 우리에게 그대로 갚지는 아니하셨으니
11 이는 하늘이 땅에서 높음 같이
그를 경외하는 자에게 그의 인자하심이 크심이로다
12 동이 서에서 먼 것 같이
우리의 죄과를 우리에게서 멀리 옮기셨으며
13 아버지가 자식을 긍휼히 여김 같이
여호와께서는 자기를 경외하는 자를 긍휼히 여기시나니
14 이는 그가 우리의 체질을 아시며
우리가 단지 먼지뿐임을 기억하심이로다
15 인생은 그 날이 풀과 같으며
그 영화가 들의 꽃과 같도다
16 그것은 바람이 지나가면 없어지나니
그 있던 자리도 다시 알지 못하거니와

기자는 이 섹션에서도 하나님의 성품과 행하시는 일에 대하여 찬양을 이어간다. 앞 섹션에서는 주로 2인칭 단수 '너'(you)를 사용하여 하나님이 자기 백성을 어떻게 대하시는가에 대해 말했다면, 이 섹션에서는 1인칭 복수인 '우리'(we)를 사용하여 찬양한다. 하나님은 무엇보다도 인간의 연약함을 아시기 때문에 많은 자비와 인내로 그를 대하신다. 하

나님이 하시는 일이 다섯 가지로 묘사되고 있다.

첫째, 하나님은 우리가 지은 죄에 따라 우리를 처벌하지 않으신다(10절). 이 말씀은 우리가 저지른 죄에 상응하는 처벌이 100이라면, 하나님은 100으로 우리를 벌하시는 것이 아니라, 그것보다 훨씬 더 수위를 낮추어 징계하신다는 의미이다. 만일 하나님이 우리가 받아야 할 처벌을 모두 내리시면 살아남을 자가 별로 없을 것이다. 주님은 자기 백성에게 서로의 죄에 대하여는 '이에는 이, 눈에는 눈'의 원리로 처벌하라고 하셨지만, 정작 하나님이 백성을 대하실 때에는 훨씬 더 자비로우시다.

둘째, 하나님은 주를 경외하는 사람들에게 참으로 큰 인자를 베푸신다(11절, cf. 13절). 하나님이 죄인들에게 '법대로'하지 않으시고 처벌을 훨씬 약하게 하시는 것은 법대로 하면 그들이 죽을 것이기 때문이기도 하지만, 하나님이 참으로 인자하신 분이기 때문이기도 하다. 본문은 '그의 인자하심'(חַסְדּוֹ)은 하늘이 땅에서 높음 같다고 한다. 이 말씀은 구원이 하늘에서 오는 것을 의미한다. 하늘에 주님의 보좌가 있기 때문이다(May).

또한 우리가 상상할 수 있는 최고의 대조법이다. 땅에서 가장 높은 곳이 하늘인 것처럼, 하나님의 인자는 도저히 헤아릴 수 없이 크다는 뜻이다. 이 놀라운 하나님의 인자하심은 모든 사람에게 동일하게 임하지 않는다. 오직 '그를 경외하는 사람들'(יְרֵאָיו)에게만 허락하신다.

셋째, 하나님은 우리의 죄 문제를 완전하게 해결해 주신다(12절). 동쪽에서 가장 먼 곳이 서쪽인 것처럼, 하나님은 용서하신 죄를 우리에게서 가장 먼 곳으로 옮기신다. 그 죄로 인해 더 이상 우리와 하나님의 관계가 영향을 받지 않도록 하신다는 뜻이다. 하나님은 용서하신 죄는 없는 것처럼 여기신다.

넷째, 하나님은 부모가 자식을 대하는 마음으로 우리를 대하신다(13절). 사랑 중에 가장 기본적이고 강한 것은 자식을 향한 부모의 마음이다. 성경은 이러한 사랑을 표현할 때 '긍휼'(רחם)이라 한다(cf. 출 33:19; 시 25:6). 주님은 이 같은 마음으로 주를 경외하는 이들을 긍휼히 여기신다. 우리는 자식이 항상 부모의 사랑을 기대하고 의지할 수 있듯, 주님의 사랑을 기대하고 의지할 수 있다.

다섯째, 하나님은 우리가 얼마나 연약한 존재인가를 아신다(14-16절). '그가 우리의 체질을 아신다'(יָדַע יִצְרֵנוּ)의 문자적 의미는 '그는 우리가 [어떻게] 만들어진 것인지를 아신다'라는 뜻이다. 주님은 우리가 흙으로 빚어졌고, 죽으면 흙으로 돌아가는 연약한 존재라는 것을 아신다(Goldingay). 하나님이 직접 우리를 빚으셨기 때문에 우리가 얼마나 연약한 존재인지(얼마나 별 볼 일 없는 재료로 만들어졌는지)를 가장 잘 아시는 것이다. 주님은 우리의 재료가 먼지(티끌, 흙, cf. 창 2:7; 3:19; 욥 4:19)라는 사실을 기억하신다. 그러므로 하나님은 혹시 연약한 우리가 부서질세라 애지중지하신다.

연약한 재료로 만들어진 인간의 수명도 허무하기는 마찬가지다. 우리의 나날들은 풀과 같고, 우리의 영화는 들의 꽃과 같다(15절). 우리의 수명은 바람이 불면 순식간에 말라 죽는 풀과 같으며, 죽으면 우리가 있던 자리가 흔적도 없이 사라진다(16절). 이처럼 연약하고 허무한 우리가 창조주 하나님의 사랑을 누릴 수 있다는 사실이 참으로 경이롭다. 하나님은 우리가 약하기 때문에 더 많은 관심을 쏟으신다.

4. 온 세상에 내리시는 헤세드(103:17-19)

[17] 여호와의 인자하심은

자기를 경외하는 자에게 영원부터 영원까지 이르며

그의 공의는

자손의 자손에게 이르리니

[18] 곧 그의 언약을 지키고

그의 법도를 기억하여 행하는 자에게로다
19 여호와께서 그의 보좌를 하늘에 세우시고
그의 왕권으로 만유를 다스리시도다

여호와는 하늘에 있는 보좌에 앉아 세상을 다스리신다(19절, cf. 시 11:4; 93:2). 하나님은 이스라엘의 하나님이실 뿐만 아니라, 온 세상을 통치하는 왕이시다(cf. 시 93:1; 96:10; 99:1). 하늘에 있는 영원한 보좌에 앉아 다스리시는 하나님은 영원에서 영원에 이르기까지 '인자'(חֶסֶד)와 '공의'(צְדָקָה)를 베풀기를 기뻐하신다(17절). 그러나 모든 사람이 하나님의 은총의 수혜자들은 아니다. 주님은 그를 경외하는 사람들(17절)과 언약을 지키고 주님의 법도를 행하는 사람들에게만(18절) 이런 은혜를 내리신다. 창조주께서는 모든 사람을 사랑하시지만, 하나님을 사랑하고 경외하는 사람들을 더욱더 사랑하신다.

그렇다면 어떤 사람이 하나님을 사랑하고 경외하는가? 주님과 맺은 언약을 지키고 법도를 기억하여 행하는 이들이다(18절). 하나님의 말씀을 바로 알고 삶에서 그 말씀대로 살려고 노력하는 이가 바로 하나님을 경외하는 사람이다. 실천이 없는 순종은 없다. 우리가 이 땅에서 하나님을 사랑할 수 있는 길은 하나님의 가르침을 잘 깨닫고 실천하는 것이다(Longman).

5. 찬양 부름(103:20-22)

20 능력이 있어 여호와의 말씀을 행하며
그의 말씀의 소리를 듣는 여호와의 천사들이여
여호와를 송축하라
21 그에게 수종들며 그의 뜻을 행하는 모든 천군이여
여호와를 송축하라

22 여호와의 지으심을 받고
그가 다스리시는 모든 곳에 있는 너희여
여호와를 송축하라
내 영혼아 여호와를 송축하라

기자는 주의 자녀들뿐만 아니라 천군 천사들에게까지 여호와를 찬양할 것을 권면한다. 그는 '천사들'(מַלְאָכִים)을 능력이 있어 여호와의 말씀을 행하는 자들, 하나님의 말씀 소리를 듣는 자들이라 한다(20절, cf. 시 91:11). 행하는 것과 듣는 것 모두 순종과 연관된 언어이다. 천사들에게도 하나님의 말씀에 순종이 요구되기는 사람들에게 요구되는 것과 별반 다르지 않다는 뜻이다. 그들도 인간들처럼 하나님이 창조하신 존재들이기 때문이다.

'천군'(צְבָאוֹת)은 하나님이 군대로 거느리시는 천사들이다(cf. 시 24:10; 단 7:10). 본문은 그들이 하나님께 수종드는 자들이며, 주님의 뜻에 따라 행동하는 이들이라고 한다(21절). 기자는 천사들과 천군에게까지 위대하신 하나님을 찬양하라고 권면한다.

만일 하나님을 가장 가까운 곳에서 섬기도록 창조된 천사와 하나님의 뜻을 이루기 위해 창조된 천군들도 하나님을 찬양해야 한다면, 하물며 이 땅에 사는 사람들은 얼마나 더 하나님을 찬양해야 하는가! 그러므로 기자는 여호와께 지으심을 받고 주님이 다스리시는 세상에서 사는 모든 사람에게 여호와를 찬양하라고 한다(22절). 끝으로 그는 자신도 온 마음을 다해 하나님을 찬양할 것을 다짐하며 노래를 마무리한다(22d절). 그는 자신의 의지를 이 노래를 시작하면서 강력하게 표현하였었다(1절). 그의 찬양과 경배가 원점으로 돌아온 것이다. 그러나 이번에는 기자뿐만 아니라, 그에게 설득된 온 세상이 함께 노래하고 있다(Kidner). 이 시편은 구약에 묘사된 하나님의 진노와 심판에 가장 강력한 대조를 이룬다(Brueggemann & Bellinger).

제104편

I. 장르/양식: 회중 찬양시(cf. 29편)

이 시는 오늘까지 교회에서 가장 많이 사용되는 시편 중 하나이지만, 동시에 가장 논쟁이 많은 시편이기도 하다(Gerstenberger). 내용에 있어서는 시편 8편과 33편과 145편과 함께 '창조의 노래'(Song of Creation)로 불리기도 하며(Brueggemann), 양식은 '서술적 찬양시'(descriptive psalm of praise)로 분류된다(McCann, Tucker & Grant, VanGemeren).

중심 주제가 창조이며 마치 창세기 1장에 음을 붙여 놓은 듯한 기분이 든다. 이 시편은 1인칭 단수로 시작하고 마무리되지만, 같은 성향을 보인 103편이 회중의 노래로 분류된 것처럼 이 노래도 회중 찬양시로 분류되어야 한다. 아마도 인도자가 1인칭 단수 부분을 말하고, 공동체가 함께 반응하는 식으로 진행되는 듯하다(Goldingay).

이 시편의 내용과 양식이 시편 103편과 비슷하다고 하여 종종 학자들은 이 두 시편을 '쌍둥이 시편'(twin psalm)이라고 부른다(deClaissé-Walford et al., Tucker & Grant, cf. VanGemeren). 이 노래가 시편들 중 유일하게 "내 영혼아 여호와를 송축하라"는 말로 시작하고(104:1) 끝이 나는 것(104:35)도 103편과 같다(103:1, 22). 심지어 두 시편이 같은 저자에 의해 집필된 것이라고 하는 이들도 있다(Kirkpatrick). 그러나 두 시편이 같은 저자에 의해 집필되었다고 보기에는 증거가 부족한 듯하다.

이 시편이 창조를 노래하는 부분에 있어서는 서술적으로 묘사된 창세기 1-3장을 시적(詩的)으로 보완하는 듯하다(Grogan, VanGemeren). 시편과 창세기의 관계에 대해 이 시편이 창세기를 인용한 것이라는 학자들이 있는가 하면(Gunkel, McCarthy), 창세기가 이 시편을 인용한 것이라는 학자들도 있다(cf. Goldingay, Hossfeld-Zenger). 또한 학자들 중에는 이 시편이 이집트와 바빌론의 창조시들과 매우 유사하다고 하는 이들이 있다(Terrien, Tucker & Grant, von Rad, cf. Allen, ANET). 그러나 대부분 학자들은 증거가 불충분하며 유사점보다는 차이점이 더 많다고 결론짓는다(Craigie, Ross, VanGemeren, Zimmerli, cf. McCann). 아마도 공통적인 주제인 창조에 대한 노래이다 보니 이런 현상이 생긴 것으로 생각된다.

언제 이 시편이 저작되었는지 알 방법이 없는 것처럼 처음에 사용된 정황에 대하여도 알려진 바가 없다(Goldingay). 이러한 상황은 이 시편이 오랜 세월 동안 여러 사람에 의해 편집되고 저작되었기 때문이라는 견해가 있다(deClaissé-Walford et al.). 일부 학자들은 가을철이면 신년 예배에서 쓰인 것이라 하지만(Terrien), 추측일 뿐 어떠한 단서도 없다.

II. 구조

이 시편의 중심 주제가 창조라는 것에 모두가 동의하지만, 구조를 파악하기는 매우 어렵다. 그러므로 대부분 학자들은 각기 다른 구조들을 제시한다(cf. Allen, deClaissé-Walford et al., Goldingay, McCann, Miller, Terrien, Tucker & Grant, VanGemeren). 이 주석에서는 다음과 같은 분석을 바탕으로 본문을 주해하고자 한다(cf. VanGemeren).

A. 왕이신 하나님 찬양(104:1-4)

　B. 천지를 창조하신 하나님(104:5-9)

C. 짐승들을 창조하심(104:10-18)

D. 창조된 세상의 질서(104:19-23)

C′. 짐승들을 창조하심(104:24-26)

B′. 천지를 지속하시는 하나님(104:27-30)

A′. 왕이신 하나님 찬양(104:31-35)

III. 주해

이 시편은 103:19-22을 확대해서 노래한 것이라는 느낌이 든다. 반면에 주제적인 차이도 있다. 103편은 구속과 연관된 헤세드가 중심 주제이지만, 이 시편의 중심 주제는 창조이다. 이 두 시편의 관계는 상호보완적으로 보는 것이 바람직하다(Limburg). 주제와 이 시편의 예술적인 면모를 고려할 때, 이 노래가 창세기 1장과 함께 읽히면 참으로 큰 시너지 효과를 발휘할 수 있다(cf. deClaissé-Walford et al.). 여호와 하나님이 창조주라는 사실은 단지 신학적인 전제가 아니라, 가장 소리가 큰 찬양과 큰 기쁨의 이유가 된다(Tucker & Grant).

1. 왕이신 하나님 찬양(104:1-4)

1 내 영혼아
여호와를 송축하라
여호와 나의 하나님이여
주는 심히 위대하시며
존귀와 권위로 옷 입으셨나이다
2 주께서 옷을 입음 같이 빛을 입으시며
하늘을 휘장 같이 치시며
3 물에 자기 누각의 들보를 얹으시며

구름으로 자기 수레를 삼으시고
바람 날개로 다니시며
4 바람을 자기 사신으로 삼으시고
불꽃으로 자기 사역자를 삼으시며

이 시편이 "내 영혼아 여호와를 송축하라"는 말로 시작하고(1절) 끝이 나는 것(35절)이 103편의 형식과 같다(103:1, 22). 시편 전체에서 이 같은 공통점을 지닌 것은 103편과 104편이 유일하다. 같은 양식의 노래이지만 103편은 구세주이신 하나님을, 104편은 창조주이신 하나님을 찬양하다 보니 빚어진 일이다.

기자는 여호와 하나님은 그의 왕이시며, 심히 위대하시고, 존귀와 권위로 옷을 입으셨다며 세 가지로 주님을 찬양한다(1절). 하나님을 송축하며 이렇게 고백하는 것은 자신이 하나님의 축복을 누리고 있으며 하나님을 구속주로 아는 이들만 할 수 있는 일이다(VanGemeren). 또한 하나님을 왕으로 고백하는 것은 모든 일에 있어서 주님께 복종하겠다는 의지의 표현이다. 백성이 왕께 복종하는 것이 당연한 것처럼 말이다. 하나님이 '심히 위대하시다'(גָּדַלְתָּ מְּאֹד)는 것은 세상에 하나님과 견줄 만한 통치자(왕)는 존재하지 않으며, 하나님의 위대하심이 날이 갈수록 더 커진다는 의미이다(cf. McCann, HALOT).

개인적인 차원에서 하나님께 경의를 표한 기자는 이어 여호와는 어떤 분이신가를 생각한다. 그는 주로 분사들(participles)을 사용하여 묵상을 이어가는데, 그가 동사에서 비롯된 분사를 주로 사용하는 것은 하나님의 속성보다는 주님이 하신 일(사역)에 초점을 맞추기 위해서이다.

고대 근동에서 옷은 입고 있는 사람의 신분을 나타냈다. 하나님이 '존귀와 권위'(הוֹד וְהָדָר)로 옷을 입으셨다는 것은 주님이 온 세상의 왕이라는 지위와 참으로 잘 어울리는 옷을 입으셨다는 뜻이다(cf. 시 8:1; 21:5; 45:3; 93:1; 96:6). 존귀는 왕의 권위를, 권위는 왕의 위엄을 상징한다(Schaefer, cf. 새번역).

여호와는 온 세상에 생명을 주시고 하늘을 창조하신 분이다(2절). 주님은 사람이 옷을 입듯 하늘을 밝히는 빛을 옷으로 입으셨다고 한다(2a절). 그 빛은 모든 생명의 근원이며 하나님의 임재와 연관되어 있다(시 4:6; 27:1; 43:3; 44:3). 하나님과 빛은 항상 함께한다(Tucker & Grant, cf. 요일 1:5). 하나님은 온 세상을 생명으로 채우신 분이며, 이러한 주님의 권위와 위엄이 온 우주에 가득하다. 하나님은 생명의 빛으로 가득한 우주에 하늘을 휘장 치듯이 치셨다(2b절). 이는 사람이 마치 텐트를 치듯 하나님이 하늘을 치셨음을 나타낸다. 텐트가 세워져야 그 안에서 사람이 살 수 있다. 그러므로 이 말씀은 하나님이 하늘을 창조하셨다(만드셨다)는 의미를 초월하여 하나님이 하늘을 세우셔서 그 밑에 사람들과 짐승이 살 수 있도록 하셨다는 의미이다(VanGemeren).

하늘과 그 아래에 있는 모든 것은 하나님이 창조하셨으며, 하나님의 활동 무대이기도 하다(3-4절). 3-4절이 언급하는 네 가지, '수레, 구름, 바람, 불'은 모두 주님의 창조 사역과 연관된 것들이다(VanGemeren). 주님은 물 위에 자기 궁궐을 지으셨다(3a절). 세상에 있는 모든 물이 하나님의 통제 아래 있다는 뜻이다. 고대 근동 사람들은 원시적인 물이 창조된 세상을 항상 위협하고 있다고 믿었는데, 본문은 물이 하나님이 다스리시는 세상을 위협할 수 없음을 암시한다.

하나님은 바다와 강과 같이 땅에 있는 물만 다스리시는 것이 아니라(cf. 시 74:12-15; 93:3-4), 하늘에 있는 물, 곧 구름도 다스리신다(3b절). 주님은 구름을 이동 수단인 수레로 삼으신다. 때로는 홍수를 일으켜 많은 생명을 앗아가는 구름마저도 하나님의 통제 아래 있다.

하나님은 바람도 자유자재로 사용하신다(3c-4a절). 주님은 바람을 날개 삼아 다니기도 하시고(3c절), 바람을 사신으로 삼아 이곳저곳에 보내기도 하신다(4a절). 본문은 바람과 불꽃을 '하나님의 사신들'(מַלְאָכָיו)이라고 하는데, 103:21-22은 같은 단어로 천사들을 칭했다. 하나님은 생명이 있는 능력(천사들)과 생명이 없는 능력(바람, 구름 등)을 주변에 두시고 마음껏 사용하시는 분이다. 바람은 하나님의 권위에 절대적으로 복종하는 자연적인 힘이다.

하나님은 천둥과 번개도 통제하시는 분이다(4b절). 본문에서 '불꽃'(אֵשׁ לֹהֵט)은 번개를 의미한다(새번역, 공동, 현대인). 하나님은 일상적으로 구름과 바람을 동반하고 온 세상에 내리는 천둥과 번개도 창조하고 통제하시는 분이다. 빛과 물과 구름과 바람과 번개 등은 가장 기본적인 자연적 요소들이며 사람들이 두려워하는 것들이기도 했다. 하나님은 이 모든 것을 창조하고 통제하시는 창조주이자 통치자이시다.

2. 천지를 창조하신 하나님(104:5-9)

5 땅에 기초를 놓으사
영원히 흔들리지 아니하게 하셨나이다
6 옷으로 덮음 같이 주께서 땅을 깊은 바다로 덮으시매
물이 산들 위로 솟아올랐으나
7 주께서 꾸짖으시니 물은 도망하며
주의 우렛소리로 말미암아 빨리 가며
8 주께서 그들을 위하여 정하여 주신 곳으로 흘러갔고
산은 오르고 골짜기는 내려갔나이다
9 주께서 물의 경계를 정하여 넘치지 못하게 하시며
다시 돌아와 땅을 덮지 못하게 하셨나이다

하나님은 하늘과 구름과 바람을 창조하신 것처럼, 땅도 창조하셨다(5a절). 하나님이 땅의 기초를 놓으실 때 얼마나 튼튼하게 하셨는지, 땅은 영원히 흔들리지 않는다(5b절). 하나님은 땅을 영구적으로, 완전하게 창조하신 것이다.

하나님은 땅의 일부를 깊은 바다로 덮으셨다(6a절). 마치 사람에게 옷을 입히듯 바다로 땅을 입히셨다. 바다가 있음으로 인해 땅도 더 아름답게 되었다는 뜻이다. 때로는 물이 자기 위치를 망각하고 육지에 오르기도 했지만, 그때마다 하나님은 물을 꾸짖으셨고, 혼줄이 난 물은 원래 하나님이 정해 주신 곳으로 돌아갔다(6b-7절).

8절의 주어가 물인지, 산인지에 대하여 다소 혼란이 있다(cf. NIV, NAS, ESV, TNK). 그러나 결과는 같다. 산은 높아지고 골짜기는 내려가는 효과가 세상에 나타났다(8b절). 하나님이 물과 땅의 경계를 확실히 정해 주셨음으로 다시는 물이 경계를 넘지 않았다(9절). 이 말씀은 창세기 1장의 창조 사건에서 바다와 육지의 경계를 정해 주신 것에 대한 시적(詩的)인 표현이지, 굳이 바알 신화(바알이 바다의 신 얌[Yam]을 물리쳐 바다와 육지의 경계가 섰다고 함)와 연결하여 해석할 필요는 없다(cf. McCann, von Rad). 하나님은 바알처럼 얌과 싸우신 적이 없고, 단지 말로 바다가 제자리로 돌아가게 하셨기 때문이다. 또한 설령 사용되었다 할지라도 이 신화들의 진실성을 전제하는 것이 아니라, 그들이 사실이 아니라며 변증론적(polemic) 의도에 따라 사용되었다(Allen).

기자는 생명이 없는 것들을 살아 움직이는 것들로 묘사하며 하나님이 세상에 있는 모든 것들이 있어야 할 자리를 정해 주셨다는 사실을 확인한다. 1-4절도 그렇지만, 이 섹션은 더욱더 하나님이 세상을 창조하신 일을 회고하고 있는 창세기 1장을 생각나게 한다.

3. 짐승들을 창조하심(104:10-18)

10 여호와께서 샘을 골짜기에서 솟아나게 하시고
산 사이에 흐르게 하사
11 각종 들짐승에게 마시게 하시니
들나귀들도 해갈하며

[12] 공중의 새들도 그 가에서 깃들이며
나뭇가지 사이에서 지저귀는도다
[13] 그가 그의 누각에서부터 산에 물을 부어 주시니
주께서 하시는 일의 결실이 땅을 만족시켜 주는도다
[14] 그가 가축을 위한 풀과 사람을 위한 채소를 자라게 하시며
땅에서 먹을 것이 나게 하셔서
[15] 사람의 마음을 기쁘게 하는 포도주와
사람의 얼굴을 윤택하게 하는 기름과
사람의 마음을 힘있게 하는 양식을 주셨도다
[16] 여호와의 나무에는 물이 흡족함이여
곧 그가 심으신 레바논 백향목들이로다
[17] 새들이 그 속에 깃들임이여
학은 잣나무로 집을 삼는도다
[18] 높은 산들은 산양을 위함이여
바위는 너구리의 피난처로다

창조주의 인간과 짐승들에 대한 배려가 교차대구법적 구조로 언급되고 있다: '산과 물과 짐승들과 새들'(10-13절, A)—'가축들과 사람들'(14-15절, B)—'산과 물과 새들과 짐승들'(16-18절, A'). 주님은 세상에 있는 모든 짐승들과 사람들을 '초월적인 후하심'(superabundant liberality)으로써 먹이시고 보살피시는 분이다(Calvin).

하나님의 사역에 따라 바닷물은 제자리를 찾았고, 다시는 육지에 범람하지 않았다. 하나님은 육지와 골짜기에 샘이 솟아나게 하셔서 각종 짐승들이 마시게 하셨다(10-11절). 들나귀와 들짐승도 마시고, 공중의 새들도 마셨다(11-12절). 물을 마시고 생기를 얻은 새들이 나뭇가지 사이에서 지저귄다. 짐승들과 새들이 마시는 물은 하나님이 물 위에 세우신 궁궐(3절)에서 나와 산을 적신 물이다(13절). 하나님이 하신 일은

땅을 만족시킨다. '만족하다'(שׂבע)는 마음껏 먹었기 때문에 더 이상 아무것도 원하지 않는 상황을 묘사한다(Goldingay, cf. HALOT).

하나님이 물로 땅을 만족하게 하시니, 만족한 땅은 짐승들이 먹을 풀과 사람들이 먹을 채소를 내놓는다(14절). 이러한 일은 저절로 된 것처럼 보이지만, 사실은 하나님이 사람과 짐승들에게 먹을 것을 주기 위해 하신 일이다(14절). 하나님은 땅에서 나게 하신 먹을 것을 짐승들과 사람들에게 주셔서 그들로 만족하게 하셨다. 기자는 하나님이 사람들에게 먹으라고 주신 음식을 완벽함을 상징하는 숫자 3을 사용하여 세 가지로 언급한다(15절): 사람의 마음을 기쁘게 하는 포도주, 사람의 얼굴을 윤택하게 하는 기름, 사람의 마음을 힘있게 하는 양식. 하나님은 참으로 우리의 모든 필요를 채우시는 분이다. 포도주는 기쁨을, 얼굴은 존엄성을, 마음은 살아갈 의욕을 상징한다.

먹을 것을 풍요롭게 주셔서 짐승들과 사람들이 만족하며 살게 하신 하나님은 짐승들에게 안식처도 주신다(16-18절). 하나님이 심고 가꾸신 레바논의 백향목들은 새들이 둥지를 트는 안식처가 되었으며, 잣나무들은 학들의 집이 되었다(16-17절). '레바논의 백향목'(אַרְזֵי לְבָנוֹן)은 성경에서 가장 장엄한 나무를 상징한다. 개역개정이 '학'으로 번역한 단어(חֲסִידָה)의 더 정확한 번역은 '황새'(stork)이다(cf. 새번역, 공동, 아가페). 황새는 이 지역의 텃세가 아니라 계절에 따라 북아프리카와 이 지역을 왕래하는 철새이다(ABD, VanGemeren). 하나님은 레바논 숲의 가장 좋은 나무들을 철새들의 임시 거처로 내주실 정도로 모든 생명을 보호하신다.

높은 산들은 산양들의 서식처가 되었고, 바위는 너구리들의 안식처가 되었다(18절). 하나님의 사람에 대한 배려는 완전 수인 3에 따라 세 가지로 묘사되었고(15절), 짐승들에게 안식처를 주시는 것은 총체성의 숫자인 4에 따라 네 가지(새들, 황새, 산양, 너구리)로 요약되었다. 하나님은 세상에 있는 모든 생명들(사람들과 짐승들)을 가장 완벽하게 소외되는 사람과 짐승이 없도록 포괄적으로 먹이시고 보살피신다. 하나님의 지혜로우심이 세상에 있는 모든 짐승들을 창조하신 일을 통해 가장 극적으로 표현되었다(Eaton).

또한 이 말씀은 하나님이 천지를 창조하실 때 이렇게 만드셨다는 뜻이며, 인간의 죄로 인해 이러한 시스템이 망가졌고 장차 종말에 가서 다시 회복될 것을 암시한다. 인간의 죄로 인해 이 땅에 사는 한 짐승들과 사람들은 언제든 굶주림에 노출될 수 있기 때문이다.

4. 창조된 세상의 질서(104:19-23)

19 여호와께서 달로 절기를 정하심이여
해는 그 지는 때를 알도다
20 주께서 흑암을 지어 밤이 되게 하시니
삼림의 모든 짐승이 기어 나오나이다
21 젊은 사자들은 그들의 먹이를 쫓아 부르짖으며
그들의 먹이를 하나님께 구하다가
22 해가 돋으면 물러가서
그들의 굴 속에 눕고
23 사람은 나와서 일하며
저녁까지 수고하는도다

하나님은 육지와 바다의 경계를 정해 주신 것처럼(cf. 5-9절), 낮과 밤의 경계와 계절의 경계를 정하셔서 사람들과 짐승들의 활동 영역을 구분해 주셨다. 해와 달을 신들로 숭배한 고대 근동의 배경에서 하나님이 이것들을 창조하셨다는 것은 과히 파격적인 주장이라 할 수 있다.

여호와께서는 달이 계절들(מוֹעֲדִים)을 주관하도록 하시고(cf. 창 1:14; 레 23:2, 4, 37, 44), 해가 지는 때를 알게 하여 낮과 밤의 변화를 주관하도록 하셨다(19절, cf. 창 1:14). 그리고 밤이 되면 숲속의 짐승들이 먹이 활동을 하도록 하셨다(20절). 이는 대부분의 육식 동물들이 낮에는 잠을 자고, 밤에 먹이 활동을 하는 것을 염두에 둔 표현이다.

인상적인 것은 기자가 사자들의 먹이 활동을 하나님께 먹이를 구하는 행위로 묘사했다는 사실이다(21절). 세상 모든 짐승이 각자 먹이 활동을 하는 것 같지만, 실제로는 창조주께 먹을 것을 구하는 행위이다. 창조주께서 그들의 먹잇감을 창조하시고 그들에게 허락하셨기 때문이다.

밤이 지나 해가 돋으면 밤새 사냥을 한 짐승들은 굴로 들어가 휴식을 취한다(22절). 사람들은 아침에 들로 나와 저녁까지 수고한다(23절). 사람들이 대낮에 농사짓는 것과 짐승들이 밤새 먹이 활동하는 것이 대조된다. 낮은 일을 하는 사람들의 활동 시간이고, 밤은 먹이를 찾는 짐승들의 활동 시간이다. 하나님은 바다와 육지의 영역을 정해 주신 것처럼 사람들과 짐승들의 활동 시간도 정해 주셔서 서로 갈등하지 않도록 하셨다. 모두 자신의 자리와 역할에 따라 활동하는 것이 창조주 하나님이 계획하시고 다스리시는 세상의 모습이다.

5. 짐승들을 창조하심(104:24-26)

24 여호와여 주께서 하신 일이 어찌 그리 많은지요
주께서 지혜로 그들을 다 지으셨으니
주께서 지으신 것들이 땅에 가득하니이다
25 거기에는 크고 넓은 바다가 있고
그 속에는 생물 곧 크고 작은 동물들이 무수하니이다
26 그 곳에는 배들이 다니며
주께서 지으신 리워야단이 그 속에서 노나이다

사람들과 짐승들이 사는 땅에 질서와 경계선을 확립하신 창조주께서 바다의 일에도 관여하셨다. 육지처럼 바다에도 온갖 생물들을 두시고 질서를 확립하셨다. 세상을 구성하고 있는 육지와 바다 모두 하나님이 창조하셨고 주님의 다스림 아래 있다.

기자는 하나님이 참으로 많고 놀라운 일을 하셨다며 창조주의 능력을 찬양함으로써 이 섹션을 시작한다(24a절). 하나님은 피조물들을 대충 만들지 않으시고 모두 지혜롭게 만드셨다(24b절). 주님이 창조하신 것들이 세상을 가득 채우고 있는데, 하나하나가 주님의 걸작품(masterpiece)이라는 뜻이다. 세상의 경이로움을 보고 탄복한 기자의 감탄이자 고백이다.

하나님이 지으신 세상에는 육지만 있는 것이 아니라 크고 넓은 바다도 있다(25a절). 주님이 창조하신 바다에는 크고 작은 동물들이 무수히 살고 있다(25b절). 당연히 창조주께서 만드신 것들이다. 짐승들이 무수히 살고 있기 때문에 질서가 파괴되어 혼돈이 있을 수 있지만, 그렇지 않다. 하나님은 바다에 사는 모든 짐승들이 자기 자리를 지키며 자기 영역에서 주님이 정해 주신 기준에 따라 활동하게 하신다.

그러므로 바다는 육지에 사는 사람들이 배를 타고 다닐 수 있는 곳이다(26a절). 심지어는 리워야단 같은 바다 괴물도 사람들이 타고 다니는 배를 공격하지 못한다. '리워야단'(לִוְיָתָן)은 고대 근동의 신화에 등장하는 7개의 머리를 지닌 괴물이란 뜻으로 사용되기도 하지만(cf. 사 27:1), 본문에서는 배를 타고 바다를 항해하는 사람들을 위협할 수 있는 큰 짐승들(고래, 바다 악어 등)을 뜻할 뿐 신화적인 의미는 없다(cf. , 시 74:12-15; 욥 41:1-11). 또한 리워야단은 위협적인 괴물이 아니라 하나님이 창조하신 바다에서 뛰노는 귀여운 짐승이다(Clifford, Levenson, Mays, Miller). 창조주 하나님이 바다에서도 육지와 같이 질서를 확립해 주셨다. 육지에 사는 사람은 바다를 항해할 때마다 창조주 하나님께 질서를 확립해 주신 것에 대해 감사해야 한다.

6. 천지를 지속하시는 하나님(104:27-30)

[27] 이것들은 다 주께서 때를 따라 먹을 것을 주시기를 바라나이다
[28] 주께서 주신즉 그들이 받으며
주께서 손을 펴신즉 그들이 좋은 것으로 만족하다가
[29] 주께서 낯을 숨기신즉 그들이 떨고
주께서 그들의 호흡을 거두신즉 그들은 죽어 먼지로 돌아가나이다
[30] 주의 영을 보내어 그들을 창조하사 지면을 새롭게 하시나이다
[31] 여호와의 영광이 영원히 계속할지며
여호와는 자신께서 행하시는 일들로 말미암아 즐거워하시리로다
[32] 그가 땅을 보신즉 땅이 진동하며
산들을 만지신즉 연기가 나는도다
[33] 내가 평생토록 여호와께 노래하며
내가 살아 있는 동안 내 하나님을 찬양하리로다
[34] 나의 기도를 기쁘게 여기시기를 바라나니
나는 여호와로 말미암아 즐거워하리로다
[35] 죄인들을 땅에서 소멸하시며
악인들을 다시 있지 못하게 하시리로다
내 영혼아 여호와를 송축하라 할렐루야

여호와께서는 육지와 바다에 사는 모든 생물들을 창조하시고 다스리실 뿐만 아니라, 그들의 생사도 주장하신다. 기자는 하나님이 하시는 일(사역)을 강조하며 이 사실을 선포한다: "주신다(27, 28절) … 펴신다(28절) … 숨기신다(29절) … 거두신다(29절) … 보내신다(30절) … 창조하신다(30절) … 새롭게 하신다(30절) … 즐거워하신다(31절) … 보신다(32절) … 만지신다"(32절). 온 우주의 생사가 하나님이 하시는 일에 달려 있다는 뜻이다. 하나님께 전적으로 의존하는 것도 찬양의 이유가 된다(Eaton).

생명이 있는 모든 것들은 주님이 그들에게 먹을 것을 주시기를 간절히 바라며 살아간다(27절). 기자는 젊은 사자들의 먹이 활동을 하나님께 먹이를 달라고 울부짖는 것으로 묘사했는데(21절), 이번에도 생명이 있는 모든 생물들의 먹이 활동을 하나님께 먹을 것을 달라고 구하는 것으로 묘사한다(27절). 하나님이 모든 생명을 먹이시기 때문이다.

하나님이 그들에게 먹이를 허락하시면 그들은 기쁘게 받으며, 주님이 주신 좋은 것들로 만족한다(28절). 세상 모든 생물들은 하나님이 주신 것을 먹으며 편안히 산다. 그러다가 주님이 낯을 숨기시면 그들은 두려워 떤다(29a절). 하나님이 낯을 숨긴다는 것은 더 이상 은혜를 베풀지 않으신다는 뜻이다. 결국 때가 되어 하나님이 그들의 호흡을 거두시면, 모든 생물은 죽어 먼지(티끌)로 돌아간다(29b절). 모든 삶의 허무함을 강조하는 표현이다.

세상에 있는 생물들이 죽었다고 절망하거나 세상이 끝났다고 생각할 필요는 없다. 하나님이 그들을 대신할 새로운 생명들을 계속 창조하실 것이기 때문이다(30절). 하나님은 자기의 '영'(רוּחַ)을 보내셔서 그들을 '창조하시고'(ברא), '새롭게 하신다'(חדשׁ). 그러므로 세상은 다시 생명으로 가득하다. 세상에 새로운 생명이 태어남은 참으로 신비롭고 경이로운 창조 사역의 결과이다(Goldingay). 하나님의 지속적이고 끊임없는 창조 사역은 세상 끝날까지 계속되며 하나님의 영광을 영원히 드러낼 것이다(31a절). 하나님은 자신이 하시는 이 모든 일을 지켜보며 즐거워하신다(31b절). 창조주 하나님은 자신이 창조하고 유지하는 세상에 대해 참으로 만족해하신다는 뜻이며 모든 것을 창조하시고 '심히 좋아하셨던' 일을 생각나게 한다(창 1:31).

주님이 땅을 보시면 땅은 진동하고, 산들을 만지시면 곧바로 불이 붙는다(32절). 하나님은 언제든 자신이 창조하신 세상에 개입하고 간섭하실 수 있다는 의미이다. 자기 백성을 축복하시고 그들의 일에 관여도 하시지만, 때로는 그들을 심판도 하신다. 그러므로 우리가 이 세상에서 일어나는 모든 일이 주님의 간섭과 통치 아래 있다는 것을 믿고 고백하는 것은 하나님이 세상을 창조하셨다는 사실을 믿는 이들에게 매우 중요하다(Calvin). 그렇다면 여호와 하나님이 세상을 창조하고 다스리신다는 사실이 우리 각 개인에게는 무슨 의미(implication)가 있는가?

첫째, 여호와가 창조주—통치자이심을 고백하는 우리는 평생토록 여호와를 노래하며 찬양해야 한다(33절). 기자는 우리의 생명이 다할 때까지 하나님을 찬양하라며 '평생토록'(בְּעוֹדִי)과 '살아 있는 동안'(בְּחַיָּי)의 두 차례 수명과 연관된 단어를 사용한다. 우리는 죽을 때까지 하나님을 창조주—왕으로 찬양해야 한다는 뜻이다.

둘째, 여호와가 창조주—통치자이심을 인정하는 우리는 주님을 의식하며 살아야 한다(34a절). 개역개정이 '기도'로 번역한 단어(שִׂיחַ)의 더 정확한 의미는 '묵상/생각하는 것'이다(HALOT, cf. 새번역, 아가페, NIV, ESV, NAS, NRS). 우리의 생각과 묵상이 주님을 기쁘게 하는 삶을 살아야 한다는 뜻이다. 우리의 생각과 묵상이 건전하고 경건하면 하나님이 기뻐하신다.

셋째, 여호와가 창조주—통치자이심을 고백하는 우리는 오직 주님으로 말미암아 기뻐해야 한다(34b절). 가장 경지에 이른 신앙은 어떤 신앙일까? 하나님께 아무것도 바라지 않고, 오직 주님 한 분으로 기뻐하고 즐거워하는 것이 아닐까?

넷째, 여호와는 죄인들이 이 땅에 발붙이지 못하게 하시고, 악인들을 제거하실 것이다(35b절). 이 땅은 창조주—통치자이신 여호와의 것이다. 그러므로 하나님은 자신이 통치하는 영토에 공의와 정의를 세우시어 악과 악인들이 설 자리를 없게 하실 것이다. 반대로 의인들은 귀하게 여기시고 그들의 삶을 축복하실 것이다. 이러한 사실을 깨달은 기자는 온몸과 마음을 다해 여호와를 송축하며 노래를 마무리한다(35c절).

제105편

I. 장르/양식: 회중 찬양시(cf. 29편)

이 시는 양식으로 회중 찬양시 형식을 취하고 있지만(deClaissé-Walford et al.), 내용에 있어서는 이스라엘의 역사를 회고하는 역사적 시편(historical psalm)으로 분류되기도 하고(Anderson, McCann, cf. 시 78, 106, 136편), 과거를 거울삼아 현재를 바꿔 가라고 권면하는 교훈적 시편(didactic hymn)으로 분류되기도 한다(Mowinckel, Murphy). 그러나 이 노래가 설령 교훈을 가르치기 위한 시편이라 할지라도, 교훈을 얻기 위해 묵상해야 할 주제가 다름 아닌 이스라엘의 역사임을 감안하면, 이 두 주제를 하나로 묶어 이 시편은 교훈을 위한 역사적 시편으로 보는 것이 바람직하다.

이 시편은 이스라엘 역사에서 가장 중요한 시기인 이집트 탈출에서 가나안 정착 때까지를 회고하고 있다. 그래서 일부 학자들은 이 시편을 선조들의 이야기를 시작하는 창세기에서 이스라엘이 가나안에 정착한 이야기로 끝나는 여호수아서에 이르기까지 내용의 요약이라고 한다(Holm-Nielsen, Stevens). 그렇다고 해서 창세기—여호수아서에 기록된 내용을 모두 요약적으로 반영하고 있지는 않다. 실제로 이 시편은 이집트를 탈출한 이스라엘이 시내 산에서 보낸 1년과 광야에서 방황한 38년을 건너뛰고 곧바로 가나안으로 향한 듯한 느낌을 준다.

그렇다고 해서 이 시편이 역사를 왜곡하고 있다고 생각되지는 않는다. 비록 시내 산을 직접적으로 언급하지는 않지만, 암시는 하고 있다. '주님의 율례와 법'(חֻקָּיו וְתוֹרֹתָיו)(45절)은 분명 시내 산 율법을 칭하는 전문적인 용어이기 때문이다. 또한 이 노래가 광야에서 이스라엘이 반역한 사건을 하나도 언급하지 않는 것은 하나님이 이스라엘이 출애굽했을 때부터 가나안에 정착할 때까지 하신 일에 초점을 맞추어 주님을 찬양하기 위해 저작되었기 때문이다(Ceresco, Clifford). 하나님의 사역과 은총에 대한 사람의 반응은 이 노래의 주제가 아니기에 이스라엘이 광야에서 하나님께 반역한 일은 언급하고 있지 않다. 그러므로 한 주석가는 기자가 창세기—여호수아서에 기록된 이스라엘의 역사에서 일부 사건들만을 선별적으로 택해 창조적으로 회고하고 있다고 말한다(McCann).

이 시편은 바로 앞의 104편과도 밀접한 연관성을 지니고 있지만(Goldingay), 다음에 등장하는 106편과 한 쌍을 이루는 듯하다. 그러므로 한 주석가는 104편과 105-106편의 관계를 '창세기의 시작부분과 나머지 오경의 관계'에 비유한다(Schaefer). 그러나 105편과 106편의 내용은 함께 출애굽 때를 회고하고 있으면서도 초점이 서로 다르다. 그래서 105편과 106편의 관계는 '이란성 쌍둥이'에 비유되기도 한다(Wilcock). 시편 105편은 하나님이 선조들과의 약속을 지키기 위해 출애굽 여정 중 이집트에서 하신 일과 광야에서 먹이신 일, 그리고 가나안 땅을 그들에게 주신 일을 회고한다. 이 모든 일이 보잘것없는 이스라엘에 임한 하나님의 은총이다. 반면에 106편은 광야에서 이스라엘이 어떻게 하나님께 범죄하여, 선조들에게 약속하심에 따라 땅을 차지하는 일이 위기에 빠졌는가에 초점을 맞춰 그 시절을 회고한다. 그러므로 105편은 하나님을 믿으라는 권면으로, 106편은 회개하라는 권면으로 이해될 수도 있다(Mays). 이 두 시편의 공통점은 하나님이 참으로 볼품없는 백성을 구원하셨다는 사실과 하나님의 구속하시는 은총을 강조함에 있다.

역대기 기자는 이 시편을 다윗이 법궤를 예루살렘으로 운반해 온 사건과 연결하여 사용한다(대상 16:8-36). 그러므로 이 시편이 다윗 왕 시대에 저작되어 전수된 것을 역대기 저자가 인용하고 있는 것이라는 해석을 전적으로 배제할 수는 없지만, 대부분 학자들은 포로기 혹은 그 이후에 저작된 것이라고 생각한다. 이 노래가 구원은 하나님께 속한 것이며, 인간의 부정적인 반응(반역)은 주님의 구원 사역에 영향을 미치지 않는다는 점을 강조하는 것을 근거로 바빌론 포로 생활 중 새로운, 혹은 제2의 출애굽을 기대하며 저작되고 사용되었을 것이라는 견해가 있다(Goldingay). 또한 106편과 함께 바빌론 포로기 때 저작된 것이라고 하는 주석가도 있다(McCann).

상당수의 주석가들이 이 시가 포로기 이후 시대(페르시아 시대)에 저작되었지만, 역대기가 인용하고 있는 것으로 보아 늦어도 주전 4세기에는 저작되었을 것이라는 추측을 내놓기도 한다(deClaissé-Walford et al., Kraus). 이 노래가 제2성전 시대(주전 516년 이후)에 저작되고 활성화된 시라는 견해도 있다(Gerstenberger). 그러나 여러 시편들처럼 이 시편도 저자와 저작 시기에 대해 구체적으로 논하기는 매우 어렵다.

II. 구조

일부 학자들은 이 시편이 교차대구법적 구조를 지니고 있다고 한다(Alden, VanGemeren). 다음은 밴게메렌(VanGemeren)이 제시한 구조이다. 아쉬운 점은 각 섹션의 텍스트 분량이 불균형적이라는 점이다. 예를 들자면 A는 6절로 구성되어 있는데, A′는 1/3절(한 단어)에 불과하다.

A. 시작하는 찬양(105:1-6)

B. 약속 언약(105:7-11)

C. 하나님의 보호(105:12-15)

D. 하나님의 배려(105:16-23)

C′. 하나님의 보호(105:24-36)

B′. 약속 이행(105:37-45b)

A′. 마무리하는 찬양(105:45c)

대부분 학자들은 이 시편이 45절로 구성된 상당히 긴 노래이다 보니 짜임새 있는 구조를 파악하는 일이 쉽지 않다고 생각한다. 본 주석에서는 다음과 같이 이 시편을 섹션화하여 본문을 주해해 나가고자 한다.

A. 위대하신 하나님 찬양(105:1-6)

B. 선조들과 언약을 맺으심(105:7-11)

C. 선조들의 가나안 여정(105:12-15)

D. 요셉이 이집트로 내려감(105:16-22)

E. 이집트 여정(105:23-25)

F. 이집트를 친 재앙들(105:26-36)

G. 유월절 사건(105:36-38)

H. 광야 여정(105:39-42)

I. 가나안을 주심(105:43-45)

III. 주해

하나님이 이스라엘을 위해 하신 가장 위대한 사역은 그들을 이집트에서 이끌고 나와 가나안에 정착하게 하신 일이다. 이 노래는 그때 일을 중점적으로 회상하면서 하나님이 하신 일만을 찬양하고자 한다. 그러므로 이 노래는 이스라엘의 실패와 불신에 대하여는 아예 언급하지 않는다. 오직 하나님이 하신 일에만 초점을 맞추면서 인간의 불신과 불

순종에 상관없이 구원을 이루시는 하나님을 찬양하기 위해서이다.

1. 위대하신 하나님 찬양(105:1-6)

[1] 여호와께 감사하고
그의 이름을 불러 아뢰며
그가 하는 일을 만민 중에 알게 할지어다
[2] 그에게 노래하며
그를 찬양하며
그의 모든 기이한 일들을 말할지어다
[3] 그의 거룩한 이름을 자랑하라
여호와를 구하는 자들은 마음이 즐거울지로다
[4] 여호와와 그의 능력을 구할지어다
그의 얼굴을 항상 구할지어다
[5] 그의 종 아브라함의 후손 곧 택하신
야곱의 자손 너희는 그가 행하신 기적과
[6] 그의 이적과 그의 입의 판단을 기억할지어다

기자는 하나님의 선하심에 참으로 감동한 상황에서 노래를 시작한다. 그는 자신의 흥분을 일곱 개의 명령문을 통해 표현한다: "감사하라(הוֹדוּ) … 부르라(קִרְאוּ) … 알게 하라(הוֹדִיעוּ) … 노래하라(שִׁירוּ) … 찬양하라(זַמְּרוּ) … 말하라(שִׂיחוּ) … 자랑하라(הִתְהַלְלוּ)"(1-3a절). 모두 복수형 명령문들이다. 저자는 온 공동체에게 권면하고 있다. 또한 이 명령문들은 모두 다 언어적인 행동과 연관된 것들이다.

이 명령어들이 강조하는 것은 크게 두 가지이다. 먼저 하나님께 찬양하고, 그 다음 하나님이 하신 일에 대해 온 세상에 알리라는 것이다. 일상적으로 시편은 순종에서 찬양으로 이어지는 흐름을 보이는

데(Brueggemann), 이 시편은 먼저 찬양하고, 그 다음 순종을 요구한다(Grogan).

하나님의 선하심을 경험한 사람은 먼저 주님께 감사하고, 그 다음 하나님이 베풀어 주신 은혜를 주변에 알려야 한다. 주님의 선하심은 우리만 누리라고 주시는 것이 아니라, 다른 사람들에게 하나님에 대하여 알릴 수 있는 기회이기 때문이다. 저자는 주의 백성들에게 네 가지를 지시한다.

첫째, 우리는 하나님이 하신 일을 알려야 한다. 저자가 만민 중에 알리라고 하는(1c절) 일은 어떤 것인가? 그는 하나님이 하신 '모든 기이한 일'(בְּכָל־נִפְלְאוֹתָיו, 2b절)과 '그가 행하신 기적'(נִפְלְאוֹתָיו אֲשֶׁר־עָשָׂה, 5b절)과 '그의 이적'(מֹפְתָיו, 6절)과 '그의 입의 판단'(מִשְׁפְּטֵי־פִיו, 6절)이라며 네 가지로 묘사한다. 이 중 세 가지는 하나님이 선조들과 이스라엘을 위해 행하신 온갖 기적들을 뜻하며, 한 가지('그의 입의 판단')는 하나님의 정의로운 판결과 연관된다. 주님의 정의로운 판결은 선조들과 이스라엘에게 때때로 내려 주신 결정과 지시로 해석될 수도 있지만, 이러한 결정과 지시가 일정한 기준과 연관이 있는 것이기 때문에 시내 산에서 주신 율법을 뜻하는 것으로 해석될 수도 있다.

개역개정이 5-6절을 구분해 놓은 것이 특이하다. 마소라 사본을 그대로 번역하면 5절은 "그가(하나님이) 행하신 기적과 그의 이적과 그의 입의 심판을 기억하라"이다. 이어 6절은 "아브라함의 자손들, 곧 그의 종들, 야곱의 자손들아, 그가 택하신 자들아!"이다. 개역개정은 주어를 정확하게 표현하기 위해 5-6절을 섞어 번역해 놓았는데, 좋은 번역은 아니다(cf. 새번역, 공동, NIV, NAS, NRS).

둘째, 우리는 하나님의 거룩한 이름을 자랑해야 한다(3a절). 우리가 천지를 창조하신 하나님이 누구신지와 주님이 하신 일이 무엇인지 뿐만 아니라 주님의 거룩한 이름을 아는 것은 자랑거리가 된다. 주님은 아무에게나 자신을 알리지 않으시고, 선택받은 사람들(בְּחִירָיו, 6절)에게

만 자기 이름을 알도록 하셨기 때문이다. 그러므로 하나님의 이름을 자랑하는 것은 우리가 주님과 특별한 관계를 유지하고 있음을 온 천하에 공표하는 일이기도 하다.

셋째, 우리는 주님을 구해야 한다(3b-4절). 기자는 우리가 하나님을 구하는 것을 세 가지로 표현한다: (1) 직접 여호와를 구함(3b절), (2) 여호와의 능력을 구함(4a절), (3) 여호와의 얼굴을 구함(4b절). '직접 여호와를 구함'은 하나님의 임재와 동행을 사모함을 뜻한다. '주님의 능력을 구함'은 주님이 우리의 삶에 온갖 이적과 기적으로 함께하시기를 바라는 것이다. '여호와의 얼굴을 구함'은 항상 하나님의 보호와 보살핌 아래 있기를 바라는 마음이다. 우리는 온전히 주님과 함께 사는 삶을 추구해야 한다.

넷째, 우리는 주님의 모든 은총을 기억해야 한다(6절). 이 권면이 이 시편의 가장 핵심 메시지다(Tucker & Grant). 하나님이 행하신 기적, 하신 말씀, 베풀어 주신 은혜는 두고두고 기념될(זכר) 때 그 진가를 드러낸다(cf. Goldingay). 주님이 이미 베풀어 주신 기적과 은총을 기념할 때마다 현재와 미래에도 주님이 함께하시며 우리를 돌보실 것이라는 확신이 서기 때문이다. 그러므로 성경은 우리 자신을 위해서라도 주님을 기념하며 살아가라고 한다.

2. 선조들과 언약을 맺으심(105:7-11)

7 그는 여호와 우리 하나님이시라
그의 판단이 온 땅에 있도다
8 그는 그의 언약
곧 천 대에 걸쳐 명령하신 말씀을 영원히 기억하셨으니
9 이것은 아브라함과 맺은 언약이고
이삭에게 하신 맹세이며

[10] 야곱에게 세우신 율례
곧 이스라엘에게 하신 영원한 언약이라
[11] 이르시기를 내가 가나안 땅을 네게 주어
너희에게 할당된 소유가 되게 하리라 하셨도다

이제부터 기자는 여호와께서 이스라엘 역사에서 그들에게 베풀어 주신 은총들 중 몇 가지를 나열하며 하나님은 참으로 온 세상의 찬양과 경배를 받을 만한 신이심을 선언한다. 그가 회고하는 중심 내용은 선조 때로 거슬러 올라가 이스라엘이 가나안 땅을 소유하게 된 과정이다. 그중 본문이 묘사하고 있는 첫 번째는 하나님이 선조들에게 땅을 약속하신 일이다.

저자는 먼저 하나님과 이스라엘의 관계를 확인하며 이 섹션을 시작한다. 여호와는 그가 속한 이스라엘의 하나님이시다(7a절). 여호와께서 그들을 다스리는 왕이 되심을 이렇게 표현한다. 또한 이스라엘의 왕이신 여호와는 온 세상의 왕이시다. 그러므로 그의 판단이 이스라엘뿐만 아니라 온 땅에 있다(7b절). '그의 판단이 온 땅에 있다'(בְּכָל־הָאָרֶץ מִשְׁפָּטָיו)는 것은 세상의 창조주—왕이신 여호와의 통치 흔적이 그가 만들고 다스리시는 온 세상에 충만하다는 뜻이다.

기자는 하나님이 아브라함 때부터 세상에 충만한 하나님의 통치 흔적의 일원으로 이스라엘에게 약속하심에 따라 가나안 땅을 그들에게 할당하셨고, 그 이후로 그 땅이 이스라엘의 소유가 된 일을 언급한다(11절). 그는 하나님의 약속은 아브라함과 맺은 '언약'(כָּרַת)이며, 이삭에게 하신 '맹세'(שְׁבוּעָה)이며, 야곱에게 세우신 '율례'(חֹק)이며, 이스라엘에게 하신 '영원한 언약'(בְּרִית עוֹלָם)이라고 한다(9–10절). 이 네 가지 모두 영원한 것들이다.

또한 이스라엘이 가나안 땅을 차지하게 된 이유는 여호와께서 선조들과 맺으신 언약을 기억하셨기 때문이다(8절). 성경에서 언약은 기억

만큼이나 중요한 단어이다(cf. Mays). 이 언약의 영원성을 강조하기 위하여 그는 '천 대에 걸쳐'(לְאֶלֶף דּוֹר)를 한 차례(8절), '영원히'(לְעוֹלָם)라는 말을 두 차례(8, 10절) 사용한다. 하나님이 맺으신 언약은 절대 다시 무르거나 무효화할 수 없다는 것을 강조한다.

그러나 주님이 선조들과 맺으신 언약이 아무리 영원한 것이라고 해도 하나님이 기억하지 않으신다면 아무 의미가 없다. 하나님과 언약을 맺은 선조들은 죽은 지 이미 오래되었기 때문이다. 그러므로 이 언약이 실현되기 위해서는 하나님이 기억하셔야 한다. 하지만 하나님은 기억하셨다! 또한 이 언약을 영원히 기억하실 것이다. 여호와께서 기억하시는 한, 선조들에게 약속하신 땅은 영원히 이스라엘의 땅이 될 것이다. 대부분 학자들이 주장하는 것처럼 이 시편이 포로기 혹은 그 이후에 저작되었다면, 이 말씀은 참으로 대단한 신앙고백이다. 이미 그들이 잃어버린 땅을 언젠가는 주님이 다시 그들에게 주실 것을 믿고 있기 때문이다.

3. 선조들의 가나안 여정(105:12-15)

12 그 때에 그들의 사람 수가 적어
그 땅의 나그네가 되었고
13 이 족속에게서 저 족속에게로,
이 나라에서 다른 민족에게로 떠돌아다녔도다
14 그러나 그는 사람이 그들을 억압하는 것을 용납하지 아니하시고
그들로 말미암아 왕들을 꾸짖어
15 이르시기를 나의 기름 부은 자를 손대지 말며
나의 선지자들을 해하지 말라 하셨도다

우리가 잘 알다시피 하나님이 처음부터 아브라함에게 가나안 땅을 차지하도록 주신 것은 아니다. 그와 그 자손들이 그 땅을 차지할 만한 민족으로 번성하지 못했기 때문이다(12a절). 결국 아브라함과 그의 후손들은 가나안 땅의 나그네가 되어 이곳저곳을 배회하며 살았다(12b-13절, cf. 창 12-35장; 신 26:5-10). 하나님께 땅을 약속 받기는 했지만, 그 약속이 실현되려면 몇백 년을 기다려야 했다.

선조들은 가나안 땅을 떠돌며 여러 가지 위험에 노출된 삶을 살았다. 그때마다 하나님은 가나안 사람들이 그들을 억압하지 못하도록 하시고, 심지어는 왕들을 꾸짖으셨다(14절). 선조들의 많은 숫자가 아니라, 하나님의 보호하심으로써 그들이 보존되고 민족으로 번성할 수 있었다. 아브라함이 이집트 왕에서 사라를 빼앗길 뻔했던 사건(cf. 창 12:17)과 아브라함과 이삭이 아내들을 아비멜렉에게 빼앗길 뻔했던 사건(cf. 창 20:3; 26:11) 등도 그들의 생존을 위협하는 사건들이다.

하나님이 가나안을 떠도는 선조들을 보호하신 이유는 그 땅을 약속하셨기 때문이기도 하지만, 그들은 하나님의 기름 부은 자들이며, 선지자들이었기 때문이다(15절). 일부 주석가들은 가나안에 떠돌아다닌 이들을 이스라엘 전체로 해석해야 한다고 하지만(Anderson), 선조들로 제한하는 것이 바람직하다. 이 섹션에서는 아직 출애굽한 이스라엘이 가나안에 입성하지 않았기 때문이다. '기름 부은 자'(מְשִׁיחַ)는 하나님이 특별히 구분하여 보호하시는 사람을 뜻하며 '메시아'가 지닌 의미이다.

선조들은 어떤 의미에서 선지자들이었는가? 아비멜렉이 사라를 아내로 취하려고 할 때 하나님은 아비멜렉에게 나타나셔서 그 일을 금하셨을 뿐만 아니라, 사라의 남편 아브라함이 아비멜렉을 위해 기도해야 문제가 해결될 것이라고 하셨다(cf. 창 20장). 아브라함은 '선지자'(נָבִיא)이기 때문이라며 아비멜렉에게 이러한 요구를 하셨다(창 20:7). 또한 이삭과 야곱도 자식들을 축복하며 기도할 때 선지자들처럼 그들의 미래에 대하여 예언을 했다. 그러므로 그들은 분명 하나님의 선지자들이었다.

4. 요셉이 이집트로 내려감(105:16-22)

16 그가 또 그 땅에 기근이 들게 하사
그들이 의지하고 있는 양식을 다 끊으셨도다
17 그가 한 사람을 앞서 보내셨음이여
요셉이 종으로 팔렸도다
18 그의 발은 차꼬를 차고
그의 몸은 쇠사슬에 매였으니
19 곧 여호와의 말씀이 응할 때까지라
그의 말씀이 그를 단련하였도다
20 왕이 사람을 보내어 그를 석방함이여
뭇 백성의 통치자가 그를 자유롭게 하였도다
21 그를 그의 집의 주관자로 삼아
그의 모든 소유를 관리하게 하고
22 그의 뜻대로 모든 신하를 다스리며
그의 지혜로 장로들을 교훈하게 하였도다

하나님은 아브라함의 후손들이 이집트로 내려가게 하기 위해 가나안 땅에 기근이 들게 하셔서 양식을 모두 끊으셨다(16절). 창세기에는 하나님이 가나안에 기근을 주신 일이 두 차례 기록되어 있다. 아브라함이 가나안에 도착한 지 얼마 되지 않아서 있었던 일이며(창 12장), 훗날 야곱의 후손들이 이집트로 내려갈 때 일이다(창 41-45장). 아브라함과 후손들이 가나안을 떠돈 이야기를 이미 언급했으니(12-15절), 이 말씀은 요셉 시대에 야곱과 가족들이 이집트로 내려가게 하신 일을 회고하고 있다.

하나님은 야곱과 가족들을 이집트로 보내시기 전에 먼저 요셉을 보내셔서 그들의 이집트 여정을 준비하게 하셨다(17a절). 그런데 하나님이 요셉을 이집트로 보내신 방법이 예사롭지 않다. 요셉이 노예로 팔려 강제로 이집트로 끌려갔기 때문이다(17b-18절). 상황이 아무리 어렵다 할지라도 하나님은 항상 자기 뜻을 이루신다(Tucker & Grant). 요셉은 참으로 억울한 일을 당했다. 그는 노예로 팔릴 만한 일을 한 적이 없는데, 형들에 의해 노예로 팔렸다.

다행인 것은 요셉이 하나님의 말씀이 응할 때까지만 노예 생활을 했다는 사실이다(19a절). 하나님이 계획하신 일을 이루기 위해 요셉이 노예 생활을 하게 하셨으니, 분명 때가 되면 요셉은 자유인이 될 것이라는 소망이 있다. 그렇다고 해서 그가 당면한 고통이 줄지는 않았을 것이다.

하나님의 때가 이를 때까지 요셉은 이집트에서 노예로 살았지만, 이 시간은 하나님의 말씀이 그를 단련하는 시간이기도 했다(19절). '단련하다'(צרף)는 용광로를 이용해 광물을 제련하는 의미를 지니고 있다(NIDOTTE). 그러므로 이 단어는 요셉이 이집트에서 참으로 혹독한 연단의 시간을 보냈다는 것을 뜻한다. 보디발의 아내의 모함을 받아 감옥에 갇힌 일이 요셉에게는 참으로 고통스러운 연단의 시간이었다. 그러나 욥이 고백한 것처럼 요셉은 "내가 가는 길을 그가 아시나니 그가 나를 단련하신 후에는 내가 순금같이 되어 나오리라"(욥 23:10)는 믿음으로 이 시간을 견뎌 냈다.

하나님이 정하신 때가 이르자 여호와께서는 다름 아닌 이집트 왕을 사용하여 요셉에게 자유를 주셨다(20절). 또한 요셉의 지혜와 능력에 탄복한 바로는 그를 자기 집의 주관자로 삼아 모든 소유를 관리하게 했다(21절). 또한 요셉이 그를 대신하여 온 나라를 가르치고 다스리는 일을 하도록 했다(22절). 바로가 다가오는 7년의 풍년과 7년의 기근에 관한 꿈을 꾼 일(창 41장) 이후로 요셉의 신변에 있었던 변화를 이렇게 요약하고 있다.

이 섹션에 기록된 요셉 이야기는 하나님의 뜻에 따라 살려고 발버둥치다가 고통의 수렁에 빠지는 사람들에게 큰 위로가 된다. 그 순간은 참으로 고통스럽고 절망스럽겠지만, 하나님이 이 모든 것을 알고 사용하시니 언젠가는 그 고통과 아픔을 통해서 주님의 뜻을 이루실 것을 확신하며 견딜 수 있는 믿음을 주기 때문이다.

5. 이집트 여정(105:23-25)

23 이에 이스라엘이 애굽에 들어감이여
야곱이 함의 땅에 나그네가 되었도다
24 여호와께서 자기의 백성을 크게 번성하게 하사
그의 대적들보다 강하게 하셨으며
25 또 그 대적들의 마음이 변하게 하여
그의 백성을 미워하게 하시며
그의 종들에게 교활하게 행하게 하셨도다

이집트의 국무총리가 된 요셉의 주선으로 야곱의 후손들은 가나안을 강타한 기근을 피해 이집트로 내려갔다. 바로가 꾼 꿈에 따라 7년 동안 지속된 기근 중 2년이 지난 때였다(창 45:6). 이렇게 해서 이스라엘이 이집트에서 나그네의 삶을 살게 되었다(23절). 훗날 이들은 이집트의 노예가 된다.

여호와께서는 이집트에 머문 야곱의 후손들을 크게 번성케 하셨다(24절, cf. 출 1:7). 이스라엘은 이집트 사람들이 두려워할 정도로 크게 번성했다. 하나님이 이스라엘을 가나안을 정복할 만한 민족으로 만들어 가신 것이다. 또한 이집트 사람들이 이스라엘을 미워하게 하셨고, 교활하게 행하게 하셨다(25절). '교활하다'(נכל)는 속임수를 쓰는 것을 뜻한다(HALOT). 이스라엘은 이집트에 머물면서 온갖 억울한 일을 당했다는 뜻이다. 하나님이 왜 이런 일을 허락하셨는가? 만일 이스라엘이 이집트에서 편안하게 살 수 있었다면, 그들은 절대 가나안을 향해 이집트를 떠나지 않았을 것이기 때문이다.

6. 이집트를 친 재앙들(105:26-36)

26 그리하여 그는 그의 종 모세와
그의 택하신 아론을 보내시니
27 그들이 그들의 백성 중에서
여호와의 표적을 보이고
함의 땅에서 징조들을 행하였도다
28 여호와께서 흑암을 보내사
그곳을 어둡게 하셨으나
그들은 그의 말씀을 지키지 아니하셨도다
29 그들의 물도 변하여 피가 되게 하사
그들의 물고기를 죽이셨도다
30 그 땅에 개구리가 많아져서
왕의 궁실에도 있었도다
31 여호와께서 말씀하신즉
파리 떼가 오며
그들의 온 영토에 이가 생겼도다
32 비 대신 우박을 내리시며
그들의 땅에 화염을 내리셨도다
33 그들의 포도나무와 무화과나무를 치시며
그들의 지경에 있는 나무를 찍으셨도다
34 여호와께서 말씀하신즉
황충과 수많은 메뚜기가 몰려와
35 그들의 땅에 있는 모든 채소를 먹으며
그들의 밭에 있는 열매를 먹었도다

[36] 또 여호와께서 그들의 기력의 시작인
그 땅의 모든 장자를 치셨도다

여호와께서는 이집트에게 억압당하고 착취당하던 이스라엘을 구원하기 위해 자기 종들인 모세와 아론을 보내셨다(26절, cf. 출 14:31). 그들은 먼저 자신들은 하나님이 보내신 사람들이라는 것을 입증하기 위해 자기 백성들에게 여호와의 표적을 보이고 징조들을 행했다(27절). 이 말씀은 이집트로 돌아온 모세와 아론이 이스라엘의 장로들 앞에서 하나님의 말씀을 전하고 이적을 행한 일을 회고하고 있다(출 4:29-31). 이때 장로들은 하나님께 엎드려 경배했다.

모세는 이집트 왕에게 이스라엘의 자유를 요구하며 10가지 재앙을 행했다(출 5-11장). 기자는 이 열 재앙 중 여덟 가지를 언급한다. 언급하지 않은 두 재앙은 가축들이 죽은 다섯 번째(cf. 출 9:1-7)와 여섯 번째 재앙인 피부병이다(cf. 출 9:8-12). 기자가 이 두 재앙이 실제로 있었던 일이라는 것을 부인해서 이곳에서 언급하지 않는 것은 아니다(cf. VanGemeren). 그가 기억에서 이 재앙들을 회고하고 있기 때문에 둘을 놓친 것으로 생각하는 것이 좋다(cf. Loewenstamm). 또한 그가 재앙들에 대한 기억을 더듬으며 노래하고 있기 때문에 언급하는 재앙들의 순서도 다르다(cf. 시 78:44-51). 다음은 출애굽기의 재앙 순서와 이 노래의 재앙 순서다. 기자가 어두움을 제일 먼저 언급하는 것은 아마도 이집트의 왕들이 자신들을 태양 신의 아들들이라고 했기 때문일 것이다(Booij, cf. Kirkpatrick). 하나님은 재앙으로 그들의 태양을 가리셨다.

출애굽기 5-11장	시편 105:28-36
1. 물이 피가 됨	1. 어두움(#9)
2. 개구리	2. 물이 피가 됨(#1)
3. 이	3. 개구리(#2)
4. 파리	4. 파리(#4)

5. 가축	5. 이(#3)
6. 피부병	6. 우박(#7)
7. 우박	7. 메뚜기(#8)
8. 메뚜기	8. 장자(#10)
9. 어두움	
10. 장자	

기자가 강조하고자 하는 것은 이 모든 재앙들이 이스라엘의 해방을 위해 하나님이 하신 일이라는 점이다. 그러므로 그는 이 모든 재앙을 하나님이 하셨다며 하나하나 하나님을 주어로 삼아 이야기를 진행한다. 하나님은 아브라함과 맺은 약속을 지키기 위해 무던히도 애를 쓰셨다.

7. 유월절 사건(105:37-38)

37 마침내 그들을 인도하여
은 금을 가지고 나오게 하시니
그의 지파 중에 비틀거리는 자가 하나도 없었도다
38 그들이 떠날 때에 애굽이 기뻐하였으니
그들이 그들을 두려워함이로다

하나님이 이집트에게 내리신 열 재앙 중 마지막 재앙이 임했을 때 바로와 이집트는 조건 없이 항복했다. 이집트 사람들의 장자와 짐승들의 맏이를 모두 죽이셨으니(cf. 36절) 얼마나 두려웠겠는가! 이 재앙을 끝으로 이스라엘은 이집트를 떠날 수 있었다. 출애굽기는 이 열 번째 재앙의 중요성을 강조하기 위해 이 재앙이 임하기 전에 미리 이 재앙에 대해 경고하고(출 11장), 유월절 등 이 재앙과 연관된 절기들에 대해 언급한 다음에(출 12:1-28) 실제로 재앙이 임한다(출 12:29-36). 이스라엘의 출애굽 역사에서 가장 중요한 일은 열 번째 재앙으로 인해 시작된 유월절 사건인 것이다.

이스라엘이 이집트를 떠나는 날, 이집트 사람들은 이스라엘 사람들이 요구한 금과 은 등 많은 것을 주면서 속히 떠나 달라고 애원했다(37절, cf. 출 12:33-36). 처음 아홉 재앙을 통해 이집트의 하나님에 대한 두려움은 극에 달했는데, 열 번째 재앙이 그들을 공포에 휩싸이게 한 것이다. 그러므로 이스라엘이 떠나자 이집트 사람들은 안도의 숨을 쉬며 기뻐했다(38a절). 이스라엘은 이집트를 두려워하며 430년을 살았는데, 그들이 떠난 날에는 이집트 사람들이 그들을 심히 두려워했다(38b절). 하나님이 이 둘의 입장을 이처럼 바꿔 놓으신 것이다.

공포와 두려움에 휩싸여 몸도 제대로 가누지 못하는 이집트 사람들과는 달리 이스라엘 사람들 중에는 비틀거리는 자가 하나도 없었다(37c절, cf. 신 8:3-4). 하나님이 얼마나 이스라엘을 잘 보살피셨는지 그들은 건강한 모습으로 이집트를 떠났다는 뜻이다(VanGemeren).

우리도 꿈을 꾸자. 언젠가는 우리가 두려워하는 것들이 오히려 우리를 두려워할 날을 꿈꾸자. 하나님이 우리와 함께 하시면 이런 날이 꼭 올 것이다.

8. 광야 여정(105:39-42)

39 여호와께서 낮에는 구름을 펴사 덮개를 삼으시고
밤에는 불로 밝히셨으며
40 그들이 구한즉 메추라기를 가져오시고
또 하늘의 양식으로 그들을 만족하게 하셨도다
41 반석을 여신즉 물이 흘러나와
마른 땅에 강 같이 흘렀으니
42 이는 그의 거룩한 말씀과

그의 종 아브라함을 기억하셨음이로다

하나님은 이집트를 탈출하는 이스라엘을 보호하시고 갈 길을 인도하시기 위해 처음부터 구름 기둥과 불 기둥으로 함께 하셨다(39절, 출 13:17-22). 낮에는 구름 기둥을 통해 그늘을 만드셔서 이스라엘이 더위에 지치지 않게 하셨다. 밤에는 기온이 뚝 떨어지는 기후에서 그들을 보호하기 위해 불 기둥으로 따뜻하게 해 주셨다. 구름 기둥과 불 기둥은 하나님의 함께하심의 증표였지만, 동시에 오늘날로 말하면 '냉·난방 서비스'도 제공했다. 구름 기둥과 불 기둥은 그들이 광야에서 살았던 40년 동안 계속 함께 있었다.

하나님은 광야에서 이스라엘을 먹이기 위해 만나와 메추라기를 주셨다(40절). 이 같은 하나님의 배려는 이스라엘이 홍해를 건너는 순간부터 시작되어 40년 동안 계속되었다(cf. 출 16:1-36; 수 5:12). 이스라엘은 하나님이 내려 주시는 음식으로 풍족하게 먹으며 만족했다.

이스라엘이 물이 필요하다고 하자 하나님은 반석을 열어 물이 나오게 하셨다(41a절). 모세가 므리바에서 바위를 쳐서 물을 낸 사건을 회고하고 있다(출 17:1-7). 모세가 내리친 바위에서 물이 얼마나 많이 나왔는지 마른 땅에 강같이 흘렀다고 한다(41b절). 충분히 가능하다. 이집트를 탈출한 이스라엘 사람들의 숫자를 200만 명으로 추정할 때, 이들이 마시고, 씻고, 옷도 빨고, 짐승들도 먹이려면 이 바위에서 하루 24시간 분(分)당 최소 10톤의 물이 흘러나와야 한다. 그러므로 바위에서 작은 강이 흘렀다고 할 수 있다.

여호와께서 이처럼 온갖 기적을 베푸시며 이집트에서 종살이하던 이스라엘을 해방시키시고 광야를 지나 가나안에 가게 하신 것은 그의 종 아브라함을 기억하셨기 때문이다. 구약에서 하나님이 '기억하시는 것'(זכר)은 은혜의 시작이다(cf. 창 8:1; 삼상 1:19). 가나안 땅을 아브라함과 그의 후손에게 주시겠다고 한 약속을 지키기 위해 이 모든 일을 하신 것이다. 하나님은 약속하신 것은 절대 잊지 않으시는 분이다. 심지어는 몇백 년이 지났는데도 이렇게 아브라함의 후손들을 찾아오셨다.

9. 가나안을 주심(105:43-45)

43 그의 백성이 즐겁게 나오게 하시며
그의 택한 자는 노래하며 나오게 하시며
44 여러 나라의 땅을 그들에게 주시며
민족들이 수고한 것을 소유로 가지게 하셨으니
45 이는 그들이 그의 율례를 지키고
그의 율법을 따르게 하려 하심이로다
할렐루야

이 섹션은 이스라엘이 가나안 땅에 정착한 일을 회고하고 있다. 기자는 그들이 반역하여 광야에서 40년을 살면서 하나님을 괴롭게 한 일을 생략하고 있다. 이 역사시의 초점이 하나님의 은혜로운 사역에 맞춰져 있기 때문에 굳이 인간의 실패는 언급할 필요가 없다.

가나안을 기업으로 받기 위해 이집트를 떠나온 이스라엘은 즐거운 마음으로 노래하며 이집트를 떠나왔다(43절). 주님은 그들에게 가나안에 있던 여러 나라들(주로 도시 국가들, cf. 수 10:16-11:15)의 땅을 주셨다(44a절). 또한 가나안 사람들이 소유하고 누리던 것을 모두 이스라엘에게 주셨다(44b절). 그들이 하나님의 율례를 지키고 율법을 따르게 하기 위함이다. 하나님은 주의 백성이 말씀에 순종하면서 살기를 기대하시며 그들에게 많은 것을 축복으로 주신다. 이 말씀은 신명기 6:1과 11-13절을 연상케 한다:

1 이는 곧 너희의 하나님 여호와께서 너희에게 가르치라고 명하신 명령과

규례와 법도라 너희가 건너가서 차지할 땅에서 행할 것이니… [11] 네가 채
우지 아니한 아름다운 물건이 가득한 집을 얻게 하시며 네가 파지 아니
한 우물을 차지하게 하시며 네가 심지 아니한 포도원과 감람나무를 차지
하게 하사 네게 배불리 먹게 하실 때에 [12] 너는 조심하여 너를 애굽 땅 종
되었던 집에서 인도하여 내신 여호와를 잊지 말고 [13] 네 하나님 여호와를
경외하며 그를 섬기며 그의 이름으로 맹세할 것이니라

제106편

I. 장르/양식: 개인 탄식시(cf. 3편)

대부분 학자들은 이 시편의 장르를 구분하기가 쉽지 않다고 토로한다. 어떤 이들은 찬양시라고 하고(cf. 1-2절), 어떤 이들은 공동체 탄식시라고 하며(cf. 4-5, 47절), 다른 사람들은 참회시라고 한다(cf. 6-7절). 또한 이 시편을 설교 혹은 강론으로 혹은 역사시로 간주하는 사람들도 있다(Brueggemann & Bellinger, cf. Goldingay, Terrien). 이처럼 다양한 의견이 제시되는 것은 이 시가 찬양과 탄식을 함께 포함하고 있기 때문이다(Allen). 또한 찬양시의 주 형태인 복수 동사와 탄식시의 주 형태인 단수 동사들이 섞여 있는 것이 어려움을 더한다. 이 주석에서는 개인 탄식시로 간주할 것이다(cf. 4절).

오래전부터 학자들은 이 시편과 105편이 한 쌍을 이룬다고 했고(McCann, Tucker & Grant), 105편과 106편을 '쌍둥이 시편'이라고 부른 이도 있다(Zimmerli). 심지어 한 학자는 105편과 106편은 원래 한 편의 노래였는데, 훗날 두 편으로 나뉜 것이라고 하기도 한다(Briggs).

이 두 편이 모두 이스라엘의 역사를 회고하고는 있지만, 내용이 확연히 다르기 때문에 일란성이 아니라 이란성 쌍둥이라고 하는 이들도 있다(deClaissé-Walford et al., Wilcock). 하나님의 신실하심을 강조하는 105편과는 달리 106편은 이스라엘의 신실하지 못함과 반역을 강조한다. 그러므로 이 시편은 105편의 메시지를 완전히 뒤집는다고 할 수 있다(Broyles, Kidner, Terrien). 또한 이스라엘의 실패와 불순종을 강조하는 면에서 78편을 보완한다(VanGemeren, cf. Goldingay, Terrien).

이처럼 이 노래는 105편과 밀접한 관계를 유지하고 있지만, 제5권을 시작하는 다음 시편(107편)과도 밀접한 연관성을 유지하고 있다. 두 편 모두 같은 찬양으로 노래를 시작하기 때문이다(McCann, cf. 106:1; 107:1).

이 시편의 전반적인 분위기도 학자들 사이에 논란이 된다. 이 노래가 하나님을 찬양하기 위해 저작된 것이므로 찬양적인 분위기를 조성하고 있다고 하는 이들도 있고(Kraus, VanGemeren), 공동체의 불만을 표현하기 위해 저작된 것이라는 주장도 있다(Allen). 이 시편은 역사시로서 이 두 가지 기능을 동시에 수행하고 있는 것으로 보는 것이 바람직하다.

대부분 주석가들은 이 시편의 저작 시기로 바빌론 포로 시대(Anderson, Goldingay, Ross), 혹은 늦은 포로 시대(Terrien), 혹은 그 이후를 지목한다(McCann). 47절이 주의 백성이 포로가 되어 열방에 흩어져 있는 것을 전제하기 때문이다.

II. 구조

다음은 밴게메렌(VanGemeren)이 제시한 교차대구법적 구조이다. 아쉬운 것은 한 중앙에 있는 D가 너무나도 많은 분량을 차지한다는 점이다.

A. 찬양 부름(106:1-2)
　B. 하나님의 구원을 위한 기도(106:3-5)
　　C. 하나님의 사랑: 구원(106:6-12)
　　　D. 이스라엘의 불신 역사와 하나님의 심판(106:13-43)
　　C'. 하나님의 사랑: 참으심(106:44-46)

B′. 하나님의 구원을 위한 기도(106:47)

A′. 찬양 부름(106:48)

대부분 학자들은 이 시에는 통일성 있는 구조가 존재하지 않는다고 생각하며, 문단으로 나누는 것도 학자들에 따라 현저한 차이를 보이고 있다(cf. deClaissé-Walford et al., Goldingay, HALOT, Ross, Terrien). 이 주석에서는 다음과 같은 분석을 바탕으로 본문을 주해해 나가고자 한다.

A. 찬양과 기도(106:1-5)
B. 이집트와 홍해에서 반역(106:6-12)
C. 광야에서 반역(106:13-18)
D. 시내 산에서 반역(106:19-23)
E. 땅 약속을 믿지 않음(106:24-27)
F. 광야에서 우상을 숭배함(106:28-33)
G. 약속의 땅을 피로 더럽힘(106:34-39)
H. 포로로 끌려감(106:40-46)
I. 귀향을 이루실 하나님 찬양(106:47)
J. 제4권을 마무리하는 찬양(106:48)

III. 주해

이 시편은 이스라엘이 출애굽 때 홍해를 건넌 시점부터 바빌론으로 포로가 되어 끌려갈 때까지 지속된 이스라엘의 불신과 실패를 회고하며 독자들에게 과거를 잊지 말 것을 권면한다. 하나님의 끊임없는 신실하심을 강조하는 105편과는 강력한 대조를 이룬다. 이 두 편은 한 쌍을 이루며 주의 백성의 구원과 보존은 그들의 반응에 의해 결정되는 것이 아니라, 하나님의 일방적인 은총과 구원하심으로 가능하다는 사실을 강조한다. 그러므로 바빌론에서 이 노래를 부른 사람들은 언젠가는 하나님이 그들의 조상 시대에 그렇게 하셨던 것처럼 그들의 삶에서도 '새로운 출애굽'을 실현하실 것을 기대한다. 그들이 과거에 베풀어 주신 주님의 은혜를 망각하지 않고 기억한다면 꼭 그렇게 될 것이라고 한다(Tucker & Grant, cf. Allen).

1. 찬양과 기도(106:1-5)

1 할렐루야
여호와께 감사하라
그는 선하시며
그 인자하심이 영원함이로다
2 누가 능히 여호와의 권능을 다 말하며
주께서 받으실 찬양을 다 선포하랴
3 정의를 지키는 자들과
항상 공의를 행하는 자는 복이 있도다
4 여호와여
주의 백성에게 베푸시는 은혜로 나를 기억하시며
주의 구원으로 나를 돌보사
5 내가 주의 택하신 자가 형통함을 보고
주의 나라의 기쁨을 나누어 가지게 하사
주의 유산을 자랑하게 하소서

시편 제4권을 마무리하고 있는 이 노래는 '할렐루야'(הַלְלוּיָהּ)로 시작하고 같은 말로 마무리된다(1, 48절). 기자가 이스라엘의 불신과 실패를 낱낱이 회고하는 노래를 '여호와를 찬양하라'는 의미를 지닌 '할렐루야'로 시작하고 끝맺는 것이 인상적이다. 하나님이 이스라엘을 버리시려고 했다면 기회가 얼마든지 있었다. 이스라엘의 역사는 불신과 실패의 연속이었기 때문이다. 그러나 주님은 그들을 버리지 않으시고 끝까지 함께하시며 그들을 품으셨다. 그러므로 기자는 백성의 지속된 불신에 개의치 않고 끝까지 신실하신 하나님은 영원히 찬양 받기에 합당하신 분이라며 이렇게 노래를 시작하고 마무리한다.

기자는 여호와께 감사하라고 하는데(1b절), '감사하다'(ידה)는 '찬양하라'는 뜻도 지녔다(cf. HALOT). 감사와 찬양은 비슷한 말이며, 뗄 수 없는 동전의 양면이다. 그는 두 가지 이유로 인해 주님을 찬양하라고 한다.

첫째, 여호와께서 선하시기 때문에 우리는 주님을 찬양해야 한다(1c절, cf. 시 100:5; 107:1; 136:1). 이스라엘이 여호와는 선하시다고 고백하는 것에는 지난 수백 년의 경험이 바탕이 되고 있다(Goldingay). 고대 근동의 신들은 인간들을 선하게 대하지 않았다. 그들은 항상 인간들을 괴롭히고 이용하려 들었다(cf. ANET). 이러한 정서에서 여호와는 선하시다는 것은 매우 파격적인 선언이다(cf. Tucker & Grant).

'선하다'(טוב)는 하나님의 가장 기본적인 속성이며, 우리가 하나님에게 좋은 일을 기대할 수 있는 근거가 된다(cf. 창 1장). 선하신 하나님은 항상 선한 것들을 자기 백성에게 주시는 분이다. 하나님의 선하심을 경험한 사람들은 자신들이 경험한 것을 주변 사람들에게 알려야 한다(cf. deClaissé-Walford et al.).

둘째, 여호와의 인자하심이 영원하기 때문에 우리는 주님께 감사해야 한다(1d절). 이 히브리어 문구(לְעוֹלָם חַסְדּוֹ)의 문자적 의미는 '그의 인자(헤세드)는 영원에 이른다'는 뜻이다. 기자가 하나님의 선하심(좋으심)을 이미 언급했으니, 이곳에서 '인자'(חֶסֶד)는 언약적 충성으로 이해되어야 한다(cf. Schaefer, Sakenfeld). 하나님은 누구와 언약을 맺으시면 그 언약을 영원히 존중하신다는 뜻이다. 하나님은 사람과 달라서 한번 언약을 맺으시면 절대 먼저 잊거나 파괴하시는 일이 없다. 이러한 면에서 1절은 이스라엘의 가장 기본적인 신앙고백이며(McCann, Tucker & Grant, cf.

대하 5:13; 7:3; 시 118:1, 29; 136:1), 106편을 지탱하는 고백이다. 이 시편의 나머지 부분이 모두 1절의 진실성을 전제하고 전개되기 때문이다(Hossfeld-Zenger). 하나님과 언약을 맺은 사람들은 끊임없이 변하고 변질하지만, 하나님은 영원히 변치 않으시는 것에 우리의 소망이 있다.

영원히 선하고 인자하신 하나님은 이때까지 자기 백성에게 수많은 자비와 은총을 베푸셨다(2절). 기자는 2절을 시작하면서 "누가 선포할 수 있느냐?"(מִי יְמַלֵּל)는 수사학적인 질문(답은 '아무도 없다')을 통해 세상 그 누구도 하나님의 권능을 모두 말할 수 없고, 주님께 드릴 찬양을 모두 선포할 수 없다고 한다(cf. Alter). 그러므로 감히 누가 여호와의 권능을 다 말하고 주님께 합당한 찬양을 모두 선포하겠는가! '여호와의 권능'(גְּבוּרוֹת יְהוָה)은 신적 전사(Divine Warrior)이신 여호와와 연관하여 흔히 전쟁에서 사용되는 용어로(VanGemeren), 하나님이 주의 백성을 위해 발휘하신 모든 능력(구원의 행위)을 뜻한다. '그에게 드릴 모든 찬양'(כָּל־תְּהִלָּתוֹ)은 여호와께서 자기 백성을 위해 베푸신 모든 구원의 은총에 합당한 경배와 찬양을 의미한다. 하나님이 행하신 권능과 베푸신 자비가 얼마나 많은지 세상 그 누구도 헤아릴 수 없다는 말로 주님께 감사하고 있다.

기자는 하나님의 선하심과 인자하심과 권능의 수혜자들(cf. 1-2절)은 참으로 복이 있다고 한다(3절). 특별히 '복 있는 사람들'(אַשְׁרֵי)(cf. 시 1:1)은 다름 아닌 정의를 지키는 자들과 공의를 행하는 자들이다. '정의를 지키는 자들'(שֹׁמְרֵי מִשְׁפָּט)에서 정의는 경건한 사회의 근간이라 할 수 있는 공평한 판결을 뜻하며, '지키는 자들'은 이것이 잘못되지 않도록 불철주야를 지키는 보초병들을 연상케 한다. '항상 공의를 행하는 자'(עֹשֵׂה צְדָקָה בְכָל־עֵת)에서 '공의'는 건전한 사회의 근간인 옳고 그름에 대한 기준을 의미한다.

복이 있는 사람은 자기 잇속을 챙기기 위해 행동하는 사람이 아니라, 하나님이 기뻐하시는 일을 행하는 사람이다(McCann). '항상 행하는 자'는 '모든 때'에 공의를 행하는 자를 뜻한다. 공의를 행할 만한 때에만 행하는 것이 아니라, 때가 적합하지 않다고 생각되어도 옳은 일이기 때문에 행하는 기지를 바탕으로 하고 있다.

그러므로 '지키는 자들'과 '항상 행하는 자'는 모두 지속성에 강조점이 있다. 공의와 정의는 한두 차례로 끝나는 것이 아니라, 평생 동안 추구하는 가치관이다. 이런 사람은 참으로 '복 있는 사람'(אַשְׁרֵי)이다. 하나님이 꼭 축복하시고 그들의 기도에 응답하실 것이기 때문이다. 기자는 이 말씀을 통해 기도가 응답 받기 위해서는 먼저 기도하는 자가 공의와 정의를 실현하는 삶을 살아야 한다는 것을 암시한다(Allen).

새번역이 4절의 의미를 정확하게 번역했다: "주님, 주의 백성에게 은혜를 베푸실 때에, 나를 기억하여 주십시오. 그들을 구원하실 때에 나를 기억하여 주십시오"(cf. NIV, NAS, ESV, NRS). '기억하다'(זכר)는 '축복하기 위하여 찾아오다'라는 뜻이다(VanGemeren, cf. NIV). 저자는 예루살렘에서 멀리 떨어진 곳에 살고 있다(Alter, cf. 47절). 그러므로 그는 자신도 하나님의 백성 중 한 사람이니, 주님이 그들에게 은혜를 베푸실 때에 자신도 꼭 그 은혜를 누릴 수 있도록 찾아오실 것을 기도한다. 그는 주님의 백성 대열에 자신이 꼭 서 있기를 바란다.

기자가 하나님이 백성에게 은혜와 구원을 베푸실 때 자기에게도 꼭 동일한 은혜를 내려 달라고 하는 이유는 세 가지이다(5절). 이 구절도 새번역이 의미를 더 확실하게 번역했다: "주님께서 택하신 백성의 번영을 보게 해 주시며, 주님 나라에 넘치는 기쁨을 함께 누리게 해 주시며, 주님의 기업을 자랑하게 해 주십시오"(cf. NIV, NAS, ESV, NRS). 첫째, 그는 주의 백성이 하나님의 축복으로 번영하고 잘되는 것을 목격하기를 원한다. 둘째, 그들과 함께 하나님을 기뻐하기를 원한다. 셋째, 주님의 유산인 주의 백성이 누리는 영광을 온 세상에 자랑하고 싶어한다. 이 세 가지를 염원하며 그는 주님이 자기 백성에게 은혜를 베푸실 때 그도 기억해 주시기를 기도하고 있다. 기자가 4-5절을 통해 경험하고 싶다는 것들은 여호와께서 허락하셔야 가능한 것들이다(Gerstenberger). 그러기 때문에 그는 하나님의 자비에 호소하고 있는 것이다.

2. 이집트와 홍해에서 반역(106:6-12)

6 우리가 우리의 조상들처럼 범죄하여
사악을 행하며 악을 지었나이다
7 우리의 조상들이 애굽에 있을 때
주의 기이한 일들을 깨닫지 못하며
주의 크신 인자를 기억하지 아니하고
바다 곧 홍해에서 거역하였나이다
8 그러나 여호와께서는 자기의 이름을 위하여
그들을 구원하셨으니
그의 큰 권능을 만인이 알게 하려 하심이로다
9 이에 홍해를 꾸짖으시니 곧 마르니
그들을 인도하여 바다 건너가기를
마치 광야를 지나감 같게 하사
10 그들을 그 미워하는 자의 손에서 구원하시며
그 원수의 손에서 구원하셨고
11 그들의 대적들은 물로 덮으시매
그들 중에서 하나도 살아 남지 못하였도다
12 이에 그들이 그의 말씀을 믿고
그를 찬양하는 노래를 불렀도다

하나님을 찬양한 기자는 이어 조상들의 일을 회고한다. 후손이 조상들의 죄를 고백하는 기도를 드림은 구약에서 종종 있는 일이다(cf. 단

9:4–20). 출애굽 때 이스라엘이 이집트와 홍해에서 어떻게 하나님이 이때까지 베풀어 주신 은총을 순식간에 망각하고 주님을 거역했는가를 회상한다. 그는 조상들의 반역을 강조하기 위해 죄와 연관된 네 개의 동사를 사용한다: '범죄하다'(חטא) … '사악을 행했다'(עוה) … '악을 지었다'(רשע) … '거역했다'(מרה)(6–7절). 숫자 4는 총체성을 상징한다. 이때 이스라엘은 완전히 죄짓는 일에만 몰두하고 있었다는 뜻이다. 기자는 하나님의 도우심으로 이집트를 탈출한 그의 조상들이 그들을 억압한 이집트 사람들과 별반 다를 바가 없었다는 것을 이렇게 회고한다. 조상들이 왜 이렇게 되었는가? 그들은 하나님이 그들을 위해 행하신 온갖 기적들의 혜택을 받았을 뿐, 이 기적들에서 깨달은 것이 없었기 때문이다(Goldingay). 이스라엘은 처음부터 하나님이 구원하실 만한 인격을 지닌 사람들이 아니었다.

특이한 것은 포로기 시대를 살아가고 있는 그가 조상들의 죄를 회고하면서 "우리가 우리의 조상들처럼 범죄하여 사악을 행하며 악을 지었다"는 말을 더한다는 것이다(6절, cf. 출 20:6; 34:7). 오경은 이스라엘이 시내 산에서 맺은 언약은 그 자리에 있었던 조상들이 맺은 것이 아니라, 그 자리에 없었던 후손들이 그곳에서 맺은 것이나 별반 다름없다고 말한다(cf. 신 4장). 이러한 정서가 이 말씀의 배경이 된다(McCann, Perowne). 기자는 주의 백성인 이스라엘이 바빌론으로 끌려오게 된 것은 자신들의 죄 때문이며, 그들의 죄의 역사는 출애굽 때부터 이미 시작되어 이때까지 지속되어 왔고, 자신들은 조상들과 별반 다를 바 없는 죄인들이라는 사실을 고백한다(Mays, Schaefer).

이러한 고백을 통해 그는 자신이 속한 공동체가 과거 조상들의 사건에서 배우지 못한 세대라는 사실을 인정한다(Tucker & Grant). 그리고 그는 예전에 형편없던 그들의 조상에게 구원의 은총을 베푸신 여호와께서 그들에게도 구원의 역사를 내려 달라는 바람과 염원을 고백한다: "우리도 조상들과 별반 다를 바 없는 죄인들입니다. 예전에 우리 조상들을 이집트에서 구원하신 것처럼, 우리를 바빌론에서 구원해 주십시오"(cf. 47절).

이스라엘은 이집트에서 종살이할 때부터 하나님의 사역을 잘 알지 못했으며 감사하지도 않았다(7절). 그들은 삶이 너무 고달파 하나님께 기도했고, 하나님은 그들을 구원하고자 모세를 보내셨다. 그러나 그들은 모세를 그다지 환영하지 않았으며, 열 재앙이 진행되는 동안에도 하나님과 모세를 원망하기 일쑤였다(cf. 출 7-10장). 하나님이 행하신 '기이한 일들'(נִפְלְאוֹת)이 누구를 위한 것인지, 또한 무엇을 위한 것인지에 대해 그다지 깊은 이해와 감사가 없었기 때문이다. 그러므로 저자는 그의 조상들이 이집트에 있는 동안에도 하나님이 하신 일들에 대해 깨달음이 부족했다고 한다(7a-b절).

하나님이 이집트에 행하신 열 재앙과 이스라엘을 특별히 배려하신 기적들은 '주님의 크신 인자'(רֹב חֲסָדֶיךָ)였다(7c절). 자기 백성을 향한 하나님의 특별한 배려였던 것이다. 그러나 이러한 사실에 대한 깨달음이 부족하니 그들은 주님의 은총을 기억하지 못했다. 결국 그들은 홍해에서 다시 주님을 거역했다(7d절).

'거역하다'(מרה)는 하나님이 그들을 모든 위기에서 구원하실 것이라는 사실을 믿지 못하고 반역했다는 뜻이다(cf. HALOT). 죄는 하나님의 속성을 기억하지 못하는 것에서 시작된다(Eaton). 이집트에서 1년에 걸쳐 열 재앙을 내리시는 동안 이스라엘에게 내려 주신 은총을 망각한 것이 하나님을 향한 반역으로 이어졌다.

이 말씀은 이스라엘이 홍해를 건널 무렵 이집트 군이 쫓아오는 것을 보고 모세에게 "우리를 광야에서 죽이려고 이집트에서 데리고 나왔느냐?"며 항의했던 일을 회고하고 있다(cf. 출 14:1-12). 지난 1년 동안 온갖 기적을 경험했던 사람들이 할 만한 말은 절대 아니다. 불신하는 이스라엘과 달리 모세는 하나님이 이번에도 역사하실 것을 확신하고 믿었다(출 14:13-14). 모세의 말대로 여호와께서는 곧바로 홍해를 갈라 이스라엘이 마른 땅을 가듯이 홍해를 지나가도록 하셨다(출 14:15-16).

시편 기자는 하나님이 홍해를 갈라 불신하고 원망하는 조상들을 구원하신 것은 두 가지 목적을 두고 하신 일이라고 한다(8절).

첫째, 하나님은 자기 이름을 위해 그렇게 하셨다(8a-b절). 이스라엘은 지난 1년 동안 하나님이 이집트에 내리신 열 재앙을 옆에서 지켜보고 혜택을 누리면서도 하나님을 알려고 하지도 않고 믿지도 않았다. 그들은 하나님이 구원해 주실만한 사람들이 아니었다. 그러므로 하나님은 자기 자신의 명예를 위해 그들을 구원하셨다. 여호와는 이스라엘의 선조들과 맺은 약속을 꼭 이루시는 분이며, 한번 구원 사역을 시작하면 끝까지 책임지시는 하나님이라는 명예를 위해 그들을 구원하셨다.

둘째, 하나님은 온 세상이 주님의 큰 권능을 알게 하시려고 그들을 구원하셨다(8c절). 주님은 온 세상을 창조하시고 통치하시는 분임으로 온 세상이 주님을 알기를 원한다. 그러므로 주님의 모든 사역은 세상이 주님에 대해 조금 더 알 수 있는 효과를 발휘한다. '큰 권능'(גְּבוּרָה)은 하나님이 행하시는 기적들 중 더욱더 큰 이적을 뜻한다. 본문에서는 주님이 홍해를 마르게 하여 이스라엘이 광야를 지나가듯이 홍해를 가게 하신 일이다(9절).

하나님이 홍해를 꾸짖으시니 홍해는 곧 마른 땅을 내주었다(9a절). '꾸짖다'(גער)는 자기의 본분을 망각한 이를 나무란다는 뜻이다(cf. HALOT). 시편 104:7은 하나님이 산을 덮은 물을 꾸짖으시자 물이 바다로 돌아갔다고 한다. 자연은 창조주께서 하시는 일에 적극적으로 협조하도록 창조되었는데, 협조하지 않으면 당연히 '꾸짖음'을 들어야 한다.

하나님의 꾸지람을 들은 홍해가 곧바로 그의 백성에게 길을 내 주었다. 이스라엘은 홍해를 건널 때 마치 광야를 지나가는 것처럼 건넜다(9b-c절). '광야'(מִדְבָּר)는 메마른 땅의 상징이며 이스라엘이 가나안 입성 전에 40년 동안 거하던 곳이다(cf. 민 21:20; 23:28). 하나님의 꾸지람에 바닷물에 잠겨 있는 땅이 메마른 광야처럼 되었다. 주의 백성은 홍해를 건너는 동안 바닷물로 인해 어떠한 어려움도 당하지 않았다는 뜻이다.

이 기적을 통해 하나님은 이스라엘을 그들을 미워하는 자, 곧 원수들의 손에서 구원하셨다(10절). 이집트의 왕과 그의 군사들의 손에서 구원하셨다는 뜻이다. 홍해 사건 이후로 이집트는 다시는 이스라엘을 예전처럼 억압하지 못했다.

하나님이 홍해에서 이루신 기적은 이스라엘을 구원하신 일로 그치지 않았다. 그들을 미워하는 원수들 곧 그들의 대적들인 이집트 군대를 수장시키는 효과도 발휘했다(11절). 주의 백성에게는 구원의 기회를 제공한 홍해가 이집트 군대에게는 심판의 장소가 된 것이다. 출애굽기 14장에 의하면 이스라엘을 추격해온 이집트 마병들은 이스라엘이 홍해를 마른 땅처럼 건너자 그들의 뒤를 쫓아 홍해로 들어갔다. 하나님이 이스라엘 사람들이 모두 건널 때까지 이집트 군의 앞을 막았다가 길을 열어 주신 것이다. 이윽고 이집트 군이 바다 한가운데 있을 때, 하나님은 양쪽에 벽을 이루고 있던 바닷물이 그들을 덮치도록 하셨다. 결국 이집트 군은 하나도 살아남지 못하고 모두 죽었다.

그들은 이스라엘의 구원과 이집트의 패배를 기념하기 위해 하나님을 찬양하는 노래를 불렀다(12절). 출애굽기 15장에는 모세와 미리암이 이때 일을 기념하며 부른 노래 두 편이 기록되어 있다. 기자는 이 노래들을 떠올리며 이렇게 증언한다. 그러나 그들의 찬양은 오래가지 못한다(cf. 13절).

3. 광야에서 반역(106:13-18)

13 그러나 그들은 그가 행하신 일을 곧 잊어버리며
그의 가르침을 기다리지 아니하고
14 광야에서 욕심을 크게 내며
사막에서 하나님을 시험하였도다

[15] 그러므로 여호와께서는
그들이 요구하는 것을 그들에게 주셨을지라도
그들의 영혼은 쇠약하게 하셨도다
[16] 그들이 진영에서 모세와
여호와의 거룩한 자 아론을 질투하매
[17] 땅이 갈라져 다단을 삼키며
아비람의 당을 덮었고
[18] 불이 그들의 당에 붙음이여
화염이 악인들을 살랐도다

홍해에서 하나님의 '큰 권능'을 경험한 이스라엘의 여호와에 대한 추억은 오래가지 않았다. 그들은 곧바로 하나님이 행하신 일을 잊어버렸으며, 주님의 가르침을 기다리지도 않았다(13절). 이스라엘의 가장 큰 영적 문제는 '망각증'이었다. '가르침'(עֵצָה)은 지시/조언을 뜻한다(cf. NIDOTTE). 그들은 하나님의 지시와 상관없이 자기들 마음대로 독립적으로 행동했다. 그들은 하나님께 명령을 받는 자들이 아니라, 하나님께 지시하는 자들이 되었다(Anderson).

이스라엘이 하나님의 지시를 거부하고 독립적으로 행동한 결과는 무엇인가? 결코 좋고 경건한 열매는 아니었다. 오히려 이스라엘은 광야에서 욕심을 크게 내고 사막에서 하나님을 시험했다(14절, cf. 시 78:18). '그들이 욕심을 크게 냈다'(וַיִּתְאַוּוּ תַאֲוָה)(14a절)는 같은 어원의 단어를 반복하며 그들이 절제되지 않은 욕망에 사로잡혔던 상황을 묘사한다. 광야에서 '그들이 욕심을 크게 냈다'는 것은 무엇을 뜻하는가? 하나님이 주시는 것들에 만족하지 못하고 끊임없이 불만을 토로했다는 의미이다(cf. 새번역, 아가페, NIV, ESV, NAS).

무엇에 대한 불만이었는가? 먹을 것을 내놓으라는 투정이었다(공동, 현대인). 하나님은 분명 그들의 필요를 채워 주셨을 것이다. 그러나 그들은 항상 기다리지 못하고 하나님이 채워 주시기 전에 먼저 불평했다. 불평하지 않고 먼저 기도하여 구했으면 참으로 좋았을 것이다. 또한 그들의 불평은 하나님을 항상 '앞서간 것'이라 할 수 있다. 이러한 이스라엘의 행동은 하나님을 시험하는 일이기도 했다(14b절, cf. 민 11:5-6). '시험하다'(נסה)는 여호와께서 자기 백성들에게 종종 행하시는 일이지만, 백성들은 하나님께 이렇게 하면 안 된다. 하나님은 백성들에게 큰 수치를 당하시면서도 그들을 끝까지 품으셨다.

여호와께서는 그들의 불평을 다 들어주시고 그들이 요구하는 것들을 모두 주셨다(15a-b절). 그러나 즐거운 마음으로 들어주신 것은 아니다. 세상에 그 누가 자기를 시험하는 사람들을 따뜻하게 대하겠는가! 하나님은 그들의 요구를 들어주시면서 동시에 그들의 영혼을 쇠약하게 하셨다(15c절). 어느덧 이스라엘의 구원자가 심판자로 변한 것이다(Allen). '영혼을 쇠약하게 했다'(וַיְשַׁלַּח רָזוֹן בְּנַפְשָׁם)의 더 정확한 번역은 '그는 생명/영혼을 수척하게 하는/단축하는 것을 보내셨다'는 뜻이다. 무엇이 사람의 생명/영혼을 수척하게 하는가? 질병이다. 그러므로 대부분 번역본들이 이 문장을 '무서운 전염병을 보내셨다'는 의미로 번역한다(아가페, 현대인, NIV, ESV, NAS, NRS). 이 말씀은 민수기 11:31-35에 기록된 사건을 연상케 한다.

하나님께 대드는 사람들이 모세와 아론을 가만히 둘 이유가 없다. 그들은 모세와 아론을 질투했다(16절). 그러나 모세와 아론은 하나님이 이스라엘 사회의 질서를 확립하기 위해 에이전트(agent)로 사용한 사람들이므로, 이들의 지위를 의심하는 것은 하나님이 세우신 사회의 근간을 흔드는 일이었다(deClaissé-Walford et al., Goldingay). 그러므로 하나님은 모세와 아론을 시기하는 사람들을 가만히 두지 않으셨다. 반역한 다단과 아비람 무리를 불로 태우시고, 그들이 서 있는 땅을 갈라 매장하셨다(17-18절, cf. 민 16:35). 이 말씀은 민수기 16장에 기록된 사건으로 레위 지파 사람 고라와 르우벤 지파 사람 다단과 아비람이 주도하고

250명이 함께한 반역을 회고하고 있다. 고라도 이때 심판을 받아 죽었지만, 기자는 어떤 이유 때문인지 그를 언급하지 않는다(cf. 신 11:7).

4. 시내 산에서 반역(106:19-23)

19 그들이 호렙에서 송아지를 만들고
부어 만든 우상을 경배하여
20 자기 영광을 풀 먹는 소의 형상으로 바꾸었도다
21 애굽에서 큰 일을 행하신 그의 구원자
하나님을 그들이 잊었나니
22 그는 함의 땅에서 기사와
홍해에서 놀랄 만한 일을 행하신 이시로다
23 그러므로 여호와께서 그들을 멸하리라 하셨으나
그가 택하신 모세가 그 어려움 가운데에서 그의 앞에 서서
그의 노를 돌이켜 멸하시지 아니하게 하였도다

이 섹션은 모세가 율법을 받기 위해 시내 산 정상으로 올라간 뒤에 한동안 돌아오지 않자 아론이 사람들에게서 모은 금으로 송아지를 만들고 그 송아지가 그들을 이집트에서 인도해 낸 여호와라고 했던 사건을 회고하고 있다(19절, cf. 출 32장; 신 9:12-17). 하나님과 언약을 맺은 곳이 어이없게 하나님을 배신하는 장소가 되었다. 이는 제2계명을 위반하는 행위였다(cf. 출 20:4-6). 아론을 중심으로 그들은 결코 해서는 안 될 일을 한 것이다. 이스라엘이 자기 영광(하나님)을 풀이나 뜯어먹는 소의 형상으로 바꾼 일이었기 때문이다(20절). 그들은 이 일을 통해 찬란히 빛나는 영광의 하나님(cf. 출 24장)을 숭배하지 않고 물질을 숭배했다(Schaefer, VanGemeren). 말을 못하는 소(송아지)는 말씀하시고 행동하시는 하나님을 절대 상징할 수 없다. 그러므로 그들이 금송아지가 바로 그들을 이집트에서 인도해내신 여호와라며 절을 했지만, 우상에게 절한 것이지 하나님을 경배한 것은 아니다(Goldingay, cf. 신 4장).

이스라엘은 어떻게 아론이 만든 금송아지가 여호와라고 생각했을까? 이집트에서 큰일을 행하신 그들의 구원자 하나님을 잊었기 때문이다(21절). 그들은 주님이 이집트에서 온갖 기적을 베푸시고, 홍해에서 상상을 초월하는 놀라운 일을 행하신 하나님을 잊었다(22절). 만일 한 순간이라도 그들이 출애굽을 이루신 하나님을 생각하고 기념했다면, 이런 일은 저지르지 않았을 것이다(Tucker & Grant). 망각이 또 죄로 연결되고 있다. 그러므로 성경은 주님을 기념하라는 권면을 자주 한다.

그들이 하나님을 완전히 잊지는 않았을 것이다. 그들은 하나님의 이름이 여호와이며, 많은 기적을 행하신 일을 직접 목격한 자들이다. 그러나 하나님에 대한 지식이 그들의 삶에 어떠한 영향을 미치지는 않았다. 그들은 예전에 이집트에서 노예로 살던 방식을 벗어나지 못했고, 하나님이 무엇을 위해 그들을 구원하셨는지 알지 못했다. 그러므로 그들은 주님을 경험하기 전과 후에 별반 다를 바 없는 삶을 살았다.

분노하신 하나님은 그들을 모두 죽이기를 원하셨다(23a절, cf. 출 32:9-10; 신 9:25). 이스라엘 사람 모두를 죽이시고 모세를 통해 새로운 민족을 시작하겠다고 하셨다. 그러나 모세가 눈물로 애원하여 아론과 백성들을 살려냈다. 기자는 이때 모세가 어려움 가운데에서 주님 앞에 서서 호소했다고 하는데, '어려움 가운데'(בַּפֶּרֶץ)는 성벽이 무너지기 전에 갈라진 틈이 생기는 현상을 묘사하는 단어이다(NIDOTTE, cf. 새번역, 현대인, NIV, NAS, ESV, NRS, TNK). 이 사건이 초래한 가장 심각한 결과는 하나님과 이스라엘 사이에 '틈'이 생긴 일이다. 모세는 마치 틈이 생긴 성벽을 적들로부터 방어하기 위해 그 틈에 서서 죽을 각오로 싸우는 군인처럼 눈물로 기도하며 '틈을 메꾼 것'이다. 모세의 용감한 기도에 감동하신 하나님이 다시 한번 그들을 용서하시고 자비를 베푸셨다(Anderson). 이 순간에도 하나님의 이 같은 용서와 자비가 가능하다는 것이 기자가 암시하는 바이다.

5. 땅 약속을 믿지 않음(106:24-27)

[24] 그들이 그 기쁨의 땅을 멸시하며
그 말씀을 믿지 아니하고
[25] 그들의 장막에서 원망하며
여호와의 음성을 듣지 아니하였도다
[26] 이러므로 그가 그의 손을 들어 그들에게 맹세하기를
그들이 광야에 엎드러지게 하고
[27] 또 그들의 후손을 뭇 백성 중에 엎드러뜨리며
여러 나라로 흩어지게 하리라 하셨도다

이 섹션은 가데스 바네아에서 있었던 반역을 회고한다(cf. 민 13-14장). 이스라엘은 지파별로 한 사람씩 선발하여 가나안으로 40일 동안 정탐을 보냈다. 정탐꾼들의 보고에 의하면 땅은 비옥한데 거주민들이 문제였다. 그들은 수도 많았지만 참으로 덩치가 큰 백성이어서 이스라엘은 그들 앞에 메뚜기와 같다고 했다.

보고를 들은 백성들은 하나님께 도움을 청하거나 주님의 약속을 믿기는커녕 오히려 주님을 원망하며 말씀을 믿지 않았다(24-25절). 이때까지 지난 2년 동안 하나님이 행하신 온갖 기적과 이적을 경험한 사람들이 왜 이렇게 하나님을 불신했을까? 게다가 그들은 홍해에서는 하나님의 약속을 믿었었다(cf. 12절). 그런데 어느덧 불신자들로 변질되었던 것이다! 홍해에서 찬양하던 그들이(12절) 이곳에서는 원망하는 자들이 되었다(25절). 역시 기적은 사람을 변화시키지 못하며, 죄 문제도 해결하지 못하는 듯하다. 기자는 이러한 행위를 '기쁨의 땅'(אֶרֶץ חֶמְדָּה)(cf. 렘 3:19; 슥 7:14), 곧 그들을 행복하게 하는 땅을 스스로 멸시한 일이라고 한다(24a절).

결국 하나님은 손을 들어 맹세하시어 원망하는 그들을 심판하셨다(cf. 민 14:22-23). 손을 들어 맹세한다는 것은 절대 되돌릴 수 없는 맹세를 뜻한다(Longman). 이때 반역한 사람들 모두가 광야에서 죽을 것이라고 하셨고, 그렇게 되었다. 40년이 지나면서 출애굽 1세대 중에서 20세 이상 성인이었던 사람들은 모두 죽었다. 유일한 예외는 다수와는 달리 긍정적인 보고를 했던 여호수아와 갈렙이었다(cf. 민 14:38).

한 가지 특이한 것은 기자가 27절을 통해 하는 말은 민수기 13-14장에는 없다는 것이다. 아마도 자기 세대가 바빌론으로 끌려와 사는 것이 옛적 가데스 바네아에서 그들의 조상이 하나님께 반역했던 일과 별반 다를 바가 없다는 의미에서 여기에 첨부하는 듯하다. 그들은 가데스 바네아에서 반역하여 약속의 땅에서 살지 못했고, 자신들은 약속의 땅에서 반역하여 약속의 땅에서 쫓겨났다. 두 그룹 모두 약속의 땅에서 살 수 없는 것이 매일반이다.

6. 광야에서 우상을 숭배함(106:28-33)

28 그들이 또 브올의 바알과 연합하여
죽은 자에게 제사한 음식을 먹어서
29 그 행위로 주를 격노하게 함으로써
재앙이 그들 중에 크게 유행하였도다
30 그 때에 비느하스가 일어서서 중재하니
이에 재앙이 그쳤도다
31 이 일이 그의 공의로 인정되었으니
대대로 영원까지로다
32 그들이 또 므리바 물에서 여호와를 노하시게 하였으므로
그들 때문에 재난이 모세에게 이르렀나니

[33] 이는 그들이 그의 뜻을 거역함으로 말미암아
모세가 그의 입술로 망령되이 말하였음이로다

본 텍스트가 회고하고 있는 반역 사건은 브올 산에서 생긴 일(민 25장)과 므리바에서 있었던 일(출 17:1-7; 민 20:1-12)이다. 기자는 이스라엘이 브올의 바알과 연합했다고 한다(28a절). '브올의 바알'(בַּעַל פְּעוֹר)은 브올 산의 주인이라는 뜻이며, 모압 사람들이 숭배하던 신들 중 하나이다. '연합하다'(צמד)는 '같이 멍에를 지다'는 뜻이다(VanGemeren, cf. HALOT). 하나님의 백성이 브올의 바알과 함께 멍에를 졌다는 것은 이 우상을 숭배하는 자들이 되었다는 뜻이다. 매우 심각한 범죄다.

더 나아가 그들은 '죽은 자들'(מֵתִים)에게 제사한 음식을 먹었다(28b절). 본문에서 '죽은 자들'은 이미 죽은 사람들을 의미할 수 있고(McCann, cf. 개역개정, 새번역, ESV, NAS, NRS, TNK), 죽은 신들(생명이 없는 신들)을 의미할 수도 있다(Allen, Hossfeld-Zenger, VanGemeren, cf. 아가페, 현대인, 공동, NIV, CSB). 둘 중 어느 해석을 택하든 별로 중요하지는 않다. 둘 다 하나님의 진노를 사기에 충분한 반역 행위이기 때문이다(29a절).

이스라엘의 어처구니없는 우상 숭배에 진노하신 하나님은 그들 중에 재앙을 내리시어 크게 유행하도록 하셨다(29절). 재앙이 걷잡을 수 없이 퍼져 나갔다는 뜻이다. 민수기는 이때 염병이 돌아 24,000명이 죽었다고 한다(민 25:8-9).

아론의 손자인 제사장 비느하스가 한 이스라엘 남자가 미디안 여자와 장막 안으로 들어가는 것을 보고 뒤쫓아가 둘을 모두 죽였다(민 25:7-8). 이 일을 계기로 하나님이 내리신 재앙이 멈췄다(30b절). 기자는 비느하스가 한 일을 하나님과 이스라엘 사이에 중재한 것이라고 한다(30a절). 비느하스는 범죄자들을 죽임으로써 하나님의 분노를 달랠 수 있었던 것이다.

비느하스가 한 일은 '공의'(צְדָקָה)로 인정되어 영원히 기념될 것이다

(31절). 일부 주석가들은 그의 공의가 대대로 인정된다는 것이 그의 제사장직이 영원히 지속될 것이라고 해석하지만(VanGemeren), 단순히 그의 의로운 행위가 두고두고 기념될 일이라는 뜻으로 해석하는 것이 바람직하다(cf. 아가페, 현대인, 공동, NIV, NAS, ESV, TNK).

이스라엘의 불신이 므리바 물과 연관된 사건은(32절) 성경에 두 차례 기록되어 있다. 그들이 홍해를 건너 시내 산으로 가는 도중 마실 물이 없다며 하나님을 원망했다가 모세가 바위에게 명령하여 물을 내게 한 곳이 므리바 혹은 맛사라고 불린다(출 17:1-7). '므리바'(מְרִיבָה)는 '다툼'이라는 의미를 지녔으며, '맛사'(מַסָּה)는 '시험함'이라는 뜻을 지녔다(cf. NIDOTTE). 이때는 모세가 하나님의 책망을 받지 않았다. 모든 것이 순조롭게 진행되었다.

모세가 바위에서 물을 내다가 하나님의 책망을 받아 가나안에 들어가지 못하게 된 사건은 민수기 20장에 기록되어 있다. 가나안 입성을 약 1년 앞둔 시점에 미리암이 가데스에서 죽었다. 이때 이스라엘 백성들이 물에 대해 모세를 원망했으며, 하나님은 모세에게 바위에게 명령하여 물을 내서 백성들이 마시게 하라고 하셨다. 그러나 화가 머리끝까지 난 모세는 바위에게 명령한 것이 아니라 가지고 있던 지팡이로 두 차례나 힘껏 내리쳤다. 바위에서 물은 나왔지만, 하나님은 모세가 바위에게 명령하지 않고 내리쳤다며 그는 가나안에 들어갈 수 없다고 선언하셨다(민 20:13). 이곳에서도 다툼이 있었다 하여 '므리바 물'(מֵי מְרִיבָה)이라고 했다. '므리바'는 다툼을 뜻하는 일반 명사이기 때문에 이 두 곳을 칭하는 지명으로 사용된 것이다.

기자가 회고하고 있는 므리바 사건은 민수기 20장에 기록되어 있는 두 번째 사건이다. 이스라엘은 이때까지 40년 동안 매일 기적을 체험하며 살아왔지만, 언제든지 이방인들의 문화와 우상 숭배를 흠모할 준비가 되어 있었다(VanGemeren). 이러한 이스라엘의 '죄 중독증'은 가나안 정착 이후에도 계속되었다(cf. 삿 2:1-3). 결국 이스라엘이 하나님을 노하게 했는데, 그 여파가 그들에게만 영향을 끼친 것이 아니라, 모세에게도 미쳤다. 모세가 그들의 불신으로 인해 자기 입술로 망령되이 말하였기 때문이다.

그때 모세는 “반역한 너희여 들으라. 우리가 너희를 위하여 이 반석에서 물을 내랴!”라고 외쳤다(민 20:10). 하나님은 모세가 이 말로 인해 이스라엘이 보는 앞에서 주님의 거룩함을 나타낼 만큼 신뢰하지 않았다며 그의 말과 행동을 문제 삼으셨다(민 20:12). 저자는 이 사건을 회고하면서 그들 때문에 재난이 모세에게 이르렀다고 한다(32절). 일부 학자들은 이 사건뿐만 아니라, 이스라엘의 지속적인 반역과 불신이 모세에게 이런 벌을 내리게 했다고 해석하기도 한다(Allen, Goldingay, Hossfeld–Zenger).

7. 약속의 땅을 피로 더럽힘(106:34–39)

34 그들은 여호와께서 멸하라고 말씀하신
그 이방 민족들을 멸하지 아니하고
35 그 이방 나라들과 섞여서
그들의 행위를 배우며
36 그들의 우상들을 섬기므로
그것들이 그들에게 올무가 되었도다
37 그들이 그들의 자녀를
악귀들에게 희생제물로 바쳤도다
38 무죄한 피 곧 그들의 자녀의 피를 흘려
가나안의 우상들에게 제사하므로
그 땅이 피로 더러워졌도다
39 그들은 그들의 행위로 더러워지니
그들이 행동이 음탕하도다

기자는 이스라엘이 약속의 땅 가나안에 입성하여 어떻게 살았는지를 요약적으로 회고하고 있다. 이 섹션은 여호수아서—열왕기에 기록된 이스라엘의 삶을 간략하게 정리하고 있다. 여호와께서는 이스라엘이 가나안에 입성하기 전에 가나안 사람들을 진멸하라고 누누이 말씀하셨다(34절). 이스라엘은 가나안 사람들과 다르게 살아야 한다는 명령을 받았다(Tucker & Grant). 만일 이스라엘이 다르게 살기를 거부하고 그들을 살려 두면 이스라엘이 그들의 우상 숭배와 죄에 동요될 것이다(35–36a절). 그러나 이스라엘은 하나님의 말씀을 거역하고 가나안 사람들 대부분을 살려 두었다(cf. 삿 1장). 다르게 살기를 거부한 것이다. 결국 이스라엘이 살려준 가나안 사람들은 이스라엘에게 올무가 되었다(36b절, cf. 삿 2장).

이스라엘이 가나안 사람들의 우상 숭배와 죄에 동요된 결과는 참혹했다. 그들은 자신들의 자녀들을 악귀들에게 희생제물로 바치기 일쑤였다(37절, cf. 레 18:21; 신 12:31; 왕하 16:3; 21:6; 23:10; 렘 7:31; 19:5). 또한 자기 자녀들의 무고한 피로 우상들에게 제사하는 일로 인해 복된 땅, 곧 약속의 땅을 피로 더럽혔다(38절, cf. 렘 2:7, 23; 겔 20:30–31, 43; 호 5:3). 결국 그들은 이처럼 야만적인 우상 숭배와 무고한 피흘림으로 스스로를 더럽혔다(39a절). 기자는 이런 그들의 행동을 음탕하다고 한다(39b절). '음탕하다'(זנה)는 '창녀 짓을 하다'라는 뜻을 지녔으며, 구약에서 민족이나 나라가 음탕하다는 것은 그들이 우상을 숭배했다는 뜻이다(cf. 출 34:15–16; 신 31:16; 사 1:21; 렘 2:20; 호 2:2–13). 이스라엘은 우상 숭배자들이 되었다.

8. 포로로 끌려감(106:40–46)

[40] 그러므로 여호와께서 자기 백성에게 맹렬히 노하시며
자기의 유업을 미워하사

41 그들을 이방 나라의 손에 넘기시매
그들을 미워하는 자들이 그들을 다스렸도다
42 그들이 원수들의 압박을 받고
그들의 수하에 복종하게 되었도다
43 여호와께서 여러 번 그들을 건지시나
그들은 교묘하게 거역하며
자기 죄악으로 말미암아 낮아짐을 당하였도다
44 그러나 여호와께서 그들의 부르짖음을 들으실 때에
그들의 고통을 돌보시며
45 그들을 위하여 그의 언약을 기억하시고
그 크신 인자하심을 따라 뜻을 돌이키사
46 그들을 사로잡은 모든 자에게서
긍휼히 여김을 받게 하셨도다

이스라엘이 약속의 땅을 우상 숭배와 죄로 물들일 때 하나님은 무엇을 하셨는가? 만일 하나님이 방관만 하셨다면 하나님에게도 어느 정도의 책임이 있다고 할 수 있다. 시내 산에서 맺어진 관계는 이스라엘이 죄를 짓고 방황하면 하나님이 그들을 쳐서라도 돌이키게 하시는 것을 전제하기 때문이다.

기자는 하나님이 할 만큼 하셨다고 회고한다. 여호와께서는 범죄한 이스라엘에게 맹렬히 노하시고 심지어 미워하기까지 하셨다(40절). 이스라엘을 이방 나라의 손에 넘겨 그들이 이스라엘을 억압하고 다스리도록 하셨다(41절). 이 말씀에는 포로기가 포함되어 있다(VanGemeren). 그러다가 이스라엘이 하나님께 부르짖으면 이방인들의 손에서 그들을 구원하기를 여러 차례 반복하셨다(43a절). 그때마다 그들은 죄와 우상 숭배로 가득한 자신들의 생각을 버리지 않고 그 생각대로 하나님을 거역하여 스스로 더 낮아졌다(43b-c절). 이스라엘은 참으로 형편없는 삶을 스스로 택하여 구원할 가치가 없는 사람들로 전락했다는 것이다.

이스라엘이 너무 고통스러워 다시 하나님께 부르짖으면, 하나님은 그들의 울부짖음에 응답하셨다(44절). 주님은 그들과 맺은 언약을 기억하시고 그들에게 큰 자비를 베푸셔서 그들을 억압하는 자들에게서 해방시키셨다(45절). 하나님은 억압하는 자들에게 억압한 자들이 자비를 베풀도록 하셨다(46절). 출애굽 사건의 시작을 연상케 하는 표현이다(cf. 출 2:23-25; 3:7-9). 하나님이 이스라엘을 아무리 구원하시고 자비를 베푸셔도 그들은 경건해지지 않았다. 오히려 시간이 지날수록 더 타락할 뿐이었다. 결국 그들의 구원은 하나님의 자비에 달린 것이지, 그들의 행실에 의해 결정되는 것이 아니었다. 우리의 삶을 돌아보게 하는 대목이다.

9. 귀향을 이루실 하나님 찬양(106:47)

47 여호와 우리 하나님이여
우리를 구원하사 여러 나라로부터 모으시고
우리가 주의 거룩하신 이름을 감사하며
주의 영예를 찬양하게 하소서

기자는 과거에 여호와께서 여러 차례 이스라엘을 용서하시고 회복시키셨던 것을 근거로(cf. 40-46절) 그가 당면하고 있는 현실적인 문제에 대해 하나님께 호소한다. 그는 지금 타국에 끌려와 살고 있다. 그러므로 그는 하나님이 옛적에 하셨던 것처럼 포로가 되어 타국으로 끌려온 주의 백성을 다시 구원하셔서 약속의 땅으로 인도하시기를 간구한다.

주님이 그렇게 해 주시는 날, 주의 백성은 주님의 거룩하신 이름에 감사하며, 주님께 영광을 돌리며 찬양할 것이다. 기자가 주의 백성의 회복을 가장 간절히 바라는 이유는 이런 일을 경험한 후 그들이 주님의 이름을 목청껏 찬양하고 주님께 마음껏 경배하고자 해서이다. 우리의 찬양을 받기를 기뻐하시는 하나님은 분명히 이러한 기자의 바람을 허락하실 것이다.

10. 제4권을 마무리하는 찬양(106:48)

48 여호와 이스라엘의 하나님을 영원부터 영원까지 찬양할지어다
모든 백성들아 아멘 할지어다
할렐루야

시편 90편으로 시작된 제4권이 마무리되고 있다. 이 말씀이 원래 106편에 속한 것인지, 혹은 편집자들이 제4권의 끝을 알리기 위해 따로 삽입한 것인지 확실하지는 않다(cf. Goldingay). 다만 106편이 '할렐루야'로 시작했고, 이 구절이 다시 '할렐루야'로 마무리되는 것으로 보아 원래 이 말씀이 106편의 일부였을 가능성을 배제할 필요는 없다(cf. VanGemeren).

제4권이 마무리되는 시점에 이스라엘은 아직도 바빌론에 억류되어 있다. 그러므로 그들의 여호와를 향한 찬양은 신뢰와 확신의 고백이다. 그들은 제4권을 통해 많은 것을 기도했다. 이제 그들은 하나님이 그들의 기도를 들으실 것을 확신하며 이 고백으로 책을 마무리하고 있다.

기자는 설령 하나님이 그들의 기도에 응답하지 않으실지라도 주의 백성들은 영원부터 영원까지 여호와를 찬양할 것을 주문한다. 권면을 받은 백성들은 아멘으로 화답할 것이다. 온 공동체가 하나가 되어 있다. 할렐루야!

시편 Ⅲ

90–150편

제5권(107–150편)

시편을 구성하고 있는 다섯 권 중 마지막 책이며, 107–150편이 이 섹션에 포함되어 있다. 제3권이 나라와 성전을 잃은 슬픔을 노래했고, 제4권이 바빌론으로부터 하나님이 '새로운 출애굽'을 이루실 것을 기대했다면, 이 섹션은 이 기대에 확신을 더한다. 그러므로 제5권은 처음 네 권보다 더 많은 찬양과 '할렐루야 시'로 구성되어 있다.

하나님이 꼭 구원을 이루실 것이라는 기대는 무엇에 근거한 것인가? 바로 하나님의 말씀이다. 그러므로 이 섹션에서는 하나님의 말씀을 상징하는 율법에 대한 찬양이 가장 장엄하게 울려 퍼진다(cf. 119편). 성경에서 찬양하면 빼놓을 수 없는 사람이 다윗이다. 그러므로 제3권과 4권에서는 거의 모습을 보이지 않던 다윗이 제5권에서는 표제에 자주 등장한다. 하나님은 자기 백성의 말씀에 대한 반응이나 순종에 관여치 않으시고 이미 선포하신 말씀에 따라 주의 백성을 구원하시고 인도하실 것이다. 말씀은 주의 백성을 구원할 능력을 지닌 것이다.

제107편

I. 장르/양식: 회중 찬양시(cf. 29편)

시편 105-107편이 서로 비슷한 언어와 주제를 사용하여 저작된 것을 보면 제4권과 제5권의 경계선은 어느 정도 유동적이라 할 수 있다(Goldingay). 105편과 106편은 이스라엘 역사에서 가장 중요한 사건에 대해 회고했다. 107편은 이 두 편이 드린 간절한 기도에 대한 응답이라 할 수 있다(Tucker & Grant). 또한 제4권처럼 제5권도 제3권이 제시한 위기에 대한 대응이라는 점도 이 두 권의 성향을 잘 보여준다(McCann).

제4권을 마무리한 시편 106:47은 주의 백성을 열방에서 모아 달라고 기도하고 있는데, 5권을 시작하는 107편에서는 이러한 기도가 응답이 된 듯하다(deClaissé-Walford et al., Goldingay, McCann, Hossfeld-Zenger). 이 시편이 여호와께서 기도를 들으시고, 바빌론 포로 생활을 끝내시고 새로운 출애굽을 이루실 것을 기대하고 있기 때문이다. 또한 106편과 107편은 같은 말로 시작한다는 공통점도 지녔다.

우리는 감사시의 가장 확실한 모델인 이 노래를 회중 찬양시로 구분하지만(Anderson, cf. Brueggemann & Bellinger), 모두 다 동의하는 것은 아니다. 개인 찬양시라는 이도 있고(McCann), 감사-지혜시(thanksgiving-wisdom psalm)라고 하는 이들도 있다(Ross, VanGemeren, cf. Beyerlin). 이 시편이 두 장르로 구성되었다고 하는 사람들은 1-32절은 선포적 찬양시(declarative praise psalm)이며, 32-42절은 지혜시(wisdom psalm)라고 한다.

시의 장르에 대해 이 같은 혼란이 초래되는 것은 이 노래가 한 곳에서 한 저자에 의해 저작되지 않았기 때문일 것이다. 일부 학자들은 이 시편 전체가 포로기 이전에 저작된 것이라 하지만(Calvin, cf. Perowne, Terrien), 대부분 학자들은 이 노래는 원래 왕정 시대에 성전에서 감사 제물을 드리며 부른 노래인 1-32절에 포로로 끌려간 사람들이 바빌론 혹은 페르시아 시대에 33-43절을 더해 자신들의 노래로 바꾼 것이라고 한다(Allen, Anderson, Kraus, deClaissé-Walford et al., cf. McCann). 또한 상당수의 학자들은 이 노래 전체가 포로기 혹은 그 이후 시대에 저작되고 사용된 것이라 하기도 한다(Goldingay, Terrien, VanGemeren).

이 시편은 어떤 정황에서 처음 사용된 것일까? 정확히 알 수는 없지만, 성전에서 진행된 예배에서 사용된 것이라고 하기도 하고(Weiser), 열방에서 예루살렘으로 모여든 순례자들의 노래라고 하기도 한다(Terrien). 2-3절을 근거로 이 노래는 예루살렘으로 돌아온 귀향민들이 성전에서 예배를 드리며 부른 노래로서 4-32절이 묘사하고 있는 네 가지 상황은 그들이 바빌론에서 돌아오면서 경험한 일들이라고 하는 학자도 있다(Snaith). 이 네 가지 상황 중 바다를 건넌 일(23-32절)은 디아스포라 유태인들이 배를 타고 고향으로 돌아온 일로 해석하는 이도 있다(Allen). 이 네 가지 상황을 상징적으로 해석해야 한다는 학자들은 이 네 가지 정황은 하나님이 자기 백성을 구원하시는 다양한 방법을 묘사할 뿐 실제적으로 있었던 일을 회고하는 것은 아니라고 한다(Goldingay, Hossfeld-Zenger, Tucker & Grant). 아마도 예루살렘으로 돌아온 귀향민들이 하나님의 구원의 범위가 얼마나 넓은 지를(cf. 4-32절) 찬양하는 노래인 듯하다.

II. 구조

이 시편을 섹션으로 구분하는 것은 쉬운 일이다. 대부분 학자들은 이 시편을 1-3절, 4-32절, 33-42절, 43절 네 파트로 구분한다. 두 번째 섹션인 4-32절은 주께서 자기 백성을 구원하시는 네 가지 시나리오를 담고 있다고 생각한다. 이 섹션은 알덴(Alden)이 제시하는 구조이다.

A. 찬양 권면(1-3절)
　B. 하나님이 사막에 있는 자들을 구원하심(4-9절)
　　C. 하나님이 어둠 속에 있는 자들을 구원하심(10-16절)
　　　D. 어리석은 자들이 회개하고 구원을 얻음(17-22절)
　　C'. 하나님이 깊은 곳에 있는 자들을 구원하심(23-32절)
　B'. 하나님이 사막에 있는 자들을 구원하심(33-42절)
A'. 지혜 권면(43절)

위 구조에 의하면 하나님이 어둠 속에 있는 자들을 구원하시는 일(C)과 깊은 곳에 있는 자들을 구원하시는 일(C')이 평행을 이루는데, 23-32절은 바다 속 깊은 곳에 있는 자들을 구원하시는 것이 아니라, 바다의 수면 위에서 항해하는 자들을 구원하시는 일을 묘사하고 있다. 따라서 둘이 대칭이 될 수는 없다. 그러므로 4-32절의 구조는 하나님이 두 가지 죄로부터 자기 백성을 구원하시는 일(10-16절, 17-22절)이 두 개의 혼돈에서 하나님이 자기 백성을 구원하시는 일(무질서를 상징하는 사막[4-9절]과 바다[23-32절])로 감싸여 있는 것으로 이해함이 바람직하다(Mejia).

또한 4-32절을 구성하고 있는 하나님의 네 가지 구원 사례는 모두 동일한 패턴에 따라 묘사되며 이 섹션의 통일성과 점집성을 유지하고 있다: (1) 위기 설명, (2) 주님께 드린 기도, (3) 구원이 임함, (4) 감사. 알덴(Alden)은 위 구조를 통해 4-42절의 통일성을 주장하지만, 이 섹션의 통일성은 32절에서 끝난다. 다음 도표를 참조하라.

	4-9절	10-16절	17-22절	23-32절
위기	4-5	10-12	17-18	23-27
기도	6	13	19	28
구원	7	14	19-20	29
감사	8-9	15-16	21-22	30-32

이러한 이해를 바탕으로 이 주석에서는 다음과 같은 구조에 따라 본문을 주해해 나갈 것이다.

A. 감사 권면(107:1-3)
B. 감사할 이유(107:4-32)
1. 광야에 임한 하나님의 구원(107:4-9)
2. 억압된 자들에게 임한 하나님의 구원(107:10-16)
3. 병든자들에게 임한 하나님의 구원(107:17-22)
4. 바다에 임한 하나님의 구원(107:23-32)
B′. 찬양할 이유(107:33-42)
A′. 지혜 권면(107:43)

III. 주해

이 노래는 창조주의 피조물에 대한 사랑, 특별히 자기 백성에 대한 사랑을 깊이 묵상하게 한다. 하나님의 사랑은 주님의 '인자하심'(חֶסֶד)으로 가장 잘 묘사되는데(cf. 1, 43절), 하나님이 언약을 맺으신 백성을 끝까지 보살피신다는 뜻이다(Tucker & Grant). 그러므로 하나님의 인자하심은 죄로 인해 주님의 도움을 필요로 하는 모든 백성에게 반드시 임한다. 시편은 이러한 사실을 노래하다가 마지막 절에서는 이 사실을 알려 주는 지혜에 순응하라고 권면한다(Gerstenberger).

1. 감사 권면(107:1-3)

> [1] 여호와께 감사하라
> 그는 선하시며 그 인자하심이 영원함이로다
> [2] 여호와의 속량을 받은 자들은 이같이 말할지어다
> 여호와께서 대적의 손에서 그들을 속량하사
> [3] 동서남북 각 지방에서부터 모으셨도다

제5권을 시작하는 이 시편의 시작은 제4권을 마무리하는 106편과 시작이 같다(1절, cf. 106:1). 이곳에서는 단지 106편을 시작했던 첫 단어 '할렐루야'(הַלְלוּיָהּ)가 빠졌을 뿐이다. 기자는 106편과의 이 같은 연결고리를 형성하여 독자들이 이 노래를 106편과 함께 읽고 묵상하기를 기대하는 듯하다(McCann, Tucker & Grant). 106편은 과거에 백성들의 지속적인 반역에도 불구하고 그들에게 끝까지 '인자'(חֶסֶד)를 베푸시고 용서하신 하나님을 찬양했다. 이 노래는 하나님의 인자하심이 포로가 되어 타국으로 끌려온 주의 백성들에게 다시 임했음을 찬양한다. 그러므로 106편이 하나님의 선하시고 인자하심이 영원할 것을 기대하며 부른 노래라면, 이 시편은 기자가 이미 경험한 일을 토대로 주님의 선하심(טוֹב)과 인자하심(חֶסֶד)이 영원하다는 확신으로 부르는 찬양이다.

하나님께 감사하라는 권면이 주님의 은혜를 체험한 모든 사람을 대상으로 하고 있지만, 여호와의 속량을 받은 자들은 더욱더 하나님께 감사해야 하며 자신들이 경험한 일을 다른 사람들에게 알려 여호와의 선하시고 인자하심에 대해 증언해야 한다(2a절). '여호와의 속량을 받은 자들'(גְּאוּלֵי יְהוָה)은 사람이 기업 무를 자의 권한을 행하여 값을 치르고 친척을 구하듯 하나님이 구원하신 이들이며, 출애굽 사건과 연관되어 자주 사용되었다(출 6:6; 15:13; 시 74:2; 77:16). 하나님이 속량하신 사람들은 원래 그들이 있어야 할 곳으로 돌아왔으며, 그들이 잃었던 유

산/기업도 되찾았다는 것을 암시한다. 그러므로 '속량을 받은 자들'은 바빌론 포로 생활에서 돌아온 사람들을 뜻할 수 있다(cf. 사 41:14; 44:6; 47:4; 48:17; 60:16; 63:16). 하나님의 구원을 경험한 사람들은 당연히 자신들이 경험한 하나님의 놀라운 은혜를 찬양해야 하며 다른 사람들이 하나님을 알도록 주님의 선하심과 인자하심을 알려야 한다.

주의 백성이 자유를 얻어 다시 각자의 기업으로 돌아온 것은 하나님이 하신 놀라운 일의 결과였다. 주님은 원수들의 손에서 그들을 속량하셨으며 동서남북 각 지방에서부터 모으셨다(2b-3절). 주의 백성을 그들을 억압하는 원수들에게서 구원하는 일은 결코 쉽지 않다. 원수들이 놓아주려 하지 않았을 것이기 때문이다. 그러므로 하나님은 원수들이 저항할 수 없는 큰 능력을 발휘하여 그들을 해방시키셨다. 출애굽 때 하나님이 이집트 왕을 꼼짝 못하게 하신 일을 생각나게 한다.

하나님은 이러한 해방 사역을 세상 모든 곳을 상징하는 '동서남북 각 지방에서' 하셨다. 마소라 사본은 '남북'대신 '북쪽과 바다쪽'(מִצָּפוֹן וּמִיָּם)이라 하지만 의미는 '남북'으로 충분하다(Jarick). 세상의 네 방향을 가리키는 동서남북은 총체성을 상징한다. 세상 어디든 주의 백성이 끌려간 곳으로 가셔서 그들을 억압하는 자들의 손에서 구원하시어 조국으로 돌아오게 하셨다는 것이다. 그러므로 이 말씀은 어느 특정한 지역에서 구원 사역을 이루신 것이 아니라 세상 모든 곳에서 자기 백성을 구원하셨다는 일반적인 내용을 회고하고 있는 것으로 해석하는 것이 바람직하다. 또한 세계 곳곳에서 자기 백성을 구원하셨다는 내용 때문에 많은 학자들은 이 시를 포로기 이후에 예루살렘으로 돌아온 사람들이 부른 노래라고 한다(cf. Allen, Grogan, McCann, VanGemeren).

2. 광야에 임한 하나님의 구원(107:4-9)

4 그들이 광야 사막 길에서 방황하며

거주할 성읍을 찾지 못하고
[5] 주리고 목이 말라
그들의 영혼이 그들 안에서 피곤하였도다
[6] 이에 그들이 근심 중에 여호와께 부르짖으매
그들의 고통에서 건지시고
[7] 또 바른 길로 인도하사
거주할 성읍에 이르게 하셨도다
[8] 여호와의 인자하심과 인생에게 행하신
기적으로 말미암아 그를 찬송할지로다
[9] 그가 사모하는 영혼에게 만족을 주시며
주린 영혼에게 좋은 것으로 채워주심이로다

기자는 앞 섹션에서 하나님이 세상 곳곳에서 이루신 구원을 찬양하라고 했다. 지금부터는 4-32절을 통해 하나님의 구원 사역이 얼마나 포괄적이고 대대적으로 이루어졌는가를 네 가지 사례를 통해 묘사한다. 이미 언급한 것처럼 이 사례들을 실제적이고 특정한 역사적 정황을 배경으로 해석하려는 것보다는 구원의 다양성과 광범위함을 상징하는 것들로 해석하는 것이 바람직하다(Beyerlin, Goldingay, Hossfeld-Zenger). 4-32절이 묘사하는 네 사례 중 두 개는 죄에서 자기 백성을 구원하시는 주님의 구원 사역을, 두 개는 위협적인 환경(무질서)에서 자기 백성을 구원하시는 하나님의 사역을 묘사하고 있다(Mejia, cf. VanGemeren). 이 중 본문은 첫 번째 위협적인 환경인 광야에서 구원을 이루시는 하나님의 자비를 찬양한다.

근동 지역 광야(사막)는 생존하기가 매우 어려워 사람들이 기피하는 곳이었다. 물이 귀하고 먹을 것도 얻기가 쉽지 않았다. 그러므로 사막에서 길을 잃고 방황하면 생명에 큰 위험을 받게 되었다. 기자는 주의 백성들이 광야에서 길을 헤매 거주할 성읍을 찾지 못하고 방황하다가 생명에 위협을 받는 순간을 묘사한다(4-5절). 이 말씀이 이집트를 떠나 40년 동안 광야를 헤맨 출애굽 1세대 이야기, 혹은 바빌론에서 광야 길 1,500킬로미터를 걸어 예루살렘으로 돌아온 귀향민들의 이야기를 배경으로 할 수도 있다.

그러나 저자는 본문을 통해 하나님은 자기 백성이 광야에서 길을 잃고 죽어갈 위기에 처한다고 할지라도 그 위험한 환경에서 그들을 구원하신다며, 메마른 광야가 하나님의 구원하시는 자비를 막을 수 없다는 것을 하나의 사례로 제시한다. 광야가 언급된다고 해서 반드시 출애굽 사건이나, 바빌론에서 돌아온 사건과 연관시킬 필요는 없다.

목이 마르고 지쳐 죽을 위기에 처한 사람들이 하나님의 구원을 얻는 방법은 매우 간단하다. 여호와께 부르짖어 자신이 처한 상황에 대해 기도하면 된다(6a절). 특히 자신이 처한 근심(고난)에 대해 하나님께 아뢰면 된다. 그렇게 하면 하나님은 '그들이 당면하고 있는 고통'(מִמְּצוּקוֹתֵיהֶם)에서 건지실 것이며(6b절), 그들이 처한 문제를 곧바로 해결해 주실 것이다. 하나님은 목이 마르고 지쳐 죽을 지경에 처한 백성이 기도하면 곧바로 그들에게 물을 주시고 생기를 북돋아 주신다.

주님은 죽을 지경에 이른 백성을 살리실 뿐만 아니라, 그들의 길도 인도해 주시어 원래 그들이 가고자 했던 성읍으로 안내하신다(7절). 한 주석가는 이 성읍이 예루살렘이라고 해석하는데(Briggs), 이 말씀을 하나의 구원 사례를 말하고 있는 것으로 간주한다면, 굳이 구체적으로 한 도시를 특정할 필요는 없다. 애초에 그들이 광야에서 길을 헤맨 것이 화근이었는데, 주님은 인도하심을 통해 그 화근을 원천적으로 차단하신다. 그러므로 하나님의 구원하시는 은혜를 체험한 사람들은 자신들이 경험한 일(하나님의 기적)을 회상하며 주님을 찬양해야 한다(8절).

또한 이 같은 간증을 들은 우리도 그들과 함께 주님을 찬양해야 한다. 하나님은 주님을 간절히 사모하는 영혼에게 만족을 주시며, 주린 영혼들을 좋은 것으로 채워 주시는 분임을 찬양해야 한다(9절). 본문에서 '만족을 주다'(שׂבע)는 목마른 영혼이 마음껏 마시도록 하신다는 뜻이다(cf. 사 66:11, 암 4:8). '채우다'(מלא)는 배고픈 사람이 좋은 것을 마음껏 먹어 배가 부르다는 뜻이다(cf. HALOT). 하나님은 우리가 만족할 때까지 우리의 필요를 넘치도록 채우시는 분이다.

3. 억압된 자들에게 임한 하나님의 구원(107:10-16)

10 사람이 흑암과 사망의 그늘에 앉으며
곤고와 쇠사슬에 매임은
11 하나님의 말씀을 거역하며
지존자의 뜻을 멸시함이라
12 그러므로 그가 고통을 주어
그들의 마음을 겸손하게 하셨으니
그들이 엎드러져도 돕는 자가 없었도다
13 이에 그들이 그 환난 중에 여호와께 부르짖으매
그들의 고통에서 구원하시되
14 흑암과 사망의 그늘에서 인도하여 내시고
그들의 얽어 맨 줄을 끊으셨도다
15 여호와의 인자하심과 인생에서 행하신
기적으로 말미암아 그를 찬송할지로다
16 그가 놋문을 깨뜨리시며
쇠빗장을 꺾으셨음이로다

앞 섹션에서는 물이 없어 생명을 위협하는 광야에서 자기 백성을 구원하시는 하나님을 찬양한 기자가 이 섹션에서는 죄로 인해 하나님께 벌을 받은 사람이 어떻게 다시 주님의 구원을 경험하게 되는가를 말한다. 그는 죄로 인해 하나님께 벌을 받은 사람을 사슬에 묶여 감옥에 갇혀 있는 자로 묘사한다(Hossfeld-Zenger). 기자는 죄인이 당면하고 있는 절망적인 속박을 강조하기 위해 고통과 억압과 연관된 다양한 표현을 사용한다: '환난, 고통, 흑암, 사망, 그늘, 얽어 맨 줄'(13-14절, cf. McCann). 속박된 사람은 어떠한 자유도 누릴 수 없는 상황이다. 사람이 죄의 노예가 되면 이렇게 된다.

기자는 비유를 곤고와 사슬에 묶여 흑암과 사망의 그늘에 앉아 있는 처량한 사람의 이야기로 시작한다(10절). 이러한 표현이 바빌론 포로생활을 뜻할 수 있지만(cf. Tucker & Grant, VanGemeren), 단순히 죄인이 죄로 인해 속박되어 있는 모습을 묘사하는 것일 수도 있다(cf. Beyerlin). 그가 전혀 움직일 수 없게 묶여 죽음의 그늘 아래 있는 것은 하나님의 말씀을 거역하고 주님의 뜻을 멸시했기 때문이다(11절). 그러므로 곤고와 쇠사슬에 묶여 사망의 그늘 아래 있는 것은 죄인에 대한 비유이지 사람이 실제로 이렇게 있다는 뜻은 아니다. 사람이 죄를 지으면 죄책감과 죄가 초래하는 부정적인 결과에 사로 잡혀 있게 된다는 사실을 비유하는 것이다.

죄인이 죄와 결과로 인해 억압을 받는 것은 하나님의 죄인에 대한 심판이기도 하다(12a절). 하나님은 겸손하게 하기 위해 죄인들에게 벌을 주신다(12b절). 결국 벌을 받은 죄인들은 엎드러져도 돕는 자가 없다(12c절). 친구들도 그들 곁을 떠난다. 하나님이 심판하셨기 때문이다. 온갖 억압과 속박으로 죄인은 외롭고 고통스럽다. 문제를 해결하기 위해 자신이 할 수 있는 일이 하나도 없다는 사실이 더욱 절망적이다.

이러한 상황에서 죄인이 할 수 있는 유일한, 또한 가장 효과적인 일은 주님께 부르짖는 것이다(13a절). 죄를 지었을 때 우리를 벌하시는 이는 하나님이시지만, 또한 우리를 죄의 억압과 속박에서 해방시키실 수 있는 유일한 분도 하나님이시다. 주님은 환난 중에서 부르짖는 백성을 모른 체하지 않으신다. 그들을 얽어 맨 줄을 끊으시고 흑암과 사망의 그늘에서 인도해 내신다(13b-14절). 죄가 죄인에게 가할 수 있는 모든 억압과 속박에서 자유하게 하시는 것이다.

그러므로 주님의 구원을 경험한 사람은 주님이 그에게 행하신 인자하심과 기적으로 말미암아 주님을 찬송해야 한다(15절). 은혜는 수혜자가 베푸는 이에게 감사할 때 배가 된다. 하나님이 부르짖는 죄인을 구원하시는 일은 언제나 가능하며, 하나님의 구원의 능력에는 한계가 없다. 주님은 세상에서 가장 크고 무거운 놋문을 깨뜨리시고 쇠빗장을 꺾으시며 갇혀 있는 자들을 구원하시는 분이기 때문이다. 언제든 주님은 자기 백성을 구원하실 능력을 갖추고 계신다. 죄는 우리를 억압하고 짓누르지만, 하나님은 그런 우리를 언제든 속박에서 해방시키실 수 있다. 하나님은 죄의 영향력보다 더 크신 분이기 때문이다.

4. 병든자들에게 임한 하나님의 구원(107:17–22)

17 미련한 자들은 그들의 죄악의 길을 따르고
그들의 악을 범하기 때문에 고난을 받아
18 그들은 그들의 모든 음식물을 싫어하게 되어
사망의 문에 이르렀도다
19 이에 그들이 그들의 고통 때문에 여호와께 부르짖으매
그가 그들의 고통에서 그들을 구원하시되
20 그가 그의 말씀을 보내어 그들을 고치시고
위험한 지경에서 건지시는도다
21 여호와의 인자하심과 인생에서 행하신 기적으로 말미암아
그를 찬송할지로
22 감사제를 드리며 노래하여
그가 행하신 일을 선포할지로다

누가 죄를 짓는가? 기자는 '미련한 자들'(אֱוִלִים)이라고 한다(17절). 죄

의 영향력이 얼마나 심각하다는 사실을 잘 아는 정직하고 지혜로운 자들은 죄를 멀리하기 때문이다(cf. 41–42절). 그러므로 죄의 영향력을 의식하지 못하여 죄를 짓는 사람들은 미련하다 할 수 있다.

때로는 죄가 사람의 영혼만 결박하고 짓누르는 것이 아니라, 육체에도 영향을 미친다. 죄인이 죄의 결과로 인해, 혹은 죄책감으로 인해 모든 음식물을 멀리하거나 먹을 수 없을 때가 있다(18절). 그러므로 죄인이 심각한 병을 앓는 자로 묘사되고 있다(Grogan). 이러한 상황이 오래 지속되면 죽음의 문턱에 이르게 된다. 우리가 이러한 상황에 처하게 되면 어떻게 해야 살 수 있는가?

기자는 이번에도 하나님의 인자하심을 믿고 주님께 부르짖는 것밖에는 방법이 없다고 한다(19a절). 죽게 된 죄인들이 하나님께 기도하면 하나님은 고통에서 그들을 구원하시고 더 나아가 자기 말씀으로 그들을 고치시고 위험한 지역에서 건져 내신다(20절). 20절의 의미를 새번역이 잘 살렸다: "단 한 마디 말씀으로 그들을 고쳐 주셨고, 그들을 멸망의 구렁에서 끌어내어 주셨다." 하나님은 죄인을 구원하시기 위해 죄인을 직접 찾아오실 필요가 없다. 자신이 계신 곳에서 한 마디만 하시면 모든 문제가 해결된다. 하나님의 한 마디 말씀은 그들을 위험에서 건지실 뿐만 아니라 그들의 병도 고치신다. 하나님의 말씀은 치유와 회복의 전령이 되는 것이다(cf. Goldingay, VanGemeren). '고치다'(רפא)는 병을 치료한다는 뜻이다. 하나님은 병석에서 부르짖는 죄인을 용서하시고 치료하신다.

그러므로 하나님의 인자하심(חֶסֶד)과 기적으로 죽음을 면하고 죄를 용서받은 사람은 당연히 주님을 찬양해야 한다(21절). 더 나아가 감사제를 드리며 하나님을 찬양하고 온 세상에 주님이 그에게 행하신 일을 알려야 한다(22절). 하나님이 우리에게 은혜를 베푸시는 일에는 그 은혜를 경험한 우리가 온 세상에 하나님이 하신 일을 알리게 하기 위한 목적도 포함되어 있다.

5. 바다에 임한 하나님의 구원(107:23-32)

23 배들을 바다에 띄우며
큰 물에서 일을 하는 자는
24 여호와께서 행하신 일들과
그의 기이한 일들을 깊은 바다에서 보나니
25 여호와께서 명령하신즉
광풍이 일어나 바다 물결을 일으키는도다
26 그들이 하늘로 솟구쳤다가 깊은 곳으로 내려가나니
그 위험 때문에 그들의 영혼이 녹는도다
27 그들이 이리저리 구르며
취한 자 같이 비틀거리니
그들의 모든 지각이 혼돈 속에 빠지는도다
28 이에 그들이 그들의 고통 때문에 여호와께 부르짖으매
그가 그들의 고통에서 그들을 인도하여 내시고
29 광풍을 고요하게 하사
물결도 잔잔하게 하시는도다
30 그들이 평온함으로 말미암아 기뻐하는 중에
여호와께서 그들이 바라는 항구로 인도하시는도다
31 여호와의 인자하심과 인생에게 행하신 기적으로 말미암아
그를 찬송할지로다
32 백성의 모임에서 그를 높이며
장로들의 자리에서 그를 찬송할지로다

기자는 4-32절에서 네 가지의 구원 시나리오를 제시하면서 제일 먼저 혹독한 자연환경을 상징하는 광야에서의 구원을 묘사했다(cf. 4-7절). 그 다음 영혼을 자유하게 하는 구원(cf. 10-16절)과 육체를 질병에

서 해방하는 구원(cf. 17–22절)을 노래했다. 이제 그는 다시 혹독한 자연 환경에서 자기 백성을 구원하시는 하나님을 찬양한다. 그러나 이번에는 물이 없는 광야가 아니라, 물이 너무 많아 위험한 바다에서의 구원이다. 그러므로 이 네 구원은 '환경(A)—죄(B)—죄(B′)—환경(A′)'의 구조를 보이고 있다(cf. Mejia). 처음 세 구원 사례(4–22절)는 시편 다른 곳에서도 언급이 되는 여호와의 구원 사례와 연관이 있지만, 바다에서 구원하시는 네 번째 사례는 시편에서 이곳이 유일하다(McCann).

광야는 물이 너무 없어 위험한 곳이지만, 바다는 물이 너무 많아 위험한 곳이다. 그러므로 광야와 바다는 한 쌍을 이루며 하나님은 어떠한 극단적인 환경에서도 자기 백성을 구원하신다는 진리를 강조한다(cf. Hossfeld–Zenger). 이 비유의 배경으로 우리가 가장 쉽게 상상할 수 있는 곳은 큰 바다인 지중해이다(cf. 23절의 '큰 물').

바다를 삶의 터전으로 삼고 살아가는 사람들은 항상 태풍과 파도의 위협에 노출되어 있다. 마치 대상(隊商, caravan)을 형성하여 광야를 오가는 사람들이 목마름의 위협에 노출되어 있는 것처럼 말이다(cf. 4–7절). 광야를 지나는 사람들이 때로는 메마른 광야에서 하나님이 하시는 기이한 일들을 경험하거나 목격하는 것처럼, 바다를 항해하는 사람들도 하나님이 하시는 기이한 일들을 깊은 바다에서 목격하거나 경험한다(23–24절). '그의 기이한 일들'(נִפְלְאוֹתָיו)은 하나님이 일상적으로 하시는 기적 같은 일들을 뜻한다. 본문에서는 광풍 등 천재지변을 의미한다.

평온한 바다에 광풍이 일 때마다 아무리 경험이 많은 선원이라 할지라도 오금이 저린다. 광풍은 곧 파도로 이어지고 큰 파도는 언제든 배를 삼킬 수 있기 때문이다(25–26절). 이런 일이 있을 때마다 양초가 녹아내리듯 선원들의 영혼은 녹아내린다. '십 년을 감수하는 경험'인 것이다. 더 커다란 문제는 광풍과 파도에 대처할 방법이 없다는 사실이다. 그저 선원들은 바다의 출렁임에 따라 이리저리 구르며 술에 취한 사람처럼 비틀거리다가 바다가 잠잠해지기를 간절히 바랄 뿐이다(27a-b절). 육체가 이처럼 구르고 비틀거릴 때에는 정신도 몽롱해진다(27c절). 영과 육에 성한 틈이 없다.

이번에도 위기를 벗어날 수 있는 유일한 방법은 하나님께 부르짖는 것이다(28절). 하나님은 그들의 신음소리를 들으시고 그들을 구원하신다(28절). 광풍과 파도로 소용돌이 치던 바다가 잔잔하도록 하시는 것이다(cf. 욘 1:15; 마 8:26). 또한 그들의 배를 목적지까지 안전하게 인도하신다(29-30절).

주님의 인자하심에 따라 구원을 입은 사람들은 자신들이 경험한 일을 생각하며 하나님을 찬송해야 한다(31절). 또한 주변 사람들에게 하나님이 그들을 위해 하신 일을 증거하며 주님을 경배해야 한다(32절). 경배와 찬양은 은혜를 입은 사람이 하나님께 보이는 당연한 반응이다.

위 네 가지 사례를 보면 공통점들이 있다. 첫째, 사람들은 자신들이 곤경에 처해야만 하나님께 부르짖는다. 미리 평온할 때에도 하나님께 간절히 기도하면 더 좋을 텐데 말이다. 둘째, 하나님은 가장 혹독한 환경에 처하거나 죄에 가장 무겁게 짓눌려 있는 사람들의 기도를 들어주는 자비를 베푸신다(cf. Mays, Tucker & Grant). 어떠한 환경에서도 여호와의 자비(헤세드)는 사람들을 구원한다(McCann). 셋째, 하나님은 곤경에 처한 사람들을 구원하실 뿐만 아니라, 그들이 가야 할 길도 인도하신다. 주님의 자비로움은 우리가 위기를 탈출하도록 하시는 일에서 멈추지 않고, 우리의 앞길도 책임져 주신다. 넷째, 은혜를 경험한 사람은 반드시 하나님의 자비에 감사하며 온 세상에 주님이 하신 일을 알려야 한다. 놀라운 은혜를 입은 사람이 먼저 은혜를 베푸신 분에게 예물을 드리며 감사하는 것은 매우 오래된 종교적 전통이다(Gerstenberger). 또한 주님이 베풀어 주시는 은총은 우리를 위한 것으로 끝날 것이 아니라, 더 나아가 세상을 가르치는 효과를 발휘해야 한다.

6. 찬양할 이유(107:33-42)

33 여호와께서는 강이 변하여 광야가 되게 하시며
샘이 변하여 마른 땅이 되게 하시며
34 그 주민의 악으로 말미암아
옥토가 변하여 염전이 되게 하시며
35 또 광야가 변하여 못이 되게 하시며
마른 땅이 변하여 샘물이 되게 하시고
36 주린 자들로 말미암아 거기에 살게 하사
그들이 거주할 성읍을 준비하게 하시고
37 밭에 파종하며 포도원을 재배하여
풍성한 소출을 거두게 하시며
38 또 복을 주사 그들이 크게 번성하게 하시고
그의 가축이 감소하지 아니하게 하실지라도
39 다시 압박과 재난과 우환을 통하여
그들의 수를 줄이시며 낮추시는도다
40 여호와께서 고관들에게는 능욕을 쏟아 부으시고
길 없는 황야에서 유리하게 하시나
41 궁핍한 자는 그의 고통으로부터 건져 주시고
그의 가족을 양 떼 같이 지켜 주시나니
42 정직한 자는 보고 기뻐하며
모든 사악한 자는 자기 입을 봉하리로다

이미 앞에서 언급한 것처럼 많은 학자들이 포로기 혹은 그 이후 시대인 왕정 시대에 저작된 1-32절에 이 섹션이 더해졌다고 생각한다(cf. McCann). 기자는 이 섹션에서 하나님의 살리고 죽이시는 절대적인 주권을 강조한다(Brueggemann & Bellinger). 창조주 하나님은 우리가 사는 환경을 언제든 바꾸실 수 있다.

첫째, 여호와께서는 강이 변하여 광야가 되게 하시고 샘이 변하여 마른 땅이 되게 하신다(33절). 자신이 사는 땅은 강과 샘이 있어 물 부족은 없다고 자만하지 말라는 경고이다. 하나님은 언제든지 강과 샘을 광야처럼 마르게 하실 수 있기 때문이다.

그렇다면 어떠한 상황에서 강과 샘이 변화하여 마른 사막으로 변하는가? 바로 그 땅에 사는 사람들이 죄를 지을 때이다(34a절). 성경은 우리가 사는 땅은 우리의 죄로 인해 오염된다는 사실을 누누이 강조한다(cf. 창 3, 4, 6-9장). 인간의 죄로 오염된 땅은 하나님의 심판을 받아 생산력을 잃거나 사람이 살 수 없는 땅으로 몰락한다. 그러므로 사람들이 죄를 지으면 하나님은 그들이 사는 땅이 옥토라 할지라도 언제든 염전으로 변하게 하실 수 있다.

둘째, 하나님은 메마른 광야와 마른 땅이 변하여 못과 샘물이 되게 하신다(35절). 하나님이 메마른 땅을 옥토로 변하게 하시는 일은 옥토를 염전으로 변하게 하시는 일만큼 쉽고 간단하다. 그렇다면 언제 메마른 땅이 옥토로 변하는가? 인간이 죄를 지으면 땅이 황폐해진다는 34절은 그 땅에 사는 사람들이 하나님께 부르짖고 회개할 때 메마른 땅이 옥토로 변하는 것을 암시한다.

하나님은 옥토로 변한 땅에 주린 자들이 살게 하신다. 그들은 그곳에 성읍을 세우고 농산물을 재배하며 풍성한 소출을 누리게 될 것이다(36-37절). '주린 자들'(רְעֵבִים)은 먹을 것이 없어서 배고픈 사람들을 뜻한다. 그들이 거하던 땅이 광야였을 때에는 먹을 것이 없었다. 이제는 양식을 걱정할 필요가 없게 되었다. 하나님은 그들에게 복을 주셔서 크게 번성하게 하시고, 그들의 가축들도 번성하게 하신다(38절). 그들이 이러한 변화를 누리게 된 것은 주님께 부르짖고 죄를 회개했기 때문이다.

자기 백성의 부르짖음에 많은 것으로 축복하신 하나님은 언제든 그들이 죄를 지으면 다시 억압하시고 그들의 숫자를 낮추실 수 있다(39절). 고관들과 상류층이라 할지라도 하나님의 심판을 피해갈 수는 없다(cf. Goldingay). 그들도 광야에서 길을 찾지 못하고 방황하며 살 수 있다(40절). 반면에 궁핍한 자는 고통에서 건져 주시고 마치 목자가 양 떼를 지키듯이 그의 가족을 지켜 주실 것이다(41절). 본문에서 '궁핍한 자'(אֶבְיוֹן)는 죄를 회개하고 하나님께 부르짖는 사람이다(cf. VanGemeren). 자신들의 영혼이 얼마나 궁핍한가를 익히 아는 사람들이다. 주님이 이런 사람은 반드시 곤경에서 구하고 보호해 주실 것이다. 그러나 회개하지 않는 자들은 고관들이라 할지라도 심판을 받을 것이다(40절).

하나님이 죄를 회개하는 자들은 반드시 구원하시고 보호하시지만, 하나님께 부르짖기를 거부하는 악인들은 신분의 높음에 상관없이 심판하시는 것을 보고 정직한 자들이 기뻐한다(42a절). 그들이 꿈꾸는 세상이기 때문이다. '정직한 자들'(יְשָׁרִים)은 곧은 길을 가는 사람들을 뜻한다. 삶에서 항상 바른 길을 추구하는 자들이다. 반면에 모든 사악한 자들은 자기 입을 닫는다(42b절). '모든 사악한 자'(כָּל־עַוְלָה)는 불의와 부정을 행하고 즐기는 자들이다(cf. NIDOTTE). 그들이 침묵하는 것은 하나님이 다스리시는 세상에 그들이 있을 만한 곳이 없다는 것을 깨달았기 때문이다.

7. 지혜 권면(107:43)

43 지혜 있는 자들은 이러한 일들을 지켜보고
여호와의 인자하심을 깨달으리로다

기자는 하나님은 온갖 어려운 환경에 처한 사람들의 부르짖음을 들으시고 구원하시며, 자기 죄를 회개하는 사람들을 해방시키고 인도하신다고 했다. 반면에 악인들은 신분이 높은 사람이라 할지라도 벌하신다고 했다. 이제 그는 우리가 하나님의 이 같은 통치 원리에서 배우기를 원한다. 특히 '여호와의 (큰) 인자하심'(חַסְדֵי יְהוָה)에 대해 깨닫기를 간절히 바란다. 만일 깨달음이 없다면 그가 이 노래를 통해 가르치고자 했던 모든 것이 허사가 되기 때문이다.

제108편

다윗의 찬송 시

I. 장르/양식: 회중 탄식시(cf. 12편)

시편의 마지막 모음집인 제5권을 시작했던 107편은 아무런 표제를 지니지 않았다. 이 시를 포함한 세 시편(108–110편)은 표제를 지녔는데, 모두 '다윗'을 언급한다. 표제가 다윗의 이름을 언급하는 시편이 그룹으로 등장하기는 제2권 이후 처음이다. 제3–4권에서는 종종 한 편씩 등장했다. 제5권 모음집의 마지막 부분이라 할 수 있는 138–145편도 다윗과 연관된 시들이다. 그러므로 제5권의 시작과 끝이 다윗과 연관된 표제들을 지닌 노래들로 구성되어 있으면서 중앙에 있는 시들을 감싸고 있다. 제4권에서 다윗과 연관된 시는 고작 둘(101편, 103편)이라는 점을 감안하면 이례적이라 할 수 있다.

이러한 현상에 대해 일부 학자들은 포로기 이후 시대가 다윗 왕조의 회복에 관심을 가지고 있었던 일을 보여주는 것이라고 해석한다(Hossfeld–Zenger). 반면에 이 모음집에서 다윗은 왕이 아니라 기도하는 사람의 모범 사례가 되고 있다며, 모든 성도가 다윗처럼 기도할 것을 권면하기 위해서 다윗의 이름이 모음집 시작과 끝에 등장한다고 한다(Wilson). 포로기 이후에는 이스라엘이 더 이상 왕의 통치에 대해 큰 관심을 갖지 않았던 점을 고려하면(cf. 역대기), 다윗과 연관된 표제들은 우리가 하나님을 어떻게 경배하고 찬양해야 하는가를 가르쳐 주는 듯하다.

이 노래는 개인 탄식시인 57편과 공동체 탄식시인 60편을 재인용하여 구성한 노래이다. 1–5절은 시편 57:7–11을, 6–13절은 시편 60:5–12을 도입했다. 이러한 현상은 당시 편집자들이 필요에 따라 일부 시편을 재구성/재인용 하는 관례를 반영하고 있다(cf. McCann). 이 시편의 분위기는 57편이나 60편의 것보다 더 밝다(Grogan).

표제는 이 노래가 "다윗의 찬송 시"(שִׁיר מִזְמוֹר לְדָוִד)라며 짤막하게 표기하고 있는데, 1–5절의 출처가 되는 57편은 "다윗의 믹담 시, 인도자를 따라 알다스헷에 맞춘 노래, 다윗이 사울을 피하여 굴에 있던 때에"라는 상당히 긴 표제를 지녔다. 또한 6–13절의 근원이 되는 60편은 "다윗이 교훈하기 위하여 지은 믹담, 인도자를 따라 수산에듯에 맞춘 노래, 다윗이 아람 나하라임과 아람소바와 싸우는 중에 요압이 돌아와 에돔을 소금 골짜기에서 쳐서 만 이천 명을 죽인 때에"라는 시편에서 가장 긴 표제를 지녔다. 두 시편의 정황은 다르지만, 모두 다윗과 연관된 표제를 지녔다는 공통점을 지니고 있다. 이 시편 기자는 57편과 60편과 연관된 긴 표제들을 무시하고 간단히 '시, 다윗의 찬송'(מִזְמוֹר לְדָוִד שִׁיר)이라며 '시'(שִׁיר)라는 새로운 장르를 시작하고 있다(Tucker & Grant).

이 시편을 편집한 저자는 언제, 어떤 목적을 가지고 이미 존재하는 노래들 중 두 섹션을 인용하여 새로운 노래를 만든 것일까? 이미 존재하는 시편들을 인용하고 재구성하여 새로운 노래를 만드는 일은 포로기 이후 시대에 종종 있었던 일이라며, 이 노래가 포로기 이후 시대에 저작된 것이라는 주장이 있다(Allen, Botha, cf. Terrien). 이 시대에 새로운 시를 저작하여 정경에 포함되도록 하는 것보다 이미 정경으로 받아들여지는 시편들을 인용하여 새로운 시를 저작하는 것이 정통성을 인정받는데 훨씬 더 쉬웠기 때문이라고 한다.

그러나 저자들이 어떠한 목적으로 이러한 유형의 시편들을 저작했는지는 도저히 알 수 없다는 비관적인 견해도 팽배하다(Kraus, cf. McCann). 이 시편 안에서 단수와 복수가 교차 사용되는 것을 근거로 이 노래를 개인 탄식시로 분류하는 사람이 있다(Terrien). 이 시가 개인 탄식시인지 혹은 회중 탄식시인지는 그다지 중요하지 않지만 이 주석에서는 회중 탄식시로 구분하여 주해해 나가고자 한다(cf. deClaissé–Walford et al.). 단수와 복수가 교차 사용되는 것은 아마도 포로기 이후 시대에 총독 등 지도자가 백성들을 대신해서 하나님께 기도하고 있기 때문일 것이다(Goldingay). 고통을 당하는 성도가 하나님을 찬양하고 하나님의 신탁을 추구하는 일은 삶에서 항상 있는 일이다. 그러므로 이 시편의 적용 범위는 영원하다고 할 수 있다.

II. 구조

이 시편이 다른 시편들을 인용하여 저작되었다는 이유로 아예 구조를 제시하기를 거부하는 학자들도 있다(Kraus). 그러나 인용도 분명 해석을 전제하며, 해석은 새로운 메시지 구상을 전제한다. 또한 메시지는 그 메시지를 담을 텍스트 구조가 있음을 암시한다. 원래는 1–5절과 6–13절이 각각 다른 시편에서 도입되었기 때문에 5절과 6절 사이에 주요 나눔(division)이 있어야 한다고 생각할 수도 있다. 그러나 내용을 보면 5절과 6절은 서로 다른 시편에서 도입되었음에도 불구하고 전혀 끊김이 없는 '호소'(petition)를 구성하고 있다. 이 주석에서는 다음과 같은 구조를 바탕으로 본문을 주해해 나가고자 한다.

A. 감사 찬양(108:1–4)
  B. 구원 간구(108:5–6)
    C. 구원하시겠다는 신탁(108:7–9)
    C′. 신탁을 실현하시기를 기도함(108:10–11)

B′. 구원 간구(108:12)
A′. 신뢰와 확신(108:13)

III. 주해

큰 어려움을 경험한 주의 백성들이 자신들의 어려운 처지에 대해 낙심하지 않고 그들을 구원하실 여호와를 찬양하며 주님께 도와 주실 것을 호소한다. 그들의 기도를 들으신 하나님은 그들을 꼭 구원하실 것이라며 신탁을 주신다. 신탁을 받은 백성들은 하나님이 속히 구원을 이루실 것을 호소한다.

1. 감사 찬양(108:1-4)

[1] 하나님이여
내 마음을 정하였사오니
내가 노래하며
나의 마음을 다하여 찬양하리로다
[2] 비파야, 수금아, 깰지어다
내가 새벽을 깨우리로다
[3] 여호와여 내가 만민 중에서 주께 감사하고
뭇 나라 중에서 주를 찬양하오리니
[4] 주의 인자하심이 하늘보다 높으시며
주의 진실은 궁창에까지 이르나이다

이 시편 기자가 찬양으로 노래를 시작하는 것은 그가 처한 상황이 평안해서가 아니다. 이 섹션이 인용하고 있는 시편 57편이 노래된 정황을 보면 그의 생명을 노리는 원수들의 온갖 방해와 위협이 사라진 것은 아니다. 단지 하나님이 그 모든 위험에서 그를 보호하실 것을 믿고 확신하니 걱정이 되지 않을 뿐이다. 그는 환란 속에서 주님만이 주실 수 있는 평안을 맛보게 되었고, 그 평안에 대해 이렇게 감사하고 있다.

저자는 세상 일로 걱정할 시간에 창조주 하나님을 찬양하기로 마음을 정했다. 그는 오로지 하나님을 찬양하겠다는 확고한 의지를 강조하기 위해 "내 마음을 정했다"(נָכוֹן לִבִּי)는 말로 노래를 시작한다(1절). 절대 흔들리지 않을 것을 각오했다는 것이다. '정하다'(כון)는 어떠한 경우에도 요지부동한 결정을 한다는 뜻이다(cf. HALOT). 그는 원수들의 공격(cf. 12-13절)에도 아랑곳하지 않고 주님을 믿고 찬양할 것을 다짐했다. 그가 처한 상황에 상관없이 하나님께 충성하기로 다짐했기 때문이다(Botha).

그는 목소리로만 주님을 노래하는 것이 아니라, 마음을 다해(1절) 온갖 악기와 함께 주님을 찬양하고자 한다(2절). 대부분 번역본들이 '마음'으로(cf. 새번역, 공동, 아가페, NIV, NAS, NRS, TNK) 번역한 '영광'(כָּבוֹד)은 생명/영혼을 의미한다. 기자는 영혼을 담은 찬양으로 주님을 경배하고자 한다.

기자는 새벽 이미지를 사용하여 노래를 이어가고 있다. 이점을 강조하기 위해 '깨우다'(עור)가 2절에서 두 차례 사용된다. 그는 악기들을 깨우고자 한다. 곧 하나님을 찬양하는 일로 새벽을 깨우려고 하는 것이다(2절). 성경에서 새벽은 하나님의 구원이 임하는 시간이다(Brueggemann & Bellinger). '새벽을 깨우다'는 무엇을 의미하는가? 일부 주석가들은 이 표현을 가나안 신화와 연결시키지만(cf. Dahood, Hossfeld-Zenger), 별 설득력이 없다. 두 가지 해석이 가능하다. 첫째, 하나님을 찬양하며 밤을 새겠다는 뜻이다(Kraus, cf. McCann). 한국 교회의 정서에 빗대자면 철야기도를 하겠다는 것이다. 둘째, 하루를 하나님에 대한 찬양으로 시작하겠다는 의미이다(Tucker & Grant, VanGemeren). 한국 교회의 정서에 빗대자면 새벽기도로 하루를 시작하겠다는 것이다.

어느 해석을 선호하든 중요하지 않다. 중요한 것은 하나님을 찬송하는 것이 그의 삶을 가득 채운다는 사실이다. 시편에서는 고통이 짙은 밤으로, 구원이 날이 밝음으로 묘사되는 경우가 여러 차례 있다(cf. 시 5:3; 30:5; 59:16; 88:13; 130:5-6). 이 사실과 연결해서 해석하면 기자는 아침이 되면 분명 하나님의 구원이 그에게 임하리라는 믿음을 근거로 새벽을 기도와 찬양으로 깨우고자 하는 것이다.

더 나아가 기자는 온 열방 앞에서도 주님께 감사하며 찬양하겠다고 서원한다(3절). '만민'(עַמִּים)과 '뭇 나라'(אֻמִּים)는 분명히 이스라엘의 범위를 초월하는 개념들이다(cf. HALOT). 그러므로 일부 주석가들은 9절이 포로기 이후 시대에 이 노래가 공동체의 노래로 개작된 증거라고 한다(Gerstenberger, Wilson). 그러나 기자가 지금은 제한된 공간인 성전에서 주님을 찬양하지만, 언젠가는 온 세상이 지켜보는 곳에서 주님의 위대하심을 노래하고자 하는 비전을 선포하는 것일 수도 있다(cf. Goldingay).

그가 찬송할 내용은 하나님의 '인자하심'(חֶסֶד)이 얼마나 큰지 가장 높은 하늘에 닿고, 주님의 '진리/성실하심'(אֱמֶת)은 궁창(대기)을 가득 채운다는 사실이다(4절). 이처럼 은혜가 끝이 없고 항상 신뢰와 믿음으로 우리의 삶을 가득 채우시는 하나님이시니 어찌 찬양하지 않을 수 있겠는가!

2. 구원 간구(108:5-6)

5 하나님이여
주는 하늘 위에 높이 들리시며
주의 영광이 온 땅에서 높임 받으시기를 원하나이다
6 주께서 사랑하시는 자들을 건지시기 위하여
우리에게 응답하사 오른손으로 구원하소서

앞 섹션에서 기자는 하나님의 인자하심이 하늘보다 높고 주님의 진실은 궁창에 이른다고 했다(cf. 4절). 이처럼 위대하신 하나님을 어찌 우리 가슴에만 품을 수 있겠는가! 그러므로 그는 하나님이 하늘보다 더 높이 들리시며, 주님의 영광이 온 세계보다 더 높아지기를 간절히 원한다(5절).

하나님을 찬양한 저자는 주님께 구원을 간구한다(6절). 모든 사람은 아니더라도 최소한 주께서 사랑하시는 자들, 곧 주님이 구원하기를 기뻐하시는 사람들을 구원해 달라는 기도다(6a절). 하나님은 사랑하는 사람이 오랫동안 곤경에 처하는 일을 결코 묵인하지 않으실 것이다.

그는 주님이 그들을 구원하실 때 오른손으로 하시라고 한다(6b절). 오른손은 두 손 중에서도 능력과 베풂의 상징이다. 기자는 하나님이 의인들을 구원하실 때 그 누구도 대항할 수 없는 확고한 능력으로 하실 것을 기도하고 있다.

3. 구원하시겠다는 신탁(108:7–9)

[7] 하나님이 그의 성소에서 말씀하시되
내가 기뻐하리라
내가 세겜을 나누며
숙곳 골짜기를 측량하리라
[8] 길르앗이 내 것이요
므낫세도 내 것이며
에브라임은 내 머리의 투구요
유다는 나의 규이며
[9] 모압은 내 목욕통이라
에돔에는 내 신발을 벗어 던질지며
블레셋 위에서 내가 외치리라 하셨도다

기자의 간절한 기도에 하나님이 응답하셨다. 이 신탁이 성전에서 일하는 제사장을 통해서, 혹은 선지자를 통해서 온 것인지는 알 수 없지만(cf. Kraus), 분명 하나님은 이 말씀을 그에게 주셨다. 그런데 메시지나 의도가 잘 이해되지 않는 신탁이다. 기자는 "그래 네가 기도한 것처럼 내가 너희를 구하겠다"식의 신탁을 기대했을 것이다. 그런데 실제로 그에게 전달된 주님의 말씀은 마치 동문서답처럼 느껴진다.

하나님은 '그의 성소에서'(בְּקָדְשׁוֹ) 말씀하셨는데, 성전 사역과 연관된 누군가가 이 말씀을 기자에게 전달해 주었다는 뜻이다. 하나님이 기도를 들으시고 말씀을 하신 것은 참으로 반갑고 좋은 일이다. 주님의 구원을 기대할 수 있기 때문이다.

개역개정은 하나님이 하신 첫 말씀(אֶעְלֹזָה)을 "내가 기뻐하리라"(7b절)로 번역했는데, 만족스러운 번역은 아니다. 새번역은 의미를 보강하기 위하여 "내가 크게 기뻐하련다"로, 공동번역은 "나 이제 흔연히 일어나리라"로, 아가페는 "전쟁에서 승리하셨으니"(cf. 현대인)로 번역했다. 이 동사(עלז)는 '승리하다'는 의미를 지녔다(HALOT). 그러므로 이 말씀은 하나님이 전쟁에 패하여 탄식하며 기도하는 주의 백성에게 그들이 두려워하는 적들과 전쟁은 주님께 전혀 문제가 되지 않으며, 하나님이 그들을 상대로 이미 승리하셨다고 선언하는 것이다.

승리하신 하나님은 세겜을 나누고 숙곳 골짜기를 측량하신다(7c-d절). 주인이 자기 땅을 마음대로 하는 모습이다. 이어 하나님은 길르앗과 므낫세도 자기 소유라고 하신다(8a-b절). 세겜과 숙곳과 길르앗과 므낫세 네 지명 모두 북 왕국 이스라엘과 연관이 있으며(cf. ABD) 이 시편에서는 이스라엘을 상징하는 총체성을 지녔다. 세겜은 요단 강 서편에, 숙곳은 바로 강 건너 동편에 위치했다. 길르앗은 요단 강 동편에, 므낫세는 동편과 서편에 땅을 받았는데, 본문에서는 서편을 염두에 두고 있다. 그러므로 이 네 지리적 이름은 요단 강 동편과 서편을 아우르는 북 왕국 전체를 상징한다. 북 왕국을 통틀어 에브라임라고도 하는

데 이 이름이 등장하는 것도 이러한 의미를 부각시키는 듯하다.

일부 주석가들은 이 지명들이 국가적인 탄식시에 언급되는 이유는 북 왕국 이스라엘이 앗시리아의 손에 멸망했기 때문이라고 한다. 이 노래는 주전 722년쯤에 북 왕국의 멸망을 배경으로 불린 노래라는 것이다. 이렇게 해석할 경우 이 섹션이 언젠가는 주께서 멸망한 북 왕국 이스라엘을 다시 회복시키실 것을 다짐하는 것으로 이해할 수 있다.

그러나 그렇게 단정할 필요는 없다. 이 도시들이 언급이 되는 것은 하나님의 그들에 대한 소유권과 특별한 관계를 강조하기 위해서이다(cf. deClaissé-Walford et al., Goldingay). 이어지는 두 행에서 에브라임은 주님의 투구로, 유다는 주님의 규에 비유되는 것을 보면 이러한 사실이 더 확실해진다(8c-d절). 투구는 전쟁 무기다. 그러므로 일부 학자들은 에브라임이 언제든 하나님이 사용하실 수 있는 무기로 존재하고 있음을 암시하는 말씀이라고 한다(Mowinckel). 권세를 상징하는 규는 하나님이 소중하게 여겨 애착을 가지고 항상 가지고 다니시는 물건이다. 반면에 모압과 에돔과 블레셋은(9절) 이스라엘의 전통적인 원수들이며(Brueggemann & Bellinger, cf. 출 15:14-15), 하나님이 이용하시고는 정복하시는 나라들이다. 그들은 하나님의 애착이 가는 소유물이 아니며, 특별한 관계를 맺은 나라들도 아니다. 게다가 10절이 에돔을 정복하는 것을 갈망하는 것으로 보아, 이 노래는 우리가 알지 못하는 에돔과 연관된 사건에 관한 노래이다.

이 말씀을 통해 하나님은 전쟁에서 패하고 돌아와 탄식하는 주의 백성들에게 염려하지 말라고 당부하신다. 주님이 자기 백성에게 패배를 안겨준 자들을 상대로 승리하실 것이기 때문이다. 이점을 강조하기 위하여 본문은 모압과 에돔과 블레셋 세 나라를 언급한다(9절). 이 나라들은 주의 백성을 계속 괴롭혀온 전통적인 적들이며 남쪽에서 주의 백성을 포위하고 있는 나라들이다(블레셋: 남서쪽, 모압과 에돔: 남동쪽). 이 세 나라 중 하나의 예로 주님은 블레셋을 격파하고 승전가를 부를 것이라고 하신다(9c절).

하나님은 정복한 모압은 목욕통으로 삼으실 것이라고 하는데(9a절), 잡일을 위해 그들을 종으로 부리실 것을 의미한다(cf. Kirkpatrick). 하나님이 에돔에게는 신발을 던지시겠다고 하는데(9b절), 신발을 누구에게 던지는 것은 그를 상대로 승리했다는 의미이다(Wilson, cf. Dahood). 하나님은 이스라엘의 전통적인 적들을 정복하셔서 목욕통을 부리는 기구들로 사용하시지만, 그들을 투구 다루듯 다루시는 에브라임과 규를 잡듯이 잡으신 유다처럼 귀하게 여기지 않으실 것이라고 한다(8c-d절).

하나님이 귀하게 여기시는 에브라임과 유다는 절대 망하지 않을 것이다. 이번의 패배는 하나의 전투에 불과하며 전쟁은 계속되고 있다. 또한 전쟁은 여호와께 속한 것이다. 전쟁을 주관하시는 하나님이 유다와 에브라임을 포기하거나 적들에게 넘겨주지 않으시고 아직도 그들을 귀하게 여기시니, 유다와 에브라임은 분명 승리할 것이다. 이 사실을 강조하기 위해 주님의 신탁은 "내가 승리하리라"(cf. 7절)로 시작하여 "블레셋을 격파하고 승전가를 부르련다"(9절, 새번역)로 끝이 난다.

이 섹션은 주의 백성에게 믿음을 요구하고 있다. 그들은 적들에게 크게 패하여 좌절하고 있다. 이런 상황에서 하나님은 그들에게 패배를 안겨준 적들을 상대로 승리할 것이라고 선언하신다. 주의 백성은 결정해야 한다. 뼈아픈 실패를 맛본 현실이 실체의 전부라고 인정할 것인가? 현실을 초월한 하나님의 말씀을 믿을 것인가? 당연히 주님의 말씀을 믿어야 된다. 우리가 접하고 보는 현실 뒤에는 그 현실을 주관하시는 하나님이 계신다.

4. 신탁을 실현하시기를 기도함(108:10-11)

10 누가 나를 이끌어 견고한 성읍으로 인도해 들이며
누가 나를 에돔으로 인도할꼬

[11] 하나님이여
주께서 우리를 버리지 아니하셨나이까
하나님이여
주께서 우리의 군대들과 함께 나아가지 아니하시나이다

신탁을 받은 기자가 자기의 고민을 털어놓는다. 그는 백성들을 이끌고 가서 에돔을 정복하고자 하지만 자신이 없다(10절). 에돔의 성들은 참으로 견고하기 때문이다. 아마도 이 시편 기자가 왕이었음을 암시하는 듯하다. 그러나 그는 홀로 군사를 이끌고 가서 에돔을 정복할 자신이 없다. 최근의 패배가 그를 더욱더 위축시켰을 것이다.

기자는 최근에 맛본 패배의 원인들 중 단연 신학적 이유를 가장 중요한 요인으로 지적한다: 하나님이 그들을 버리셨기 때문이다(11절). 원래 이스라엘의 전쟁은 하나님이 함께 하시고 인도하시는 성전(聖戰)인데, 이번 전쟁은 그렇지 않았다는 것이다. 하나님이 그들의 군대와 함께 가지 않으신 것이다. 결국 이스라엘은 하나님의 도우심 없이 홀로 전쟁을 했고 적에게 패했다. 기자는 이러한 사실을 전쟁이 시작되기 전에는 의식하지 못했고 패배한 후에나 비로소 깨달았을 것이다. 하나님이 함께하시지 않는 전쟁을 시행하는 것은 어리석고 무모한 일이기 때문이다.

살면서 우리도 항상 염려해야 할 이슈는 하나님이 정작 우리와 함께 하시는가 이다. 조금이라도 의심의 여지가 있거나, 하나님이 함께하지 않으신다는 생각이 들면 하던 일을 멈추고 이 시편 기자처럼 하나님이 다시 우리와 함께하신다는 확신을 얻을 때까지 기도하고 주님의 임재를 사모해야 한다. 하나님이 함께하지 않으시면 함께하실 때까지 하던 일을 멈추고 아무것도 하지 않는 것이 좋다.

5. 구원 간구(108:12)

[12] 우리를 도와 대적을 치게 하소서
사람의 구원은 헛됨이니이다

실패를 맛본 기자가 하나님의 도움을 청한다. 그는 하나님이 함께하심과 도우심으로 원수들을 치기를 간절히 소망한다. 이 말씀은 이스라엘 군대가 아직도 존재하며 하나님의 지휘를 바란다는 뜻이다. 그러므로 이 노래는 북 왕국 멸망과 상관 없는 노래다(Weiser).

저자는 하나님의 도우심을 간절히 바라는 이유를 분명히 말하고 있다: "사람의 구원은 헛되다." 하나님의 도우심에 비교할 때 사람들의 도움은 별 도움이 되지 않는다는 것이다. 역사를 살펴보면 나라나 개인이 사람을 의존했다가 낭패를 본 사례가 수도 없이 많다. 기자가 외치는 대로 사람의 구원(도움)은 헛되다!

기자는 오직 하나님만이 그를 도우실 수 있으며, 하나님의 도우심만이 중요하다며 주님의 도우심을 사모하고 있다. 자신이 처한 위기를 정치적/군사적으로 해결하지 않고, 신앙적으로 해결하려는 그의 믿음이 돋보인다. 하나님이 그들을 버리셨다고 확신하는 상황에서 만일 주님이 그들을 도우신다면, 주님의 도움은 군사적인 도움으로만 의미 있는 것이 아니다. 주님이 그들과 함께하신다는 뜻이 되기 때문이다. 기자는 참으로 지혜로운 기도를 하고 있다.

6. 신뢰와 확신(108:13)

[13] 우리가 하나님을 의지하고 용감히 행하리니
그는 우리의 대적들을 밟으실 자이심이로다

기자는 하나님이 다시 그들과 함께해 주시면, 어떻게 적들과 싸울 것인가에 대한 포부를 말하고 있다. 그는 함께하시는 하나님을 의지하여 용감하고 장렬하게 싸울 것을 다짐한다. 이러한 기자의 다짐에는 하나님께 한 번만 더 기회를 달라는 염원이 서려 있다.

그가 용맹스럽게 싸울 의지를 다지는 것은 전쟁에 함께하시는 주님이 원수들을 짓밟으실 것을 믿고 확신하기 때문이다. 만일 이스라엘이 전쟁에서 승리한다면 그 승리는 어느 정도 그들의 노력과 능력의 대가이겠지만, 궁극적으로 그 승리는 그들과 함께하시며 적들을 밟으신 하나님이 이루신 승리이다. 우리도 이 신적 용사가 속히 오셔서 우리의 삶에서 승리하시기를 꾸준히 바라며 기도해야 한다.

제109편

다윗의 시, 인도자를 따라 부르는 노래

I. 장르/양식: 개인 탄식시(cf. 3편)

우리는 이 시편을 개인 탄식시로 구분하지만(cf. deClaissé-Walford et al., Tucker & Grant, VanGemeren), 전쟁에서 패배한 공동체가 하나님께 드리는 기도라며 회중 탄식시로 구분하는 이들도 있다(Birkeland, Eaton, Goulder, Mowinckel). 또한 이 시가 처음에는 개인 탄식시로 저작되었지만, 훗날 공동체가 부른 노래로 읽히고 사용된 것이라는 견해도 있다(Croft). 이처럼 다양한 견해가 존재하는 것은 이 시가 단수와 복수가 교차하며 진행되기 때문이다. 이 같은 인칭 변화의 중요성에 대하여는 야노스키(Janowski)를 참조하라.

양식은 개인 탄식시이지만, 내용은 분명 저주시(imprecatory psalm)이다. 시편들 중 상당 수의 탄식시가 조금이나마 원수들에 대한 저주를 포함하고 있다(시 17:13; 31:17; 35:4; 59:11-13; 70:2-3). 또한 전체적인 분위기가 원수들에게 저주를 선포하는 시들도 있다(시 12, 58, 83, 137, 139편)(Hossfeld-Zenger). 이러한 시들 중 이 시편은 가장 강력한 저주시로서(Grogan, Gunkel, cf. Gerstenberger), 저주는 10-11절에서 극에 달한다(Goldingay). 그러므로 하나님은 사랑이심으로 주의 백성은 원수들을 무

조건 용서해야 한다고 생각하는 사람들에게는 가장 당혹스러운 시편이다(Brueggemann & Bellinger).

대부분의 학자들은 이 노래가 참으로 억울한 일을 당한 사람이 성전으로 나아가 그곳에서 사역하는 제사장—재판관(priestly judge)에게 자신의 억울함을 호소하며 드린 기도라고 한다(Allen, Seybold, Terrien, Wright). 그러나 시편 기자가 당한 억울한 일이 아니라, 그가 당면한 질병으로 인해 이 노래를 부른 것이라는 해석도 있다(Goldingay, cf. 23-24절). 본문을 종합적으로 분석해볼 때 전자의 해석이 더 어울린다. 또한 이 시의 특징은 '신실한 언약적 스피치'(faithful covenantal speech)와 '절제되지 않은 복수 촉구'(free unrestrained speech of rage seeking vengeance)가 절묘한 균형을 이루고 있지만, 끝에 가서는 항상 후자가 전자에게 종속되는 것에 있다(Brueggemann).

원수에게 저주를 비는 이 시편과 신약의 원수를 사랑하라는 말씀은 서로 대립되는 듯하다. 따라서 이 시편은 기독교 역사에서 상당히 등한시되거나 무시되었다(deClaissé-Walford et al., Tucker & Grant). 심지어는 3년 주기로 거의 모든 시편이 읽히도록 한 영국 성공회의 기도책(lectionary)에서도 이 시편은 제외되었다(Tucker & Grant). 신약에서도 베드로가 8절을 가롯 유다의 죽음을 설명하면서 사용한 것 외에는(행 1:20) 인용되지 않는다.

이 시의 저작 시기는 왕정 시대가 끝날 무렵이라는 주장이 있는가 하면, 더 구체적으로 예레미야가 저자일 가능성을 조심스럽게 제시하는 학자도 있다(Terrien). 이 시편의 내용이 예레미야 18:19-23과 비슷하다는 생각에서 비롯된 추측이다. 또한 포로기 이후 시대에 저작된 것이라는 견해도 있다(Anderson). 그러나 대부분 학자들은 저작 시기와 정황에 대하여는 말을 아낀다. 추측하기가 어렵기 때문이다.

II. 구조

학자들은 이 시편의 구조를 분석하는 일은 고사하고, 본문을 문단으로 섹션화 하는 일에도 이견을 보인다(cf. Allen, deClaissé-Walford et al., McCann, Terrien, VanGemeren). 이 노래는 구조와 흐름을 파악하기가 어려운 시라는 점을 암시한다. 이 주석에서는 다음과 같은 구분을 바탕으로 본문을 주해해 나가고자 한다.

A. 침묵하지 마소서(109:1-5)
B. 저주를 내리소서(109:6-15)
C. 악인들의 삶을 보소서(109:16-20)
D. 악인들의 손에서 구하소서(109:21-25)
E. 원수들의 저주를 축복으로 바꾸소서(109:26-31)

III. 주해

이 시편은 가장 강력한 언어로 원수들을 벌하라고 기도한다. 원수를 끝까지 사랑하라는 신약의 가르침과 상반된 것이라 할 수도 있겠지만, 사실은 이러한 기도가 진정한 용서의 첫걸음이다. 사람이 감정을 정리하지 않고는 원수를 용서할 수 없기 때문이다. 그러므로 이 시편 같은 기도문을 통해 하나님께 우리의 상한 심령을 토로하고 나면 감정이 어느 정도 추슬러지며, 이때부터 용서가 시작된다.

1. 침묵하지 마소서(109:1-5)

[1] 내가 찬양하는 하나님이여
잠잠하지 마옵소서
[2] 그들이 악한 입과 거짓된 입을 열어 나를 치며

속이는 혀로 내게 말하며
3 또 미워하는 말로 나를 두르고
까닭 없이 나를 공격하였음이니이다
4 나는 사랑하나 그들은 도리어 나를 대적하니
나는 기도할 뿐이라
5 그들이 악으로 나의 선을 갚으며
미워함으로 나의 사랑을 갚았사오니

이 섹션은 모두 스피치(말)에 관한 내용을 담고 있다. 기자는 여호와를 '내가 찬양하는 하나님'(אֱלֹהֵי תְהִלָּתִי)이라고 부르며 노래를 시작한다. 하나님은 지난날들에 그의 삶에서 행하신 일들을 통해 영원히 그의 찬양을 받기에 합당한 분임을 드러내셨다는 뜻이다(VanGemeren). 그는 이처럼 성실하시고 공평하신 하나님, 곧 정의로 그의 삶과 세상을 다스리시는 하나님의 성품에 위배되는 일을 경험했으니 잠잠하지 마시라는 기도로 노래를 시작한다.

'잠잠하다'(חרשׁ)는 귀머거리가 듣지 못해 침묵하는 상황을 묘사한다(Tucker & Grant, cf. 사 42:18). 자신은 참으로 억울한 일을 당했으니 하나님이 꼭 그의 기도를 듣고 개입하셔서 자신과 가해자(들) 사이에 공평한 판결을 내려 달라는 호소이다. 비록 이 노래가 탄식시이지만, 그는 하나님이 그의 기도를 꼭 들어주실 것을 믿고 확신하기 때문에 찬양으로 시작한다(Dahood).

찬양을 시작하자마자 다윗은 원수들에 당한 억울함과 그들에 대한 분노를 쏟아낸다. 그는 쉽게 이런 말을 할 사람이 아니다. 그는 원수들에게 참으로 억울한 일들을 많이 당해오면서도 참고 참았지만, 드디어 억눌렀던 감정을 표현하며 그들에게 입은 상처를 드러내고 있다(Kidner). 그는 하나님께 원수들이 그에게 저지른 일을 만수(滿數)인 일곱 가지로 고발한다. 대부분이 그들의 입(말)과 관련된 서운함이다. 또한 몇 가지는 서로 중복된다고 할 수 있다.

첫째, 그들은 입을 열어 악하고 거짓된 말로 그를 쳤다(2a절). ‘악한 입’(פִּי רָשָׁע)은 하나님이 죄로 판단하실 말을 했다는 뜻이다. ‘거짓된 입’(פִּי־מִרְמָה)은 시편에서 독특한 표현이다. 그들이 속이는 말을 했다는 뜻이다(cf. HALOT). 악인들은 이같이 악한 말로 그를 공격했다.

둘째, 그들은 속이는 말을 했다(2b절). 이곳에서 ‘속이는 혀’(לְשׁוֹן שָׁקֶר)는 주변 사람들에게 기자에 대해 나쁜 말을 퍼트린다는 의미로 사용되고 있다(cf. 새번역, 아가페, 현대인). 아가페 성경이 2절의 의미를 잘 표현하고 있다: “악하고 거짓말하는 자들이 그들의 입을 열어 거짓된 혀로 나에 대해 나쁘게 말하고 있습니다.”

셋째, 그들은 미워하는 말로 그를 둘렀다(3a절) ‘미워하는 말’(דִּבְרֵי שִׂנְאָה)은 강력한 적대적인 감정이 실린 말을 뜻한다(cf. NIDOTTE). ‘두르다’(סבב)는 감싼다는 의미다. 악인들의 악한 말이 어디를 가든 기자를 포위하고 있다. 그러므로 사람들은 오로지 악인들의 말을 통해 그를 보며 편견적인 판단을 내린다.

넷째, 그들은 이유 없이 그를 공격했다(4b절). ‘공격하다’(לחם)는 군사적인 언어로 싸운다는 뜻을 지녔다(Tucker & Grant). 그들은 매우 공격적으로 기자를 괴롭혀 생명을 위협하고 있다(Davidson). 기자가 가장 황당한 것은 그는 그들에게 이러한 공격을 받을 만한 일을 한적이 없다는 사실이다. ‘까닭 없이’(חִנָּם)는 합당한 이유가 전혀 없다는 뜻이다(HALOT). 그는 참으로 억울한 일을 당하고 있다. 인간은 종종 고통 속에서 신음하는 사람들을 이유 없이 공격하는 잔인성을 보인다(Gerstenberger, cf. Brueggemann & Bellinger).

다섯째, 그들은 사랑을 악으로 갚았다(4a절). 기자는 그들에게 ‘사랑’(אַהֲבָה)을 베풀었다. 사랑은 좋은 감정을 전제한다. 그는 그들을 참으로 따뜻하고 선하게 대했다는 뜻이다. 그러나 그들은 그를 ‘원수로 삼았다’(יִשְׂטְנוּנִי). ‘대립하다/원수가 되다’(שׂטן)는 매우 강력한 단어로, 이 동사에서 고유명사 '사탄'이 파생했다. 너무나도 황당한 일을 당한 기자는 그저 묵묵히 주님께 기도할 뿐이다(4b절). 이런 상황에서는 하나님께 기도하는 일 외에는 방법이 없다.

여섯째, 그들은 악으로 선을 갚았다(5a절). '선'(טוֹבָה)과 '악'(רָעָה)은 서로 반대되는 말이다. 악인들은 기자가 그들에게 행한 모든 선한 일을 악으로 되갚았다. 이들은 선을 베풀 만한 사람들이 절대 아니다.

일곱째, 그들은 미움으로 사랑을 갚았다(5b절). 이 말씀은 다섯째(4a절)와 같은 말이다. 기자가 원수들에 대해 가장 어처구니없다고 생각하는 부분이다. 사람의 탈을 쓰고 어찌 사랑을 미움으로 되갚을 수 있냐는 것이다. 그러므로 그는 두 차례 이 사실을 하나님께 아뢰며 자신의 상처받은 감정을 표현하고 있다.

2. 저주를 내리소서(109:6–15)

6 악인이 그를 다스리게 하시며
사탄이 그의 오른쪽에 서게 하소서
7 그가 심판을 받을 때에 죄인이 되어 나오게 하시며
그의 기도가 죄로 변하게 하시며
8 그의 연수를 짧게 하시며
그의 직분을 타인이 빼앗게 하시며
9 그의 자녀는 고아가 되고
그의 아내는 과부가 되며
10 그의 자녀들은 유리하며 구걸하고
그들의 황폐한 집을 떠나 빌어먹게 하소서
11 고리대금하는 자가 그의 소유를 다 빼앗게 하시며
그가 수고한 것을 낯선 사람이 탈취하게 하시며
12 그에게 인애를 베풀 자가 없게 하시며

그의 고아에게 은혜를 베풀 자도 없게 하시며
13 그의 자손이 끊어지게 하시며
후대에 그들의 이름이 지워지게 하소서
14 여호와는 그의 조상들의 죄악을 기억하시며
그의 어머니의 죄를 지워 버리지 마시고
15 그 죄악을 항상 여호와 앞에 있게 하사
그들의 기억을 땅에서 끊으소서

이 시편 해석에서 가장 논쟁이 되는 이슈는 일명 '미움의 노래'(song of hate, Brueggemann)라고 불리는 6-19절이 누구의 스피치인가? 이다. 학자들은 둘로 나뉘어 있다. 첫째는 기자가 그를 괴롭히는 원수들을 비난하는 스피치로 간주하는 것이다(Althann, Calvin, McCann, VanGemeren, Wright, Ward). 둘째는 기자가 원수들의 스피치를 이곳에 인용하는 것으로 해석하는 것이다(Allen, Booij, Brueggemann, Creager, deClaissé-Walford et al., Goldingay). 번역본들도 둘로 나뉘어 있다. 기자가 원수를 비난하는 스피치로 간주하는 번역본들에는 개역개정, 아가페, NIV, ESV, NAS 등이 있다. 기자가 원수들이 한 말을 인용하는 것이라고 하는 번역본들에는 새번역, 공동, 현대인, NRS 등이 있다.

기자가 원수들의 말을 인용하고 있다는 해석에 가장 큰 영향을 행사한 것은 경건한 주의 자녀는 6-19절이 묘사하는 저주를 입에 담을 수 없다는 전제이다(cf. deClaissé-Walford et al., Gerstenberger, Tucker & Grant). 또한 기자는 바로 앞 섹션에서 '원수들'(복수)에 대해 탄식했는데(1-5절), 이 섹션에서는 '원수'(단수)를 상대로 저주를 선포하는 것을 보면(cf. 6절) 이 섹션은 기자가 원수들의 말을 인용하는 것으로 보인다. 기자에게는 여러 원수들이 있지만, 원수들에게는 한 원수(기자)가 있을 뿐이기 때문이다(McCann). 그러나 31절에서 기자는 "하나님이 자기 오른쪽에 계신다"는 말을 하는데, 6절은 사탄이 원수의 오른 쪽에 서 있게 해 달라고 하는 것을 보면, 6-19절은 기자가 원수들에 대해 선포하는 저주이다. 이 주석에서는 기자의 스피치로 간주하여 해석해 나갈 것이다.

기자는 앞 섹션에서 악인들이 까닭 없이 그를 괴롭힌다며 하나님께 결코 잠잠하지 마시라고 기도했다(cf. 1절). 이제 그는 하나님이 그들에게 내려 주시기를 바라는 저주들을 나열한다. 이 섹션이 복수인 '원수들'이 아니라 단수인 '원수'로 진행된다 해서 문제될 것은 없다. 히브리어 성경에서 대표성(모형)을 논할 때는 단수를 사용하기 때문이다(Janowski). 저자는 그를 괴롭히는 모든 원수들을 '한 원수'로 싸잡아 저주를 선언하고 있는 것이다. 그는 악인들에 대한 저주 여덟 개를 선언한다.

첫째, 기자는 악인들이 원수들을 다스리게 되기를 소망한다(6절). 앞에서 그를 괴롭히는 원수들은 '악한 입'(פִּי רָשָׁע)을 가졌다고 했다(2절). 이제 그는 원수들이 그들처럼 '악한 사람'(רָשָׁע)들의 다스림을 받게 되기를 바란다. 그래야 그들도 기자의 억울한 심정을 어느 정도 헤아리게 될 것이다.

'다스리다'로 해석된 동사(פקד)는 '(심판하기 위하여) 찾아가다'는 뜻이다(NIDOTTE). 본문의 의미는 분명하다. 악인들이 그를 괴롭히는 악인들을 찾아가 악으로 심판해주기를 바란다. 또한 그는 '사탄'이 그의 오른쪽에 서게 하도록 해 달라고 하는데(6b절), '사탄'(שָׂטָן)은 '비난자'(accuser)라는 뜻을 지닌 일반명사다(McCann, Tucker & Grant, cf. 아가페, 공동, 현대인, NAS, NIV, ESV, RSV, TNK). 원래 오른쪽은 가까이 지내며 도움을 받을 수 있는 사람을 세우는 곳이다. 그런데 기자는 하나님이 원수들의 오른쪽에 그들을 비난할 자들/괴롭힐 자들을 세우시기를 기원한다. 그들이 혹독한 곤경에 처하게 되기를 바라는 기도이다.

둘째, 기자는 악인들이 유죄 판결을 받기를 원한다(7절). 그들이 행한 모든 일이 재판 받게 되기를 바라며, 그 재판의 결과로 유죄가 선언되기를 희망하고 있다. 만일 세상이 그들을 재판하지 않으면 하나님이 하실 것이다. 이때 악인들의 기도가 죄로 변하게 해 달라는 부탁은 그들이 아무리 간절히 재판장(하나님)께 기도해도 그들의 기도가 무시되어 유죄 판결에 변함이 없도록 해 달라는 뜻이다(VanGemeren).

셋째, 기자는 악인들의 수명이 짧고 사회적 지위를 빼앗기기를 기도한다(8절). 장수가 사람이 누릴 수 있는 가장 큰 축복이라고 생각했던 사회에서 제명을 다 살지 못하게 수명을 단축시켜 달라는 것은 매우 강력한 저주다. 게다가 악인들이 장수하며 누릴 사회적 지위도 모두 빼앗기도록 기도한다. 악인들에 대한 기억이 단명으로 인해 빨리 사라질 뿐만 아니라, 그들의 영향력도 사회에서 신속하게 없어지도록 해 달라는 기도이다.

넷째, 기자는 악인들의 집이 완전히 망해 사라지기를 소망한다(9-10절). 악인들이 빨리 죽으면(cf. 8절), 어느 정도 기대되는 결과이다. 그들의 자녀들은 아버지를 잃은 고아들이 될 것이며, 그들의 아내들은 남편 잃은 과부들이 될 것이다(9절). 악인들의 집안에 임할 수 있는 가장 큰 사회적인 수치와 수모이다(cf. VanGemeren). 가장이 사라지니 집안이 순식간에 망한다. 결국 황폐한 집에서 더 이상 나올 것이 없으면, 자녀들은 이곳저곳을 떠돌며 구걸하여 생명을 연장하게 된다. 이것이 저자가 바라는 시나리오다(cf. Guillaume). 상당수의 주석가들이 이 저주와 다음 저주(#5)를 기자의 가장 비(非)기독교적 언행이라고 생각한다(Kirkpatrick).

다섯째, 기자는 악인들의 재산이 모두 엉뚱한 사람들에게 넘어가기를 기원한다(11절). 수고하고 노력하여 얻은 부가 한 순간에 고리대금업자에게 넘어가고 낯선 사람이 빼앗아가는 시나리오이다. 사실 세우기는 어려워도 무너지는 것은 한 순간이다. 기자는 악인들의 모든 수고의 열매가 고리대금업자와 낯선 사람 등 참으로 어이없는 사람들에게 넘어가기를 바라고 있다. 의인들은 악인들의 재산을 가지면 안 되기 때문이다.

여섯째, 기자는 그 누구도 악인들과 그들의 자식들에게 인애와 은혜를 베풀지 않기를 바란다(12절). 본문에서 '인애'(חֶסֶד)와 '은혜'(חוֹנֵן)는 비슷한 말로 쓰이고 있으며 그 누구도 그들을 불쌍히 여기지 않기를 바란다는 뜻이다. 두 번째 행이 고아들을 언급하는 것을 보면 이 말씀은 이미 죽은 악인들과 살아 있는 그들의 자식들에게 선을 베풀지 말라는 의미를 지녔다. 산 자들과 죽은 자들에게 은혜를 베풀지 말라고 한다.

일곱째, 기자는 악인들의 자손이 끊어져 그 집안의 이름이 지워지기를 기도한다(13절). 고대 사회에서 자손을 낳는 가장 큰 이유는 이름을 남기기 위해서였는데, 자손들이 없어 이름이 기억되지 않게 해 달라고 하는 것은 참으로 강력한 저주이다(cf. Childs).

여덟째, 기자는 하나님이 악인들의 조상들의 죄를 기억하셔서 그들의 조상들에 대한 기억도 끊으시기를 바란다(14-15절). 하나님은 용서받지 않은 죄는 영원히 기억하신다(Anderson). 그러므로 하나님이 악인들의 조상들의 죄를 기억하셔서 벌로 그들의 이름도 땅에서 영원히 잊혀지게 해 달라는 기도이다. 그러므로 조상—악인—자손 세 세대가 완전히 잊혀지게 해 달라고 한다.

3. 악인들의 삶을 보소서(109:16-20)

16 그가 인자를 베풀 일을 생각하지 아니하고
가난하고 궁핍한 자와 마음이 상한 자를
핍박하여 죽이려 하였기 때문이니이다
17 그가 저주하기를 좋아하더니
그것이 자기에게 임하고 축복하기를 기뻐하지 아니하더니
복이 그를 멀리 떠났으며
18 또 저주하기를 옷 입듯 하더니
저주가 물 같이 그의 몸 속으로 들어가며

기름 같이 그의 뼈 속으로 들어갔나이다

[19] 저주가 그에게는 입는 옷 같고

항상 띠는 띠와 같게 하소서

[20] 이는 나의 대적들이

곧 내 영혼을 대적하여 악담하는 자들이

여호와께 받는 보응이니이다

기자는 위 섹션(6-15절)에서 그를 괴롭히는 악인들에게 가장 강력한 저주를 내려 달라고 하나님께 기도했다. 이 섹션에서는 왜 그들이 하나님의 저주를 받아야 하는지를 말한다. 그는 자신의 기도가 그들에 대한 감정에 근거한 것이 아니라 팩트(fact)에 근거한 사실을 강조하기 위해 '왜냐면'(יַעַן)이라는 단어로 이 섹션을 시작한다. 기자는 악인들이 저주를 받기에 합당하다며 네 가지 이유를 제시한다.

첫째, 악인들은 그 누구에게도 인자를 베풀지 않는 삶을 살았다(16a절). '인자'(חֶסֶד)는 하나님의 속성 중 가장 기본적인 것이며, 하나님이 사람에게 베푸시는 모든 은총을 이 단어로 요약할 수 있다. 하나님이 우리에게 자비를 베푸시는 이유는 주님의 자비를 경험한 우리가 서로에게 자비를 베풀며 살게 하기 위해서이다(cf. Mays). 그러나 악인들은 남들에게 자비를 베푸는 일을 아예 마음에 두지도(생각지도) 않는 삶을 산다. 이러한 행위는 하나님과 맺은 언약을 위반하는 행위이기도 하다(레 19:18; 미 6:8). 그러므로 그들은 하나님의 저주를 받을 만하다는 것이 기자의 주장이다.

둘째, 악인들은 약자들을 핍박하고 죽이려 했다(16b-c절). '가난한 자'(אִישׁ־עָנִי)는 재산이 전혀 없어 경제적으로 매우 어려운 사람을, '궁핍한 자'(אֶבְיוֹן)는 억압을 받거나 비참한 상황에 처한 사람을, '마음이 상한 자'(נִכְאֵה לֵבָב)는 환난 등으로 인해 마음이 위축된 사람을 뜻한다(NIDOTTE, HALOT). 이러한 약자들은 사회와 이웃의 보호와 격려가 필요하다. 그러나 악인들은 그들을 핍박하고 죽이려 했다. '핍박하다'(רדף)는 해를 끼치기 위해 일부러 쫓아가는 것을 뜻한다. 악인들은 불쌍한 사람들을 모른 척하는 것이 아니라, 일부러 쫓아가 그들을 '죽을 때까지'(לְמוֹתֵת) 괴롭혔다. 그러므로 그들은 저주를 받을 만하다. 잠시 후 기자는 자신도 궁핍하고 가난한 자라고 한다(22절). 그러므로 악인들이 괴롭히는 약자들에는 그도 포함이 되어 있다.

셋째, 악인들은 남을 저주하기를 좋아하고 축복하기를 싫어했다(17절). 새번역이 이 구절의 의미를 정확하게 표현하고 있다: "그가 저주하기를 좋아하였으니, 그 저주가 그에게 내리게 하십시오. 축복하기를 싫어하였으니, 복이 그에게서 멀어지게 하십시오."(cf. 아가페, 현대인, 공동, NIV). 한마디로 말해서 악인들이 심은 대로 거두게 하시라는 기도이다. 주님의 자녀들은 하나님처럼 사람들을 축복하기를 기뻐하고 저주는 삼가야 하는데, 악인들은 정반대로 살고 있다. 그들은 남을 축복하는 일에는 인색하고, 저주를 내리는 일을 즐겼다. 그러므로 저자는 그들이 남들을 저주한 것처럼 하나님이 그들을 저주하시라고 기도한다.

넷째, 악인들은 저주하기를 옷 입듯 했다(18-19절). 저주가 그들의 살과 뼈에 배어 있다(18절). 기자는 그들의 일상이 남을 저주하는 일로 가득했다는 것을 뜻하며 비유적으로 말하고 있다(Kitz). 자나 깨나, 앉으나 서나 그저 남에게 피해를 입히고, 악을 행하는 자들의 삶은 참으로 주변 사람들을 괴롭게 한다. 그러므로 기자는 평생 남을 저주하며 살던 악인들이 이제는 평생 저주받은 인생을 살게 되기를 기원한다(19절). '물과 기름'(18절)은 그들이 사람들을 저주하기 위해 행했던 마술이나 주술에서 사용한 것을 의미할 수 있다(Anderson). 혹은 목마른 사람이 물을 순식간에 마시고 병든 사람이 몸에 기름을 바르듯, 악이 그들 몸의 일부가 되어 오래 머물러 있다는 뜻일 수도 있다(Briggs, cf. Tucker & Grant). 이 네 번째 이유는 세 번째 것과 중복되는 부분이 있다. 그러나 세 번째 보다 더 강력한 저주이다.

기자는 위 네 가지 이유를 말하면서 그를 괴롭히는 대적들이 꼭 하나님의 심판을 받아 저주를 경험하기를 바란다(20절). 새번역이 20절의 의미를 정확하게 번역했다: "주님, 나를 고발하는 자와, 나에게 이런 악담을 퍼붓는 자들이 오히려 그런 저주를 받게 해주십시오." 원수들이 기자를 악하게 대했으니, 그 악인들이 행한 대로 그들에게 갚아 달라는 기도이다. 기자는 원수들에게 참으로 억울하고 원통한 일을 당했다. 그러므로 그는 그를 괴롭힌 자들에 대하여 원한이 사무쳐 있다.

일부 주석가들은 19-20절을 따로 구분하여 선지적인 선언으로 간주한다(Kidner, VanGemeren). 16-18절은 원수들이 하는 짓들을 고발했는데, 19-20절은 하나님이 이러한 행위를 심판하실 것이라며 선지자가 선포하는 신탁이라는 것이다. 충분히 가능한 해석이다.

4. 악인들의 손에서 구하소서(109:21-25)

21 그러나 주 여호와여
주의 이름으로 말미암아 나를 선대하소서
주의 인자하심이 선하시오니 나를 건지소서
22 나는 가난하고 궁핍하여
나의 중심이 상함이니이다
23 나는 석양 그림자 같이 지나가고
또 메뚜기 같이 불려 가오며
24 금식하므로 내 무릎이 흔들리고
내 육체는 수척하오며
25 나는 또 그들의 비방거리라
그들이 나를 보면 머리를 흔드나이다

원수들에게 벌을 내리라고 기도했던 기자는 이 섹션에서 자신은 전혀 다르게, 하나님이 자비와 은혜로 대해 주시기를 기도한다. 그는 하나님과 특별한 관계를 맺고 있기 때문에, 하나님은 그와의 관계를 생각해서라도 그의 일에 개입하셔야 한다(Tucker & Grant). 이처럼 대조적인 상황을 강조하기 위해 이 섹션은 강조형 대조 ‘그러나 주 여호와여’(וְאַתָּה יְהוִה אֲדֹנָי)로 시작한다(21절). 원수들의 죄를 고발한 저자가 이제 모든 것을 하나님의 판결에 넘긴다는 신호이기도 하다(McCann).

인상적인 것은 그가 하나님의 은총을 바라는 근거가 자신의 의로움이나 원수들에게 억울하게 당한 일이 아니라, 하나님의 이름과 인자하심과 선하심이다(21절). 하나님의 ‘이름’(שֵׁם)은 하나님의 모든 속성과 인품의 결정체다. 그러므로 그는 하나님이 사람들을 축복하는 일을 즐거워하시며 공의와 정의를 사랑하신다는 사실에 호소하고 있다. 또한 ‘인자하심’(חֶסֶד)과 ‘선하심’(טוֹב)은 하나님의 가장 기본적인 속성들이다. 그는 이 세 가지를 나열함으로써 그가 은총을 바라는 유일한 근거는 오직 하나님이심을 고백한다.

저자는 자신의 처지를 스스로는 도저히 탈출할 수 없는 상황으로 묘사한다. 그러므로 그는 하나님이 그를 건지시기를 바란다(21c절). ‘건지다’(נצל)는 ‘잡아채다’는 의미를 지녔다. 하나님이 그를 구출해 주셔야만 그가 처한 곤경에서 빠져나올 수 있다.

그는 하나님의 도움을 구하면서 자신의 어려운 처지를 솔직하게 고백한다. 그는 가난하고 궁핍하고 중심이 상했다(22절). ‘가난’(עָנִי)과 ‘궁핍’(אֶבְיוֹן)은 16절에서 악인들(하나님의 저주를 받을 자들)이 핍박하는 불쌍한 사람들을 묘사하며 사용된 단어들이다. 또한 ‘중심이 상하다’(בְּקִרְבִּי לִבִּי חָלַל)는 16절의 ‘마음이 상한 자’(נִכְאֵה לֵבָב)와 표현이 조금 다르기는 하지만 같은 의미를 지녔다(cf. 시 69:26; 사 53:5). 그러므로 기자는 악인들이 무자비하게 공격하고 어떠한 자비도 베풀지 않았던 사람들 중에 자신이 속해 있음을 고백한다. 구약에서 하나님은 가난한 자들과 궁핍한 자들을 특별히 보호하는 왕이시다. 그러므로 이 말씀은 하나님의 개입을 강력하게 요구하는 기도다(Tucker & Grant). 악인들에게 받지 못한 '자비'(חֶסֶד)를 하나님께 기대하고 있다.

기자는 생명에 위협을 느끼고 있다. 현대어 성경이 23절의 의미를 잘 번역했다: "이 몸은 저녁 해거름처럼 점점 사위어 가고 메뚜기처럼 바람에 휩쓸려 갑니다"(새번역, 아가페, 공동, NIV, NAS, cf. 욥 17:7; 시 102:11). 메뚜기 비유는 고대 사람들이 이른 아침이면 식물에 붙어 있는 메뚜기들을 흔들어 떨어뜨려 삶아 먹거나 기름에 튀겨 먹었던 일을 배경으로 하고 있다(Tucker & Grant). 그는 하나님이 개입하지 않으시면 곧바로 죽을 수도 있다고 고백하고 있다.

저자는 생명에 위협을 느끼고 있을 뿐만 아니라, 육체도 건강하지 못하다. 그의 무릎은 흔들리고, 육체는 살이 쭉 빠져 수척해졌다(24절, cf. 시 31:10; 107:12). '무릎이 흔들린다'(בִּרְכַּי כָּשְׁלוּ)는 것은 '배가 고파 무릎이 주저앉다/쓰러진다'는 뜻이다(Goldingay). 그가 건강한 상태에서 금식을 하여 이렇게 된 것인지, 혹은 병을 다스리려고 금식을 하다 이렇게 된 것인지 정확히 알 수는 없다. 그러나 결과는 같다. 그의 몸은 생명에 위협을 받을 정도로 건강하지 못하다.

이러한 그의 모습을 보고 사람들은 비아냥거리며 머리를 흔든다(25절, cf. 시 22:6-7). 만일 그가 금식을 하다 몸이 망가졌다면, 사람들은 그가 금식을 하면서까지 드린 기도를 하나님이 응답하지 않으셨다며 비아냥거리는 상황이다. 만일 그가 병으로 인해 몸이 수척해진 것이라면, 하나님을 잘 믿는 사람이 몹쓸 병에 걸렸다며 비아냥거리고 있는 것이다.

5. 원수들의 저주를 축복으로 바꾸소서(109:26-31)

26 여호와 나의 하나님이여
나를 도우시며

주의 인자하심을 따라 나를 구원하소서
27 이것이 주의 손이 하신 일인 줄을 그들이 알게 하소서
주 여호와께서 이를 행하셨나이다
28 그들은 내게 저주하여도 주는 내게 복을 주소서
그들은 일어날 때에 수치를 당할지라도 주의 종은 즐거워하리이다
29 나의 대적들이 욕을 옷 입듯 하게 하시며
자기 수치를 겉옷 같이 입게 하소서
30 내가 입으로 여호와께 크게 감사하며
많은 사람 중에서 찬송하리니
31 그가 궁핍한 자의 오른쪽에 서사
그의 영혼을 심판하려 하는 자들에게서 구원하실 것임이로다

기자는 하나님이 그의 삶에 개입하셔서 은총을 베풀기를 다시 한번 간곡히 기도한다. 그는 여호와께서 그와의 관계를 근거로 도우실 것을 기대하며 여호와를 '나의 하나님'(אֱלֹהָי)이라고 한다(26a절). 또한 21절에서 고백한 것처럼 이번에도 자신의 의가 아니라, '주의 인자하심에 따라'(כְחַסְדֶּךָ) 구원해 주실 것을 호소한다(26c절). 그는 자신과 하나님이 맺은 언약적 관계에 근거하여 도와주실 것을 청하고 있다(Tucker & Grant).

하나님이 그를 도우시면 그를 괴롭히는 원수들도 주께서 그를 구원하셨다는 사실을 깨달을 것이다(27절). 원수들이 이 같은 사실을 깨달으면, 여호와께서 보호하시는 그를 함부로 하지 않을 것이다. 또한 하나님에 대한 두려움이 그들 안에 생길 수도 있다.

기자는 더 나아가 하나님의 축복을 갈망한다. 설령 원수들이 그를 저주할지라도 그들의 저주가 아무런 효력을 발휘하지 못하고, 그가 오히려 하나님의 축복을 받아 행복한 삶을 살게 될 것을 확신한다(28절). 하나님이 그를 축복하시면 그를 보고 고개를 저으며 비웃는 자들도(cf. 25절) 그를 하나님의 은총을 입은 자로 인정할 것이다. 반면에 악인들은 그들의 저주가 실현되지 않으면 큰 수치를 당할 것이다. 이 시편에서 축복과 저주만큼 강력한 대조가 명예와 수치이다(Tucker & Grant).

저자는 원수들이 온갖 수치와 수모를 옷 입듯 하게 되기를 기도한다(29절). 원수들은 저주를 옷 입듯 했다(18–19절). 그들이 심은 대로 거두게 해 달라는 기도이다. 또한 그동안 그가 원수들에게 당했던 수치와 수모가 모두 그들에게 되돌아가기를 원한다.

저자는 그와 원수들의 상황이 바뀔 것을 꿈꾸며 확신한다. 그러므로 그는 여호와께 감사하며 많은 사람들 앞에서 주님의 선하심을 찬양하는 순간을 꿈꾼다(30절, cf. Goulder). 그가 이같이 확신하는 것은 여호와가 어떤 분이신가를 확실히 알기 때문이다. 하나님은 궁핍한 사람의 오른쪽에 서서 원수들의 손에서 그를 구원하는 분이시기 때문이다. 기자가 원수들의 오른쪽에는 '고발하는 자'(שָׂטָן)가 서 있기를 빈 것과는 대조적이다(cf. 6절). '궁핍한 자'(אֶבְיוֹן)는 이미 기자가 자신을 묘사하며 사용한 단어이며, 억울하게 억압을 당하는 사람을 뜻한다(cf. 22절). 정의로우신 하나님이 억울한 일을 당한 사람을 구원하실 것이며, 까닭없이 그를 괴롭게 한 자들을(cf. 3절) 오히려 괴롭게 하실 것이라는 믿음이다.

제110편

다윗의 시

I. 장르/양식: 왕족시(cf. 2편)

이 시는 왕족시가 확실하다(Brueggemann & Bellinger, Grogan, McCann, Tucker & Grant, VanGemeren, cf. 시 2, 18, 20, 21, 72, 101, 132, 144편). 또한 신약이 가장 많이 인용하는 시편이다(마 22:44; 26:64; 막 12:36; 14:62; 16:19; 눅 20:42-44; 22:69; 행 2:34-35; 롬 8:34; 고전 15:25; 엡 1:20; 골 3:1; 히 1:3, 13; 5:6; 7:17, 21; 8:1; 10:12-13; 12:2; 벧전 3:22). 이러한 사실을 근거로 초대교회 시대부터 이 노래는 예수님의 사역과 밀접한 연관이 있는 메시아의 노래(messianic psalm)로 해석되어 왔다(Hay). 시편 2편이 메시아 사역의 예언과 연관이 있고 시편 89편이 거부당한 메시아를 슬퍼하는 노래라면, 이 시편은 승리한 메시아의 노래이다(Mays, Mitchell).

이 시편은 7절로 구성된 짧은 노래이지만, 텍스트가 잘 보존되지 않아 번역과 해석이 어려운 시편들 중 하나에 속한다(cf. Allen, Goldingay, Hossfeld-Zenger). 이러한 사실은 새번역에도 반영되어 있다. 새번역은 이 시편에 대하여 13개의 각주를 지니고 있다.

번역과 해석이 어려운 만큼 이 시편이 언제 누구에 의해 저작되었고 어떤 정황에서 사용되었는가에 대해서도 매우 다양한 해석이 존재한다. 저작 연대에 대한 학자들의 견해는 다윗 시대에서부터 마카비 시대까지 800년 이상의 차이를 보인다.

다윗 시대에 저작된 것으로 생각하는 사람들도 정황에 대해서는 다양한 추측을 내놓았다. 다윗이 오랜 내란 끝에 드디어 12지파를 모두 다스리게 된 통일 왕국의 왕이 된 것과 사독과 그의 자손들을 대 제사장직으로 임명한 일을 기념하는 노래라는 견해가 있다(Rowley). 이 시편이 예루살렘의 왕이자 제사장이었던 멜기세덱(4절)을 언급한다 하여 다윗이 예루살렘을 정복한 때 저작한 것이라고 주장하는 이가 있다(Ross). 이 경우 이 노래가 왕권보다는 제사장직을 강조하기 때문에 다윗은 멜기세덱의 대를 잇는 제사장이 된다(Allen). 이 시편이 예언적 성향을 지니고 있다고 생각하는 이들은 이 노래가 사무엘하 23장에 기록된 다윗의 노래와 비슷하다 하여 이 시를 다윗이 남긴 마지막 예언으로 간주한다(Delitzsch). 이 시편이 아카디아에서 왕에게 선포된 예언(Akkadian prophecies)과 매우 비슷하다는 연구도 있다(Hilber).

다윗이 통일 왕국의 왕으로 취임했을 때 예루살렘을 정복하고 부른 노래라는 해석이 있다(Brueggemann & Bellinger). 그러나 그가 죽은 후 왕정 시대에 예루살렘 성전에서 새 왕이 취임하는 예식에서 사용된 노래라는 해석이 지배적이다(Booij, Eaton, Gilbert & Pisano, Hardy, Jefferson, Nel, Terrien). 왕의 취임식과는 잘 어울리지 않는 내용이 있다 하여 이 시는 전쟁을 준비하거나 전쟁에서 승리한 왕을 기념하는 노래라는 주장도 있다(cf. McCann). 정확히 어떤 정황에서 사용된 것이었는지 도대체 알 수 없다고 하는 이들도 있다(Goldingay, VanGemeren).

이 노래가 이스라엘이 사회적—정치적으로 매우 어려운 시기를 살고 있을 때 하나님의 신실하심을 고백하는 노래로 저작되었다며(Allen) 포로기 이후 시대에 다윗 집안 사람 중 하나가 다윗 왕조를 이어갈 것을 갈망하며 부른 노래라고 하는 이들도 있다(Goulder, Schreiner). 마카비 시대에 저작된 것이라는 견해도 있다(Treves, Gerleman).

일부 독일 학자들(Ballhorn, Leuenberger)은 시편에 등장하는 가난하고 불쌍한 자들이 이 노래에서는 존귀함을 받는 왕이라고 한다. 언젠가는 하나님이 그들을 메시아처럼 대해 주실 것을 노래하고 있다는 것이다(cf. Tucker & Grant). 이 노래가 처음에는 어떠한 정황에서 사용되었는지 알 수 없지만 종말론적인 관점을 반영하고 있으며(Kidner), 왕의 즉위식으로 설명되지 않는 부분들이 많으니, 메시아적으로 해석되어야 한다(Terrien). 이 시편은 맨 처음 사용된 역사적 정황을 초월하여 장차 오실 메시아에 대한 예언적 노래인 것이다(Kidner, Kissane, cf. Hay).

II. 구조

다음은 알덴(Alden)이 제시한 구조이다. 교차대구법적 구조를 지향하다 보니 실제 각 구절이 말하고자 하는 것과 그의 요약이 잘 어울리지 않는다. 다소 억지스러운 부분이 있다.

A. 여호와께서 왕을 세우심(1절)
  B. 정복하라는 권면(2절)
    C. 능력의 날(3절)
      D. 여호와께서 맹세하심(4절)
    C′. 진노의 날(5절)
  B′. 그는 정복할 것(6절)
A′. 여호와께서 왕을 세우심(7절)

대부분 학자들은 이 시편을 1-3절과 4-7절 두 주요 파트로 나눈다(deClaissé-Walford et al., Goldingay, Terrien, Tucker & Grant). 각 파트를 조금 더 세분화하면 다음과 같은 구조가 역력하다(cf. deClaissé-Walford et al., VanGemeren).

A. 주님의 첫 번째 말씀(110:1)

B. 말씀의 실현(110:2-3)
A′. 주님의 두 번째 말씀(110:4)
B′. 말씀의 실현(110:5-7)

III. 주해

하나님은 다윗과 그의 후손들이 주의 백성을 영원히 통치하게 하실 것이라는 약속을 주셨다(삼하 7장). 이 시편은 그 약속이 어떻게 메시아를 통해 최종적으로 성취될 것인가를 노래한다. 하나님이 온 세상을 정복하셔서 메시아에게 복종하게 하신다. 그러므로 관점은 상당 부분 종말론적이라 할 수 있다.

1. 주님의 첫 번째 말씀(110:1)

[1] 여호와께서 내 주께 말씀하시기를
내가 네 원수들로 네 발판이 되게 하기까지
너는 내 오른쪽에 앉아 있으라 하셨도다

이 말씀의 내용은 간단하다. 여호와께서 '내 주'께 말씀하시기를 주님이 직접 '내 주'의 원수들을 정복하여 복종시킬 때까지 주님의 오른쪽에 앉아 있으라고 하셨다는 것이다. 이 말씀을 전하는 사람(내레이터)은 예배를 인도하는 제사장이거나 신탁을 선언하는 선지자이다. 그러므로 그는 하나님의 말씀을 받는 이를 '내 주'(אֲדֹנִי)라고 부른다.

"여호와께서 말씀하시기를…"(נְאֻם יְהוָה)은 선지서들 중에서도 예레미야서와 에스겔서에서 매우 자주 사용되는 표현이지만(cf. 렘 2:3, 9, 12, 19, 22, 29; 겔 14:11, 14, 16, 18, 20, 23), 시편에서는 이곳이 유일하다. 예레미야와 에스겔 모두 이 노래에 등장하는 왕처럼 제사장이었기 때문일 수도 있다(Goldingay). 또한 이 두 선지서에서는 하나님 스피치의 끝부분에 자주 등장하지만, 이곳에서는 스피치를 시작하면서 사용되고 있다. 1절은 여호와께서 직접 말씀하신 것이라는 점을 강조하기 위해서이다(Tucker & Grant).

일부 학자들은 여호와께서 '내 주'를 오른쪽에 앉히는 것이 이집트에서 신과 왕이 섭정하는 것을 배경으로 하는 것이라 하지만(Hossfeld-Zenger, Keel), 단순히 하나님은 '내 주'를 참으로 친밀하게 여기시고 존귀하게 생각하시기 때문에 오른쪽에 앉아 있으라고 하신다. 구약에서 밧세바가 솔로몬 왕의 오른쪽에 대비(大妃)의 자격으로 앉았다고 하는 것이 유일한 사례이다(왕상 2:19). 이는 매우 막강한 권력을 상징한다(Goldingay).

문제는 '내 주'가 누구냐는 것이다. 여호와께서 누구에게 이 말씀을 하시는가? 일부 학자들이 주장하는 것처럼 고난을 겪고 있는 가난한 사람들을 뜻하는가?(cf. Ballhorn, Leuenberger) 그런 것 같지는 않다. 만일 이 시가 왕들의 취임식에서 사용된 것이라면, 여호와께서 새로 취임하는 다윗 왕조의 왕에게 원수들이 새 왕에게 복종하도록 해 주시겠다는 약속이다(cf. VanGemeren). 그러나 앞에서 본 것처럼 왕들의 취임식에서 이 시가 사용된 것이 확실하지 않고, 이 시의 상당 부분이 종말론적이며(cf. Kidner), 신약이 이 말씀을 예수님과 연관시켜 인용하는 것을 감안하면 여호와께서 메시아에게 하신 말씀으로 해석하는 것이 바람직하다. 여호와 말씀의 대상인 '내 주'는 곧 메시아 예수이신 것이다.

하나님은 메시아의 원수들, 그러므로 여호와의 원수들이기도 한 사람들을 모두 발판이 되게 하실 것을 선언하신다. '발판'(הֲדֹם)은 법궤를 지탱하고 있는 다리를 뜻하기도 하고(대상 28:2; 시 99:5; 132:7), 세상(사 66:1)과 시온(애 2:1)을 의미하기도 하지만, 이곳에서는 승리하신 하나님이 보좌에 앉아 발을 올려놓는 것이다. 고대 근동에서는 전쟁에서 승리한 왕이 패배한 왕의 목을 밟는 기념식이 있었다. 이러한 풍습을 배경으로 성경에서는 발판을 밟는 모습이 생겨났다(VanGemeren, cf. 수 10:24; 왕상 5:3; 사 51:23). 그러므로 원수들을 발판으로 삼는다는 것은 주님의 절대적인 다스림을 상징한다.

종말이 되면 하나님이 세상 모든 사람을 정복하여 복종시킬 것이다. 시편 2편에서 하나님은 다윗 왕조의 왕에게 온 세상을 다스리는 권리를 약속하신다(시 2:8-9). 그때까지 여호와께서 귀하게 여기시는 메시아는 주님의 오른쪽에 앉아 있으면 된다. 여호와께서 모든 여건을 만들어서 비로소 메시아에게 넘기실 것이다. 고린도전서 15:25는 이 말씀을 예수님의 메시아적 권위의 근거로 삼는다.

2. 말씀의 실현(110:2-3)

2 여호와께서 시온에서부터 주의 권능의 규를 내보내시리니
주는 원수들 중에서 다스리소서
3 주의 권능의 날에
주의 백성이 거룩한 옷을 입고
즐거이 헌신하니
새벽 이슬 같은 주의 청년들이 주께 나오는도다

하나님은 세상을 정복하셔서 메시아가 다스리게 하시겠다고 했는데(1절), 과연 어떻게 이 일이 실현될 것인가? 이 섹션은 군사적인 언어를 사용하여 전쟁이 있을 것이고, 그 전쟁에서 여호와께서 승리하실 것이라고 한다. 여호와께서는 원수들을 상대로 전쟁하기 위해 시온을 떠나지 않으신다. 단지 주의 권능의 규를 메시아에게 주셔서 하나님을 대신하여 메시아가 원수들을 다스리게 하신다(2절). 전쟁은 어떠한 어려움도 없이 시작하자마자 곧바로 끝이 난다는 뜻이다. '다스리다'(רדה)는 제압한다는 뜻을 지녔다. 원수들은 억지로라도 메시아의 다스림을 받아야 한다(Goldingay, cf. HALOT).

3절을 정확히 번역하고 해석하는 것이 매우 어렵다(cf. Allen, Grogan, Hossfeld-Zenger). 이러한 어려움은 여러 번역본들의 다양한 번역에도 반영되어 있다. 게다가 영어 번역본들도 같은 것이 하나도 없다. '권능의 날'이 왕이 취임하는 날을 뜻한다는 해석이 있지만(Anderson), 큰 설득력이 있는 주장은 아니다. 이 날은 전쟁하는 날로 해석해야 한다(Weiser).

주의 권능의 날에 주의 백성이 거룩한 옷을 입고 즐거이 헌신하니 새벽 이슬 같은 주의 청년들이 주께 나오는도다	개역개정
임금님께서 거룩한 산에서 군대를 이끌고 전쟁터로 나가시는 날에, 임금님의 백성이 즐거이 헌신하고, 아침 동이 틀 때에 새벽 이슬이 맺히듯이, 젊은이들이 임금님께로 모여들 것입니다.	새번역
주의 백성이 스스로 원하여, 주의 권능의 날에 참여할 것입니다. 거룩하고 위엄 있게 단장한 새벽에 맺히는 이슬처럼 신선한 청년들이 주님께 나올 것입니다.	아가페
주께서 군대를 이끌고 거둥하시는 날 싸움터에 나서시는 날 주님의 백성들은 기꺼이 나서리이다. 이른 아침 초롱초롱 빛나는 이슬처럼 주님의 젊은이들이 거룩한 언덕으로 주님 앞에 나오리이다. 싸우러 나오리이다.	현대인
네가 나던 날, 모태에서부터, 네 젊음의 새벽녘에 너는 이미 거룩한 산에게 왕권을 받았다.	공동
영광스러운 성도들 중에 임할 너의 권능의 날에 왕권이 너와 함께 할 것이다. 아침이 되기 전에 내가 너를 모태에서 나오게 했다.	칠십인역 (LXX)

이 말씀이 전쟁 이미지를 배경으로 하고 있다는 것을 바탕으로 간단하게 정리하는 것이 바람직하다(VanGemeren). 첫째, 이 전쟁에 참여하는 사람들은 자원해서 싸우러 나올 것이다(cf. 삿 5:2, 9). 둘째, 그들은 적들과 싸울 만반의 준비를 하고 나온다. 셋째, 그들은 왕을 온전히 섬길 준비를 하고 나온다. 넷째, 그들은 새벽 이슬처럼 많을 것이다(cf. 삼하 17:12). 다섯째, 그들은 젊기 때문에 장렬하게 싸울 준비를 하고 나온다. 이 전쟁을 통해 왕은 어두움으로 상징되는 적들을 물리치고 새벽빛처럼 세상을 밝힐 것이다(Booij, Davidson).

3. 주님의 두 번째 말씀(110:4)

4 여호와는 맹세하고 변하지 아니 하시리라
이르시기를 너는 멜기세덱의 서열을 따라
영원한 제사장이라 하셨도다

하나님은 약속하시면 영원히 그 약속을 지키시는 분이다(4a절). 본문은 어떤 약속을 염두에 두고 이렇게 말하는가? 하나님은 사무엘하 7장에서 선지자 나단을 통해 다윗에게 그와 그의 후손들이 영원히 주의 백성을 다스릴 것이라고 하셨다. 우리는 이것을 '다윗 언약'이라고 한다. 이 약속에 따라 메시아는 다윗의 후손으로 오게 되었다. 본문은 이 언약을 염두에 둔 말씀이다(Tucker & Grant, VanGemeren).

하나님은 다윗의 후손으로 오시는 메시아를 멜기세덱의 서열을 따라 영원한 제사장으로 삼으실 것이다. 멜기세덱은 아브라함이 전쟁 포로로 끌려가는 롯을 구해 오는 길에 만난 사람이었다(cf. 창 14장). 창세기는 그의 신상에 대해 아무런 정보도 제공하지 않는다. 단지 그는 지극히 높으신 하나님의 제사장이자 살렘(예루살렘)의 왕이었다. 메시아가 멜기세덱 서열의 제사장이라는 것은 아마도 그가 '왕—제사장'의 모형이었기 때문인 듯하다(Paul). 법궤가 예루살렘으로 들어올 때 다윗 왕은 제사장이 해야 할 일을 했다(cf. 삼하 6장). 솔로몬 왕도 제사장이 해야 할 일을 스스로 했다(왕상 8장). 메시아는 '왕—제사장—선지자'이다. 그러므로 멜기세덱은 이 세 가지 직분 중 왕과 제사장직을 겸한 메시아의 부분적인 모형이라 할 수 있다(cf. 슥 6:13; 히 5:6-10; 7:22).

4. 말씀의 실현(110:5-7)

5 주의 오른쪽에 계신 주께서

그의 노하시는 날에
왕들을 쳐서 깨뜨리실 것이라
6 뭇 나라를 심판하여 시체로 가득하게 하시고
여러 나라의 머리를 쳐서 깨뜨리시며
7 길 가의 시냇물을 마시므로
그의 머리를 드시리로다

메시아가 세상 정복에 나서는 날, 하나님은 그의 오른쪽에 서서(cf. 시 16:8; 109:31; 121:5) 왕들을 복종시키실 것이다(5절). 1절에서 오른쪽은 특별한 관계와 명예를 상징했는데, 이 말씀에서는 보호와 지원을 상징한다(Tucker & Grant). 하나님께 반역하는 자들은 모조리 심판을 받아 죽임을 당할 것이기 때문에 온 세상이 시체로 가득하며, 나라들의 우두머리(왕)는 모두 제거될 것이다(6절). 고대 근동에서 흔히 있었던 전쟁의 참담한 모습이다(McCann). 세상 왕들이 범우주적 왕이신 여호와께서 세상을 다스리시는 원리(공의와 정의)에 따라 자기 백성을 다스리지 않았기 때문이다(Hossfeld–Zenger).

그가 길가의 시냇물에서 마신다고 하는데(7절), 주어가 누구인지 확실하지 않다(cf. McCann, VanGemeren). 이 노래가 여호와께서 메시아를 위해 싸워 주시는 일을 배경으로 하고 있기 때문에 아마도 승리한 메시아를 이 절의 주어로 보는 것이 바람직하다. 전쟁은 하나님이 하시는 일이기 때문에(cf. 시 2:5) 메시아는 특별히 싸우지 않았다.

그런데도 이 7절은 메시아에게 승리를 보장하는 행위로 시냇물을 마시는 것을 들고 있다(Allen). 한 주석가는 이 일을 솔로몬이 기혼 샘에서 왕이 된 것과 연결하여 해석하는데(Goldingay), 문제는 메시아가 왕이 되는 것이 이 말씀의 포인트가 아니라 승리한 것이 강조점이다. 기드온이 수많은 사람들 중에 그와 함께 전쟁에 나아가 승리할 300명을 물 마시는 일로 구분했던 일을 연상케 하는 표현일 수도 있다(Allen,

VanGemeren, cf. 삿 7:6). 그때도 하나님이 전쟁에 참여한 300명에게 이미 승리를 준비해 주셨다. 아마도 전쟁의 승자가 패한 왕의 땅에서 물을 마심으로써 자신의 승리와 권리를 확인하는 행위일 것이다(van der Meer, cf. McCann).

제111편

I. 장르/양식: 회중 찬양시(cf. 29편)

이 시편은 일인칭 단수를 사용한다 하여 개인 감사시(thanksgiving psalm)로(deClaissé-Walford et al.), 혹은 찬양시(hymn of praise)로 구분한다(Brueggemann & Bellinger). 그러나 이 개인이 온 회중을 인도하고 있기 때문에 회중의 고백적인 찬양시(confessional hymn)로 간주하는 것이 바람직하다(Goldingay).

이 시편과 바로 뒤를 잇는 112편은 알파벳 시이며, 둘이 한 쌍을 이룬다. 두 편 모두 처음 8절은 각각 히브리어 알파벳 두 개를, 9-10절은 각각 세 알파벳으로 시작하는 문장들로 구성되어 있다.

111편은 하나님의 위대한 사역을, 112편은 111편 마지막 부분(10절)이 언급하는 여호와를 경외함을 테마로 발전시켜 유기적인 관계를 유지한다. 하나님이 이루신 출애굽(3-6절)과 율법을 주신 일(7-9절)을 기념하는 111편은 신학을, 하나님이 하신 일에 대한 인간의 반응을 기록하고 있는 112편은 인간론을 제시하는 것으로 해석되기도 한다(Hossfeld-Zenger, cf. Brueggemann & Bellinger) 또한 111편은 하나님의 의로우심을, 112편은 인간의 의로움을 중점적으로 노래한다(Tucker & Grant).

이러한 연관성 때문에 이 두 시편이 같은 저자에 의해 저작되었을 수도 있다는 추측도 있다(VanGemeren). 심지어 한 학자는 111-112편을 한 편으로 간주해 통일된 구조를 제시하기도 한다(Alden).

111-112편 다음으로 등장하는 알파벳 시는 119편이다. 이 둘 사이에 이집트 찬양시(Egyptian Hallel Psalms) 모음집이라고 하는 113-118편이 끼어 있다. 이집트 찬양시들은 유월절을 기념하며 부른 노래들이다. 그렇다면 현재 구조는 이집트 찬양시들이 토라를 기념하는 시들(111-112, 119편) 사이에 있으면서 율법을 주신 하나님을 찬양하라는 듯하다.

대체적으로 학자들은 알파벳 시들이 포로기 이후에 저작된 것이라고 생각한다. 그러므로 이 시도 알파벳 시라는 이유로 포로기 이후 시대, 더 구체적으로는 페르시아 시대 저작된 것이라 하기도 한다(Terrien). 그러나 이 시편이 왕정 시대에 저작되었다는 것을 부인할 만한 증거는 없다(Ross). 대부분 학자들은 이 시의 저작 연대를 도무지 알 수 없다고 한다(Goldingay).

이 시편이 사용된 정황으로는 언약을 기념하는 가을 축제라는 견해도 있고(Terrien), 유월절 혹은 장막절에 사용되었을 것이라는 추측도 있다(Goldingay). 그러나 대부분 학자들은 구체성을 피하면서 이스라엘 예배나 예식에서 사용되었을 것 정도로 추정한다(Dahood, Kraus, Weiser).

II. 구조

학자들에 따라 이 시를 섹션화 하는 것이 매우 다양하다(cf. Alden, Allen, deClaissé-Walford et al., Goldingay, McCann, VanGemeren). 이 주석에서는 다음과 같은 분석을 바탕으로 본문을 주해해 나가고자 한다.

A. 감사 다짐(111:1)

B. 하나님의 사역 찬양(111:2–4)

B′. 하나님의 사역 설명(111:5–9)

A′. 찬양 권면(111:10)

III. 주해

이 노래는 하나님이 행하신 일, 특히 출애굽을 이루신 일과 율법을 주신 일을 묵상하고 찬양한다. 하나님이 이처럼 위대하신 일을 했으니 주님을 영원히 찬양하고 경배하는 것은 당연한 일이다. 토라를 이해하려면 여호와를 경외함이 필요하다. 여호와를 경외하는 것이 지혜의 근본이기 때문이다.

1. 감사 다짐(111:1)

[1] 할렐루야,
내가 정직한 자들의 모임과 회중 가운데에서
전심으로 여호와께 감사하리로다

기자는 '할렐루야'로 노래를 시작하는데, 앞으로 112편과 113편도 같은 단어로 노래를 시작한다. 할렐루야는 이 시편 전체의 분위기를 조성한다. 하나님께 감사하고 주님을 찬양하는 시라는 것이다. 히브리어 알파벳 중 첫 글자(א)로 시작하는 문장은 "전심으로 여호와께 감사하리로다"이다. 우리말과 히브리어 문장 구조가 다르기 때문에 순서가 뒤바뀐 것이다.

저자는 온 마음을 다해 여호와께 감사하겠다고 하는데, '감사하다'(ידה)는 '고백하다' 혹은 '선포하다'는 의미도 지녔다(Allen, Goldingay, cf. NIDOTTE). 이 시편이 하나님께 드리는 찬양이 아니라, 하나님에 대해 증거하는 찬양이라는 점을 감안하면 '선포하다, 고백하다'가 더 정확한 표현이다(Tucker & Grant). 그는 여호와 하나님이 너무 좋아서 다른 사람들에게도 주님에 대해 알리려고 한다. 그는 특히 '회중'(עֵדָה)과 '정직한 자들의 모임에서'(בְּסוֹד יְשָׁרִים) 주님을 찬양하고 싶어 한다. 일부 학자들은 이 두 그룹을 구별하려고 하지만(Allen, Goulder, Kraus), 본문에서는 이러한 구별이 별 의미는 없어 보인다. 회중과 정직한 사람들은 악인들과 대조되는 사람들이며 선한 이들, 또한 여호와를 경외하는 사람이 바로 그가 함께 하나님을 찬양할 사람들이다. 찬양은 매우 개인적인(personal) 것이지만, 사적인(private) 것일 필요는 없다(McCann).

2. 하나님의 사역 찬양(111:2-4)

2 여호와께서 행하시는 일들이 크시오니
이를 즐거워하는 자들이 다 기리는도다
3 그의 행하시는 일이 존귀하고 엄위하며
그의 공의가 영원히 서 있도다
4 그의 기적을 사람이 기억하게 하셨으니
여호와는 은혜로우시고 자비로우시도다

이 시편의 중심 주제인 '여호와께서 행하시는 일들'(מַעֲשֵׂי יְהוָה)이 소개되고 있다(2절). 그는 여호와께서 하시는 일들이 크다고 하는데, 고대 근동에서 '크다'(גְּדֹלִים)는 주로 신적 왕(divine king)이 하는 일을 묘사하는 데 사용되었다(Hossfeld-Zenger, McCann, cf. 시 47:2; 48:1; 95:3). 기자는 하나님을 이스라엘의 왕으로 찬양하고 있는 것이다(Tucker & Grant).

신적 왕이신 여호와께서 하시는 큰 일들을 즐거워하는 사람들은 여호와의 놀라운 일들을 즐거워하며 기다린다(2b절). '즐거워하다'(חָפֵץ)는 시편 1:2에서 사용된 단어이며, 여호와의 말씀을 주야로 묵상하기를 즐거워하는 자는 복이 있다고 한다(cf. 시 112:1; 119:35). 우리가 주님이 하신 일들은 '기릴수록'(דְּרוּשִׁים), 곧 깊이 묵상하고 생각할수록 더 큰 은혜를 경험하게 하기 때문이다.

여호와의 일을 깊이 묵상하는 사람들은 주님이 하시는 일이 얼마나 존귀하며 엄위한지 안다(3a절). 일상적으로 '존귀'(הָדָר)와 '엄위'(הוֹד)는 왕권과 연관된 명예(honor)와 위풍(majesty)에 관한 언어들이다(cf. 시 21:5; 96:6; 104:1; 145:5). 그러나 본문에서는 이 단어들이 여호와께서 행하시는 일들을 수식한다. 하나님은 존귀와 엄위로 가득한 왕이시므로, 하시는 일들도 주님의 왕권에 걸맞은 존귀와 엄위를 지녔다는 것이다. 주님은 세상을 다스리는 왕에 걸맞은 사역을 하신다.

하나님이 하시는 일은 모두 의롭다(3b절). 여호와께서 행하시는 일은 모두 주님의 의로움을 반영하고 있다는 것이다(Tucker & Grant). 그러므로 하나님이 사역하시는 한 주님의 공의는 주님의 일을 통해 영원히 서 있다.

여호와께서는 '자신이 행하신 기적들'을 사람들이 기억하게 하셨다(4a절). '주님이 행하신 기적들'(נִפְלְאֹתָיו)이 이 시편에서는 하나님의 사역에 대한 전반적인 묘사로 사용되고 있지만, 구약에서는 출애굽 사건을 의미하며 자주 사용된다(출 3:20; 15:11; 34:10; 시 77:11, 14; 78:4; 105:5; 106:22; 136:4). 하나님은 사람들이 주님이 행하신 기적들을 잊지 않고 기억하도록 하셨다. 예배는 사람이 하나님을 기억하는 일이 아니라, 하나님이 우리가 주님을 기억하도록 하신 일이다(Kraus).

자기 백성을 위해 놀라운 일들을 행하시고 그것을 기념하게 하시는 여호와는 참으로 은혜로우시고 자비로우시다(4b절). '은혜'(חַנּוּן)와 '자비'(רַחוּם)는 하나님이 아론의 금송아지 사건을 용서하시면서 스스로에 대해 하신 말씀에 포함되어 있다: "여호와라 여호와라 자비롭고 은혜롭고 노하기를 더디하고 인자와 진실이 많은 하나님이라"(출 34:6). 여호와께서 하시는 일들은 주님의 능력을 천하에 드러내는 것에 멈추지 않는다. 주님이 하시는 일들은 이스라엘과 언약을 맺으신 여호와께서 참으로 자신이 주장하시는 대로 자비롭고 은혜롭고 노하기를 더디 하시고 인자와 진실이 많으신 하나님임을 입증한다.

3. 하나님의 사역 설명(111:5-9)

5 여호와께서 자기를 경외하는 자들에게 양식을 주시며
그의 언약을 영원히 기억하시리로다
6 그가 그들에게 뭇 나라의 기업을 주사
그가 행하시는 일의 능력을 그들에게 알리셨도다
7 그의 손이 하는 일은 진실과 정의이며
그의 법도는 다 확실하니
8 영원무궁토록 정하신 바요
진실과 정의로 행하신 바로다
9 여호와께서 그의 백성을 속량하시며
그의 언약을 영원히 세우셨으니
그의 이름이 거룩하고 지존하시도다

여호와의 자비롭고 은혜로우심은 자기 백성을 보살피는 일에서도 역력하게 드러났다. 하나님은 주님을 경외하는 사람들에게 양식을 주셨다(5a절). 광야생활 40년 동안 만나와 메추라기로 이스라엘을 먹이신 일을 회상하는 말씀이다(deClaissé-Walford et al., Tucker & Grant, cf. 출 16장; 민 11장). 또한 누구와 언약을 맺으시면 그 언약을 영원히 기억하신다(5b절, cf. 새번역, 현대인, 공동). 하나님은 아브라함과의 약속을 실현하기 위해 그의 후손들을 이집트에서 인도해 내셨다. 여호와께서 백성들을 먹이고 보살피시는 것도 자비와 은혜이지만, 한번 약속하시면 절대 잊지 않고 기억하시는 것도 은혜이며 자비이다.

구조적으로 6절은 이 시편의 한 중심에 있다. 이 절을 중심으로 앞뒤에 각각 10행이 있다(Gerstenberger). 하나님은 그를 경외하는 자기 백성에게 뭇 나라의 기업을 주셨다(6a절). 이스라엘에게 가나안을 주신 일을 회상하는 말씀이다(cf. 신 6-7장). 가나안을 이스라엘에게 주신 것은 하나님이 하시는 일의 능력을 그들에게 알리는 계기가 되었다(6b절). ‘능력’(כֹּחַ מַעֲשָׂיו)은 출애굽기 9:16과 15:6에서도 하나님의 위대하심을 묘사하면서 사용되었다. 출애굽 모티프가 계속되고 있다.

하나님이 이스라엘에게 땅을 주신 일이 이 노래의 한 중앙에 위치했다는 것은 하나님이 하신 일들 중 땅을 주신 일이 가장 중요하고 위대한 업적임을 암시한다(Gerstenberger, McCann). 무한한 능력을 지니신 하나님이 아브라함과 약속하신 것을 지키기 위해 가나안 사람들을 몰아내고 그 땅을 이스라엘에게 주신 것은 이스라엘이 누구를 섬기고 사랑해야 하는가를 확실하게 알려 주신 사건이었다.

7절에서는 하나님이 하시는 일이 주님의 법도로 대체되고 있다(McCann). 진실과 정의는 여호와께서 하시는 일을 통해서도 드러나지만(7a절), 법도를 통해 더 확실해지기 때문이다(7b절). ‘법도’(פִּקּוּדִים)는 하나님이 시내 산에서 주신 율법을 의미한다(deClaissé-Walford et al., cf. McCann). 하나님은 왜 우리에게 말씀을 주셨는가? 진실과 정의로 행하도록 하기 위해서다(8절). 아가페 성경이 8절 후반부를 정확하게 번역했다: “신실함과 올바름 가운데서 행해지고 있습니다”(NIV, ESV, NRS, NAS). 강조점이 실천에 가 있는 것이다(Allen). 기자는 2절에서 하나님이 하신 일을 깊이 연구하고 묵상하라고 했다. 이제 그는 묵상에서 실천으로 이어갈 것을 주문하고 있다(Tucker & Grant).

여호와는 그의 백성을 속량하셨다(9a절). ‘속량’(פְּדוּת)은 노예 생활에서 구원하는 일을 의미한다(deClaissé-Walford et al., Tucker & Grant). 그러므로 이 말씀도 출애굽과 연관이 있다. 하나님이 이집트에서 종살이하던 이스라엘을 속량하셨기 때문이다.

하나님은 속량한 이스라엘과 언약을 영원히 세우셨다(9b절). 혹독한 노예 생활에서 해방시켜 주신 것도 감사한데, 시내 산에서 언약을 맺어 그들을 자기 백성으로 삼으신 것이다. 그러므로 기자는 이처럼 놀라운 일을 하신 하나님의 이름은 거룩하고 지존하다고 한다(9c절). '지존하다'(נוֹרָא)는 다음 절에서 '경외하다'로 번역된 단어와 같은 어원(ירא)에서 비롯된 단어이다. 그러므로 '지존하다'보다는 '두렵게 하다'(terrible, awe-inspiring)가 더 정확한 번역이다(새번역, TNK, CSB, cf. NIV, NAS, ESV, RSV). 여호와처럼 존귀하고 두려움을 자아내는 신은 없다는 뜻이다. 하나님의 존귀하심과 두렵게 하심은 우리가 주님이 이루신 놀라운 구원을 예배와 삶에 반영하도록 하기 위한 것이다(Brueggemann & Bellinger).

4. 찬양 권면(111:10)

10 여호와를 경외함이 지혜의 근본이라
그의 계명을 지키는 자는 다 훌륭한 지각을 가진 자이니
여호와를 찬양함이 영원히 계속되리로다

하나님이 행하신 일과 주신 법도를 깊이 묵상하고 실천하라고 한 기자가 여호와를 경외하라는 권면으로 노래를 마무리한다. 주님이 하신 일에 대해 많이 알고 주님의 법도에 대해 깊은 이해가 있어도 여호와를 경외하는 마음이 없으면 아무 소용이 없기 때문이다(cf. 잠 1:7; 9:10). 그러므로 그는 여호와를 경외하는 것이 모든 지혜(우리가 하나님이 하신 일과 말씀을 묵상함으로써 얻고자 하는 것)의 근본이라고 한다.

하나님을 경외함이 있는 지혜는 실천적이어서 주님의 계명을 지키려고 한다. 참 지혜는 실천을 유도한다. 기자는 주님의 말씀대로 살려고 하는 사람들을 훌륭한 지각을 가진 사람이라 한다. 하나님이 사역과 말씀을 통해 우리에게 주시고자 하는 깨우침을 깨달은 사람이라는 뜻이다.

사람이 하나님을 경외하는 것과 상관없이 여호와를 찬양하는 일은 이 땅에서 영원히 계속될 것이다. 혹은 이 말씀을 기자의 기도로 간주할 수도 있다: "여호와를 찬양함이 영원히 계속되기를!"(Dahood). 하나님을 찬양하는 일에 기꺼이 동참하는 사람은 지혜롭다. 또한 하나님을 찬양하는 것은 오직 여호와를 경외하는 사람만이 누릴 수 있는 특권이다.

제112편

I. 장르/양식: 회중 찬양시(cf. 29편)

이 시편도 111편처럼 알파벳 시이며 각 문장은 첫 글자로 히브리어 알파벳 22개를 순서적으로 사용한다. 학자들은 111편과 112편의 관계를 '쌍둥이'로(Zimmerli), '삼촌—조카'로(Goldingay), 혹은 '원작—속편'(Terrien)으로 표현한다. 이 두 시편이 같은 저자에 의해 저작되었다고 하는 이들도 있고(Kraus, Ross), 112편 기자가 111편을 모델로 삼아 자신의 시를 저작한 것이라는 견해도 있다(Goldingay, Terrien, cf. Allen). 심지어는 이 두 편을 묶어 한 편의 시로 취급하는 이도 있다(Alden).

학자들이 이처럼 111편과 112편의 특별한 관계를 강조하는 것은 111편이 "여호와를 경외함이 지혜의 근본이라. 그의 계명을 지키는 자는 다 훌륭한 지각을 가진 자이니 여호와를 찬양함이 영원히 계속되리라"(10절)로 마무리 되었는데, 112:1이 "여호와를 경외하며 그의 계명을 크게 즐거워하는 자는 복이 있도다"라며 111:10의 흐름을 그대로 이어 가기 때문이다. 또한 111편을 구성한 언어 중 11개의 단어와 표현이 112편에서 사용되었다(deClaissé-Walford et al., Tucker & Grant).

	112편	111편
경외(יָרֵא)	1	5, 10
즐거워함(חָפֵץ)	1	2
정직한 자들(יְשָׁרִים)	2, 4	1
잘됨(טוֹב)	5	10
공의가 영원히 서 있으리로다	3b, 9b	3b
자비롭고 긍휼이 많음	4b	4b
정의로 행함	5b	7a
기억됨	6b	4a
견고함	8a	8a
주다	9a	5a
영원히	6b	5, 8, 9

특이한 점은 111편은 이 단어들의 상당 수를 여호와께 적용하는데, 112편은 의로운 사람을 묘사하는 일에 사용한다는 점이다. 이러한 이유로 인해 111편은 신론을(theology), 112편은 인간론(anthropology)을 중심 주제로 삼고 있다고 하는 이들도 있다(Seybold, Tucker & Grant). 111편은 하나님을 찬양하는 것이 목적이었다면, 112편은 하나님을 경외하는 사람의 삶을 노래하고 있다는 것이다. 의인의 삶을 노래하고 있다 보니 1장과의 연결성도 자연스럽다(Brueggemann & Bellinger, Mays).

우리는 이 시가 취하는 양식을 회중 찬양시로 구분하지만(cf. Goldingay, Goulder), 내용이 여호와를 경외하는 이의 삶에 초점이 맞춰져 있기 때문에 지혜시(wisdom psalm)로 구분되는 것도 좋다(Brueggemann & Bellinger, Ross, Thomas, VanGemeren). 이 지혜시가 추구하는 지혜는 하나님의 말씀에서 오는 '토라 지혜'(Torah wisdom)이다(VanGemeren). 여러 지혜시들이 그런 것처럼, 이 시편도 종말론적 관점을 반영하고 있다(Kuntz, McCann). 언젠가는 하나님이 분명 여호와를 경외하는 사람들을 인정하시고, 악인들을 벌하실 것이다.

이 시의 저작 시기에 대해서는 다양한 추측이 있다. 왕정 시대에 왕족시로 저작된 것이라고 생각하는 이들은 이 시편이 노래하고 있는 여호와를 경외하는 사람은 다름 아닌 왕이라고 한다(Sherwood). 그러나 대부분 학자들은 포로기 이후 시대를 저작 시기로 보며(VanGemeren), 더 구체적인 시기를 제시하는 사람들은 페르시아 시대를 지목한다(Allen, Kraus, Terrien).

II. 구조

다음은 밴게메렌(VanGemeren)이 제시한 구조이다. 이 짧은 시의 구조 분석으로는 지나치다는 생각이 든다. 또한 원 저자가 이처럼 복잡한 구조를 추구하며 이 노래를 저작했을까? 라는 의구심이 든다.

A. 지혜를 기뻐하는 자들이 누릴 축복(1절)
  B. 의인들이 누릴 축복(2-3절)
    C. 곤경에 임하는 축복(4절)
  B′. 자비와 인애를 베푸는 자들에 임하는 축복(5절)
    C′. 곤경에 임하는 축복(6-8절)
  B″. 의인들이 누릴 축복(9절)
A′. 악인들의 갈망에 임할 저주(10절)

대부분 학자들은 이 시편은 이렇다 할 구조를 지니지 않았다고 생각하거나 아예 구조 분석이 불가하다고 생각한다. 이러한 상황은 알파벳 시의 특징이라고 할 수 있다. 이 주석에서는 다음과 같은 분석을 바탕으로 본문을 주해해 나갈 것이다. 이 시편의 중심 주제는 여호와를 경외하는 이의 삶이다.

A. 경외하는 이가 누릴 복(112:1-3)
B. 경외하는 이의 일상(112:4-6)

C. 경외하는 이의 두려움이 없는 삶(112:5-9)
D. 경외하지 않는 자는 멸망함(112:10)

III. 주해

이 시편은 여호와를 경외하는 사람이 누리는 축복을 노래한다. 그의 신앙과 지혜는 공의와 정의를 사랑하시는 하나님이 하신 일과 그의 말씀을 묵상하는 것에서 시작한다. 여호와를 경외하는 삶이 누리는 축복은 이 땅에서만 실현되는 것이 아니라, 종말까지 이어진다. 끝날에 가서 하나님은 의인은 높이시고, 악인들은 모두 멸망시키실 것이기 때문이다.

1. 경외하는 이가 누릴 복(112:1-3)

1 할렐루야,
여호와를 경외하며
그의 계명을 크게 즐거워하는 자는 복이 있도다
2 그의 후손이 땅에서 강성함이여
정직한 자들의 후손에게 복이 있으리로다
3 부와 재물이 그의 집에 있음이여
그의 공의가 영구히 서 있으리로다

이 시편도 111편처럼 '할렐루야'로 시작하며 노래의 성향을 알려준다. 이 시편은 찬양시라는 것이다(Goldingay, Goulder). 기자는 시편 111:10의 내용과 연결하여 노래를 시작한다. 여호와를 경외하고 주님의 계명을 크게 즐거워하면 '복이 있다'(אַשְׁרֵי)며 시편 1편을 연상케 한다(cf. McCann). 시편에서 총 26차례 사용되는 이 단어는 우리가 이스라엘의 지혜에 대한 가르침을 접하고 있다는 신호이다(deClaissé-Walford et al.). 111편은 하나님이 하신 일을 즐거워하라고 했는데, 이 시편은 주님의 말씀을 기뻐하라라고 한다.

주님의 계명을 '크게 즐거워한다'(חָפֵץ מְאֹד)는 것은 하나님의 율법을 추구하며 그 말씀에 따라 살기를 매우 기뻐한다는 뜻이다. 그에게는 율법대로 사는 것이 짐이 아니라 특권이기 때문이다. 여호와를 경외하는 지식의 실천적인 면모이다. 안다는 것은 곧 그 지식을 지침으로 삼아 행동하는 것이다.

여호와를 경외하고 주님의 계명을 즐거워하는 사람들이 누릴 축복은 크게 세 가지이다.

첫째, 그들의 후손들은 이 땅에서 강성할 것이다(2절). '강성하다'(גִּבּוֹר)는 군사적인 언어이지만 비유적인 언어로 사용될 때는 큰 영향력을 행사하는 것을 의미한다(Tucker & Grant, cf. 잠 31:23). 자손들이 강성하게 되는 것은 경건하게 사는 삶에 임하는 포상이 아니라, 경건한 삶의 결과이다(Tucker & Grant). 우리가 하나님을 경외하는 삶을 살면 우리 자손들에게 큰 영향을 미친다.

둘째, 부와 재물이 그들의 집에 있다(3a절, cf. 잠 1:13). 하나님이 의인들에게 복을 주셔서 궁핍함이 없게 하실 것이라는 뜻이다. 하나님을 경외하는 삶은 우리의 현실(재물과 집)에도 영향을 미친다. 중요한 것은 의인이 하나님이 그에게 축복으로 내려 주신 부와 재물을 어디에 쓰느냐 이다. 4절과 9절은 그가 이웃들과 가난한 사람들을 위해서 쓴다고 한다.

셋째, 그들의 공의가 영구히 서 있을 것이다(3b절). 하나님이 그들의 의를 인정하시는 축복이 그들과 함께할 것이다. 하나님을 경외하는 삶은 우리의 영원한 미래에도 영향을 미친다.

2. 경외하는 이의 일상(112:4-6)

4 정직한 자들에게는 흑암 중에 빛이 일어나나니
그는 자비롭고 긍휼이 많으며 의로운 이시로다
5 은혜를 베풀며 꾸어 주는 자는 잘 되나니
그 일을 정의로 행하리로다
6 그는 영원히 흔들리지 아니함이여
의인은 영원히 기억되리로다

앞 섹션(1-3절)은 복 있는 사람, 곧 하나님을 경외하는 사람이 누리는 축복에 대해 말했다. 이 섹션은 의인이 그와 같은 축복을 누리게 된 이유를 설명한다. 그의 일상이 참으로 경건하고 거룩하기 때문에 하나님이 그를 보호하시고 복을 내리실 수밖에 없다는 논지다.

여호와를 경외하는 사람들에게는 흑암 중에도 빛이 일어난다(4a절). 참으로 어려운 상황에 처하더라도 분명 구원이 그에게 임할 것이라는 뜻이다. 흑암 중에 일어나는 '빛'(אוֹר)이 누구 혹은 무엇을 의미하는가는 학자들 사이에 상당한 논쟁거리다(Goldingay, cf. deClaissé-Walford et al., Tucker & Grant). 빛이 실제적인 빛인지, 혹은 의인인지, 혹은 하나님인지가 이슈다. 하나님이 어려움에 처한 의인을 돕기 위해 일어나시는 모습이다(cf. 시 27:1; 37:6; 미 7:8).

의인들이라 해서 살면서 어려움을 겪지 않는 것은 아니다. 그러나 그들이 곤경에 처하면 하나님이 나서서 그들을 도우신다. 그러므로 그들은 자비롭고 긍휼이 많은 의로운 삶을 계속할 수 있다(4b절). 개역개정은 4b절의 주어를 하나님으로 해석했는데, 거의 모든 번역본이 정직한 자들을 주어로 해석한다(새번역, 현대인, 공동, NIV, NAS, NRS, ESV, TNK). 하나님이 정직한 자들에게 빛이 되어 주시어 그들이 계속 자비롭고 긍휼이 많은 의로운 삶을 살 수 있도록 하신다는 의미이다. 정직한 자들은 자비와 긍휼이 많고 의로우신 하나님을 닮은 삶을 살아간다(cf. 시 111:8).

여호와를 경외하는 정직한 사람들은 자비롭고 긍휼이 많고 의로운 삶을 산다고 하는데(4절), 이러한 사람들은 삶에서 어떻게 열매를 맺는가? 그들은 이웃에게 은혜를 베풀기를 기뻐하며, 꾸어 주기도 잘한다(5a절, 출 22:24–26; 레 25:35–38; 신 24:6, 10–14; cf. Hossfeld–Zenger, 시 34:8–10; 37:21; 이자를 받지 않고 빌려주는 것이 얼마나 중요한가는 느헤미야 5장을 참조하라). 의인들은 자신들이 하나님께 경험한 긍휼과 은혜를 이웃들에게 흘려보낸다. 새번역이 5절의 의미를 잘 표현하고 있다: "은혜를 베풀면서 남에게 잘 꾸어 주는 사람은 모든 일이 잘 될 것이다. 그런 사람은 일을 공평하게 처리하는 사람이다." 남을 배려하는 것이 손해 보는 것 같지만, 하나님이 그를 축복하시니 오히려 더 잘된다. 하나님을 경외하는 사람은 항상 옳은 결정을 한다(Kidner).

하나님이 남에게 선을 행하기를 기뻐하는 사람은 특별히 보호하시기 때문에 그 누구도 그를 흔들 수 없다(6절). '흔들리다'(מוט)는 시편 46:6에서 중심을 잡지 못해 좌우로 요동하는 열방을 묘사하며 사용되었다. 반면에 하나님의 도성은 절대 흔들리지 않는다고 했다(시 46:5). 의인은 요동치는 세상에서도 하나님의 도성처럼 영원히 흔들리지 않을 것이다. 또한 그가 의로운 삶을 살았으므로 사람들은 오랫동안 그를 기억할 것이다: "그런 사람은 영원히 흔들리지 않을 것이다. 의로운 사람은 영원히 기억된다"(새번역).

3. 경외하는 이의 두려움이 없는 삶(112:5–9)

7 그는 흉한 소문을 두려워하지 아니함이여
여호와를 의뢰하고 그의 마음을 굳게 정하였도다
8 그의 마음이 견고하여 두려워하지 아니할 것이라

그의 대적들이 받는 보응을 마침내 보리로다
9 그가 재물을 흩어 빈궁한 자들에게 주었으니
그의 의가 영구히 있고
그의 뿔이 영광 중에 들리리로다

기자는 여호와를 경외하며 의로운 삶을 사는 자는 절대 흔들리지 않을 것이라고 했다(cf. 6절). 이 섹션에서는 어떠한 상황에서도 흔들리지 않는 의인들의 삶을 두 가지로 묘사한다. 포로기 이후에 이 시편이 저작된 것이라고 하는 이들은 이 말씀이 불안해하는 당시 공동체에 큰 위로를 주었을 것이라고 한다(Tucker & Grant).

첫째, 여호와를 경외하는 사람들은 흉한 소문을 두려워하지 않는다(7a절). 시기와 질투가 만연한 세상에서 사람들은 의롭고 경건하게 사는 사람들을 가만히 두지 않는다. 자신들이 의롭게 살지 못하는 것에 대해 경건한 사람들에게 자극을 받아 더 거룩하게 살면 될 것을 자신들이 그렇게 살지 못하면 남들도 그렇게 살면 안 된다고 생각하기 일쑤다. 결국 그들은 의인들을 시기하고 질투하여 온갖 험담과 '악한 소문들'(מִשְּׁמוּעָה רָעָה)을 생산해 낸다. 그러므로 이 세상에서 경건하고 의롭게 사는 일은 참으로 힘이 든다.

그러나 의인들은 선을 행하는 일을 그만두거나 지치지 않는다. 그들은 오직 여호와를 의뢰하고 마음을 굳건하게 하기 때문이다(7b절). '여호와를 의뢰하다'(בָּטֻחַ בַּיהוָה)는 하나님이 그들이 의를 행하며 사는 것을 기뻐하시고 인정하신다는 것을 믿고 확신한다는 뜻이다. 의인들이 선을 행하면서 사는 것은 처음부터 세상 사람들에게 인정받기 위한 것이 아니라, 하나님의 말씀과 권위에 복종하는 행위였다. 그들은 오직 삶에서 여호와를 예배하기 위해 의롭게 살아온 것이다. 그들은 하나님이 인정하시면 된다는 각오로 살아간다. 그러므로 세상 사람들이 아무리 악한 소문을 퍼뜨린다 해도, 그들의 마음은 굳건하다.

둘째, 여호와를 경외하는 사람들은 두려워하지 않는다(8a절). '그의 마음이 견고하다'(סָמוּךְ לִבּוֹ)는 것은 어떠한 일로도 마음이 흔들리지 않는 꾸준함이 있다는 뜻이다. 이러한 일이 가능한 것은 의인들은 자신들이 왜 경건하고 거룩한 삶을 추구해야 하는가에 대한 확고한 믿음과 확신이 있기 때문이다. 하나님이 이런 일을 기뻐하시고, 그들이 이렇게 사는 것을 귀하게 여기신다는 믿음과 확신이다. 그들의 삶이 바로 여호와를 경외하는 삶이기 때문이다. 우리가 하나님이 인정하시는 삶을 살 때, 우리는 모든 두려움을 떨치고 평안을 누릴 수 있다.

의인들이 악인들이 조성하는 두려움에 흔들리지 않고 당당하게 살면 그들을 괴롭히던 악인들이 오히려 '흔들리는' 것을 보게 될 것이다(8b절). 8절의 의미는 새번역이 잘 살렸다: "그의 마음은 확고하여 두려움이 없으니 마침내 그는 그의 대적이 망하는 것을 볼 것이다." 하나님이 원수들이 의인들을 두려워하고, 그들에게 복종하도록 하신다.

기자는 여호와를 경외하는 삶이 무엇이며, 하나님이 왜 그들을 귀하게 여기시는지 다시 한번 하나의 예를 들어 설명한다(9절). 그들은 하나님이 주신 물질적인 축복(cf. 3절)을 어려운 이웃들을 위해 기꺼이 사용한다(9a절, cf. 5절). 그들이 누구든 어려운 사람을 보면 대가를 바라거나 아끼지 않고 돕는 것을 강조하기 위해 기자는 '(자유로이/마음껏) 흩어 준다'(פִּזַּר נָתַן)는 말을 사용한다(cf. 새번역, 아가페, 현대인, NIV, NAS, TNK, ESV, NRS). 그들이 이런 일을 할 수 있는 것은 하나님이 그들에게 주신 축복이 이웃들을 돕기 위한 것이라는 사실을 알기 때문이다. 그들은 자신들을 하나님의 축복을 흘려보내는 축복의 통로로 생각한다.

하나님은 이처럼 아름다운 삶을 사는 사람들을 존귀하게 여기신다. 그러므로 그들은 영원히 기억되며(9b절), 그들의 뿔이 더 높이 들리게 하실 것이다(9c절). '뿔'(קֶרֶן)은 힘과 능력의 상징이다. 하나님이 악한 세상에서 위축되고 소심해질 수 있는 의인들을 더 축복하셔서 더 강성하게 하실 것이라는 뜻이다. 그들은 하나님의 더 큰 축복으로 더 많은 사람들을 도울 것이다.

4. 경외하지 않는 자는 멸망함(112:10)

10 악인은 이를 보고 한탄하여
이를 갈면서 소멸되리니
악인들의 욕망은 사라지리로다

하나님이 그를 경외하는 삶을 사는 사람들은 영원히 복을 주시고 존귀하게 여기시지만, 악인들은 망하게 하신다. 악인들은 죽는 순간까지 시기와 질투로 가득한 사람들이다. 하나님이 의인들을 보호하시고 축복하시는 것을 보고 한탄한다. '한탄하다'(כעס)는 '화를 낸다'는 뜻이다(새번역, 아가페, 공동, NIV, NRS, ESV, NAS). 의인들이 하나님의 복을 받는 모습을 보고 회개하기는커녕 오히려 분통을 터트린다. 비뚤어져도 참으로 많이 비뚤어진 사람들이다. 의인과 악인의 차이는 상당 부분 마음가짐에서 비롯되는 듯하다.

결국 화로 가득한 악인들은 이를 갈며 소멸될 것이다. 이를 가는 것은 아무것도 할 수 없는 사람의 분노 표현이다(Anderson). '소멸하다'(מסס)는 전쟁과 연관된 것이며 싸울 의욕을 완전히 잃는다는 뜻에서 마음이 '녹아내리다'는 뜻을 지녔다(수 2:11; 5:1; 7:5; 겔 21:7; 미 1:4). 의인들의 빛은 더 빛을 발하고, 악인들은 음지에서 조용히 사라진다(Tucker & Grant). 악인들에게는 끝까지 회개라는 것은 없다. 하나님이 벌하실 만한 자들이다. 악인들이 죽으니 그들의 '욕망들'(תַּאֲוַת)도 그들과 함께 사라진다. 아마도 의인들을 해하려는 욕망들일 것이다(Hossfeld-Zenger). 악한 사람들에게서 선한 것들이 나올 리 없다. 그러므로 하나님이 그들을 죽이실 때 그들의 악한 욕망도 함께 사라지게 하신다.

악인들이 남을 돕는 일에 인색한 의인들의 후손들이라는 해석이 있다(Terrien). 그러나 8절 후반부가 대적들을 언급하는 것으로 보아 가능성이 별로 없다. 악인들은 의인들을 시기하고 질투한 나쁜 사람들이다.

시편 113-150편

시편 113-150편은 대부분 찬양시라는 주제로 하나로 묶이며, 크게 세 섹션으로 구분된다.

첫째, 시편 113-118편은 일명 '이집트 찬양시'(Egyptian Hallel) 혹은 '유월절 찬양시'(Passover Hallel)로 불리며, 유월절을 기념하며 불렸다(deClaissé-Walford et al., VanGemeren). 오늘날 유태인들은 113-114편은 유월절 음식을 먹기 전에, 115-118편은 먹은 후에 읽는다(Goldingay, cf. 마 26:30; 막 14:26). 뒤를 잇는 119편은 토라시(Torah)로 따로 구분된다.

둘째, 시편 120-134편은 '위대한 찬양시'(Great Hallel)로 불렸으며, 예루살렘 성전을 찾아가는 순례자들이 부른 노래들이다. 뒤를 잇는 135-136편은 '찬양 파트너들'(partners in praise)로 불리기도 하며 위대한 찬양시들에 대한 적절한 결론으로 생각된다(Mays). 뒤를 잇는 137편은 회중 탄식시로 따로 구분된다. 138-145편은 모두 다윗의 시로 구성되어 있다.

셋째, '최종 찬양시'(Final Hallel)는 시편 146-150편으로 구성되어 있다. 이 마지막 찬양시들은 성도들이 일상에서 부른 노래들로 알려져 있다. 특히 성전이 파괴된 주후 70년 이후에는 회당에서 매일 드리는 기도의 일원으로 사용되었다(VanGemeren). 이 같은 세 주요 찬양시 섹션을 염두에 두고 각 시편을 주해해 나가고자 한다.

제113편

I. 장르/양식: 회중 찬양시(cf. 29편)

유월절을 기념하며 부른 '이집트 찬양시'(Egyptian Hallel, 113-118편) 모음집에 속한 첫 번째 시편이며, 서술적 찬양시(descriptive praise psalm)이다(Ross, VanGemeren, cf. Brueggemann & Bellinger). 유태인들은 오늘날에도 이 시편과 다음 시편(114편)을 유월절 음식을 먹기 전에 묵상하거나 부른다. 이러한 이유로 인해 이 시편은 유대교와 기독교의 찬양 전통에서 매우 특별한 자리를 차지하게 되었다(Craigie). 교회는 오랜 세월 동안 이 시편과 114편, 그리고 118편을 부활절을 기념하며 묵상했다(McCann, Ross).

우리는 이 시를 회중 찬양시로 분류하지만(cf. deClaissé-Walford et al.), 찬양시(praise psalm)와 증거시(testimony psalm)를 합한 것이라는 견해도 있다(Goldingay). 이 시는 '할렐루야'로 시작하여(1절) '할렐루야'로 마무리하며(9절) 이 두 할렐루야가 노래를 감싸고 있다. 중심 내용은 몇 번의 높낮이를 반복하며 진행된다(Graber).

이 시가 예루살렘 성전으로 순례를 떠난 사람들이 부른 노래라는 견해가 있는가 하면(Terrien), 유월절 예배에서 두 성가대가 교창적으로 부른 노래라는 추측도 있다(Kraus). 윌리스(Willis)는 이 노래가 원래 전쟁에서 승리한 후 이스라엘이 부른 노래였는데, 훗날 실로에서 불리기 시작했다고 한다.

저작 시기에 대하여도 매우 다양한 견해가 존재한다. 이 시편과 한나의 노래(삼상 2장)의 유사성을 근거로 왕정 시대에 이스라엘의 북쪽 지방에서 저작되었다고 하는 학자가 있다(Willis). 심지어는 왕정 시대 이전인 주전 12세기에 저작된 노래라는 이도 있다(Freedman). 그러나 대부분 학자들은 이 시편이 포로기 이후에 저작되었다고 생각하며(Anderson, Kirkpatrick), 구체적으로 페르시아 시대를 지목하는 이도 있다(Terrien). 이 시편이 한순간에 저작된 것이 아니라, 오랜 세월을 지나며 여러 사람들에 의하여 계속 수정되었다는 주장도 있다(Allen). 저작 시기에 대하여는 도대체 알 수가 없다.

II. 구조

이 시편을 두 파트로 구분하는 이들도 있지만(McCann, Terrien), 대부분 학자들은 세 파트로 구분한다. 이 주석에서도 다음과 같이 세 섹션으로 구분하여 본문을 주해해 나가고자 한다(cf. Ross, Tucker & Grant, VanGemeren).

A. 위대하신 하나님 찬양(113:1-3)
B. 낮은 곳에 임하는 높으신 하나님(113:4-6)
C. 낮은 자들을 구원하시는 하나님(113:7-9)

III. 주해

여호와 하나님은 참으로 위대하시고 높으신 분이다. 그런데 그분은 세상에서 가장 낮은 자들을 찾아오셔서 구원을 베풀기를 즐겨하신다. 그러므로 하나님의 높으심과 인간의 낮음이 대조되며 극명한 대조를 이루는 노래이다.

1. 위대하신 하나님 찬양(113:1-3)

1 할렐루야,
여호와의 종들아 찬양하라
여호와의 이름을 찬양하라
2 이제부터 영원까지
여호와의 이름을 찬송할지로다
3 해 돋는 데에서부터 해 지는 데에까지
여호와의 이름이 찬양을 받으시리로다

'할렐루야'로 시작하는 세 시편(111-113편) 중 세 번째 것이다. 이 시를 끝맺는 마지막 단어도 '할렐루야'이다. 두 할렐루야가 내용을 감싸며 이 시편은 분명 찬양시라는 점을 확실하게 한다. 기자는 찬양의 중요성을 강조하기 위해 이 짧은 섹션에서 '찬양하다'(הלל)를 네 차례나(1절[3x], 3절) 사용한다. 개역개정이 2절에서 '찬송하다'로 번역한 히브리어 동사(ברך)의 본 의미는 '축복하다'이지만, 인간이 하나님을 축복할 수 있는 것은 아니기 때문에 '찬송하다/송축하다'로 번역함이 옳다(cf. Goldingay). 저자는 '여호와의 종들'(עַבְדֵי יְהוָה)에게 찬양하라고 하는데, 제사장들과 레위 사람들뿐만 아니라 모든 주의 백성에게 주는 권면이다(VanGemeren). 주의 백성들은 종들이 주인의 권위에 복종하는 마음으로 여호와를 찬양해야 한다(Kidner).

무엇을 찬양해야 하는가? 본문은 '여호와의 이름'(שֵׁם יְהוָה)을 세 차례(1, 2, 3절) 언급하면서 주님의 이름을 찬양할 것을 주문한다. 여호와의 이름은 주님이 행하신 모든 일과 자신에 대해 주신 계시의 결정체이다

(deClaissé-Walford et al., cf. 출 3:16; 6:7; 겔 36:28; 37:23). 여호와 하나님의 모든 것을 찬양하라는 권면이다(cf. Kraus). 여호와의 속성과 하시는 일은 모두 선하기 때문이다.

언제 여호와의 이름을 찬양해야 하는가? 기자는 '이제부터 영원까지'(מֵעַתָּה וְעַד־עוֹלָם) 찬양하라 한다(2절). 찬양이 끊이는 일이 없도록 지속적으로 찬양하라는 것이다. 우리를 위한 하나님의 은총과 자비가 끊이지 않는 한, 우리의 찬송도 계속되어야 한다(VanGemeren). 또한 영원히 끊이지 않는 찬양은 앞으로 시편 모음집에서 매우 중요한 주제로 부상한다(Hossfeld-Zenger). 하나님을 찬양하려면 주님이 하신 일과 속성에 대해 깊은 묵상과 그 묵상에서 일어나는 감동이 있어야 한다. 그러므로 이 말씀은 항상 하나님을 마음에 두고 살라는 권면이기도 하다.

어디서 여호와의 이름을 찬양해야 하는가? 저자는 '해 돋는 데에서부터 해 지는 데에까지'(מִמִּזְרַח־שֶׁמֶשׁ עַד־מְבוֹאוֹ) 세상 모든 곳에서 하나님을 찬양할 것을 권면한다. 남녀노소 가릴 것 없이 주님의 자녀들은 세상 어디에서 살든 항상 주님을 찬양하는 찬송 소리가 온 세상(해 뜨는 곳에서부터 해지는 곳까지)에서 끊이지 않도록 해야 한다. 기자는 2-3절을 통해 여호와를 향한 경배와 찬양은 시간과 공간을 초월하여 계속되어야 한다고 한다(Goldingay). 한 주석가는 이러한 상황을 '초우주적인 여호와의 위엄'(super cosmic majesty of YHWH)을 노래하는 것이라고 한다(Terrien).

2. 낮은 곳에 임하는 높으신 하나님(113:4-6)

4 여호와는 모든 나라보다 높으시며
그의 영광은 하늘보다 높으시도다
5 여호와 우리 하나님과 같은 이가 누구리요
높은 곳에 앉으셨으나
6 스스로 낮추사

천지를 살피시고

하나님은 참으로 위대하시다. 세상 모든 나라가 주님 아래 있다(4a절). 여호와께서 온 세상을 다스리신다는 의미이다. 또한 하나님의 영광은 하늘보다 높다(4a절). 하나님은 주님께 가장 잘 어울리는 보좌에서 세상뿐만 아니라 하늘도 다스리신다(Nasuti). 하나님은 우리의 상상을 초월하는 가장 영광스럽고 존귀하신 분이다.

그러므로 여호와 우리 하나님 같으신 분은 그 어디에도 없다(5a절). 여호와는 그 누구와도 비교가 불가능한 특별한 신이시다(cf. 출 15:11; 신 3:24; 사 40:18; 시 35:10). 감격스러운 것은 이처럼 위대하신 여호와가 바로 '우리 하나님'(אֱלֹהֵינוּ)이라는 사실이다. 하나님은 우리와 매우 특별한 관계를 맺으셨다.

하나님은 모든 면에서 가장 위대하고 특별한 신이시며 높은 보좌에 앉아 계시는 왕이시다(5b절). 또한 여호와는 세상과 그 안에 사는 자기 백성들에 대해 매우 관심이 많으시다. 그러므로 세상에서 가장 높은 곳에 계시는 하나님은 스스로 자신을 낮추시어 세상을 두루 살피신다(6절). 이때까지 시편에서 하나님은 사람들을 시험하기 위해 세상을 살피셨는데(시 11:4; 14:2; 17:2-3), 이 시편에서는 사람들을 돕기 위해 살피신다(Anderson). 또한 높으신 하나님이 낮은 곳으로 임하시는 것은 주님의 위대하심을 좀먹는 것이 아니라 더 드높이는 일이다(Slotki).

3. 낮은 자들을 구원하시는 하나님(113:7-9)

7 가난한 자를 먼지 더미에서 일으키시며
궁핍한 자를 거름더미에서 들어 세워
8 지도자들
곧 그의 백성의 지도자들과 함께 세우시며

[9] 또 임신하지 못하던 여자를 집에 살게 하사
자녀들을 즐겁게 하는 어머니가 되게 하시는도다
할렐루야

여러 학자들이 이 시편과 사무엘상 2장에 기록된 한나의 노래의 연관성을 지적했는데, 바로 이 섹션 때문이다. 한나는 임신하지 못하는 여인이었는데 하나님이 그녀에게 아들 사무엘을 주셨다. 또한 한나는 하나님을 찬양하면서 주님은 가장 낮은 자들을 가장 높은 곳으로 높이시는 분이라며 주님의 절대적인 주권을 찬양하는데(삼상 2:8), 바로 이 섹션도 이러한 내용을 담고 있다.

앞에서 기자는 하나님이 자기 백성들을 돕기 위해 세상을 살피시는 것을 암시했을 뿐(6절), 구체적으로 표현하지는 않았다. 이 섹션은 하나님이 자기 백성을 도우시는 일을 두 가지 예를 들어 설명한다. 두 사례 모두 여호와는 사람들을 차별하지 않으실 뿐만 아니라 오히려 가장 낮은 자들의 운명을 바꿔 놓으시는 '낮은 자들의 하나님'이심을 선언한다. 다음 두 사례는 하나님이 어떤 분이신가를 정의한다고 할 수 있다(Craigie).

첫 번째 사례는 하나님이 가난한 자를 존귀하게 하시는 일이다(7-8절). '가난한 자'(דַּל)는 경제적인 어려움에 처한 사람을 의미하는 여러 단어들 중 가장 절박한 사람들을 뜻한다(Tucker). 이 사람들은 자신들이 처한 경제적인 어려움을 스스로 극복할 만한 여력이 없는 사람들이다(Goldingay, Tucker & Grant). 그러므로 하나님이 도우시지 않으면 어떠한 소망도 없다. 하나님은 이처럼 절박한 사람을 먼지 더미에서 일으키신다(רום). '일으키다'(רום)는 4절에서 하나님의 '높으심'(רום)을 선언하며 사용된 단어이다. 그러므로 언어유희가 사용되고 있다. 세상에서 가장 높으신(רום) 분이 가장 낮은 자를 높이신다(רום)(McCann).

'궁핍한 자'(אֶבְיוֹן)는 주변의 도움이 필요한 자(needy)를 의미하며, 겨우 생존하는 사람들이다(Tucker & Grant). '거름더미'(אַשְׁפֹּת)는 쓰레기를 버리는 장소를 뜻한다(HALOT). 궁핍한 자들이 이곳에 있다는 것은 그들이 경제적으로 가난할 뿐만 아니라 사회적으로 소외당하고 따돌림을 당하고 있음을 암시한다(VanGemeren). 이들의 유일한 소망도 하나님이 도우시는 것이다. 하나님은 이 사회적 약자들을 높여 '지도자들'(נָדִיב)과 어깨를 나란히 하게 하신다. 사무엘서에서는 이러한 사회적 변화가 다윗을 통해 가장 확실하게 드러난다.

두 번째 사례는 하나님이 임신하지 못하는 여인을 임신하게 하시는 일이다(8절). 이 말씀 또한 사무엘의 어머니 한나와 직접적으로 연관이 있는 말씀이다(cf. 삼상 1장). 고대 근동 사회, 특히 이스라엘에서 아이를 낳는 것은 여성들에게 가장 영광스러운 일로 여겨졌다. 반대로 여자가 아이를 낳지 못하는 것은 큰 수치가 되어 사회에서 소외되기 일쑤였다. 그러므로 이 말씀은 하나님이 여자의 삶에 큰 반전을 이루신다는 뜻이다. 사무엘서에서는 한나가 이러한 경험을 했다. 여호와의 특별하심은 위대한 위상에 있는 것이 아니라, 힘없는 사람들의 삶을 변화시키는 것에 있다(Brueggemann).

제114편

I. 장르/양식: 회중 찬양시(cf. 29편)

'이집트 찬양시' 모음집(113-118편)의 두 번째 노래이다. 고대 번역본들(LXX, Syriac, Vulgate)은 114-115편을 하나로 취급하지만, 두 시편의 내용이 많이 다르기 때문에 하나로 취급하는 것은 바람직하지 않다(VanGemeren). 이 시편은 광야에서 이스라엘과 함께하시고 요단 강을 건너게 하신 하나님의 현현을 회고하는 서술적 찬양시(descriptive praise psalm)형식을 지녔다. 그러므로 유월절을 기념하기에 참으로 좋은 시라고 생각된다.

우리는 이 시편을 회중 찬양시로 구분하지만(cf. deClaissé-Walford et al.), 찬양하라는 권면이 없는 것이 독특하다(McCann, Tucker & Grant). 내용은 이스라엘의 역사를 회고하는 역사시(historical psalm)이지만(Brueggemann & Bellinger, Ross), 출애굽 사건이 다른 노래들에서처럼 일정한 속도를 유지하며 기념되는 것이 아니라, 마치 천둥이 치는 것처럼, 혹은 지진이 땅을 가르는 것처럼 순식간에 있었던 일로 묘사된다(Geller, Kidner, Weiser). 이 노래는 출애굽 사건 자체보다는 그 사건을 상징하는 시적 언어가 하나님이 주권적으로 역사와 자연을 다스리시는 것을 묘사하는 수단으로 사용되기 때문이다(Weiser).

이 시편의 저작 시기를 왕정 시대로 추측하는 사람들은 사마리아가 멸망한 주전 722년을(Anderson), 혹은 그보다 늦은 시기를 지목한다(Weiss). 이 시편을 여호수아 3-5장과 연결하여 길갈 전승(Gilgal tradition)의 일부로 간주하는 이들도 있다(Kraus). 또한 이 시는 북 왕국의 벧엘에서 유래한 것이며, 요시야 시대에 남 왕국 유다의 관점인 2절이 삽입된 것이라는 견해도 있다(Ruppert, cf. Ross). 포로기 혹은 이후 시대의 신학을 반영하고 있다고 하여(cf. Gerstenberger) 포로기 이후 시대를 저작 시기로 보는 이들도 있다(Goldingay). 그러나 이 시편이 언제, 어떤 상황에서 저작되었는지에 대하여는 도저히 알 수가 없다는 것이 대부분 사람들의 입장이다(cf. McCann). 이 시편에 대한 모든 것이 불확실한 수수께끼 같은 시라고 하는 이도 있다(Terrien).

저작 시기는 알 수 없지만, 이 시편이 처음 저작되었을 때는 아마도 예배나 예식에서 사용되었을 것이다. 유태인들이 113편과 함께 이 시편을 유월절 음식을 먹기 전에 읽고 묵상하는 것을 보면 유월절 절기에 사용하기 위해 저작된 것이 거의 확실하다. 세월이 지나면서 이 시는 이스라엘 역사를 바꿔 놓은 출애굽 전통과 그 전통이 주는 생명에 참여하도록 새로운 세대를 초청하는 역할을 한 시편이다(Brueggemann).

II. 구조

대부분 학자들은 이 시편을 네 섹션으로 구분한다(Allen, deClaissé-Walford et al., McCann, Ross, Tucker & Grant). 이 주석에서도 다음과 같은 구조를 바탕으로 본문을 주해해 나가고자 한다.

A. 하나님의 주권 아래 있는 유다와 이스라엘(114:1-2)

    B. 바다와 강과 산들과 언덕들의 반응(114:3-4)

    B′. 바다와 강과 산들과 언덕들의 반응에 대한 질문(114:5-6)

A′. 하나님의 주권 아래 있는 세상(114:7-8)

III. 주해

유다와 이스라엘이 하나님의 주권 아래 있는 것처럼 온 세상이 하나님의 통치 아래 있다. 그러므로 하나님은 언제든 세상을 자기가 원하는 대로 변화시키고 사용하실 수 있다. 산과 바다 등 자연을 형성하고 있는 것들도 이러한 사실을 알고 있다. 기자는 이스라엘의 출애굽과 가나안 정착 사건을 회상하면서 이러한 사실을 노래한다.

1. 하나님의 주권 아래 있는 유다와 이스라엘(114:1-2)

[1] 이스라엘이 애굽에서 나오며
야곱의 집안이 언어가 다른 민족에게서 나올 때에
[2] 유다는 여호와의 성소가 되고
이스라엘은 그의 영토가 되었도다

출애굽은 이스라엘이 하나님의 언약 백성으로 태어난 생일이다(Kirkpatrick). 이스라엘이 태어나던 날, 그들은 이방 나라에서 구출되었으며, 언어가 다른 민족에게서 나왔다(1절, cf. 출 42:23). '언어가 다른 민족'은 주의 백성이 받은 억압을 생각나게 한다(Tucker & Grant, cf. 출 20:2; 신 6:21; 사 28:11; 렘 5:15). 출애굽은 노예 생활을 하던 이스라엘이 억압하는 자들의 압박에서 풀려나 자유를 누리게 된 날이다.

출애굽을 통해 노예 생활에서 해방된 주의 백성은 여호와의 성소가 되고 영토가 되었다(2절). 이 시편이 북 왕국이 망한 주전 722년 이후에 저작된 것이라고 생각하는 사람들은 유다만 존재하는 상황에서 이스라엘이 유다를 의미하는 비슷한 말로 사용되고 있다고 하지만(Allen),

기자는 두 이름을 사용하여 이 두 나라가 모두 여호와의 백성임을 강조한다(Dahood, Kirkpatrick).

이 두 나라 중에서도 유다가 여호와의 성소라고 하는 것은 성전이 예루살렘에 있다는 사실을 확인하며(Allen), 이스라엘과 유다 중 유다가 하나님과의 관계에서 더 특별한 위치(성전이 예루살렘에 있으므로)를 누리고 있다는 것을 의미할 수도 있지만(Weiss, cf. 시 78:68-69), 이 말씀에서는 유다와 이스라엘이 평행을 이루며 함께 하나님의 기업임을 의미하는 것으로 해석하는 것이 바람직하다(Hossfeld-Zenger, McCann, cf. 출 19:5-6).

2. 바다와 강과 산들과 언덕들의 반응(114:3-4)

3 바다가 보고 도망하며
요단은 물러갔으니
4 산들은 숫양들 같이 뛰놀며
작은 산들은 어린 양들 같이 뛰었도다

하나님이 이스라엘을 이집트에서 구원해 내신 날, 바다가 보고 도망쳤다(3a절). 이미지는 바다가 무언가를 보고 혼비백산하여 줄행랑을 치는 모습이다. 홍해가 주의 백성에게 길을 내어준 일을 염두에 둔 회고이다(cf. 출 14-15장). 요단 강도 순식간에 물러갔다(3b절). 여호수아가 백성들과 함께 이른 봄 홍수로 범람하는 요단 강을 마른 땅 건너듯이 건넌 일을 회상한다(cf. 수 3-4장). 왜 홍해와 요단 강이 도망한 것일까? 7절은 그들이 하나님의 현현을 보았기 때문이라고 한다. 파도가 출렁이는 바다와 홍수로 범람하는 강도 하나님을 보자 도망가기에 바빴다는 것이다(cf. 수 4:23).

바다와 요단 강은 옛 창조의 일부였다. 하나님이 이스라엘을 자기 백성으로 삼으시는 새 창조를 시작하자 옛 창조물들은 도망하기에 바쁘다. 옛 창조는 하나님의 새로운 창조를 방해하거나 막을 수 없기 때문이다(Broyles, Ross). 하나님의 새로운 창조인 구원 사역은 천지를 창조하신 옛 창조 사역보다 훨씬 더 위대하고 놀라운 일이다.

산들과 언덕들도 주님을 보자마자 뛰놀았다(4절). 주의 백성의 길을 가로막은 물들은 도망했지만(3절), 산들은 숫양들과 어린 양들처럼 기뻐 뛰었다(Hossfeld-Zenger). 산들이 기뻐 뛰논 것은 산에서 하나님이 이스라엘에게 율법을 주셨기 때문이다(Tucker & Grant). 하나님이 이스라엘과 언약을 맺기 위해 시내 산에 임하셨을 때 땅이 흔들리고 우레가 임한 것을 이렇게 표현하고 있다(cf. 출 19장).

3. 바다와 강과 산들과 언덕들의 반응에 대한 질문(114:5-6)

5 바다야 네가 도망함은 어찌함이며
요단아 네가 물러감은 어찌함인가
6 너희 산들아 숫양들 같이 뛰놀며
작은 산들아 어린 양들 같이 뛰놂은 어찌함인가

기자는 출애굽 사건을 떠올리며 상당히 흥분하고 즐거워한다(Weiss). 그의 질문에는 이러한 분위기가 반영되어 있다. 그는 먼저 홍해와 요단 강이 순식간에 도망한 이유를 묻는다(5절). 홍해와 요단 강은 하나님의 백성이 가야 하는 길을 막아 섰다가 두려워 혼비백산하여 도망했다. 창조주의 출현(cf. 7절)에 피조물들은 심히 두려워 자리를 피한 것이다. 이어 기자는 산들은 왜 숫양들과 어린 양들처럼 뛰놀았는지 묻는다(6절). 그들은 하나님이 이스라엘과 언약을 맺기 위해 시내 산에 임하셨을 때 기뻐 뛰었다.

바다와 요단 강과 산들과 작은 산들에 대하여는 이미 3-4절이 똑같은 내용을 언급했다. 단지 이곳에서는 수사학적인 질문들로 바꿔 놓은 것뿐이다. 그러나 중요한 차이가 한 가지 있다. 3-4절은 과거형으로 기록되어 옛적에 있었던 일을 추억하는 반면 이 섹션은 현재형으로 진행되었다는 사실이다(Nelson). 이러한 변화를 통해 기자는 독자들을 출애굽 사건이 진행되던 현장으로 돌아가 선조들의 경험이 그들의 경험이 되도록 유도한다(Allen). 또한 출애굽 사건과 이에 대한 자연의 반응은 옛 추억으로 머무는 것이 아니라, 이 순간에도 특별한 의미로 주의 백성에게 다가오고 실현되어야 한다는 것을 암시한다(Nelson).

4. 하나님의 주권 아래 있는 세상(114:7-8)

7 땅이여
너는 하나님 앞에서 떨지어다
8 그가 반석을 쳐서 못물이 되게 하시며
차돌로 샘물이 되게 하셨도다

개역개정의 7절 번역이 다소 아쉽다. 마소라 사본을 번역하면 "땅이여 주 앞에서 떨어라, 야곱의 하나님 앞에서 떨어라"가 된다(cf. 새번역, 아가페, 현대인, 공동, NIV, NAS, NRS, ESV, TNK). '떨다'(חיל)는 산모가 아이를 낳을 때 고통으로 몸을 비트는 모습이다(HALOT, cf. 시 97:4). 바다와 강이 참으로 고통스러웠다는 뜻이다.

7절이 두 차례 사용하는 '앞에서'(מִלִּפְנֵי)는 하나님의 현현이 임했음을 의미한다(cf. Tucker & Grant, VanGemeren). 5-6절은 왜 바다와 강이 도망하고, 왜 산이 뛰놀았는지를 질문했는데, 7절이 이 질문들에 답하고 있다. 그들은 하나님의 현현을 목격했기 때문에 급히 도망했다.

하나님은 출애굽의 역사를 이루실 때 반석을 쳐서 못물이 되게 하셨으며, 차돌로 샘물이 되게 하셨다(8절). 모세가 르비딤과 가데스에서 바위를 쳐 물을 내게 한 일을 회고하고 있다(cf. 출 7:1-7; 민 20:2-13). 저자는 하나님이 광야에서 물을 주신 사건을 분사(participle)들을 사용하여 현재에도 계속되고 있는 것처럼 묘사한다(VanGemeren). 과거에 바위를 쳐서 물을 주신 하나님이 아직도 축복의 물이 흐르도록 하실 수 있다는 점을 강조하기 위해서이다(Kirkpatrick). 또한 온 세상을 두려워 떨게 하시는 하나님이 자기 백성을 자상하게 보살피시며 그들의 필요를 채우시는 모습이 인상적이다.

제115편

I. 장르/양식: 회중 찬양시(cf. 29편)

옛 번역본들은 이 시편을 114편과 하나로 취급했다(LXX, Vulgate). 아마도 두 가지가 작용한 것 같다. 첫째, 111-113편에서 각 시편을 나누는 역할을 하던 '할렐루야'가 114-115편 사이에는 없다. 둘째, 114:7이 온 세상에게 주님 앞에서 두려워 떨 것을 요구하는데, 115편이 그들이 왜 떨어야 하는지 그 이유를 말하며 114:7을 확대 설명하는 듯한 느낌을 준다. 그러나 114편과 115편은 서로 독립된 노래라는 것이 학자들의 견해이다(cf. deClaissé-Walford et al., McCann, Hossfeld-Zenger, VanGemeren).

이 시편의 양식을 구분하기가 쉽지 않다. 한 시에서 매우 다양한 유형의 스피치가 사용되고 있기 때문이다: '애가, 찬양, 신탁, 권면, 찬양'(Tucker & Grant, cf. Brueggemann & Bellinger, McCann). 우리는 이 시를 회중 찬양시로 분류하지만(cf. Anderson, deClaissé-Walford et al., Ross), 회중 확신시(communal confidence psalm)로 구분하는 이들도 있다(Goldingay, VanGemeren). 회중 확신시는 공동체의 필요를 설명하며 하나님이 그들의 필요를 채우실 것이라는 확신을 표현한다. 시편 115, 125, 129편이 확신시로 구분된다(VanGemeren). 이 세 편의 확신시들 중 115편을 빼고, 46편을 추가하는 이도 있다(Kraus). 확신시는 찬양시뿐만 아니라 탄식시하고도 매우 비슷하다(VanGemeren). 그러므로 이 시편을 회중 탄식시로 구분하는 이도 있다(Allen).

이 시편의 저작 시기도 확실히 알 수 없다(cf. Luke). 우상들에 대한 논쟁적인 성향을 근거로 포로기 이후 시대로 보는 이들이 있다(Brueggemann & Bellinger, McCann, cf. Terrien). 더 구체적으로 시기를 언급하는 사람들은 주전 5세기에 예루살렘의 회복된 공동체에서 불린 노래이며, 우상 숭배의 어리석음을 가르치기 위해서 저작된 것이라고 한다(Goldingay). 그러나 우상 숭배에 대한 경고는 이미 오래전부터 수없이 많이 나오기 때문에 이 시편이 우상 숭배의 어리석음을 경고한다 해서 포로기 이후로 볼 필요는 없다.

학자들은 이 노래가 성전에서 진행된 예배나 예식에서 인도자와 예배자들이 교창적으로 불렀을 것으로 생각한다(Luke, cf. McCann, Tucker & Grant). 구체적으로 어떤 예배나 예식이었는지는 전혀 알 수 없다(Kraus). 그러므로 본문이 주는 메시지에 치중하는 것이 현명하다(Hossfeld-Zenger). 유태인들은 오늘날에도 이 시편을 유월절 음식을 먹은 다음에 묵상한다.

II. 구조

거의 모든 학자들이 교차대구법적 구조를 제시한다. 그러나 문단 나누기와 문단 메시지 요약에서는 현저한 차이를 보인다(cf. Alden, Allen, Tucker & Grant, VanGemeren). 이 주석에서는 다음과 같은 구조를 바탕으로 본문을 주해할 것이다.

A. 하나님께 호소함(115:1-3)

B. 우상들의 무능함(115:4-8)

C. 여호와를 의지하라(115:9-11)

C'. 여호와께서 복을 주신다(115:12-14)

B'. 여호와의 능력(115:15-16)

A'. 하나님을 찬양함(115:17-18)

III. 주해

기자는 이스라엘의 하나님 여호와가 우상들과 얼마나 다른 가를 묘사한다. 여호와는 모든 면에서 열방의 신들과 비교할 수 없는 신이시다. 그러므로 모든 영광과 찬양을 주님께만 돌리는 것은 물론이요, 하나님만 의지하라고 한다. 우리가 하나님을 의지하면, 주님은 우리에게 많은 은혜로 화답하실 것이다.

1. 하나님께 호소함(115:1-3)

[1] 여호와여
영광을 우리에게 돌리지 마옵소서
우리에게 돌리지 마옵소서
오직 주는 인자하시고 진실하시므로
주의 이름에만 영광을 돌리소서
[2] 어찌하여 뭇 나라가
그들의 하나님이 이제 어디 있느냐
말하게 하리이까
[3] 오직 우리 하나님은 하늘에 계셔서
원하시는 모든 것을 행하셨나이다

주의 백성이 참으로 고통스러운 일을 경험했다. 그들의 불행을 지켜보던 세상 사람들이 비아냥거리면서 "너희들의 하나님은 어디 있느냐?"고 묻는다(2절, cf. 출 32:12; 시 42:3; 79:10; 욜 2:17; 미 7:10). 고대 사회에서 이러한 질문은 전쟁에서 주로 사용되었다(Kidner, Tucker & Grant, cf. 사 36:13-20). 열방의 질문은 매우 의미심장하다(Hossfeld-Zenger). 그들이 숭배하는 우상들은 능력 여부에 상관없이 물리적인 모습을 취한다(cf. 4-7절). 반면에 이스라엘의 신은 이 세상에서 어떠한 물리적인 모습도 지니지 않았다. 여호와는 하늘에 계시기 때문이다(3절). 열방의 질문은 포로기 혹은 그 이후 시대 이스라엘의 어려운 형편을 반영하고 있는 듯하다(Goldingay, Kraus, cf. Anderson).

세상 사람들에게 온갖 수모를 당하던 사람들이 하나님께 호소한다(1절). 그들은 여호와께서 그들에게 영광을 돌리지 말고 오직 하나님 자신에게 돌리라고 한다. 이 말씀은 자신들은 무능하고 무기력하여 땅에 떨어진 하나님의 영광과 명예를 높이기 위해 어떠한 일도 할 수 없으니 여호와께서 스스로 회복하시라는 간절한 바람이다(Anderson, deClaissé-Walford et al., Ross, Tucker & Grant). 하나님의 '영광'(כָּבוֹד)은 주의 백성의 번영과 직접 연관이 있다(VanGemeren, cf. McCann).

이러한 간구는 주의 백성들의 슬픔을 잘 표현하고 있다. 그들은 수치와 모욕은 자신들만 당했으면 한다. 그러나 그들이 여호와의 백성이라는 이유로 사람들은 하나님도 욕되게 한다. 안타까운 것은 그들이 하나님의 명예를 회복시키기 위해 할 수 있는 일이 아무것도 없다는 사실이다. 그러므로 그들은 하나님께 주님의 명예와 이름을 회복하라고 간절히 기도한다.

주의 백성은 이처럼 안타까운 기도를 드리면서도 주님이 꼭 그들의 기도를 들으시고 자기 명예를 회복하실 것을 확신한다. 주님은 인자하시고 진실하시기 때문이다(1절). '인자'(חֶסֶד)와 '진실'(אֱמֶת)은 하나님의 속성들 중 가장 기본적이고 중요한 것들이다(cf. 출 34:6). 그러므로 기자는 땅에 떨어진 명예와 영광을 회복하라며 하나님을 자극하는 기도를 드리고 있다.

이 노래를 부르는 공동체는 여호와는 하늘에 계시면서 역사하시는 하나님이심을 고백한다(3절). 하나님의 사역이 하늘로 제한된 것은 아니다. 하늘은 여호와의 범우주적 주권을 상징한다(McCann, cf. 시 113:4-5).

하나님이 그들의 삶에 대해 침묵하신다 해서 그들을 버리거나 더 이상 사역을 하지 않으시는 분이 아니다. 하나님은 이 순간에도 하늘에 계시면서 원하시는 일이라면 무엇이든지 이루신다(3절). 하나님은 자기 백성들을 돕는 일이라면(Krawelitzski) 어떤 일이든 하실 수 있는 능력(Hurvitz)과 자유(Seybold)를 지니셨다는 뜻이다. 심지어는 은혜를 베푸시는 것을 보류하는 것도 하나님의 자유이다(Calvin). 하나님의 자유는 주의 백성들이 경험하고 있는 여호와의 부재를 상당 부분 설명한다.

"너희 하나님이 어디 있느냐?"라는 열방의 질문(2절)은 여호와의 무능함을 전제한다(Tucker & Grant). 이에 대해 주의 백성들은 여호와는 세상 그 어느 신들보다도 능력이 큰 신이라는 사실을 확신한다. 여호와께서 하늘에서 사역하신다는 것은 주님이 이 세상에 머무는 신들(cf. 4-8절)과는 질적으로 다르다는 것을 의미하기 때문이다(Weiser).

2. 우상들의 무능함(115:4-8)

4 그들의 우상들은 은과 금이요
사람이 손으로 만든 것이라
5 입이 있어도 말하지 못하며
눈이 있어도 보지 못하며
6 귀가 있어도 듣지 못하며
코가 있어도 냄새 맡지 못하며
7 손이 있어도 만지지 못하며
발이 있어도 걷지 못하며

목구멍이 있어도 작은 소리조차 내지 못하느니라

8 우상들을 만드는 자들과

그것을 의지하는 자들이 다 그와 같으리로다

이스라엘의 하나님 여호와는 하늘에 계시며 무엇이든 이루시는 분이라고 고백한 기자가 이스라엘에게 "너희 하나님이 어디 있느냐?"고 묻는 이방인들이 신이라고 숭배하는 것들은 어떠한가를 지적한다. 이 섹션은 이스라엘의 하나님 여호와와 열방의 신들을 가장 극명하게 대조하며 열방은 이스라엘에게 "너희 하나님이 어디 있느냐?"고 물을 자격이 전혀 없다고 한다(Kraus). 열방은 참으로 어이없는 물건들을 신으로 숭배한다며 오히려 그들의 어리석음을 비난한다.

기자는 먼저 우상들은 사람의 손이 조각하고 만들어 낸 은과 금덩어리에 불과하다고 한다(4절). 여호와는 사람들을 창조하시는데, 우상들은 사람들에 의해 제조된다(McCann). 그는 이방인들이 신으로 숭배하는 '신들'을 비(非)신격화(de-divinization) 하고 있다(Hossfeld-Zenger). 우상들의 재료에 나무와 돌을 더할 수 있다. 우상들은 타락한 인간들이 상상력을 발휘하여 생산한 '신들'이다. 그러므로 우상들은 신들이 아니기 때문에 우상들이 사람들을 타락시키는 것이 아니라, 타락한 인간들이 만들어 내는 것이 우상이다. 기자도 이러한 사실을 분명히 하고 있다. 우상들은 그들을 제조해 낸 인간보다 능력이 더 약하다.

이어 그는 우상들이 할 수 없는 것들을 만수(滿數)인 7가지로 나열하며 우상들의 허무맹랑함을 고발한다(cf. 시 135:15-18; 사 44:9-20; 46:6-7). 열방은 자신들의 우상을 능력을 지닌 '왕'이라고 하는데, 이 섹션은 그들의 우상들은 무능한 '벌거벗은 왕'이라고 한다(Kidner). 우상들은 대체적으로 사람이나 짐승 형태를 취하기 때문에 우리가 지니고 있는 기관(장기)들을 지니고 있다. 다만 이것들은 무용지물이다. 장식용에 불과한 것이다(5-7절): (1) 입, (2) 눈, (3) 귀, (4) 코, (5) 손, (6) 발, (7) 목구멍. 이 일곱 가지는 말하는 기관(입, 5a절)으로 시작하여 소리를 내는 기관(목구멍, 7c절)으로 마무리되며, 우상들의 가장 큰 문제는 말이나 소리를 낼 수 없음에 있다는 사실을 강조한다. 반면에 우리 하나님은 말씀으로 자기 백성과 교통하신다.

우상들은 사람이 손으로 만든 것이라는 말로(4절) 이 섹션을 시작한 기자는, 우상들을 만드는 자들과 그것들을 의지하는 자들은 그들이 숭배하는 우상들과 별반 다를 바가 없다는 사실로 마무리한다(8절). 우상들과 숭배자들은 둘 다 어리석기는 마찬가지며, 영적인 지각이 없는 것도 같다는 의미의 저주다(Kraus, cf. 왕하 17:15; 사 44:9-20; 렘 2:5). 결국 우상과 숭배자들은 함께 망하게 될 것을 경고한다.

3. 여호와를 의지하라(115:9-11)

9 이스라엘아
여호와를 의지하라
그는 너희의 도움이시요
너희의 방패시로다
10 아론의 집이여
여호와를 의지하라
그는 너희의 도움이시요
너희의 방패시로다
11 여호와를 경외하는 자들아
너희는 여호와를 의지하여라
그는 너희의 방패시로다

기자는 이스라엘(9a절)—아론의 집(10a절)—여호와를 경외하는 자들(11a절)을 순차적으로 언급하면서 여호와를 의지할 것을 세 차례 권면한다(9b, 10b, 11b절). 일부 학자들은 '여호와를 경외하는 자들'을 유대교로 개종한 이방인들이라고 하지만(Hossfeld–Zenger, cf. deClaissé–Walford et al.), 전혀 설득력이 없는 해석이다. 이는 주의 백성들을 의미한다(Gerstenberger, McCann, Tucker & Grant).

8절은 우상을 '의지하는'(בטח) 자들은 모두 망할 것이라고 했다. 반면에 여호와를 '의지하는'(בטח) 자들은 살 것이다. 저자는 같은 단어를 사용하여 우상 숭배자와 여호와를 의지하는 이들의 대조적인 운명을 강조한다.

열방이 아무리 빈정대도 이스라엘이 의지할 분은 여호와뿐이다. 열방의 신들은 모두 인간들이 조각해 낸 우상들이며, 아무런 능력도 지니지 않았기 때문이다(4–8절). 반면에 여호와는 하늘에 머무시면서 원하는 일은 마음대로 하시는 능력의 신이다(3절). 그러므로 하나님은 그를 경외하는 사람들에게 도움을 주시고, 방패가 되어 주신다. 이스라엘이 처한 상황이 아무리 어렵다 해도 분명 구원하시고 보호하실 것이다.

그는 하나님이 그들의 도움이시라는 말도 두 차례 반복한다(9c, 10c절). '도움'(עֵזֶר)은 힘을 뜻한다(HALOT). 하나님은 결정만 하시면 언제든 그들을 도우실 힘과 능력을 지니고 계신다. 그러므로 이스라엘이 해야 할 일은 주님의 능력을 의심하는 것이 아니라, 주님이 사역하시기를 간절히 구하는 것이다.

저자는 '여호와는 그들을 돕는 방패이시다'라는 말도 세 차례 언급한다(9d, 10d, 11c절). '방패'(מָגֵן)는 방어용 무기이다. 주님은 분명 자기 백성의 방패가 되시어 적들의 공격에서 그들을 안전하게 보호하실 것이다. 또한 하나님은 분명 주님을 의지하는 그들을 구원하실 것이다. 주님은 인자하시고 진실하시기 때문이다(1절).

4. 여호와께서 복을 주신다(115:12-14)

12 여호와께서 우리를 생각하사 복을 주시되
이스라엘 집에도 복을 주시고
아론의 집에도 복을 주시며
13 높은 사람이나 낮은 사람을 막론하고
여호와를 경외하는 자들에게 복을 주시리로다
14 여호와께서 너희를 곧 너희와 너희의 자손을
더욱 번창하게 하시기를 원하노라

앞 섹션(9-11절)은 여호와를 의지하라는 권면을 세 차례나 했다. 이 섹션은 여호와께서 주를 의지하는 사람들에게 복을 내려 달라는 기도로 구성되어 있다. 하나님이 주를 의지하는 사람들에게 복을 주시기로 결정만 하시면 그들의 어려운 형편이 반전될 것이다(12절).

앞 섹션에서 '이스라엘—아론의 집—여호와를 경외하는 자들' 순서로 주님을 의지하라고 했는데(9-11절), 이 섹션에서도 기자가 복을 빌어 주는 순서가 동일하게 전개된다. 다만 여호와를 경외하는 자들을 설명하면서 "높은 사람이나 낮은 사람을 막론하고"라는 말을 더하고 있다(13절). 하나님은 어떠한 차별도 하지 않으시고 주님을 의지하는 사람들은 모두 선대하신다. 또한 이 말씀은 사람이 노력하여 하나님의 복을 버는 것이 아니라, 은혜(선물)로 받는 것을 암시한다(McCann).

하나님이 복을 내려 주시면 이스라엘의 삶에는 어떤 변화가 생길까? 그들과 그들의 자손이 더욱 번창하게 될 것이다. 이 말씀이 늘어나는 주의 백성이 이방인 개종자들을 포함할 것을 의미한다는 해석도 있다(cf. Goldingay). 이스라엘이 심각하게 위축된 상황에서 공동체로써 그들이 바랄 수 있는 가장 큰 축복이다.

5. 여호와의 능력(115:15-16)

[15] 너희는 천지를 지으신 여호와께
복을 받는 자로다
[16] 하늘은 여호와의 하늘이라도
땅은 사람에게 주셨도다

잘 깨닫지 못해서 그렇지 주의 백성들은 이미 창조주이신 여호와께 복을 받은 자들이다(15절). 주님의 축복은 이 순간에도 계속되고 있으며, 하나님이 가장 멀리 계신다고 생각될 때에도 주님의 복은 우리와 함께한다. 우리는 창조주께서 창조하시고 다스리시는 세상에서 살고 있다. 또한 우리는 그 창조주를 의지하고 있다. 그러므로 하나님이 우리에게 복을 주시는 것은 당연한 일이다. 단지 우리가 복을 복으로 깨닫지 못하고 있을 뿐이다.

창조주께서는 하늘에 거하시며 사역하신다(16a절, cf. 3절). 땅은 우리에게 주셨다(16b절, cf. 창 1장). 여호와께서 세상에 내린 축복을 마음껏 누리며 살아가라는 의미이다(cf. Calvin).

6. 하나님을 찬양함(115:17-18)

[17] 죽은 자들은 여호와를 찬양하지 못하나니
적막한 데로 내려가는 자들은 아무도 찬양하지 못하리로다
[18] 우리는 이제부터 영원까지 여호와를 송축하리로다
할렐루야

하나님은 주를 의지하는 사람들을 도우시고 보호하신다(9-11절). 또한 주님은 그를 의지하는 자들에게 복을 주시어 번성케 하신다(12-14

절). 주님이 창조하신 세상도 마음껏 누리라며 우리에게 주셨다(16절). 이러한 하나님의 은혜에 우리는 어떻게 반응해야 하는가?

기자는 열심히 주님을 찬양하라고 한다. 죽어 스올로 내려가는 사람들은 여호와를 찬양할 수 없다(17절, cf. 시 94:17). 그러므로 살아 있는 동안 열심히 찬양하고 경배해야 한다. 우리가 살아 있다는 것은 하나님을 찬양한다는 것을 의미하며(Tucker & Grant), 우리가 찬양을 이어가는 한 우리는 살아 있다(Hossfeld-Zenger). 죽으면 주님을 찬양할 수 없기 때문이다. 여호와를 '축복하라'(ברך)는 단어가 사용되고 있지만(18절), '송축하다/찬송하다'로 번역하는 것이 적절하다. 우리는 이제부터 영원까지 여호와를 찬양하고 경배할 특권을 누리고 있다.

제116편

I. 장르/양식: 개인 찬양시(cf. 11편)

거의 모든 학자들이 이 노래는 큰 위기에서 구원해 주신 하나님께 드리는 개인 감사시(thanksgiving hymn)라고 한다(Brueggemann & Bellinger, McCann, Tucker & Grant, VanGemeren). 감사시의 요소들인 감사, 기도, 탄식, 확신, 서원을 포함하고 있기 때문이다. 다만 이 요소들이 일정한 순서를 따르지 않고 섞여 있어서 논리적인 문단 나누기와 구조를 파악하는 일은 거의 불가능하다(Gerstenberger, McCann).

게다가 칠십인역(LXX)과 라틴어 버전(Vg.) 등 옛 번역본들은 116편을 1-9절과 10-19절 둘로 구분하여 각각 독립적인 시편으로 취급하여 혼란을 더한다. 그러나 반복적으로 사용되는 단어들 등 이 두 섹션을 독립적인 시로 간주하기 보다는 통일성 있는 한편의 시로 취급하게 하는 증거들이 더 많다(Tucker & Grant).

이 노래가 성전을 말하고(19절) 제물을 드리는 일(13, 17절)을 언급하는 것으로 보아 예루살렘 성전에서 예배를 드리거나 예식을 치르며 사용된 것은 확실하다(McCann). 그러나 저작 시기를 파악하는 일은 쉽지 않다. 대부분 학자들은 포로기 이후를 저작 시기로 본다. 주전 6세기 말에 예루살렘 성전이 재건된 직후에 저작된 것이라는 견해가 있고(Terrien), 단순히 페르시아 시대라는 주장도 있다(Goldingay). 대부분 주석가들은 저작 시기에 대해 이렇다 할 언급을 하지 않는다.

이 시편이 어떤 정황에서 사용되었는가도 확실하지 않다. 죽을 뻔한 질병에서 회복된 사람이 부른 노래라는 이들이 있다(Terrien, cf. McCann). 또한 어느 시점에 이 노래가 이집트 찬양시(113-118편) 모음집에 포함되게 되었는지도 알 수 없다. 유태인들은 유월절 음식을 먹고 난 다음에 이 노래를 묵상했다.

II. 구조

다음은 밴게메렌(VanGemeren)이 제시한 구조이다. 한마디로 말해서 너무 복잡하다. 저자가 이처럼 복잡한 구조를 염두에 두고 이 시편을 집필하지는 않았을 것으로 생각된다.

I: A. 감사(1-2절)
  B. 구원의 필요성(3절)
    C. 구원하시는 하나님(4-6a절)
II: A′. 감사(6b-7절)
    C′. 구원하시는 하나님(8-11절)
  B′. 감사 서원(12-14절)
III: B″. 감사 서원(13-14절)
    C″. 구원하시는 하나님(15-16절)
  A″. 감사 서원(17-19절)

이 시의 구조를 파악하기는 거의 불가능하다는 것이 학자들의 생각이다(Gerstenberger, cf. McCann, Tucker & Grant). 이 시를 두 섹션으로 나누는 사람들은 1-11절과 12-19절로 나누는가 하면(Hossfeld-Zenger,

Janowski), 1–9절과 10–19절로 나누는 이들도 있다(Barré, cf. LXX, Vg.).

많은 주석가들이 이 시를 1–7절과 8–14절과 15–19절 세 파트로 나눈다(Allen, Mays, McCann, Brueggemann & Bellinger). 이 주석에서는 다음과 같은 분석을 바탕으로 본문을 주해해 나가고자 한다.

A. 종이 평생 기도할 것을 다짐함(116:1–2)
B. 종이 주님께 구원을 기도함(116:3–6)
C. 주님이 종을 구원하심(116:7–9)
D. 종이 고통 속에서 주님을 신뢰함(116:10–11)
E. 종이 베푸신 은혜에 감사(116:12–14)
F. 하나님은 종의 죽음을 소중히 여기심(116:15–16)
G. 종이 감사제를 드림(116:17–19)

III. 주해

생사를 좌우하는 큰 위기에 처했던 사람이 주님께 드리는 감사와 기도에 관한 노래이다. 기자는 자신이 경험한 은혜가 큰 만큼 평생 주님만을 찬양하며 의지하고 살 것을 다짐한다. 또한 그는 평생 자신의 기도가 끊이지 않을 것도 서원한다. 하나님의 사랑(은혜)과 성도의 신뢰는 신앙의 가장 기본적인 두 요소이다.

1. 종이 평생 기도할 것을 다짐함(116:1–2)

1 여호와께서 내 음성과 내 간구를 들으시므로
내가 그를 사랑하는도다
2 그의 귀를 내게 기울이셨으므로
내가 평생에 기도하리로다

이 섹션이 정확히 어떻게 번역되어야 하는가에 대해 상당히 논란이 있다(cf. deClaissé-Walford et al.). 주어가 여호와인지 혹은 기자인지, 또한 목적어가 누구인지가 확실하지 않기 때문이다(cf. Terrien). 그러나 전반적인 의미는 확실하다. 기자는 하나님이 그의 기도를 들어주셨다는 말을 반복하며 감사를 표시한다. 이 시편은 하나님이 그의 기도에 응답해 주신 일에 대한 감사 찬송임을 암시한다. 그는 여호와께서 그의 음성과 간구를 '들으시고'(1a절), 그에게 '귀를 기울이셨다'(2b절)며 여호와는 자기 백성의 기도를 들으시는 자상한 분이심을 찬양한다. 하나님은 우리의 가장 작은 신음에도 응답하시는 분이다.

우리의 기도에 귀를 기울이시는 하나님에 대한 우리의 반응은 어떠해야 하는가? 기자는 두 가지로 말한다.

첫째, 하나님을 사랑하라(1b절). 이 사실을 강조하기 위해 '내가 사랑합니다'(אָהַבְתִּי)가 강조형으로 이 시편의 첫 단어로 등장한다(VanGemeren, cf. Tucker & Grant). '사랑하다'(אהב)는 사람이 사랑하는 이를 만날 때 숨이 가빠지는 것을 묘사하는 감정적인 단어이다(cf. HALOT, NIDOTTE). 우리는 하나님을 진심으로, 열정적으로 바라보고 섬겨야 한다.

둘째, 더 열심히 기도하라(2b절). '기도하다'로 번역된 동사(קרא)의 기본적인 '부르다'이다. 그래서 일부 주석가들은 본문에서 이 단어가 여러 사람들에게 선포하겠다는 의미를 지니고 있다고 한다(Allen). 그러나 이 섹션의 주제는 우리의 기도에 응답하시는 하나님이다. 그러므로 이웃들을 불러 그들에게 이 사실에 대해 증거하는 것도 의미가 있겠지만, 하나님께 더 열심히, 꾸준히 기도하겠다는 취지로 해석하는 것이 더 설득력이 있다.

하나님은 우리의 기도를 하나도 놓치지 않으시고 모두 들으시고 적절하게 응답하시는 분이다. 그러므로 우리는 더욱더 기도해야 한다. 일종의 선순환이 제시되고 있다. 우리의 기도가 하나님께 열납될 때 우리는 더 적극적으로 기도할 힘이 생긴다.

2. 종이 주님께 구원을 기도함(116:3–6)

3 사망의 줄이 나를 두르고
스올의 고통이 내게 이르므로
내가 환난과 슬픔을 만났을 때에
4 내가 여호와의 이름으로 기도하기를
여호와여 주께 구하오니
내 영혼을 건지소서 하였도다
5 여호와는 은혜로우시며 의로우시며
우리 하나님은 긍휼이 많으시도다
6 여호와께서는 순진한 자를 지키시나니
내가 어려울 때에 나를 구원하셨도다

일부 학자들은 기자가 질병으로 인해 고통을 당하는 중 하나님이 그의 기도에 응답하셔서 치유하신 것으로 생각하지만(Terrien, cf. McCann), 정확히 어떤 일이 있었는지는 알 수 없다. 한 가지 확실한 것은 그가 경험한 위기가 그의 생명을 위협했다는 사실이다.

상황이 얼마나 위협적이었는지, 저자는 사망의 줄이 그를 둘렀고, 스올의 고통이 그에게 이르렀다고 한다(3절). '사망의 줄'(חֶבְלֵי־מָוֶת)이 그를 둘렀다는 것은 그가 죽음의 올무에 걸려 결코 빠져나올 수 없었던 상황을 묘사한다. 마치 올무에 걸린 새처럼 죽음을 기다리는 절박한 상황이었기에 그는 '스올의 고통'(מְצָרֵי שְׁאוֹל), 곧 '죽을 것이라는 공포'에 휩싸였다(cf. Allen).

이처럼 절망적인 상황에서(3c절) 그는 소망의 끈을 놓지 않았다. 그는 여호와께 간절히 기도했다(4절). 그는 주님께 그의 영혼을 구원해 달라고 호소했다(4c절). 살려 달라고 기도한 것이다(공동, 현대인, TNK, NRS). 상황이 절박한 만큼 그는 더 간절한 기도를 드릴 수 있었을 것이다.

끝까지 포기하지 않고 기도한 것이 그를 살렸다. 여호와께서 그에게 응답하신 것이다(5-6절). 기자는 그의 기도를 들으신 하나님의 성품을 은혜로우시고, 의로우시며, 긍휼이 많으시다며 세 가지로 묘사한다(5절). '은혜'(חַנּוּן)는 하나님의 용서와 백성들을 보존하시는 일과 연관이 있다(cf. 시 103:8; 111:4). 하나님의 '의'(צַדִּיק)는 언약과 약속을 지키시는 일에서 가장 빛난다(VanGemeren). '긍휼'(מְרַחֵם)은 하나님이 인간의 연약함과 한계를 이해하시고 자상하게 대하시는 것을 의미한다(cf. 103:13-14). 하나님의 속성들 중 일부인 이 세 가지는 일명 '은혜 공식'(the grace formula)으로 알려진 출애굽기 34:6-7의 일부이다(Janowski). 시편은 이 은혜 공식을 다양하게 인용하는데, 이 말씀도 그중 하나이다(cf. 시 103편; 111:4; 112:4; 145:8-9).

은혜로우시고, 의로우시며, 긍휼이 많으신 여호와는 순진한 자를 지키신다(6a절). '순진한 자들'(פְּתָאִים)은 어리거나 지식과 경험이 많지 않아 쉽게 유혹되는 사람들을 뜻한다(Anderson, HALOT). 이런 사람들은 배울 의지가 있음으로 가르치면 된다(cf. Tucker & Grant, NIDOTTE). 기자는 자신이 이 순진한 자들 중 하나였다고 한다. 그러므로 하나님이 어려움에 처한 그를 구원하셨다(6b절). 만일 순진한 자가 어리거나 지식과 경험이 많지 않은 사람이라면, 그가 처한 어려움이 질병이나 건강 문제는 아니었을 것이다.

3. 주님이 종을 구원하심(116:7-9)

7 내 영혼아
네 평안함으로 돌아갈지어다
여호와께서 너를 후대하심이로다
8 주께서 내 영혼을 사망에서,
내 눈을 눈물에서,

내 발을 넘어짐에서 건지셨나이다
9 내가 생명이 있는 땅에서
여호와 앞에 행하리로다

여호와의 도움으로 위기를 넘긴 기자는 예전에 누리던 평온한 삶으로 속히 돌아가기를 소망한다(7a-b절). 그는 하나님의 응답을 통해 주님이 그와 함께하신다는 사실을 깨달았다. 그러므로 주변이 아직 완전히 평온하지 않을지라도 그는 정상적인 삶을 살고자 한다. '평안함'(מְנוֹחַ)은 안식처를 뜻한다(HALOT). 한때는 스올(무덤)로 내려갈 뻔했던 사람이 이제는 안식처로 돌아가는 것을 꿈꾸고 있다. 그가 누리고자 하는 평안함은 하나님이 그를 후대하신 결과이다(7c절). '후대하다'(גמל)는 부족한 부분을 채운다는 의미를 지녔다(HALOT). 여호와께서 기자의 삶에서 부족한 부분(안식이 없는 부분)을 채우신 것이다.

기자는 하나님이 그의 기도에 응답하시어 도우신 일을 세 가지로 묘사한다(8절).

첫째, 하나님은 그의 영혼을 사망에서 구하셨다(8a절). 그는 죽을 뻔했다. 위기의 상황에서 주님이 그에게 구원의 팔을 내미신 것이다.

둘째, 하나님은 그의 눈에서 눈물이 멈추게 하셨다(8b절). 자신이 처한 어려움으로 인해 기도하면서 우느라 그의 눈에서 눈물이 그치지 않았다. 그러나 이제 하나님이 그의 눈에서 눈물을 모두 씻어 주셨다.

셋째, 하나님은 그의 발이 넘어지지 않도록 하셨다(8c절). 모든 것을 포기하여 넘어지거나 주저 앉을 수 있었는데, 하나님은 그에게 서서 걸을 수 있는 힘을 주시고, 바른 길을 가도록 인도하셨다.

이러한 은혜를 경험한 기자는 자기가 살아 있는 동안 여호와 앞에서 살 것을 다짐한다(9절). 이 말씀에도 사람이 죽으면 아무것도 할 수 없는 무기력한 존재가 된다는 것을 전제한다. 그러므로 그는 이 땅에 사는 동안 진실하고 정직한 삶, 곧 하나님이 인정하시는 삶을 살겠다고 한다. 하나님의 도움으로 실족하지 않고 계속 길을 걷는 사람(cf. 8c절)의 당연한 결단이다.

4. 종이 고통 속에서 주님을 신뢰함(116:10–11)

[10] 내가 크게 고통을 당하였다고 말할 때에도
나는 믿었도다
[11] 내가 놀라서 이르기를
모든 사람이 거짓말쟁이라 하였도다

기자는 자신이 큰 고통 중에도 하나님에 대한 믿음을 버리지 않았던 일을 회고한다. 그의 고백은 1–2절에 묘사된 그의 절대적인 하나님에 대한 신뢰를 바탕으로 하고 있다. 그가 당면한 어려움이 참으로 컸기 때문에 그는 '내가 참으로 큰 고통을 당한다'(אֲנִי עָנִיתִי מְאֹד)며 당혹해 했다(10a절). 그럼에도 불구하고 그는 하나님을 믿었다(10b절). '믿다'(אמן)는 '아멘'이 유래한 어원으로, 하나님은 신실하시고 믿을 수 있는 분이셔서 선한 것들로 자기 백성을 도우심을 고백하는 행위이다(Kirkpatrick). 기자는 자신이 처한 상황이 너무나도 어려웠지만, 하나님은 이 모든 것을 통제하시고 다스리셔서 그가 다시 평안을 찾을 수 있도록 하실 것이라는 확신을 가지고 주님을 바라보았다.

기자는 자신이 경험한 어려움을 통해 삶에 대해 한 가지 교훈을 얻었다. 인간은 절대 신뢰할 만한 존재들이 아니라는 사실이다(11절). 일부 주석가들은 이 말씀이 상당히 과장된 것이라 하지만(Booij, Goldingay), 그렇지 않다. 우리의 고통 중 상당 부분은 대인관계에서 유래한다. 이럴 때면 우리는 사람에 대해 실망한다. 또한 우리가 곤경에 처했을 때 사람들은 매우 잔인하게 우리를 대한다. 게다가 도와주겠다고 나서는 사람들 중에 상당 수가 절대 믿거나 의지해서는 안 될 사람들이다. 그러므로 기자는 자기 일을 경험하면서 사람들은 절대 신뢰할 수 없음으로 의지하면 안 된다는 사실을 깨달았다(cf. Allen). 결국 우리가 믿고 의지할 수 있는 이는 하나님 한 분이다.

5. 종이 베푸신 은혜에 감사(116:12-14)

12 내게 주신 모든 은혜를
내가 여호와께 무엇으로 보답할까
13 내가 구원의 잔을 들고
여호와의 이름을 부르며
14 여호와의 모든 백성 앞에서
나는 나의 서원을 여호와께 갚으리로다

하나님의 은혜로 죽음을 모면한 기자는 주님께 어떻게 감사를 표할 것인가를 고민한다(12절): "내가 여호와께 무엇으로 보답할까?" 이 질문은 수사학적인 질문이다. 인간이 하나님의 은혜에 보답하는 방법은 없기 때문이다(VanGemeren). 그러므로 그는 하나님의 성전을 찾아가 주님께 제물을 드리며 예배를 통해 조금이나마 감사한 마음을 표하고자 한다(13-14절). 그는 구원의 잔을 들고 여호와의 이름을 부르겠다고 한다(13절). 구원의 잔은 하나님의 도움을 통해 죽지 않게 된 것과 이후 하나님의 꾸준하신 보호를 상징한다(Janowski). 또한 일상적으로 여호와의 이름을 부르는 것은 기도를 통해 하나님께 무엇을 부탁한다는 의미인데(cf. 4절), 이 말씀에서는 단지 그가 성전에 가서 하나님의 선하심과 인자하심에 대해 묵상하며 감사 예배를 드리겠다는 의미이다(cf. Kraus, 출 29:40; 민 28:7).

또한 그는 모든 백성이 지켜보는 가운데 자신이 서원한 것을 주님께 갚을 것을 다짐한다(14절). 이 또한 공개적인 예배와 연관된 것이다

(Gerstenberger). 하나님이 그가 서원한 바를 이루어 주셨다는 사실을 사람들에게 알리기 위해서다. 그가 곤경에 처했을 때 주님께 어떠한 서원을 했을 것이고(cf. 시 50:14; 56:12; 욘 2:9), 그 서원을 갚겠다고 한다. 이 또한 성전을 찾아 여호와께 예배를 드리겠다는 뜻이다. 서원은 성전에서 갚는 것이기 때문이다.

6. 하나님은 종의 죽음을 소중히 여기심(116:15-16)

15 그의 경건한 자들의 죽음은
여호와께서 보시기에 귀중한 것이로다
16 여호와여
나는 진실로 주의 종이요
주의 여종의 아들 곧 주의 종이라
주께서 나의 결박을 푸셨나이다

초대교회 교부들 중 상당 수가 15절을 순교에 관한 말씀으로 간주했다(cf. Wesselschmidt). 하나님은 순교자들을 가장 귀하게, 아름답게 여기신다는 것이다. 그러나 구약은 어떠한 경우라도 죽음을 그다지 좋은 것으로, 혹은 아름다운 것으로 간주하지는 않는다. 이러한 문제를 해결하기 위해 학자들은 1행의 '죽음'(מָוֶת)을 '믿음'으로 바꾸거나(Barré), 2행의 '귀중한 것'으로 번역된 히브리어 단어(יָקָר)를 '커다란 대가'(costly)로 번역하기를 제한한다(Janowski, McCann, Tucker & Grant, cf. deClaissé-Walford et al.). 그러므로 번역본들은 성도들의 죽음은 하나님 보시기에 '통탄할 것'(grievous)이라고 번역한다(현대인, NRS, TNK, cf. Emerton). '주님의 경건한 자들'(חֲסִידָיו)이 죽는 것은 사람의 생명을 귀하게 여기시는 하나님이 치르시기에도 큰 대가이기 때문에 주님이 쉽게 허락하시는 일이 아니며, 성도의 때 이른 죽음도 하나님이 주저하시는 일이다

(VanGemeren).

하나님은 경건한 종들이 죽는 것보다 살기를 더 기뻐하시는 분이다. 그러므로 기자는 주님의 진실한 종으로 살려고 노력하는 자신을 하나님이 살도록 결박을 풀어주셨다며 하나님을 찬양한다(16절). '여종의 아들'은 아버지가 자유인이 되어도 주인의 집을 떠나지 못하는 종을 의미한다(Dahood, cf. 출 21:4). '결박'(מוֹסֵר)은 멍에를 뜻한다. 멍에는 기자가 스스로 노력해서 풀 수 있는 것이 아니었다(Kraus). 하나님이 속박하는 것들에게서 그를 자유롭게 하신 것이다.

7. 종이 감사제를 드림(116:17–19)

17 내가 주께 감사제를 드리고
여호와의 이름을 부르리이다
18 내가 여호와께 서원한 것을
그의 모든 백성이 보는 앞에서 내가 지키리로다
19 예루살렘아,
네 한가운데에서
곧 여호와의 성전 뜰에서 지키리로다
할렐루야

기자는 13–14절에서 하나님의 성전을 찾아가 제물을 드리며 주님을 예배할 것을 다짐했다. 자신이 경험한 은혜에 대해 하나님께 보답할 길이 없으니 이렇게라도 해서 고마움을 표시하겠다고 했다. 그는 노래를 마무리하는 이 섹션에서 자신의 다짐을 재차 확인한다.

앞에서는 구원의 잔을 들고 주님의 이름을 부를 것이라고 했는데(13절), 이번에는 감사제를 드리며 주님의 이름을 부르겠다고 한다(17절). '잔'(13절)이 곧 '감사제'의 일부인 것이다(cf. 레 7:12; 22:29). 이어 그는 자신이 여호와께 서원한 것을 모든 백성이 보는 앞에서 지킬 것이라고 하는데(18절), 14절에서 다짐한 것을 재차 확인하고 있다. 이번에는 예루살렘에게도 자기가 감사제를 드리고 서원을 지키는지를 지켜보라고 한다(19절). 그는 무슨 일이 있어도 꼭 성전을 찾아 주님께 감사제를 드리고 자신이 서원한 것을 갚을 것이다.

제117편

I. 장르/양식: 회중 찬양시(cf. 29편)

이집트 찬양시(113-118편)의 다섯 번째 노래이다. 두 절로 구성된 가장 짧은 시편이지만, 참으로 위대한 메시지를 담고 있다(Grogan, cf. Brueggemann & Bellinger). 이 노래는 찬양의 노래(deClaissé-Walford et al., McCann, Tucker & Grant) 혹은 서술적 찬양시(descriptive psalm of praise)로 구분된다(Ross, VanGemeren). 다른 시편들과의 연관성에 있어서는 할렐루야 시편들로 구성된 111-116편을 마무리하는 축도로 간주되기도 한다(Ross).

히브리어 사본들 중 36개는 116편과 117편을 한편의 시로 묶어 놓았고, 중세기에 출판된 시편 모음집들도 이 둘을 하나로 묶어 놓았다(Tucker & Grant). 그러나 내용과 주제를 고려할 때 116편과 117편은 서로 독립적인 시로 취급되어야 한다. 116편은 공동체가 함께 주님을 찬양하게 하며, 117편은 온 열방을 가상적인(hypothetical) 청중으로 동원하는 차이점도 보인다.

이 짧은 노래는 여러 예배에서 송영처럼 사용된 것으로 생각되나, 구체적으로 어떤 예배에서 사용된 것인지는 알 수 없다(Goldingay). 오늘날 유태인들은 유월절 예식에서 음식을 먹고 예식을 마무리하기 위해 네 번째 축하 잔을 마신 후 이 말씀을 읽거나 묵상한다(deClaissé-Walford et al.).

저작 시기로는 주전 7-6세기 왕정 시대로 보는 이들이 있다(Dahood). 그러나 대부분 학자들은 포로기 혹은 그 이후 시대를 저작 시기로 생각한다(Goldingay).

Ⅱ. 구조

두 절로 이루어진 이 시편은 여호와를 찬양하라는 권면(1절)과 찬양할 이유(2절)로 구성되어 있다.

A. 여호와 찬양 권면(117:1)

B. 여호와를 찬양할 이유(117:2)

Ⅲ. 주해

이 노래는 하나님의 인류 구원 계획이 처음부터 이방인들을 포함하고 있었다는 사실을 선포한다. 그러므로 이 가장 작은 시편의 규모(scale)는 가장 크고 넓다고 할 수 있다(Dahood, Kidner). 가장 진귀한 보석처럼 빛나는 노래이다.

1. 여호와 찬양 권면(117:1)

[1] 너희 모든 나라들아 여호와를 찬양하며
너희 모든 백성들아 그를 찬송할지어다

기자는 온 열방에게 하나님을 찬양하라고 권면한다(1절). '모든 나라들'(כָּל־גּוֹיִם)과 '모든 백성'(כָּל־הָאֻמִּים)은 세상에 있는 모든 민족들을 뜻한다. 로마서 15:11도 이러한 의미로 이 구절을 인용한다. 하나님은 이스라엘이 독점할 수 있는 분이 아니다. 그렇게 하기에는 너무나도 위대한 창조주이시다. 하나님은 이스라엘도 만드셨지만, 온 열방도 지으신 분이다. 그러므로 그는 당연히 온 열방에게 그들의 창조주이신 여호와를 찬양하라고 한다.

이 말씀은 상당 부분 종말론적인 비전을 내포하고 있다. 비록 현실은 열방이 하나님을 모르지만, 언젠가는 온 세상이 하나님을 알게 될 때가 올 것을 확신하고 있기 때문이다. 그러므로 이 말씀은 일종의 선교적 선포라고 할 수 있다. 기자는 이스라엘 백성으로 구성된 자기 청중에게 언젠가는 이런 시대가 오는 것이 하나님의 비전이라며 이방인들의 전도에도 힘써야 한다는 것을 암시한다(cf. Hossfeld-Zenger). 기자의 이러한 비전이 상당 부분 오늘날 교회를 통해 성취되었다.

2. 여호와를 찬양할 이유(117:2)

2 우리에게 향하신 여호와의 인자하심이 크시고
여호와의 진실하심이 영원함이로다
할렐루야

이어 저자는 온 세상이 왜 하나님을 찬양해야 하는지를 설명한다(2절). 우리(온 열방을 포함)에게 향하신 하나님의 인지하심이 크고, 진실하심이 영원하기 때문이다. 시편에서 '인자하심'(חֶסֶד)과 '진실하심'(אֱמֶת)은 이미 수차례 함께 등장했으며 하나님의 가장 기본적인 속성을 묘사하는 개념들이다(시 25:10; 36:5; 40:10; 57:10; 85:10; 86:15; 89:14; 92:2; 98:2; 100:5; 108:4; cf. 출 34:6). 여호와께서는 온 세상을 꾸준한 사랑으로 다스리신다(McCann). 하나님의 온 인류를 향한 사랑은 참으로 크고 영원하다.

인자하심은 자비와 인애를, 진실하심은 꾸준하심(성실하심)을 뜻한다. 하나님은 변함없는 사랑으로 꾸준히 인간들을 사랑하신다. 그러므로 이스라엘뿐만 아니라, 주님께 지음을 받은 모든 민족은 하나님께 감사와 경배를 드려야 한다는 것이 저자의 주장이다. '할렐루야'는 대체적으로 주의 백성에게 주어지는 권면이지만, 이번에는 온 열방도 그들의 찬양에 함께할 것을 권면한다(Goldingay).

제118편

I. 장르/양식: 개인 찬양시(cf. 11편)

'이집트 찬양시'(113-118편)의 마지막 노래로서 여러 정형화된 표현들(cf. 20, 26절)을 포함하는 듯한 느낌을 주는(Terrien, Westermann, cf. Gerstenberger) 시이며 내용은 감사시(song of thanksgiving)다(Brueggemann & Bellinger, Grogan, McCann). 이 시편은 단수와 복수를 함께 사용하고 있기 때문에 단수를 사용하는 5-19, 21, 28절을 근거로 개인 찬양시(deClaissé-Walford et al., Tucker & Grant)로 혹은 복수를 사용하는 1-4, 22-25, 27, 29절을 바탕으로 공동체 찬양시로 구분되기도 한다(Ross, cf. Tucker & Grant).

이 시편이 교창적(antiphonal)이고 인도자(I)를 왕으로 간주하는 이들은 다윗 계열의 왕이 전쟁에서 승리를 거두고 예루살렘으로 돌아와 여호와께 감사 예식을 드릴 때 사용한 노래라고 한다(Eaton, Kidner, McCann, cf. 대하 20:27-28). 그러나 이 노래가 바빌론 포로기 이후 상황을 반영하고 있다는 것이 대부분 학자들의 주장이다(cf. Anderson, McCann, Ross, Tucker & Grant, VanGemeren). 이들은 왕이 아니라 제사장이 예배를 인도하는 자라고 생각한다. 또한 왕정 시대에 유래한 오래된 시편을 훗날 사람들이 자신들이 처한 상황에 적절하게 재활용하고 있다고 생각한다(Anderson, McCann, Tucker & Grant).

이 시편이 사용된 정황에 대하여도 다양한 추측이 있다. 바빌론의 손에 함락된 성전을 귀향민들이 건축한 다음(주전 520–520년) 이 노래를 부른 것이라고 한다(Terrien). 가을 축제 때 사용되었으며 성전 밖에서 부른 노래라고 하는 이들도 있다(Anderson, Mowinckel). 이 시편을 사용한 절기나 예식에 대해 구체적으로 제안하지는 않지만, 1–18절과 19–29절 두 섹션으로 구분하여 1–18절은 성전 앞에서 진행된 행진 예식(liturgical procession)에서 사용되었고, 19–29절은 그 행렬이 성전 안으로 들어와 뜰에서 부른 노래라는 해석이 지배적이다(Allen, deClaissé–Walford et al., Kraus, Tucker & Grant). 오늘날 유태인들은 이 노래를 유월절과 연결하여 사용하지만, 탈무드는 장막절 중에 이 시편을 묵상했다고 한다(b. Sukkoth 45:a–b).

초대교회는 이 시편에서 예배를 인도하는 이가 다름 아닌 예수님이라고 했다(McCann). 이 시를 전적으로 메시아와 연관하여 해석한 것이다. 그럴만한 이유가 있다. 신약에서 이 시편이 자주 예수님과 연관하여 사용되기 때문이다. "여호와의 이름으로 오는 자가 복이 있음이여"(26절)는 종려 주일(Palm Sunday)과 연관하여 네 복음서에서 모두 인용된다(마 21:9; 막 11:9–10; 눅 19:38; 요 12:13). "건축자가 버린 돌이 집 모퉁이의 머릿돌이 되었나니"(22절)는 예수님이 마가복음 12:10에서 직접 인용하신다. 베드로도 사도행전 4:11에서 이 말씀을 인용하고 있고, 바울도 에배소서 2:20–21에서 이 말씀을 배경으로 삼았다. "여호와는 내 편이시라 내가 두려워하지 아니하리니 사람이 내게 어찌할까"(6절)는 로마서 8:31과 히브리서 13:6에서 인용된다.

II. 구조

테리엥(Terrien)은 이 시편에 대하여 다음과 같은 교차대구법적 구조를 제시한다. 그러나 텍스트를 문단화 하는 작업과 각 문단의 요약이 그다지 설득력이 있어 보이지는 않는다.

I. 여호와는 선하시다(1-4절)
　II. 곤경에서 주님께 부르짖음(5-7절)
　　III. 좋은 피난처가 되신 주님(8-9절)
　　　IV. 이방 나라가 패함(10-12절)
　　　　V. 여호와는 나의 힘(13-14절)
　　　IV′. 여호와의 오른손(15-18절)
　　III′. 나를 위하여 문을 열라(19-21절)
　II′. 모퉁이 돌은 기적(22-24절)
I′. 여호와는 선하시다(25-29절)

대부분 학자들은 이 시편에 대해 이렇다 할 구조를 제시하지 않고 단지 문단화 하여 본문을 주해한다. 그만큼 구조를 파악하기 어렵고 내용이 다양하여 섹션화 하기가 쉽지 않기 때문이다. 이 주석에서는 다음과 같은 분석을 바탕으로 본문을 주해해 나갈 것이다.

A. 하나님의 선하심과 인자하심(118:1-4)
　B. 나를 구원하신 하나님(118:5-18)
　B′. 우리를 구원하신 하나님(118:19-28)
A′. 하나님의 선하심과 인자하심(118:29)

III. 주해

이 노래는 큰 위기에서 하나님의 구원을 경험한 사람이 드리는 노래이다. 그는 하나님의 선하심과 인자하심을 개인적인 차원에서 감사하는 것에서 멈추지 않고, 주님의 구원을 경험한 공동체가 함께 주님을 예배하도록 유도한다. 그의 감사와 간증이 공동체로 확대되고 있는 것이다. 또한 이 시는 신약에서 메시아이신 예수께 적용되는 말씀들을 포함하고 있다.

1. 하나님의 선하심과 인자하심(118:1-4)

[1] 여호와께 감사하라
그는 선하시며 그의 인자하심이 영원함이로다
[2] 이제 이스라엘은 말하기를
그의 인자하심이 영원하다 할지로다
[3] 이제 아론의 집은 말하기를
그의 인자하심이 영원하다 할지로다
[4] 이제 여호와를 경외하는 자는 말하기를
그의 인자하심이 영원하다 할지로다

하나님의 특별한 은총을 경험한 기자는 흥분된 어조로 노래를 시작한다. 그는 제일 먼저 감사하며 찬양하고자 하는 하나님의 속성 두 가지를 나열한다. 하나님의 선하심과 인자하심이다(1절, cf 시 106:1; 107:1; 136:1). '선하심'(טוֹב)과 '인자하심'(חֶסֶד)은 하나님이 자기 백성을 대하실 때 어떻게 하시는가를 가장 잘 표현하는 개념들이다. 주님은 자기 백성을 참으로 좋게, 인자하게 대하신다. 또한 이러한 하나님의 선하심과 인자하심은 '영원히'(לְעוֹלָם) 지속된다. 하나님은 인간처럼 변하는 분이 아니시다.

이후 기자는 이스라엘 '공동체(2a절)—아론의 집(3a절)—여호와를 경외하는 자들(4a절)'을 순서적으로 지적하며 그들의 찬양을 통해 여호와의 인자하심이 영원하다는 사실을 고백할 것을 권면한다(cf. 시 115:9-11). 그래서 이 섹션에서는 "그의 인자하심이 영원하다 할지로다"는 말씀에 세 차례 후렴이 되어 반복된다(2b, 3b, 4b절, cf. 1b절).

기자가 '이스라엘—제사장들—여호와를 경외하는 자들'에게 여호와를 찬양하라며 순차적으로 권면하는 것은 '이스라엘'과 '여호와를 경외하는 자들'(יִרְאֵי יְהוָה)은 분명 구별되어야 하며, 다른 부류의 사람들임을 전제한다. 만일 같은 사람들이라면 '이스라엘'에 이미 포함되었음으로 굳이 따로 분류할 필요가 없기 때문이다. 그러므로 '여호와를 경외하는 자들'은 이방인들 중 주의 백성이 된 사람들을 의미한다(Calvin). 기자는 언젠가는 온 세상 사람들 중에 여호와를 경외할 자들이 많이 나올 것을 확신한다. 그러므로 신약 저자들은 더욱더 이 시편의 일부를 예수님께 적용한 것이다. 우리가 바로 주님의 인자하심이 영원하다며 주님을 찬양하는 '여호와를 경외하는 자들'이 된 것이다.

2. 나를 구원하신 하나님(118:5-18)

5 내가 고통 중에 여호와께 부르짖었더니
여호와께서 응답하시고
나를 넓은 곳에 세우셨도다
6 여호와는 내 편이시라
내가 두려워하지 아니하리니
사람이 내게 어찌할까
7 여호와께서 내 편이 되사
나를 돕는 자들 중에 계시니
그러므로 나를 미워하는 자들에게 보응하시는 것을
내가 보리로다
8 여호와께 피하는 것이 사람을 신뢰하는 것보다 나으며

[9] 여호와께 피하는 것이 고관들을 신뢰하는 것보다 낫도다
[10] 뭇 나라가 나를 에워쌌으니
내가 여호와의 이름으로 그들을 끊으리로다
[11] 그들이 나를 에워싸고 에워쌌으니
내가 여호와의 이름으로 그들을 끊으리로다
[12] 그들이 벌들처럼 나를 에워쌌으나
가시덤불의 불 같이 타 없어졌나니
내가 여호와의 이름으로 그들을 끊으리로다
[13] 너는 나를 밀쳐 넘어뜨리려 하였으나
여호와께서는 나를 도우셨도다
[14] 여호와는 나의 능력과 찬송이시요
또 나의 구원이 되셨도다
[15] 의인들의 장막에는 기쁜 소리, 구원의 소리가 있음이여
여호와의 오른손이 권능을 베푸시며
[16] 여호와의 오른손이 높이 들렸으며
여호와의 오른손이 권능을 베푸시는도다
[17] 내가 죽지 않고 살아서
여호와께서 하시는 일을 선포하리로다
[18] 여호와께서 나를 심히 경책하셨어도
죽음에는 넘기지 아니하셨도다

기자는 어떤 고통 중에 하나님의 선하심과 인자하심을 경험한 것일까? 정확히 알 수는 없지만 10-12절이 열방이 그를 에워쌌다고 하는 것으로 보아 큰 국가적인 위기였던 것이 분명하다. 그가 국가적인 위기 중 주의 백성의 지도자였음을 암시하기 때문에 일부 학자들은 기자가 다윗 계열의 왕이었다고 한다.

그가 고통 중에 여호와께 부르짖었다는 것은(5a절) 그와 백성이 당면

한 위기가 매우 심각했음을 암시한다. 기자는 그들이 처했던 위기를 매우 좁은 공간에 갇혔던 일로 묘사한다(cf. Tucker & Grant). 그러므로 하나님이 그의 기도를 응답하실 때 그가 갇혀 있던 비좁은 곳을 탈출하여 '넓은 곳'(מֶּרְחָב)에 세우셨다고 한다(5b-c절). 성경은 하나님의 구원을 '넓은 곳'으로 옮기는 것으로 묘사하고는 한다(Hossfeld-Zenger, Janowski, cf. 시 18:19; 31:8). 본문에서는 적들에게 포위된 상황에서 그 포위가 풀렸다는 뜻으로 해석될 수도 있다.

하나님의 도우심으로 큰 위기를 탈출한 기자는 이 일로 인해 여호와가 그의 편이라는 사실을 새로이 깨달았다(6a절). '내 편'(לִי)(6, 7절)이라는 말의 더 정확한 의미는 '나와 함께하신다'는 뜻이다(cf. 아가페, 현대인, NIV, NAS). '내 편'은 주님이 맹목적으로 내 편이 되어 주신다는 오해를 불러일으킬 수 있기 때문에 '함께하신다'로 번역하는 것이 좋다.

기자가 하나님이 그와 함께하신다는 사실을 깨달으니 세상에 두려울 것이 없다(6-7절). 하나님이 그와 함께하시니 그를 가장 두렵게 했던 사람들도 더 이상 두렵지 않다(6절). 기자는 6절을 '여호와'(יְהוָה)로 시작하여 '사람'(אָדָם)으로 마무리하여 하나님과 사람 사이에 최대한 많은 공간을 둔다(Dahood). 하나님과 인간에 대한 가장 강력한 대조를 유도하기 위해서다.

기자는 하나님이 그를 괴롭히는 자들에게 보응하시는 것을 직접 보게 될 것이라는 믿음도 생겼다(7절). 그는 밝은 미래도 기대하게 된 것이다. 이 모든 일이 하나님이 그와 함께하시면서 그를 도우시기 때문에 가능하다.

하나님께 부르짖어 구원을 경험한 기자가 자신이 깨달은 진리를 선언한다(8-9절). 여호와께 피하는 것이 사람을 신뢰하는 것보다 낫다(8절). 심지어는 고관들(왕자들, 권세가들)을 신뢰하는 것보다 여호와께 피하는 것이 더 낫다(9절). '…보다 낫다'는 잠언과 전도서에서 자주 사용되는 표현이며 이 시편이 사람들에게 지혜를 주기 위한 목적을 지니고 있음을 암시한다(deClaissé-Walford et al., Goldingay, cf. 잠 15:16; 16:8; 19:1).

'사람'(אָדָם)과 '고관들'(נְדִיבִים)은 한 쌍을 이루며 신분의 높낮이에 상관없이 인간들은 의지할 만한 존재들이 아니라는 사실을 지적한다. 하나님의 능력과 사람들의 능력은 결코 비교될 수 없으며, 하나님의 선하심과 인자하심도 그들의 것과 비교될 수 없기 때문이다. 인간은 신분적 높낮이에 상관없이 신뢰할 만한 자들이 아니라는 선언이 세상에 믿을 만한 사람이 하나도 없다고 했던 시편 116:11을 연상케 한다.

기자가 경험했던 위기는 어떠한 것이었는가? 그는 온 열방이 그를 에워쌌다고 한다(10절). 그들은 그를 에워싸고 에워쌌으며(11a절), 벌들처럼 그를 에워쌌다(12a절, cf. 신 1:44; 사 7:18). '에워싸고 에워쌌다'(סַבּוּנִי גַם־סְבָבוּנִי)는 자력으로는 도저히 빠져나갈 수 없는 포위된 상황을 묘사하는 듯하다. 혹은 이스라엘을 에워싸고 있는 주변 나라들이 모두 정치적인 적들이라 할 수 있는 상황을 이렇게 묘사할 수도 있다(느 6장, cf. Kraus).

그러나 기자는 원수들의 이 모든 에워쌈을 여호와의 이름으로 끊을 수 있었다(10b, 11b, 11c절). 개역개정은 이 섹션에서 동사 '끊다'(מוּל)가 미래형으로 번역되는 미완료형(אֲמִילַם)으로 사용되었다 하여 '그들을 끊으리로다'로 번역한다. 그러나 이 말씀에서는 이미 일어난 일을 묘사하고 있는 완료형 기능으로 해석되어야 한다. 그는 이미 하나님의 이름으로 적들의 포위를 모두 끊은 것이다(새번역, 아가페, 현대인, 공동, NIV, NAS, ESV, NRS).

그가 '하나님의 이름으로'(בְּשֵׁם יְהוָה) 포위망을 끊었다는 것은 하나님이 도우셨기 때문에 가능했다는 의미를 지니고 있다. 하나님의 이름은 여호와의 구원하시기 위한 임재를 상징하기도 하지만, 본문에서는 적들을 공격하는 무기를 상징한다(Kraus). 하나님이 그를 도우시니 겹겹이 에워싼 적들의 포위가 한 순간에 불타버린 가시덤불처럼 흔적도 없이 사라졌다(12b절). 하나님이 절대적으로 승리하신 것이다.

결국 전쟁은 적들이 원하는 대로 되지 않았다. 그들은 기자를 '밀어 넘어뜨리려고' 왔지만, 여호와께서 그를 도우셨기에 그는 든든히 서 있을 수 있었다(13절). 하나님이 그가 서 있는 반석이 되신 것이다. 그러므로 그는 여호와께서 그의 능력과 찬송과 구원이 되어 주신 것을 찬양한다(14절, cf. 출 15:2; 사 12:2). 그가 이 순간 살아 주님을 찬양하고 있는 것이 모두 주님이 하신 일이며 베푸신 은총이다.

저자는 이 일을 통해 한 가지 교훈을 깨달았다. 여호와께서는 의인들에게 구원을 베푸신다는 사실이다. 그러므로 의인들의 장막에는 기쁜 소리, 곧 여호와의 구원의 소리가 끊이지 않는다(15a절). 의인들이 자신들이 경험한 하나님의 은총을 서로에게 증언하는 소리로 가득하다는 뜻이다. 그들은 여호와의 능력의 상징인 '오른손'이 높이 들려 권능을 베푸셔서 그들을 구원하신 일을 세 차례나 증거한다(15b–16b절). 기자는 자신이 경험한 주님의 구원을 온 의인 공동체가 찬양할 주제로 승화시키고 있다.

기자도 자기 생명이 다할 때까지 주님이 하시는 일을 온 세상에 알리겠다고 다짐한다(17절). 그는 한때 죽음이 참으로 그의 가까운 곳에 도달했다는 생각을 했지만, 죽지 않고 살았다(17a절). 여호와께서 그를 심히 경책하신 것이 사실이지만, 그를 죽음에 넘기지는 않으셨기 때문이다(18절). 그는 원수들이 그를 에워싸고 에워싼 일(10–12절)을 하나님이 그를 경책하신 일로 생각한다. 한 주석가는 이러한 상황을 두고 '고난에 대한 하나님 중심적 이해'(theocentric understanding of suffering)라고 한다(Kraus).

'심히 경책하다'(יַסֹּר יִסְּרַנִּי)는 징계를 하시고 또 하셨다는 뜻이다. 그가 무슨 죄로 인해 하나님의 경책을 받은 것인지는 알 수 없다. 한 가지 확실한 것은 그는 자신이 경험한 군사적 위기를 주님이 경책하신 일이라며 스스로 깨닫고 있다는 사실이다. 하나님이 때로는 자기 자녀들을 경책하시지만, 죽도록 하시지는 않는다. 하나님은 항상 회복을 염두에 두고 자기 백성들을 부모가 자식을 징계하듯 하시기 때문이다.

3. 우리를 구원하신 하나님(118:19-28)

19 내게 의의 문들을 열지어다
내가 그리로 들어가서 여호와께 감사하리로다
20 이는 여호와의 문이라
의인들이 그리로 들어가리로다
21 주께서 내게 응답하시고
나의 구원이 되셨으니
내가 주께 감사하리이다
22 건축자가 버린 돌이
집 모퉁이의 머릿돌이 되었나니
23 이는 여호와께서 행하신 것이요
우리 눈에 기이한 바로다
24 이 날은 여호와께서 정하신 것이라
이 날에 우리가 즐거워하고 기뻐하리로다
25 여호와여 구하옵나니
이제 구원하소서
여호와여 우리가 구하옵나니
이제 형통하게 하소서
26 여호와의 이름으로 오는 자가 복이 있음이여
우리가 여호와의 집에서 너희를 축복하였도다
27 여호와는 하나님이시라
그가 우리에게 빛을 비추셨으니
밧줄로 절기 제물을 제단 뿔에 맬지어다
28 주는 나의 하나님이시라

내가 주께 감사하리이다
주는 나의 하나님이시라
내가 주를 높이리이다

여호와의 큰 구원을 경험한 기자가 성전으로 나아가 주님을 예배하기를 원한다. 그러므로 그는 의의 문들이 그에게 열려 그 문들을 지나 주님께 감사드리기를 원한다(19절). '의의 문들'(שַׁעֲרֵי־צֶדֶק)은 성도가 성전 뜰로 들어가기 위해 통과해야 하는 성전 문들이다. 이 문들은 여호와의 문들이며(20a절), 주님을 예배하기 위해 성전으로 들어가려면 지나가야 하는 문이기도 하다(20b절). 하나님의 선하심과 인자하심에 올바르게 반응하는 의로운 사람들만(cf. 1, 29절) 지나갈 수 있기 때문에 '의의 문들'이다(Hossfeld-Zenger, VanGemeren).

저자는 성전 뜰에 서서 주님께 감사 예배를 드리기를 원한다(21c절). 여호와께서 그에게 응답하시어 그를 큰 위기에서 구원하셨기 때문이다(21a-b절). 그는 하나님이 그를 구원하신 일을 건축자가 버린 돌이 집 모퉁이의 머릿돌이 된 일에 비유한다(22절). "건축자가 버린 돌이 집 모퉁이의 머릿돌이 되었다"는 당시 유태인들의 건축방식에서 유래한 격언이었을 것이다(Tucker & Grant). 머릿돌은 두 줄의 돌들이 만나는 코너에 세워지거나, 건축물의 기둥을 지탱하는 돌이다. 그러므로 건축에 매우 중요한 돌이며 건축물의 완성을 상징했다(Hossfeld-Zenger). 하나님은 볼품없는 그를('건축자가 버린 돌') 구원하셔서 존귀한 자('모퉁이의 머릿돌')가 되도록 하셨다는 뜻이다. 이 말씀은 예수님의 삶에 참으로 적절하게 적용된다(cf. 마 21:42; 막 12:10; 눅 20:17; 행 4:11; 엡 2:20; 벧전 2:7). 세상은 예수님의 가치를 알아보지 못하고 십자가에 버렸다. 그러나 주님은 예수님을 세상의 모퉁이 돌로 세우셨다(엡 2:20).

이런 일은 우리 주변에서 찾아보기 힘들다. 그러므로 그는 주께서 이처럼 놀라운 구원을 베푸시고 또한 그를 존귀하게 하신 것은 하나님이 하신 참으로 기이한 일이라고 한다(23a절). '기이한 일'(נִפְלָאת)은 하나님이 행하시는 기적을 의미하며 시편에서 이미 여러 차례 사용되었다(시 9:2; 26:7; 75:2; 78:4; 96:3; 105:2; 107:8, cf. 출 15:11; 34:10).

적들에게 포위되어 죽음을 기다리던 때에는 하나님의 은혜로 그가 살게 될 뿐만 아니라 여호와의 성전을 찾아와 주님께 감사하며 예배드리는 날이 올 것이라고는 상상도 못했다. 그러므로 기자는 이날을 여호와께서 정하신 날, 곧 여호와께서 성전에서 그의 예배를 받으시기로 정하신 날이라고 한다(24a절). 그러므로 그는 이날 마음껏 즐거워하고 기뻐하자며 함께 예배를 드리는 사람들을 권면한다(24b절).

한때 원수들의 손에 죽을 뻔한 기자는 하나님의 도움으로 구원을 받고 성전까지 찾아와 예배를 드리는 감격을 누리고 있다. 그러나 그에게는 아직도 해결되지 않은 문제들도 있다. 이 문제들이 해결되려면 하나님의 도움이 필요하다. 그러므로 그는 기쁨과 즐거움으로 여호와께 예배를 드리면서 간구를 곁들인다. 그는 여호와께 모든 일이 형통하도록 구원을 베풀어 달라고(도와 달라고) 기도하고 있다(25절). '이제 구원하소서'(הוֹשִׁיעָה נָּא)는 제발 구원해 주시기를 간절히 바라는 표현으로 신약의 '호산나'이다(마 21:9; 막 11:9-10).

기자는 하나님께 예배를 드리기 위해 그와 함께 성전 뜰에 모여 있는 성도들을 축복하고, 또한 그들이 서로를 축복하기를 원한다(26b절). 그가 그들에게 사용하고, 그들이 서로에게 사용할 축복은 "여호와의 이름으로 오는 자가 복이 있다"이다(26a절). 이 축복은 '여호와의 이름으로' 성전에 들어온 자들에게만 유효하다(Allen, VanGemeren). 신약은 이 축복을 예수님께 적용한다. 예수님도 여호와의 이름으로 오셨기 때문이다.

축복을 받은 사람들이 감격으로 반응한다: "여호와는 하나님이시라. 그가 우리에게 빛을 비추셨다"(27a-b절). '그가 우리에게 빛을 비추셨다'(וַיָּאֶר לָנוּ)의 문자적 의미는 '그가 우리에게 빛이 되셨다'이다. 백성들은 주님이 직접 우리의 생명과 구원이 되신 것을 고백한다.

"밧줄로 절기 제물을 제단 뿔에 맬지어다"(27c절)의 정확한 번역과 해석은 난제로 남아 있다(cf. Allen, Anderson, Goldingay, McCann). 그러나 전반적인 의미는 확실하다. 그들은 하나님과 성전을 향한 자신들의 충성에 변함이 없을 것이라며 확고히 다짐하였던 것이다(cf. VanGemeren).

청중들로부터 찬양과 다짐의 바통을 이어받은 기자가 개인적인 고백과 다짐으로 이 섹션을 마무리 한다(28절). 그는 평생 여호와만이 그의 하나님이심을 고백하며 살 것이다(28a, 28c절, cf. 출 15:2). 또한 그는 평생 주님께 감사할 것이며(28b절), 오직 주님만을 높이며 살 것이다(28d절).

4. 하나님의 선하심과 인자하심(118:29)

29 여호와께 감사하라
그는 선하시며
그의 인자하심이 영원함이로다

기자는 이 시편을 시작했던 권면으로(cf. 1절) 노래를 마무리한다. 하나님의 선하심과 인자하심이 영원함을 감사하며 살라는 권면이다. '감사하라'(הוֹדוּ)는 1, 19, 21, 28절에 이어 다섯 번째로 사용되고있으며 '고백하라'는 의미로 해석될 수 있다(Goldingay, Hossfeld-Zenger). 하나님의 선하심과 인자하심에 대해 증언/간증하라는 요구를 내포하고 있는 것이다(Tucker & Grant). 여호와의 선하심과 인자하심은 세상 모든 사람에게 찬양과 경배를 받기에 합당하기 때문이다.

제119편

I. 장르/양식: 토라시(cf. 1편)

한 학자는 이 시편이 개인 탄식시라고 하지만(Soll), 이 노래는 히브리어 알파벳 22개를 순서적으로 사용해 제작한 지혜시다(deClaissé-Walford et al., VanGemeren, cf. 1-3절). 알파벳 시들은 각 알파벳을 한 차례씩 사용하여 진행되는 것이 일상적인데(cf. 34, 111, 112, 145편), 이 시편은 각 알파벳을 연이어 8차례씩 사용하여 총 176절로(=22x8) 구성되어 있어 가장 긴 시이다. 길이뿐만 아니라, 작품성에 있어서도 알파벳 시의 절정이다(cf. Kraus, McCann). 그러므로 한 주석가는 이 시를 여호와께서 이스라엘에게 주신 계시(말씀)에 대한 '문학적 기념비'(a literary monument)라고 한다(Allen).

이 시는 사람이 하나님에 대해(about), 혹은 하나님께 드리는(to) 찬양과 간증과 항의와 신뢰와 호소와 결단과 고백과 순종 다짐 등 매우 다양한 요소들로 구성되어 있다(Goldingay). 그러므로 학자들은 이 시편을 토라 신앙의 매우 중요한 부분으로 간주한다(Hossfeld-Zenger, Mays, Westermann).

오래전부터 유태인들은 이 시편을 오순절과 연관시켜 왔다(Grogan).

이유는 분명하다. 이 노래는 바로 앞에 등장하는 '이집트 찬양시' 모음집(113-118편)과 바로 뒤에 등장하는 '순례자의 노래' 모음집(120-134편) 사이에 있다. 이집트 찬양시들은 유월절을 기념하는 노래이다. 순례자의 노래들은 예루살렘 성전과 연관된 노래들이다. 이스라엘 종교에서 매우 중요한 것들이며 이 시편은 이 두 그룹 사이에서 율법의 중요성을 강조한다. 또한 오순절은 오래전부터 율법과 연관된 절기였다(Grogan).

히브리어 알파벳을 순서적으로 사용하여 노래를 진행하다 보니 일정한 흐름이 있는 것이 아니라 율법의 아름답고 위대함을 찬양하고, 율법을 지킬 것을 다짐하고, 순종을 소망하는 일이 반복된다. 그렇다 보니 일부 학자들은 이 시는 일정한 구조나 흐름이 없이 무작위적으로 저작된 노래라고 하기도 하고(Allen), 노래의 흐름을 도대체 예측할 수 없다고 하기도 한다(Freedman).

이 시편의 내용을 혹평하는 사람들은 성경 문서 중에 내용이 가장 없는 것이라고 하고(Duhm), 깊은 생각과 가르침을 반영하는 노래가 아니라 별 내용이 없는 참으로 인위적인 시라고 하기도 한다(Sabourin, Weiser). 그러나 이 시편이 많은 것을 반복하고 있지만, 이 단조로운 반복도 인상적인 것으로 평가된다(Anderson, Dahood). 또한 이 시편은 여호와를 믿는 이와 토라를 공부하는 이의 모델을 제시한다는 이들도 있고(Gerstenberger, Reynolds), 성경적 지성의 위대한 업적이라고 하는 이들도 있다(Brueggemann).

특별한 전개나 흐름이 없이 같은 내용이 지속적으로 반복되는 것에 대해 학자들은 이 시편이 처음부터 강해자는 필요 없고 읽는 이와 듣는 이가 필요한 작품으로 저작되었기 때문이라고 한다(Augustine, cf. Goldingay). 시편을 연구하는 학자들이라 할지라도 이 시편만큼은 내용을 연구하기 위해 공부하지 말고, 단순히 읽고 묵상하며 즐기도록 제작되었다는 것이다. 그러므로 학자들은 이 노래가 끊임없이 '읽히고 묵상 되어야 할'(lectio divina) 시편이라 하기도 하고(Levenson), '묵상적인 시'라고 한다(Whybray).

한 학자는 이 시편은 주전 597년에 바빌론으로 끌려간 여호야긴 왕이 다윗 왕조의 회복을 꿈꾸며 저작한 것이라고 하는데(Soll), 그렇게 결론짓기에는 왕권에 대한 내용이 부족하다. 대부분 사람들은 이 시가 알파벳 시라는 사실을 근거로 포로기 이후 시대에 저작된 것으로 간주한다(cf. McCann). 알파벳 시는 이스라엘 문학에서 상대적으로 늦게 개발된 것으로 생각되기 때문이다.

옛적에 이 시편이 어떤 용도로 사용되었는가에 대하여는 알려진 바가 없다. 오늘날 유태인들은 이 시편을 모세를 통해 주신 율법을 기념하는 오순절 때 묵상한다(deClaissé-Walford et al.). 이 노래가 요시야 왕 시대(주전 622년)에서 예루살렘이 망하던 때(주전 586년) 사이에 저작된 것이라고 하는 이들도 있지만(Terrien), 알파벳 시들이 대체적으로 포로기 이후에 저작된 것이라는 점을 근거로 포로기 이후 시대를 저작 시기로 지목하는 이들도 있다(VanGemeren).

II. 구조

저자는 하나님의 율법을 지칭하는 단어로 총 8개를 사용한다(deClaissé-Walford et al., Kidner, VanGemeren, cf. Freedman). 이 단어들이 강조하는 바는 각각 조금씩 다르지만(cf. Kidner), 이 시편에서는 모두 율법을 칭하는 비슷한 말로 사용된다(Grogan). 다음은 각 단어들의 빈도수이다. 다양한 단어들이 반복적으로 사용되면서 이 노래에 점집성과 통일성을 더한다. 우리말 번역본들은 같은 히브리어 단어를 다르게, 혹은 다른 단어들을 같은 말로 번역하기도 하기 때문에 번역본을 보고는 구분하기가 쉽지 않다.

율법(תּוֹרָה)	25x
판단(מִשְׁפָּט)	23x
증거(עֵדֻת)	23x
율례(חֹק)	22x
말씀(דָּבָר)	22x
계명(מִצְוָה)	22x
법도(פִּקּוּד)	21x
약속(אִמְרָה)	21x

율법을 칭하는 8개의 비슷한 단어들은 참으로 골고루 이 시편 전체에 분포되어 있다. 다음은 총 8개의 단어들 중 각 섹션이 사용하는 단어들의 숫자를 정리해 놓은 것이다(deClaissé-Walford et al.).

1-8절	8개 중 7개
9-16절	8개 중 7개
17-24절	8개 중 6개
25-32절	8개 중 7개
33-40절	8개 중 8개
41-48절	8개 중 8개
49-56절	8개 중 6개
57-64절	8개 중 8개
65-72절	8개 중 6개
73-80절	8개 중 8개
81-88절	8개 중 8개
89-96절	8개 중 6개
97-104절	8개 중 7개
105-112절	8개 중 6개
113-120절	8개 중 7개
121-128절	8개 중 7개
129-136절	8개 중 8개

137–144절	8개 중 7개
145–152절	8개 중 7개
153–160절	8개 중 8개
161–168절	8개 중 7개
169–176절	8개 중 7개

이 시편이 이처럼 다양한 단어들을 사용하여 지속적으로 '토라'를 정의하고 있는 것을 고려하면 이 시편에서 토라(Torah)는 하나님이 시내 산에서 모세를 통해 이스라엘에게 주신 율법이나 심지어는 모세 오경으로 제한될 수 없는 것이 확실하다. 넓은 의미에서 구약에 기록된 하나님의 모든 말씀을 염두에 둔 것으로 해석되어야 한다(cf. Levenson). 기자는 여러 차례 토라가 우리에게 길을 제시한다고 하는데, 길은 성도들이 취해야 할 삶의 방식을 뜻한다는 것도 이러한 해석을 지지하는 듯하다. 시내 산에서 선포된 말씀만이 아니라 구약을 구성하고 있는 하나님의 모든 말씀이 우리에게 지침이 되기 때문이다.

이 시편은 히브리어 알파벳 22개의 순서에 따라 각각 8절씩 22섹션으로 구성된 것 외에는 이렇다할 구조는 없다(cf. Allen, Freedman). 그러므로 이 주석에서는 다음과 같은 분석을 바탕으로 본문을 주해해 나갈 것이다.

A. 알레프(א)(119:1–8)
B. 베이트(ב)(119:9–16)
C. 기멜(ג)(119:17–24)
D. 달레트(ד)(119:25–32)
E. 헤(ה)(119:33–40)
F. 바브(ו)(119:41–48)
G. 자인(ז)(119:49–56)
H. 헤트(ח)(119:57–64)
I. 테트(ט)(119:65–72)

J. 요드(י)(119:73-80)
K. 카프(כ)(119:81-88)
L. 라메드(ל)(119:89-96)
M. 멤(מ)(119:97-104)
N. 눈(נ)(119:105-112)
O. 사멕(ס)(119:113-120)
P. 아인(ע)(119:121-128)
Q. 페(פ)(119:129-136)
R. 짜데(צ)(119:137-144)
S. 코프(ק)(119:145-152)
T. 레쉬(ר)(119:153-160)
U. 신(ש)(119:161-168)
V. 타브(ת)(119:169-176)

III. 주해

이 시편은 율법(말씀)의 놀라움과 실용성을 찬양한다. 율법은 하나님이 주신 것이기 때문에 아름답다. 사람들이 율법을 묵상하며 율법대로 살면 율법은 그들에게 생명을 주며 참으로 행복하게 살게 할 것이다. 이 시편의 가장 기본적인 목적은 '율법 신앙'(Torah piety)의 복됨을 가르치기 위한 것이다(Brueggemann & Bellinger).

이미 언급한 것처럼 이 시편은 특별한 전개나 흐름이 없이 비슷한 내용을 지속적으로 반복한다(Calvin). 그러므로 많은 학자들이 이 시편의 경우 본문의 의미를 해석하고 설명해 주는 강해자보다는 읽고 묵상하고 즐기는 묵상자가 필요하다고 한다. 이 주석에서도 이 시편의 경우 단순히 묵상하고 이 노래의 풍요로움을 즐기고자 한다.

1. 알레프(א)(119:1-8)

1 행위가 온전하여
여호와의 율법을 따라 행하는 자들은
복이 있음이여
2 여호와의 증거들을 지키고
전심으로 여호와를 구하는 자는
복이 있도다
3 참으로 그들은 불의를 행하지 아니하고
주의 도를 행하는도다
4 주께서 명령하사
주의 법도를 잘 지키게 하셨나이다
5 내 길을 굳게 정하사
주의 율례를 지키게 하소서
6 내가 주의 모든 계명에 주의할 때에는
부끄럽지 아니하리이다
7 내가 주의 의로운 판단을 배울 때에는
정직한 마음으로 주께 감사하리이다
8 내가 주의 율례들을 지키오리니
나를 아주 버리지 마옵소서

성경에서 가장 긴 장(章)이자 위대한 율법시인 이 시편의 대장정은 '복이 있는 사람은'(אַשְׁרֵי)이라는 말로 시작한다(1c절, 우리 말과 히브리어의 어순이 다르기 때문에 마소라 사본에서는 이 단어가 이 시편을 시작하지만, 우리 말 번역본에서는 1c절에 옴). '복이 있는 사람'은 지혜문헌에서 자주 등장하며, 하나님께 신실한 이들이 지녀야 할 말과 행동을 지닌 사람들을 의미한다(Tucker & Grant, cf. 욥 5:17; 시 1:1; 2:12; 32:1; 33:12; 34:8; 잠 3:13;

8:32; 14:21; 16:20; 20:7; 전 10:17).

이 노래는 시편 1편처럼 행복한 삶을 사는 지혜를 주는 시라는 것을 암시한다. 기자는 행위가 온전한 사람들은 복이 있다고 하는데(1a절), '행위가 온전한 자들'(תְמִימֵי־דָרֶךְ)의 문자적 의미는 '온전한(흠이 없는) 길을 가는 자들'이다(창 17:1; 잠 11:20; cf. 아가페, NIV, NAS, ESV). 삶이 길을 가는 일에 비유되고 있다.

그렇다면 사람이 어떻게 온전한 삶을 살 수 있는가? 저자는 '여호와의 율법에 따라 행하는 것'이라고 한다(1b절). '행하다'(הלךְ)는 '걷다/가다'라는 뜻을 지녔다. 1a절은 우리의 삶을 길을 가는 일에 비유하더니, 이번에는 걷는 것에 비교하고 있다. 삶은 긴 여정이며, 하나님의 말씀에 따라 이 여정을 가는 사람이 행복하다는 것이다. 율법은 우리의 삶이 어떤 가치관과 방식을 추구해야 하는가를 가르쳐줄 뿐만 아니라, 우리가 가는 길이 옳다는 사실을 확인해 준다.

2절도 '복이 있는 사람은'(אַשְׁרֵי)이라는 말로 시작한다. 복은 하나님이 인간에게 내려 주시는 것이다. 그러므로 주님의 말씀대로 사는 것은 우리의 노력의 결과이기도 하지만, 근본적으로 하나님이 내려 주시는 축복이다. 사람은 율법에 따라 사는 일을 스스로 결정하고 실천할 만한 의지가 약하므로 주님이 이러한 결단과 의지를 주셔야 가능하기 때문이다(cf. 4절).

그렇다면 과연 어떤 사람이 복이 있는 사람인가? 여호와의 증거들을 지키는 사람은 복이 있다(2a절). '증거들'(עֵדוּת)은 '증언/간증'을 뜻하며 본문에서는 하나님의 말씀을 두고 하는 말이다. 하나님의 말씀은 여호와는 우리의 하나님이시며 우리와 함께하신다는 증거이다. 그러므로 오경에서 성막은 하나님의 임재를 상징하는 '증거막'(אֹהֶל עֵדוּת)으로 언급된다(민 9:15; 17:2; 18:2).

순종하는 삶을 사는 것은 곧 하나님이 우리와 함께하신다는 증거이며, 이렇게 사는 사람들은 복이 있다. 이러한 삶을 사는 사람들은 '온 마음을 다해'(בְּכָל־לֵב) 여호와를 구하는 사람들이기 때문이다(2b절). '구하다'(דרשׁ)는 진솔한 마음으로 찾는다는 뜻이다(VanGemeren). 그러므로 주님이 이러한 사람을 축복하시는 것은 당연한 일이다.

하나님의 말씀대로 사는 사람은 참으로 복이 있는 사람이라고 한 기자는 3절에서부터 본격적으로 말씀에 따라 사는 사람이 누릴 축복과 특권에 대하여 말하기 시작한다.

첫째, 율법은 우리가 불의를 행하지 않도록 하는 기준이다(3절). 율법을 삶의 기준으로 삼는 사람들은 불의를 행하지 않는다(3a절). 율법이 불의한 일을 행하지 않도록 제지하기 때문이다. '불의'(עַוְלָה)는 남에게 해를 끼치는 일을 의미한다(cf. HALOT). 우리가 하나님의 말씀이 제시하는 길에 따라 사는 일(3b절)의 가장 기본적인 언행은 어떠한 해가 될 만한 일을 하지 않는 것이다. 우리는 하나님의 축복의 통로가 되도록 부르심을 입었기 때문이다.

둘째, 하나님의 말씀은 우리가 그 말씀대로 살 수 있도록 하는 하나님의 도우심을 동반한다(4절). '법도'(פִּקּוּדִים)는 하나님의 통치권과 연관되어 있는 단어이다(Kidner). 기자가 이웃들에게 불의를 행하지 않고 살 수 있었던 것은 여호와께서 법도를 주시며 성실하게 지키라고 하셨을 뿐만 아니라 잘 지킬 수 있도록 도우셨기 때문이다. 그는 하나님의 다스림에 호응하는 차원에서 더욱더 선을 행하며 살고 있다. 그는 하나님의 말씀을 통해 어떻게 살 것인가를 배웠고, 말씀은 그가 순종할 수 있도록 도왔다며 경건한 삶에 대한 모든 영광을 하나님께 돌리고 있다.

셋째, 하나님의 말씀은 앞으로도 우리가 말씀을 성실하게 지킬 수 있도록 붙잡아 주실 것이다(5절). 기자는 하나님이 도와주셔야 그가 경건한 삶을 살 수 있다는 것을 확신한다. 그러므로 이때까지 그를 지켜 주신 것처럼 앞으로도 그렇게 하실 것을 기대한다.

넷째, 하나님의 말씀대로 살면 우리의 삶은 부끄럽지 않다(6절). '부끄럽다'(בושׁ)는 구약에서 하나님이 원수들을 버려 완전히 망하도록 한다는 의미를 지녔다(VanGemeren, cf. 시 6:10; 25:2; 83:17). 하나님의 말씀은 경건하고 거룩한 삶의 기준이다. 그러므로 우리가 조심해서 주님의 '모든'(כֹּל) 말씀대로 살려고 노력하면 우리는 하나님께 버림받아 부끄럽게 되는 죄를 짓지 않으면서 살 수 있다.

다섯째, 하나님의 말씀은 우리에게 의로운 판단을 가르쳐 준다(7a절). '의'(מִשְׁפָּט)는 옳고 그름에 대한 판단 기준을 의미하는데(Delitzsch), 사람이 스스로 옳고 그름을 판단하는 것은 쉽지 않다. 그러나 하나님의 율법을 판단 기준으로 삼으면 쉬워진다. 하나님의 말씀은 우리에게 지혜를 주신다. 옳은 판단을 할 수 있는 지혜를 얻은 사람은 '정직한 마음으로'(בְּיֹשֶׁר לֵבָב, 굽지 않고 곧은 마음으로) 그 지혜에 대해 하나님께 감사할 것이다(7b절).

여섯째, 하나님의 말씀은 하나님의 함께하심을 동반한다(8절). 주의 자녀에게 가장 두려운 것은 하나님께 버려지거나 멀리 떨어져 있는 일이다. 기자는 자신이 율법대로 사는 한 주님이 항상 그와 함께할 것을 기대한다. 우리가 말씀에 순종하며 사는 한 하나님은 항상 우리와 함께하시며 보호하실 것이다.

2. 베이트(ב)(119:9–16)

9 청년이 무엇으로 그의 행실을 깨끗하게 하리이까
주의 말씀만 지킬 따름이니이다
10 내가 전심으로 주를 찾았사오니
주의 계명에서 떠나지 말게 하소서
11 내가 주께 범죄하지 아니하려 하여
주의 말씀을 내 마음에 두었나이다
12 찬송을 받으실 주 여호와여
주의 율례들을 내게 가르치소서

[13] 주의 입의 모든 규례들을
나의 입술로 선포하였으며
[14] 내가 모든 재물을 즐거워함 같이
주의 증거들의 도를 즐거워하였나이다
[15] 내가 주의 법도들을 작은 소리로 읊조리며
주의 길들에 주의하며
[16] 주의 율례들을 즐거워하며
주의 말씀을 잊지 아니하리이다

첫째, 하나님의 말씀은 우리의 행실을 깨끗하게 한다(9절). 기자는 지혜를 가르치는 선생처럼 수사학적인 질문을 던진다: “청년이 무엇으로 그의 행실을 깨끗하게 할 수 있을까?”(cf. 시 34:11; 잠 1:4; 25:12-13; 전 11:9; 12:1) ‘깨끗하다’(זכה)는 죄와 죄의 영향력을 벗어나 있는 상태를 뜻한다(Delitzsch). 기자는 앞 섹션에서 우리의 삶을 ‘길’(דֶּרֶךְ)에 비유했는데 이번에는 ‘행실’(אֹרַח)에 비유한다. 이 둘 다 비슷한 비유이지만, ‘길’(road)은 사람이 다니는 길을, ‘행실/길’(path)은 삶의 여정에 대한 비유(metaphor)이다(Tucker & Grant). 본문의 ‘청년’은 스승에게 교훈을 받는 학생으로, 잠언의 ‘내 아들’과 같다(VanGemeren).

율법은 인간의 삶에서 가장 유혹이 많은 시기인 청년 때에도 우리가 죄를 짓지 않고 깨끗하게 살 수 있게 한다. ‘깨끗하다’(זכה)는 도덕적으로 흠이 없다는 뜻이다(HALOT). 우리가 주님의 말씀을 지키려고 노력하면 평생 경건하고 거룩하게 살 수 있다.

둘째, 하나님의 말씀은 주님을 찾는 사람들이 하나님을 떠나지 않도록 지켜 준다(10절). 우리가 전심으로 주님을 찾는 것은 곧 하나님의 말씀에서 떠나지 않는 것을 의미한다. 하나님의 임재와 보호가 주님의 말씀 안에서 거할 때 우리와 함께하기 때문이다. 그러므로 기자는 주님께 말씀을 떠나는 일이 없도록 지켜 달라고 기도한다.

셋째, 하나님의 말씀은 우리가 죄를 짓지 않도록 우리 마음을 보호한다(11절). 기자는 자신이 어떠한 죄도 짓지 않으려고 하나님의 말씀을 자기 마음에 두었다고 한다. '두다'(צפן)는 원래 '숨기다'는 뜻을 지녔는데(HALOT), 이 곳에서는 '저장하다/쌓아 두다'는 의미로 사용되고 있다(Tucker & Grant). 그의 마음에는 온갖 하나님의 말씀이 언제든 꺼내 쓸 수 있도록 저장되어 있다. 또한 이 말씀은 기자가 하나님의 말씀을 단순히 외우고 묵상하는 것이 아니라 주님을 경외하는 삶도 살고 있다는 것을 뜻한다(VanGemeren, cf. 신 6:4-9; 30:14; 렘 31:33). 우리의 마음과 삶이 율법으로 가득하면 악한 생각이나 행실이 틈을 탈 수 없기 때문이다.

넷째, 하나님의 말씀은 우리가 주님을 찬송하도록 한다(12절). 우리가 율법을 배우면 하나님이 얼마나 놀라운 분이신가를 깨닫게 된다. 하나님의 놀라우심을 깨닫게 되면 우리는 새로운 노래로 주님의 위대하심을 찬양하게 된다. 또한 기자가 주님께 율법을 가르쳐 달라고 기도하는 것은 그가 배울 마음 자세가 되어 있음을 암시한다. 그는 율법을 배우기 전에 선생이신 하나님을 먼저 찬양하여 이러한 마음 자세를 표현한다(VanGemeren). 찬양하고 싶으면 주님의 말씀을 배우고 깊이 묵상하면 된다.

다섯째, 하나님의 말씀은 배운 사람들이 주님을 선포하게 한다(13절). 주님의 말씀은 복된 것으로, 이 축복은 우리가 서로와 나눌 때 배가 된다. 또한 하나님의 말씀은 의롭고 경이로워 배운 이가 홀로 가슴에 품고 살기에는 너무나 아깝다. 그러므로 주님의 말씀은 배우면 배울수록 다른 사람들에게 더 많이 증거하게 한다.

여섯째, 하나님의 말씀은 우리에게 기쁨을 준다(14절). 기자는 부자가 많은 재물로 인해 기뻐하는 것처럼 자기는 주님의 말씀을 즐거워한다고 한다. 그는 하나님의 말씀으로 매우 만족하고 있다(cf. 16절). 만족함은 내적으로 경건한 사람의 진실된 표현이다(VanGemeren). 그가 세상에서 그 무엇으로도 얻을 수 없는 하나님의 진리를 얻었으니 얼마나 기쁘고 즐겁겠는가! 하나님의 말씀은 우리의 삶에 참 기쁨을 더하여 우리가 참으로 행복하도록 한다.

일곱째, 하나님의 말씀은 우리에게 깊은 묵상에 젖어 들게 한다(15절). '작은 소리로 읊조리다'(שׂיח)는 곰곰이 생각하며 숙고한다는 의미를 지녔다(HALOT, NIDOTTE). 하나님의 말씀을 이해하는 일이 때로는 쉽지 않다. 또한 하나님의 말씀을 우리의 삶에 적용하는 일도 쉽지 않다. 그러므로 우리를 깊은 묵상에 빠지게 하기도 한다.

여덟째, 하나님의 말씀은 영원히 기억되어야 한다(16절). 기자는 그에게 행복을 주는 하나님의 율법들을 절대 잊지 않겠다고 다짐한다. 말씀은 잊기에는 너무나 놀랍고 좋은 것이기 때문이다. 또한 말씀을 기억하는 것은 하나님을 생각하는 것이다(VanGemeren). 그러므로 우리는 평생 하나님과 주님의 말씀을 생각하며 기쁨으로 살아야 한다.

3. 기멜(ג)(119:17-24)

[17] 주의 종을 후대하여 살게 하소서
그리하시면 주의 말씀을 지키리이다
[18] 내 눈을 열어서
주의 율법에서 놀라운 것을 보게 하소서
[19] 나는 땅에서 나그네가 되었사오니
주의 계명들을 내게 숨기지 마소서
[20] 주의 규례들을 항상 사모함으로
내 마음이 상하나이다
[21] 교만하여 저주를 받으며
주의 계명들에서 떠나는 자들을
주께서 꾸짖으셨나이다

[22] 내가 주의 교훈들을 지켰사오니
비방과 멸시를 내게서 떠나게 하소서
[23] 고관들도 앉아서 나를 비방하였사오나
주의 종은 주의 율례들을 작은 소리로 읊조렸나이다
[24] 주의 증거들은 나의 즐거움이요
나의 충고자니이다

첫째, 하나님의 말씀은 주님이 우리를 후대하는 증거다(17절). 기자는 먼저 자신을 '주의 종'이라며 하나님과 그의 관계를 강조한다(cf. 시 36:1). 그는 하나님께 충성하는 종이며, 하나님은 그의 주인이시다. '후대하다'(גמל)는 삶을 풍요롭게 한다는 의미를 지녔다(cf. HALOT). 기자는 하나님이 선처를 베푸실 때 비로소 우리는 말씀대로 살 수 있다고 한다. 하나님의 선처는 사람이 율법대로 살려고 하는 이유가 되며 동시에 율법대로 살 수 있도록 능력도 주신다는 뜻이다.

둘째, 하나님의 말씀은 참으로 놀랍다(18절). 사람이 아무리 주님의 율법을 주야로 묵상해도 완전히 깨달을 수는 없다. 또한 하나님의 말씀이 지닌 신비로움과 놀라움을 모두 헤아릴 수도 없다. 그러므로 기자는 하나님께 그의 눈을 열어주시어 율법의 놀라운 것들을 보게 해 달라고 기도한다. 그에게 유일한 삶의 의미는 하나님의 말씀을 알고 순종하는 일이다(Briggs).

셋째, 하나님의 말씀은 우리가 가야 할 길을 알려준다(19절). 기자는 이 땅에서의 삶을 나그네의 삶이라고 한다. '나그네'(גֵּר)는 목적지도 모른 채 정처 없이 떠도는 삶을 살 수 있다(cf. 시 39:12-13). 그러므로 그는 하나님이 말씀을 그에게서 숨기지 않을 것을 기도한다. 하나님의 말씀은 가야 할 길로 우리를 인도하기 때문이다.

넷째, 하나님의 말씀은 우리가 쉽게 얻을 수 있는 것이 아니다(20절). 기자는 하나님의 말씀을 간절히 사모하다가 마음이 쇠약해졌다고 한다. 죽을 지경에 이르렀다는 것이다(Anderson). 많이 지친 사람의 모습이다. 우리도 하나님의 말씀이 쉽게 깨달아지지 않을 때가 있다. 이럴 때는 시간을 두고 깊이 묵상하고 연구해야 한다. 우리는 진리를 습득하기 위해서 때로는 많은 노동을 해야 한다.

다섯째, 하나님의 말씀을 떠나는 것은 저주를 받을 일이다(21절). 사람들이 왜 하나님의 말씀을 떠나는가? 교만해서다(21a절). 그들은 자신들의 능력을 믿기 때문에 하나님의 말씀을 멀리한다. 그러나 그들의 이 같은 행위는 스스로 저주를 받을 일이며, 하나님은 분명 그들에게 벌을 내려 꾸짖으실 것이다(21c절). 율법은 사람이 살아갈 기준인데, 그 기준을 거부했으니 그에 상응하는 응징이 임할 것이다.

여섯째, 하나님의 말씀은 우리에 대한 비방과 멸시가 사라지게 한다(22-23절). 우리가 율법대로 살면 당연히 경건하고 의로운 삶을 살게 될 것이다. 우리가 이렇게 살면 사람들은 바르게 살지 않는다며 우리를 비방할 수 없다. 우리가 주님의 말씀을 조용히 묵상하며 실천하면 일반인들보다 판단력이 훨씬 더 정확한 고관들의 비방도 사라질 것이다(23절). 율법은 경건하게 살지 못하는 것에 대한 비방을 사라지게 한다. 기자와 그를 멸시하는 자들과 교만한 자들의 차이는 하나님의 말씀을 붙드느냐 버리느냐의 차이이다.

일곱째, 하나님의 말씀은 우리의 조언자이다(24절). 우리는 삶에서 많은 선택과 결정을 해야 한다. 말씀을 많이 알고 있으면, 우리가 선택하고 결정할 때 율법은 큰 조언자가 되어 우리가 바른 결정과 선택을 하도록 도울 것이다. 말씀의 도움을 받아 올바른 선택과 결정을 하게 된 우리는 말씀을 더욱더 기뻐하며 즐거움으로 삼게 된다.

4. 달레트(ㄱ)(119:25-32)

25 내 영혼이 진토에 붙었사오니

주의 말씀대로 나를 살아나게 하소서
26 내가 나의 행위를 아뢰매
주께서 내게 응답하셨사오니
주의 율례들을 내게 가르치소서
27 나에게 주의 법도들의 길을 깨닫게 하여 주소서
그리하시면 내가 주의 기이한 일들을 작은 소리로 읊조리리이다
28 나의 영혼이 눌림으로 말미암아 녹사오니
주의 말씀대로 나를 세우소서
29 거짓 행위를 내게서 떠나게 하시고
주의 법을 내게 은혜로이 베푸소서
30 내가 성실한 길을 택하고
주의 규례들을 내 앞에 두었나이다
31 내가 주의 증거들에 매달렸사오니
여호와여 내가 수치를 당하지 말게 하소서
32 주께서 내 마음을 넓히시면
내가 주의 계명들의 길로 달려가리이다

첫째, 하나님의 말씀은 우리를 살린다(25절). 기자는 자기 영혼이 진토에 붙었다고 하는데, 땅은 죽은 사람을 묻는 곳이다(cf. 시 7:5; 22:15, 29; 44:25). 그러므로 그는 죽음에 임박했다며 주님이 그를 살려주시기를 간절히 기도한다. 주님의 말씀이 생명을 살리는 능력이 있어서 일 수도 있고(cf. 신 8:3; 30:6; 32:47), 혹은 하나님이 말씀을 통해 그에게 생명을 약속하신 것을 지키시라는 뜻일 수도 있다(시 71:20; 80:18; 85:6; 138:7, cf. 새번역, 현대인).

둘째, 하나님은 말씀을 통해 우리에게 응답하신다(26절). 기자는 그동안 자신이 어떻게 살아왔는가를 하나님께 말씀드렸더니, 주께서 그에게 응답하셨다고 한다. 그는 기도를 통해 진솔하게 자신의 삶을 하

나님께 보여드린 것이다(VanGemeren). 그러면서 주님의 율례들을 더 가르쳐 달라고 하는 것으로 보아, 주님이 말씀을 통해 그에게 응답하셨음을 암시한다. 우리가 하나님의 말씀을 많이 알고 묵상하면, 주님은 묵상과 말씀을 통해 우리의 기도에 응답하시기도 한다. 또한 이런 일을 경험하면 우리는 더욱더 하나님의 말씀을 배우려고 하게 된다.

셋째, 하나님의 말씀은 주님이 행하시는 온갖 기적들에 대해 깊이 묵상하게 한다(27절). 우리가 하나님의 말씀을 통해 주님이 어떤 분이시며 어떤 일을 하시는가를 깨달으면, 하나님이 행하시는 '기적들'(נִפְלְאוֹת)이 단순히 사건으로 끝나지 않는다. 하나님이 기적을 행하실 때에는 분명 이유가 있을 것이기 때문이다. 그러므로 하나님의 말씀을 많이 알면, 그것을 근거로 하나님이 행하신 기적들이 상징하는 바와 의미를 묵상을 통해 깨닫게 된다. 이러한 묵상은 하나님을 더욱더 의지하게 한다. 하나님이 행하신 가장 위대한 기적은 창조 사역과 구속 사역이다(VanGemeren).

넷째, 하나님의 말씀은 우리의 영혼을 소생시킨다(28절). '녹다'(דלף)는 눈물을 흘린다는 의미를 지녔으며(HALOT), 슬픔을 뜻하는 '눌림'(תּוּגָה)과 함께 사용되고 있다(cf. Allen). 슬퍼서 쓰러졌다는 의미이다(Dahood). 우리의 영혼이 슬픔에 잠겨 눈물을 흘리며 절망할 때, 곧 죽음이 가까이 다가와 있음을 느낄 때(cf. 창 42:38; 44:31; 시 31:10; 116:3), 하나님의 말씀은 우리를 살리고 세우신다. '세우다'(קוּם)는 일어나게 한다는 뜻이다. 주님의 말씀은 슬픔으로 인해 쓰러진 우리가 다시 두 발로 설 수 있도록 한다.

다섯째, 하나님의 말씀은 우리에게 내려 주시는 은혜이다(29절). 하나님은 아무에게나 자기 말씀을 주시지 않는다. 거짓을 행하는 자들에게는 주시지 않고 오직 은혜를 입은 사람들에게 주신다. '거짓'(שֶׁקֶר)은 속이는 말뿐만 아니라, 어떠한 가치도 없는(worthless) 말과 무의미한 말(pointless)도 포함한다(Anderson). 은혜를 많이 경험한 사람일수록 가치

있고 의미 있는 진실된 말로 가득하다. 주님의 은혜로운 말씀이 그러하기 때문에 말씀으로 가득하면 거짓된 행실을 멀리하게 된다.

여섯째, 하나님의 말씀은 우리가 성실한 길을 가게 한다(30절). 말씀에 충만한 사람은 삶에 성실하게 임한다. '성실'(אֱמוּנָה)은 꾸준하여 믿을 만하다는 뜻이다(HALOT). 성실은 하나님의 가장 기본적인 속성이기도 하다. 그러므로 우리가 신앙과 삶에 성실하게 임하는 것은 곧 하나님을 닮아 가는 것이다.

일곱째, 하나님의 말씀은 우리가 수치를 당하지 않게 해준다(31절). 기자는 자신이 하나님의 증거들(증언, 말씀)에 매달렸다고 한다. 간절히 사모하는 마음으로 강하게 붙들었다는 뜻이다. 하나님의 말씀은 진실하기 때문에 주님의 말씀을 붙잡고 사는 사람들은 진실하게 살 것이며, 진실하게 살면 수치를 당할 일이 없다는 뜻이다.

여덟째, 하나님의 말씀은 우리의 마음을 넓힌다(32절). 말씀은 우리에게 깨달음을 주며(cf. 새번역, 새번역), 깨달음은 우리의 이해력을 높인다. 결과적으로 우리의 마음이 넓어지는 것이다. 또한 성경은 사람이 곤경에 처하는 것을 좁은 곳에 갇히는 일로 묘사한다(cf. 시 116, 140편). 그러므로 이곳에서 그가 말씀을 통해 넓은 곳에 있다는 것은 구원을 경험했다는 뜻일 수도 있다(Tucker & Grant).

5. 헤(ה)(119:33-40)

33 여호와여 주의 율례들의 도를 내게 가르치소서
내가 끝까지 지키리이다
34 나로 하여금 깨닫게 하여 주소서
내가 주의 법을 준행하며 전심으로 지키리이다
35 나로 하여금 주의 계명들의 길로 행하게 하소서
내가 이를 즐거워함이니이다

36 내 마음을 주의 증거들에게 향하게 하시고
탐욕으로 향하지 말게 하소서
37 내 눈을 돌이켜 허탄한 것을 보지 말게 하시고
주의 길에서 나를 살아나게 하소서
38 주를 경외하게 하는 주의 말씀을
주의 종에게 세우소서
39 내가 두려워하는 비방을 내게서 떠나게 하소서
주의 규례들은 선하심이니이다
40 내가 주의 법도들을 사모하였사오니
주의 공의로 나를 살아나게 하소서

히브리어 알파벳 '헤'(ה)는 여러 사역동사(causative verbs)를 시작하는 글자이다(Wilcock). 그러므로 이 섹션이 하나님의 가르치시고 지시하시고 재조정하시는 사역을 강조하는 것은 당연한 일이다(Grogan). 기자는 우리의 모든 순종이 하나님의 가르치심과 지시하심에 근거하고 있다는 점을 암시한다.

첫째, 우리는 하나님의 말씀을 평생 실천해야 한다(33절). 기자는 하나님의 율법을 간절히 사모하며 주님이 가르쳐 주시기를 바란다. 말씀은 하나님이 설명하시고 가르쳐 주셔야 우리의 것이 되기 때문이다(VanGemeren). 그는 하나님께 배운 율법을 평생 지키고자 한다. 그는 끝까지 말씀을 지키겠다고 하는데, '끝'(עֵקֶב)은 '보상'(reward)를 뜻한다(Anderson, Briggs, Weiser). 그는 하나님의 말씀이 주께서 그에게 주시는 보상이라며, 평생 주신 말씀에 순종하며 살겠다고 다짐하고 있다. 주의 자녀들에게는 하나님의 말씀 자체가 보상이다(Briggs).

둘째, 우리는 하나님의 말씀을 온 마음을 다해 실천해야 한다(34절). 33절은 시간(평생)을 강조했다면, 이 말씀은 전심으로 순종할 것을 강조한다. 기자는 하나님의 율법을 '온 마음으로'(בְּכָל־לֵב) 지켜 행하려 한다. 그러므로 그는 여호와께 율법에 대한 깨달음을 구한다. 율법은 깨달을수록 더 확실하게 순종할 수 있기 때문이다.

셋째, 우리는 기쁜 마음으로 하나님의 말씀을 실천해야 한다(35절). 기자는 하나님의 도우심을 받아 주님의 율법대로 살기를 간절히 소망한다. 그가 율법에 순종하는 일을 기뻐하기 때문이다. 율법은 하나님이 우리에게 짐으로 지어 주신 것이 아니다. 소수에게만 허락하신 특권이다. 이러한 사실을 이해하면 하나님의 말씀에 따라 사는 것은 복되고 즐거운 일이다.

넷째, 하나님의 말씀은 우리가 탐욕을 부리지 않도록 한다(36절). '탐욕'(בֶּצַע)은 불법적인 이익이나 개인적인 잇속을 뜻한다(HALOT, cf. 아가페, NIV, NRS, ESV). 우리가 이 땅에서 우리 중심적으로 살지 않고 이웃을 배려하며 더불어 살아가기 위해서는 하나님의 말씀이 기준이 되어야 한다.

다섯째, 하나님의 말씀은 우리를 우상 숭배에서 보호해 준다(37절). 구약에서 '허탄한 것'(שָׁוְא)은 어떠한 가치도 없는 것(worthless/valueless)을 뜻하기도 하지만(cf. Allen), 종종 우상을 의미하기도 한다(렘 10:15; 18:15; cf. NIDOTTE). 기자는 조금이라도 우상에게 한눈을 팔지 않기를 간절히 소망한다. 이렇게 살 수 있는 방법은 하나님의 말씀에 충만하여 주님의 길에서 살아가는 것이다.

여섯째, 하나님의 말씀은 주님을 경외하게 한다(38절). '경외'(יִרְאָה)는 우리 모두에게 필요한 건전한 두려움이다. 하나님의 말씀은 알면 알수록 하나님이 어떤 분이신가를 깨닫게 한다. 깊이 알면 알수록 하나님은 우리를 두렵게 한다. 하나님이 주신 말씀과 기준대로 살기가 쉽지 않기 때문이다. 또한 하나님의 거룩한 속성도 알면 알수록 우리의 고개가 숙여진다.

일곱째, 하나님의 말씀은 우리의 두려움을 없애 준다(39절). 기자는 사람들이 그를 비방하는 것을 참으로 두려워한다. 아마도 그들은 그가 율법을 지키려고 노력하는 일을 비방하거나(Kirkpatrick), 자신들이 사는 것처럼 살지 않는다고 비방하는 것일 것이다(Briggs). 그는 하나님의 율법이 그가 두려워하는 모든 비방을 없애 줄 것을 확신한다. 하나님의 율법은 참으로 선한 것이기 때문에, 만일 그가 그 선한 율법대로 살면 사람들이 그를 비방할 이유가 없을 것이다. 말씀대로 사는 선이 두려운 악을 물리치고 있다. 이후 율법은 우리 안에 경건한 두려움을 생성할 것이다.

여덟째, 하나님의 말씀은 우리에게 생명을 준다(40절). 기자는 자신이 하나님의 율법을 사모했으니 주께서 공의로 그에게 생명을 주시기를 바란다. '공의'(צְדָקָה)는 의로운 삶을 살기 위해 꼭 필요한 가이드라인이다. 하나님은 율법을 통해 우리가 의롭게 살 수 있도록 생명(생기)을 주신다. 이 말씀은 또한 의로 인해 고통을 당하고 있는 사람들에게 하나님의 의로운 심판이 임하여 그들의 억울함을 헤아려 달라는 기도이기도 하다(Anderson).

6. 바브(ו)(119:41–48)

41 여호와여 주의 말씀대로 주의 인자하심과
주의 구원을 내게 임하게 하소서
42 그리하시면 내가 나를 비방하는 자들에게
대답할 말이 있사오리니
내가 주의 말씀을 의지함이니이다
43 진리의 말씀이 내 입에서 조금도 떠나지 말게 하소서
내가 주의 규례를 바랐음이니이다
44 내가 주의 율법을 항상 지키리이다
영원히 지키리이다
45 내가 주의 법도들을 구하였사오니

자유롭게 걸어갈 것이오며
46 또 왕들 앞에서 주의 교훈들을 말할 때에
수치를 당하지 아니하겠사오며
47 내가 사랑하는 주의 계명들을 스스로 즐거워하며
48 또 내가 사랑하는 주의 계명들을 향하여
내 손을 들고 주의 율례들을 작은 소리로 읊조리리이다

첫째, 하나님의 말씀에는 주의 인자하심과 구원이 있다(41절). '인자하심'(חֶסֶד)은 하나님의 가장 기본적인 속성이며, 사람을 선처 하시는 것을 묘사한다. 하나님의 말씀은 어떻게 주의 인자하심과 구원이 우리에게 임하는지를 알려준다. 그러므로 기자는 하나님의 말씀대로 인자하심과 구원이 그에게 임하기를 기원한다.

둘째, 하나님의 말씀은 우리를 변론한다(42절). 기자는 바로 앞 절(41절)에서 하나님의 인자하심과 구원이 그에게 임하기를 간절히 기도했다. 하나님이 말씀을 통해 약속하신 것이 이루어지기를 소망한 것이다. 하나님의 인자하심이 그에게 임하는 날, 그는 비방하는 자들에게 할말도 생긴다. 그들은 아마도 "네가 믿는 하나님이 어디 있느냐?"라는 식으로 그를 비방했을 것이다(cf. 시 42:4, 11; 115:2). 하나님의 말씀을 의지한 것이 헛되지 않았고, 그를 구원에 이르게 했다는 말로 그들에게 당당하게 변론할 것이다.

셋째, 하나님의 말씀은 우리가 진리의 말을 하게 한다(43절). '진리'(אֱמֶת)는 시간이 아무리 지나도 변하지 않는 진실을 의미한다(HALOT). 기자는 우리가 하나님의 율법을 따르면 우리 입에는 항상 진리가 머문다고 한다. 하나님의 말씀이 바로 진리이기 때문이다. 우리가 진리를 말할 때 우리의 삶도 진실하다. 또한 우리가 진리를 추구하는 한 하나님의 신실하심을 끊임없이 찬양할 수 있다(cf. Anderson). 하나님은 우리에게 진리를 주시는 분이기 때문이다.

넷째, 하나님의 말씀은 우리가 영원히 지키도록 주신 것이다(44절). 율법이 얼마나 아름답고 놀라운 것인가를 깨달은 기자는 항상 율법을 지킬 것을 다짐한다. 그는 '영원히'(עוֹלָם) 세상이 '끝날 때'(עַד)까지 말씀을 지키며 살 것이다. 우리도 이러한 각오로 하나님의 말씀을 우리의 삶의 기준으로 삼았으면 좋겠다.

다섯째, 하나님의 말씀은 우리가 세상을 자유롭게 살 수 있도록 한다(45절). 율법은 삶의 방식을 정의한다. 그러므로 우리가 말씀을 기준으로 삼아 세상을 살면 말씀은 우리가 죄를 짓지 않으면서도 마음껏 세상을 즐기며 살 수 있는 길을 제시한다. 이러한 삶이야 말로 하나님이 기뻐하시는 자유로운 삶이다.

여섯째, 하나님의 말씀은 왕들도 감동시키는 지혜를 지녔다(46절). 고대 근동의 문화적 정서에 의하면 왕들이 가장 지혜로운 자들이다(cf. 솔로몬). 신들은 특별히 선택한 자들에게만 지혜를 주었는데, 왕들이 바로 신들의 선택을 받은 자들이라고 생각했기 때문이다. 그러므로 백성이 왕 앞에 서서 지혜를 말하는 것은 수치를 당할 수밖에 없는 일이었다. 기자는 하나님의 말씀이 얼마나 아름답고 지혜로운지 그가 왕들 앞에서 율법을 말해도 전혀 수치를 당하지 않을 것을 자신한다. 하나님의 말씀은 왕들이 자기 신들에게서 받을 수 없었던 지혜를 담고 있기 때문이다.

일곱째, 하나님의 말씀은 말씀을 사랑하는 이들을 기쁘게 한다(47절). 기자는 하나님의 말씀을 참으로 사랑한다. 하나님의 계명들을 참으로 사랑하다 보니 기쁨과 즐거움이 생긴다. 하나님의 말씀은 읽고 묵상하는 자들을 감동시키는 능력을 지녔기 때문이다.

여덟째, 하나님의 말씀은 우리를 기도하게 한다(48절). 기자는 손을 들고 율례들을 묵상할 것이라고 하는데, 손을 드는 것은 기도하는 자세이다(Delitzsch, Kidner, cf. 시 28:2; 사 1:15). 그는 자신이 사랑하는 계명들을 하나하나 깊이 묵상하며 기도하고자 한다. 하나님의 말씀은 우리에게 참으로 적절하며(41절), 신뢰할 만하기에(42–43절), 순종해야 하고(44절), 추구해야 하며(45절), 사랑해야 한다(47–48절)(Kidner). 우리도 빈말로 기도하는 것이 아니라, 하나님의 말씀을 묵상하는 기도를 드리면 좋겠다.

7. 자인(ז)(119:49–56)

[49] 주의 종에게 하신 말씀을 기억하소서
주께서 내게 소망을 가지게 하셨나이다
[50] 이 말씀은 나의 고난 중의 위로라
주의 말씀이 나를 살리셨기 때문이니이다
[51] 교만한 자들이 나를 심히 조롱하였어도
나는 주의 법을 떠나지 아니하였나이다
[52] 여호와여 주의 옛 규례들을 내가 기억하고
스스로 위로하였나이다
[53] 주의 율법을 버린 악인들로 말미암아
내가 맹렬한 분노에 사로잡혔나이다
[54] 내가 나그네 된 집에서
주의 율례들이 나의 노래가 되었나이다
[55] 여호와여 내가 밤에 주의 이름을 기억하고
주의 법을 지켰나이다
[56] 내 소유는 이것이니
곧 주의 법도들을 지킨 것이니이다

첫째, 하나님의 말씀은 우리에게 소망을 가지게 한다(49절). 기자는 옛적에 하나님이 그에게 하신 말씀을 추억한다. 그는 그때 매우 어려운 상황에 처해 있었으며, 어떠한 소망도 없는 듯했다. 이러한 상황에서 하나님의 말씀은 그에게 위로가 되었을 뿐만 아니라, 미래를 기대하는 소망이 되었다. 하나님의 말씀을 기억하는 것은 절망하는 우리에게 소망하게 하는 능력을 지녔다.

둘째, 하나님의 말씀은 죽게 된 사람을 살린다(50절). 이 말씀도 기자의 지난 일에 대한 회고이다. 그가 참으로 힘들고 어려웠을 때, 하나님의 말씀은 그에게 위로가 되었다. 또한 주님의 말씀은 그를 살렸다. 하나님의 말씀에는 죽게 된 사람도 살리는 힘이 있기 때문이다.

셋째, 하나님의 말씀이 때로는 우리를 조롱거리로 만든다(51절). 기자는 이번에도 자기 경험을 말한다. 그는 하나님의 법을 끝까지 붙든다는 이유로 교만한 자들(하나님을 의지 않고 자신들을 믿으며 사는 사람들)에게 심히 조롱을 당한 적이 있다. 사람이 여호와를 섬기며 사랑하는 일은 참으로 좋은 것이지만, 이러한 사실을 이해하지 못하는 사람들은 우리의 이 신앙으로 인해 우리를 조롱하는 것과 비슷하다. 그러나 세상이 조롱한다고 주님을 떠날 우리가 아니다!

넷째, 하나님의 말씀은 우리를 위로한다(52절). 삶에 지치고 세상에 치였을 때, 하나님의 말씀은 우리가 스스로를 위로하는 도구가 된다. 그러므로 우리가 하나님의 말씀을 붙잡고 있는 한, 주님의 말씀으로 다시 설 수 있고 삶의 치열한 도전을 받아들일 수 있다.

다섯째, 하나님의 말씀은 우리를 분노케 한다(53절). 하나님의 말씀은 참으로 아름다우며 우리의 삶을 풍요롭게 하는 능력을 지녔다. 이러한 말씀을 받아들이기를 거부하는 사람들이 너무 안타깝다. 그런데 종종 하나님의 말씀을 받아들이기를 거부하는 것을 초월하여 노골적으로 하나님의 말씀을 대적하거나 비아냥거리는 자들이 있다. 기자는 우리가 이런 사람들을 보게 되면 분노해야 한다고 한다. '맹렬한 분노'(זַלְעָפָה)는 흔한 단어가 아니며, 모든 풀을 순식간에 말려버리는 사막에서 불어오는 바람(sirocco)를 뜻한다는 것이다(Briggs). 다행인 것은 이런 삶들을 접할 때 우리는 더욱더 하나님을 신뢰하고 바라게 된다

(VanGemeren). 예수님이 성전 앞에서 화를 내신 일을 생각나게 한다(cf. 마 21:12-13). 우리에게 거룩한 분노는 필요하다.

여섯째, 하나님의 말씀은 우리의 고단한 삶 중에 노래가 된다(54절). 기자는 자신의 삶을 이곳저곳을 떠도는 나그네의 삶으로 묘사한다(cf. 새번역). 지친 몸을 이끌고 세상 이곳저곳을 헤매는 그에게 삶을 포기하지 않고 오히려 더 열심히, 성실하게 살도록 하는 힘은 주님의 율법에서 온다. 율법이 그의 찬송과 기쁨이 되기 때문이다. 또한 '나그네 된 집'(בֵּית מְגוּרָי)을 포로로 끌려가 이방인들의 땅에 사는 주의 백성으로 해석하는 것도 가능하다(Levenson). 이 경우 이 말씀은 이스라엘 영토의 회복을 구하는 기도가 된다. 우리는 처한 경제적 여건과 상관없이 하나님의 말씀으로 행복할 수 있다.

일곱째, 하나님의 말씀은 어두운 밤에도 우리를 지켜 준다(55절). 기자는 삶의 가장 혹독한 순간을 어두운 밤에 비유하고 있다. 다윗의 '사망의 음침한 골짜기'를 생각나게 한다(시 23:4). 친구들과 가족들도 모두 떠나고 홀로 흐느끼는 밤에 주님의 말씀은 그와 함께하며 보호하고 위로했다. 세상이 우리에게서 모든 것을 앗아갈 수 있어도, 우리 안에 있는 하나님의 말씀은 빼앗을 수 없기 때문이다.

여덟째, 하나님의 말씀은 우리를 축복한다(56절). 이 문장을 정확히 번역하기는 쉽지 않다(cf. 새번역, 아가페, 새번역, 공동, NIV, NAS, NRS). 기자는 "이것이 나에게 있다"(זֹאת הָיְתָה־לִּי)고 하는데, '이것'이 무엇인지 알 수 없기 때문이다. 아마도 하나님의 말씀대로 사는 삶에 임하는 축복을 두고 하는 말씀일 것이다(아가페, ESV, NAS, NRS, TNK). 하나님의 말씀은 지키려고 하는 이들에게 복을 내려준다는 뜻이다.

8. 헤트(ח)(119:57-64)

57 여호와는 나의 분깃이시니

나는 주의 말씀을 지키리라 하였나이다
58 내가 전심으로 주께 간구하였사오니
주의 말씀대로 내게 은혜를 베푸소서
59 내가 내 행위를 생각하고
주의 증거들을 향하여 내 발길을 돌이켰사오며
60 주의 계명들을 지키기에 신속히 하고
지체하지 아니하였나이다
61 악인들의 줄이 내게 두루 얽혔을지라도
나는 주의 법을 잊지 아니하였나이다
62 내가 주의 의로운 규례들로 말미암아
밤중에 일어나 주께 감사하리이다
63 나는 주를 경외하는 모든 자들과
주의 법도들을 지키는 자들의 친구라
64 여호와여 주의 인자하심이 땅에 충만하였사오니
주의 율례들로 나를 가르치소서

첫째, 하나님의 말씀은 주님이 우리의 기업이 되시는 증거이다(57절). 기자는 바로 앞 섹션(cf. 54절)에서 자기는 이 땅에서 나그네의 삶을 산다고 했다. 그는 나그네로 사는 이 땅에 어떠한 분깃도 가지지 않았고, 오직 주님이 그의 분깃이라고 고백한다. 그가 평안히 거할 '집'은 오직 하나님이시라는 뜻이다(cf. McCann). '분깃'(חֵלֶק)은 유산을 두고 하는 말이다(NIDOTTE). 여호수아서는 모든 이스라엘 사람들이 가나안에 분깃을 받을 것이라고 한다(수 15:13; 18:7; 19:9). 그러므로 그는 분명 분깃을 받았을 것이다. 그러나 그는 물리적인 분깃으로 만족하지 못한다. 그는 하나님이 그의 분깃이 되어 주실 때 비로소 만족할 것이다. 하나님은 그의 분깃 되심의 증표로 말씀을 주셨다. 그러므로 하나님을 자기 분깃으로 고백하는 사람들은 모두 하나님의 말씀을 지켜 행해야 한다.

둘째, 하나님의 말씀은 주님께 간구하는 자들에게 은혜를 베푼다(58절). 말씀은 우리에게 어떻게 기도하고, 어떻게 간구해야 하는가를 가르쳐 준다. 그러므로 우리가 하나님의 말씀에 따라 주님께 기도하면, 간구를 들으신 주님은 은혜로 화답하신다. 이 은혜도 말씀을 통해 올 수 있다.

셋째, 하나님의 말씀은 우리의 삶을 돌이키게 한다(59절). 하나님의 말씀이 제시하는 기준과 가치관에 따라 우리의 삶을 평가해보면 우리가 옳은 방향으로 가지 않고 있다고 생각할 수 있다. 이럴 때는 하나님의 말씀으로 방향을 조정해야 한다. 하나님으로부터 자꾸 멀어지는 방향으로 가고 있다는 생각이 들 때는 발길을 돌이켜 주님께 돌아와야 한다.

넷째, 하나님의 말씀은 신속한 순종을 요구한다(60절). 이 말씀은 바로 앞절(59절)과 연결되어 있다. 기자는 하나님으로부터 점점 멀어지고 있는 자신의 삶을 보고 돌아섰다(59절). 이 구절은 그가 지체하지 않고 하나님의 말씀에 순종했다고 한다. 그는 신속하게 발걸음을 돌이켰으며, 이것이 회개의 열매이다(Briggs).

다섯째, 하나님의 말씀은 악인들의 밧줄에서 우리를 구원한다(61절). 기자가 사용하는 이미지는 원수들에 의해 꼼짝 못하도록 온갖 밧줄로 묶인 사람의 모습이다. 악인들이 악한 말과 음모와 억압으로 지배하는 상황을 묘사하고 있다(VanGemeren). 그는 원수들에게 묶인 상황에서도 하나님의 말씀을 기억하고 묵상한다. 자기 스스로는 아무것도 할 수 없는 상황에서 말씀을 통해 하나님의 구원을 기대하는 것이다.

여섯째, 하나님의 말씀은 항상 감사하도록 한다(62절). 기자는 한밤중에 일어나 하나님의 율법을 생각하며 감사한다고 한다. 주님의 말씀이 너무나도 놀랍고 아름다워 낮이나 밤이나 생각하면 감사가 저절로 나온다는 뜻이다.

일곱째, 하나님의 말씀은 주를 경외하는 사람들을 이어준다(63절). 누구든 하나님의 율법을 지키는 사람들은 동료의식을 느끼며 서로 친구가 된다. 말씀은 사람과 사람을 이어주는 역할을 하는 것이다.

여덟째, 하나님의 말씀은 가르침에 적합하다(64절). 창조주 하나님의 선하심이 온 세상을 채우고 있다. 하나님의 말씀이 얼마나 선하고 아름다운가에 감동한 기자는 하나님이 자비를 베푸시기를 간절히 바란다. 어떤 자비인가? 그에게 율법을 가르쳐 주시는 은혜이다.

기자의 삶에서 가장 중요한 것은 하나님의 말씀을 깨닫고 순종하는 일이다(Delitzsch). 그러나 그는 더 많이 사모한다. 그는 단순히 배우고 묵상하는 것을 통해 얻는 깨달음이 아니라, 선생이신 하나님만이 그에게 직접 주실 수 있는 깨우침을 바라고 있다(Goldingay). 창조주 하나님은 아무것도 요구하지 않은 세상을 좋은 것으로 채우시는데, 하물며 자녀들의 기도와 바람을 무시하시겠는가! 기자는 하나님의 말씀을 배울 만반의 준비가 되어 있다. 그리고 주님의 가르침을 사모한다.

9. 테트(ט)(119:65–72)

65 여호와여 주의 말씀대로 주의 종을 선대하셨나이다
66 내가 주의 계명들을 믿었사오니
좋은 명철과 지식을 내게 가르치소서
67 고난 당하기 전에는 내가 그릇 행하였더니
이제는 주의 말씀을 지키나이다
68 주는 선하사 선을 행하시오니
주의 율례들로 나를 가르치소서
69 교만한 자들이 거짓을 지어 나를 치려 하였사오나
나는 전심으로 주의 법도들을 지키리이다
70 그들의 마음은 살져서 기름덩이 같으나

나는 주의 법을 즐거워하나이다
71 고난 당한 것이 내게 유익이라
이로 말미암아 내가 주의 율례들을 배우게 되었나이다
72 주의 입의 법이 내게는 천천 금은보다 좋으니이다

첫째, 하나님의 말씀은 우리를 선대한다(65절). 기자는 하나님이 그를 선대했다고 하는데, '선대하다'(טוֹב עָשִׂיתָ)는 하나님이 그를 위해 좋은 일을 하셨다는 뜻이다(cf. VanGemeren). 신명기에서 '선'(טוֹב)은 하나님이 생명을 유지하도록 주시는 축복을 뜻하기도 한다(신 10:13). 하나님이 그를 선하게 대하신 것은 말씀을 통해 약속하신 것을 이행하는 일이었다. 하나님의 말씀은 주님이 우리를 선대하시겠다는 약속을 담고 있다. 하나님은 약속하신 것은 모두 지키시는 분이다. 그러므로 말씀은 우리를 선대한다.

둘째, 하나님의 말씀은 명철과 지식을 준다(66절). 기자는 하나님의 계명들을 통해 좋은 명철과 지식을 배우기를 원한다. '좋은 명철'(טוּב טַעַם)은 누구에게 답할 때 선한 판단력을 가지고 반응하는 것이다(NIDOTTE, cf. HALOT). 기자는 남들에게 좋은 조언자가 되기를 희망하고 있다. 또한 그는 하나님의 말씀이 우리가 습득해야 할 온갖 지식으로 가득하다는 사실을 알고 있다.

셋째, 하나님의 말씀은 우리가 옳은 길을 가게 한다(67절). 기자는 자신이 그릇 행하였다고 하는데, '그릇 행하다'(שׁגג)는 길을 잃고 헤매거나 길을 잘못 들다는 뜻이다(HALOT). 그는 마음대로 살다가 길을 잃고 헤맸으며, 그 일로 인해 매우 힘든 시간을 보냈다. 다행히 그는 고난 중에 하나님을 만났다(cf. 시 94:12; 욥 5:17; 잠 3:11-12; 애 3:25-30; 히 12:4-11). 기자는 과거를 거울삼아 다시는 방황하고 싶지 않다. 그러므로 그는 하나님의 말씀을 붙들고 살 것이다. 말씀은 그를 바른 길로 인도하기 때문이다. 또한 말씀은 그에게 생명을 준다(Hossfeld-Zenger).

넷째, 하나님의 말씀은 선하다(68절). 하나님은 선하시며 선을 행하기를 기뻐하시는 분이다. 이처럼 선하신 하나님이 주신 것이 율법이다. 그러므로 율법은 선하다. 기자는 율법을 열심히 배우고 묵상하여 선하신 하나님을 더 깊이 알아가기를 원한다.

다섯째, 하나님의 말씀은 교만한 자들의 공격에서 우리를 보호한다(69절). '교만한 자들'(זֵדִים)의 더 정확한 의미는 '무례하고 건방진 자들'이다(HALOT). 그들은 하나님을 의지하지 않고 자신들을 믿고 살아가는 자들이다. 이런 사람들은 하나님을 경외하는 사람을 보면 견디지 못해 온갖 거짓을 지어내 공격해 댄다. 기자는 이런 자들의 공격이 있을 때면 주님의 율법을 더 깊이 묵상하고 지키려 한다. 하나님의 말씀은 이런 자들의 공격에서 보호하는 능력이 있으며, 우리의 마음을 평안하게 하기 때문이다.

여섯째, 하나님의 말씀은 우리의 마음을 건강하게 한다(70절). 기자는 무례하고 건방진 자들(cf. 69절)의 '마음은 살이 쪄서 기름덩이'(לִבָּם טָפַשׁ כַּחֵלֶב) 같다고 하는데, 분별력과 감정을 상실한 마음을 두고 하는 말이다(cf. 새번역, 아가페, NIV, ESV). 그는 자신의 마음 건강을 위해서라도 율법을 즐거워하며 배우기를 힘쓴다. 하나님의 말씀은 그의 마음을 건강하게 지켜 줄 것이기 때문이다.

일곱째, 하나님의 말씀은 고난을 배움의 도구로 사용한다(71절). 이 말씀은 기자가 고난을 당하기 전에는 자기 마음대로 행하다가 그릇된 길로 가게 되었다고 했던 67절과 연관이 있다. 그때 그는 고난을 통해 하나님의 말씀의 소중함을 깨달았다. 이 말씀은 그때 일을 회고하면서 고난으로 인해 그가 하나님의 율법을 배우게 되었으니, 고난도 그에게 유익했다고 한다. 때로는 우리도 고난을 당한 후에야 비로소 하나님의 말씀에 대한 열정이 살아난다. 그러므로 이런 경우에는 고난도 유익하다. 하나님의 말씀을 배우게 되는 도구가 되기 때문이다.

여덟째, 하나님의 말씀은 소중한 보배이다(72절). 기자는 하나님의 율법이 수천 개의 금과 은보다 좋다고 한다. 하나님의 말씀이 얼마나 귀한 것인가를 깨달은 사람의 고백이다. 하나님은 이처럼 소중한 보배를 우리에게 공짜로 주셨다. 그러므로 누구든 하나님을 사모하는 사람들은 세상에서 가장 소중한 보배를 마음껏 누릴 수 있다.

10. 요드(י)(119:73-80)

73 주의 손이 나를 만들고 세우셨사오니
내가 깨달아 주의 계명들을 배우게 하소서
74 주를 경외하는 자들이 나를 보고 기뻐하는 것은
내가 주의 말씀을 바라는 까닭이니이다
75 여호와여 내가 알거니와 주의 심판은 의로우시고
주께서 나를 괴롭게 하심은 성실하심 때문이니이다
76 구하오니 주의 종에게 하신 말씀대로
주의 인자하심이 나의 위안이 되게 하시며
77 주의 긍휼히 여기심이 내게 임하사
내가 살게 하소서
주의 법은 나의 즐거움이니이라
78 교만한 자들이 거짓으로 나를 엎드러뜨렸으니
그들이 수치를 당하게 하소서
나는 주의 법도들을 작은 소리로 읊조리리이다
79 주를 경외하는 자들이 내게 돌아오게 하소서
그리하시면 그들이 주의 증거들을 알리이다
80 내 마음으로 주의 율례들에 완전하게 하사
내가 수치를 당하지 아니하게 하소서

첫째, 하나님의 말씀은 세상을 창조하신 창조주에 관한 이야기다(73

절). 그러므로 일부 학자들은 저자가 이 섹션을 기록할 때 창세기 1-3장을 염두에 두고 한 것이라고 하기도 한다(Davidson). 기자는 하나님이 그를 만들고 세우셨다고 한다. 그러므로 그가 창조주 하나님을 알고 싶어하는 것은 당연한 일이다. 그는 율법에 자신이 주님에 대해 알고 싶은 것이 모두 담겨있다는 사실을 안다. 하나님의 말씀은 주님이 어떻게 세상과 인간을 만드셨는가를 기록하고 있기 때문이다. 그러므로 그는 하나님에 대한 이야기이자 자신에 대한 이야기인 말씀을 배우기를 간절히 사모한다. 창조주께서 피조물의 행복, 곧 하나님의 말씀을 알고 깨닫는 일을 거부하실 이유는 없다(Delitzsch).

둘째, 하나님의 말씀은 주를 경외하는 자들이 함께 기뻐하게 한다(74절). 세상에서 하나님을 경외하는 자들은 항상 소수이다. 또한 처한 환경에서 홀로 주님을 사랑한다는 느낌을 받을 때도 있다. 이런 상황에서 누가 하나님을 섬기고 주님의 말씀을 간절히 사모하는 것을 보면 큰 위로와 격려가 된다. 기자는 이러한 상황을 묘사하며 자기가 하나님의 말씀을 간절히 바라는 것이 여호와를 경외하는 자들에게 큰 기쁨이 된다고 한다. 우리가 하나님의 말씀을 열심히 공부하는 것이 주변에 있는 경건한 사람들에게 큰 기쁨과 즐거움이 된다.

셋째, 하나님의 말씀은 주님의 심판이 의롭다는 사실을 깨닫게 한다(75절). 기자는 앞 섹션에서 죄로 인해 고난을 당한 일을 회고했다(cf. 67, 71절). 이번에도 그 경험과 연결하여 증언한다. 우리가 하나님의 심판을 당할 때는 아프고 고통스럽지만, 일단 지나고 나서 말씀을 묵상해보면 하나님의 심판은 곧 주님의 의(義)를 드러내신 일이라는 사실을 깨닫는다. 우리는 혹독한 고통 중에 비로소 하나님 말씀의 가치와 주님의 능력을 실감하게 된다(Delitzsch).

'의'(מִשְׁפָּט)는 올바른 판결을 뜻한다. 하나님은 우리에게 잘못된 판결을 내리시는 재판관이 아니다. 또한 하나님이 심판을 통해 우리를 괴롭게 하시는 것은 주의 성실하심(אֱמוּנָה)의 증거이기도 하다. 하나님이 우리와 맺으신 관계가 지닌 의무 사항(예, 우리가 잘못된 길을 가면 쳐서 돌이키게 하시는 일)에 성실하게 임하시는 것이기 때문이다.

넷째, 하나님의 말씀은 우리에게 위안이 된다(76절). 삶에 지쳐 위로가 필요할 때, 우리는 주님의 말씀을 찾아야 한다. 주님이 인자하심으로 우리를 보살피시고, 우리를 얼마나 사랑하시는가를 가장 잘 표현하고 있기 때문이다. 그러므로 기자도 힘이 들 때면 하나님의 말씀을 통해 위로를 받는다.

다섯째, 하나님의 말씀은 우리를 살게 한다(77절). 말씀은 우리가 왜 살아야 하는가에 대해 알려준다. 주님이 우리를 긍휼히 여기시기 때문이다. '긍휼'(רַחֲמִים)은 부모의 자식에 대한 사랑이다(NIDOTTE, cf. HALOT). 부모는 자식이 살기를 간절히 바란다. 그러므로 우리가 하나님의 말씀을 알면 알수록 창조주 하나님이 얼마나 우리가 살기를 바라는가를 깨닫게 된다. 또한 말씀은 주님이 우리가 행복하고 즐겁게 살기를 바란다는 사실을 깨닫게 한다.

여섯째, 하나님의 말씀은 교만한 자들이 수치를 당하게 한다(78절). 앞 섹션(cf. 69절)에서 언급한 것처럼 '교만한 자들'(זֵדִים)은 무례하고 건방진 자들을 두고 하는 말이다. 이런 사람들이 의인들을 엎드러뜨리는 유일한 방법은 거짓을 꾸며 대는 것이다. 하나님은 자기 자녀가 억울하게 당하는 것을 결코 묵인하지 않으실 것이다. 주님은 분명 그들이 계획한 수치가 그들에게 임하게 하실 것이다. 말씀이 이러한 약속을 하고 있기 때문이다. 그러므로 억울한 일을 당한 기자는 잠잠히 하나님의 율법을 묵상할 뿐이다. 그가 이러한 상황에서 하나님의 말씀을 묵상하고 주님만을 바라보는 것은 주님에게 나서서 그들을 치시라는 간접적인 압력으로 작용한다. 하나님의 말씀이 진실됨을 보여주셔야 하기 때문이다.

일곱째, 하나님의 말씀은 우리가 증거하도록 한다(79절). 기자는 주를 경외하는 자들이 모두 그를 떠난 이미지를 사용한다. 아마도 오해와 헛소문으로 인해 그를 멀리하는 상황일 것이다. 그러므로 그는 그들이 다시 그의 곁으로 돌아오게 해 달라고 기도한다. 그는 그들이 돌아와 하나님의 증거들(말씀)을 알기를 원한다. 그는 그들이 하나님이 말씀에 따라 얼마나 신실하게 그를 대하시고 선처하셨는가에 대해 알기를 바란다. 모든 오해와 헛소문으로 인한 편견이 사라지기를 꿈꾸는 것이다.

여덟째, 하나님의 말씀은 수치를 당하지 않게 한다(80절). 기자는 율법을 통해 '그의 마음이 온전해지기를'(יְהִי־לִבִּי תָמִים) 소망한다. 어떠한 흠이나 책잡힐 일이 없기를 바라는 것이다. 이렇게 살면 우리는 수치를 당할 일이 없다. 물론 마음이 비뚤어지거나 하나님을 미워하는 자들은 시기와 질투로 인해 우리를 비난할 것이다. 그러나 하나님과 주의 자녀들은 모두 우리를 인정할 것이다.

11. 카프(כ)(119:81–88)

81 나의 영혼이 주의 구원을 사모하기에 피곤하오나
나는 주의 말씀을 바라나이다
82 나의 말이 주께서 언제나 나를 안위하실까 하면서
내 눈이 주의 말씀을 사모하기에 피곤하니이다
83 내가 연기 속의 가죽부대 같이 되었으나
주의 율례들을 잊지 아니하나이다
84 주의 종의 날이 얼마나 되나이까
나를 핍박하는 자들을 주께서 언제나 심판하시리이까
85 주의 법을 따르지 아니하는 교만한 자들이
나를 해하려고 웅덩이를 팠나이다
86 주의 모든 계명들은 신실하니이다
그들이 이유 없이 나를 핍박하오니 나를 도우소서

[87] 그들이 나를 세상에서 거의 멸하였으나
나는 주의 법도들을 버리지 아니하였사오니
[88] 주의 인자하심을 따라 나를 살아나게 하소서
그리하시면 주의 입의 교훈들을 내가 지키리이다

한 학자는 이 섹션을 근거로 이 시편이 개인 탄식시라고 한다(Soll). 그는 또한 이 섹션이 이 시편의 핵심 내용을 담고 있다고 한다. 기자가 가장 낮은 곳(절망적인 곳)에서 주님께 부르짖고 있다.

첫째, 하나님의 말씀은 우리가 소망하도록 한다(81절). 기자는 주님의 구원을 사모하는 일에 지쳤다고 한다. 아무리 간절히 바라고 기도해도 주님의 구원이 지연되고 있는 것에 대한 탄식이다. 그럼에도 불구하고 그는 계속 하나님의 말씀에 소망을 둔다. 하나님의 구원이 말씀을 통해서만 임하기 때문이다. 우리도 때로는 하나님의 구원이 지체될 수 있다는 사실을 염두에 두고 기다림의 미학을 배워야 한다.

둘째, 하나님의 말씀은 우리를 위로한다(82절). 이번에도 기자는 지연되는 하나님의 위로에 지쳐 있다. 그러나 그는 주님의 말씀을 통한 위로에 희망의 끈을 놓지 않는다. 하나님의 위로가 얼마나 놀라운가를 예전에 맛보았기 때문이다. 게다가 하나님의 위로가 지연된다고 해서 우리가 바라볼 수 있는 곳이 있는가? 없다. 우리의 유일한 위로는 하나님의 말씀을 통해 임할 것이기 때문이다.

셋째, 하나님의 말씀은 혹독한 고난을 견디게 해 준다(83절). 기자는 자신의 경험을 불에 던져진 가죽부대에 비교한다. 가죽부대가 불에 던져지면 처음에는 쪼글쪼글해지다 결국에는 불에 타 없어진다. 연기에 그을리고 불에 타는 가죽부대는 아무런 매력도 없는 무용지물이다(VanGemeren). 그는 혹독한 고난을 이렇게 묘사한다. 그가 이처럼 견디기 힘든 고난을 이겨낼 수 있었던 것은 율법을 잊지 않았기 때문이다. 하나님의 말씀이 고난을 견디게 한 것이다.

넷째, 하나님의 말씀은 주님의 오래 참으심이다(84절). 기자는 자기가 살날이 얼마 남지 않았다며 주님께 원수들을 벌해 달라고 호소한다. 살아 있는 동안 그들이 하나님의 벌을 받는 것을 보고 싶기 때문이다. 그러나 주님은 악인들에게도 충분한 기회를 주기를 원하신다. 그러므로 오래 참으시며 그들이 회개하기를 기다리신다. 끝까지 돌아오지 않으면 비로소 말씀에 따라 심판하신다.

다섯째, 하나님의 말씀은 우리가 핍박을 당하게 한다(85절). 기자는 하나님의 말씀을 따르지 않는 자들이 그를 해하려고 웅덩이를 팠다고 한다. 그들이 그를 해하려는 이유는 단 한 가지, 그가 하나님의 말씀을 사랑하기 때문이다. 우리도 때로는 하나님을 경외한다는 사실 하나로 핍박을 당하고 손해를 보지 않는가!

여섯째, 하나님의 말씀은 우리의 억울함을 헤아려 준다(86절). 이 말씀은 바로 앞 구절(85절)과 연관되어 있다. 기자는 하나님의 말씀을 사랑한다는 이유로 악인들에게 핍박을 당했다. 그러나 그는 핍박이 오래 가지는 않을 것으로 기대한다. 주님이 우리의 억울함을 헤아리시고 도우실 것이기 때문이다. 주님은 이러한 상황에서 우리를 도우실 것을 말씀을 통해 약속하셨다. 그러므로 기자는 주님의 말씀이 이루질 것을 믿고 확신하며 주님의 율법은 신실하다고 한다.

일곱째, 하나님의 말씀은 어떠한 핍박도 견디어 낼 힘이다(87절). 이 말씀도 기자가 악인들의 핍박에 대해 호소하는 85-86절과 연관이 있다. 핍박자들이 그를 거의 죽이다시피 했지만, 그는 끝까지 하나님의 말씀을 붙들었다. 하나님의 말씀에는 생명이 있고, 또한 악인들에 대한 심판이 있기 때문일 것이다. 때로는 단순히 견디는 것이 승리하는 비법이다.

여덟째, 하나님의 말씀은 우리를 소생시킨다(88절). 기자는 핍박을 받아 거의 죽을 지경에 처했다(cf. 87절). 그래도 그가 오직 하나님의 말씀만 붙든 것은 율법에는 생명이 있고, 그를 소생시킬 능력이 있기 때문이다. 그러므로 원수들의 핍박이 강해질수록 그는 하나님의 말씀을 더 소망한다.

12. 라메드(ל)(119:89-96)

89 여호와여
주의 말씀은 영원히 하늘에 굳게 섰사오며
90 주의 성실하심은 대대에 이르나이다
주께서 땅을 세우셨으므로 땅이 항상 있사오니
91 천지가 주의 규례들대로 오늘까지 있음은
만물이 주의 종이 된 까닭이니이다
92 주의 법이 나의 즐거움이 되지 아니하였더면
내가 내 고난 중에 멸망하였으리이다
93 내가 주의 법도들을 영원히 잊지 아니하오니
주께서 이것들 때문에 나를 살게 하심이니이다
94 나는 주의 것이오니 나를 구원하소서
내가 주의 법도들만을 찾았나이다
95 악인들이 나를 멸하려고 엿보오나
나는 주의 증거들만을 생각하겠나이다
96 내가 보니 모든 완전한 것이 다 끝이 있어도
주의 계명들은 심히 넓으니이다

첫째, 하나님의 말씀은 주님이 온 세상을 다스리시는 도구다(89절). 이 구절에서 '말씀'(דָּבָר)은 하나님의 속성과 목적과 의지와 선포된 말씀을 의미한다(Anderson). 기자는 하나님의 말씀이 하늘에 영원히 굳게 섰다고 하는데, 하늘은 하나님이 세상을 다스리시는 곳이다. 그러므로 그는 하나님이 말씀을 통해 세상을 다스리신다는 사실을 선포하고자 한다. 하나님은 영원히 말씀을 통해 세상을 다스리실 것이다(cf. 91절). 세상이 영원한 것은 하나님의 신실하심의 표징이자 보장이다(Kirkpatrick).

둘째, 하나님의 말씀은 세상 끝날까지 우리와 함께 있을 것이다(90절). 바로 앞 89절은 하나님의 말씀이 영원히 세상을 다스릴 것이라고 했는데, 이 구절은 하나님의 성실하심이 이러한 사실을 보장한다고 한다. 또한 땅이 영원한 것처럼 율법도 영원할 것이다.

셋째, 하나님의 말씀은 주의 종들을 위한 것이다(91절). 온 세상은 하나님의 율법에 따라 운영된다. 만물이 주님의 종이 되어 하나님의 말씀을 따르고 있기 때문이다. 하나님의 말씀은 주의 종들에게 준수하라고 주셨다.

넷째, 하나님의 말씀은 고난 중에 있는 사람의 생사를 결정한다(91절). 기자는 그가 혹독한 고난 중에 있었던 일을 회고한다. 만일 하나님의 율법이 없었더라면 그는 이미 죽었을 것이라고 한다. 율법에 대한 사모함과 즐거움이 그가 생명을 붙들게 하여 그를 살린 것이다. 하나님의 말씀이 없으면 사람은 소망이 없이 죽는다.

다섯째, 하나님의 말씀은 영원히 기억되어야 한다(93절). 죽을 고비에서 말씀을 통해 살게 된 기자는(cf. 91절), 앞으로 평생 주님의 율법을 잊지 않고 살겠다고 다짐한다. 하나님이 말씀을 통해 그에게 생명을 주셨기 때문이다. 말씀에는 우리를 살게 하는 능력이 있다.

여섯째, 하나님의 말씀은 우리가 주의 소유가 됨을 확인한다(94절). 기자는 자신이 율법을 사모하는 것은 곧 자신이 하나님의 소유임을 확인하는 것이라고 한다. 그러므로 그는 주인이신 하나님께 주님의 소유물인 그를 구원하시기를 기도한다. 오직 그의 주인이신 하나님만이 그를 구원할 수 있다(Hossfeld-Zenger).

일곱째, 하나님의 말씀은 악인들의 음모에서 우리를 보호한다(95절). 기자는 자신이 당하고 있는 고난이 악인들의 공격임을 밝힌다(Briggs).

악한 사람들이 기자를 죽이려는 음모를 꾸미고 기회를 엿보고 있다. 그러나 그는 그들의 음모나 악한 의도를 생각하며 시간을 허비하는 것이 아니라, 오직 주님의 율법을 묵상하며 살겠다고 다짐한다. 악인들의 음모는 죽이는 것이 목적이지만, 하나님의 말씀은 살리는 힘이 있기 때문이다.

여덟째, 하나님의 말씀은 영원하다(96절). 아무리 좋고, 완벽한 것이라도 모두 끝이 있다. 그러나 하나님의 말씀은 완전하면서도 끝이 없다. 세상의 완벽한 것들은 모두 끝이 나지만, 하나님의 말씀은 세상의 것이 아니라, 하늘에 계시는 하나님이 주신 것이기 때문이다. 이 말씀은 전도서의 요약으로도 손색이 없다(Kidner).

13. 멤(מ)(119:97–104)

97 내가 주의 법을 어찌 그리 사랑하는지요
내가 그것을 종일 작은 소리로 읊조리나이다
98 주의 계명들이 항상 나와 함께 하므로
그것들이 나를 원수보다 지혜롭게 하나이다
99 내가 주의 증거들을 늘 읊조리므로
나의 명철함이 나의 모든 스승보다 나으며
100 주의 법도들을 지키므로
나의 명철함이 노인보다 나으니이다
101 내가 주의 말씀을 지키려고 발을 금하여
모든 악한 길로 가지 아니하였사오며
102 주께서 나를 가르치셨으므로
내가 주의 규례들에서 떠나지 아니하였나이다
103 주의 말씀의 맛이 내게 어찌 그리 단지요
내 입에 꿀보다 더 다니이다

104 주의 법도들로 말미암아 내가 명철하게 되었으므로
모든 거짓 행위를 미워하나이다

첫째, 하나님의 말씀은 우리가 사랑할 것이다(97절). 기자는 율법을 얼마나 사랑하는지 하루 종일 묵상한다. 지속되는 묵상이 하나님과 말씀을 사랑하는 증거가 된다. 또한 하나님의 말씀은 묵상하면 묵상할수록 더 사랑하게 된다. 이 세상 그 무엇과도 바꿀 수 없는 것이 하나님의 말씀이기 때문이다.

둘째, 하나님의 말씀은 우리를 지혜롭게 한다(98절). 기자는 자신이 율법과 함께하는 한 항상 원수들보다 더 지혜롭다고 한다. 말씀은 그를 지혜롭게 하기 때문이다. 당연하다. 율법은 세상에서 가장 지혜로우신 주님의 말씀이기 때문이다. 세상에서 주님의 말씀보다 더 지혜로운 것은 없다.

셋째, 하나님의 말씀은 우리를 명철하게 한다(99절). 기자는 자신이 스승들보다 더 명철하다고 한다. '명철하다'(שׂכל)는 '통찰하다'는 뜻을 지녔다. 사람이 공부하는 이유 중 통찰력을 높이는 것은 매우 중요한 목적이다. 기자는 자기의 통찰력이 스승들보다 낫다고 자부한다. 교만해서가 아니다. 스승들의 가르침이 하나님의 말씀에 근거하지 않았음을 의미할 수도 있고(Goldingay), 혹은 그가 주야로 하나님의 말씀을 묵상해서 스승들보다 더 깊은 통찰력을 얻었다는 뜻일 수도 있다. 하나님의 말씀은 세상 그 어떤 스승보다도 우리를 명철하게 한다.

넷째, 하나님의 말씀은 우리가 이해하도록 한다(100절). 기자는 앞절에서 사용한 '명철'이란 의미의 단어(שׂכל)와 다른 단어(בין)를 사용하고 있다. 학습을 통해 얻는 명철(שׂכל)은 이론적인 면모가 있다면, 본문의 명철(בין)은 실용적인 면모를 강조한다. 이런 이해력과 포용력은 삶의 연륜에서 묻어나는 것이다. 그러므로 기자는 하나님의 말씀을 통해 자신이 삶의 경험이 많은 노인들보다 더 명철하다고 한다. 이 또한 교만의 말이 아니다. 하나님의 말씀은 삶의 경험에서도 얻을 수 없는 포용력과 이해력을 준다는 뜻이다.

다섯째, 하나님의 말씀은 우리가 악한 길을 가는 것을 금한다(101절). 하나님의 말씀은 긍정적인 것들을 추구하고 지향하지만, 악한 것들을 제지하는 힘도 있다. 기자는 하나님의 말씀을 지키느라 악한 길을 가지 않았다고 한다. 하나님의 말씀은 이처럼 선과 악에서 선택을 요구하며 악을 배척하도록 하는 능력이 있다.

여섯째, 하나님의 말씀은 우리에게 주신 가르침이다(102절). 하나님이 말씀을 주신 목적은 분명하다. 선과 악에 대해 우리를 가르치기 위해 주셨다. 그러므로 우리가 율법을 배워 선에 대해 알게 되면 우리는 더 간절한 마음으로 하나님의 말씀을 떠나지 않으려 한다.

일곱째, 하나님의 말씀은 참으로 달콤하다(103절). 기자는 주의 말씀이 꿀보다 더 달다고 한다. 율법을 통해 하나님의 선하심을 경험한 사람의 고백이다. 하나님의 말씀이 달게 느껴지는 순간부터는 순종이 참으로 쉬워진다. 순종하면 순종할수록 더 달콤한 것이 하나님의 말씀이기 때문이다.

여덟째, 하나님의 말씀은 모든 악한 길을 미워하게 한다(104절). '거짓 행위'(אֹרַח שָׁקֶר)는 위선적인 삶의 방식을 의미한다. 기자는 율법을 통해 얻은 깨달음으로 자신의 삶의 방식을 완전히 바꿨을 뿐만 아니라, 모든 악한 삶의 방식을 미워한다고 한다. 그는 하나님의 말씀을 통해 진실되고 선한 삶이 얼마나 귀한 것인가를 깨달은 것이다.

14. 눈(נ)(119:105–112)

105 주의 말씀은 내 발에 등이요
내 길에 빛이니이다
106 주의 의로운 규례들을 지키기로 맹세하고

굳게 정하였나이다
107 나의 고난이 매우 심하오니
여호와여 주의 말씀대로
나를 살아나게 하소서
108 여호와여 구하오니
내 입이 드리는 자원제물을 받으시고
주의 공의를 내게 가르치소서
109 나의 생명이 항상 위기에 있사오나
나는 주의 법을 잊지 아니하나이다
110 악인들이 나를 해하려고 올무를 놓았사오나
나는 주의 법도들에서 떠나지 아니하였나이다
111 주의 증거들로 내가 영원히 나의 기업을 삼았사오니
이는 내 마음의 즐거움이 됨이니이다
112 내가 주의 율례들을 영원히 행하려고
내 마음을 기울였나이다

첫째, 하나님의 말씀은 우리의 길을 밝혀 주는 등불이다(105절). 기자가 사용하는 이미지는 깜깜한 밤에 길을 가는 사람이다. 삶을 칠흑 같은 어두움으로 묘사한다. 이러한 어두움을 두려워하지 않는 것은 그가 혼자가 아니기 때문이다. 주의 말씀이 등불이 되어 그가 가야 할 길을 밝혀준다. 하나님의 말씀은 우리가 살면서 당면하는 선택에서 항상 옳은 선택, 혹은 윤리적인 선택을 하도록 해 줄 것이다(cf. Kidner).

둘째, 하나님의 말씀은 우리에게 결단을 요구한다(106절). 기자는 율법을 지키기로 맹세하고 굳게 결정했다고 한다. 하나님의 말씀이 아무리 아름답고 좋은 것이라도 순종하기는 쉽지 않다는 사실을 암시한다. 세상이 우리를 내버려두지 않을 것이기 때문이다. 그러므로 그는 맹세하고 굳게 정했다. 비장한 각오로 하나님의 말씀대로 살기로 결정한

것이다. 우리도 경건한 삶을 살려면 이러한 각오로 하나님의 말씀을 대해야 한다.

셋째, 하나님의 말씀은 고난 중에 있는 사람을 살린다(107절). 기자는 어떤 고난을 당하고 있는지 설명하지 않는다. 그가 '당하고 있는 고난은 참으로 혹독하다'(נַעֲנֵיתִי עַד־מְאֹד)고 하는 것으로 보아 생명을 위협할 정도이다. 그럼에도 불구하고 그는 하나님의 말씀을 바라본다. 주님이 그를 살리시겠다고 약속하셨기 때문이다. 그러므로 그는 말씀을 통해 그를 살려 달라고 기도한다.

넷째, 하나님의 말씀은 공의롭다(108절). '공의'(מִשְׁפָּט)는 지혜로운 판단/판결과 연관된 개념이다. 하나님의 말씀은 우리가 현명한 판단을 하도록 한다. 그러므로 기자는 이러한 사실에 감사하여 '자원제물'(נִדְבוֹת)을 드리며 주님을 경배하고자 한다. 또한 하나님의 공의로운 말씀을 더 사모한다.

다섯째, 하나님의 말씀은 어떠한 상황에서도 기념되어야 한다(109절). 기자는 마치 추격자들에게 쫓기는 도망자의 삶을 사는 듯하다. 그는 자신의 생명이 자기 손에(בְכַפִּי) 있다고 하는데, 언제든 적들에게 빼앗길 수 있는 위태로운 상황을 묘사한다(Kirkpatrick). 엄청난 스트레스와 긴장 속에 하루하루를 살고 있다. 이러한 상황에서도 그는 하나님의 말씀을 절대 잊지 않을 것을 다짐한다. 그는 쫓기는 삶을 살면서도 항상 주님의 말씀을 묵상할 것이다. 이것이 그나마 그가 살 수 있는 비법이고, 그의 삶의 의미이기 때문이다.

여섯째, 하나님의 말씀은 악인들의 올무를 벗어나게 한다(110절). 악인들은 온갖 음모와 권모술수로 하나님의 백성을 공격한다. 그러나 우리가 하나님의 말씀 안에 거하는 한 그들은 성공하지 못할 것이다. 주님이 우리를 보호하시고 구원하실 것이기 때문이다.

일곱째, 하나님의 말씀은 우리의 영원한 기업이다(111절). '기업'(נָחַל)은 자손대대로 물려주는 유산이다. 기자는 하나님의 율법이 얼마나 놀랍고 좋은지 영원히 자기 기업으로 삼았다고 한다. 하나님의 말씀이 자손대대로 물려줄 신앙의 유산이 된 것이다. 그를 행복하게 하는 말씀은 그렇게 할만한 가치가 있기 때문이다.

여덟째, 하나님의 말씀은 우리가 영원히 행한다(112절). 기자는 율법을 영원히 행하기로 결심했다. 하나님의 말씀은 한두 차례 순종하고 떠나는 것이 아니기 때문이다. 하나님의 말씀이 우리의 삶에서 효과를 발휘하여 열매를 맺으려면 지속적으로 순종해야 한다.

15. 사멕(ס)(119:113–120)

113 내가 두 마음 품는 자들을 미워하고
주의 법을 사랑하나이다
114 주는 나의 은신처요 방패시라
내가 주의 말씀을 바라나이다
115 너희 행악자들이여 나를 떠날지어다
나는 내 하나님의 계명들을 지키리로다
116 주의 말씀대로 나를 붙들어 살게 하시고
내 소망이 부끄럽지 않게 하소서
117 나를 붙드소서
그리하시면 내가 구원을 얻고
주의 율례들에 항상 주의하리이다
118 주의 율례들에서 떠나는 자는
주께서 다 멸시하셨으니
그들의 속임수는 허무함이니이다
119 주께서 세상의 모든 악인들을 찌꺼기 같이 버리시니
그러므로 내가 주의 증거들을 사랑하나이다
120 내 육체가 주를 두려워함으로 떨며

내가 또 주의 심판을 두려워하나이다

첫째, 하나님의 말씀은 하나된 마음으로 지켜야 한다(113절). 기자는 두 마음을 품는 자들을 미워한다고 하는데, 여기서 '두 마음을 품는 자들'(סֵעֲפִים)은 구약에서 이곳에서만 사용된 단어이다. 때로는 율법을 지키고, 때로는 거역하며 사는 사람들을 뜻한다. 사람은 간사하기 때문에 이런 짓을 한다(cf. 아가페). 하나님이 제시하신 기준보다는 자기 잇속을 염두에 두고 결정하는 사람들의 모습이다. 기자는 한결같이 한마음으로 오직 주님의 말씀을 사랑하겠다고 다짐한다. 삶에서 모든 결정을 하나님의 말씀에 따라 하겠다는 의지를 다지고 있다.

둘째, 하나님의 말씀은 우리의 보호막이다(114절). 은신처와 방패는 둘 다 공격과 상관없는 방어와 연관된다. 기자는 세상과 악인들이 어떠한 공격을 해 온다 할지라도, 오직 주님의 말씀만을 바라볼 것이다. 주님은 말씀을 통해 그의 은신처와 방패가 되실 것이기 때문이다.

셋째, 하나님의 말씀은 의인들에게서 악인들이 떠나게 한다(115절). 기자는 자신은 하나님의 율법대로 살겠다며 악인들에게 그를 떠나라고 한다. 의인과 악인의 차이는 가치관과 행실의 차이이다. 그러므로 경건한 사람들이 악한 사람들과 계속 함께할 수는 없다. 같이하면 항상 부딪칠 것이기 때문이다. 언젠가는 물과 기름처럼 나뉘게 된다. 우리도 주님의 자녀가 되기 전과 후에 어울리는 사람들이 다르지 않은가!

넷째, 하나님의 말씀은 우리의 소망이 진실됨을 확인한다(116절). 기자는 온갖 악인들로 가득한 세상에서 그들의 가치관과 다른 기준인 하나님의 말씀에 따라 살고 있다. 그러므로 온갖 비아냥과 야유가 있는 것이 당연하다. 그럼에도 불구하고 그는 말씀대로 살면 언젠가는 하나님이 그의 삶을 인정하실 것이라는 소망을 품고 있다. 그는 이 소망이 실현되는 날을 꿈꾸고 있다.

다섯째, 하나님의 말씀은 주님이 도우셔야 지킬 수 있다(117절). 기자는 하나님이 그를 붙드시기를 간절히 소망한다. 그래야 그가 율법을 지킬 수 있기 때문이다. 우리가 아무리 원해도 하나님이 도우시지 않으면 우리는 말씀대로 살 수 없다.

여섯째, 하나님의 말씀은 악인들을 심판한다(118절). 악인들이 심판을 받는 이유는 두 가지다. 그들이 하나님의 말씀을 떠났기 때문이며, 하나님의 말씀을 떠난 후 꾸며낸 일들이 모두 속임수이고 허무한 것들이기 때문이다. 기자는 언젠가는 하나님의 심판이 악인들에게 분명히 임할 것을 경고한다.

일곱째, 하나님의 말씀은 악인들을 찌꺼기로 취급한다(119절). '찌꺼기'(סִגִים)는 은을 제련하고 남은, 쓰레기로 버리는 찌끼를 뜻한다. 하나님은 악인들을 보존할 가치가 없는 찌꺼기로 취급하시지만, 의인들은 이 찌꺼기들이 제거된 다음에 남은 순수한 은을 대하듯이 하신다는 뜻이다. 악인과 의인의 차이는 무엇인가? 하나님의 말씀을 미워하는 것과 사랑하는 것의 차이다.

여덟째, 하나님의 말씀은 거룩한 두려움을 생성한다(120절). 기자는 자신이 하나님을 두려워하며, 주의 심판도 두려워한다고 한다. 거룩한 두려움이다. 경건한 사람들도 이러한 두려움 속에 살 필요가 있다. 그래야 죄를 덜 지으며 살 수 있기 때문이다. 말씀은 이러한 두려움을 생성한다.

16. 아인(ע)(119:121-128)

121 내가 정의와 공의를 행하였사오니
나를 박해하는 자들에게 나를 넘기지 마옵소서
122 주의 종을 보증하사 복을 얻게 하시고
교만한 자들이 나를 박해하지 못하게 하소서
123 내 눈이 주의 구원과 주의 의로운 말씀을

사모하기에 피곤하니이다
124 주의 인자하심대로 주의 종에게 행하사
내게 주의 율례들을 가르치소서
125 나는 주의 종이오니 나를 깨닫게 하사
주의 증거들을 알게 하소서
126 그들이 주의 법을 폐하였사오니
지금은 여호와께서 일하실 때니이다
127 그러므로 내가 주의 계명들을 금
곧 순금보다 더 사랑하나이다
128 그러므로 내가 범사에 모든 주의 법도들을 바르게 여기고
모든 거짓 행위를 미워하나이다

첫째, 하나님의 말씀은 우리를 억압하는 자들에게서 보호한다(121절). 기자는 하나님의 말씀에 따라 의롭게 살아왔다며 주님께 그를 박해하는 자들에게 넘기지 말라고 기도한다. 경건하게 살아온 것에 일종의 보상을 기대하는 기도라 할 수 있다. 특별한 경우가 아니라면 하나님이 의인들의 길을 축복하실 것을 말씀을 통해 약속하시기 때문이다. 하나님은 말씀대로 살아온 자녀를 정당한 이유가 없이 억압을 당하도록 하지 않으실 것이다.

둘째, 하나님의 말씀은 우리를 보증한다(122절). '보증하다'(ערב)는 누구를 책임진다는 뜻이다(HALOT). 하나님은 말씀을 통해 우리를 책임지신다. 복을 얻게 하시며, 교만한 자들이 우리를 억압하지 못하도록 보호하신다. 그러나 하나님의 이 같은 보호가 항상 곧바로 임하는 것은 아니다. 기자도 다음 절에서 그가 하나님의 구원을 기다리다가 지쳤다고 한다.

셋째, 우리는 하나님의 말씀을 간절히 사모해야 한다(123절). 기자는 하나님의 구원과 의로운 말씀을 사모하느라 참으로 피곤하다고 한

다. '구원'(יְשׁוּעָה)은 우리의 일상적인 필요를 채우시는 것도 포함한다(VanGemeren). 그가 피곤한 것은 매우 오랫동안 간절히 바랐기 때문이다. 하나님이 말씀과 구원이 때로는 상당히 지체될 수 있음을 암시한다. 그러나 하나님의 말씀은 우리가 열정적으로 사모할 만한 가치가 있다.

넷째, 하나님의 말씀은 주님의 인자하심이 임할 때에만 배울 수 있다(124절). 기자는 하나님께 인자하심을 베풀어 달라고 한다. 그래야 그가 하나님의 율법을 배울 수 있기 때문이다. 하나님의 말씀은 우리가 원해서 배울 수 있는 것이 아니라, 하나님이 은혜를 베푸셔야 배울 수 있다. 또한 주님이 은혜를 베푸실 때 배우려고 하는 마음 자세가 있어야 배울 수 있다.

다섯째, 하나님의 말씀은 주의 종들을 위한 것이다(125절). 기자는 자신이 주님의 종이라고 고백하며 하나님과의 관계를 확인하고, 하나님께 자신을 복종시킨다. 그래야만 율법을 배우고 깨달음을 얻을 수 있기 때문이다. 그는 '알다/배우다'(ידע)라는 동사를 사용해 자신은 하나님이 율법을 통해 하신 말씀을 모두 그대로 받아들이고 순종하겠다는 의지를 표현한다(Anderson).

여섯째, 하나님의 말씀을 폐하면 심판이 임한다(126절). 악인들이 율법을 폐했다고 하는데, '폐하다'(פרר)는 지키지 않아 아무런 의미나 효력이 없다는 뜻이며(HALOT), 하나님과 맺은 언약을 파괴하는 일을 의미한다(Anderson, Tucker & Grant, cf. 사 24:5; 33:8; 렘 11:10; 31:32). 하나님의 말씀은 주의 백성에게 주신 것이므로 주님을 거부하는 사람들은 당연히 주님의 율법도 거부한다. 그러므로 기자는 이제는 하나님이 일하실 때라고 한다. 하나님은 말씀을 거부한 사람들을 분명히 심판하신다. 그러므로 기자는 지금이 주님이 일하실 때라고 한다. 말씀을 폐한 사람들은 벌하시고, 순종한 사람들은 축복하실 때가 되었다는 뜻이다.

일곱째, 하나님의 말씀은 순금보다 더 가치가 있다(127절). 기자는 율법이 수천 개의 은과 금보다 더 가치가 있다고 한 적이 있는데(72절), 이번에는 순금보다 가치가 있다고 한다. 하나님의 말씀은 세상에서 가장 진귀한 보배이다. 악인들이 하나님의 말씀을 미워하고 거부할수록 기자는 주님의 율법을 더 사랑하게 된다고 고백하고 있다(Kirkpatrick).

여덟째, 하나님의 말씀은 진실한 행위를 지향한다(128절). 하나님의 말씀으로 무장한 기자는 주님의 율법은 모두 옳게 생각한다. 말씀이 진리라는 것이다. 진리를 알고 나니 모든 거짓 행위를 미워하게 되었다. 말씀은 우리의 마음 자세를 바꿔 놓는다.

17. 페(פ)(119:129–136)

129 주의 증거들은 놀라우므로
내 영혼이 이를 지키나이다
130 주의 말씀을 열면 빛이 비치어
우둔한 사람들을 깨닫게 하나이다
131 내가 주의 계명들을 사모하므로
내가 입을 열고 헐떡였나이다
132 주의 이름을 사랑하는 자들에게 베푸시던 대로
내게 돌이키사 내게 은혜를 베푸소서
133 나의 발걸음을 주의 말씀에 굳게 세우시고
어떤 죄악도 나를 주관하지 못하게 하소서
134 사람의 박해에서 나를 구원하소서
그리하시면 내가 주의 법도들을 지키리이다
135 주의 얼굴을 주의 종에게 비추시고
주의 율례로 나를 가르치소서
136 그들이 주의 법을 지키지 아니하므로
내 눈물이 시냇물 같이 흐르나이다

첫째, 하나님의 말씀은 참으로 놀라운 것들이다(129절). 구약에서 '놀라운 것들'(פְּלָאוֹת)은 출애굽과 연관된 일들을 포함한다(cf. 출 15:11). 하나님의 말씀은 이처럼 가장 귀하고 아름다운 기적들을 담고 있으니 놀랍다(cf. Hossfeld-Zenger). 기자는 율법에 감격하여 온 마음(영혼)을 다해 말씀을 지키기를 원한다. 참으로 귀한 것을 깨달았음으로 그 깨달음을 실천하고 싶은 열망이 생긴 것이다.

둘째, 하나님의 말씀은 어리석은 사람들도 깨닫게 한다(130절). 지혜로운 사람들에게 더없이 좋은 것이 말씀이지만, 어리석거나 단순한 사람들에게도 빛(지혜와 생명)을 비춰줄 수 있다. 여호와를 경외하는 것이 지식의 근본이기 때문이다.

셋째, 우리는 하나님의 말씀을 간절히 사모해야 한다(131절). 기자는 하나님의 율법을 사모하기를 헐떡일 때까지 했다고 한다. 여기서 '헐떡이다'(שׁאף)는 숨을 가쁘게 쉰다는 뜻이다. 그가 얼마나 말씀을 사모했는지 숨이 넘어갈 정도라고 한다. 우리도 이러한 간절함으로 주님의 말씀을 사모했으면 좋겠다.

넷째, 하나님의 말씀은 주를 사랑하는 이들에게 내려 주신 은혜이다(132절). 기자는 하나님이 다른 사람들에게 베푸시는 은혜만큼 자기에게도 베푸시기를 바란다. 그는 하나님의 말씀을 사랑하기 때문에 주님의 은혜를 받을 만한 사람이라고 생각한다.

다섯째, 하나님의 말씀은 우리가 죄를 짓지 못하게 한다(133절). 말씀을 알면 알수록 악과 죄에 대해 알게 된다. 그러므로 죄악을 행할 가능성이 현저하게 줄어들 것이다. 기자는 자신은 말씀 위에 굳게 섰으니 죄악이 그를 지배하지 못하도록 해 달라고 기도한다.

여섯째, 하나님의 말씀은 사람들의 박해에서 우리를 구원한다(134절). 박해는 잘못된 것이다. 그러므로 진리이고 바른 하나님의 말씀은 박해에서 우리를 구원할 것이다. 하나님의 은혜를 입으면 우리는 하나님의 말씀을 더욱더 지키려는 열정을 얻게 된다.

일곱째, 하나님의 말씀은 우리의 형편을 헤아린다(135절). 기자는 하나님께 얼굴을 자기에게 비춰 달라고 하는데, 하나님의 얼굴이 사람을 비춘다는 것은 주님이 그의 형편을 헤아리시는 것을 뜻한다(cf. 시 31:16; 민 6:24-26). 기자는 그의 형편을 하나님이 헤아리시게 하는 말씀을 배우기를 소망한다.

여덟째, 하나님의 말씀은 우리를 긍휼하게 한다(136절). 기자는 율법을 지키지 않는 자들을 생각하며 눈물을 흘린다. 그들이 주님을 모르고 계속 죄를 짓는 것이 안타깝기 때문이다. 이처럼 율법은 우리 마음에 조금이나마 하나님의 긍휼한 마음이 생기게 한다.

18. 짜데(צ)(119:137-144)

137 여호와여 주는 의로우시고
주의 판단은 옳으니이다
138 주께서 명령하신 증거들은 의롭고
지극히 성실하니이다
139 내 대적들이 주의 말씀을 잊어버렸으므로
내 열정이 나를 삼켰나이다
140 주의 말씀이 심히 순수하므로
주의 종이 이를 사랑하나이다
141 내가 미천하여 멸시를 당하나
주의 법도를 잊지 아니하였나이다
142 주의 공의는 영원한 공의요
주의 율법은 진리로소이다
143 환난과 우환이 내게 미쳤으나
주의 계명은 나의 즐거움이니이다
144 주의 증거들은 영원히 의로우시니

나로 하여금 깨닫게 하사 살게 하소서

이 섹션의 핵심은 하나님의 의로우심이다. 주님이 주신 율법도 의로우며, 이 의로움은 주님의 약속이 꼭 지켜질 것을 보증한다(Grogan).

첫째, 하나님의 말씀은 의롭고 옳은 판단력이다(137절. cf. 137, 138, 142, 144절). 기자는 하나님은 의로우시고 주님의 판단력은 옳다고 하는데, 주님의 판결과 경우에 따라 심판하시는 일이 모두 정당하다는 뜻이다(VanGemeren, cf. 시 116:5-6; 147:17-20; 사 11:4). 하나님의 의로우심은 우주의 통치자로서 주님이 계획하고 실행하시는 정책을 정의하기 때문이다(McCann). 그가 하나님의 의와 판결을 접하는 방법은 딱 한 가지, 말씀을 통해서이다. 그는 율법을 통해 드러나는 하나님의 의로우심과 옳은 판단력을 사모하며 자신도 주님 닮아 가는 삶을 살기를 소망한다.

둘째, 하나님의 말씀은 주님의 의로우심과 성실하심을 선포한다(138절). 기자는 율법은 의롭고 지극히 성실하다고 한다. 말씀이 하나님의 영광을 반영하고 있기 때문이다. '의'(צֶדֶק)와 '성실'(אֱמוּנָה)은 하나님의 속성들 중 가장 기본적인 것들이다(cf. Kirkpatrick).

셋째, 하나님의 말씀은 우리를 분노케 한다(139절). 기자는 주님의 말씀을 무시하는 원수들에 대해 매우 강한 분노를 느낀다. 세상에서 제일 좋은 것이 하나님의 말씀인데, 그들은 그 사실을 인정하지 않기 때문이다. 의인과 악인의 가장 기본적인 성향 차이는 하나는 하나님의 말씀을 사랑하지만, 다른 하나는 하나님의 말씀을 인정하지 않음에 있다(Tucker & Grant). 우리도 때로는 하나님의 말씀을 무시하는 사람들을 보고 분노를 느끼지 않는가! 이런 경우 분노는 안타까움의 절정이다.

넷째, 하나님의 말씀은 순수하다(140절). '순수하다'(צרף)는 제련과정에서 이물질이 완전히 제거되어 순도 100퍼센트 광물이 남은 상황을 묘사하는 단어이다(HALOT). 하나님의 말씀은 오랜 세월을 지나며 수

많은 연단과 시험을 거쳐 완전히 진실하다는 사실이 입증되었다는 뜻이다(cf. NIV, ESV).

다섯째, 하나님의 말씀은 미천한 자들을 존귀하게 대한다(141절). 기자는 자신은 세상에서 별 볼 일 없는 사람이라 멸시를 당하지만, 끝까지 하나님의 말씀을 잊지 않고 기념한다고 한다. 율법은 그를 존귀한 자로 대하기 때문이다. 하나님의 말씀은 신분이나 사회적 지위에 따라 사람을 차별하지 않는다.

여섯째, 하나님의 말씀은 영원한 진리이다(142절). 세상은 변하고 사람도 변할 것이다. 그러나 하나님의 말씀은 세월이 지나도 변하지 않는 진리이다. 그러므로 기자는 말씀을 통해 드러난 하나님의 공의는 영원하다고 한다. 그는 세상의 그 어떠한 영화도, 혹은 세상의 혹독한 핍박도 절대 그를 하나님의 영원한 말씀에서 떼어놓을 수 없을 것이라고 다짐한다(Kirkpatrick).

일곱째, 하나님의 말씀은 환난 중에도 기쁨을 준다(143절). 기자는 온갖 환난과 우환으로 힘들어 한다. 그럼에도 그는 하나님의 율법을 포기하지 않고 계속 묵상한다. 주님의 말씀이 어려운 환경에 처한 그에게는 유일한 기쁨이기 때문이다. 삶이 아무리 힘이 들어도 말씀을 묵상하면 잠시나마 세상 그 무엇을 통해서도 맛볼 수 없는 환희와 기쁨을 누릴 수 있다.

여덟째, 하나님 말씀의 의로움은 영원하다(144절). 기자는 하나님의 말씀 때문에 악인들에게 무시당하고 핍박을 당한다. 율법을 범하는 악인들은 율법을 사랑하고 순종하는 그가 밉기 때문에 온갖 핍박을 가한다(Briggs). 그러나 그는 하나님과 주님의 율법이 의롭다는 것을 확신한다(cf. 137절). 그러므로 기자는 자신이 하나님의 말씀을 온전히 알지 못하니 주님의 영원히 의로운 말씀을 더 깊이, 많이 깨달을 수 있도록 기도한다. 의는 핍박에 상관없이 우리가 삶에서 추구해야 하는 것으로 생각하기 때문이다. 그는 주님의 말씀에 따라 살기를 소망한다. 말씀이 그를 영원히 지켜 줄 것이다.

19. 코프(ק)(119:145-152)

145 여호와여 내가 전심으로 부르짖었사오니
내게 응답하소서
내가 주의 교훈들을 지키리이다
146 내가 주께 부르짖었사오니
나를 구원하소서
내가 주의 증거들을 지키리이다
147 내가 날이 밝기 전에 부르짖으며
주의 말씀을 바랐사오며
148 주의 말씀을 조용히 읊조리려고
내가 새벽녘에 눈을 떴나이다
149 주의 인자하심을 따라 내 소리를 들으소서
여호와여 주의 규례들을 따라 나를 살리소서
150 악을 따르는 자들이 가까이 왔사오니
그들은 주의 법에서 머니이다
151 여호와여 주께서 가까이 계시오니
주의 모든 계명들은 진리니이다
152 내가 전부터 주의 증거들을 알고 있었으므로
주께서 영원히 세우신 것인 줄을 알았나이다

첫째, 하나님의 말씀은 순종을 요구한다(145절). 기자는 율법을 온전히 실천할 것을 다짐하면서 주님이 그의 부르짖음에 응답하시기를 간절히 구한다. '부르짖다'(קרא)는 애가에서 자주 사용되는 탄식의 표현이다(Tucker & Grant, VanGemeren). 그는 하나님께 슬프고 겸손한 사람이 울부짖듯 부르짖고 있다. 하나님이 말씀을 아무에게나 주시는 것이 아니라, 순종하겠다며 겸손한 자세로 간절히 부르짖는 사람들에게만 주시는 은총이기 때문이다.

둘째, 하나님의 말씀은 구원에 이르는 길이다(146절). 기자는 율법에 전적으로 순종할 것을 다짐하며 하나님이 그를 구원해 주실 것을 호소한다. 하나님의 말씀은 우리를 구원에 이르게 하는 능력이 있다.

셋째, 하나님의 말씀은 우리가 새벽에 묵상하기에 좋은 것이다(147-148절). 기자는 하루가 시작되기 전인 새벽에 일어나 주님의 말씀을 묵상하며 기도한다고 한다. 새벽은 우리가 하루를 시작하기 전에 묵상하고 기도하기에 좋으며, 주님의 도우심을 기대하기에도 좋은 때이기 때문이다(cf. 시 130:6). 이처럼 말씀을 사모하는 마음으로 하루를 시작하는 사람이 추구하는 것은 딱 한 가지, 하루 종일 하나님의 말씀대로 살아가는 일이다. 묵상이 없는 순종은 있을 수 없기 때문이다.

넷째, 하나님의 말씀은 우리를 살린다(149절). 기자는 하나님께 그의 기도를 들으시고 율법에 따라 그를 살려 달라고 한다. 하나님의 말씀은 우리를 살리는 능력을 지녔기 때문이다.

다섯째, 하나님의 말씀은 의인들이 가까이한다(150절). 기자는 악인들은 율법에서 멀리 떨어져 있다고 한다. 뒤집어 말하면 경건하고 거룩한 사람들은 율법을 가까이한다는 뜻이다. 하나님의 말씀은 오직 의인들 옆에 있다. 악인들은 말씀을 기업으로 받지 못한다.

여섯째, 하나님의 말씀은 우리 곁을 지키는 진리이다(151절). 앞절(150절)에서 율법은 악인들에게서 멀리 있다고 한 기자가, 이 구절에서는 하나님의 말씀이 그의 곁에 있다고 한다. 또한 바로 앞절에서 악인들이 그를 해하려고 가까이 왔다고 하는데, 이 구절에서 그는 주님의 말씀이 그의 곁에 머물며 그를 지켜 준다고 고백한다. 주님의 말씀이 그의 곁을 지키는 한, 악인들은 더 이상 다가오지 못할 것이다. 악인들이 가까이 오는 것은 잠시, 일시적인 현상이지만, 하나님의 말씀이 우리의 삶에 가까이 있는 것은 영원하다. 또한 말씀은 그의 곁에 머물면서 그에게 무엇이 진리인지를 가르쳐 준다. 하나님의 말씀이 진리와 거짓을 판단하는 기준이 되기 때문이다.

일곱째, 하나님의 말씀은 영원하다(152절). 기자는 하나님의 율법은 주님이 세우신 영원한 규례라고 한다. 악인들의 협박과 무시는 최근에 일어난, 잠시 그의 곁을 머물다가 곧 떠날 일이다. 반면에 하나님의 말씀은 '영원하다'(לְעוֹלָם). 주님의 말씀은 태초에도 있었고 세상 끝날까지 영원히 우리와 함께할 것이다. 세상은 없어져도 하나님의 말씀은 없어지지 않는다.

20. 레쉬(ר)(119:153-160)

153 나의 고난을 보시고 나를 건지소서
내가 주의 율법을 잊지 아니함이니이다
154 주께서 나를 변호하시고
나를 구하사 주의 말씀대로 나를 살리소서
155 구원이 악인들에게 멀어짐은
그들이 주의 율례들을 구하지 아니함이니이다
156 여호와여 주의 긍휼이 많으오니
주의 규례들에 따라 나를 살리소서
157 나를 핍박하는 자들과 나의 대적들이 많으나
나는 주의 증거들에서 떠나지 아니하였나이다
158 주의 말씀을 지키지 아니하는 거짓된 자들을
내가 보고 슬퍼하였나이다
159 내가 주의 법도들을 사랑함을 보옵소서
여호와여 주의 인자하심을 따라 나를 살리소서
160 주의 말씀의 강령은 진리이오니

주의 의로운 모든 규례들은 영원하리이다

첫째, 하나님의 말씀은 우리를 고난에서 건진다(153절). 기자는 자신이 큰 고난 중에 있다고 한다. 그럼에도 불구하고 좌절하지 않고 오히려 율법을 붙드는 것은 하나님이 그를 건지실 것을 확신하기 때문이다. 하나님의 말씀은 고난 중에 있는 성도를 구원하는 힘이 있다.

둘째, 하나님의 말씀은 우리를 변호한다(154절). 기자는 하나님이 그를 변호하시고 살려 달라고 호소한다. 말씀은 우리가 의롭게 살다가 곤경에 처할 때 주님이 구원하실 것을 약속하신다. 그러므로 의를 행하다가 생명을 위협하는 곤경에 처한 그가 하나님께 약속하신 대로 살려 달라고 기도하고 있다. 또한 그는 하나님이 반드시 그의 기도를 들으시고 구원하실 것을 확신한다. 그의 소망이 변하지 않는 하나님의 말씀에 근거하고 있기 때문이다(Tucker & Grant).

셋째, 하나님의 말씀은 구하는 자들과 함께한다(155절). 기자는 악인들이 구원에서 멀어져 있는 이유를 그들이 율법을 구하지 않기 때문이라고 한다. 뒤집어 말하자면 하나님의 구원은 말씀을 가까이하는 자들과 함께한다는 뜻이다. 하나님의 말씀은 구하는 자들에게 평생 동반자가 되어 그들의 길에 함께한다. 하나님의 말씀은 우리가 구원에 이르는 길(하나님께 나아가는 길)을 제시하기 때문이다.

넷째, 하나님의 말씀은 생명이다(156절). 기자는 하나님께 율법에 따라 그를 살려 달라고 기도한다. 하나님의 말씀에는 사람을 살리는 힘이 있기 때문이다. 그는 생명을 위협하는 곤경에 처해있다. 이런 상황에서 그에게 유일한 소망은 오직 말씀뿐이다.

다섯째, 하나님의 말씀은 헌신을 요구한다(157절). 기자는 온갖 원수들에게 시달리고 있다. 그들이 그에게 원하는 유일한 것은 율법을 떠나는 일이다. 하나님을 부인하라는 뜻이다. 그러나 핍박이 강해질수록 말씀을 떠나지 않겠다는 그의 각오도 강해진다. 말씀은 경우에 따라 온갖 희생을 요구하기 때문이다.

여섯째, 하나님의 말씀은 죄인들을 슬퍼한다(158절). 말씀에 흠뻑 젖어 사는 기자를 슬프게 하는 자들이 있다. 하나님의 말씀을 지키지 않는 자들이다. 앞에서 기자는 이들의 행동에 대해 분노한적이 있는데, 이번에는 슬퍼한다. 하나님의 말씀은 우리가 죄인들을 정죄하기보다는 안타까워하기를 원하기 때문이다.

일곱째, 하나님의 말씀은 우리를 살린다(159절). 기자는 하나님이 그가 주님의 율법을 얼마나 사랑하는지 헤아리시고 그를 살려 달라고 한다. 말씀에는 사람을 살리는 힘이 있기 때문이다. 또한 기자는 죽은 사람은 아무것도 못한다는 사실을 잘 알고 있기 때문에 살아서 하나님의 말씀을 더 사랑하고 더 순종하기를 원한다.

여덟째, 하나님의 말씀은 영원하다(160절). 주님의 말씀은 진리이다. 또한 하나님의 모든 율법은 의롭다. 하나님의 의로운 진리인 말씀은 영원히 있을 것이다.

21. 신(ש)(119:161–168)

161 고관들이 거짓으로 나를 핍박하오나
나의 마음은 주의 말씀만 경외하나이다
162 사람들이 많은 탈취물을 얻은 것처럼
나는 주의 말씀을 즐거워하나이다
163 나는 거짓을 미워하며 싫어하고
주의 율법을 사랑하나이다
164 주의 의로운 규례들로 말미암아
내가 하루 일곱 번씩 주를 찬양하나이다
165 주의 법을 사랑하는 자에게는 큰 평안이 있으니
그들에게 장애물이 없으리이다

[166] 내가 주의 법도들과 증거들을 지켰사오니
나의 모든 행위가 주 앞에 있음이니이다
[167] 내 영혼이 주의 증거들을 지켰사오며
내가 이를 지극히 사랑하나이다
[168] 내가 주의 법도들과 증거들을 지켰사오니
나의 모든 행위가 주 앞에 있음이니이다

첫째, 하나님의 말씀은 의로운 핍박을 안겨주기도 한다(161절). 기자는 고관들(왕자들)이 이유없이 그를 핍박한다고 한다(23절, cf. 시 35:7, 19; 69:5; 109:3). 그들의 핍박이 거세질수록 말씀을 경외하는 마음이 커진다고 하는 것으로 보아, 그들이 그를 핍박하는 이유는 단 한 가지, 하나님의 말씀대로 살지 말라고 하기 위해서다. 말씀은 세상의 권세가들이 지닌 권력보다 더 큰 권위를 지녔다. 그러므로 그는 핍박을 각오하고 계속 하나님의 말씀을 사모한다. 세상의 어떤 핍박이라도 말씀이 주는 기쁨을 그에게서 앗아갈 수 없기 때문이다.

둘째, 하나님의 말씀은 참으로 큰 기쁨을 준다(162절). 기자가 사용하는 이미지는 전쟁에 참여한 군인의 모습이다. 군인이 가장 기쁠 때는 전쟁이 승리로 끝나(살아 있음의 증거) 약탈물을 나눠 가질 때이다. 기자는 군인들(용병들)이 노획물을 기뻐하는 것처럼 자기는 하나님의 말씀을 기뻐한다고 한다. 주님의 말씀은 우리에게 기쁨의 샘이 되기 때문이다.

셋째, 우리는 하나님의 말씀을 선택하고 사랑해야 한다(163절). 세상은 항상 우리에게 선택을 요구한다. 때로는 거짓과 진실 중 하나를 선택하라고 하기도 한다. 이럴 때마다 우리는 진실을 선택해야 한다. 우리가 가장 소중하게 여기는 하나님의 말씀이 진실되고, 그 말씀이 진실을 선택할 것을 유도하기 때문이다. 진실을 택하며 거짓은 미워해야 한다.

넷째, 하나님의 말씀은 끊임없는 찬양을 유도한다(164절). 하나님의 말씀은 참으로 놀랍고 아름답다. 그러므로 말씀을 묵상할수록 더 많이, 자주 찬양하게 된다. 기자는 율법으로 인해 하루 일곱(만수) 번씩 찬양한다며 그의 입술에서 온종일 찬양이 끊이지 않는다고 고백한다. 말씀을 통해 표현된 하나님의 의로우심이 언젠가는 그를 구원할 것이기 때문이다(VanGemeren). 베네딕트 사제들(Benedictine monks)은 이 말씀을 바탕으로 매일 7차례 주님의 말씀을 송영하는 전통을 세웠다고 한다(Tickle).

다섯째, 하나님의 말씀은 우리에게 큰 평안을 준다(165절). 군인들은 약탈물을 나눠가질 때 일시적인 평안을 누리지만, 주님만이 주실 수 있는 '큰 평안'(שָׁלוֹם רָב)은 율법을 사랑하는 자들에게만 임한다. 하나님이 하시는 일이니 누구도 방해하지 못하며, 참 평안이 우리에게 오는 것을 막을 만한 장애물도 없다.

여섯째, 하나님의 말씀은 우리를 구원한다(166절). 개역개정은 166절과 168절에 똑같은 말씀이 나오는 것으로 번역했다. 그러나 대부분 번역본들은 "주여, 나는 주님의 구원을 소망하며 계명들을 지켰습니다"로 표기한다(새번역, 아가페, 공동, NIV, NAS, ESV). 히브리어 사본들 중 차이를 나타내 빚어진 일이다. 저자가 똑같은 문장을 한 절 건너 다시 사용했을 가능성은 별로 없기 때문에 대부분 번역본들이 채택한 본문을 수용하는 것이 바람직하다. 하나님은 말씀에 순종하는 자들을 구원하신다는 의미다.

일곱째, 하나님의 말씀은 지킬수록 더 사랑하게 된다(167절). '사랑하다'(אהב)가 이 섹션에서 세 차례 사용되며(163, 165, 167절), 중심 테마임을 암시한다. 기자는 자기가 온 마음을 다해 율법을 지켰다고 한다. 지키고 나니 말씀을 더 사랑하게 되었다. 주님의 말씀은 지킬수록 더 사랑하게 하는 매력이 있다. 하나님의 말씀을 사랑하고 순종하면 주님의 말씀을 더 사랑하고 순종하고픈 선순환이 생긴다.

여덟째, 하나님의 말씀은 우리의 행위를 판단하는 기준이다(168절). 기자는 그가 율법을 지킨 일이 모두 주님 앞에 있다고 한다. 하나님이 말씀에 대한 순종 여부를 판단하신다는 것이다. 물론 말씀이 기준이 되어 순종과 불순종을 판단할 것이다.

22. 타브(ת)(119:169–176)

169 여호와여
나의 부르짖음이 주의 앞에 이르게 하시고
주의 말씀대로 나를 깨닫게 하소서
170 나의 간구가 주의 앞에 이르게 하시고
주의 말씀대로 나를 건지소서
171 주께서 율례를 내게 가르치시므로
내 입술이 주를 찬양하리이다
172 주의 모든 계명들이 의로우므로
내 혀가 주의 말씀을 노래하리이다
173 내가 주의 법도들을 택하였사오니
주의 손이 항상 나의 도움이 되게 하소서
174 여호와여 내가 주의 구원을 사모하였사오며
주의 율법을 즐거워하나이다
175 내 영혼을 살게 하소서
그리하시면 주를 찬송하리이다
주의 규례들이 나를 돕게 하소서
176 잃은 양 같이 내가 방황하오니
주의 종을 찾으소서
내가 주의 계명들을 잊지 아니함이니이다

첫째, 하나님의 말씀은 우리에게 깨달음을 준다(169절). '이르게 하다'(קרב)는 전문적인 용어로 하나님께 제물을 드릴 때 사용되는 단어이다(VanGemeren). 그러나 기자는 더 이상 하나님께 드릴 제물이 없다. 그가 드릴 수 있는 유일한 제물은 부르짖음뿐이다. 기자는 하나님이 그에게 말씀에 대한 깨달음을 주시기를 간절히 바란다. 말씀에서 얻은 깨달음을 바탕으로 기도하기를 원하며, 이런 기도는 반드시 하나님 앞에 이를 것을 확신하기 때문이다.

둘째, 하나님의 말씀은 우리가 하나님의 구원을 경험하게 한다(170절). 바로 앞절에서는 '부르짖음'을 제물로 드린 기자가, 이 구절에서는 '간구'를 제물로 드려 주님께 '이르게 한다.' 주님의 말씀을 근거로 드리는 그의 간구는 제물이 되어 하나님 앞에 이를 것이다. 하나님 앞에 이르는 기도는 기도하는 자를 구원하는 능력이 있다. 그러므로 하나님의 말씀은 우리가 주님의 구원을 경험하는 지름길이다.

셋째, 하나님의 말씀은 우리가 주님을 찬양하게 한다(171절). 기자는 율법을 배울수록 하나님을 더욱더 찬양하게 된다고 한다. 진리를 깨달으니 당연한 일이다. 하나님의 말씀은 중독성이 강하다.

넷째, 하나님의 말씀은 우리가 부를 노래이다(172절). 기자는 주님의 말씀을 노래로 부르겠다고 한다. 실제적으로 노래 가사로 사용할 것을 의미할 수도 있지만, 그의 입술에서 말씀이 떠나지 않게 하겠다는 뜻으로 풀이될 수도 있다. 노래를 부르듯 하나님의 말씀을 온종일 흥얼거리면, 우리에게 임하는 은혜는 배가 될 것이다.

다섯째, 하나님의 말씀은 우리를 돕는 주님의 손길이다(173절). 기자는 자신이 율법을 택했으므로 하나님의 도움의 손길이 항상 그와 함께하기를 기대한다. 말씀은 하나님의 손이 우리를 돕는 보증수표이다.

여섯째, 하나님의 말씀은 우리에게 구원의 즐거움을 준다(174절). 기자는 율법을 매우 즐거워한다. 하나님의 말씀 안에 주님의 구원과 살리는 능력이 있기 때문이다. 그러므로 그는 말씀이 약속한 구원이 속히 임하기를 간절히 사모한다.

일곱째, 하나님의 말씀은 우리가 살아 있는 한 끊임없이 찬양하는 것이다(175절). 기자는 하나님이 그의 영혼을 계속 살게 하시기를 기도한다. 살아 있는 사람만이 하나님을 찬양할 수 있기 때문이다. 구약 성도들은 사람이 죽어 스올로 가면 아무것도 할 수 없는 무기력에 빠진다고 생각했다. 그러므로 그는 하나님의 말씀이 평생 그를 도우며 그를 살리기를 원한다. 그래야 하나님을 더 찬양할 수 있기 때문이다.

여덟째, 하나님은 말씀을 통해 우리를 찾으신다(176절). 기자는 자신은 어리석고 미련한 양 같아서 방황을 그칠 수 없다고 한다(cf. 렘 50:6; 겔 34:4-6, 16). 마치 우리의 지조 없는 삶을 묘사하는 듯하다. 그러므로 그는 하나님이 그를 찾으셔서 방황을 그치도록 해 주시기를 원한다. '찾다'(בקשׁ)는 발견한다는 뜻이다. 기자는 자신은 하나님을 찾아갈 능력이 없으니, 주님께서 그를 찾아 주셔야 자신이 살 수 있다고 고백하고 있다. 주님께 목자가 되어 길을 잃은 양과 같은 자기를 찾아 달라고 부탁한다(cf. 눅 15:4-7). 하나님이 그의 목자가 되실 때 비로소 그는 하나님의 말씀대로 살 수 있다. 하나님께 가장 가까이 있는 사람들은 스스로 부족함과 연약함을 느끼고 주님께 도움을 청한다(Davidson).

제120편

성전에 올라가는 노래

I. 장르/양식: 순례시

유태인들의 전승은 120-136편을 '위대한 찬양시'(Great Hallel psalms)라고 불렀다. 이 모음집의 대부분을 차지하는 120-134편은 모두 표제에 '성전에 올라가는 노래'(שִׁיר הַמַּעֲלוֹת)라는 공통적인 문구를 담고 있다. 이 시편들의 내용을 분석해 보면 개인 혹은 공동체 탄식시(120, 123, 126, 130편)와 개인 혹은 공동체 찬양시(121, 122, 124, 125, 129, 131, 134, 135, 136편)와 지혜시(127, 128, 133편)와 왕족시(132편)가 포함되어 있다. 그럼에도 불구하고 모두 성전에 올라가는 노래로 표기가 되어 있다. 또한 이 모음집에서 성전이 있는 시온과 예루살렘이 총 12차례 언급되며 모음집의 통일성을 암시한다(Grogan). 그러므로 이 주석에서는 이 노래들의 장르를 모두 '순례시'로 간주하고 소(小)장르로 탄식시인지, 혹은 찬양시인지를 언급하고자 한다.

총 15편으로 구성된 이 모음집에 공통적으로 붙여진 '성전에 올라가는 노래'라는 표제가 정확히 무엇을 의미하며, 어떤 정황에서 사용되었는지에 대하여는 별로 알려진 바가 없다. 흔히 이 시편들은 '순례자들의 노래'라고 하지만, '단계적 노래'(Gradual Psalm, Song of Degree)로 불리기도 한다. 유태인들의 성경해석 전승인 미쉬나(Mishnah)에 의하면 '성전에 올라가는 노래'를 구성하고 있는 15편의 시편들은 레위 사람들이 15개로 구성된 성전 계단에 서서 부른 노래들이다(Middoth 2.5, cf. 느 3:15; 12:37; 겔 40:6).

그러나 이 시편들이 평범한 성도들의 삶에서 찾아볼 수 있는 것들—거주지(120:5–6), 일상(121:8; 127:2; 128:2), 가족의 중요성(128:3–4), 친척들과 친구들(122:8; 133:1)—을 언급하는 것을 보면 이 노래들은 성도들이 사용한 것이지 레위 사람들이 부른 노래는 아닌 것으로 생각된다(McCann). 또한 공동체가 함께 부를 만한 노래들(123–126, 130–132, 134편)은 이 모음집이 절기 때 사용되었음을 암시한다.

학자들은 이 모음집이 예루살렘과 시온을 자주 언급하는 것(122, 125–126, 128–129, 132–134편)과 단수와 복수가 자주 교차하면서 사람들의 반응을 끌어내는 점을 감안하여 매년 세 주요 절기 때(cf. 출 23:14–17; 신 16:16) 순례자들이 예루살렘 성전으로 올라가는 길에 부른 노래로 간주한다(Goldingay, McCann, Mowinckel). 그러므로 '올라가는'(מַעֲלוֹת) 노래로 불리는 것이다(VanGemeren). 그러나 이 시편들이 처음부터 이러한 사용을 염두에 두고 저작된 것은 아니다. 이미 언급한 장르의 다양성을 감안할 때, 세월이 지나면서 이 모음집에 속하게 되었고, 하나님의 성전이 있는 예루살렘이 주의 백성의 모임 장소라는 점을 강조하기 위한 목적으로 사용되었다(deClaissé–Walford et al.). 더 구체적으로 이 모음집이 느헤미야의 리더십으로 예루살렘 성벽이 완성된 주전 445년 장막절에 처음 사용되기 시작되었다는 주장이 있다(Goulder, Wilcock). 미쉬나는 제2성전 시대에 이 노래들이 성전 예배에서 정기적으로 사용되었다고 한다.

'성전으로 올라가는 노래' 모음집의 첫 번째 노래인 120편의 장르에 대해서는 다소 논란이 있다. 이 시 전체를 과거로 해석하여 개인 감사시 혹은 찬양시로 구분하는 이들이 있다(Anderson, Kraus). 반면에 이 노래에서 사용되는 동사들을 현재와 미래로 해석하여 개인 탄식시로 해석하는 이들이 주류를 이룬다(Allen, Brueggemann & Bellinger, Goldingay, Keet, Kirkpatrick, McCann, Tucker & Grant, Weiser, cf. RSV). 시제를 과거로 볼 것인가 혹은 현재로 간주할 것인가에 따라 탄식시가 될 수도 있고, 감사시가 될 수도 있는 것이다. 이 주석에서는 개인 탄식시로 간주하여 본문을 주해해 나가고자 한다.

120편이 언제쯤 어떤 용도로 처음 저작되었는지는 알 수 없다. 120-134편이 모두 포로기 시대에 저작된 것이라고 하는 사람들(Press)도 있고, 제2성전 시대에 사용된 레위 사람들의 설교 모음집이라고 하는 이들도 있다(Seidel, cf. VanGemeren). 그러나 일부는 포로기 이전에 저작되었을 가능성이 다분하다(Ross).

한 주석가는 120편을 포함한 모음집 전체가 세상 곳곳에 흩어져 사는 디아스포라 유태인들이 예루살렘으로 순례를 가면서 부른 노래라고 한다(Perowne). 여러 종교들 사이에서 갈등하는 성도가 하나님의 용서를 구하며 새로운 마음과 각오로 주님을 섬길 것을 다짐하는 노래라는 해석도 있다(Terrien). 그러나 이러한 해석은 추측일 뿐, 이렇다할 증거는 없다.

II. 구조

주석가들은 이 시를 매우 다양하게 문단으로 나눈다(cf. deClaissé-Walford et al., McCann, Ross, VanGemeren). 그만큼 각 섹션으로 구분하기가 어렵다는 뜻이다. 이 주석에서는 다음과 같은 구조를 바탕으로 본문을 주해해 나가고자 한다.

A. 기도에 응답하시는 하나님(120:1)
B. 구원을 위한 기도(120:2)
C. 원수들에게 임할 벌(120:3-4)

D. 절망과 좌절(120:5–7)

III. 주해

순례자가 예루살렘으로 가면서 부르는 첫 번째 노래는 약속과 성취를 계속 오가는 노래이다(Allen). 기자는 자신이 당면한 원수들의 비방과 그로 인한 어려움과 절망을 표현하고 있다. 그가 아무리 평화를 원해도 원수들은 싸우자고 대든다. 기자는 낙심하여 하나님을 더욱더 간절히 찾는다. 원수들의 비방이 그가 하나님의 성전으로 순례를 떠나게 하는 하나의 자극이 된 것이다.

1. 기도에 응답하시는 하나님(120:1)

1 내가 환난 중에 여호와께 부르짖었더니
내게 응답하셨도다

마소라 사본은 일상적으로 문장 중간에 오는 목적어 '여호와께'(אֶל־יְהוָה)를 가장 앞에 두어 기자가 다름 아닌 여호와께 부르짖고 있다는 점을 드러내고자 한다(Hossfeld–Zenger, VanGemeren). 이 문장은 부르짖는 사람이 아니라, 여호와께 부르짖는 일을 강조하는 것이다. 그는 '환란 중'(בַּצָּרָתָה)에 하나님께 부르짖었다고 하는데, 매우 비좁은 공간에 갇힌 사람의 모습이다(Tucker & Grant, cf. 시 118:5). 하나님이 그를 구원하시면 그는 넓은 공간에서 주님을 찬양할 것이다.

이 구절의 시제를 과거로 혹은 현재로 해석하느냐에 따라 노래의 장르가 바뀐다. 만일 1절을 개역개정이 한 것처럼 과거로 해석하면 이 노래는 감사시가 되고(cf. 새번역, 아가페, 현대인, 공동, ESV, NAS, TNK), 현재로 혹은 미래로 해석하면 탄식시가 된다(cf. NIV, NRS, RSV). 대부분 학자들은 시제를 현재로 취급하며, 이 구절이 탄식시 형식을 지녔다고 한다(cf. 시 3:4; 18:6; 22:21; 66:14; 118:21). 가장 큰 이유는 2-3절과 7절은 절대 과거가 될 수 없으며 기자가 현재 당면하고 있는 상황을 묘사하고 있기 때문이다.

시제를 현재로 번역하면 이 구절은 하나님이 어떤 분이신지에 대하여 원리를 말하고 있다: "내가 환난 중에 여호와께 부르짖으면, 주님은 내게 응답하신다." 하나님은 우리의 기도를 꼭 들어주시는 분이라는 것이다. 혹은 1절을 과거에 기자가 경험한 일로 간주하여, 기도의 응답을 경험한 기자가 그 경험을 토대로 하나님께 부르짖고 있는 것으로 해석할 수 있다(cf. VanGemeren). 이러한 해석에 따라 우리는 이 노래를 개인 탄식시로 구분했다.

2. 구원을 위한 기도(120:2)

2 여호와여
거짓된 입술과 속이는 혀에서
내 생명을 건져 주소서

1절에서처럼 이 구절에서도 기자는 '여호와여'를 문장의 맨 앞에 두고 있다. 그는 자신이 하나님께 부르짖고 있음을 강조하고자 한다(Tucker & Grant). 학자들 사이에 이 구절의 시제는 현재라는 것에는 이의가 없다. 심지어는 1절을 과거로 해석하는 사람들도 모두 이 구절은 현재라는 것을 인정한다. 그렇다면 그들은 1절이 과거로 시작했는데, 2절이 현재를 언급하는 것을 어떻게 설명하는가? 그들은 이 구절이 과거에 기자가 드렸던 기도를 회상하고 있기 때문이라고 한다. 기자가 과거에 "여호와여 거짓된 입술과 속이는 혀에서 나를 구원하소서"(2절)라고 기도한 것을 주님께서 들으시고 구원하셨다는 것이다(1절).

그러나 더 자연스러운 해석은 1절을 하나님은 기도를 들으시는 분이심을 선언하는 것으로 간주하고, 기자가 그 선언을 바탕으로 2절에서 주님께 도움을 청하는 것으로 해석하는 것이 바람직하다. 한 주석가는 '거짓된 입술과 속이는 혀'가 저자가 사는 사회의 전반적인 성향을 묘사하고 있다고 하지만(Clifford), 그가 생명을 위협받고 있는 상황이라는 점을 감안하면 악의적인 비방과 모함으로 해석하는 것이 바람직하다. 일부 주석가들은 느헤미야가 산발랏 일당들에게 당한 일을 회고하고 있는 것으로 이해한다(Goulder, Grogan, Wilcock).

저자는 악인들의 심한 비방과 모함으로 인해 생명에 위협을 느낄 정도로 고통스러워하고 있다. 일상적으로 평범한 신분을 지닌 악인들의 말이 생명을 위협하지는 않는다. 그러므로 기자가 생명에 위협을 느끼고 있다는 것은 그에 대해 비방하고 모함하는 자들의 신분이 상당히 높다는 것을 암시한다. 그들은 음모와 모함으로 사람을 죽일 수도 있는 사회적 위치에 있는 자들이다. 더욱이 기자가 평민이었다면, 그들의 말은 매우 위협적인 결과를 초래했을 것이다.

3. 원수들에게 임할 벌(120:3-4)

3 너 속이는 혀여
무엇을 네게 주며
무엇을 네게 더할꼬
4 장사의 날카로운 화살과
로뎀 나무 숯불이리로다

원수들에게 억울하게 당하고 있는 기자가 보복할 수 있다면 그들에게 내리고 싶은 벌을 생각해 본다. 그는 그들의 음모와 모함으로 인해 생명에 위협을 느끼는 고통을 당하고 있다. 그러므로 그는 가능하다면 그들의 혀에 큰 벌을 내리고 싶어한다. 어떤 벌인가?

기자는 그들의 혀에 화살이 관통했으면 좋겠다고 한다. 더욱이 장사(무사)의 날카로운 화살이 그것들을 찌르고, 로뎀 나무 숯불이 그 혀들을 태웠으면 한다. 우리나라에서 로뎀 나무에 가장 가까운 것은 싸리나무이다(cf. 새번역). 마른 싸리 나무는 가늘지만 나무가 단단하여 매우 오래 타는 나무로 알려져 있다(Kraus). 또한 잎이 많아서 순식간에 불이 붙어 활활 타오른다. 기자는 그들이 받을 심판이 곧 임하여 그들을 순식간에 태우기 시작하여 오랫동안 지속적으로 때웠으면 한다.

그의 이러한 바람은 그들을 저주하라는 기도이기도 하다(Hossfeld-Zenger, Weiser, cf. 삼상 3:17; 14:44; 삼하 3:9; 왕상 2:23). 하나님이 그의 원수들을 가장 날카로운 화살로 찌르고, 가장 강렬한 불로 다 태워 주시기를 원한다. 원수들이 계획하고 있는 모든 것들이 그들에게 임하기를 바라는 무서운 저주이다(Keet). 우리는 남들의 마음을 상하게 하면 이런 저주를 받을 수도 있다는 것을 기억하며 살아야 한다.

4. 절망과 좌절(120:5-7)

5 메섹에 머물며
게달의 장막 중에 머무는 것이
내게 화로다
6 내가 화평을 미워하는 자들과 함께
오래 거주하였도다
7 나는 화평을 원할지라도
내가 말할 때에 그들은 싸우려 하는도다

기자는 당장 성전으로 나아가 위와 같이(2-4절) 주님께 기도하고 싶지만 성전에서 멀리 떨어져 사는 자신이 원망스럽다. 그는 자신이 '메섹'(מֶשֶׁךְ)에 머물고 있다고 하는데, '머물다'(גור)는 단어가 특이하다. 이 단어는 이방인이 되어 잠시 머문다는 뜻이다(NIDOTTE). 저자는 의도적으로 이 단어를 사용하여 자신을 악인들이 득실거리는 세상에서 한곳에 정착하지 못하고 이곳저곳 떠도는 사람처럼 묘사하고 있다(VanGemeren).

메섹은 흑해의 남서쪽에 위치한 코사서스(Caucasia) 산 지역과 그곳에 사는 사람들을 의미한다(HALOT, cf. 창 10:2; 겔 38:2). 오늘날의 터키에 속한 지역 사람들이다(Goldingay). '게달'(קֵדָר)은 이집트와 에돔 사이를 떠도는 유목민들을 뜻한다(HALOT, cf. 사 21:16–17; 렘 2:10; 49:28; 겔 27:21). 가나안에서 남동쪽에 위치해 있다. 그렇다면 메섹은 이스라엘 영토에서 북쪽으로, 게달은 남동쪽에 있다.

그래서 대부분 주석가들은 기자가 북쪽의 메섹과 남쪽의 게달을 언급하는 것은 그가 성전으로 쉽게 나올 수 없는 먼 곳에 살고 있다는 것을 뜻하는 상징적인 의미로 해석한다. 혹은 설령 저자가 예루살렘에 사는 사람이라고 할지라도, 그는 메섹과 게달 사람들 같은 야만인들 사이에 살고 있어서 주님께 나오기가 쉽지 않다는 것을 표현한다(Allen, Anderson, Briggs, cf. Kraus). 요즘 말로 하자면, '나는 테러리스트들 중에 살고 있다'는 표현이다(Ross). 이 두 곳이 이스라엘의 영토 밖에 있다는 것을 감안하여 기자를 타국에서 예루살렘으로 순례를 떠나는 사람으로 간주하기도 한다(deClaissé-Walford et al., Goldingay, cf. Dahood, Mays). 그러나 이 말씀을 비유적으로 해석하는 것이 바람직하다. 기자는 자신이 당면하고 있는 원수들이 적대적인 이방 야만인들과 별반 다를 바가 없다는 것을 이렇게 표현하고 있다(Allen).

저자는 '평화'(שָׁלוֹם)를 사랑한다고 하는데(cf. 시 109:4; 119:165), 소망적이고 풍요로운 삶을 살고 싶다는 뜻이다(Mays). 그는 다른 사람들과도 화평하기를 원한다. 서로 존중하고 행복하게 살고 싶은 것이다. 문제는 그가 살고 있는 곳에 사는 사람들은 화평을 싫어한다는 사실이다.

그가 아무리 평화를 원해도 그들은 그와 싸우려 할 뿐, 그의 말을 들으려 하지 않는다. 가장 신실한 사람이라 할지라도 주변에 있는 악인들이 허락하지 않으면 평안을 누릴 수 없는 것이 현실이다(Weiser). 기자와 원수들의 이 같은 대립은 매우 오래된 일이다(McCann).

이런 사람들과는 평화를 협상할 방법이 없다. 그러므로 그는 참 평화를 주시는 여호와께 나아가 그의 어려움에 대해 호소하고자 순례길을 가고 있다. 그가 순례를 마치고 집으로 돌아올 때까지는 주님이 주시는 참 평안을 누릴 수 있을 것이다. 기자가 온 세상 사람들과 화평하기를 원한다 하여 그를 다윗 왕조의 왕으로 간주하는 주석가도 있다(VanGemeren).

제121편

성전에 올라가는 노래

I. 장르/양식: 순례시

이 시편은 성전에 올라가는 노래 모음집(120-134편)의 두 번째 노래이다. 이 시는 시편 23편과 함께 가장 사랑받는 시편이기도 하다(Brueggemann & Bellinger). 어떤 이는 이 노래를 지혜시(wisdom psalm)로 분류하기도 하지만(Willis), 하나님의 보호를 기념하는 확신시(Grogan, Tucker & Grant) 혹은 주님의 보호를 감사하는 감사시인 것이 확실하다(deClaissé-Walford et al.).

이 시는 앞줄의 중요 단어를 다음 줄 앞 부분에서 반복 사용하는 전사반복(anadiplosis) 형식을 취하고 있다(cf. Broyles). 예를 들자면 1b절은 '나의 도움'(עֶזְרִי)이라는 단어로 마무리되는데, 다음 라인인 2a절은 '나의 도움'(עֶזְרִי)으로 시작한다. 이러한 현상이 이 시편 안에서 지속적으로 관찰된다. 학자들은 이러한 기법을 '계단식'(stair-step)이라고 하기도 한다(Tucker & Grant). 이 시편이 성전에 '올라가는' 노래라는 점을 감안할 때 매우 적절한 문학적 기법이라 할 수 있다.

학자들은 이 시편이 쌍방이 주고받는 대화로 구성되어 있다고 한다. 기자가 1-2절을 말하고, 그의 말에 반응하는 사람들의 말이 3-8절을 형성한다고 생각한다(cf. Limburg). 기자인 왕과 반응하는 제사장들이 주고 받은 노래라고 하기도 하고(Goldingay), 기자가 예루살렘을 향해 순례길을 떠날 때 배웅하는 자들과 나눈 대화라는 해석도 있다(Limburg). 순례길을 갈 때 함께한 일행과 나눈 대화, 혹은 그가 예루살렘에 도착한 후 제사장들 혹은 다른 순례자들과 나눈 것이라는 해석도 있다(deClaissé-Walford et al.). 순례자가 예배를 마치고 집으로 돌아갈 때 제사장과 나눈 대화로 구성되었다는 주장이 있다(Goldingay). 기자가 자신과 대화를 주고받는 독백(monologue)으로 구성되어 있다는 견해도 있다(VanGemeren).

이 노래가 이 같은 용도로 사용된 것은 '성전에 올라가는 노래'로 분류된 이후부터 있었던 일이다. 이 시편이 이 모음집에 속하기 전에는 어떤 정황에서 저작되고 불렸을까? 이 노래가 언덕과 산을 언급한다고 해서 전쟁에 참여하는 용사가(Ceeresko), 혹은 전쟁터로 떠나는 왕이 부른 노래라는 견해가 있다(Goldingay).

일부 학자들은 이 노래가 포로기 이후에 저작된 것이라 하지만(Anderson), 대부분 학자들은 왕정 시대에 저작된 것이라고 한다(Ceresko, Goldingay, Terrien). 그러나 이 시편이 어떤 정황에서 누구에 의해 처음 저작되고 사용되었는가에 대하여는 알려진 바도, 알 수도 없다는 것이 최종 결론이다(McCann).

II. 구조

일부 학자들은 이 시편을 1-2절과 3-8절 두 파트로 구분할 것을 제안하지만(deClaissé-Walford et al., Goldingay), 대부분 주석가들은 1-2절, 3-4절, 5-6절, 7-8절 네 섹션으로 나누는 것을 선호한다(McCann, Ross, Tucker & Grant, Terrien, VanGemeren). 이 주석에서는 다음과 같은 분석을 바탕으로 본문을 주해해 나가고자 한다.

A. 도우시는 여호와(121:1-2)
B. 보호하시는 여호와(121:3-4)
C. 그늘 되신 여호와(121:5-6)
D. 지키시는 여호와(121:7-8)

III. 주해

이 시편에서는 '지키다'(שמר)가 반복적으로 사용되며 중심 테마를 형성하고 있다. 5절을 시작하는 '(여호와는) 너를 지키시는 이'(שֹׁמְרֶךָ)가 이 시편의 한 중앙에 있는 단어라는 사실도 이 개념이 중심 테마임을 암시한다(Ceresko). 여호와는 우리를 지키시는(보호하시는) 하나님이시다. 기자는 주님의 지키심을 확신하며 순례길을 가고 있다.

1. 도우시는 여호와(121:1-2)

1 내가 산을 향하여 눈을 들리라
나의 도움이 어디서 올까
2 나의 도움은 천지를 지으신
여호와에게서로다

이스라엘의 역사에서 전투는 주로 산에서 일어나는 것이라는 사실에 근거하여(cf. 삼상 31장), 이 시편이 전쟁으로 떠나는 장수나 왕이 부른 노래라는 해석이 있다(Ceresko). 또한 산은 산적들과 위험이 도사리고 있고, 우상들이 숭배되던 곳이라 해서 부정적인 의미로 해석하는 이들도 있다(Brueggemann & Bellinger, Grogan, Keet, Morgenstern, Pollock, Terrien, Willis). 그러나 기자가 1절의 수사학적인 질문을 통해 2절의 답을 기대하게 하는 것을 보면(Mays), 이 시가 산을 언급하는 것을 부정적으로 볼 필요는 없다(cf. 시 18:2). 이 노래는 순례자의 노래이다. 또한 그가 산을 향해 도움을 기대하고 있는 것은 그가 마음에 둔 산은 여호와께서 거하시는 시온 산이 확실하다(Goldingay, Hossfeld-Zenger, Mitchell). 또한 눈을 든다는 것은 사모함의 표현이지 두려움의 표현이 아니다(Tucker & Grant, cf. 창 39:7; 겔 18:6; 렘 3:2; 시 123:1).

기자는 그의 도움이 천지를 지으신 창조주 여호와에게서 올 것을 확신하는데, 구약에서는 곤경에 처한 사람이 도움을 바랄 때 가장 흔히 언급하는 것이 창조주이기 때문이다(cf. 욥기, 이사야 40-55장). 그는 그를 도울 수 있는 유일한 이는 천지를 지으신 여호와시라고 확신한다. '천지를 지으신 이'(the Maker of heaven and earth)는 훗날 사도신경의 일부가 된다(cf. 창 14:19; 시 124:8; 134:3; 146:6).

순례자의 노래로 사용된 이후 이 노래는 순례자가 예루살렘에 거의 도달할 때쯤 불렀을 것으로 생각된다(cf. deClaissé-Walford et al.). 그는 먼 발치에서 시온 산을 바라보며 그를 도우실 하나님이 그곳에 계심을 이렇게 노래를 시작하여 표현했을 것이다. 그가 기대하는 '도우심'(עֵזֶר)은 보호와 인도하심과 축복을 의미한다(VanGemeren). 시온 산에 계시는 이스라엘의 하나님은 여호와시며 창조주시다. 그는 창조주 앞에 나아가기를 간절히 소망하여 먼 길을 왔다.

2. 보호하시는 여호와(121:3-4)

3 여호와께서 너를 실족하지 아니하게 하시며
너를 지키시는 이가 졸지 아니하시리로다
4 이스라엘을 지키시는 이는 졸지도 아니하시고
주무시지도 아니하시리로다

인칭이 1인칭(나)에서 2인칭(너)으로 바뀌고 있다. 그래서 대부분 학자들이 1-2절은 저자가 한 말이며, 3-8절은 다른 사람(들)이 저자의 말에 반응하는 것으로 해석한다. 기자는 자기를 도울 수 있는 '유일한 보호자'(cf. Hossfeld-Zenger)는 창조주이신 여호와라고 고백하고 있고, 그의 고백을 들은 사람들이 그 고백의 근거를 말함으로써 그를 격려하고 있다.

이 섹션은 여호와의 보호하심을 네 가지로 노래한다.

첫째, 하나님은 우리가 실족하지 않게 우리가 가는 길을 예비하고 살피신다(3a절, cf. 시 55:22; 66:9). 순례자가 이때까지 하나님의 보호 아래 예루살렘에 무사히 도착한 일을 염두에 둔 말씀이다. 또한 집으로 돌아가는 길도 보호하실 것을 기대한다(Davidson, Grogan).

둘째, 하나님은 졸지 않고 우리를 지키신다(3b절). 하나님의 보호와 인도하심에는 빈틈이 없다. 주님은 피곤하면 조는 사람과는 다르시다. 그러므로 끊임없이 우리를 보호하실 수 있다.

셋째, 우리를 지키시는 하나님은 우리가 속한 공동체도 지켜 주신다(4a절). 하나님은 기자만 지켜 주시는 것이 아니라, 그가 속한 이스라엘도 지켜 주신다. 기자를 지키실 때 졸지 않으신 것처럼, 이스라엘을 지키실 때에도 졸지 않으신다. 빈틈이 없이 완벽하게 보호하신다.

넷째, 우리를 지키시는 하나님은 주무시지도 않고 보호하신다(4b절). '조는 것'(נוּם)이 일시적인 현상이라면, '잠을 자는 것'(יָשֵׁן)은 상당한 시간 동안 진행되는 현상이다. 잠시 혹은 오랜 시간 동안 하나님이 우리를 보호하지 않으시는 일은 없다는 뜻이다. 고대 근동의 신들은 잠을 자기도 했다(Batto, cf. 왕상 18:27). 우리 하나님 여호와는 조시거나 주무시거나 무엇을 드실 필요도 없으신 분이다. 하나님은 항상 우리를 보호하신다.

3. 그늘 되신 여호와(121:5-6)

5 여호와는 너를 지키시는 이시라
여호와께서 네 오른쪽에서 네 그늘이 되시나니
6 낮의 해가 너를 상하게 하지 아니하며
밤의 달도 너를 해치지 아니하리로다

하나님의 보호하심이 그늘에 비교되고 있다. 주님은 그늘이 되시어 낮과 밤에 상관없이 항상 우리를 보호하신다(cf. 시 17:8; 36:7; 57:1; 63:7; 사 51:16). 출애굽 때 구름 기둥과 불 기둥을 연상케 하는 말씀이다(cf. 민 14:9; 시 91:1; 렘 48:45). 근동 지역의 여름은 참으로 혹독하다(cf. Goldingay). 대낮에 길을 걷는 일은 살인적이라 할 수 있다. 여호와는 그늘이 되셔서 자기 백성이 상하지 않도록 보호하신다.

그늘 되신 하나님의 보호를 받는 백성은 밤에도 염려할 필요가 없다. 6절이 '밤의 달'을 해하는 것으로 묘사하는 것에 대해 어떤 이들은 바빌론 신화가 배경이 되고 있다고 한다. 바빌론의 달(moon) 신의 이름은 신(Sin)이었는데, 이 신은 열병과 문둥병 등 몇 가지 질병을 주는 신으로 알려졌다. 이 말씀의 배경이 바로 이 신과 연관된 재앙들이라는 것이다(Kraus). 그러나 그렇게 해석할 필요는 없다. 구름이 없는 근동의 낮이 혹독한 만큼 밤도 매우 춥다(Calvin). 다행히 그늘 되신 하나님이 자기 백성을 보호하신다. 하늘에서 내려오는 찬기에서 그들을 가리시는 것이다. 하나님의 보호는 낮으로만 제한되지 않고, 밤에도 유효하다는 뜻이다(Kidner, cf. Tucker & Grant).

이 말씀은 예루살렘에 도달한 기자가 집을 떠난 후 어떤 기후적 여건을 지나 시온 산까지 오게 되었는가를 잘 묘사하고 있다. 그는 하나님의 보호하심 없이는 오기 어려운 길을 왔다.

4. 지키시는 여호와(121:7–8)

7 여호와께서 너를 지켜 모든 환난을 면하게 하시며
또 네 영혼을 지키시리로다
8 여호와께서 너의 출입을
지금부터 영원까지 지키시리로다

기자가 예루살렘으로 오는 동안 경험한 하나님의 보호는 앞으로도 계속될 것이다(Davidson, Grogan). 여호와께서는 그를 '모든 형태의 환난'(כָּל־רָע)에서 보호하실 것이다. 또한 그의 영혼도 지켜 주실 것이다. 그는 주님 안에서 참 평안을 누리며 살 것이라는 의미다.

뿐만 아니라 하나님은 그의 출입도 지켜 주실 것이다. 기자가 집에 있든, 혹은 길을 떠나든 항상 그와 함께하시며 그를 지키실 것이다(cf. 신 28:6; 31:2; 수 14:11; 왕상 3:7). 주님의 이 같은 보호는 일시적인 것이 아니라 영원히 지속될 것이다. 이 말씀은 성전에서 예배를 드리고 자기 집으로 돌아가는 순례자에게 매우 적절한 축복으로 생각된다.

제122편

다윗의 노래 곧 성전에 올라가는 노래

I. 장르/양식: 순례시

이 시편은 '시온의 노래'(Song of Zion, cf. 46, 48, 76, 84, 87, 132편)로 분류되는 시들 중 하나이다(Tucker & Grant, VanGemeren). 그러나 다른 시온의 노래들처럼 예루살렘을 이상화하거나 상징적인 언어로 묘사하지 않는다. 이 시편은 실제적이고 물리적인 예루살렘의 모습을 기념하고 찬양한다(Goldingay). 그러므로 이 시편에는 '여호와의 집'(1, 9절), '성문'(2절), '보좌'(5절), '성과 궁중'(7절) 등 예루살렘과 연관된 물리적인 공간과 물체들이 언급된다. 이런 면에서 48편과 상당히 비슷하다고 할 수 있다.

기자가 예루살렘의 물리적인 형상에 감탄하다 보니 이 노래에서는 시온에서 여호와를 예배하는 일보다 예루살렘의 물리적인 놀라움에 감탄을 금치 못하는 일이 중심이 되고 있다(Terrien, cf. Goldingay). 그러므로 이 시는 가장 확실한 순례시라 할 수 있다(cf. Brueggemann & Bellinger). 표제는 이 시편이 다윗에게서 비롯되었다고 하는데, 확실하지는 않다. 표제가 아예 없는 사본들과 옛 번역본들이 많기 때문이다(Ross).

대부분 학자들은 120-122편의 순서가 의도적으로 정해졌다고 생각한다(cf. Crow). 지리적 상황이 변하고 있기 때문이다. 120편에서 순례자들은 열방에 흩어져 있다. 121편에서는 순례자들이 시온을 향해 순례길을 가고 있다. 122편에서는 순례자들이 예루살렘에 도착했다. 그러므로 이 세 편은 먼 곳—여정—도착의 순서로 구성되어 있다는 것이다(cf. Goldingay, McCann, Tucker & Grant).

학자들은 '성전에 올라가는 노래' 모음집(120-134편) 중 이 시편이 유일하게 순수한 '순례자의 노래'라고 한다(McCann, Tucker & Grant, Westermann). 이 시는 늦은 다윗 시대에 저작되었다고 하고(Ross), 포로기 이후 시대에 저작된 것이라 하기도 한다(Goldingay, Tucker & Grant).

II. 구조

이 시편이 사용하고 있는 주요 개념들과 단어들을 바탕으로 분석하면 다음과 같은 교차대구법적 구조가 드러난다(McCann).

A. 순례자와 '여호와의 집'(1-2절)
    B. 예루살렘(3-4절)
        C. 다윗의 집(5절)
    B'. 예루살렘(6-7절)
A'. 순례자와 '여호와의 집'(8-9절)

많은 주석가들은 이 시를 1-2절, 3-5절, 6-9절 세 파트로 구분하여 본문을 주해한다(deClaissé-Walford et al., Hossfeld-Zenger, Ross, Tucker & Grant, VanGemeren). 이 주석에서도 다음과 같이 세 섹션으로 구분하여 본문을 주해해 나가고자 한다.

A. 예루살렘의 현재(122:1-2)
B. 예루살렘의 과거(122:3-5)
C. 예루살렘의 미래(122:6-9)

III. 주해

이 노래는 순례자가 목적지인 예루살렘에 드디어 도착한 상황(1-2절)으로 시작하여 예루살렘에 하나님의 심판과 평화가 영원히 함께하기를 기도하는 종말론적인 비전으로 마무리된다(5-9절). 우리가 항상 예루살렘의 평안을 위해 기도해야 하는 것은 주님이 종말 때 그곳에 임하여 온 세상을 심판하실 것이기 때문이다.

1. 예루살렘의 현재(122:1-2)

1 사람이 내게 말하기를
여호와의 집에 올라가자 할 때에
내가 기뻐하였도다
2 예루살렘아
우리 발이 네 성문 안에 섰도다

어디서 시작되었는지 알 수 없지만, 드디어 기자의 순례길이 마무리되었다. 그와 일행의 발이 예루살렘 성문 안에 서 있기 때문이다. 그러므로 그가 순례길을 오는 동안 안전하게 지켜 주신 여호와의 은혜를 마음껏 기뻐할 때이다. '그가 기뻐했다'(שָׂמַחְתִּי)(1절)는 것이 이 시편의 전체적인 분위기가 어떤 것인지를 암시하고 있다. 저자는 기쁨으로 이 노래를 부른다. 예루살렘을 생각하며 기쁨으로 노래하는 그와는 달리 먼 훗날 예수님은 예루살렘을 바라보고 눈물을 흘리며 슬퍼하셨다(눅 19:42-44).

'사람이 내게 말하기를'(בְּאֹמְרִים לִי)은 반복적인 의미를 지니고 있기 때문에, '사람들이 내게 말할 때마다'로 해석해야 한다(VanGemeren). 기자는 사람들이 여호와의 집에 올라가자고 말할 때마다 기뻐했던 일을 추억하고 있다. 그는 예루살렘 순례를 항상 마음에 두고 살았고, 사람들이 순례길을 떠나자고 할 때마다 흥분했다며 드디어 그가 항상 하고자 했던 일을 하게 되었다며 기뻐한다. 중요한 것은 저자가 큰 도시에 도착해서 기뻐하는 것이 아니라, 하나님의 집에 도착했기 때문에 기뻐한다는 것이다(Goldingay). 우리가 예배 처소를 찾을 때마다 이런 마음으로 임할 수 있으면 얼마나 좋을까!

율법은 이스라엘 성인 남자들에게 매년 무교절과 칠칠절과 초막절이면 성전으로 순례를 가라고 한다(신 16:16). 무교절은 유월절과 연관된 초봄에 있는 절기이며 봄 추수의 시작을 알리는 절기이기도 하다. 이때부터 50일이 지나면 봄 수확을 마무리하는 칠칠절이다. 가을 추수가 끝나면 초막절이 온다. 이스라엘 남자들은 이 세 절기 때에는 성전으로 순례를 떠났다. 기자도 이 세 절기 중 하나에 예루살렘을 찾았을 것이다.

2. 예루살렘의 과거(122:3-5)

3 예루살렘아
너는 잘 짜여진 성읍과 같이 건설되었도다
4 지파들 곧 여호와의 지파들이
여호와의 이름에 감사하려고
이스라엘의 전례대로 그리로 올라가는도다
5 거기에 심판의 보좌를 두셨으니
곧 다윗의 집의 보좌로다

예루살렘 성 안에 서 있는 기자가 이 도성의 지난날들을 세 가지로 회상한다.

첫째, 예루살렘은 참으로 잘 갖추어진 성읍이다(3절). 고대 근동에서 성읍은 사람들의 생존과 직접 연관된 것이었다. 그러므로 이 말씀은 예루살렘이 모든 면에서 하나도 부족하거나 아쉬운 것이 없어 주민들을 완벽하게 보호할 수 있는 성읍이라는 뜻이다(Goulder). 그러므로 공동번역은 “과연 수도답게 잘도 지어졌구나”로 번역하고 있다. 시온의 노래들이 예루살렘의 완벽함을 노래하는 것을 감안하면 저자의 말에 충분히 동의할 수 있다.

둘째, 예루살렘은 역사와 전통이 있는 이스라엘의 모임 장소이자 예배처소이다(4절). 이스라엘은 예배를 통해 연합과 통일성을 유지했다(Calvin). 이스라엘의 모든 지파가 여호와께 감사하려고 예루살렘으로 모여든다(cf. 출 23:17; 34:23; 신 16:16). 예루살렘이 잘 짜인 성읍인 것처럼, 이스라엘의 열두 지파들도 연합이 잘된 예배자들이다(VanGemeren). ‘이스라엘의 전례대로’(עֵדוּת לְיִשְׂרָאֵל)는 ‘이스라엘에게 주신 말씀에 따라’라는 의미를 지녔다. 여호와의 지파들이 예배를 위해 예루살렘으로 모여드는 것은 사람들이 정한 전통에 의한 것이 아니라, 하나님이 정해주신 것이라는 뜻이다.

셋째, 예루살렘은 다윗 왕조의 통치가 계속되는 곳이다(5절, cf. 왕상 7:7). 왕이신 하나님의 백성 통치가 예루살렘에서 진행되고 있는데, 다윗 왕조를 통해서 이루어지고 있다. 일명 다윗 언약이라고 하는 사무엘하 7장이 이 말씀의 배경이 되고 있다. 아마도 지방에서 올라온 순례자들은 자신들이 사는 지역에서 해결하지 못한 법적인 이슈들을 이때 가져와 주님의 공평한 판결을 받기도 했을 것이다(Mays). 앞으로도 하나님의 통치는 예루살렘에서 계속될 것이며 이 도성에 정의와 번영을 안겨줄 것이다. 예루살렘은 이스라엘의 종교적 중심일 뿐만 아니라, 정치적 중심이기도 하다.

3. 예루살렘의 미래(122:6-9)

[6] 예루살렘을 위하여 평안을 구하라
예루살렘을 사랑하는 자는 형통하리로다
[7] 네 성 안에는 평안이 있고
네 궁중에는 형통함이 있을지어다
[8] 내가 내 형제와 친구를 위하여 이제 말하리니
네 가운데에 평안이 있을지어다
[9] 여호와 우리 하나님의 집을 위하여
내가 너를 위하여 복을 구하리로다

앞 섹션에서 예루살렘은 이스라엘 역사에서 매우 중요한 성지라는 사실을 묵상한 기자가 이 도성은 앞으로도 영원해야 한다고 복을 빌어 주며 순례자들에게 예루살렘의 영원한 미래를 위해 기도하고 축복할 것을 몇 가지로 당부한다. 핵심은 '평화'(שָׁלוֹם)다.

첫째, 예루살렘의 평안을 위해 기도하라(6절). '예루살렘'(יְרוּשָׁלַם)은 '평화 위에 세워진 도성'이라는 뜻이다(HALOT). 그러나 예루살렘은 이름과 걸맞지 않은 온갖 고통과 어려움을 경험한 도시이다. 기자는 이름에 걸맞게 예루살렘에 항상 평화가 깃들기를 기도하라고 한다. 그의 권면은 그가 예루살렘을 방문했을 때에는 도성이 평안하지 않았던 것을 암시할 수도 있다(McCann). 오직 여호와만이 이 도성에 참 평안을 주실 수 있다. 또한 그는 예루살렘을 사랑하는 마음으로 이 도성을 위해 기도하는 사람들은 모두 형통할 것이라며 복을 빌어 주고 있다.

둘째, 많은 사람들이 기도하고 축복하는 것에 따라 예루살렘은 항상 평안하고 형통한 성읍이 될 것이다(7절). 평안하고 형통한 도성 예루살렘은 기자가 꿈꾸는 이 도시의 이상적인 모습이다(VanGemeren). 하나님은 이 도성을 사랑하는 자들의 기도를 들으시고, 예루살렘에 평안과 형통함의 복을 내려 주실 것이다.

셋째, 예루살렘의 평안을 위해 기도하는 사람들에게도 평안을 빌어 주라(8절). 기자는 자기와 함께 예루살렘의 평안을 위해 기도하고 도성을 축복하는 사람들에게 평안을 빌어준다. 하나님의 도성을 위해 기도하고 복을 비는 사람은 주님의 복을 받을 만한 자격이 있기 때문이다. 또한 그들이 하나님의 도성에 평안을 빈 것처럼, 평안이 그들에게 임할 것이다.

넷째, 성전과 예배자들을 위해 복을 구하라(9절). 기자는 하나님의 백성들이 하나님의 처소인 성전에서 하나되는 꿈을 꾸고 있다. 그러므로 그는 앞으로도 주님의 집과 주의 성도들을 위해 계속 복을 구할 것을 다짐한다. 하나님의 성전이 복된 것처럼 주의 백성도 복되기를 바라는 염원이다.

제123편

성전에 올라가는 노래

I. 장르/양식: 순례시

이 시편은 기도시(a prayer psalm)이며(cf. Goldingay, Clifford, Ross), 성경에 기록된 가장 사랑스러운 기도문 중 하나이다(Brueggemann & Bellinger). 또한 '성전에 올라가는 노래' 모음집에서 처음으로 등장하는 '온전한 기도'(complete prayer)라 할 수 있다(McCann). 더 구체적으로는 단수(1절)와 복수(2-4절)로 드리는 기도다. 단수가 복수로 바뀌는 것은 순례자가 예루살렘으로 홀로 가다가 여럿이 함께 가게 되는 상황과 잘 어울린다(McCann). 또한 단수가 복수로 바뀌는 것을 느헤미야 같은 공동체 지도자나 레위 사람이 예배를 인도하며 사용한 증거로 생각하는 이들도 있다(Goldingay).

비록 1절이 단수를 사용하지만, 이 노래는 분명 공동체 탄식시이다(cf. deClaissé-Walford et al., Tucker & Grant). 또한 이 노래는 하나님의 개입이나 응답을 받지 못하고 마무리되는 탄식시이다(Crow). 하나님께 기도는 하지만, 정작 하나님이 어떻게 반응하실지는 확실하지 않은 상황에서 마무리된다.

이 노래가 저작되고 불린 정황은 포로기 이후 시대라는 것이 대부분 학자들의 결론이다(Goldingay, McCann, Terrien, cf. 느 2:19; 4:4). 심지어 이 시편은 예루살렘을 재건하려고 페르시아를 떠난 귀향민들이 순례길에 부른 노래라고 하는 이도 있다(Terrien). 그러나 정확한 저작 시기와 정황은 알 수 없다. 단지 억압과 핍박의 시대에 부른 노래인 것은 확실하다.

II. 구조

이 시편은 상대적으로 짧은 노래이지만, 여러 단어들의 반복적인 사용으로 구조가 역력하게 드러나는 시이다. 이 주석에서는 다음과 같이 두 파트로 구분하여 본문을 주해해 나갈 것이다.

A. 주님을 바라며 기다림(123:1-2)

B. 간절히 은혜를 구함(123:3-4)

III. 주해

기자는 주의 백성이 당면한 멸시와 비아냥이 크다며 주님의 개입을 위해 기도한다. 그는 여호와께서 꼭 그의 기도를 들어주시어 그들을 이 같은 수모에서 구원하실 것을 확신한다. 그러나 그것은 그의 희망사항일 뿐 정작 하나님은 침묵하신다.

1. 주님을 바라며 기다림(123:1-2)

1 하늘에 계시는 주여
내가 눈을 들어 주께 향하나이다
2 상전의 손을 바라보는 종들의 눈 같이,
여주인의 손을 바라보는 여종의 눈 같이
우리의 눈이 여호와 우리 하나님을 바라보며

우리에게 은혜 베풀어 주시기를 기다리나이다

기자는 눈을 들어 하늘에 계시는 주님을 바라본다(1절, cf. 시 2:4; 11:4; 115:3, 16). '눈을 들다'(נָשָׂאתִי אֶת־עֵינַי)는 사모함을 표현한다(창 39:7; 겔 18:6; 시 121:1). 그는 간절한 마음으로 주님이 계시는 곳을 바라보고 있다. 이 시편이 순례자의 노래인 데도 그가 하늘에 계시는 하나님을 찾는 것을 보면, 그는 이 기도를 성전 뜰에서 드리는 듯하다. 비록 성전이 하나님이 이스라엘 중에 거하시는 것을 상징하지만, 솔로몬이 수차례 기도한 것처럼 하나님은 하늘에 계시기 때문이다(cf. 왕상 8장).

저자는 자기와 함께한 사람들에게 한마음이 되어 주님을 간절히 사모하자고 한다(2절). 그가 사용하는 이미지는 종들이 간절한 마음으로 왕(주인)을 바라보는 것이다. 종들은 스스로는 그 어떠한 일도 할 수 없다(Hossfeld-Zenger). 그들은 전적으로 주인을 의지해야 한다. 종들이 오직 주인을 바라보는 것처럼, 그들도 주인이신 여호와를 바라보고 있다. 손은 행동과 실천의 상징이다. 간절히 주님을 바라보면 여호와께서는 분명 그들에게 은혜를 베풀어 주실 것이다.

2. 간절히 은혜를 구함(123:3-4)

3 여호와여
우리에게 은혜를 베푸시고
또 은혜를 베푸소서
심한 멸시가 우리에게 넘치나이다
4 안일한 자의 조소와
교만한 자의 멸시가
우리 영혼에 넘치나이다

기자는 하나님이 그들에게 은혜를 베푸시고 또 베푸시기를 기도한다(3절). 그들이 당면한 멸시와 비웃음이 참으로 크기 때문에 스스로 감당하기가 어렵다(3d-4d절). 그러므로 그는 '넘치다'(שׂבע)를 두 차례 반복하여 자신들의 어려움을 토로한다(3d, 4d절). 원수들의 조롱과 멸시가 도저히 견딜 수 없는 수위에 도달했다는 뜻이다(cf. Dahood). 확실하지는 않지만, 그들의 조롱은 "너희의 신은 어디 있느냐?"라는 질문을 포함할 수 있다(Mays, cf. 42:11; 115:2). 포로기 이후 느헤미야 시대와 잘 어울리는 상황이다(McCann, cf. 느 2:19; 4:1, 4).

'안일한 자/거만한 자'(לַעֲג)는 경제적으로 부유한 사람을 뜻한다(Brueggemann & Bellinger, cf. 암 6:1). '교만한 자'(גְּאֵיוֹן)는 자격도 없으면서 험담하고 남을 비꼬는 자들을 뜻한다. 기자가 이 둘을 비슷한 말로 사용하여 같은 부류를 지적하는 것은 교만한 자들의 교만이 그들의 경제적인 부유함에서 비롯되었음을 암시한다(Calvin). 기자는 자신들이 억울하게 당하고 있음을 하소연한다. 또한 하나님은 이런 자들을 가장 싫어하신다. 그러므로 비록 하나님이 그들을 벌하실 것에 대해 구체적으로 언급되어 있지는 않지만, 충분히 기대할 수 있는 상황이다.

제124편

다윗의 노래 곧 성전에 올라가는 노래

I. 장르/양식: 순례시

이 시편은 공동체 감사시(communal psalm of thanksgiving)라는 것이 대부분 학자들의 결론이다(Grogan, McCann, Ross, Tucker & Grant, VanGemeren). 그러나 전형적인 공동체 감사시 양식을 따르지 않는 특징을 갖고 있다. 심지어는 사용하는 단어들과 표현들도 공동체 감사시와 많이 다르다. 아마도 개인 찬양시를 감사시로 변형하여 사용하는 과정에서 발생한 현상일 것이다(Goldingay). 원래는 찬양시였던 것으로 감사시로 바꿔 사용하다 보니 이 시편은 내용에 있어서 찬양시에 더 가깝다(Ross).

대부분의 공동체 감사시는 공동체가 경험한 하나님의 은혜에 대한 찬양으로 시작한다(Tucker & Grant, cf. 118:4-14). 반면에 이 시편은 다르게 시작한다. 기자는 하나님이 개입하시지 않았더라면 일어났을 일을 회고하는 것으로 노래를 시작한다.

이 시편의 내용은 바빌론 포로 생활을 마치고 돌아오는 귀향민들이 부를 만한 노래이다(Allen, McCann, Terrien). 또한 히스기야 시대에 있었던 산헤립의 침략이 수포로 돌아간 이후에도 부르기에 적합한 노래였다(Goldingay). 만일 표제가 말하는 대로 이 시편이 다윗 시대에 불린 노래라면, 아마도 블레셋 사람들의 침략이 있은 다음에 불렀을 것이다 (Grogan, cf. 삼하 5장).

이처럼 다양한 정황이 가능하기 때문에 이 시편의 저작 시기와 삶의 정황을 논하는 것은 매우 어려운 일이다. 원래는 순례자의 노래가 아니었는데, 하나님이 자기 백성에게 구원을 베푸셨다는 내용이 이러한 용도로 사용되게 한 것으로 생각된다(Goldingay).

II. 구조

밴게메렌(VanGemeren)은 이 시편에 대해 다음과 같이 세부적인 교차대구법적 구조를 제시하는데, 그다지 설득력이 있어 보이지는 않는다. 가장 큰 문제는 함께 취급되어야 할 같은 구절을 자꾸 다른 섹션으로 나누는 것이다.

A. 여호와의 임재(124:1-2a)
  B. 위험에서 보호(124:2b-5)
    C. 여호와 찬양(124:6a)
  B′. 위험에서 보호(124:6b-7)
A′. 여호와의 임재(124:8)

대부분 학자들은 이 시편을 1-5절과 6-8절 두 파트로, 혹은 두 번째 섹션(6-8절)을 6-7절과 8절로 구분하여 세 단락으로 나눈다(cf. Allen, Goldingay, McCann, Ross, Tucker & Grant). 이 주석에서는 다음과 같은 분석을 바탕으로 본문을 주해해 나가고자 한다.

A. 여호와의 구원(124:1-5)
B. 여호와의 구원 찬양(124:6-7)
C. 여호와 신뢰 선언(124:8)

III. 주해

이 시편은 하나님이 과거에 구원을 베풀지 않으셨다면 어떻게 되었을까? 하는 가상 시나리오로 시작한다. 끔찍한 결과를 초래했을 것이라는 결론이다. 그러므로 구원을 베푸신 여호와를 찬양하며 앞으로도 주님만을 의지할 것을 선언한다.

1. 여호와의 구원(124:1-5)

1 이스라엘은 이제 말하기를
여호와께서 우리 편에 계시지 아니하셨더라면
우리가 어떻게 하였으랴
2 사람들이 우리를 치러 일어날 때에
여호와께서 우리 편에 계시지 아니하셨더라면
3 그 때에 그들의 노여움이 우리에게 맹렬하여
우리를 산채로 삼켰을 것이며
4 그 때에 물이 우리를 휩쓸며
시내가 우리 영혼을 삼켰을 것이며
5 그 때에 넘치는 물이
우리 영혼을 삼켰을 것이라
할 것이로다

이 섹션은 '만일… 아니하셨더라면'이라는 가상 시나리오를 두 차례 반복하며 시작한다(1, 2절, cf. 창 31:42; 43:10; 신 32:29; 삼상 25:34). 하나님이 하신 일을 강조하기 위해서다(cf. 129:1-2). 기자는 여호와께서 한 순간이라도 자기 백성에게서 눈을 돌리시면, 그들은 원수들에게 심각한 공격을 받아 모두 멸망할 것이라는 사실을 고백한다(Kraus).

'우리와 함께 하셨다'(הָיָה לָנוּ)는 '임마누엘'(하나님이 우리와 함께하신다)의 과거형이며(VanGemeren), 군사적으로 대립하는 상황에서 사용되는 표현이다(Hossfeld-Zenger, cf. 창 31:42; 삼상 17:46; 시 56:10; 118:6-7). 기자가 묘사하고 있는 상황은 원수들로 부터 군사적인 침략을 받은 사건이다(Tucker & Grant).

나머지 섹션(3-5절)은 '…되었을 것이다'라며 참혹한 상황을 묘사한다. 기자는 이러한 기법으로 하나님이 그들을 구원하지 않으셨다면 그들이 얼마나 어려운 상황에 처했을 것인가를 회상하며 감사를 표한다. 하나님이 함께하시면 축복을 기대해도 좋은데, 주님의 축복은 구원을 포함한다.

기자는 사람들에게 상상력을 동원하여 하나님의 구원이 얼마나 놀라운 은혜인가를 생각해보라고 도전한다(1-2절). 그들은 공격해오는 자들을 물리칠만한 능력이 없다. 이런 상황에서 만일 원수들이 그들을 쳤고, 여호와께서 그들 편에 계시지 않으셨다면 그들은 어떻게 되었을까? 기자는 두 가지로 이 질문에 답을 한다.

첫째, 불과 같은 원수들의 노여움이 그들을 산채로 삼켰을 것이다(3절). '삼키다'(בלע)는 죽음을 뜻하는 비유이다(VanGemeren, cf. 시 55:15; 잠 1:12; 렘 51:34-35). 고라와 도단과 아비람이 모세를 비방했다가 땅이 갈라지며 그들과 가족들을 삼킨 일에서 사용되었다(민 16:34). 이미지는 모든 것을 태우는 불이다. 원수들이 그들을 모두 태워 죽였을 것이라는 결론이다.

둘째, 넘치는 물과 같은 원수들이 그들을 휩쓸었을 것이다(4-5절). '넘치는'(הַזֵּידוֹנִים)은 성경에서 단 한 번 사용되는 단어(hapax legomenon)이지만, 의미는 확실하다. '걷잡을 수 없이 거세다'는 뜻이다(HALOT). 돌발 홍수(flash flood)가 자주 발생했던 고대 근동 사람들은 이러한 물이 얼마나 무서운지 익히 알고 있었다(Keel). 이미지는 모든 것을 휩쓸어 가는 홍수다(cf. Arnold & Beyer). 홍수는 지나가는 길에 있는 모든 것을 쓸어 가는 파괴의 상징이다(시 18:16; 42:7; 69:1-2). 맹렬한 불을 피한 사람들(3절)을 홍수가 휩쓸어 가는 모습이다. 그러므로 기자는 생존자가 거의 없는 혹독한 재앙을 묘사하고 있다.

여호와께서 그들의 편에 서서 원수들과 싸워 주지 않으셨다면 그들은 이렇게 되었을 것이다. 공동체는 이 같은 가상 시나리오를 생각하며 하나님의 구원이 얼마나 놀라운 일인가를 묵상하며 감사한다. 그들은 자신들의 감사함을 표현하기 위해 이 노래를 순례자의 노래로 삼았을 것이다.

2. 여호와의 구원 찬양(124:6-7)

6 우리를 내주어 그들의 이에 씹히지 아니하게 하신
여호와를 찬송할지로다
7 우리의 영혼이 사냥꾼의 올무에서 벗어난 새 같이 되었나니
올무가 끊어지므로 우리가 벗어났도다

앞 섹션(1-5절)에서 하나님이 걷잡을 수 없는 불과 무시무시한 홍수에 비교되는 원수들의 공격에서 구원하신 일을 회상한 기자가 이 섹션에서는 한 걸음 더 나아가 그들을 구원하신 여호와께 영광을 돌리며 찬양한다. 이번에도 그는 두 개의 비유를 사용하여 주님께 감사한다.

첫째, 하나님은 그들이 원수들의 먹잇감이 되지 않도록 하셨다(6절). 기자가 사용하는 이미지는 닥치는 대로 이빨로 씹어 대는 들짐승들의 모습이다(VanGemeren). 만일 여호와께서 그들의 일에 개입하지 않으시고 지켜만 보셨다면, 그들은 분명 원수들의 이빨에 질근질근 씹혔을 것이라는 고백이다. 원수들에게 패하는 것도 고통스러운 일인데, 오로지 그들의 먹잇감으로 전락했다면 더 괴로웠을 것이다.

둘째, 하나님은 그들이 갇혀 있던 올무를 찢고 구원하셨다(7절, cf.

시 119:110). 고대 근동에서는 새들을 잡기 위해 그물을 덫으로 사용했다. 새가 그물에 걸리면 탈출할 가능성이 없다. 움직일수록 그물이 몸을 더 조여 오기 때문이다. 그러므로 올무에 걸린 새는 죽음을 상징한다(Tucker & Grant). 이러한 위기감은 주전 701년에 앗시리아 왕 산헤립이 히스기야를 예루살렘 성에 가둔 일을 생각나게 한다(Brueggemann & Bellinger, cf. 왕하 18장). 기자는 자신들은 마치 올무에 걸린 새처럼 탈출할(살아날) 소망이 없었는데, 하나님이 그들을 붙잡고 있던 그물을 찢으시고 그들을 탈출시키셨다고 한다. '우리가 벗어났도다'는 '우리가 자유인이 되었다'(we are free!)라는 의미를 지녔다(Kraus). 죽을 수밖에 없는 생명을 구원하셨다는 것이다. 그러므로 그들을 구원하신 여호와께서 그들의 찬송을 받는 것은 당연하다.

3. 여호와 신뢰 선언(124:8)

8 우리의 도움은 천지를 지으신
여호와의 이름에 있도다

하나님의 도우심으로 큰 위기를 모면한 공동체는 그들을 구원하신 하나님을 앞으로도 영원히 신뢰하고 의지할 것을 다짐한다. 여호와 하나님은 천지를 지으신 창조주이며, 자신의 이름(명예)을 생각해서라도 주님과 특별한 관계를 맺은 사람들을 반드시 구원하실 것이기 때문이다. 과거에 경험한 은혜가 앞으로도 더욱더 은혜를 소망하며 살겠다는 의지로 이어지고 있다.

제125편

성전에 올라가는 노래

I. 장르/양식: 순례시

'성전에 올라가는 노래' 모음집(120-134편) 중 여섯 번째 노래인 이 시편은 공동체 탄식시로 구분되기도 하고(Allen, Dahood, Reynolds), 공동체 확신시(Brueggemann & Bellinger, Broyles, Gerstenberger, Goldingay, Kraus, McCann, Ross, Tucker & Grant, VanGemeren)로 구분되기도 한다. 이러한 혼란은 확신시와 탄식시가 상당히 비슷하기 때문에 빚어지는 현상이다(cf. Gerstenberger, VanGemeren).

시온시(psalm of Zion)로도 구분되는 이 시편은(Grogan) 분명 주의 백성이 당면하고 있는 위기에 대해 탄식한다. 그러나 언어가 구체적이지 않아서 어느 시대에 처음 저작되어 불린 것인지가 명확하지 않다. 일부 학자들은 포로기 이전을 지목하고(Ross), 심지어는 주전 7세기 말이나 6세기 초 바빌론의 유다에 대한 억압이 최고조에 달할 때 저작된 것이라고 하기도 한다(Terrien).

그러나 내용이 열방에게 다스림을 받은 포로기 이후 시대의 정황과 잘 어울린다는 것이 대부분 학자들의 결론이다(Allen, Anderson, McCann, Reynolds). 언제 저작된 것인지 알 수는 없지만, 바빌론이 이스라엘을 없애 버리려고 했으나 하나님의 신실하심이 그들을 보존하고 지켰다는 사실을 기념하기 위해 사용되었을 가능성이 크다. 이 노래는 지혜시적인 성향도 지녔다(Crow).

II. 구조

대체적으로 학자들은 이 시편을 1-2절, 3절, 4-5절 세 파트로 구분한다(deClaissé-Walford et al., Goldingay, McCann, Ross, Tucker & Grant). 이 주석에서는 다음과 같은 분석을 바탕으로 본문을 주해하고자 한다.

A. 신뢰 선언(125:1-2)
B. 악인들 심판 확신(125:3)
C. 선대를 구함(125:4-5)

III. 주해

이 시편은 상황이 아무리 어려워도 주의 백성은 분명 여호와의 보호 아래 있음을 강조한다. 그들은 마치 하나님이 거하시는 시온 산이 어떠한 상황에서도 요동치 않는 것처럼 주님의 보호 아래 영원히 있을 것이다.

1. 신뢰 선언(125:1-2)

1 여호와를 의지하는 자는
시온 산이 흔들리지 아니하고 영원히 있음 같도다
2 산들이 예루살렘을 두름과 같이
여호와께서 그의 백성을 지금부터 영원까지 두르시리로다

기자는 여호와를 의지하는 사람들은 절대 흔들리지 않을 것이라고 한다(1절). '의지하다'(בטח)가 이 모음집에서 처음으로 사용되고 있다. 전적으로 신뢰한다는 뜻이다. 하나님의 성전이 있는 시온 산이 절대 없어지지 않고 그곳에 영원히 있는 것처럼 여호와를 의지하는 사람들도 절대 사라지지 않을 것이다. 시온의 완벽함과 영원함을 노래하는 '시온의 노래들'(Songs of Zion, cf. 46, 48, 76, 84, 87, 122편)을 생각하면 이 말씀의 의미가 새롭게 느껴진다. 이 노래들에서 시온은 단순한 언덕이 아니다. 하나님의 도움(시 121:1-2; 124:8)과 축복과 보호(시 76:6-9; 132:13-16)를 상징한다. 그러므로 시온 산이 무너지면, 하나님의 모든 축복과 약속이 무너진다(Weiser).

시온 산은 절대 사라지지 않고 영원하다(시 16:8; 46:5; 93:1; 112:6-7). 여호와께서 그곳에 머무시며 보호하시기 때문이다. 시온이 하나님께 영원한 것처럼 주님을 신뢰하는 사람들도 하나님께 영원하다(Goldingay). 그들은 고난과 역경이 와도 이기고 견딜 수 있다. 폭풍우가 몰아칠 때는 세상에 남아 있을 것이 하나도 없을 것 같지만, 지나고 나면 시온 산이 제자리에 있는 것처럼 주님의 보호가 그들을 꼭 지켜 줄 것이다.

온갖 환란에도 주님의 성도들이 건재한 또 한 가지 이유는 산들이 예루살렘을 에워싸고 보호하는 것처럼 여호와께서 자기 백성을 영원히 보호하시기 때문이다(2절). 예루살렘은 더 높은 산들로 겹겹이 쌓인 언덕이다(Tucker & Grant). 이 말씀은 더 높은 산들이 예루살렘을 병풍처럼 둘러싸고 침략자들에게서 보호하는 것처럼, 하나님의 보호막이 그의 백성들을 두르고 있다는 뜻이다. 그러므로 주의 백성은 해를 두려워할 필요가 없다.

2. 악인들 심판 확신(125:3)

> [3] 악인의 규가 의인들의 땅에서는
> 그 권세를 누리지 못하리니
> 이는 의인들로 하여금
> 죄악에 손을 대지 아니하게 함이로다

하나님은 의인들을 보호하시는 분이다. 그러므로 하나님은 악인들의 규가 의인들이 사는 땅에서는 권세를 누리지 못하도록 하신다. '규'(שֵׁבֶט)는 통치의 상징이다. 일부 주석가들은 '악인들'을 이스라엘을 괴롭히는 이방인들과 그들의 수종들로 제한하지만(Allen, VanGemeren), 이스라엘 사람들 중 악한 사람들을 포함하는 것으로 보는 것도 괜찮다(Hossfeld-Zenger). 하나님의 통치는 공의와 정의 위에 세워져 있기 때문이다. 악인들은 주의 백성을 억압하고 심지어 일부를 타국으로 끌고 가기도 하지만(cf. 시 124:2-5), 그들의 억압이 영원하지는 않다. 주의 백성이 하나님을 의지하고 신뢰하는 한 언제든 악인들의 통치는 끝이 날 것이라는 소망이 있다. 그러므로 이 말씀은 하나님의 보호하심을 부정적인 언어('악인들은 권세를 누리지 못한다')를 통해 확신하고 있다(Goldingay).

악인들이 의인들을 오랫동안 다스리게 되면 부작용이 생긴다. 악인들의 지배를 받는 의인들이 악인들처럼 되고자 하는 유혹을 받을 수 있다(Goulder, cf. 느 5장). 공의와 정의로 심판하시는 하나님이 악인들의 행위로 가려져 있기 때문이다. 그러므로 의인들이 악인들로 전락하는 일을 막기 위해서라도 하나님은 악인들이 의인들을 지배하는 일이 지속되지 않도록 하신다. 한 학자는 이 말씀이 이 노래의 핵심 메시지라고 한다(Reynolds).

3. 선대를 구함(125:4-5)

4 여호와여
선한 자들과 마음이 정직한 자들에게 선대하소서
5 자기의 굽은 길로 치우치는 자들은
여호와께서 죄를 범하는 자들과 함께 다니게 하시리로다
이스라엘에게는 평강이 있을지어다

하나님에 대한 신뢰와 확신으로 시작된 노래가 의인들을 선대해 달라는 기도로 마무리되고 있다(4절). '선대하다'(יטב)는 '좋은/선한 일을 하다'는 의미를 지녔으며 흔히 언약에서 약속하신 것을 근거로 하나님이 베풀어 주시는 은혜이다(Harman). 기자는 여호와께서 마음이 착하고 정직한 사람들, 곧 여호와를 경외하여 곧은 길(straight path)을 가기를 사랑하는 주의 자녀들을 언약적 관계를 근거로 축복해달라고 기도하고 있다.

반면에 굽은 길로 치우치는 자들은 죄인들과 동일하게 취급하시기를 기도한다(5절). 굽은 길로 치우친다는 것은 곧게 펼쳐져 있는 주요 도로를 가지 않고 굽은 샛길을 간다는 의미이다(VanGemeren, cf. 삿 5:6). 이는 악인들은 분명히 벌을 받도록 해 달라는 기도이다. 의인이 복을 받고 악인들이 벌을 받는 것은 세상을 다스리시는 이가 누구인가와 연관된 이슈다(McCann). 하나님은 자신이 세상을 다스리신다는 사실을 확인하기 위해서라도 악인들을 벌하시고 선한 사람들을 선처하실 것이다.

마지막으로 기자는 "이스라엘에게는 평강이 있을 지어다"라는 축도로 노래를 마무리하고 있다. '이스라엘에게 임하는 평강'이 이 노래의 중심 주제이다(Crow, Kraus). 하나님이 이 공동체를 좋게 대하시면 그들에게 '평강'(שָׁלוֹם)이 임할 것이다(5c절). 주의 백성은 하나님이 그들을 선하게 대하실 때 비로소 평강을 누리게 된다.

제126편
성전에 올라가는 노래

I. 장르/양식: 순례시

이 시편을 공동체 감사시로 분류하는 이들도 있지만(Gerstenberger), 대부분 학자들은 공동체 탄식시로 구분한다(Allen, Grogan, Tucker & Grant, VanGemeren). 이러한 혼란은 감사시와 탄식시가 그다지 다르지 않다는 것에서 비롯된다(cf. VanGemeren).

이 시편은 이스라엘의 왕정 시대에 저작된 것이라고 하기도 하지만(Dahood), 1-3절이 포로 생활에서 조국으로 돌아가는 일을 언급하고 있는 것으로 보아 포로기 이후 시대에 저작된 것이 확실하다(Goldingay, Ross). 더 구체적으로 제1차 귀향민들이 바빌론에서 예루살렘으로 돌아온 때인 주전 538년쯤에 저작된 것이라고 하는 이들도 있다(Clifford, Kraus, McCann, VanGemeren).

귀향민들은 유토피아를 꿈꾸며 예루살렘으로 돌아왔지만, 얼마 지나지 않아 그들은 혹독한 현실에 좌절했다(cf. 에스라—느헤미야). 이 시편이 절망적인 분위기를 전혀 반영하고 있지 않은 것으로 보아 이 같은 현실이 그들을 괴롭히기 전에 저작되었을 것이다(Broyles, Harman).

귀향민들은 맨 처음 이 노래를 신년 예배 혹은 장막절에 사용했을 것이다(Goldingay, Mowinckel). 세월이 지나면서 '성전으로 올라가는 노래' 모음집에 속하게 되었다.

II. 구조

밴게메렌(VanGemeren)은 이 시편을 다음과 같이 다섯 섹션으로 나눈다. 고작 여섯 절로 구성된 노래를 다섯 파트로 나누는 것이 그다지 설득력이 있어 보이지는 않는다. 게다가 특별한 상황이 아니면 같은 절을 각기 다른 섹션으로 나누는 일은 바람직하지 않다.

A. 하나님의 백성의 기쁨(1-2a절)
　B. 열방을 향한 선언(2b절)
　　C. 감사(3절)
　　　D. 기도(4절)
　　　　E. 기도 응답 확신(5-6절)

일부 학자들은 이 시편을 1-3절, 4절, 5-6절 세 파트로 구분한다(Anderson, deClaissé-Walford et al., Kraus). 그러나 대부분 주석가들은 1-3절, 4-6절 두 단락으로 나누는 것을 선호한다(Goldingay, Hossfeld-Zenger, McCann, Ross, Tucker & Grant). 이 주석에서는 다음과 같은 분석을 바탕으로 본문을 주해해 나가고자 한다.

A. 기쁨으로 가득한 귀향(126:1-3)
B. 지연되지 않는 축복 간구(126:4-6)

III. 주해

이스라엘이 바빌론으로 끌려온 지 수십 년이 지났다. 때가 되면 하나님이 다시 그들을 약속의 땅으로 불러들이실 것이라는 선지자들의 예언이 점점 잊혀가고 있다. 이러한 상황에서 하나님은 놀라운 일을 하셨다. 그들을 예루살렘으로 돌려보내신 것이다. 이 시편은 기대에 찬 귀향과 성공적인 정착을 노래하고 있다.

1. 기쁨으로 가득한 귀향(126:1-3)

[1] 여호와께서 시온의 포로를 돌려 보내실 때에
우리는 꿈꾸는 것 같았도다
[2] 그 때에 우리 입에는 웃음이 가득하고
우리 혀에는 찬양이 찼었도다
그 때에 뭇 나라 가운데에서 말하기를
여호와께서 그들을 위하여 큰 일을 행하셨다 하였도다
[3] 여호와께서 우리를 위하여 큰 일을 행하셨으니
우리는 기쁘도다

도저히 믿기지 않는 일이 현실로 드러났다. 바빌론으로 끌려간 유다 사람들이 시온으로 돌아오게 된 것이다(1절). 기자는 귀향을 과거 일로 회상하고 있다(Goldingay). 그러므로 분위기는 마치 어린아이가 흥분된 어조로 하나님이 이루신 놀라운 일을 되뇌는 것 같다(Davidson).

사실은 이미 선지자들이 오래전에 예언한 대로 실현된 것뿐이다(사 14:1-2; 44:24-45:25; 48:20-21; 렘 29:14; 30:3; 33:7, 10-11; 암 9:14). 그러나 백성들이 선지자들의 메시지를 알고 있다고 해서 기쁨이 덜하는 것은 아니다. 그들은 참으로 열광하고 있다.

고레스 통도장(Cyrus Cylinder)에 기록된 바에 의하면 역사는 이 일이 페르시아 왕 고레스가 별 어려움 없이 바빌론을 정복한 일을 기념하기 위해 바빌론 사람들이 바빌론으로 잡아온 민족들을 각자 조국으로 돌려보낸 것이라고 한다(cf. 대하 36:22-23; 스 1:1-4). 그러나 기자는 여호와께서 하신 일이라고 한다(1a절). 이 역사적 사건에 신학적인 해석을 더하고 있는 것이다. 이사야는 하나님이 고레스를 자기 종(도구)으로 사용하여 이루신 일이라고 한다(사 45장).

주의 백성은 너무나도 기뻐서 꿈을 꾸는 듯한 느낌이다(1b절). 그들의 입에는 웃음이 가득하고(2a절), 놀라운 일을 하신 여호와에 대한 찬양이 그들의 입에서 끊이지 않는다(2b절). 그들은 온 세상이 여호와께서 그들을 위해 하신 일을 알기를 원한다. 그러므로 그들은 뭇 나라들 가운데서 여호와께서 큰 일을 행하셨다고 증언하며, 열방도 여호와께서 자기 백성을 위해 큰 일을 하셨다는 사실을 인정한다(2c-d절). 예전에 "너희의 신은 어디있느냐?"고 조롱했던 것과 사뭇 다르다(cf. 시 42:3; 79:10; 115:2). 하나님이 그들을 위해 큰 일을 행하셨으므로 그들은 참 기쁘다(3절).

이 섹션의 분위기는 흥분과 기쁨이다(cf. deClaissé-Walford et al.). 당연한 일이다. 전혀 상상할 수 없었던 일, 이때까지 그 누구도 들어보지 못했던 일, 곧 나라를 잃은 지 수십 년 만에 다시 찾았으니 참으로 기쁜 일이 아니겠는가! 여호와께서 이 일을 이루셨다. 그러므로 주님은 찬양을 받기에 합당하신 분이다.

2. 지연되지 않는 축복 간구(126:4-6)

4 여호와여
우리의 포로를 남방 시내들 같이 돌려 보내소서
5 눈물을 흘리며 씨를 뿌리는 자는
기쁨으로 거두리로다
6 울며 씨를 뿌리러 나가는 자는
반드시 기쁨으로 그 곡식 단을 가지고 돌아오리로다

앞 섹션이 온 세상을 배경으로 하고 있다면, 이 섹션은 공동체에 속한 사람들의 일상을 배경으로 하고 있다(Hossfeld–Zenger). 4절을 번역하기가 쉽지 않다 보니 우리말 번역본들은 제각각 다르게 번역한다. 새번역은 "네겝 시내들에 다시 물이 흐르듯이 포로로 잡혀간 자들을 돌려보내 주십시오"로, 아가페 성경은 "네게브 사막을 흐르는 시내처럼 자유롭게 해 주소서"로, 현대인 성경은 "단비 내려 메마른 강바닥에 다시 물 흐르듯 우리 땅 우리에게 다시 주소서"로 번역했다. 공동은 전혀 다른 번역을 제시한다: "저 네겝 강바닥에 물길 돌아 오듯이 우리의 포로들을 다시 데려 오소서."

개역개정이 '돌려 보내다'로 번역한 히브리어 단어(שׁוב)는 '회복하다'로 해석될 수 있다. 그래서 거의 모든 영어 번역본들은 "우리의 (어려운) 형편을 회복하소서"(restore our fortunes, cf. 시 14:7)로 번역한다(NIV, NRS, RSV, ESV, TNK, CSB). 그렇다면 네겝(남방) 시내들처럼 그들의 형편이 회복된다는 것은 무엇을 뜻하는가?

가나안 남쪽 지역은 1년 내내 거의 비가 내리지 않는다. 그러므로 이곳에 있는 시내들은 항상 말라 있다. 그러나 겨울에 비가 내리면 순식간에 갑자기 불어난 물로 범람한다. 그러므로 이곳에서 '바짝 메마른' 그들의 형편을 남방 시내들처럼 회복시켜 달라는 기도는 그들의 어려운 형편이 순식간에 나아질 수 있도록 복을 내려 달라는 간구이다(McCann, Tucker & Grant, VanGemeren, Weiser). 그들은 오랜 시간에 거쳐 임하는 '잔잔한 물 같은 축복'이 아니라 당장, 화끈하게 임하는 축복이 필요하다는 것이다. 귀향민들이 예루살렘에 도착했을 때 그들을 기다리고 있던 혹독한 현실을 감안하면(cf. 시 85편, 학개서, 에스라—느헤미야) 이 기도는 참으로 적절한 기도였다.

하나님이 곧바로 복을 주시면 그들은 이 순간 눈물을 흘리며 씨를 뿌리고 있지만, 곧 기쁨으로 거둘 것을 확신한다(5절). 이 표현이 비가 처음 내릴 때는 '눈물'처럼 찔끔 내리지만, 곧 장대비로 변하는 상황을 묘사하는 것으로 풀이하는 이가 있다(Shaefer). 그러나 농부가 눈물로 씨를 뿌린다는 것은 어떤 수확이 나올지 알 수 없는 상황에서 만일 작황이 좋지 않으면 경제적인 손실을 감수해야 하는 부담을 안고 씨앗을 뿌리는 상황을 묘사한다(VanGemeren, cf. Brueggemann & Bellinger, Gerstenberger, Mays).

그들은 예루살렘으로 돌아오기 위해 참으로 많은 것을 포기했다. 또한 바빌론에서 예루살렘까지의 1,500킬로미터의 여정도 참으로 어려운 길이었다. 이런 것들은 모두 그들이 주님의 나라를 재건하기 위해 '눈물로 씨를 뿌린 일'이라 할 수 있다(cf. Delitzsch). 하나님은 그들이 눈물을 흘리며 뿌린 씨가 많은 열매를 맺어 그들에게 곡식 단이 되어 돌아오게 하실 것이다(6절). 이 시편은 하나님에 대한 기대와 밝은 미래에 대한 확신으로 가득 차 있다.

제127편

솔로몬의 시 곧 성전에 올라가는 노래

I. 장르/양식: 순례시

이 시편은 '성전에 올라가는 노래' 모음집(120–134편) 중 한 중앙에 위치한 여덟 번째 순례자의 노래이다. 또한 모음집에 등장하는 첫 번째 지혜시다(Allen, deClaissé–Walford et al., Grogan, Tucker & Grant, VanGemeren, cf. 128, 133편). 모든 학자들이 이 시편을 지혜시로 구분하는 것은 1절과 4절과 5절을 격언으로 간주하기 때문이다(Kraus, cf. Tucker & Grant). 여기에 2절을 더하는 이들도 있다(Hossfeld–Zenger, cf. 잠 5–7장).

이 시편이 지혜시이고, 이 노래가 성전으로 순례길을 떠나는 사람들이 부른 노래이다 보니 이스라엘 역사에서 지혜와 성전과 가장 깊은 관계가 있었던 솔로몬이 표제에 언급이 되는 것은 당연한 일이다(cf. Tucker & Grant). 이 노래가 솔로몬과 연관된 시라는 표제를 액면 그대로 수용하는 사람들은 이 시편이 처음 사용된 것은 솔로몬이 성전을 헌당할 때라고 한다(Perowne, Ross, cf. Eaton, Miller).

모빙클(Mowinckel)은 "주님께서 집을 세우지 아니하시면"(1절)을 솔로몬의 성전 헌당 사건의 미드라쉬(midrash)로 간주하여 이 시편은 왕정시대에 저작된 것이라 한다. 더 구체적으로 히스기야 시대를 저작 시기로 지목하는 이도 있다(Terrien).

늦은 저작 시기를 제시하는 사람들은 성전이 재건될 필요가 있었던 포로기 이후 시대를 지목한다(Kirkpatrick). 재건된 성전에서 장막절 때 사용된 노래라는 견해도 있다(Anderson). 오늘날 유태인들은 아이가 태어난 다음에 감사 예배에서 이 노래를 사용한다(VanGemeren).

II. 구조

학자들은 모두 이 시편을 1-2절과 3-5절로 구분하는 것에 동의한다. 그러나 주제가 서로 상이하게 다르다 하여 일부 학자들은 원래 두 개의 독립적으로 존재했던 노래들(1-2절과 3-5절)이 하나로 묶인 것이라고 한다(Keet). 그러나 대부분 주석가들은 통일성을 강조하며 원래부터 1-5절이 한 편의 시였음을 주장한다(Anderson, Goldingay, Miller, Schaefer). 이 주석에서는 다음과 같이 두 섹션으로 구분하여 본문을 주해해 나가고자 한다.

A. 여호와를 모르는 허무한 삶(127:1-2)

B. 여호와를 아는 복된 삶(127:3-5)

III. 주해

이 시편은 사람들의 일상을 통해 여호와를 모르고 살아가는 사람들의 허무한 삶과 여호와에 대한 믿음으로 살아가는 사람들의 복된 삶을 대조한다. 이 노래는 집을 세우시고, 성을 지키시고, 사람의 노력과 수고를 축복하시고, 각 가정에 자녀들을 주시는 것 등 우리가 일상에서 접하는 하나님의 숨겨진 사역을 노래한다.

1. 여호와를 모르는 허무한 삶(127:1-2)

[1] 여호와께서 집을 세우지 아니하시면
세우는 자의 수고가 헛되며
여호와께서 성을 지키지 아니하시면
파수꾼의 깨어 있음이 헛되도다
[2] 너희가 일찍이 일어나고 늦게 누우며
수고의 떡을 먹음이 헛되도다
그러므로 여호와께서 그의 사랑하시는 자에게는
잠을 주시는도다

이 지혜시는 두 개의 조건 문구(אִם, if/unless…)로 시작한다. 첫 번째 문장은 여호와께서 집을 세우지 아니하시면 세우는 자들의 수고가 헛되다고 한다(1a-b절). '집'(בַּיִת)이 예루살렘 성전으로 해석되기도 하지만(deClaissé-Walford et al.), 본문에서 집은 사회의 가장 기본적인 단위인 가정을 상징한다(Grogan, Hossfeld-Zenger, Ross, VanGemeren). 하나님을 의지하여 믿음으로 가정을 세워 나가지 않으면 세우려는 자들(가족의 구성원들)의 수고가 모두 헛되다. '헛되다'(שָׁוְא)는 '속임수, 사기극'이라는 뜻이다(HALOT). 하나님을 의지하지 않고 인간적인 노력으로만 세우는 가정은 '헛수고/소용없는 일'(cf. 현대인)이기에 무언가 선한 것을 기대하며 가정을 세우고자 하는 자들은 스스로를 속이는 일이다(cf. Tucker & Grant). 그들이 얻고자 하는 결과(행복과 평안)가 결코 허락되지 않을 것이기 때문이다. 하나님이 축복하시고 그들과 함께 집을 세워 주셔야 그들이 가정을 통해 얻고자 하는 모든 것들을 얻을 것이다. 하나님 안에서 세워지는 가정만이 구성원들이 추구하는 기쁨과 건강과 행복을 누릴 수 있다. 우리의 가정은 주님 안에서 잘 세워져 가고 있는가 되돌아보자.

두 번째 문장은 여호와께서 성을 지키지 아니하시면 파수꾼의 깨어 있음이 헛되다고 하는데(1c-d절), 성은 여러 가정들이 모여 이루는 공동체와 사회를 상징한다(Hossfeld-Zenger, VanGemeren). 하나님이 세우지 아니하셨기에 무의미한 가정들이 모여 공동체를 이룬다면, 그 공동체도 무의미하기는 마찬가지이다. 그러므로 이 말씀은 하나님이 세우신 가정이 주님의 축복 안에 있는 것처럼, 공동체/사회도 하나님이 지켜 주셔야 여러 가지 축복으로 인해 건강한 공동체가 될 수 있다. 하나님이 지켜 주지 않으시면, 성을 지키려는 모든 사람의 노력이 다 헛되다. 심지어는 파수꾼들이 불철주야로 성을 지키려고 깨어 있어도 지키지 못한다. 건강한 공동체가 유지되려면 하나님의 보호와 축복이 반드시 있어야 한다. 우리가 속한 공동체가 무엇을 바탕으로 세워지는 것을 바라는가를 생각하게 하는 말씀이다.

기자는 2절에서 하나님을 의지하며 사는 사람이 누리는 축복과 그렇게 하지 않는 사람의 허무한 수고를 대조한다. 하나님이 세우지 않으신 집에서 살고, 하나님이 지키지 않으시는 성에서 사는 사람의 모든 수고는 헛되다(2a-b절). 아무리 일찍 일어나 늦은 시간에 잠자리에 들기까지 하루 종일 열심히 일하고 수고해도 헛되다. 그들의 모든 노력이 의미 있는 결실을 맺지 못하고 낭비될 뿐이다.

반면에 하나님의 축복 안에 거하는 사람의 수고와 노력은 어떠한가? 매우 의미 있고 효과적인 수고와 노력이다. 하나님이 주님을 사랑하는 자들을 축복하시고 함께하시기 때문에 그들도 아침 일찍 일어나 밤늦게까지 열심히 일하지만, 헛수고가 아니다(2c-d절). 그들의 노력은 분명 의미 있는 노동이 되어 가정과 사회를 통해 세우고 이루고자 하는 일들을 모두 성취할 것이다(Goldingay). 그러므로 기자는 하나님이 주님을 사랑하는 자들에게 잠을 주신다고 한다. 편안한 마음으로 쉬고 잠을 자면서도 헛되이 수고하는 자들보다 훨씬 더 복된 삶을 살 것이다. 여호와께서 그들의 수고와 노동에서 '무의미'를 지워 주실 것이기 때문이다(Tucker & Grant).

2. 여호와를 아는 복된 삶(127:3-5)

3 보라 자식들은 여호와의 기업이요
태의 열매는 그의 상급이로다
4 젊은 자의 자식은
장사의 수중의 화살 같으니
5 이것이 그의 화살통에 가득한 자는 복되도다
그들이 성문에서 그들의 원수와 담판할 때에
수치를 당하지 아니하리로다

앞 섹션에서 집과 성을 언급한 기자가 가정과 성문에 대한 이야기를 이어 간다.

첫째, 하나님이 세우시는 집에 태어나는 자식들은 여호와의 기업이며, 주님이 주시는 상급이다(3절). '기업'(נַחֲלָה)은 땅 등 자식이 부모에게 유산으로 받은 것을 뜻한다(Kraus, cf. 수 14:9, 13; 15:20; 16:5). '상급'(שָׂכָר)은 일상적으로 노동에 대한 대가를 뜻한다. 그러나 이곳에서는 선물을 의미한다(Tucker & Grant, cf. NIDOTTE). 자식들은 하나님이 부모들에게 내려 주시는 가장 큰 유산이자 선물이다. 그러나 이 말씀은 주님을 믿는 사람들에게나 의미 있는 것이지, 주님을 의지하지 않거나 믿지 않는 자들에게는 별 의미가 없다. 그들은 여호와께서 그들에게 자식들을 기업으로 주셨다는 사실을 믿지 않을 것이기 때문이다.

둘째, 하나님이 세우시는 가정들의 자식은 든든한 무기와 같다(4절). 기자가 사용하는 이미지는 '노련한 군인'(גִּבּוֹר)이 지닌 화살이다. 자식들은 부모에게 파괴력을 지닌 무기와 같다는 뜻이다. 중요한 것은 이 문장의 정황이 부모들의 '화살 통'을 '예리한 화살들'(자녀들)로 채우는 이는 부모가 아니라, 하나님이시라는 사실이다(Allen). 원수들과 싸워야 할 때 자식들은 부모들이 믿고 사용할 만한 무기가 되어 줄 것이다.

셋째, 하나님이 세우시는 집의 자식들은 부모의 든든한 지원자들이 될 것이다(5절). 자식들은 부모를 지켜 줄 무기와 같으니, 자식이 많은 사람들은 복되다. 살다 보면 원수들과 다툴 때가 생기는데, 이럴 때면 자식들이 부모의 가장 든든한 지원군이 되어 그들의 옆을 지키며 부모들이 수치를 당하지 않도록 보호해 줄 것이다. 성문은 소송과 재판이 이루어지는 곳이다(신 17:5; 21:19; 22:15; 암 5:12; 시 69:12). 그러므로 이 말씀은 부모가 누군가와 법적인 다툼을 벌일 때, 자식들은 그들이 의지할 만한 아군이 되어줄 것이며 부모들이 공평한 판결을 받게 할 것이라는 의미이다(Tucker & Grant, cf. VanGemeren). 부모와 자식이 함께 이루는 가정이 어떠해야 하는가를 생각하게 하는 말씀이다.

제128편

성전에 올라가는 노래

I. 장르/양식: 순례시

이 시편은 '복이 있도다'(אַשְׁרֵי)로 시작하는 지혜시다(Brueggemann & Bellinger, Goldingay, Tucker & Grant, VanGemeren). 옛 이스라엘에서 공동체가 함께 드린 예배나 예식에서 사용된 노래로 생각된다(Goldingay, Weiser). 내용에 있어서는 제사장의 축도(민 6:24-26)를 바탕으로 한 노래다(VanGemeren).

이 시편은 127편과 쌍을 이루고 있다(Grogan). 일부 학자들은 포로기 이후에 저작된 것이라 하지만, 이렇다 할 증거는 없는 추측일 뿐이다(cf. Ross).

II. 구조

이 노래를 각각 '복이 있도다'(אַשְׁרֵי)로 시작하는 1-3절과 4-6절로 구분하기도 하지만(Allen), 대부분 주석가들은 지혜를 가르치는 1-4절과 축복을 선언하는 5-6절로 구분한다(Davidson, deClaissé-Walford et al., Hossfeld-Zenger, Kraus, Mays, Terrien, Tucker & Grant, VanGemeren). 이 주석

에서는 다음과 같은 분석을 바탕으로 본문을 주해해 나가고자 한다.

A. 지혜로운 가르침(128:1-4)

B. 지혜로운 축복(128:5-6)

III. 주해

지혜시는 보통 악인과 의인의 삶을 대조하는데, 이 노래는 오로지 여호와를 경외하는 사람의 복된 삶과 그가 누릴 축복만을 노래한다. 악인과 그의 삶은 이 노래의 배경도 되지 못한다. 하나님은 오로지 의인에게만 온갖 복과 은혜를 내리신다.

1. 지혜로운 가르침(128:1-4)

1 여호와를 경외하며
그의 길을 걷는 자마다 복이 있도다
2 네가 네 손이 수고한 대로 먹을 것이라
네가 복되고 형통하리로다
3 네 집 안방에 있는 네 아내는
결실한 포도나무 같으며
네 식탁에 둘러 앉은 자식들은
어린 감람나무 같으리로다
4 여호와를 경외하는 자는
이같이 복을 얻으리로다

이 섹션은 복이 있는 사람에 대한 이야기로 시작하여(1절), 그는 꼭 복을 얻으리라는 말로 끝이 난다(4절). 가운데 부분(2-3절)은 그가 누릴 복이 어떤 것인지를 설명한다. a-b-a′ 구조를 지닌 것이다. 또한 127

편이 사용하는 주요 단어들이 이 섹션에서도 사용된다(deClaissé-Walford et al.): '복 있는'(אַשְׁרֵי), '집'(בַּיִת), '자녀들'(בָּנִים), '보라!'(הִנֵּה, 4절을 시작하는 단어이지만, 개역개정에서는 번역이 되지 않음, cf. 공동, 현대인).

어떤 사람이 복이 있는 사람인가? 기자는 '복 있는 사람'(אַשְׁרֵי)(시 1:1-2; 112:1)이 지닌 성향을 두 가지로 정의한다(1절). 첫째, 여호와를 경외하는 사람이다. 하나님에 대한 경건한 두려움을 가지고 자신의 삶을 온전히 주께 의지하며 사는 사람을 두고 하는 말씀이다(시 2:11; 25:14; 31:19; 33:18; 34:9). 둘째, 주님의 길을 걷는 사람이다(cf. 시 25:9-10). 주님의 길을 걷는 것은 하나님을 경외하는 삶을 산다는 의미를 지녔기 때문에 이 둘은 평행을 이룬다(McCann). 하나님을 경외하면 하나님이 싫어하시는 일(죄)을 기피하고, 하나님이 좋아하시는 일(선행)을 하며 살려는 노력이 따른다. 또한 선을 행하려는 노력은 평생 우리가 추구해야 할 삶의 방식이다. 그러므로 성경은 하나님의 말씀에 순종하며 경건하게 사는 것을 사람이 길을 가는 일에 비유한다. 우리의 삶과 신앙은 여정이라는 뜻이다.

하나님을 경외하고 주님의 말씀에 따라 사는 복이 있는 사람이 누릴 축복은 어떤 것인가?

첫째, 그는 자신의 노동과 노력에 대한 정당한 대가를 누리며 살 것이다(2절, cf. 시 127:2). 죄가 만연한 세상에서는 사람이 노동한 만큼 대가를 얻지 못할 때가 많다. 그러므로 성경은 노동에 대한 정당한 대가를 누리지 못하는 것은 하나님의 불편한 심기의 표현이라고 한다(신 28:33; 시 78:46; 109:11). 창조주이자 통치자이신 하나님이 주님을 경외하고 하나님의 방식대로 살려고 노력하는 사람들에게 복을 주시면 그들이 자신들의 수고에 대한 정당한 대가를 누리게 된다. 그러므로 그의 삶은 복되고 형통할 것이다. '형통하다'(טוֹב לָךְ)는 좋은 일들이 많이 있을 것이라는 뜻이다.

둘째, 행복하고 번성하는 가정이다(3절). 기자는 복 있는 사람의 아내를 포도나무로, 자식들을 감람나무로 비유하는데, 포도나무와 감람나무는 번성과 번영의 상징이다(Keel, cf. 왕상 4:25). '집안에 있는 아내'는 하나님의 가장 큰 축복이며 음녀(잠 7:11-12)와 강력한 대조를 이룬다(Davidson). 성경에서 자식이 없는 것은 하나님의 무관심의 표현이다(창 30:1-2; 삼상 1:5). 반면에 번성한 집안은 하나님의 축복이다(cf. 시 115:13). 아내와 자식들이 있어야 가정이 형성될 수 있는 것처럼, 고대 근동에서는 포도나무와 감람나무가 있어야 생명을 유지할 수 있었다(Goldingay, Weiser).

또한 포도나무와 감람나무는 메시아 시대와 연관된 축복이기도 하다(미 4:4; 슥 3:10). 그러므로 포도나무와 감람나무 아래 있는 것은 평화와 번영의 상징이다(VanGemeren). 치열한 세상에서 아내와 자식들이 있는 가정은 참된 안식처요, 메시아가 주실 평화와 기쁨의 상징이다. 사람이 주님을 경외하고 말씀대로 살면 그가 경외하고 순종하는 하나님이 이런 기쁨을 그에게 축복으로 주신다(4절).

2. 지혜로운 축복(128:5-6)

5 여호와께서 시온에서 네게 복을 주실지어다
너는 평생에 예루살렘의 번영을 보며
6 네 자식의 자식을 볼지어다
이스라엘에게 평강이 있을지로다

기자는 앞 섹션에서 복이 있는 사람에 대해 말했다. 이 섹션에서는 그 사람에게 복을 주시는 이는 다름 아닌 여호와라는 사실을 선언한다(Goldingay). 그는 여호와를 경외하고 주님의 길을 걷는 복이 있는 사람에게 더 많은 여호와의 복을 빌어 주고 있다. 일종의 축도이다(Brueggemann & Bellinger). 그러므로 이 말씀이 제사장의 축도로 알려진 민수기 6:24–26과 연결하여 설명되기도 한다(cf. McCann).

여호와께서 시온에서 그에게 더 많은 복을 주실 것이다. 시온은 여호와의 거처이기 때문에 시온이 언급되고 있다. 이 말씀은 예루살렘과 시온으로 모여든 순례자들을 격려하기 위한 축도이며(Tucker & Grant), 이곳으로 순례 오는 명분이기도 하다(Grogan). 그들이 시온으로 순례를 온 것이 결코 헛되지 않았음을 선언한다.

하나님의 거처인 시온이 예루살렘에 있기 때문에, 예루살렘은 앞으로도 계속 번영할 것이라고 한다. 이런 면에서 이 시는 시온의 노래와 비슷한 성향을 지니고 있다. 예루살렘의 번영은 여호와의 임재와도 연관이 있다. 하나님의 임재가 예루살렘에 머물면, 그 도성은 번영할 것이다. 반면에 하나님의 임재가 그곳을 떠나면 예루살렘은 가나안의 한 평범한 도성으로 전락한다.

제129편

성전에 올라가는 노래

I. 장르/양식: 순례시

학자들은 이 시편의 장르에 대해 다양하게 제안한다. 어떤 이들은 공동체 확신시(communal confidence, cf. 115, 125편)라고 하고(VanGemeren), 확신이 중심이 되는 기도시(prayer psalm)라고 하는 이들도 있다(Kraus). 이 시편은 저주시(imprecatory psalm)(deClaissé-Walford et al.), 혹은 감사시(Brueggemann & Bellinger, Grogan, Westermann), 혹은 감사시와 탄식시가 섞인 노래로 분류되기도 한다(Tucker & Grant).

학자들이 이처럼 다양한 장르를 제안하는 것은 1-4절은 감사시가 확실한데, 5-8절은 탄식시가 확실할 뿐만 아니라, 더 나아가 저주시로 간주될 수 있기 때문이다(cf. Gerstenberger). 노래 자체가 여러 양식을 취하고 있는 것이다. 게다가 확신시와 감사시와 탄식시는 상당 부분 비슷한 내용을 담고 있는 것도 장르를 구분하는 일에 이슈로 작용한다(cf. VanGemeren).

이 시편은 포로기 이후 시대에 저작된 것이라고 하는 이들이 있다(Terrien). 예배나 예식에서 이스라엘을 미워하는 자들에게 저주를 선포하며 사용된 노래라는 주장이 있다(Weiser). 그러나 훗날 이런 용도로 사용되었을지 몰라도, 원래는 공동체가 당면한 위기에서 하나님의 구원을 바라는 노래로 저작되고 사용되었다는 견해도 있다(Van der Wal).

Ⅱ. 구조

이 시편은 두 가지의 농사와 연관된 이미지가 주류를 이룬다(Tucker & Grant). 첫 번째 섹션인 1-4절은 쟁기질 이미지를 중심으로 구성되어 있으며, 두 번째 섹션인 5-8절은 추수 이미지를 중심으로 구성되어 있다. 그러므로 이 시편을 이 두 이미지를 바탕으로 두 섹션으로 구분하는 것이 바람직하다(cf. Goldingay, McCann, Ross, Tucker & Grant). 이 주석에서는 다음과 같은 구조를 바탕으로 본문을 주해해 나가고자 한다.

A. 억압자들에 대한 회고(129:1-4)
B. 억압자들에 대한 저주(129:5-8)

Ⅲ. 주해

일상적으로 씨 뿌리는 일과 수확은 긍정적인 의미를 지녔지만(cf. 126편), 이 노래에서는 부정적인 의미로 사용된다. 기자는 하나님께 주의 백성을 괴롭히는 자들에게 벌을 내리실 것을 호소한다. 원수들에게 보복해 달라는 기도이다(cf. Allen).

1. 억압자들에 대한 회고(129:1-4)

1 이스라엘은 이제 말하기를
그들이 내가 어릴 때부터
여러 번 나를 괴롭혔도다
2 그들이 내가 어릴 때부터

여러 번 나를 괴롭혔으나
나를 이기지 못하였도다
[3] 밭 가는 자들이 내 등을 갈아
그 고랑을 길게 지었도다
[4] 여호와께서는 의로우사
악인들의 줄을 끊으셨도다

기자는 이스라엘의 지난날 회고를 어릴 때부터 이때까지 원수들에게 지속적으로 괴롭힘을 당해온 한 사람의 목소리로 묘사한다(1절, cf. 시 124:1-2, 3-5; 121:7-8; 122:8-9; 132:3-4). 그러므로 이 시편이 단수를 사용하지만, 공동체의 고백으로 이해되어야 한다(Gunke). 그는 두 차례나 원수들이 어린 시절부터 이스라엘을 괴롭혔고(1, 2절, cf. 렘 2:2; 겔 23:3; 호 2:3, 15; 11:1), 그들이 여러 번 이스라엘을 괴롭혔다는 말도 두 차례 반복하고 있다(1, 2절). 이스라엘의 '어린 시절'(נְעוּרִים)은 한 나라로 출범할 때를 뜻한다. 예레미야와 호세아는 이 단어를 회상하여 이스라엘이 이집트를 탈출하여 광야에서 머물던 때를 회상한다(렘 2:2; 호 2:17). 원수들은 이스라엘의 초창기 때부터 이때까지 괴롭혀 왔다는 뜻이다. '괴롭히다'(צרר)는 정치적 혹은 군사적 억압과 공격을 의미한다(HALOT, cf. 민 10:9; 25:17; 사 11:13). '여러 번'(רַבַּת)은 시도 때도 없이 기회가 있을 때마다 그들을 괴롭혔다는 사실을 강조한다(cf. Tucker & Grant).

다행인 것은 비록 그들이 오랜 세월 동안 수차례 이스라엘을 괴롭혔지만, 그들을 이기지는 못했다는 사실이다(2c절). 그들이 처한 상황이 어려울 때마다 하나님이 기적을 베푸셨기 때문이다(VanGemeren).

원수들은 이스라엘의 등을 밭 가는 사람이 밭을 갈아엎듯 갈아서 밭고랑을 만들었다(3절). 게다가 그들이 '밭'을 갈기 위해 사용한 짐승은 이스라엘이었다(Allen). 이스라엘 사람들과 영토를 자신들의 이익을 위해 원하는 대로 마음껏 이용했다는 뜻이다. 힘이 약한 이스라엘은 이러한 상황을 지켜볼 수밖에 없었다. 원수들로 인해 이스라엘이 힘들었던 순간들은 참으로 많았고, 때로는 그들의 지배를 받았지만, 그들이 이스라엘을 완전히 제압하여 망하게 하지는 못했다.

원수들의 혹독한 억압을 받으면서도 이스라엘이 망하지 않았던 이유는 여호와께서 개입하셨기 때문이다(4절). 주님의 '의로우심'(צַדִּיק)이 원수들이 이스라엘에게 불의를 행하는 것을 용납하지 않으셨다. 그러므로 하나님이 원수들이 이스라엘을 부리기 위해 쟁기/멍에에 묶은 줄을 끊으셨다(Grogan, Keel, cf. 렘 30:8). 원수들이 주의 백성을 미워하는 것은 곧 하나님을 미워하는 것이기 때문이다(Kraus). 하나님은 이스라엘을 원수들의 억압과 통치에서 구원하셨다.

2. 억압자들에 대한 저주(129:5-8)

5 무릇 시온을 미워하는 자들은
수치를 당하여 물러갈지어다
6 그들은 지붕의 풀과 같을지어다
그것은 자라기 전에 마르는 것이라
7 이런 것은 베는 자의 손과
묶는 자의 품에 차지 아니하나니
8 지나가는 자들도
여호와의 복이 너희에게 있을지어다 하거나
우리가 여호와의 이름으로 너희에게 축복한다
하지 아니하느니라

5-8절은 보는 시각에 따라 예언 혹은 희망사항으로 해석될 수 있다(cf. McCann). 정황을 고려하면 원수들에게 선포하는 저주가 확실하다

(Clifford, Kraus, Mays). 주의 백성을 괴롭히는 원수들이 북 왕국 사람들이라는 해석이 있지만(Weiser), 설득력이 없다. 이방인들을 두고 하는 말이다. 누구든 시온을 미워하는 자들은 수치를 당하고 물러갈 것이다(5절). '수치를 당하다'(בּושׁ)와 '물러가다'(סוג)는 둘 다 군사적/정치적 격변(upheaval)과 연관된 단어들이다(Goldingay). 원수들은 원하는 바를 이루지 못하고 퇴치될 것이다. 시온을 미워하는 것은 곧 그곳에 거하시는 하나님을 미워하는 것이므로 하나님이 이러한 상황을 묵인하지 않으실 것이기 때문이다.

시온을 미워하는 자들은 지붕의 풀과 같다(6절, cf. 왕하 19:26; 사 37:27). 가나안 지역 집들은 흙이나 돌을 사용하여 평평한 지붕을 만들었는데, 이런 곳에서 풀이 자라는 것은 매우 어렵다. 더욱이 비가 별로 오지 않는 기후이기에 더욱더 그렇다. 그나마 우기 때 잠시 싹이 튼 것은 자라기 전에 말라 죽기 일쑤다. 하나님과 그의 백성을 미워하는 자들은 이 풀처럼 자라기도 전에 말라 죽을 것이다. 설령 그것들이 자란다 해도 풀을 베고 묶는 사람들이 관여할 만큼 자라지도, 양이 많지도 않다(7절).

지나가는 사람들도 이 형편없는 풀의 양과 질을 보며 수고하는 자들에게 여호와의 축복을 선언할 수 없다(8절, cf. 룻 2:4). 고대 사람들은 풀은 짐승들의 먹이가 되기 때문에 풀을 수확하는 사람들을 축복하고는 했다. 그러나 이 풀은 얼마나 빈약한지 도저히 축복의 말이 나오질 않는다. 주의 백성을 괴롭히는 원수들을 어떠한 쓸모도 없는 쓰레기로 전락하게 해 달라는 저주이다.

제130편
성전에 올라가는 노래

I. 장르/양식: 순례시

이 시편은 일곱 개의 참회시(penitential psalm) 중 하나이다(cf. 6, 32, 38, 51, 102, 130, 143편). 이 시편들은 주후 6세기에 카시오도루스(Cassiodorus)의 시편 주석에서 처음으로 참회시로 구분되기 시작했다(Bautch). 내용을 살펴보면 이 시는 '개인 탄식시'다(Anderson, VanGemeren). 그러나 학자들은 '신뢰시'라고 하기도 하고(Denton, Ross), '기도시'라고 하기도 한다(Goldingay, cf. Brueggemann & Bellinger). 보는 각도에 따라서 어느 정도 유동적인 면모를 지닌 시편인 것이다.

이 노래가 죄와 고백과 용서에 대한 확신을 강조하고 있다해서 종교개혁자 루터는 이 시편을 '바울적인 성향이 다분한 시'(Paluline Psalm)라고 불렀다(Ross). 역대기 기자는 2절을 솔로몬의 헌당 기도를 마무리하면서 인용한다(cf. 대하 6:40).

이 시편이 왕정 시대에 저작된 것이라고 하는 이들도 있지만(Dahood), 대부분 학자들은 포로기 이후 시대를 저작 시기로 지목한다(Allen, Bautch, Brueggemann & Bellinger, deClaissé-Walford et al., VanGemeren). 하나님을 뵙기 위해 성전으로 순례를 떠나는 길에 죄를 회개하게 하는 시로 매우 적절하다 할 수 있다.

II. 구조

대부분 학자들은 이 시편을 1-2절, 3-4절, 5-6절, 7-8절 네 섹션으로 구분한다(deClaissé-Walford et al., Goldingay, Ross, Terrien, Tucker & Grant, VanGemeren). 이 주석에서는 다음과 같은 분석을 바탕으로 본문을 주해해 나가고자 한다.

A. 간구(130:1-2)
B. 신뢰(130:3-4)
C. 기대(130:5-6)
D. 권면(130:7-8)

III. 주해

구체적으로 밝히지는 않지만 기자는 자신이 지은 죄로 인해 고통을 받고 있다. 그는 또한 하나님이 그를 용서하시고 회복시킬 것을 확신한다. 기자는 이러한 상황을 세상의 가장 낮은 곳에 있는 사람이 가장 높은 곳으로 올라가는 이미지를 사용하여 설명한다(Kidner). 그러므로 그는 주변 사람들에게 은혜가 풍성하신 여호와를 의지할 것을 권면한다.

1. 간구(130:1-2)

1 여호와여
내가 깊은 곳에서 주께 부르짖었나이다
2 주여
내 소리를 들으시며

나의 부르짖는 소리에 귀를 기울이소서

기자는 자신을 깊은 바다 혹은 수렁에 빠져 밖에서 누군가가 도와주지 않으면 죽을 수밖에 없는 절박한 사람으로 묘사한다(1절, cf. 시 69:1-2, 14). 아무것도 아닌 사람(nobody)이 별 볼 일 없는 곳(nowhere)에서 부르짖고 있다(Brueggemann). 깊은 곳에 빠져 있다는 것은 죽음과 파괴가 임박했다는 부정적인 뉘앙스를 지니고 있다(사 51:10; 겔 27:34; cf. McCann). 그러므로 라틴어 버전(Vg.)은 이 시편에 'De profundis'(out of the depths, 깊은 곳에서)라는 이름을 붙여 주었으며, 많은 문화권에서 장례식 초청장을 이 이름으로 부른다(Terrien). 주님께서 그들이 깊은 곳(죽음)에서 부르짖는 소리를 들어 달라는 취지에서다(deClaissé-Walford et al.).

또한 이 말씀은 하나님께도 단절된 상황을 묘사한다(VanGemeren). 그가 어떤 일로 인해 곤경에 처했는지는 알 수 없지만, 자신을 가장 겸손하게 낮추고 있다. 이러한 상황에서 그가 유일하게 할 수 있는 일은 위쪽(하늘)을 향해 부르짖는 일이다.

그러므로 그는 그와 특별한 관계를 맺으신 여호와가 계시는 하늘을 향해 자기의 부르짖음에 귀를 기울여 달라고 호소한다(2절, cf. 대하 6:40; 7:15; 느 1:6, 11). 저자가 사용하는 이미지는 주인—종 관계에 근거해 종이 자기 주인에게 호소하는 모습이다(Allen, Kraus). 그의 주인이신 하나님이 도우시지 않으면 그에게는 어떠한 소망도 없다.

기자가 이처럼 절박하게 자기 자신을 묘사하는 것은 그가 당면한 문제가 매우 심각하여 하나님이 돕지 않으시면 헤어날 가능성이 없음을 뜻할 수 있고, 혹은 주변에 그를 도울 자가 아무도 없기 때문에 오직 주님이 도와주시기를 바라는 기도일 수도 있다. 중요한 것은 그는 매우 절망적인 상황에 처해 있다는 것이다.

2. 신뢰(130:3-4)

3 여호와여

주께서 죄악을 지켜보실진대

주여 누가 서리이까

4 그러나 사유하심이 주께 있음은

주를 경외하게 하심이니이다

만일 하나님이 각 사람이 지은 모든 죄에 대하여 '기록해 두시고/지켜보시고'(שׁמר) 책임을 물으신다면 어떻게 될까? 기자는 하나님 앞에 '서 있을 수'(עמד) 있는 사람은 하나도 없다고 한다(3절). 주님 앞에 죄에 대해 떳떳할 수 있는 사람은 없다. 우리 모두는 죄를 지으며 살기 때문에, 심판자이신 하나님 앞에서 당당할 수 있는 사람은 없다는 뜻이다. 기자는 이 고백을 통해 자신도 죄를 지었기 때문에 하나님 앞에 설 수 없음을 시인한다. 그는 자신이 당하고 있는 고통이 그의 죄로 인해 비롯된 하나님의 벌일 수도 있다는 가능성에 대해 생각하고 있다. 하나님의 용서하심은 항상 이처럼 경외로운 두려움을 자아내게 한다(Grogan).

다행인 것은 하나님이 죄를 심판하시는 분이지만, 또한 용서하시는 분이라는 사실이다(4절). 비록 저자가 하나님과 그의 관계를 '주인—종' 관계로 묘사하여 노래를 진행하고 있지만, 잘못을 저지른 종이 주인이 그를 용서해 줄 것을 막연히 바라며 호소하는 것은 아니다. 그는 주인이 종의 어떠한 죄도 용서해 줄 것이라는 확신과 믿음을 바탕으로 기도한다(Calvin, Goldingay). 그러므로 기자는 사유하심이 주님께 있다는 사실을 위로와 소망으로 삼는다. 이 사실을 바탕으로 그는 간접적으로 용서를 구하는 기도를 드리고 있다(Anderson).

'사유하심'(סְלִיחָה)은 '용서'(pardon)를 의미한다(HALOT, cf. 단 9:9). 기자

가 하나님은 용서하시는 분이라는 직접적인 선언보다 '사유하심이 주께 있다'라고 하는 것은 '사유하심'을 주어로 만들어 용서하심의 중요성을 강조하기 위해서다(Goldingay). 주님께 심판만 있는 것이 아니라, 용서도 있다. 심판만 하시는 것이 아니라 용서도 하시는 것이 창조주 여호와의 위대하심이다(Weiser). 그러므로 우리는 용서하시는 주님을 더욱더 경외하게 되며, 하나님의 용서하심은 우리의 삶을 영원히 바뀌게 하신다(Davidson).

3. 기대(130:5-6)

5 나 곧 내 영혼은 여호와를 기다리며
나는 주의 말씀을 바라는도다
6 파수꾼이 아침을 기다림보다
내 영혼이 주를 더 기다리나니
참으로 파수꾼이 아침을 기다림보다 더하도다

하나님은 우리의 모든 죄를 용서하시는 분이기에 기자는 주님을 간절히 바라보며 말씀을 기다린다(5a절). 그는 여호와를 기다리는 일은 또한 '주의 말씀을 바라는 일'이라 한다(5b절). 그는 하나님이 그의 죄를 용서하셨다고 선언하는 말씀을 간절히 사모하고 있다(Kraus, Tucker & Grant). 소망 신학(theology of hope)의 죄 용서를 소망하는 것과 죄 사함을 얻은 것이 긴장관계를 조성하고 있다(Gerstenberger, Goldingay, cf. Weiser). 죄를 지은 사람에게 가장 중요한 것은 하나님의 용서를 선언하는 말씀이다.

그는 자신이 하나님의 말씀을 얼마나 사모하는지 비유로 말한다(6절). 파수꾼이 아침을 기다리는 것보다 더 간절히 주님의 말씀을 기다린다. 우리는 밤새 불침번을 서는 파수꾼이 얼마나 간절한 마음으로 날이 밝아 오기를 기다리는지 어느 정도 상상을 할 수 있다. 칠흑같이 어두운 밤에 적들이 어디에서 그를 노려보고 있는지도 모르는 상황에서 보초를 선다는 것은 참으로 두려운 일이다. 그러므로 파수꾼은 자신의 목숨을 보존하기 위해 날이 밝기를 얼마나 간절히 소원하겠는가!(cf. Clifford, Gerstenberger).

다행히 파수꾼의 간절한 바람은 동이 틀 때마다 성취된다. 이와 같이 하나님을 간절히 바라는 사람들도 반드시 만족하게 될 것을 암시한다(Anderson). 그러므로 우리는 항상 간절한 사모함으로 주님의 말씀을 바라고 기다리면 반드시 구원을 경험할 것이다.

4. 권면(130:7–8)

7 이스라엘아
여호와를 바랄지어다
여호와께서는 인자하심과 풍성한 속량이 있음이라
8 그가 이스라엘을
그의 모든 죄악에서 속량하시리로다

하나님이 그를 도우시고 용서하실 죄는 용서하실 것이라고 확신하는 기자가 온 이스라엘 사람들에게 확신에 찬 권면을 한다. 아무것도 바라지 말고 오직 여호와를 바라라는 권면이다(7a–b절). 오직 하나님만을 그들의 소망으로 삼으라는 것이다. 일부 학자들은 이 시편이 원래 1–6절로 구성되었는데, 여기에 편집자들이 7–8절을 더한 것이라고 한다(Crow). 그러나 이 주장을 뒷받침할 만한 역사적 증거는 없다.

그가 이처럼 확신을 가지고 권면하는 것은 주님 안에는 인자하심과 풍성한 속량이 있기 때문이다(7c절). '인자하심'(חֶסֶד)은 시편에서 이미 수차례 사용된 단어로 하나님의 선하신 속성을 총체적으로 묘사한다

(cf. NIDOTTE). '속량'(פְּדוּת)은 대가를 치르고 누구를 구원한다는 뜻이다(Hossfeld-Zenger, cf. HALOT). 여호와는 참으로 인자하셔서 필요하다면 값을 치르면서까지 자기 백성을 구원하는 하나님이시다. 주님은 사람들이 의지할 수 있는 구원주이신 것이다.

이스라엘이 주님을 의지하면, 주님은 분명 그들을 모든 죄악에서 반드시 구원하실 것이다(8절). 그러므로 기자는 그들에게 오직 여호와를 바라라고(소망하라고) 권면한다(7절). 하나님은 절대 우리를 실망시키는 분이 아니시다. 누구든 주님을 의지하는 자는 반드시 구원을 얻을 것이다.

제131편

다윗의 시 곧 성전에 올라가는 노래

I. 장르/양식: 순례시

불과 3절로 구성되어 있는 이 시편은 150편의 시편들 중 두 번째로 짧은 노래이다. 노래가 매우 짧다 보니 장르를 논하는 것은 별 의미가 없다고 하는 이들도 있다(Crow). 그러나 많은 학자들이 이 노래가 지니고 있는 양식을 논한다.

표제가 다윗의 이름을 언급하고 있다 하여, 이 시를 왕족시로 보는 이들이 있다(Dahood, cf. Robinson). 그러나 대부분 학자들은 '개인 확신시' 혹은 '신뢰시'로 분류한다(Brueggemann & Bellinger, deClaissé-Walford et al., Grogan, Ross, Tucker & Grant, VanGemeren). 이 시편을 '기도시'로 분류하는 이들도 있다(Kraus).

이 시편이 매우 짧은 것은 아마도 더 큰 시의 일부였는데, 나머지 부분이 잊혔기 때문이라는 추측이 있다(Crow). 짧음에도 불구하고 메시지와 문장력에 있어서 이 시편은 '단순함의 보석'(a jewel of simplicity)이라는 평가를 받는다(Gerstenberger). 포로기가 끝난 지 얼마 되지 않은 페르시아 시대에 순례자들이 예루살렘을 향해 가면서 부른 노래이다(Terrien).

Ⅱ. 구조

이 시편은 다음과 같은 순서로 진행된다.

A. 겸손 고백(131:1)

B. 신뢰 고백(131:2)

C. 소망 권면(131:3)

Ⅲ. 주해

기자는 자신의 삶은 세상이 줄 수 있는 것들(교만, 거짓 평안 등)을 멀리하고 겸손히 주님 만이 주실 수 있는 평안을 추구하며 살고 있다고 선언한다. 이어 그는 주의 백성에게 자기처럼 겸손하게 여호와만을 바라보며 살아갈 것을 권면한다.

1. 겸손 고백(131:1)

[1] 여호와여
내 마음이 교만하지 아니하고
내 눈이 오만하지 아니 하오며
내가 큰 일과 감당하지 못할
놀라운 일을 하려고 힘쓰지 아니하나이다

기자는 '마음'(לֵב), '눈'(עַיִן), '영혼'(נֶפֶשׁ)(2절)의 사람 몸을 구성하고 있는 기관들을 사용해 노래를 진행한다. 여기에 '힘쓰지 않는다'(לֹא־הִלַּכְתִּי)는 문자적으로 '걷지 않는다'는 뜻을 지녔다. 다리/발 사용을 전제하고 있는 것이다. 그러므로 그는 총체성의 상징인 4가지를 사용하여 자신의 삶 전체가 어떠한가를 말하고자 한다.

그는 자신의 삶의 모든 영역에서 교만과 오만의 세상 가치와 삶의 방식을 거부한다고 선언한다. '교만하다'(גָּבַהּ)는 자랑하는 것을, '오만하다'(רוּם)는 스스로 높아져 남을 내려다 본다(무시한다)는 뜻을 지녔다(HALOT, NIDOTTE). 그는 또한 자신이 감당할 수 없는 일, 곧 그의 능력 밖에 있는 일을 하려고 무리하지 않는다. 시편에서 '큰 일'(גְּדֹלוֹת)과 '놀라운 일/무리한 일'(נִפְלָאוֹת)은 하나님이 자기 백성을 위해 하시는 기적적인 일들을 묘사하는 데 자주 사용되었다(시 40:6; 72:18; 86:10; 98:1; 106:22; 136:4; 145:5–6). '힘쓰지 않는다'(לֹא־הִלַּכְתִּי)는 '가지 않는다'는 의미를 지녔다. 자기가 감당할 수 있는 일(길)의 범주를 벗어나는 일은 없다는 뜻이다(Shoemaker). 기자는 자신은 하나님이 아니라는 고백을 간접적으로 하고 있다(Harman).

기자는 참으로 자기 자신을 잘 아는 사람이다. 세상은 자꾸 이러한 것들—교만, 오만, 한계를 벗어나는 일—을 행하며 살라고 하지만, 그는 세상이 아니라, 주님의 기준에 따라 살고자 한다.

2. 신뢰 고백(131:2)

2 실로 내가 내 영혼으로 고요하고 평온하게 하기를
젖 뗀 아이가 그의 어머니 품에 있음 같게 하였나니
내 영혼이 젖 뗀 아이와 같도다

세상의 교만하고, 오만하고, 무리한 것들을 추구하라는 유혹을 물리친 기자는 하나님이 주시는 참 평안과 보호를 누리고 있다. 그가 하나님 품에서 누리는 평안과 만족감을 어머니 품에 안겨 있는 젖 뗀 아이와 비교한다. 어머니의 품에서 사랑과 보호를 받는 아이가 행복한 것처럼 그도 하나님의 사랑과 보호를 마음껏 누리고 행복하다는 뜻이다(cf. Brueggemann & Bellinger, Goldingay, Keet). 일부 학자들은 본문이 어머니의 품 이미지를 사용한다 하여 이 시편이 여성에 의해 저작된 것이라고 하지만(cf. Allen, deClaissé–Walford et al., Goldingay, McCann), 별 의미 없는 주장이다.

'고요하다'(שוה)는 높낮이가 없이 평탄한 곳에 있는 것을, '평온하다'(דמם)는 움직이지 않고 가만히 있다는 것을 뜻한다(HALOT). 이 시편이 예배와 예식에서 사용된 것이라고 하는 사람들은 이 말씀이 예배자가 엎드려 겸손을 표현하는 자세를 묘사하고 있다고 한다(Crow). 그러나 사람이 세상에서 누릴 수 있는 가장 따뜻하고 포근한 곳의 이미지의 상징으로 간주함이 바람직하다. 세상은 창조주께서 인간들에게 정해 주신 길을 벗어나면서까지 무리하게 활동하라 하지만, 우리는 오직 주님 안에 있는 고요함과 평온함을 추구하고 누려야 한다.

3. 소망 권면(131:3)

3 이스라엘아
지금부터 영원까지
여호와를 바랄지어다

오직 하나님만이 주실 수 있는 고요함과 평온함을 누리고 있는 기자가 자신의 경험을 토대로 주의 백성을 권면한다. 그는 이 순간부터 영원까지 오직 주님을 바라라고 한다. 사람은 결코 영원하지도, 온전하지도 않은 고요함과 평온함을 찾기 위해 몸부림친다. 참 평온을 경험한 저자는 주님 안에 그들이 찾는 것들이 모두 있다며, 오직 주님을 바라라고 한다. '바라다'(יחל)는 소망한다는 뜻이다. 우리가 주님을 간절히 사모하면, 하나님은 분명히 우리가 추구하는 것들을 허락하실 것이다. 여호와는 우리에게 참 평온을 주시는 분이다.

제132편

성전에 올라가는 노래

I. 장르/양식: 순례시

이 시편은 '성전에 올라가는 노래' 모음집(120-134편)에 속한 노래 중 가장 긴 것이며 18절로 구성되어 있다. 이 노래가 모음집에서 가장 길다는 것이 이 시편의 중요성을 암시하는 듯하며(McCann), 모음집의 마지막 부분에 등장하는 것도 이 시편의 역할을 고려할 때 참고할 만한 사항이다. 그러나 다윗이 법궤를 예루살렘으로 모셔온 일(삼하 6장)과 그가 하나님께 언약을 받은 일(삼하 7장)을 회고하는 오래된 시가 페르시아 시대 이후에 형성된 모음집에 속하게 된 것은 아직도 풀지 못한 수수께끼로 남아 있다(VanGemeren, cf. Davidson).

이 시편의 장르와 저작 시기를 파악하는 것은 매우 어렵다(Fretheim). 상당 수의 학자들이 이 시편을 '시온의 노래'(Zion song)라고 한다(Gunkel, VanGemeren). 왕족시라고 하는 이들도 많다(deClaissé-Walford et al., Hillers, Terrien). 기도시라고 하는 이들도 있고(Goldingay), 시온의 노래와 왕족시 중간쯤에 속한다는 주장도 있다(Allen, Kraus). 이 시편의 장르에 대하여 의견이 분분하다. 저자와 정황을 파악하는 것이 참으로 어려운 일일뿐만 아니라, 규명하는 일이 지나치게 소모적이니 차라리 이처럼 무의미한 노력을 포기하라는 제안까지 있다(Goldingay).

전통적인 견해에 따르면 이 시는 다윗이 하나님께 언약을 받은 사무엘하 7장 이후에 다윗이 저작한 시이다. 그러므로 이 시가 주전 10세기에 다윗에 의해 저작된 것이라는 사람들이 있다(Ross, Terrien, VanGemeren, cf. Dahood). 왕정 시대에 저작된 것은 맞지만, 솔로몬 이후 시대라고 주장하는 이들도 있다(Anderson).

저작 시기를 논할 때 한 가지 고려할 사항이 있다. 역대기 저자는 132:8-10을 솔로몬의 헌당 기도에 인용한다(대하 6:41-42). 그러나 열왕기에 기록된 기도문(cf. 왕상 8장)에는 132:8-10이 등장하지 않는다. 그러므로 이 시편이 왕정 시대에 저작되었다고 단정하기가 어렵다고 하는 이들이 많다(cf. Goldingay). 그렇다 보니 이 시편의 저작 시기를 바빌론 포로 시대로(Laato), 혹은 그 이후, 심지어는 주전 2세기 마카비 시대로 제안하는 이들이 있다(Bee, Houk).

이 시편이 처음 사용된 정황에 대하여도 의견이 분분하다. 다윗 왕조의 왕이 취임할 때마다 예식에서 사용된 노래라고 하는 이들이 있고(Hillers), 여호와가 왕 되심을 기념하는 축제에서(Porter), 혹은 성전과 왕궁이 완공된 다음에 매년 헌당식을 기념하는 축제에서 부른 노래라는 주장도 있다(Gunkel). 포로기 이후 편집자들에 의해 순례시로 분류되어 이 모음집에 편입이 된 것 외에는 이 시편이 언제 저작되었고, 어떤 정황에서 처음 사용되었는지에 대하여는 별로 알려진 바가 없다.

II. 구조

대체적으로 학자들은 이 시편을 1-10절과 11-18절 두 파트로 나눈다(deClaissé-Walford et al., McCann, Tucker & Grant). 첫 번째 파트(1-10절)는 다윗에 초점을 맞추고, 두 번째 파트(11-18절)는 그의 후손들에게 초점을 맞추어 진행된다(Wilcock). 이 두 섹션은 다음과 같이 평행을 이룬다.

1-10절	11-18절
A. 다윗이 하나님께 맹세함(1-5절) B. 법궤 이야기 회상(6-8절) C. 제사장들과 백성을 위한 기도(9절) D. 다윗을 위한 기도(10절)	A'. 하나님이 다윗에게 맹세하심(11-12절) B'. 법궤 이야기에 대한 하나님의 반응(13-15절) C'. 제사장들과 백성을 위한 기도(16절) D'. 다윗을 위한 기도에 대한 하나님의 반응(17-18절)

이 주석에서는 각 섹션의 마지막 부분(C-D와 C′-D′)을 하나로 묶어 다음과 같은 구조를 바탕으로 본문을 주해해 나가고자 한다.

A. 다윗이 하나님께 맹세함(132:1-5)
B. 법궤 이야기 회상(132:6-8)
C. 예배자들을 위한 기도(132:9-10)
A′. 하나님이 다윗에게 맹세하심(132:11-12)
B′. 법궤 이야기에 대한 하나님의 반응(132:13-15)
C′. 기도에 대한 하나님의 응답(132:16-18)

III. 주해

순례시들은 순례자들이 예루살렘으로 순례를 가며 부른 노래들인데, 이 노래는 왜 예루살렘으로 순례를 가야 하는지를 설명한다. 시온은 하나님이 선택하신 곳이므로 하나님의 임재의 상징인 법궤가 있는 곳이다. 또한 그곳에는 다윗의 보좌가 있다. 하나님은 다윗 왕조를 통해 자기 백성을 통치하시겠다고 했는데(cf. 삼하 7장), 하나님의 통치가 바로 그곳에서 이루어지고 있기 때문이다.

1. 다윗이 하나님께 맹세함(132:1-5)

[1] 여호와여

다윗을 위하여
그의 모든 겸손을 기억하소서
2 그가 여호와께 맹세하며
야곱의 전능자에게 서원하기를
3 내가 내 장막 집에 들어가지 아니 하며
내 침상에 오르지 아니하고
4 내 눈으로 잠들게 하지 아니하며
내 눈꺼풀로 졸게 하지 아니하기를
5 여호와의 처소
곧 야곱의 전능자의 성막을
발견하기까지 하리라 하였나이다

기자는 여호와께 기억하라는 호소로 노래를 시작한다(1절). '기억하다'(זכר)는 단순히 옛일을 추억하는 것에서 멈추지 않는다. 성경에서 하나님이 기억하시는 것은 곧 은혜를 베푸시는 것을 의미한다(Childs, cf. 느 5:19; 13:14, 22, 31). 하나님이 불임으로 괴로워하는 한나를 기억하시고(זכר) 그에게 사무엘을 아들로 주신 것처럼 말이다(삼상 1장, cf. 출 6:5; 32:13; 레 26:42; 신 9:27).

그는 하나님께 무엇을 기억하시라고 하는가? 곧 어떤 복을 내려달라고 하는가? 저자는 하나님께 다윗의 겸손을 헤아리시고 복을 주시기를 간구한다. '겸손'(עֻנּוֹת)은 자신을 크게 책망한다는 뜻이다(HALOT). 다윗이 자신을 크게 책망하면서까지 하나님 앞에 겸손히 엎드린 일을 생각하시고 그에 상응하는 복을 내려 달라는 기도이다.

다윗이 도대체 어떤 일을 했기에 기자는 이렇게 말하는 것일까? 다윗의 맹세와 서원 때문이다(2절). 그는 이스라엘과 특별한 관계를 맺으신 하나님 '여호와'(יהוה), 곧 '야곱의 전능자'(אֲבִיר יַעֲקֹב)께 법궤를 예루살렘으로 모셔 오고 법궤를 위해 성전을 짓겠다고 맹세하고 서원을 했다. 이 섹션에서 다윗이 예루살렘 성전을 세운 일이 중점적으로 조명을 받고 있다(Tucker & Grant). 사무엘서는 다윗이 법궤와 성전에 대해 서원하고 맹세했다는 말이 나오지는 않지만, 기자는 그 일을 회고하면서 다윗의 강한 의지를 이렇게 표현한다(cf. Anderson).

'야곱의 전능자'(2, 5절)는 창세기 49:24에서 온 것으로 하나님이 야곱을 어떻게 보호하시고 인도하시며 축복하셨는가를 요약하는 성호이다. 시편에서는 하나님을 위대하신 신적 전사(Divine Warrior)로 묘사하며 사용된다(VanGemeren). 다윗은 그에게 승리를 주신 이 위대하신 전사에게 성전을 짓기를 원했다. 그는 이 일을 하기 위해 금 10만 달란트(=3,500톤)와 은 100만 달란트(=35,000톤)와 셀 수 없이 많은 동과 철을 준비했다(대상 22:15).

그래서 다윗은 '야곱의 전능자'(אֲבִיר יַעֲקֹב)의 성막, 곧 여호와의 처소를 발견하기까지(5절) 자신은 결코 잠을 자지 않겠다고 서원하고 맹세했다(3-4절). 일부 학자들은 다윗이 3절에서 '집에 들어가지 않고, 침상에 오르지 않을 것'을 맹세하는 것이 아내들과 부부관계를 갖지 않겠다는 의지의 표현으로 해석하지만(Anderson), 3절을 4절과 함께 읽으면 그런 의미는 전혀 없다.

다윗이 하나님의 법궤가 머물도록 천막을 예루살렘에 두었던 점을 고려하면(삼하 6:17), 본문에서 '성막'(מִשְׁכָּן)은 장차 솔로몬이 지을 성전을 뜻한다(Huweiler, cf. Briggs). 이 단어는 5, 7, 8, 15절에서 사용되면서 노래에 통일성과 점집성을 더한다(deClaissé-Walford et al.). '발견하다'(מצא)는 잃은 것을 찾는 것이 아니라, 적합한 장소를 정한다는 뜻이다(HALOT, cf. 새번역, 아가페, 현대인, 공동, NIV, NAS, NRS, ESV, TNK). 기자는 다윗이 하나님의 성전으로 적합한 장소를 정할 때까지 온갖 수고와 열정을 아끼지 않겠다고 했던 그의 의지를 강조하고 있다.

2. 법궤 이야기 회상(132:6-8)

6 우리가 그것이 에브라다에 있다 함을 들었더니
나무 밭에서 찾았도다
7 우리가 그의 계신 곳으로 들어가서
그의 발등상 앞에서 엎드려 예배하리로다
8 여호와여 일어나사
주의 권능의 궤와 함께 평안한 곳으로 들어가소서

앞 섹션에서 다윗이 열정과 헌신으로 하나님의 법궤가 머물 만한 성전터를 정한 일을 회고한 기자가 이번에는 어떻게 다윗이 법궤를 예루살렘으로 모셔왔는가를 회고한다. 이때까지 다윗 입장에서 단수로 노래를 진행해 왔던 기자가 이 섹션에서는 복수로 진행한다. 다윗이 한 일에 기자와 그의 청중이 함께 동참한 효과를 발휘하기 위해서다(Huweiler, McCann). 과거에 있었던 일이 기자의 현재에도 효력을 발휘하고 있다(Tucker & Grant).

번역본들은 6a절을 두 가지로 해석한다. 첫째, 다윗과 그의 사람들이 에브라다에 있을 때 법궤에 대한 소식을 접했다(새번역, 현대인, 공동, NIV, ESV, NAS, NRS). 둘째, 그들은 법궤가 에브라다에 머물고 있다는 소식을 들었다(개역개정, TNK). 법궤가 에브라다에 머문 기록이 없다는 사실을 고려할 때 다윗 일행이 에브라다에 머물고 있을 때 법궤에 대한 소식을 접한 것으로 해석해야 한다. 에브라다는 베들레헴 근처에 있는 곳이며 다윗이 에브라다에서 태어났다(삼상 17:12; cf. 룻 4:11). 한 주석가는 본문의 에브라다가 한때 법궤가 머물렀던 실로를 의미한다고 하지만(Weiser), 설득력이 없는 제안이다.

개역개정은 칠십인역(LXX)의 선례에 따라 그들이 법궤를 '나무 밭에서 찾았다'(τοῖς πεδίοις τοῦ δρυμοῦ)고 하는데(6절), '나무'(יָעַר)를 일반명사로 간주한 번역이다. 일부 학자들은 '나무'(יַעַר)가 8절의 '법궤'(אֲרוֹן)를 의미한다고 한다(Tucker & Grant). 그러나 대부분 번역본들과 학자들은 이 단어를 고유명사로 간주하여 '야아르(들판)'로 해석했다(새번역, 아가페, 현대인, 공동, NIV, ESV, NRS, NAS, TNK). 사무엘서에 의하면 법궤가 기럇여아림(삼상 6:21–7:2)에 머물렀고, 여아림(יְעָרִים)은 '야아르'(יַעַר)의 복수형임을 감안할 때 고유명사로 남겨두는 것이 바람직하다. 에브라다에 머물던 다윗이 법궤가 기럇여아림에 있다는 소식을 듣고 그곳으로 내려가 법궤를 모셔온 것이다(cf. Allen, Goldingay, Grogan, McCann)..

다윗은 기럇여아림에 있던 법궤를 주님이 계신 곳으로 모셨다(7절). 주님이 '계신 곳'(מִשְׁכָּן)은 5절에서 예루살렘 성막을 의미했다. 그러므로 이 말씀은 다윗이 법궤를 예루살렘으로 모셔온 일을 회고하고 있다. 다윗이 법궤를 모시기 위하여 세운 예루살렘 장막은 주님이 계신 곳이며, 백성들은 그곳에서 주님의 발등상 앞에 엎드려 예배했다. '주님의 발등상'(רַגְלָיו)은 하나님이 세상을 통치하시는 곳, 곧 법궤를 뜻한다(cf. 민 10:35–36; 대하 6:41–42; 시 99:1–2).

다윗은 법궤를 예루살렘 성막으로 모셔 오면서 여호와께 일어나셔서 법궤와 함께 평안한 곳으로 들어가시라고 기도했다(8절). 광야 생활 중 신적 전사(Divine Warrior)이신 여호와의 법궤가 움직일 때마다 백성들이 "여호와여 일어나소서"라고 외쳤던 일을 연상케 한다(민 10:35–36). 다윗과 백성들이 법궤를 예루살렘으로 모신 이유 중 하나는 신적 전사이신 여호와께서 그들을 위해 싸워 주셔서 원수들로부터 평안을 주실 것을 기대했기 때문인 것이다(VanGemeren).

3. 예배자들을 위한 기도(132:9–10)

9 주의 제사장들은 의를 옷 입고
주의 성도들은 즐거이 외칠지어다

[10] 주의 종 다윗을 위하여
주의 기름 부음 받은 자의 얼굴을 외면하지 마옵소서

기자는 제사장들과 백성들을 위해 기도한다.

첫째, 그는 주의 제사장들이 의를 옷으로 입기를 간절히 소망한다(9a절). 제사장들이 부정과 불의에 오염되지 않고 의롭고 경건한 예배자들이 되어 이스라엘의 예배를 잘 인도할 수 있도록 기도한다.

둘째, 그는 성도들이 하나님이 계시는 곳에서 즐거이 외칠 수 있기를 기도한다(9b절). 마음껏 찬양하고, 마음껏 기도할 수 있는 여건이 조성되어 그들이 기쁜 마음으로 하나님을 예배하는 일을 꿈꾼다.

셋째, 다윗 왕조를 위해 기도한다(10절). 하나님은 다윗에게 그와 그의 자손이 영원히 주의 백성을 통치하게 할 것을 약속하셨다(cf. 삼하 7장). 이제 그 약속을 영원히 지켜 달라고 간구한다. 다윗과의 약속을 생각하셔서 주의 기름 부음을 받은 자들, 곧 다윗의 왕위에 앉은 그의 후손들의 얼굴을 외면하지 말라고 호소한다. 그들의 기도를 들어주셔서 그들이 주의 백성을 영원히 통치할 수 있도록 보호해 달라는 기도이다.

4. 하나님이 다윗에게 맹세하심(132:11–12)

[11] 여호와께서 다윗에게 성실히 맹세하셨으니
변하지 아니하실지라
이르시기를 네 몸의 소생을 네 왕위에 둘지라
[12] 네 자손이 내 언약과
그들에게 교훈하는 내 증거를 지킬진대
그들의 후손도 영원히 네 왕위에 앉으리라 하셨도다

기자는 하나님이 다윗과 맺으신 언약, 곧 다윗 언약(cf. 삼하 7장)을 회상한다. 하나님은 성실하게 그때 맹세하셨다(11절). '성실'(אֱמֶת)은 진실을 뜻하기도 하지만(cf. 새번역), 강조점은 시간이 지나도 변하지 않는 것(마음이 바뀌지 않는 것)에 있다(cf. 아가페, 현대인). 그러므로 하나님이 다윗에게 하신 "네 몸의 소생을 네 왕위에 둘지라"라는 말씀은 영원히 변하지 않고 그대로 지속될 것임을 의미한다.

그러나 다윗 언약이 맹목적으로 영원히 지켜지는 것은 아니다. 언약이 유지되려면 한 가지 조건이 충족되어야 한다. 다윗의 후손들이 지속적으로 하나님의 교훈과 증거를 지켜야 하는 것이다(12절). 시편에서 '언약'(בְּרִית)과 '증거'(עֵדוּת)는 율법을 의미하며 이미 수차례 사용되었다(cf. 시 119편). 하나님이 그들에게 교훈하신(가르치신) 율법을 지키는 한 다윗의 후손들은 영원히 그 왕위에 앉을 것이다.

5. 법궤 이야기에 대한 하나님의 반응(132:13-15)

13 여호와께서 시온을 택하시고
자기 거처를 삼고자 하여 이르시기를
14 이는 내가 영원히 쉴 곳이라
내가 여기 거주할 것은 이를 원하였음이로다
15 내가 이 성의 식료품에 풍족히 복을 주고
떡으로 그 빈민을 만족하게 하리로다

하나님은 다윗과 그의 후손들이 주의 백성을 영원히 다스릴 수 있는 언약을 주시고, 다윗이 보좌를 둔 예루살렘에 있는 시온 산을 자기 처소로 삼으셨다(13절). 하나님은 시온을 자신의 영원한 안식처로 삼으셨으며, 그곳에 거주하기를 원하신다(14절). 세상 그 어느 곳도 주님의 거처가 될 수 없이 초라하지만, 그나마 주님이 시온을 자기 거처로 원하셨다. 하나님이 시온을 택하심도 은혜인 것이다.

하나님이 시온에 거하시면 주변 백성에게도 큰 혜택이 임한다. 시온이 있는 성 예루살렘은 식량이 풍족할 것이며, 빈민들도 배불리 먹게 될 것이다(15절). 풍요로운 생명의 하나님이 시온 주변에 사는 자기 백성의 의식주를 책임져 주신다. 당연히 하나님이 그곳에 머무시는 동안에만 있는 일이다. 주전 586년에 있었던 일(cf. 애가)이 증언하는 것처럼 하나님의 영광이 그곳을 떠나면 굶주림과 질병이 그곳에서 창궐한다.

6. 기도에 대한 하나님의 응답(132:16-18)

16 내가 그 제사장들에게 구원을 옷 입히리니
그 성도들은 즐거이 외치리로다
17 내가 거기서 다윗에게 뿔이 나게 할 것이라
내가 내 기름 부음 받은 자를 위하여 등을 준비하였도다
18 내가 그의 원수에게는 수치를 옷 입히고
그에게는 왕관이 빛나게 하리라 하셨도다

기자는 9-10절에서 제사장과 백성들과 왕에 대한 기도를 드렸다. 이 섹션은 하나님의 기도에 대한 응답이다.

첫째, 제사장들에게 '의의 옷을 입혀달라'(יִלְבְּשׁוּ־צֶדֶק)고 했던 기도(9절)가 주님이 그들에게 '구원의 옷을 입히시겠다'(אַלְבִּישׁ יֶשַׁע)는 응답을 받고 있다(16a절). 의의 옷을 입는 것은 의로운 일을 하는 것을 의미하고, 구원의 옷을 입는 것은 사람들을 구원의 길로 인도한다는 뜻이다. 제사장들의 사역은 의를 행하는 것이고, 그들이 의를 행함은 곧 사람들을 구원하는 것이라는 의미이다.

둘째, '주의 성도들이 즐거이 외치게 해 달라'(חֲסִידֶיךָ יְרַנֵּנוּ)고 했던 기도(9절)가 '그들은 참으로 즐거이 외칠 것'(חֲסִידֶיהָ רַנֵּן יְרַנֵּנוּ)이라는 말씀으로 응답 받고 있다(16b절). 하나님은 기자의 즐거이 외치게 해달라는 기도에 같은 동사의 부정사(רַנֵּן)를 더하여 꼭 그렇게 하실 것을 약속하신다. 주의 백성들이 즐거이 외칠 날이 오고 있다.

셋째, 다윗을 생각하셔서 앞으로도 그의 보좌에 앉는 왕들의 얼굴을 외면하지 말아 달라는 기도(10절)에 하나님은 세 가지로 답하신다. 제일 먼저 하나님은 시온에서 다윗에게 뿔이 나게 하실 것이다(17a절). 뿔은 강인함을 상징한다. 다윗의 왕조는 하나님이 계시는 시온에서 나온 것이므로 강인할 것이다. 하나님이 다윗 왕권을 통해 자기 백성을 다스리실 것을 의미한다(VanGemeren).

이어 하나님은 다윗의 대를 이어 왕이 될 그의 후손들을 위해 등을 준비하셨다고 한다(17b절). '등'(נֵר)은 선지자 아히야가 솔로몬의 죄로 인해 왕국에서 10지파가 떨어져 나가겠지만, 한 지파는 두어 다윗의 등불을 유지하도록 하시겠다는 하나님의 신탁을 선포할 때 다윗 왕조의 지속성을 상징하며 사용했다(왕상 11:36). 기자는 하나님이 왕들의 얼굴을 외면하지 말아 달라며 왕조가 끊기지 않게 해 달라고 호소했는데, 하나님은 다윗 집안에서 등불이 계속 타오를 것이라고 말씀하신다.

마지막으로 하나님은 다윗은 존귀하게 하시고, 그의 원수들은 수치를 당하도록 하실 것을 약속하신다(18절). 그의 왕관은 빛이 날 것이고, 원수들은 수치의 옷을 입을 것이라고 하셨는데, 이는 다윗이 승승장구할 것이며, 그의 원수들은 모두 그에게 패할 것을 의미한다.

제133편
다윗의 시 곧 성전에 올라가는 노래

I. 장르/양식: 순례시

학자들은 이 시편이 짧고 간단하면서도 매우 복잡한 시라고 하고(Goldingay), 분명한 시작은 있지만, 끝맺음이 없는 시라고 하기도 한다(Zevit). 내용은 축복송(song of blessing)이라는 이들이 있지만(Anderson, Kraus), 지혜시(wisdom psalm)라는 견해가 주류를 이룬다(Allen, Brueggemann & Bellinger, Crow, deClaissé-Walford et al., Grogan, Gunkel).

표제는 이 시를 다윗과 연관시키지만, 다윗을 저자로 보는 이들은 거의 없다. 이 시편이 포로기 이후 시대에 저작된 것이라는 주장이 있다(Anderson). 반면에 왕정 시대를 제안하기도 하고(Terrien), 더 구체적으로는 히스기야 시대를 지목하는 이들도 있다(Norin, cf. VanGemeren). 히스기야는 주전 722년에 망한 북 왕국 이스라엘의 남은 사람들을 유다에 편입시키려고 했는데, 이때 '형제의 연합'이 아름답다며 북 왕국 사람들을 설득하기 위해서 사용한 노래라는 것이다.

정확히 언제쯤인지 확실하지는 않지만, 남북이 통일되지 않은 시대에 통일을 염원하며 부른 노래라고 하는 이들도 있다(Berlin). 훗날 포로기 이후 시대에는 사마리아 사람들과 유다 사람들의 통일을 염원하며 사용되었다는 주장이 있다(Goldingay).

II. 구조

이 시편은 매우 짧은 시이지만 확실한 구조를 지니고 있다. 이 주석에서는 다음과 같은 구조를 바탕으로 본문을 주해해 나가고자 한다.

A. 형제의 아름다운 동거(133:1)

B. 보배로운 기름처럼(133:2)

B′. 헤르몬 산의 이슬처럼(133:3a)

A′. 형제의 복받은 동거(133:3b)

III. 주해

이 시편은 형제들이 한마음을 지니고 함께 사는 것이 얼마나 복된 일인가를 노래한다. 하나님은 형제들의 동거에 복을 더하시어 그들의 삶을 더욱더 행복하고 값지게 하신다.

1. 형제의 아름다운 동거(133:1)

1 보라
형제가 연합하여 동거함이
어찌 그리 선하고 아름다운고

이 말씀은 일종의 격언이라는 것이 대부분 학자들의 주장이다(cf. Allen, Crow, McCann, Tucker & Grant). 그래서 대부분의 학자들이 이 시편을 지혜시로 분류한다. 형제의 동거가 참으로 아름답다는 점을 강조하기 위해 기자는 '보라!'(הִנֵּה)라는 감탄사로 이 구절을 시작한다. 본문에서 이 단어는 '복이 있다'라는 의미로 사용되고 있다(Bellinger, cf. 잠 15:23; 16:16; 욥 34:4; 전 6:12).

고대 근동에서는 여러 세대가 함께 사는 대가족들 몇이 모여 공동체를 이루는 구조였다. 그러므로 본문에서 함께 연합하는 형제들의 이야기는 분명 가족 단위에서 시작되었을 것이다(cf. Kraus). 그러나 '형제'(אַחִים)는 매우 다양한 의미를 지닌 단어이기 때문에 같은 부모에게서 태어난 자들로 해석할 필요는 없으며 훨씬 더 넓은 범위의 연합체제들에게 적용될 수 있다(Kidner, cf. HALOT). 그러므로 일부 학자들이 이 시편을 이미 망한 북 왕국 이스라엘의 생존자들과 남 왕국 유다 사람들의 연합을 도모하는 노래라고 하는 것이다(Berlin, cf. Gerstenberger). '연합'(יָחַד)은 함께 공동체를 이룬다는 뜻이며, '동거하다'(ישׁב)는 자리를 함께한다는 뜻이다.

다양한 사람들이 서로의 차이를 내려놓고 함께 모여 공동체를 이루어 같은 비전을 추구하며 사는 것은 참으로 선하고 아름답다. '선'(טוֹב)은 좋은 일이라는 뜻으로 하나님의 은총을 의미하며 성경에서 자주 사용된다. '아름답다'(נָעִים)는 감정에 초점을 맞춘 단어로 '즐거운, 사랑스런, 기분이 좋은'이라는 의미를 지녔다. 주님 안에서 형제가 연합하여 한 공동체를 이루며 사는 일은 참으로 우리를 행복하게 해 준다는 뜻이다. 이 시편이 순례시 모음집에 속하게 된 것은 시온으로 순례를 가는 동안에 모든 순례자들이 같은 목적지를 향해 행복하고 즐거운 시간을 갖게 되기 때문일 것이다(VanGemeren).

2. 보배로운 기름처럼(133:2)

2 머리에 있는 보배로운 기름이
수염 곧 아론의 수염에 흘러서
그의 옷깃까지 내림 같고

기자는 1절에서 형제의 동거는 '선하다'(טוֹב)고 했는데, 이번에는 '보배로운'(טוֹב) 기름과 같다며 동일한 단어를 사용하여 좋은 일임을 강조한다. 기자는 공동체의 구성원들이 서로의 차이점을 내려놓고 한마음으로 행복하게 사는 것은 곧 아론의 머리에서 흘러내려 그의 옷깃까지 적시는 보배로운 기름과 같다고 한다.

이 '기름'(שֶׁמֶן)은 제사장들을 안수할 때 사용된 것으로 성막에서만 제조되고 사용되는 거룩하고 특별한 기름이다(cf. 출 30:22-33). 더욱이 이 기름이 다름 아닌 이스라엘의 초대 대제사장 아론의 머리에서 흘러내린다. 대제사장 아론이 언급되는 것은 아마도 제사장 제도를 통해 용서와 축복이 임하기 때문일 것이다(cf. 출 29:44-46; 레 9:22-24; 민 6:24-26).

기자는 아론이 살아 있던 광야 생활 중에 이스라엘 12지파가 하나되어 하나님의 복을 누렸던 일을 회상하고 있다(cf. Goldingay). 또한 주의 백성이 언제든 하나가 되면 주님이 아론의 머리에 거룩한 기름으로 안수하셔서 복을 주신 것처럼, 그들에게도 복을 주실 것을 확신한다. 아론의 머리에 부은 기름이 그의 옷깃까지 내리는 모습은 하나님이 복을 주시되 넘치게 주실 것을 암시한다. 성경에서 기름은 기쁨을 상징하기도 한다.

3. 헤르몬 산의 이슬처럼(133:3a)

3 헐몬의 이슬이 시온의 산들에 내림 같도다

형제의 연합의 복됨을 기름에 비교한 기자가 이번에는 이슬에 비교한다. 그것도 헤르몬 산의 이슬이다. 헤르몬 산은 예루살렘에서 북쪽으로 약 200킬로미터 떨어진 곳에 위치했으며 해발 3,000미터에 달하는 높은 산이다. 지중해에서 오는 구름이 이 높은 산을 넘지 못하고 이슬이 되어 적시다 보니 헤르몬 산에는 건기 때에도 항상 물과 초원이 있었다(ABD). 헤르몬 산의 이슬은 생명과 풍요의 상징이었던 것이다 (Goldingay, cf. Anderson).

기자는 형제의 연합은 그 산을 풍요로운 생명의 근원으로 만든 헤르몬 산의 이슬이 시온의 산들에 내리는 것과 같다고 한다. 일부 학자들은 서로 멀리 떨어진 시온과 헤르몬 산이 문제가 된다 하여 시온을 헤르몬 산 밑자락에 위치한 마을 이욘(Ijon)으로 바꿀 것을 제안한다(cf. Crow). 그러나 이 시편이 형제의 연합에 임하는 하나님의 축복(이슬, 비)을 강조하기 때문에, 하나님이 계시는 시온을 그대로 유지하는 것이 바람직하다(cf. Hossfeld-Zenger).

기자는 주의 백성이 시온에서 연합을 하면 그들의 삶이 항상 생명이 넘치고 풍요로울 것이라 한다. 이 시편이 추구하는 연합의 한 중심에는 여호와께 드리는 예배가 있다(Goldingay). 이스라엘의 남자들이 성전을 찾아야 하는 세 절기 중 둘은 건기(4-10월)에 있다. 5-6월에 있는 칠칠절과 9월에 있는 장막절이다. 건기를 맞이하여 메마른 대지를 걸어 예루살렘으로 순례 가던 사람들에게 헤르몬 산의 이슬은 참으로 좋은 상상을 하게 했을 것이다.

4. 형제의 복받은 동거(133:3b)

3b 거기서 여호와께서 복을 명령하셨나니
곧 영생이로다

기자는 하나님이 '그곳'(שָׁם)에서 복을 명령하셨다고 한다. 그러면 그곳은 어디인가? 일부 주석가들은 시온이라고 하고(Kirkpatrick), 다른 사람들은 시온과 연관된 형제의 연합이라고 하기도 한다(Dahood, VanGemeren). 중요한 것은 형제가 함께 시온에 계시는 주님 앞에 설 때 복을 누린다는 것이다.

그들이 누릴 축복은 '영생'(חַיִּים עַד־הָעוֹלָם)이다. 마치 헤르몬 산의 이슬이 온 세상에 생명을 주는 것처럼 형제의 연합은 많은 사람에게 생명을 줄 것이다(Tucker & Grant). 본문의 영생은 내세와는 상관없는 것이며, 이 땅에서 오래(마치 영원하다고 느낄 정도) 살게 될 것이라는 뜻이다. 무병장수가 절대 쉽지 않았던 시대를 살았던 고대 사람들에게 가장 매력적인 축복이었을 것이다. 주님은 연합하는 형제들에게 이 같은 복을 명령하셨다. 반드시 임할 축복이라는 뜻이다.

제134편

성전에 올라가는 노래

I. 장르/양식: 순례시

이 시편은 '성전에 올라가는 노래' 모음집(120-134편)의 마지막 노래이다. 모음집이 시작할 때 노래들이 예배자들을 위협하는 사람들과 상황에 초점을 맞추었는데, 모음집을 마무리하는 시들은 시온과 시온으로 순례 온 사람들이 누리는 축복을 부각시킨다(Hossfeld-Zenger). 또한 120편은 성전에서 멀리 떨어져 있는 사람들이 시작한 순례시였는데, 이 노래는 성전 뜰에 있는 사람들의 노래이다. 이 노래는 순례시 모음집에 매우 적절한 결론이 되고 있는 노래인 것이다.

이 시편도 워낙 짧기 때문에 장르를 논하는 것이 별 의미는 없다. 그럼에도 불구하고 이 시편을 종말론적인 소망을 노래하는 왕족시라고 하는 이도 있고(Terrien), 공동체 찬양시로 분류하는 일들도 있다(Brueggemann & Bellinger, deClaissé-Walford et al., VanGemeren). 예배 중 사용된 미니 예식(liturgy in miniature)으로 부르는 이도 있다(Anderson).

133편이 주의 백성이 시온에 모인 것을 기념하는 노래였다면, 이 시편은 그들이 온 목적을 이루는 노래이다(McCann). 그들이 시온으로 온 이유는 여호와를 찬양하기 위해서다(cf. 1-2절). 장막절에 성전을 찾아와 여호와를 예배하고(Grogan) 성전을 떠나는 성도들에게 빌어준 제사장의 축도가 3절을 구성하고 있다(Auffret, McCann, Tucker & Grant).

II. 구조

이 주석에서는 다음과 같은 구분을 바탕으로 본문을 주해해 나가고자 한다.

A. 예배 부름(134:1-2)

B. 제사장의 축도(134:3)

III. 주해

1. 예배 부름(134:1-2)

1 보라
밤에 여호와의 성전에 서 있는
여호와의 모든 종들아
여호와를 송축하라
2 성소를 향하여 너희 손을 들고
여호와를 송축하라

이 노래는 시온으로 모여든 순례자들이 모든 예배를 마치고 집으로 떠나는 날 전야에 성전에서 부른 노래이다. 그들은 한동안 못 볼 성전을 떠나면서 한 번 더 예배의 제단을 쌓기를 원한다. 기자는 성전 뜰에 모인 사람들에게 하나님을 송축하라고 하는데, '송축하다'(ברך)는 축복하다는 뜻을 지녔으며 사람이 하나님을 축복할 때는 '찬양하다'는 의미를 지닌다(cf. 아가페, 현대인, 공동, NIV).

이스라엘뿐만 아니라 고대 근동 사회에서 사람이나 공동체의 삶에 신(들)의 축복보다 더 중요하고 결정적인 것은 없었다(NIDOTTE). 시온에서 하나님의 임재와 축복을 경험하고 집으로 돌아가는 사람들이 마음을 합해 그들에게 복을 주시는 여호와께 한 번 더 찬양을 통해 감사를 표현한다.

함께 모여 하나님을 찬양하는 '여호와의 모든 종들'(כָּל־עַבְדֵי יְהוָה)은 누구인가? 제사장들과 레위 사람들이 성전에 사역하는 것을 성경이 종종 '서 있다'(עמד)고 하고(신 10:8; 18:7; 대상 23:20; 시 135:2) '밤'(לַיְלָה)에 성전 뜰에서 하나님을 찬양한다 해서(cf. 대상 9:33; 23:26, 30) 이들은 성전에서 사역하는 제사장들과 레위 사람들이라고 하는 이들이 있다(Dahood, VanGemeren). 그러나 이 노래가 순례자들의 마지막 노래이고, 성경에서 '서 있다'가 온 회중에게 적용되기도 한다(cf. 레 9:5; 렘 7:10). 또한 성도가 밤새 예배를 드리는 것도 종종 있던 일이며(van der Toorn, cf. 사 30:29; 시 3:5), '종'(עֶבֶד)이 일반인을 의미하기도 한다는 점을 고려할 때(cf. 시 132:10), 이 노래에서 여호와를 찬양하는 모든 종들은 예루살렘으로 모여든 순례자들이다(Allen, deClaissé-Walford et al., Grogan, McCann, Tucker & Grant).

기자는 곧 성소를 떠날 예배자들에게 성전을 향해 손을 들고 여호와를 송축하라고 한다(2절, cf. 왕상 8:30). 성전은 하나님이 머무시는 곳이다. 한동안 다시 뵙지 못할 하나님의 임재를 향해 존귀와 영광의 표시로 손을 들고 찬양하고 감사하라는 뜻이다.

2. 제사장의 축도(134:3)

3 천지를 지으신 여호와께서
시온에서 네게 복을 주실지어다

성전을 떠나 각자 집으로 돌아가야 하는 순례자들에게 제사장들이 복을 빌어준다(Auffret, cf. 민 6:24-25; 신 21:5; 삼하 2:20; 시 118:26). '축복하다'(ברך)가 이 짧은 시에서 세 번째 사용되고 있다. 처음 두 차례는 순례자들이 하나님을 경배하는 일에 사용되었고, 이번에는 제사장이 하나님의 이름으로 예배자들을 축복하는 데 사용되고 있다.

그들에게 복을 주시는 이는 천지를 지으신 여호와시다. 창조주 하나님만이 주실 수 있는 종합적인 복을 빌고 있다(Habel). 주님은 시온에서 그들에게 복을 내리신다. 하나님은 앞으로도 시온에 거하시며, 그곳에서 자기 백성을 지키시고 보호하실 것이다.

제135편

I. 장르/양식:

비록 '성전으로 올라가는 노래' 모음집(120–134편)은 끝났지만, 이것이 '순례시' 모음집(120–136편)인 '위대한 찬양시'(Great Hallel psalms)의 일부임을 감안할 때, 135–136편은 분명 '성전으로 올라가는 노래' 모음집과 연관성이 있다. 학자들은 135–136편이 이 모음집과 언어적으로, 또한 주제적으로 깊은 연관성이 있다고 생각한다(cf. Kidner, McCann, Tucker & Grant, VanGemeren). 가장 확실한 연관성은 134편은 여호와를 송축하라고 했는데, 이 시편들은 하나님을 어떻게 송축할 것인가를 설명하고 있는 듯하다는 것이다.

이스라엘의 역사 일부를 회고하고 있다고 해서 이 시편을 역사시(historical psalm)라고 하는 이들도 있지만(Brueggemann & Bellinger), 대체적으로 학자들은 이 노래를 공동체 찬양시(deClaissé–Walford et al., Ross)로 분류한다. 더 구체적으로는 서술적 찬양시(descriptive praise psalm)이다(VanGemeren).

이 시는 포로민들을 위로하기 위해 포로기나 그 이후에 저작된 것이라고 하는 이가 있다(Terrien). 정확하게 언제쯤인지는 알 수 없지만,

이스라엘 역사에서 매우 늦게 저작된 시라는 것에는 대부분 동의한다(Goldingay, Tucker & Grant).

이 시가 이스라엘이 이집트에서 탈출하여 가나안에 정착하게 된 것을 회고하고 있다고 해서 유월절에 사용된 것이라는 주장이 있다(Ross). 그러나 대부분 학자들은 이 노래가 어느 특정한 종교 절기와 연관된 시편인 것은 확실하지만, 정확히 어떤 절기인지는 도저히 알 수 없다고 결론짓는다(cf. VanGemeren).

이 시편의 특징은 구약의 여러 텍스트를 인용하거나 떠오르게 한다는 것이다. 이스라엘의 역사와 전통을 잘 알고 있던 기자가 당시 일상화된 문구들로 이 시편을 채웠기 때문에 빚어진 현상이다(Anderson, Goldingay). 다음 도표를 참조하라(Broyles, Kidner, Tucker & Grant, cf. Allen, Goldingay, Kirkpatrick, McCann, Terrien).

시편 135편	구약
1-2절	시 113:1; 134:1-2; 116:19
3절	시 133:1; 147:1
4절	신 7:6; 14:2
5절	출 18:11
6절	시 115:3
7절	렘 10:13
8절	출 12:29
9절	신 6:22; 34:11
10-12절	시 136:17-22
13절	출 3:15
14절	신 32:36
15-18절	시 115:4-8
19-21절	시 115:9-11
21절	시 133:3; 134:3

II. 구조

학자들은 이 시편을 1-4절, 5-7절, 8-14절, 15-18절, 19-21절 다섯 섹션으로 구분한다(Tucker & Grant, VanGemeren). 이 시를 시작하고 마무리하는 '할렐루야'(הַלְלוּ יָהּ)를 독립적인 섹션으로 따로 취급하면 일곱 섹션이 된다(Allen). 이 주석에서는 노래의 시작과 끝에 있는 '할렐루야'를 독립적으로 취급하지 않을 것이다. 또한 8-14절을 8-9절, 10-12절, 13-14절 세 섹션으로 구분하여 다음과 같은 분석을 바탕으로 본문을 주해해 나가고자 한다.

A. 이스라엘을 택하신 여호와 찬양(135:1-4)
  B. 창조주 여호와의 능력(135:5-7)
    C. 역사를 주관하시는 여호와 찬양(135:8-14)
      1. 이집트를 벌하심(135:8-9)
      2. 가나안을 정복하심(135:10-12)
      3. 백성을 보살피심(135:13-14)
  B′. 우상들의 무능함(135:15-18)
A′. 시온에 계시는 여호와 찬양(135:19-21)

III. 주해

이 시편은 여호와가 온 세상의 창조주이시며 시온에 거하심을 찬양한다. 창조주는 이스라엘을 자기 백성 삼으신 분이기도 하다. 여호와의 창조 사역은 이스라엘을 이집트에서 구원하셔서 그들이 새로운 나라가 되게 하시고 그들에게 거할 땅을 주신 일에서도 계속되었다. 반면에 열방이 신들로 숭배하는 우상들은 무능하여 이스라엘의 하나님과 강력한 대조를 이룬다.

1. 이스라엘을 택하신 여호와 찬양(135:1-4)

1 할렐루야
여호와의 이름을 찬송하라
여호와의 종들아 찬송하라
2 여호와의 집 우리 여호와의 성전
곧 우리 하나님의 성전 뜰에서 있는 너희여
3 여호와를 찬송하라
여호와는 선하시며
그의 이름이 아름다우니
그의 이름을 찬양하라
4 여호와께서 자기를 위하여 야곱 곧 이스라엘을
자기의 특별한 소유로 택하셨음이로다

기자는 1절에서 '여호와'(יהוה)를 두 차례, 여호와의 약식형 '야'(יָהּ)를 한 차례, 이스라엘과 언약을 맺으신 하나님의 성호 '여호와'를 세 차례 언급한다. 이 시편은 하나님이 이스라엘과 맺으신 특별한 관계를 바탕으로 진행되고 있으며, 우상들과 비교할 수 없는 하나님의 고귀한 명예를 보존하는 것에 목적이 있다(McCann, cf. 3절).

'여호와를 찬양하라'는 의미를 지닌 '할렐루야'(הַלְלוּ יָהּ)는 시편에서 총 75차례 사용되는데, 그 중 54차례가 제5권(107-150편)에서 사용된다(deClaissé-Walford et al.). 제5권이 여호와를 찬양하기 위해 모아진 시편들이라는 것을 잘 보여주고 있다. 이 섹션에서 '찬양하라'(הַלְלוּ)도 세 차례 사용되고 있다. 그는 주의 종들에게 여호와의 이름을 찬양하라고 한다. 마치 종들이 주인에게 예를 취하는 것처럼 하나님을 주인 대하듯 대하라는 뜻이다.

'여호와의 종들'(עַבְדֵי יְהוָה)는 누구인가? 2절은 그들이 여호와의 집, 곧 성전 뜰에 서 있는 자들이라고 한다. 일부 주석가들이 주장하는 것처럼 이 시편을 134편과 연계해 해석한다면, 성전 뜰에 서 있는 주의 종들은 여호와를 예배하기 위해 각지에서 몰려든 순례자들이다. 여호와의 종들은 제사장들과 레위 사람들을 포함한 모든 주의 백성인 것이다(cf. Tucker & Grant). 그러나 이들이 뜰에 있다 해서 제사장들과 레위 사람들로 제한하는 해석도 있다(VanGemeren). 온 백성으로 보는 것이 바람직하다.

개역개정은 2절을 "여호와의 집, 우리 여호와의 성전, 곧 우리 하나님의 성전 뜰…"로 번역하여 마치 저자가 같은 공간을 세 차례 언급하는 것처럼 말하지만, 마소라 사본은 두 차례밖에 언급하지 않는다: "여호와의 집, 우리 하나님의 성전 뜰…" 중간에 등장하는 "우리 여호와의 성전"이라는 말이 없다(cf. 새번역, 아가페, 현대인, 공동, NIV, NAS, NRS, TNK).

여호와의 성전 뜰에 서 있는 주님의 종들, 곧 예배자들은 무엇을 찬양해야 하는가? 저자는 3-4절에서 세 가지를 찬양하라고 한다.

첫째, 우리는 여호와의 선하심을 찬양해야 한다(3b절). '선하다'(טוֹב)는 하나님의 가장 기본적인 속성이며 주님이 자기 백성을 대하시는 모습이다. 우리는 여호와께서 본질적으로 선하시며, 자기 백성을 선처하시는 하나님이심을 찬양해야 한다.

둘째, 우리는 주님의 아름다운 이름을 찬양해야 한다(3c-d절). 성경에서 이름은 그 이름으로 불리는 존재가 어떠한가를 가장 잘 요약한다. '아름답다'(נָעִים)는 '행복하다/기분이 좋다'는 뜻을 지녔다(HALOT). 하나님의 이름 여호와는 생각하는 이들을 행복하게 하고 기분이 좋아지게 한다. 그러므로 우리가 주님의 이름을 찬양할수록 우리도 더 행복해진다.

셋째, 주의 백성은 하나님의 특별한 소유가 되었음을 찬양해야 한다(4절). 하나님은 이스라엘을 자기의 특별한 소유로 택하셨다. '특별한 소유'(סְגֻלָּה)는 가장 귀한 소유물을 뜻한다(NIDOTTE, 출 19:5; 신 7:6; 14:2; cf. 새번역, 아가페, NAS, NIV, TNK). 우리는 여호와께서 가장 아끼고 소중히 여기시는 자들이다. 그러므로 세상에서 우리를 가장 존귀한 소유물로 여겨 주시는 하나님께 감사의 찬양을 드리는 것이 당연하다. 하나님이 우리와 맺으신 특별한 관계는 우리가 주님께 드리는 찬양의 가장 기본적이고 중요한 이유가 되고 있다.

2. 창조주 여호와의 능력(135:5-7)

5 내가 알거니와 여호와께서는 위대하시며
우리 주는 모든 신들 보다 위대하시도다
6 여호와께서 그가 기뻐하시는 모든 일을
천지와 바다와 모든 깊은 데서 다 행하셨도다
7 안개를 땅 끝에서 일으키시며
비를 위하여 번개를 만드시며
바람을 그 곳간에서 내시는도다

기자는 여호와께서 참으로 위대하시다는 사실을 개인적인 차원에서 고백한다: '나는 안다'(אֲנִי יָדַעְתִּי)(5a절). 인칭 대명사 '나'(I)가 강조형으로 등장하고 있다. 그러므로 더 정확한 번역은 '나는 스스로 안다'(I myself know), 혹은 '나는 참으로 잘 안다'(I truly know)가 되어야 한다. 공동체와 함께 하나님의 선하심과 아름다움을 찬양한 일이 개인적인 차원의 확신에 찬 고백으로 바뀌고 있다(VanGemeren). 그는 자신이 이때까지 경험한 바를 바탕으로 이처럼 단호하게 선언한다. 세상 그 어디에도 여호와 같으신 분은 없다. 그러므로 그는 하나님은 열방의 모든 신들보다 위대하시다는 사실을 확신한다(5b절). 저자는 그와 함께한 공동체가 함께 여호와의 위대하심을 확신하고 고백할 것을 요구한다(Goldingay).

여호와의 능력이 어느 정도이기에 세상의 모든 신들보다 위대하다고 하는가? 저자는 두 가지로 하나님의 무한한 능력을 묘사한다.

첫째, 하나님의 창조와 통치 능력에는 한계가 없다(6절). 하나님은 자신이 뜻하시는 것이면 무엇이든, 어디서든 다 하시는 분이다. 하나님은 자신이 기뻐하시는 일(하고자 하시는 일)을 하늘과 땅과 바다와 가장 깊은 곳에서 제한을 받지 않고 모두 행하신다.

둘째, 하나님은 날씨를 주관하시는 분이다(7절). 때로는 땅끝에서 안개를 일으키시며, 비를 내리신다. 번개를 만드시고, 바람을 조정하신다. 건기와 우기가 뚜렷하게 구분되는 근동 기후에서 날씨를 조정하는 것은 신들의 능력 중 가장 중요한 능력으로 간주되었다(cf. Hossfeld-Zenger). 바알이 가장 능력 있는 신으로 숭배된 것도 그가 날씨를 조정한다고 믿었기 때문이다. 기자는 분명히 선언한다. 바알이 날씨를 조정하는 것이 아니라, 이스라엘의 하나님 여호와께서 비와 번개와 바람과 안개를 조정하신다. 6절이 하나님의 사역 공간을 네 가지(하늘, 땅, 바다, 깊은 곳)로 언급한 것처럼 하나님의 날씨 조정도 안개, 비, 번개, 바람 네 가지로 언급한다. 숫자 '4'는 총체성, 포괄성을 상징한다. 하나님은 날씨를 조정하시는 유일한 분이다.

3. 이집트를 벌하심(135:8-9)

8 그가 애굽의 처음 난 자를
사람부터 짐승까지 치셨도다
9 애굽이여
여호와께서 네게 행한 표적들과 징조들을
바로와 그의 모든 신하들에게 보내셨도다

앞 섹션에서 세상을 자유자재로 조정하시는 창조주 여호와의 능력을 찬양한 기자가 하나님과 그의 특별한 소유인 이스라엘의 관계를 생각해 본다. 여호와와 이스라엘의 관계를 생각하면 절대 빠질 수 없는 것이 출애굽 사건이다. 이스라엘에게 여호와의 능력을 가장 인상적으로 나타내신 일이기 때문이다.

하나님이 이집트에게 이스라엘을 내보내라고 하실 때, 그들은 순순히 말을 듣지 않았다. 엄청난 손실이 우려되었기 때문이다. 그러므로 하나님은 이집트가 이스라엘을 스스로 내보낼 때까지 온갖 재앙으로 치셨다. 열 번째 재앙이 이집트 사람들과 짐승들의 장자들을 모두 죽이고 나서야 이스라엘은 이집트를 떠날 수 있었다.

기자는 그 역사적인 순간을 회상하면서 그 열 번째 재앙을 떠올린다(8절). 열 재앙의 절정이었고, 가장 두려운 재앙이었으며 이 일이 있은 후에 바로가 곧바로 이스라엘을 내보냈기 때문이다. 이집트 사람과 짐승의 장자들을 모두 죽인 일은 하나님이 그들에게 보내신 '표적'(אֹתוֹת)이자 '징조'(מוֹפֵת)이다(9절, cf. 신 6:22; 26:8; 29:2). 세상을 자기 마음대로 조정하시는 여호와께서 행하신 기적이라는 뜻이다. 또한 이집트 왕 바로와 그의 신하들에게 보내신 일이기도 하다. 창조주께서 그들에게 보내신 일이라는 것은 언제든지 다시 보내실 수 있다는 경고성을 포함하고 있다. 하나님은 언제든 자기 백성을 위하여 열방에 재앙을 보내실 수 있는 분이다. 그러므로 열방은 주의 백성을 억압하지 않도록 주의해야 한다.

4. 가나안을 정복하심(135:10-12)

10 그가 많은 나라를 치시고
강한 왕들을 죽이셨나니
11 곧 아모리인의 왕 시혼과 바산 왕 옥과
가나안의 모든 국왕이로다

[12] 그들의 땅을 기업으로 주시되
자기 백성 이스라엘에게 기업으로 주셨도다

하나님의 이스라엘을 위한 사역은 그들이 자유의 몸으로 이집트를 탈출하게 하신 일로 끝나지 않았다. 이 시편은 생략하고 있지만, 시내 산으로 데리고 가 그곳에서 자기 백성으로 삼으셨다. 이어 가나안을 정복하셨다. 오래전에 그들의 조상 아브라함과 이삭과 야곱과 하신 약속, 곧 그들의 후손들이 큰 민족이 되어 이집트를 떠날 때쯤 그들에게 가나안 땅을 주시겠다고 하신 약속을 지키기 위해서였다.

여호와께서는 가나안을 이스라엘에게 기업으로 주시기 위해 여러 나라를 치시고 수많은 가나안 왕을 죽이셨다(10절). 그들은 모두 이스라엘보다 강한 상대들이어서 하나님이 돕지 않으시면 이길 수 없었다. 모세는 이스라엘이 요단 강을 건너기 전에 먼저 싸움을 걸어온 시혼과 바산 왕 옥을 죽였다(민 21:21-35; 신 2:26-3:11; 시 136:17-20). 여호수아는 이스라엘이 요단 강을 건넌 후에 31명의 가나안 왕들을 죽였다(11b절, cf. 수 12:7-24). 기자는 이 사건들을 회고하면서 모세와 여호수아가 아니라 하나님이 그들을 죽이셨다고 한다(11절). 하나님이 모세와 여호수아를 통해 그들을 죽이신 것이다.

하나님은 이렇게 해서 가나안 땅을 정복하신 후 자기 백성 이스라엘에게 기업으로 주셨다(12절). 이 일로 여호와의 명성은 더없이 높아졌다(McCann). 가나안 땅은 하나님이 이스라엘에게 주신 선물임을 암시한다. '기업'(נַחֲלָה)은 자손 대대로 대물릴 유산이라는 뜻이다. 기자는 하나님이 자기 백성을 위해 하신 놀라운 일들을 회고하면서 출애굽과 가나안 정착만을 언급한다. 중간 단계인 시내 산 언약과 광야 40년 동안 보살펴 주신 일은 생략하고 있다. 출애굽 여정의 시작과 끝만 회고하고자 했기 때문이다.

5. 백성을 보살피심(135:13-14)

13 여호와여
주의 이름이 영원하시니이다
여호와여
주를 기념함이 대대에 이르리이다
14 여호와께서 자기 백성을 판단하시며
그의 종들로 말미암아 위로를 받으시리로다

자기 백성에게 큰 은총을 베푸신 여호와의 이름은 영원히 기억될 것이다(13b절). 이 말씀에서 '이름'은 명성(fame)을 의미한다(Anderson). 하나님의 명성은 영원히 기념될 것이다. 주의 백성이 대대로 주님의 이름을 묵상할 것이기 때문이다(13d절). 은혜를 입은 사람이 은혜를 베푼 이를 두고두고 기념하는 것은 당연하다. 이와 같이 하나님의 은혜를 입은 주의 백성은 두고두고 하나님의 이름을 기념하고 기억해야 한다.

우리가 기념해야 하는 것은 주님이 이때까지 내려 주신 은총만은 아니다. 장차 오셔서 행하실 일도 기대해야 한다(14절). 여호와께서 언젠가는 자기 백성을 판단해 주실 것이다. '판단하다'(דין)는 변호하다는 뜻이다(HALOT). 개역개정은 주님이 그의 종들로 말미암아 위로를 받으실 것이라고 하는데, '위로를 받다'(נחם)는 '위로하다/자비를 베풀다'로 해석되어야 한다(cf. 새번역, 아가페, 현대인, NIV, NAS, ESV, NRS). 하나님이 위로를 받기 위해 오시는 것이 아니라, 위로하기 위해 오시는 것이다. 그러므로 우리는 미래에 임할 하나님의 위로를 기대하며 살아야 한다.

6. 우상들의 무능함(135:15-18)

15 열국의 우상은 은 금이요
사람의 손으로 만든 것이라
16 입이 있어도 말하지 못하며
눈이 있어도 보지 못하며
17 귀가 있어도 듣지 못하며
그들의 입에는 아무 호흡도 없나니
18 그것을 만든 자와 그것을 의지하는 자가
다 그것과 같으리로다

위에서 기자는 이스라엘의 하나님 여호와는 열방의 신들과 질적으로 다르다고 선언했다(cf. 5절). 그는 이제 그 이유를 말한다. 우상들은 아무런 능력을 지니지 않은 사람들의 조각품이기 때문이다. 먼저 그는 우상의 재질을 논한다(15절). 우상은 스스로 존재하는 신이 아니라 사람이 손으로 만든 은조각이며 금조각이다. 그들에게는 생명력이 전혀 없다. 선지자들은 끊임없이 말한다. 우상들이 사람을 타락시키는 것이 아니라, 타락한 인간들이 만들어 내는 것이 우상이라는 사실을 말이다(cf. 사 2:21; 44:9-17).

저자는 우상이 가지고 있는 장기 네 가지를 지적하며 한결같이 무용지물이라고 한다(16-17절). 포괄성과 총체성의 상징인 숫자 4를 사용하여 그는 우상이 전적으로 무능한 존재라는 사실을 강조한다. 첫째, 우상은 입이 있어도 말을 못한다(16a절). 둘째, 우상은 눈이 있어도 보지 못한다(16b절). 셋째, 우상은 귀가 있어도 듣지 못한다(17a절). 넷째, 우상의 입에는 호흡이 없다(cf. 렘 10:14; 시 135:17). 생명이 없다는 뜻이다.

반면에 여호와 하나님은 입으로 말하시고, 눈으로 보시고, 귀로 들으시고, 생명력이 항상 입안에 있으신 분이다. 그러므로 사람을 만드실 때 흙으로 빚은 인간에게 호흡을 불어넣어 살게 하셨다(cf. 창 2장). 하나님은 모든 면에서 우상들과 강력한 대조를 이루신다.

우상은 아무런 능력이 없다. 인간이 만들어낸 조각품에 불과하기 때문이다. 그런데도 사람들은 자신의 손이 빚어낸 우상을 신이라 하여 숭배한다. 그들의 숭배가 우상들에게 생명을 불어넣을 수 있는가? 아니다. 우상을 만들고 신이라며 의지하는 자들은 우상들이 아무런 능력이 없기에 그 어떠한 것도 얻지 못할 것이다(18절). 우상들과 우상 숭배자들은 함께 망할 것이라는 뜻이다.

7. 시온에 계시는 여호와 찬양(135:19-21)

19 이스라엘 족속아
여호와를 송축하라
아론의 족속아
여호와를 송축하라
20 레위 족속아
여호와를 송축하라
여호와를 경외하는 너희들아
여호와를 송축하라
21 예루살렘에 계시는 여호와는
시온에서 찬송을 받으실지어다
할렐루야

기자는 이 섹션에서 '축복하다'(ברך)를 다섯 차례 사용하며 위대하신 여호와를 찬송할 것을 권면한다. 개역개정은 19-20절에서 네 차례 사용되는 이 단어를 모두 '송축하다'로 번역했다. 사람이 하나님을 축복한다는 것이 다소 부적절하다고 생각했기 때문이다. 마지막 사용이 21

절에 수동태로 등장하기 때문에 '찬송을 받다'로 번역했다. 이 섹션은 우상들과 질적으로 다르신 하나님을 찬송할 것을 강력하게(5차례) 요구한다.

여호와를 찬송하라는 명령을 받은 사람들은 '이스라엘 족속—아론 족속—레위 족속—여호와를 경외하는 자들' 네 부류이다(cf. Brueggemann & Bellinger). 온 이스라엘이 제일 먼저 언급되는 것으로 보아 '여호와를 경외하는 자들'(יִרְאֵי יְהוָה)은 이방인 개종자들(proselytes)을 의미하는 것으로 보인다(cf. Grogan, Hossfeld-Zenger). 하나님을 경배하고 찬양하는 특권이 이스라엘 사람들과 그들의 종교 지도자들에게만 제한된 것이 아니라, 세상 만민 중 여호와를 경외하는 모든 사람에게 주어졌다는 것이다. 이런 면에서 이 시편은 종말론적인 비전을 나타내고 있다. 언젠가는 이방인 성도들도 주를 마음껏 경배하는 때가 올 것임을 암시한다.

제136편

I. 장르/양식: 회중 찬양시(cf. 29편)

이 시편은 '위대한 찬양시'(Great Hallel psalms, 120–136편) 모음집의 마지막 노래이다. 탈무드 등 일부 유태인 전승은 이 노래가 유일한 '위대한 찬양시'라고 하기도 한다(cf. Ross). 공동체 찬양시로서 신년 축제나 장막절 때 불렸을 가능성이 있지만(Ross), 유월절 절기와 연관된 노래라는 것이 다수의 의견이다(cf. Goldingay, VanGemeren). 특히 이 시편이 하나님의 사역에 대한 역사적 회고(historical recital)라는 점을 감안하면 (Brueggemann & Bellinger) 하나님의 특별한 사역을 기념하는 유월절과 밀접한 연관이 있었을 것으로 생각된다.

135편과 136편은 매우 밀접하게 연관되어 있다 하여 이 두 시편을 '찬양 파트너들'(partners in praise)이라 하기도 한다(Mays, cf. McCann). 공동체 찬양시인 이 노래는 구성이 교창적(antiphonal hymn)이다(Allen, Grogan, Ross, cf. McCann). 우리 예배에서는 인도자와 회중이 번갈아 가며 한 소절씩 읽는 교독문 낭독에 가장 가깝다.

저작 시기는 포로기 이후가 많은 학자들의 추측이다(Terrien). 이 노래가 처음으로 불린 때는 귀향민들이 예루살렘에 도착했을 때라고 하는 이들도 있다(Grogan, cf. McCann).

II. 구조

이 시편의 목적은 하나님의 여러 가지 속성을 찬양하는 일에 있다는 것이 찬양에 흔히 등장하는 분사(participle)의 지속적인 사용에서 역력히 드러난다(4–10, 13, 16–17, 25절). 또한 1–3절과 26절은 찬양하라는 권면이며 이 시편을 감싸는 괄호 역할을 한다. 중간에 있는 4–25절은 히브리어 알파벳의 숫자인 22절로 구성되어 있어 알파벳 시의 느낌을 준다(Gerstenberger, Tucker & Grant). 여호와 하나님을 포괄적으로 찬양하고 있는 노래인 것이다. 이 주석에서는 다음과 같은 분석을 바탕으로 이 시편을 주해해 나가고자 한다.

A. 위대하신 하나님(136:1–3)
  B. 창조주 하나님(136:4–9)
    C. 구원하신 하나님(136:10–15)
    C'. 기업을 주신 하나님(136:16–22)
  B'. 보호하신 하나님(136:23–25)
A'. 하늘에 계신 하나님(136:26)

III. 주해

이 시편은 여호와께서 그의 백성에게 베푸신 은총을 예로 삼아 온 세상에 내려 주시는 여러 가지 은혜에 감사하고 찬양한다. 인도자가 감사할 이유를 한 가지씩 말하면 예배자들이 '그 인자하심이 영원함이로다'로 답례하는 교독문 형식을 띄고 있다.

1. 위대하신 하나님(136:1-3)

1 여호와께 감사하라 그는 선하시며
그 인자하심이 영원함이로다
2 신들 중에 뛰어난 하나님께 감사하라
그 인자하심이 영원함이로다
3 주들 중에 뛰어난 주께 감사하라
그 인자하심이 영원함이로다

기자는 여호와께 감사하라는 말로 시 전체를 시작하며 이 노래가 무엇을 목적으로 하고 있는가를 정확히 밝힌다(1a절). 이 말씀은 하나님이 하신 일을 묵상하고 감사하기 위해 저작된 것이다. '감사하다'(ידה)의 기본적인 의미는 '찬양하다'이지만, 이 시편에서처럼 히필(hiphil)로 사용될 때에는 '고백하다, 증언하다'는 뜻이 된다(HALOT, NIDOTTE). 그러므로 일부 주석가들은 '감사하라'를 모두 '고백하라/증언하라'로 바꿀 것을 제안한다(Goldingay, Mays). 좋은 제안이지만 이 주석에서는 개역개정의 '감사하라' 혹은 '찬양하라'는 의미를 유지할 것이다. 감사와 찬양에 고백과 증언(간증)이 포함되어 있기 때문이다.

후렴으로 사용되는 "그 인자하심이 영원하리로다"에 등장하는 '그의 인자하심'(חַסְדּוֹ)은 관계적인 언어이며 언약을 맺은 자에게 충성할 것을 의미한다(Sakenfeld). 그러므로 학자들은 이 말씀을 '그의 언약적 충성'(his covenant loyalty)(Anderson) 혹은 '서약'(commitment)(Goldingay)으로 번역할 것을 제안한다. 하나님은 한번 관계를 맺으시면 그 관계에 영원히 성실하실 것이다.

기자는 하나님은 우리의 찬양을 받기에 합당하신 분이라는 것을 세 가지로 선언하며 노래를 시작한다.

첫째, 우리가 주님을 찬양할 이유는 여호와는 선하시기 때문이다(1a

절, cf. 135:3). '선하다'(טוֹב)는 하나님의 가장 기본적이자 포괄적인 속성이기도 하다. 하나님이 하시는 일은 모두 좋다. 인도자의 이 같은 선언에 회중은 "그(주님)의 인자하심이 영원하다"고 답례한다. '인자하심'(חֶסֶד)과 '영원함'(עוֹלָם)은 이미 수차례 시편에서 사용되었으며, 주님이 베푸시는 은총은 매우 특별하며, 한순간에 끝나는 것이 아니라 영원히 지속되고 반복된다는 것을 강조하는 표현이다.

둘째, 우리가 여호와를 찬양할 이유는 그분은 신들 중에 뛰어난 하나님이시기 때문이다(2절). '신들 중에 뛰어난 하나님'(אֱלֹהֵי הָאֱלֹהִים)은 '신들 중에 신'이라는 뜻이며 여호와 하나님은 세상 그 어떤 신들하고 비교할 수 없는 위대하신 분이라는 것을 선포한다. 그러므로 '모든 신들 가운데 가장 크신 하나님'(새번역) 혹은 '모든 신 위에 뛰어나신 하나님'(아가페)으로 해석된다.

셋째, 우리가 여호와를 찬양할 이유는 주님은 주들 중에 뛰어난 주이시기 때문이다(3절). '주들 중에 뛰어난 주'(אֲדֹנֵי הָאֲדֹנִים)도 '신들 중 신'과 비슷한 표현이다. 세상에는 자신을 주(인)라고 하는 이들이 많지만, 여호와께 비교될 만한 주인은 없다. 하나님은 '지극히 높으신 주님'(현대인)이시기 때문이다. 이 두 성호가 함께 사용되는 사례는 신명기 10:17이 유일하다. 신명기 10:14은 26절에서 사용되는 성호 '하늘의 하나님'도 사용한다.

기자는 주님을 찬양하라는 권면을 시작하면서 하나님의 성호 세 가지를 활용하여 주님의 특별하심을 강조한다. 주님은 자기 백성과 특별한 관계를 맺으신 여호와(יהוה)이시며, 신들 중에 신이시며(אֱלֹהֵי הָאֱלֹהִים), 주들 중에 주(אֲדֹנֵי הָאֲדֹנִים)이시다. 비교를 불허하는 참으로 위대하신 하나님이시다. 그러므로 우리가 이 놀라운 하나님의 영원한 인자하심을 찬송하고 감사하는 것은 당연한 일이다.

2. 창조주 하나님(136:4–9)

4 홀로 큰 기이한 일들을 행하시는 이에게 감사하라
그 인자하심이 영원함이로다
5 지혜로 하늘을 지으신 이에게 감사하라
그 인지하심이 영원함이로다
6 땅을 물 위에 펴신 이에게 감사하라
그 인자하심이 영원함이로다
7 큰 빛들을 지으신 이에게 감사하라
그 인자하심이 영원함이로다
8 해로 낮을 주관하게 하신 이에게 감사하라
그 인자하심이 영원함이로다
9 달과 별들로 밤을 주관하게 하신 이에게 감사하라
그 인자하심이 영원함이로다

기자는 이 섹션에서 이스라엘의 하나님 여호와가 창조주이심을 찬양하라고 권면하며 창세기 1장을 떠올리게 한다. 그는 하나님의 창조 사역을 구체적으로 논하기 전에 먼저 창조주 하나님이 어떤 분이신가를 요약적으로 선포한다. 여호와는 홀로 큰 기이한 일들을 행하시는 분이다(4절). '큰 기이한 일들'(נִפְלָאוֹת גְדֹלוֹת)은 이미 시편에서 여러 차례 하나님만이 하실 수 있는 기적의 의미로 사용되었다(cf. Hossfeld–Zenger). 하나님의 능력에는 한계가 없다는 것을 강조한다. 또한 주님이 위대한 일들을 '홀로'(בַד) 하신다. 그 누구의 도움도 받지 않으시고 수많은 기적들을 행하시는 하나님이다. 그러므로 이처럼 능력이 충만하신 하나님이 창조하신 세상은 얼마나 아름답고 놀랍겠는가! 저자는 하나님의 창조 사역에 대해 몇 가지를 지적하며 주님을 찬양한다.

첫째, 우리는 하나님이 지혜로 하늘을 지으신 일을 찬양해야 한다(5

절). 기자가 사용하는 이미지는 사람이 천막을 펼치는 일이다. 하나님이 천막을 펼치듯 하늘을 펼치신 것이다(Briggs, cf. 사 42:5; 44:24). '지혜'(תְּבוּנָה)는 이해력(understanding)과 기술(skill)을 의미한다(HALOT). 하나님은 세상을 창조하실 때 자신의 모든 통찰과 실력을 동원해 만드셨다(cf. 잠 8장). 하나님이 심혈을 기울여 만드셨기 때문에 세상은 아름답고 놀라운 곳이다. 그러므로 이 아름다운 세상에서 사는 사람들은 모두 하나님께 감사해야 한다.

둘째, 우리는 하나님이 육지와 바다를 창조하신 것에 감사해야 한다(6절). '펴다'(רקע)는 '망치로 두들겨 펼치다'는 의미를 지녔다(Anderson, Human, cf. 사 42:5; 44:24). 하나님은 육지를 바다 위에 세우실 때 단단하게 세우시기 위해 망치로 쇠덩어리를 펴듯 펼치셨다. 이는 인간이 사는 좋은 곳이 되었다. 그러나 만일 바닷물이 시시때때로 범람하여 땅을 휩쓴다면 우리는 결코 이 땅에서 살 수 없다. 그러므로 하나님은 바다와 육지의 경계선을 정하셔서 바다가 육지에 범람하지 못하도록 하셨다. 하나님은 우리가 이 땅에서 평안히 살 수 있도록 모든 여건을 마련해 주셨다. 하나님이 바다와 육지를 나누신 일도 우리가 감사해야 할 일이다.

셋째, 우리는 하나님이 큰 빛들을 지으신 것을 감사해야 한다(7-9절, cf. 창 1:16). 주님이 지으신 큰 빛들은 해와 달과 별들이다. 이것들이 있어야 계절의 순환이 가능하고, 사람이 살 수 있다. 또한 이것들은 계절과 이스라엘의 종교 절기를 주관하는 것들이기도 하다. 하나님께 예배드리는 일을 가능하게 하는 것이 바로 이 천체들이다. 그러므로 하나님이 천체들을 창조심은 공간과 물건만이 아닌 시간도 주님의 피조물임을 암시한다(Allen).

하나님이 해로 낮을 주관하게 하신 것도 감사할 이유이다(8절). 해가 있음으로 우리는 따스함을 누리고, 그 빛으로 인해 낮에 활동할 수 있기 때문이다. 해는 모든 짐승과 식물에 생명을 선사한다.

하나님이 달과 별들로 밤을 주관하게 하신 것을 감사해야 한다(9절). 어두운 밤길을 갈 때 달과 별은 우리의 벗이 되어 가는 길을 밝혀 주며, 우리가 잠든 동안에도 세상을 밝히고 지켜 준다. 그러므로 우리는 해와 달과 별들을 생각할 때마다 하나님께 감사할 이유가 생긴다. 해와 달과 별은 창조주께서 온 인류에게 내려 주신 보편적인 은혜이다.

3. 구원하신 하나님(136:10–15)

10 애굽의 장자를 치신 이에게 감사하라
그 인자하심이 영원함이로다
11 이스라엘을 그들 중에서 인도하여 내신 이에게 감사하라
그 인자하심이 영원함이로다
12 강한 손과 펴신 팔로 인도하여 내신 이에게 감사하라
그 인자하심이 영원함이로다
13 홍해를 가르신 이에게 감사하라
그 인자하심이 영원함이로다
14 이스라엘을 그 가운데로 통과하게 하신 이에게 감사하라
그 인자하심이 영원함이로다
15 바로와 그의 군대를 홍해에 엎드러뜨리신 이에게 감사하라
그 인자하심이 영원함이로다

창조주를 찬양했던 바로 앞 섹션에서 이 섹션으로 넘어오는 것은 마치 창세기 1장에서 출애굽기로 점프한 느낌을 준다(Grogan). 온 세상을 창조하신 하나님은 자기 백성을 특별히 사랑하셨다. 그래서 주님은 그들을 억압자들의 손에서 구원하셨다. 이 섹션은 하나님이 이스라엘을 이집트의 손에서 구원하신 일을 회고하며 감사한다(cf. 시 135:8–12).

첫째, 우리는 억압자들에게서 구원하시는 하나님께 감사해야 한다

(10절). 이집트는 이스라엘을 보내려 하지 않았다. 수백 년 동안 노예로 부리며 노동력을 착취하는 일에 익숙해지다 보니 이스라엘 노예가 없는 삶을 상상할 수 없었기 때문이다. 하나님은 이집트가 이스라엘을 내보낼 때까지 그들에게 온갖 재앙을 내리셨다. 드디어 열 번째 재앙이 그들과 가축들의 장자들을 치자 비로소 이스라엘을 내보냈다.

'치다'(נכה)는 전쟁에서 한쪽이 다른 쪽을 공격하는 일을 묘사한다(cf. 창 14:7, 15, 17; 36:35; 민 14:45; 신 29:6; 수 11:10-12). 하나님은 바로와 이집트를 치시기를 마치 전쟁에서 적들을 치듯이 치신 것이다(Human, cf. Hossfeld-Zenger). 결국 열 재앙을 통해 드러난 하나님의 끈질긴 사역이 이스라엘을 해방시켰다. 하나님은 우리를 절대 포기하지 않으시는 분이다.

둘째, 우리는 길을 인도하시는 하나님께 감사해야 한다(11-12절). 열 번째 재앙을 통해 모든 장자를 잃은 이집트는 큰 고통과 혼란에 빠졌다. 하나님은 엄청난 혼돈에 휩싸인 나라에서 자기 백성을 인도해 내셨다. 드디어 이스라엘이 노예의 땅을 떠날 때가 되었기 때문이다.

'인도하다'(יצא)는 출애굽 이야기에서 자주 사용되는 단어이다(cf. 출 12:17, 51). 이집트가 겪은 혼란이 매우 컸기 때문에 하나님의 리더십도 더욱더 컸다. 그러므로 기자는 하나님의 강한 손과 펴신 팔이 그들을 인도해 내셨다고 한다(12절). 하나님은 가장 혼란스러운 세상에서도 우리의 갈 길을 인도하시는 분이다.

셋째, 우리는 걸림돌을 제거하시는 하나님께 감사해야 한다(13-15절). 이스라엘이 430년만에 노예의 땅 이집트를 떠나자 마자 그들의 앞길을 막는 것이 있었다. 바로 홍해였다. 이러한 사실을 알아차린 이집트 왕 바로는 그들을 죽이려고 큰 군대를 보냈다. 진퇴양난(進退兩難)의 위기였다. 하나님은 주의 백성이 나아갈 길을 막는 홍해를 가르셨다(13절). '가르다'(גזר)는 '조각내다'는 의미를 지녔다(Human, Tucker & Grant). 하나님이 홍해를 가르신 일이 이스라엘을 삼킬 듯이 버티고 있는 괴물을 조각내신 일로 묘사되고 있다(cf. Kraus, Tucker & Grant). 그들의 여정에서 걸림돌을 제거하신 것이다.

이스라엘은 하나님이 홍해를 가르신 바닷길을 무사히 통과했다(14절, cf. 출 14:23). 홍해를 가르시고 길을 내어 주신 일도 기적이었지만, 그 깊고 넓은 바닷길을 하룻밤 사이에 그 수많은 백성이 건넌 것도 기적이었다. '홀로 기이한 일들을 행하시는'(4절) 하나님이 이런 일을 행하셨다.

그러나 이스라엘에게는 생명의 길이었던 홍해 바다의 길이 바로와 이집트 군대에게는 죽음을 안겨 주었다(15절, cf. 출 14:27). 이성을 잃은 이집트 군이 여호와께서 자기 백성을 위해 베푸신 기적을 이용하려 했다. 그들은 이스라엘을 추격하기 위해 여호와께서 홍해를 가르고 내신 길을 병거를 몰고 가다가 참변을 당했다. 모두 바닷물에 수장된 것이다. 그들이 주님이 자기 백성을 구원하기 위해 내신 길을 이용하려 든 것은 참으로 어리석은 생각이었고, 그들은 혹독한 대가를 치렀다.

4. 기업을 주신 하나님(136:16-22)

16 그의 백성을 인도하여 광야를 통과하게 하신 이에게 감사하라
그 인자하심이 영원함이로다
17 큰 왕들을 치신 이에게 감사하라
그 인자하심이 영원함이로다
18 유명한 왕들을 죽이신 이에게 감사하라
그 인자하심이 영원함이로다
19 아모리인의 왕 시혼을 죽이신 이에게 감사하라
그 인자하심이 영원함이로다
20 바산 왕 옥을 죽이신 이에게 감사하라
그 인자하심이 영원함이로다

21 그들의 땅을 기업으로 주신 이에게 감사하라
그 인자하심이 영원함이로다
22 곧 그 종 이스라엘에게 기업으로 주신 이에게 감사하라
그 인자하심이 영원함이로다

하나님은 혹독한 노예 생활에서 자기 백성을 해방시키셨고, 그들의 길을 막는 홍해를 갈라 길을 내셨다. 더 나아가 큰 왕들이 다스리던 가나안 땅에서 왕들을 내치시고 그들의 땅을 빼앗아 자기 백성에게 주셨다. 이 섹션은 이스라엘의 광야 여정과 가나안 정착을 기념하며 주님께 감사할 것을 주문한다.

첫째, 우리는 생명을 위협하는 곳을 무사히 통과하게 하시는 하나님께 감사해야 한다(16절). 홍해를 건넌 이스라엘은 광야를 걸어 시내 산으로 갔다. 그곳에서 1년을 머물며 율법을 받은 후에 다시 광야를 걸어 가데스 바네아로 갔다. 안타깝게도 그곳에서 큰 죄를 저질러 벌로 38년을 더 광야에 머물렀다. 음식과 물이 없는 광야에서 그들이 유일하게 살 수 있는 길은 하나님이 매일 행하시는 기적이었다. 기자는 자세한 과정을 생략하고 하나님이 그들의 생명을 위협하는 광야를 무사히 통과하게 하신 일을 감사하라고 한다(cf. 신 8:15). 주님은 오늘날도 광야를 가는 길과 같은 우리의 삶에서 우리를 보호하시고 인도하신다.

둘째, 우리는 자기 백성을 살리기 위해 세상 권력을 치신 하나님께 감사해야 한다(17-20절). 하나님은 이스라엘의 앞길을 막고 방해하는 자들을 용납하지 않으셨다. 방해자들이 큰 권력을 가진 왕들이라도 예외는 아니었다. 가나안 정복에 나선 여호수아와 이스라엘은 31명의 왕을 죽였다(수 12:7-24). 여기에 요단 강 동편에서 죽인 시혼과 옥을 더하면 33명이 된다.

기자는 그 일을 되돌아보면서 하나님이 이 왕들을 치셨다고 한다(17절). 그는 이 왕들을 '큰 왕들'이고 '유명한 왕들'이라고 한다(17-18절).

'크다'(גָּדוֹל)는 것은 위대함을, '유명한'(אַדִּיר)은 유능하다는 의미를 지녔다(NIDOTTE). 그들은 이스라엘이 자력으로는 결코 이길 수 없는 권력자들이었음을 암시한다. 하나님이 자기 백성을 위해 그들을 죽이신 것이다. 앞으로도 하나님은 자기 백성을 해하거나 방해하는 모든 권세를 제거하실 것이다(Tucker & Grant).

저자는 하나님이 죽이신 33명의 왕들 중 시혼과 옥을 본보기로 언급한다(19-20절). 이 왕들이 따로 언급되는 것은 이 왕들이 죽게 된 과정이 성경에 가장 잘 기록되어 있기 때문이다(cf. 민 21장). 또한 이 두 왕은 이스라엘의 화평을 받아들이지 않고 스스로 이스라엘을 치러 나온 왕들이다. 그러므로 기자는 이 두 사람을 언급하여 누구든 하나님의 백성을 해하려고 하는 자들은 가장 큰 권력을 가진 왕이라 할지라도 온전하지 못할 것을 경고한다. 하나님이 그들을 치실 것이기 때문이다.

셋째, 우리는 기업을 주신 하나님께 감사해야 한다(21-22절). 하나님은 그 수많은 왕들을 죽이시고 그들의 땅을 자기 백성에게 기업으로 주셨다. '기업'(נַחֲלָה)은 유산을 의미한다. 하나님은 가나안을 이스라엘에게 영원히 경작하고 살도록 기업으로 주신 것이다. 여호수아서에 의하면 이스라엘 사람들이 전쟁을 해서 땅을 쟁취했는데, 기자는 사실 하나님이 그들에게 그 땅을 선물(유산)로 주셨다고 한다. 모든 것이 하나님의 은혜인 것이다.

5. 보호하신 하나님(136:23-25)

23 우리를 비천한 가운데에서도 기억해 주신 이에게 감사하라
그 인자하심이 영원함이로다
24 우리를 우리의 대적에게서 건지신 이에게 감사하라
그 인자하심이 영원함이로다

[25] 모든 육체에게 먹을 것을 주신 이에게 감사하라
그 인자하심이 영원함이로다

기자는 이 모든 일을 되돌아보며 하나님이 자기 백성을 위해 하신 일을 요약한다.

첫째, 하나님이 비천한 우리를 기억해 주심을 감사해야 한다(23절). '비천하다'(שֵׁפֶל)는 전혀 보잘것없다는 의미를 지녔다(NIDOTTE). 주의 백성은 하나님이 구원하실 만한 가치나 존귀함을 지닌 사람들이 아니다. 그런데도 하나님은 그들을 기억하셨다. 성경에서 하나님이 기억하시는(זכר) 것은 흔히 구원으로 연결된다. 하나님이 구원하실 가치가 없는 사람들을 원수들에게서 구원하셨기에(24절) 구원을 입은 사람들은 하나님의 놀라운 구원을 감사하고 찬양해야 한다. 하나님이 우리를 구원하실 때에는 자격을 따지지 않고 구원하신다.

둘째, 하나님이 우리를 보호하심을 감사해야 한다(25절). 하나님은 자신이 창조하신 모든 피조물을 먹이시고 보살펴 주신다. 우리가 먹는 음식도 모두 하나님이 주신 것이고, 우리가 마시는 물도 하나님이 주셨다. 주님은 구원만 하신 것이 아니라, 우리의 일상도 보호하시고 필요를 모두 채우신다. 하나님의 '인자하심'(חֶסֶד)에는 우리의 일상에 대한 배려도 포함되어 있는 것이다(Mays). 그러므로 이처럼 자상하고 은혜로운 하나님을 우리가 어찌 찬양하지 않겠는가!

6. 하늘에 계신 하나님(136:26)

[26] 하늘의 하나님께 감사하라
그 인자하심이 영원함이로다

이때까지 매 절에서 하나님께 감사하라며 여러 가지 이유를 주었던 기자가 한 번 더 총체적으로 하나님께 감사하라는 권면으로 노래를 마무리한다. 그는 이 노래를 시작하는 2-3절에서 하나님을 '신들의 신'과 '주들의 주'라고 불렀다. 노래를 마무리하며 그는 '하늘의 하나님'(אֵל הַשָּׁמָיִם)이라는 성호를 추가하고 있다. 시편에서 이 성호가 사용되는 사례는 이곳이 유일하며 포로기 이후에 사용되는 표현이다(Harman, cf. 스 1:2; 느 1:4). 우리가 생각하고 묵상하면 주님께 감사할 이유는 무궁무진하다. 그러므로 우리는 항상 감사하면서 살아야 한다. 하나님의 인자하심이 우리의 삶의 모든 영역에 배어 있으므로 우리는 항상 하나님만 의지하며 살아야 한다(Human, McCann).

제137편

I. 장르/양식: 회중 탄식시(cf. 12편)

이 시편을 분석해 보면 탄식시(1-4절)와 시온의 노래(5-6절)와 저주시(7-9절)가 섞여 있는 듯하다. 그러므로 학자들은 이 시를 공동체 탄식시(Anderson, deClaissé-Walford et al., Ross) 혹은 '수정된 시온의 노래'(modified song of Zion)(Allen) 혹은 '심판 신탁이 포함된 국가적 탄식시'(Ogden) 혹은 저주시(imprecatory psalm)라고 한다(VanGemeren). 다른 학자들은 원래 시온의 노래는 기쁨과 찬양으로 부르는 노래인데, 이 시는 시온을 노래하면서도 슬픔과 침묵(찬양을 상징하는 수금을 나뭇가지에 걸어 둠, 2절)이 중심을 이룬다 하여 '뒤집어진 시온의 노래'(inverted version of a Zion psalm)라고 하고(Goldingay), '시온의 노래를 예루살렘 탄식으로 바꿔 놓은 노래'라고도 한다(Berlin, cf. Brueggemann & Bellinger).

이 시편이 저작된 장소를 논할 때 학자들은 '그곳'(שָׁם)(1, 3절)과 '그 중'(בְּתוֹכָהּ)(2절)에 큰 의미를 부여한다. 1-3절은 모두 바빌론에서 벌어진 일이며, '그곳'에서 있었던 일이다. 그러나 '이곳'에 있는 기자는 '그곳'(바빌론)에 있지 않다. 그러므로 그는 바빌론이 망한 후 다른 곳(예루살렘)에서 이 노래를 부르고 있다(Goldingay, Hossfeld-Zenger).

시편은 역사적 정황을 언급하지 않는 것이 보편적인데, 이 시편은 매우 예외적이다. 본문이 예루살렘 멸망과 바빌론의 건재함을 전제하기 때문에 많은 학자들이 이 시편은 주전 598–539년 사이에 바빌론에서 저작된 것이라 한다(deClaissé–Walford et al., Kraus, Ross, Seybold, cf. Terrien). 바빌론 포로생활이 끝난 직후를 저작 시기로 지목하는 이들도 있다(Anderson, Goldingay, McCann, VanGemeren, cf. Kellermann).

II. 구조

이 시편은 탄식시(1–4절)와 시온의 노래(5–6절)와 저주시(7–9절)로 구성되어 있다. 그러므로 이 주석에서는 다음과 같은 구조를 바탕으로 본문을 주해해 나가고자 한다.

A. 시온을 잃은 백성의 탄식(137:1–4)
B. 예루살렘은 영원하리(137:5–6)
C. 파괴한자들에 대한 저주(137:7–9)

III. 주해

바빌론으로 끌려온 유다 사람들은 조국으로 돌아갈 날을 꿈꾸며 살았다. 그러나 그날은 쉽게 오지 않았고, 사람들은 점점 더 지쳐만 갔다. 그러다가 예루살렘이 함락되었다는 소식이 들려왔다(7절). 탄식과 분노로 가득찬 그들은 절대 예루살렘을 잊지 않을 것을 다짐하며, 여호와께 그들의 조국을 파괴한 자들에게 저주를 내리실 것을 간절히 기도한다.

1. 시온을 잃은 백성의 탄식(137:1–4)

1 우리가 바벨론의 여러 강변 거기에 앉아서

시온을 기억하며 울었도다
[2] 그 중의 버드나무에
우리가 우리의 수금을 걸었나니
[3] 이는 우리를 사로잡은 자가 거기서
우리에게 노래를 청하며
우리를 황폐하게 한 자가
기쁨을 청하고 자기들을 위하여
시온의 노래 중 하나를 노래하라 함이로다
[4] 우리가 이방 땅에서
어찌 여호와의 노래를 부를까

이 노래를 부른 기자는 아마도 주전 538년에 스룹바벨이 인도한 제1차 귀향민들과 함께 예루살렘으로 돌아온 사람이었을 것이다. 그는 유다 사람들이 바빌론 여러 강변에 앉아 눈물을 흘렸던 일을 회상한다(1절). 본문에서 '앉았다'(ישב)는 망연자실하여 땅바닥에 주저앉은 모습을 묘사한다(Briggs). 그때 기자도 포로가 되어 '거기'(שָׁם)에 있었다(1, 3절, cf. deClaissé-Walford et al., Mays). 이 섹션에서는 1인칭 복수접미사(נוּ-)가 9차례 사용되며 극에 달한 슬픔과 바빌론에 끌려온 모든 유다 사람들의 슬픔을 묘사하고 있다(Allen).

그들이 흘린 눈물이 빈곤과 굶주림에서 비롯된 것은 아니었다. 바빌론은 유프라테스 강과 티그리스 강이 합해지는 곳에 위치했으며, 이 강들의 물을 이용한 수많은 수로가 뻗어 있었다. 그러므로 기자도 이 수로들을 떠올리며 바빌론의 '여러 강변'(עַל נַהֲרוֹת)에 앉아 있는 주의 백성을 회상한다(1절). 이 수로들로 인해 바빌론은 농사짓기에 매우 적합했으므로 참으로 풍요로운 곳이었다. 이스라엘 사람들도 샛강(수로) 중 하나인 그발 강가에 정착하고 살았다(겔 1:1; 3:15). 유다 사람들은 조국에서 보다 바빌론에서 더 큰 풍요를 누렸다(Bar-Efrat, cf. VanGemeren).

예레미야는 이 실향민들에게 마음을 가다듬고 바빌론에 정착하여 바빌론의 평화와 안정을 위하여 기도하며 평안히 살 것을 권했다(렘 29:4-9). 선지자가 편지를 보낸 때부터 하나님이 그들을 다시 조국으로 데리고 오실 때까지 많은 세월이 지나야 했기 때문이다. 선지자의 이 같은 편지를 받았다 해서 조국에 대한 그리움이 지워지지는 않았다. 실향민들은 망해버린 조국(cf. 7절), 돌아갈 수 없는 조국에 대한 향수에 젖어, 하나님이 계시는 시온을 그리워하며 눈물을 흘렸다. 시온은 완전히 메마른 곳이고 바빌론은 물이 많은 곳인데 조국을 잃은 슬픔으로 물이 많은 바빌론에서 메마른 시온을 생각하고 눈물을 흘리는 것이 매우 인상적인 대조를 이루고 있다(Bar-Efrat). 아마도 시온하고 전혀 다른 바빌론의 지형이 시온을 더욱더 생각나게 했을 것이다(McCann).

유다 사람들은 수금을 강변에 있는 버드나무에 걸었다(2절). 조국이 망해 사라진 일로 가뜩이나 슬퍼 노래할 수가 없는데, 바빌론 사람들은 유다 사람들에게 시온의 노래 중 하나를 해보라고 청했기 때문이다(3절). '우리를 사로잡은 자들'(שׁוֹבֵינוּ)은 정치적—군사적 억압이 함축된 개념이다(cf. 왕상 5:2; 렘 41:10, 14; 대상 5:21; 대하 6:36). 또한 '우리를 황폐하게 한 자들'(תוֹלָלֵינוּ)은 성경에서 이곳에 단 한 번 사용되는 단어이며, '통곡하게 하는 자'라는 의미를 지녔다(Hossfeld-Zenger, cf. Allen). 이 두 개념은 전쟁에 패해 다른 나라의 억압을 받고 사는 사람들의 애환을 잘 표현하고 있다(Becking).

승자인 바빌론 사람들은 패자인 유다 사람들에게 시온의 노래를 해보라고 하는 것이 당연한 일이라고 생각했을 것이다. 그러나 조국을 잃고 포로로 끌려와 바빌론에 정착해 사는 유다 사람들에게는 상처가 되는 일이었으므로 그들의 요구를 즐거운 마음으로 받아들일 수는 없었다. 게다가 바빌론 사람들의 요구는 '너희 하나님(신)은 어디에 있냐?'는 비아냥을 내포하고 있다(Goldingay, McCann, cf. 시 42:3, 10; 79:10; 115:2). 수금은 축제 등 좋은 일을 기념하는 행사에서 자주 사용된 음악

기구이다(cf. 느 12:27; 욥 21:12; 시 98:5; 147:7).

그러므로 어찌 바빌론 사람들의 요구에 따라 시온의 노래를 부를 수 있으랴!(4절) 더욱이 바빌론은 이방 땅이고, 시온의 노래는 그들의 하나님 여호와의 위대하심과 능력을 찬양하는 노래가 아닌가!(cf. 시 46, 48, 76, 84, 87, 122편). '이방 땅'(אַדְמַת נֵכָר)에서 '이방'(נֵכָר)은 지리적인 것뿐만 아니라 영적인 괴리감을 의미한다(Tucker & Grant, cf. 창 35:2; 35:4; 신 31:16; 32:12; 수 24:20, 23; 삿 10:16; 삼상 7:3; 렘 5:19; 8:19; 말 2:11). 시온의 노래는 바빌론같이 천박하고 영적으로 황폐한 이방 땅에서 부르기에는 너무 거룩하다는 것이 포로민들의 생각이었다(Anderson, cf. Hossfeld-Zenger, McCann). 게다가 바빌론 사람들은 빈정거리며 이런 요구를 하고 있다(cf. 시 42:3, 10; 79:10; 115:2). 그러므로 억압자들의 땅에서는 아예 노래를 부르지 않으려고 수금을 버드나무에 걸었다. 절대 노래하지 않겠다는 의지의 표현이다. 기자는 이미 바빌론을 떠나 조국으로 돌아와 있다. 그러므로 그는 그때 그곳에서 있었던 일을 이렇게 회고하고 있다.

2. 예루살렘은 영원하리(137:5-6)

5 예루살렘아
내가 너를 잊을진대
내 오른손이 그의 재주를 잊을지로다
6 내가 예루살렘을 기억하지 아니 하거나
내가 가장 즐거워하는 것 보다 더 즐거워하지 아니할진대
내 혀가 내 입천장에 붙을지로다

바빌론에서는 다시는 시온의 노래를 부르지 않겠다고 다짐한 포로민들은 예루살렘을 절대 잊지 않고 영원히 기억할 것도 다짐했다. 또한 이 다짐은 예루살렘으로 돌아온 현실에서도 유효한 다짐이다(Tucker & Grant). 하나님을 사랑하는 것은 곧 시온을 사랑하는 것이고, 시온을 기억하는 것은 곧 하나님을 기억하는 것이었기 때문이다(VanGemeren). 그들은 자신들에게 저주를 내렸다. 만일 그들이 예루살렘을 잊는다면, 그들의 오른손도 모든 재주를 잊게 될 것이라고 했다(5절). 마소라 사본은 단순히 '내 오른손이 잊을 것'(תִּשְׁכַּח יְמִינִי)이라 한다.

무엇을 잊는다는 말인가? 그러므로 개역개정은 '재주'를 더하여 번역했다. 새번역은 "내 오른손아, 너는 말라비틀어져 버려라"라며 이 말씀이 저자의 자신에 대한 저주인 것을 확실하게 표현한다. 또한 오른손이 잊는 것이 마치 풍을 맞아 손을 쓰지 못하게 되는 사람처럼 될 것을 의미하는 것으로 해석했다. 오른손이 재주를 잃는 것은 수금을 타지 못하게 되는 일도 포함되어 있다(Weiser).

포로민들이 스스로 저주를 내리는 상황이 두 가지가 더 있다(6절). 첫째 상황은 예루살렘을 기억하지 않는 것이다. 세월이 지나며 예루살렘을 점점 기억 속에서 지우는 것을 의미한다. 그러므로 그들은 죽는 순간까지 절대 예루살렘을 기억하지 않는 일은 없을 것이라 한다. 둘째 상황은 자신들이 가장 즐거워하는 것보다 예루살렘을 덜 즐거워하는 것이다. 그들이 좋은 일을 떠올릴 때 예루살렘은 항상 가장 큰 기쁨을 줄 것이다. 만일 이 두 가지 다짐 중 하나라도 실현되지 않으면, 그들은 자신들의 혀가 입천장에 붙어버리라는 저주를 자신들에게 내렸다(cf. 애 4:4; 겔 3:26). 아예 말을 하지 못하게 되기를 바란다는 저주이다(cf. Bar-Efrat, Hossfeld-Zenger). 망한 조국을 떠나 사는 실향민들의 한 맺힌 다짐이었다.

3. 파괴한자들에 대한 저주(137:7-9)

7 여호와여

예루살렘이 멸망하던 날을 기억하시고
에돔 자손을 치소서
그들의 말이 헐어 버리라 헐어 버리라
그 기초까지 헐어 버리라 하였나이다
8 멸망한 딸 바벨론아
네가 우리에게 행한 대로
네게 갚는 자가 복이 있으리로다
9 네 어린 것들을
바위에 메어치는 자는 복이 있으리로다

이 섹션은 예루살렘이 바빌론 군에게 함락되던 날을 회상한다. 개역개정은 '예루살렘이 멸망하던 날'로 번역하고 있지만(7절), 마소라 사본은 '예루살렘의 날'(יוֹם יְרוּשָׁלָם)로 되어 있다. 그러나 나머지 부분을 감안하면, 이 '예루살렘의 날'은 바로 그 도성이 함락되던 날이 확실하다(cf. 새번역, 아가페, 현대인, NIV, NRS, TNK).

기록에 의하면 바빌론이 예루살렘을 정복했다. 그런데 기자는 왜 그 날에 있었던 일을 근거로 하나님께 에돔을 치라고 기도하는가?(7절) 예루살렘이 함락될 때 에돔 사람들이 앞장서서 바빌론 사람들을 도왔기 때문이다(cf. 애 4:21; 겔 25:12-14; 35:5-15). 그들은 유다를 항상 숙적으로 생각했으므로 바빌론이 예루살렘을 공략할 때, 가장 앞에서 성을 공격했다. 그들은 '헐어 버리라'(עָרָה)라고 외쳤는데, 이 동사는 사람의 옷을 완전히 벗기는 일을 묘사한다(Goldingay, cf. 레 20:19; 사 3:17; 애 4:21). 또한 바빌론 사람들에게 예루살렘을 '그 기초까지'(הַיְסוֹד בָּהּ) 헐어 버리라고 했다고 하는데, 이 단어(יְסוֹד)는 단순히 성을 무너뜨리라는 것이 아니라, 하나님이 세우신 나라인 유다의 근간을 아예 없애 버리라는 뜻을 지녔다(VanGemeren). 에돔 사람들은 이 두 단어를 사용해 유다의 치부를 드러내고 다시는 나라로 서지 못하도록 하라고 한 것이다.

다른 나라도 아니고 에돔이 이렇게 행한 것은 심각한 도덕적 문제를 지닌다. 에돔은 이스라엘의 유일한 형제 나라였기 때문이다. 에돔의 조상 에서는 야곱의 쌍둥이 형이었다. 그러므로 유다 사람들이 에돔에 대해 큰 배신감을 느낀 것은 당연한 일이다.

기자는 또한 유다의 숨통을 끊어 놓은 바빌론도 숨통이 끊기기를 기도한다(8절). 개역개정은 바빌론이 이미 멸망한 것으로 번역했지만, 대부분 번역본들은 앞으로 바빌론이 멸망할 것으로 번역한다(cf. 새번역, 아가페, 현대인, ESV, NIV, NAS, NRS). 예루살렘으로 돌아와 있는 기자는 이미 바빌론의 멸망을 목격한 사람이지만, 이 시는 바빌론에서 억압된 삶을 살고 있던 유다 사람들의 감정을 묘사하고 있다. 바빌론에서 바빌론 사람들의 억압을 받으며 살던 사람들의 입장에서 바빌론은 머지않아 망해야 할 권력이다. 그러므로 미래형 '멸망할 바빌론'으로 번역하는 것이 옳다. 세월이 지나며 바빌론과 에돔은 주의 백성을 괴롭히는 나라들의 상징이 되었다(Goldingay).

이 시편은 바빌론의 어린 아이들을 바위 위에다 메어치는 자는 복이 있다는 말로 마무리된다(9절). 가장 혹독한 저주이며 두 가지 의미를 지녔다.

첫째, 아이들이 없는 것은 미래가 없다는 뜻이다(Brueggemann & Bellinger, McCann). 그러므로 이 말씀은 바빌론이 완전히 망해 다시는 부활하지 못하도록 아이들까지 없애 버리라는 무서운 저주이다. 그들이 다른 민족들에게 행한 것처럼 그들도 같은 일을 경험하게 해 달라는 기도이다(McCann, Tucker & Grant).

둘째, 바빌론이 전쟁으로 멸망할 뿐만 아니라, 가장 잔혹한 일을 경험하도록 해 달라는 기도이다. 고대 근동에서는 전쟁에서 승리한 자들이 패한 자들의 남자를 모두 죽이는 만행을 저지르곤 했다(cf. Briggs, Kraus, Ogden). 그래서 남자들은 나이에 상관없이 모두 죽였고, 심지어는 임신한 여자의 배까지 갈랐다(cf. 신 32:25; 왕하 8:12; 호 14:1; 암 1:12;

나 3:10). 혹시 그 안에 남자 아이가 있을까를 염려해서이다. 이러한 과정에서 어린 아이들은 높은 곳에서 바위에 떨어뜨려 죽이기도 하고, 자루에 담아 바위에 내리쳐 죽이고는 했다(ABD). 유다 사람들은 이 잔인한 방법을 동원하여 바빌론의 아이들을 바위에 내리치는 사람은 복이 있다고 한다! 그들의 분노가 극에 달했다. 137편은 가장 사랑받는 문장으로 시작하지만, 가장 충격적인 문장으로 마무리된다(Clifford, Kirkpatrick).

제138편

다윗의 시

I. 장르/양식: 개인 찬양시(cf. 11편)

이 시편은 제5권에 속한 '다윗 모음집'(138-145편) 중 처음 노래이다. 단수와 복수가 함께 사용되고 있기 때문에 이 노래를 공동체 감사시라고 하는 이들이 있지만(Anderson, Kirkpatrick), 대부분 학자들은 개인 감사시로 구분한다(Brueggemann & Bellinger, deClaissé-Walford et al., Grogan, McCann, Ross, VanGemeren). 일부 학자들은 같은 시편에서 단수와 복수가 함께 사용되는 것은 찬양시의 소(小)장르인 감사시의 특징이라고 한다(Mowinckel, cf. Goldingay). 그러나 이 시를 왕족시라고 하는 이들도 있다(Eaton, Dahood).

대부분 학자들은 이 시를 찬양시라고 한다. 그러나 일부 학자들은 이 노래에서 사용되는 '찬양하다'(ידה)(1, 2, 4절)를 '증언하다/증거하다'로 해석하여(cf. HALOT) 간증시(psalm of testimony)로 구분할 것을 제안한다(Goldingay, Tucker & Grant, cf. deClaissé-Walford et al.). 충분한 설득력이 있는 제안이다.

이 시편의 저작 시기로는 포로기 이후로 보는 학자들이 주류를 이룬다(Anderson, Brueggemann & Bellinger, Goldingay, Kirkpatrick, Mays, McCann,

Terrien). 일부 칠십인역(LXX) 사본들은 표제에 '다윗' 대신 '학개와 스가랴' 혹은 '스가랴'를 표기한다(cf. Goldingay, Kirkpatrick, Ross). 아마도 이 노래가 포로기 이후에 예루살렘에 공동체를 다시 세운 것을 기념하는 시로 간주했기 때문에 빚어진 일일 것이다(Ross). 이 시를 왕족시라고 하는 이들은 이스라엘의 왕정 시대를 저작 시기로 본다(Eaton, Dahood).

이 시편은 다른 시편의 문장들을 인용하는 특징을 지녔다. 다음은 이 시편을 구성하고 있는 구절들과 다른 시편들의 유사성을 정리한 것이다(Goldingay, Tucker & Grant).

138편	다른 시편
1a절	9:1
2a절	5:7
4-5절	102:15
6절	113:5-6
8a절	57:2
8b절	136편 후렴

II. 구조

학자들이 제안한 것처럼 '찬양하다'(ידה)(1, 2, 4절)를 '증언하다/증거하다'로 해석하면(Goldingay, Tucker & Grant), 다음과 같은 구조가 가능하다. 그러므로 이 주석에서는 다음과 같은 구조를 바탕으로 본문을 주해해 나갈 것이다(cf. deClaissé-Walford et al.).

A. 신들 앞에서 여호와를 증거(138:1-3)

B. 세상 왕들 앞에서 여호와를 증거(138:4-6)

C. 원수들 앞에서 여호와를 증거(138:7-8)

III. 주해

기자는 하나님의 신실하심을 온 세상에 선포하고 알리고자 한다. 그는 신들 앞에서 여호와를 증거할 것이며, 왕들 앞에서도 증거할 것이다. 심지어는 그를 괴롭히는 원수들 앞에서도 하나님의 신실하심을 선언할 것이다.

1. 신들 앞에서 여호와를 증거(138:1-3)

1 내가 전심으로 주께 감사하며
신들 앞에서 주께 찬송하리이다
2 내가 주의 성전을 향하여 예배하며
주의 인자하심과 성실하심으로 말미암아 주의 이름에 감사하오리니
이는 주께서 주의 말씀을 주의 모든 이름보다 높게 하셨음이라
3 내가 간구하는 날에 주께서 응답하시고
내 영혼에 힘을 주어 나를 강하게 하셨나이다

기자는 온 마음과 정성을 다해 주님께 감사하겠다는 말로 노래를 시작한다(1a절, cf. 왕상 8:23; 시 9:1; 119:2, 10, 34, 58, 69; 렘 3:10; 24:7). 그는 이 섹션에서 하나님을 지칭하는 2인칭 인칭 대명사를 11차례 사용해 자신은 전적으로 하나님을 바라보며 주님께 말하고 있음을 강조한다(deClaissé-Walford et al.). '감사하다'(ידה)는 '찬양하다' 혹은 '선포하다/증언하다'는 의미로 해석될 수도 있다(Tucker & Grant, cf. HALOT, NIDOTTE). 그는 여호와의 능력과 자비를 경험하고 확신하는 사람이다. 그러므로 그는 세상 모든 '신들'(אֱלֹהִים) 앞에서도 오직 주님을 찬송하겠다고 다짐한다(1b절). 기자가 신들 '앞에서'(נֶגֶד) 여호와를 증거하겠다고 하는 것은 신들을 자극할 뿐만 아니라 무시하는 행위이다(cf.

McCann). 세상에 여호와 같으신 분은 없으며 다른 신들과 비교 불가능하다는 것을 지켜보는 신들에게 선포할 것이다. 또한 고대 근동에서는 신들과 나라들이 매우 밀접하게 연관되어 있었던 점을 고려하면, 기자는 여호와가 모든 신들보다 위대하신 것처럼 주의 백성도 주변 민족들보다 더 위대함을 선언하고 있었던 것이다(Tucker & Grant).

저자는 하나님이 계시는 성전을 향해 예배하겠다고 다짐한다(2a절). 기자는 모든 신들 앞에서 여호와를 찬양하는(증거하는) 당당함을 보이지만, 하나님께는 엎드려 경배하는 겸손함을 보이고 있다(Kidner). 이 말씀을 기자가 성전 뜰에서 엎드렸다는 의미로 해석하는 이들도 있지만(Ross), 솔로몬의 헌당 기도(왕상 8:46-49)에 따라 포로로 끌려간 타국(바빌론)에서 성전을 향해 기도하고 예배하는 것으로 해석할 수도 있다.

그는 주님의 이름에 감사하겠다고 한다(2b절). 성경에서 이름은 그 이름을 지닌 사람의 인격과 능력을 상징한다고 할 수 있다. 그러므로 기자가 주님의 이름에 감사한다는 것은 하나님의 모든 속성과 존재(being)에 깊이 매료되었다는 뜻이다. 그는 구체적으로 하나님의 속성 두 가지를 떠올린다. '인자하심'과 '성실하심'이다. '인자하심'(חֶסֶד)은 하나님이 자기 백성과 맺으신 관계를 근거로 그들을 선하게 대하시는 것을 의미한다(cf. Sakenfeld). '성실하심'(אֱמֶת)은 하나님의 속성 중 가장 중요한 것 중 하나로 주님은 참으로 꾸준하신 분이기에 우리의 믿음의 근거가 되신다.

기자가 하나님의 성실하심과 인자하심을 묵상하며 주님의 이름에 감사하는 이유가 2c절에 기록되어 있는데, 번역이 쉽지 않다. 그러므로 번역본들은 이 문장을 서로 다르게 번역해 놓았다. 다음은 각 번역본들이 반영한 의미를 정리해 놓은 것이다.

개역개정, 공동, NIV	하나님이 이미 선포하신 말씀을 스스로 주의 모든 이름(명성)보다 높게 하셨다.

새번역, LXX, 아가페, ESV, NRS, TNK, CSB	하나님이 자기 이름과 말씀을 세상의 모든 것들보다 높이셨다.
현대인	하나님의 이름은 이미 선포하신 말씀에서 묘사된 것처럼 참으로 위대하시다.
NAS	하나님은 이미 알려진 이름과 약속보다 훨씬 더 위대하시다.

의미적으로 볼 때 여호와는 약속하신 모든 것을 지키심으로써 이때까지 주신 모든 계시보다 자기 자신을 더 높이셨다는 의미에서 두 번째(새번역) 번역이 가장 합리적인 것으로 보인다(cf. Allen). 그러나 마소라 사본에 가장 가까운 번역은 첫 번째(개역개정) 것이다. 하나님이 자기의 모든 명예를 걸고 옛적 말씀(약속)을 꼭 지키실 것이라는 의미로 해석한다면, 첫 번째 번역을 유지하는 것이 바람직하다(cf. Kidner).

그렇다면 하나님이 자기 모든 명성보다 더 중요시 여기는 옛적 말씀(약속)은 어떤 것인가? 3절의 내용을 보면 주의 백성이 기도하면 반드시 응답하셔서 힘을 주실 것을 약속하신 것이다. 기자는 자신의 경험을 회고하고 있다. 그가 간구할 때마다 주님은 그에게 응답하셨고, 그에게 힘을 주셔서 강하게 하셨다. 그가 당면했던 모든 곤경과 역경을 견뎌내게 하셨다는 뜻이다.

2. 세상 왕들 앞에서 여호와를 증거(138:4–6)

4 여호와여
세상의 모든 왕들이 주께 감사할 것은
그들이 주의 입의 말씀을 들음이오며
5 그들이 여호와의 도를 노래할 것은
여호와의 영광이 크심이니이다
6 여호와께서는 높이 계셔도 낮은 자를 굽어살피시며
멀리서도 교만한 자를 아심이니이다

NIV는 4-5절을 기원(wish)으로 간주하여 '세상의 모든 왕들이 주께 감사하게 될 것을 바란다'는 의미로 번역했다(cf. 아가페). 별로 설득력이 있는 번역은 아니다. 다른 번역본들처럼 단순한 선언문으로 번역하는 것이 바람직하다. 신들 앞에서 여호와를 찬양한 기자가 이제는 그 신들을 숭배하는 왕들에게 이스라엘의 하나님을 찬양할 것을 선언한다.

세상의 왕들이 하나님의 놀라운 말씀을 듣고는 감사한다(4절). '감사하다'(ידה)는 1절에서처럼 '증거하다'로 번역될 수 있다(cf. HALOT). 이때까지 그들은 주님의 말씀처럼 선하고 인자한 것을 경험해 보지 못했기 때문이다. 그러므로 그들은 새로이 경험하게 된 하나님의 말씀에 참으로 감격한다.

왕들이 말씀을 들으니 하나님이 어떤 분이신가를 확실히 깨닫는다. 그러므로 그들은 하나님의 '도'(ways)를 노래할 것이다(5절). '여호와의 도'(דַּרְכֵי יְהוָה)는 하나님이 삶에서 실천하시는 기준을 뜻한다. 주님은 참으로 모든 면에서 완벽하고 사랑이 넘치는 삶을 사심으로 이런 하나님(신)에 대하여 들어 보지 못했던 왕들이 참으로 큰(위대하신) 주님의 영광에 매료되어 여호와를 찬양한다(cf. Allen).

기자는 하나님의 여러 가지 기준 중에 한 가지를 예로 제시한다. 하나님은 겸손한 자와 교만한 자를 구분하시는 분이다(6절). 가장 높은 곳에 계시면서도 가장 낮은 자를 굽어살피시고, 가장 먼 곳에 계시면서도 교만한 자를 알아보신다. 하나님은 분명 겸손한 자들을 축복하시고, 교만한 자들을 벌하실 것이라는 의미를 함축하고 있다. 그러므로 왕들은 여호와는 가까운 곳도 보지 못하는 우상들과 참으로 다르다는 사실을 깨닫을 것이다.

3. 원수들 앞에서 여호와를 증거(138:7-8)

7 내가 환난 중에 다닐지라도 주께서 나를 살아나게 하시고

주의 손을 펴사 내 원수들의 분노를 막으시며
주의 오른손이 나를 구원하시리이다
8 여호와께서 나를 위하여 보상해 주시리이다
여호와여
주의 인자하심이 영원하오니
주의 손으로 지으신 것을 버리지 마옵소서

기자는 하나님은 낮은 자들은 굽어살피시지만, 교만한 자들은 심판하시는 분이라고 했다(6절). 그러므로 그는 원수들을 두려워하지 않는다. 그는 삶에서 환난으로 인해 낮아지기도 하지만, 그때마다 주께서 그를 살게 하실 것이기 때문이다(7a절, cf. 시 119:25; 143:11). 또한 교만한 원수들에게는 손을 펴시어 그들의 분노를 막으신다(7b절). 그들이 낮은 자를 해하지 못하도록 하신다는 뜻이다. 그러므로 저자는 주님이 능력의 상징인 그의 오른손을 내밀어 그를 붙잡고 구원하실 것을 확신한다(7c절, cf. 시 60:5; 139:10).

기자가 하나님이 원수들의 분노에서 그를 구원하실 것을 확신하는 것은 주님이 그를 보상해 주실 것이라는 믿음이 있기 때문이다(8a절). '보상하다'(גמר)는 '목적을 달성하다'는 의미도 지니고 있다(cf. HALOT, NIDOTTE). 그러므로 많은 번역본들이 이 문장을 '여호와는 나를 위해 주의 목적을 이루실 것이다'로 번역한다(아가페, 현대인, ESV, NAS, NRS, CSB, cf. VanGemeren). 주님이 끝까지 우리와 함께 하시면서 뜻을 이루신다는 의미로 해석하는 것이 바람직하다.

하나님이 그와 끝날까지 함께하실 것을 확신하는 기자가 그러므로 주님의 인자하심이 영원하다며 찬양한다(8c절). 또한 주님이 손수 지으신 피조물인 그를 절대 버리지 마시라는 기도로 이 노래를 마무리한다(cf. 신 4:31; 31:6; 수 1:5). 주님은 자신이 창조하신 피조물에게 항상 진실하신 분이기 때문이다(Hossfeld-Zenger).

제139편

다윗의 시, 인도자를 따라 부르는 노래

I. 장르/양식: 개인 탄식시(cf. 3편)

이 시편은 제5권의 '다윗 모음집'(138-145편)의 두 번째 노래이며 이 모음집에서 가장 유명한 노래이다. 한 편의 시 안에 찬송과 감사와 탄식의 여러 양식을 지녔기 때문에 학자들은 이 시편을 다양하게 취급한다. 또한 이 노래는 1-18절과 19-24절이 다른 분위기를 반영하고 있다.

우리는 19-24절을 근거로 이 시편을 개인 탄식시로 구분하지만(cf. Allen), 다른 학자들은 개인 찬양시로(Grogan, Gunkel, Westermann), 혹은 억울한 일을 당한 사람의 기도로(Coote, Goldingay), 혹은 우상을 숭배했다고 비난을 받은 사람이 자신의 억울함을 호소하는 노래로 간주한다(McCann). 이 시편이 '알다'(ידע)를 7차례나 사용한다 하여(1, 2, 4, 6, 14, 23[2x]절) 지혜 묵상시(wisdom meditation)로 구분하는 이들도 있다(Gerstenberger, Hossfeld-Zenger).

저작 시기로는 예루살렘이 멸망할 때쯤을 제안하기도 하고(Terrien), 포로기 이후로 보기도 한다(Goldingay). 이 시편이 어떤 정황에서 사용된 것인가에 대하여는 아무도 확고한 제안을 하지 못한다. 그러므로 학자들은 이 시편의 '삶의 정황'(Sitz im Leben)은 도저히 알 수 없다고 단정한다(Goldingay, Tucker & Grant).

II. 구조

이 시편은 1-18절과 19-24절 두 섹션으로 구분된다. 또한 1-18절은 주제에 따라 세 파트로 나눌 수 있다. 본 주석에서는 다음과 같은 분석을 바탕으로 본문을 주해해 나가고자 한다.

A. 하나님이 나를 아심(139:1-6)
B. 하나님이 나를 살피심(139:7-12)
C. 하나님이 나를 창조하심(139:13-18)
D. 하나님께 드리는 기도(139:19-24)

III. 주해

이 시편에서는 동사 '알다'(ידע)가 7차례 사용되며(1, 2, 4, 6, 14, 23[2x]절) 하나님이 우리를 철저히 알고 계신다는 사실을 강조한다. 또한 기자는 자신과 하나님의 관계를 지속적으로 '나—당신'(I-You)의 관계로 묘사하여 창조주 하나님과 맺은 특별한 관계를 중점적으로 부각시킬 뿐만 아니라 노래 전체에 통일성을 더한다(Holman, Tucker & Grant).

1. 하나님이 나를 아심(139:1-6)

1 여호와여
주께서 나를 살펴 보셨으므로
나를 아시나이다
2 주께서 내가 앉고 일어섬을 아시고
멀리서도 나의 생각을 밝히 아시오며

3 나의 모든 길과 내가 눕는 것을 살펴보셨으므로
나의 모든 행위를 익히 아시오니
4 여호와여
내 혀의 말을 알지 못하시는 것이 하나도 없으시니이다
5 주께서 나의 앞뒤를 둘러싸시고
내게 안수하셨나이다
6 이 지식이 내게 너무 기이하니 높아서
내가 능히 미치지 못하나이다

기자는 하나님이 그에 대해 모든 것을 아신다는 사실을 고백하며 노래를 시작한다(1절). 그가 오직 하나님께 인정받기를 사모하는 것을 강조하기 위해 그는 1-6절에서 하나님의 성호 '여호와'(יְהוָה)를 두 차례, 하나님을 칭하는 인칭 대명사를 10차례 사용한다(deClaissé-Walford et al.). 또한 기자는 자신을 11차례 언급하며 하나님의 관계를 강조하기 위해 지속적으로 '나—당신'(I-You)을 사용하여 시편을 이어간다(Brueggemann, Miller).

주님은 자기 백성과 소유물에 대해 확실히 아시는 분이다. 여호와께서 그를 살펴보셨다고 하는데, 여기서 '살펴보다'(חקר)는 반대심문(cross-examination)을 뜻한다(HALOT). 하나님은 우리를 참으로 세심하고 확실하게 살피신다. '알다'(ידע)는 관찰 등을 통해 지식을 습득하는 것을 의미하는 관계적인 단어이다(VanGemeren). 그러므로 하나님이 우리를 아시는 것이 항상 좋은 일만은 아니고, 때로는 위협으로 느껴질 수도 있다(Calvin). 그러나 안다는 것은 '보살피다'는 의미도 포함하고 있기 때문에 굳이 불안해할 필요는 없다(cf. 시 144:3). 하나님은 우리가 우리 자신을 아는 것보다 우리를 더 잘 아신다.

하나님은 우리에 대해 무엇을 알고 계시는가? 기자는 나머지 섹션에서 네 가지로 하나님의 우리에 대한 완벽한 지식을 찬양한다.

첫째, 주님은 우리의 앉음과 일어섬을 아신다(2a절, cf. 시 1:6). 기자는 하나님이 아신다는 사실을 강조하기 위해 2인칭 남성 단수 대명사(אַתָּה)를 강조형으로 사용해 2절을 시작한다. 하나님은 우리가 앉아 있는 때와 일어설 때를 확실히 아신다. 우리의 모든 활동은 주님의 살피심 아래 있다. 창조주께서 우리의 상황을 헤아리신다는 사실은 참으로 감격스러운 일이다.

둘째, 하나님은 우리의 모든 생각을 아신다(2b절). '밝히 알다'(בין)는 이해한다는 의미를 지녔다(HALOT). 하나님은 우리가 생각하는 바를 모두 꿰뚫는 통찰력을 지니셨다. 심지어는 멀리서도 우리의 생각을 모두 아신다. 대부분 주석가들은 '멀리서'(מֵרָחוֹק)를 공간적으로 이해하지만, 시간적으로('아주 오래전부터') 해석하는 것도 가능하다(Booij). 우리가 경건하고 선한 생각만을 품고 살아야 하는 이유이다.

셋째, 주님은 우리의 모든 길과 눕는 것을 살피신다(3a절). 이 말씀은 하나님이 우리의 앉고 일어섬을 아신다는 2a절과 연관이 있다. 앉음은 눕는 것과, 일어섬은 길을 가는 것과 연관이 있기 때문이다. 그러므로 하나님은 우리의 모든 행위를 익히 아신다(3b절).

넷째, 하나님은 우리가 하는 말도 모두 아신다(4절). 주님은 우리의 생각과 움직임뿐만 아니라, 우리가 하는 말까지 하나도 모르는 것이 없으시다. 우리의 지정의가 모두 하나님의 관찰과 보호 아래 있다는 의미이다. 이러한 사실은 우리에게 우리의 생각과 행동과 말이 모두 경건해야 한다는 부담감을 가지게 한다. 또한 앞으로 기자가 드릴 기도(19-24절)의 근거가 되고 있다. 하나님이 그를 철두철미하게 살피셨는데, 어떠한 문제나 죄도 발견하지 않으셨으므로 그의 억울함을 헤아려 달라는 기도를 드리는 것이다.

하나님은 우리를 철두철미하게 알고 헤아리신 다음 우리를 보호하시고 축복하신다(5절). 주님은 우리를 보호하기 위해 우리의 앞뒤를 둘러싸셨다. 원수들의 칼과 창이 우리를 해하지 못하도록 방어막을 치셨다. 또한 우리에게 안수하신다. 안수는 보호와 축복을 의미한다(VanGemeren, cf. 창 48:14, 17; 출 33:22). 우리는 주님의 백성이며 하나님의 확실한 보호와 축복을 받는 사람들이다.

이러한 사실(지식)을 깨닫고 난 기자는 그저 감개무량할 뿐이다(6절). 그러므로 그는 감격하여 하나님이 그를 아시고, 보호하시고, 축복하신다는 지식이 너무 기이하며 높다고 감탄한다. '기이하다'(פְּלִיאָה)와 '높다'(נִשְׂגָּבָה)는 사람은 절대 할 수 없는 일과 갈 수 없는 높은 곳, 오직 하나님만 하실 수 있는 일과 거하실 수 있는 곳을 의미한다(cf. HALOT). 그러므로 저자는 하나님에 대한 지식은 그가 절대 미치지 못할 것이라고 고백한다. '미치지 못한다'(לֹא־אוּכַל)는 너무도 깊고 오묘해서 감히 측량할 수조차 없다는 뜻이다(Holman, cf. 새번역, 아가페).

2. 하나님이 나를 살피심(139:7-12)

7 내가 주의 영을 떠나 어디로 가며
주의 앞에서 어디로 피하리이까
8 내가 하늘에 올라갈지라도 거기 계시며
스올에 내 자리를 펼지라도 거기 계시니이다
9 내가 새벽 날개를 치며
바다 끝에 가서 거주할지라도
10 거기서도 주의 손이 나를 인도하시며
주의 오른손이 나를 붙드시리이다
11 내가 혹시 말하기를 흑암이 반드시 나를 덮고
나를 두른 빛은 밤이 되리라 할지라도
12 주에게서는 흑암이 숨기지 못하며
밤이 낮과 같이 비추이나니
주에게는 흑암과 빛이 같음이니이다

앞 섹션(1-6절)에서 하나님의 전지(全知, omniscience)에 대해 감탄한 기자가 이 섹션에서는 주님의 편재(遍在, omnipresence)에 대해 노래한다. 세상 어디를 가도 주님이 그곳에 계신다. 그러므로 그는 주님을 떠나 어디로 가도 주님을 피할 수 없다고 고백한다(7절).

첫째, 하나님은 하늘에 계신다(8a절). 저자는 자신이 주님을 떠나 세상의 가장 높은 곳으로 올라가더라도, 하나님은 그곳에 계신다고 한다. 세상에서 가장 높은 곳도 하나님의 눈 밖에 있지 않다는 뜻이다.

둘째, 하나님은 가장 낮은 곳에 계신다(8b절). 스올은 죽음을 뜻하기도 하기 때문에 이 말씀이 부활의 근거로 해석되기도 한다(Hossfeld-Zenger). 그러나 본문에서는 세상의 가장 낮은 곳을 의미한다(cf. Tucker & Grant). 저자는 설령 그가 하나님을 피해 세상의 가장 낮은 곳으로 내려가도 주님은 그곳에 계신다고 한다. 가장 높은 곳이 하나님의 시야 안에 있는 것처럼, 가장 낮은 곳도 하나님의 시야 안에 있다.

셋째, 하나님은 새벽 날개를 치는 곳에도 계신다(9a절). 새벽이 날개를 치는 곳은 동쪽을 의미한다(VanGemeren). 해가 동쪽에서 뜨기 때문이다. 기자는 빛의 속도로 동쪽 끝으로 날아가도 하나님은 그곳에 계시기 때문에 주님의 영역을 벗어나지 못한다고 한다(Calvin).

넷째, 하나님은 바다 끝에도 계신다(9b절). 이스라엘의 위치에서 바다(지중해)는 서쪽 끝이다. 그러므로 그는 동쪽의 정반대인 서쪽 끝으로 가도 주님이 그곳에 계신다고 한다. 그렇다면 8-9절은 하나님이 가장 높은 곳(하늘)에도, 가장 낮은 곳(스올)에도, 동쪽 끝(새벽이 날개 치는 곳)에도, 서쪽 끝(바다 끝)에도 계신다며 세상은 모두 하나님의 시야 안에 있다는 것을 강조한다.

하나님은 우리가 세상 어디로 가든, 어디에 있든 우리를 붙드시고 인도하신다(10절). 주님이 우리를 오른손으로 붙드신다는 것은 보호와 인도하심의 상징이다(시 73:23). 우리를 자녀 삼으신 하나님은 언제, 어디서든 부모가 자녀를 보호하듯 우리를 인도하신다. 우리는 항상 주님의 보살피심 아래 있다.

세상에서 가장 큰 어두움도 주님의 보호에서 우리를 가릴 수 없다(11–12절). '흑암과 빛', '낮과 밤'은 강력한 대조를 이루는 쌍 단어(pair-word)이다. 빛은 하나님의 임재를 상징한다(민 6:25–26; 시 4:6; 27:1, 8–9; 44:3; 89:15). 반면에 기자가 11–12절에서 네 차례 사용하고 있는 '흑암'(חֹשֶׁךְ)은 무질서와 죽음을 상징한다(McCann, Tucker & Grant, cf. 욥 12:22; 17:12–13; 시 23:4; 88:6, 12, 18). 하나님께 밤은 낮과 다름없으며, 흑암은 빛과 같다. 그러므로 우리가 아무리 어둠에 숨으려 해도 숨을 수 없다. 우리는 죄를 짓고 어두움에 숨으려 하지 말고, 주님의 빛 아래서 경건하게 사는 것을 기뻐해야 한다.

3. 하나님이 나를 창조하심(139:13–18)

13 주께서 내 내장을 지으시며
나의 모태에서 나를 만드셨나이다
14 내가 주께 감사하옴은 나를 지으심이 심히 기묘하심이라
주께서 하시는 일이 기이함을 내 영혼이 잘 아나이다
15 내가 은밀한 데서 지음을 받고
땅의 깊은 곳에서 기이하게 지음을 받은 때에
나의 형체가 주의 앞에 숨겨지지 못하였나이다
16 내 형질이 이루어지기 전에 주의 눈이 보셨으며
나를 위하여 정한 날이 하루도 되기 전에 주의 책에 다 기록이 되었나이다
17 하나님이여
주의 생각이 내게 어찌 그리 보배로우신지요
그 수가 어찌 그리 많은지요
18 내가 세려고 할지라도 그 수가 모래보다 많도소이다
내가 깰 때에도 여전히 주와 함께 있나이다

하나님의 전지(全知)와 편재(遍在)를 노래한 기자가 이 섹션에서는 하나님의 섬세하고 아름다운 창조를 찬양한다. 그는 자신을 예로 들어 하나님의 창조 사역을 묵상하며 자신은 창조주께서 만들어낸 하나의 제품(product)이 아니라 심혈을 기울여 만드신 걸작품(masterpiece)이라고 한다. 그는 하나님이 사람을 빚으시는 일을 다음과 같이 네 가지로 묘사한다.

첫째, 하나님은 우리가 어머니의 태 속에 있을 때부터 우리를 빚기 시작하셨다(13절, cf. 시 22:10). 기자는 주님이 그의 가장 깊은 곳(장기와 내장)을 지으셨다고 한다(cf. 새번역, 아가페). '짓다/만들다'(קנה)가 다른 곳에서는 하나님이 자기 백성을 은혜와 자비로 세우신(값을 치르고 사신) 일을 묘사한다(출 15:16; 시 74:2; 신 32:6) 가장 깊은 곳을 지으신 이가 또한 옅은 곳(겉모습)을 지으시는 것은 당연한 일이다. 그러므로 기자는 그가 모태에서 머물렀던 9개월을 창조주께서 그를 빚으신 시간이라 한다. 우리가 어머니의 뱃속에서 보낸 시간은 하나님이 우리를 창조하신 시간인 것이다.

둘째, 하나님은 우리를 참으로 놀랍고 기묘하게 만드셨다(14절). 기자는 하나님이 그를 '심히 기묘하게 만드셨다'고 하는데, '심히 기묘하다'는 히브리어 문구(נוֹרָאוֹת נִפְלֵיתִי)의 정확한 번역이 아니다. 기자는 하나님이 그를 만드신 일은 참으로 '기묘한 일'(פלה)이라고 하는데(2x), 시편에서 이미 하나님이 행하시는 기적의 묘사로 자주 사용된 표현이다. '심히'(ירא)는 너무나도 경이로워서 두려움을 자아낸다는 뜻이다. 그러므로 이 둘을 합하면 하나님이 사람을 빚으심은 '두려움을 자아내는 기묘한 일'이라는 의미가 된다. 하나님이 사람을 어떻게 만드시는 가는 오직 하나님만 아시는 신비(mystery)와 놀라운(wonder) 일이다(Mays). 기자는 이러한 사실을 알기에 하나님이 하시는 일은 기이하다고 고백한다. 하나님은 우리를 경이롭고 특별하게 만드셨다.

셋째, 하나님은 우리의 형체가 생성되는 것도 지켜보셨다(15절). 기자는 사람이 모태에서 만들어지는 것을 '은밀한 곳에서 지음을 받고, 땅의 깊은 곳에서 지음을 받은 일'로 묘사한다. '지음을 받다'(רקם)는 사람이 여러 가지 실을 사용하여 옷감을 만들어 내는 섬세한 작업을 묘사한다(HALOT, cf. 출 26:36; 27:16; 28:39; 35:35). 하나님은 참으로 섬세하게 우리를 빚으셨다.

은밀한 곳과 땅의 깊은 곳의 어두움은 자궁의 어두움을 묘사한다. 일부 학자들은 이 비유가 고대 근동 신화에서 비롯된 것이라 하지만(Kraus), 설득력이 없다. 이 말씀은 단순히 사람이 어머니의 태 속에서 형성되는 일은 세상에서 가장 깊은 어두움에 가려진 일임으로 사람이 도저히 알 수 없다는 것을 의미한다(cf. McCann). 그러나 하나님은 우리의 창조 과정을 모두 지켜보고 계셨다. 그러므로 주님께는 숨겨진 일도, 비밀에 붙여질 일도 아니다. '형체'(עָצְם)는 성경에서 단 한 번 사용되는 단어이며, '뼈들'을 뜻한다(cf. HALOT). 뼈들의 집합체를 '형체(뼈대)'라 할 수 있기 때문에 '형체'로도 번역이 가능하다.

넷째, 하나님은 우리의 수명을 우리가 태어나기도 전에 정하셨다(16절). 기자는 하나님이 형질이 이루어지 전에 그를 보셨다고 하는데, '형질'(גֹּלֶם)은 성경에서 단 한 번 사용되는 단어로 아직 형체를 지니지 않은 상태(formless)를 뜻한다(HALOT). 그러므로 형체와 형질은 우리가 어머니 태 속에서 태아(embryo) 형태로 있는 모습을 묘사한다(Hossfeld-Zenger).

저자는 우리가 어머니의 태 속에서 사람의 모습을 갖추기 전부터 주님은 우리의 날(수명)을 정하셨으며, 태어나기 전에 이미 주님의 책에 기록해 두었다고 한다(cf. 출 32:32-33; 시 56:8; 69:28; 단 12:1; 말 3:16). 우리의 수명은 태어나기 전부터 정해진 것이며 하나님은 이 모든 것을 기록해 두셨다. 이러한 사실은 우리에게 위로가 되어야 한다. 하나님이 정하신 날이 올 때까지, 우리는 이 땅에서 계속 살 것이기 때문이다. 어떠한 해(害)도 하나님이 정하신 바를 위반하면서까지 우리를 죽일 수는 없다.

기자는 하나님이 그를 어떻게 빚으셨는가를 묵상한 후 경이롭고 놀랍다는 생각을 한다. 그러므로 그는 이 모든 일을 이루신 하나님의 생각이 참으로 보배롭다고 한다(17b절). '보배롭다'(יקר)는 질에 관한 단어로 숫자가 많지 않아 매우 진귀하다는 의미를 지니기도 하지만, 이해하기가 어렵다는 뜻을 지녔다(HALOT). 그는 하나님의 생각은 참으로 어렵고 귀하기 때문에 인간이 도저히 헤아릴 수 없다는 사실을 고백한다(cf. 6절). 그는 하나님의 생각의 수가 참으로 많다고 감탄을 하기도 한다(17c절). '수가 많다'(עָצְמוּ)는 도저히 헤아릴 수 없을 정도로 (생각이) 깊다는 뜻이다. 그러므로 아무리 세려고 해도 바다의 모래알보다 많기 때문에 도저히 셀 수가 없다(18a절). 주님의 생각은 매우 깊어서 우리는 도저히 가늠할 수 없다.

그가 한 가지 확신하는 것은 그가 깨어날 때에도 하나님은 그와 함께하실 것이라는 사실이다(18b절). 그런데 이때까지 그가 잠을 자는 일이나, 이 노래를 부르는 시각이 밤이라는 말을 한 적이 없다. 그러므로 학자들은 '깨어나다/일어나다'(קיץ)를 '끝내다/끝이나다'로 번역할 것을 제안한다(cf. Allen, Hossfeld–Zenger). 기자는 자신의 삶이 끝이 나는 순간까지, 혹은 하나님의 모든 생각이 끝나는 순간까지 주님이 그와 함께하신다고 고백하고 있는 것이다(Tucker & Grant). 창조주께서 심혈을 기울여 만든 걸작품인데 어찌 그를 떠나실 수 있겠는가! 우리도 주님이 항상 함께하심을 기대하고 확신할 수 있다.

4. 하나님께 드리는 기도(139:19–24)

19 하나님이여
주께서 반드시 악인을 죽이시리이다
피 흘리기를 즐기는 자들아 나를 떠날지어다

20 그들이 주를 대하여 악하게 말하며
주의 원수들이 주의 이름으로 헛되이 맹세하나이다
21 여호와여
내가 주를 미워하는 자들을 미워하지 아니하오며
주를 치러 일어나는 자들을 미워하지 아니하나이까
22 내가 그들을 심히 미워하니
그들은 나의 원수들이니이다
23 하나님이여
나를 살피사 내 마음을 아시며
나를 시험하사 내 뜻을 아옵소서
24 내게 무슨 악한 행위가 있나 보시고
나를 영원한 길로 인도하소서

하나님은 세상에서 일어나는 모든 일을 아시는 전지(全知, omniscience)하신 분이며(1-6절), 세상 어디에도 계시는 편재(遍在, omnipresence)하신 분이다(7-12절). 또한 세상 모든 것을 창조한 창조주이시다. 피조물 중에서 인간은 하나님이 특별히 심혈을 기울여 만드신 걸작품이다(13-18절). 이러한 사실을 바탕으로 기자는 이 섹션에서 하나님께 드리고자 했던 기도를 드디어 시작한다. 그의 기도는 간구(19-20절)—헌신 확신(21-22절)—결론적 호소(23-24절)로 구성되어 있다(Goldingay).

기자의 기도는 하나님은 악을 미워하시고 선을 기뻐하신다는 사실을 근거로 한다. 그는 전지하시고, 편재하신 창조주이며, 권선징악(勸善懲惡)을 지향하시는 하나님께 기도하고 있다. 이 섹션에 기록된 기도로 인해 이 시편은 개인 탄식시로 구분된다. 이 섹션은 곤경에 처한 사람이 하나님께 도움을 청하는 간절한 기도이기 때문이다.

기자가 하나님께 벌하시기를 기도하는 악인들은 어떤 사람들인가?

첫째, 그들은 피 흘리기를 즐기는 자들이다(19절). '피 흘리기를 즐기는 자들'(אַנְשֵׁי דָמִים)의 문자적 의미는 '피의 사람들'이다. 이 표현은 시편 1-2권의 애가에서 자주 사용되는 개념이다(Tucker & Grant, cf. 시 5:6; 26:9; 55:23; 59:2). 남의 피를 흘리는 자들을 뜻한다. 이들은 생명의 존엄성을 인정하지 않고 공의와 정의에 대한 개념도 없는 자들이다(cf. 시 5:6; 잠 29:10). 물론 하나님에 대한 존경심도 없다(20절). 창조주께서 섬세하고 자상하게 만드신 인간의 피를 타당한 이유 없이 흘리는 자들은 분명히 적합한 응징을 받을 것이다. 주님이 그들을 죽이실 것이기 때문이다.

둘째, 악인들은 하나님에 대해 악의적으로 말한다(20a절). 이 말씀을 통해 기자의 원수들이 하나님의 원수들로 바뀌고 있다. 그가 하나님을 칭하면서 '당신'(you)을 뜻하는 접미사(ךָ)들을 사용하고 있기 때문이다. 그의 원수들은 곧 하나님을 대적하는 자들인 것이다. 피조물인 그들은 창조주 하나님을 모욕하는 말을 서슴지 않는 어리석고 미련한 자들이다(cf. 새번역).

셋째, 악인들은 하나님의 이름으로 헛되이 맹세하는 자들이다(20b절). 이 구절의 의미가 확실하지가 않다. 마소라 사본 자체가 혼란스럽기 때문이다. 그래서 일부 번역본들은 "그들은 당신(하나님)을 상대로 악을 행하러 일어섰습니다"로 번역한다(NRS, RSV). 심지어 칠십인역(LXX)은 "당신의 도시들을 정복하겠다는 허무한 생각을 가졌습니다"로 번역했다. 사람이 아무리 악해도 창조주 하나님을 상대로 싸우겠다는 생각을 갖는 것은 좀처럼 이해하기가 쉽지 않은 일이다. 그러나 다음 절(21절)이 같은 내용을 한 번 더 반복하는 것을 보면 개역개정의 번역을 유지하는 것이 바람직하다.

기자는 그를 괴롭히는 악인들(19절)은 하나님에 대해 악의적으로 나쁜 말을 하는 자들이라고 했다(20절). 이제 그는 하나님과 자신은 하나임을 강조한다(21-22절). 그는 하나님을 미워하는 자들을 미워하며(21b절), 하나님을 치러 일어나는 자들을 미워한다(21c절). '미워하다'(שׂנא)

는 관계적인 언어다(Tucker & Grant). 그러므로 '하나님을 미워하는 자들'(מְשַׂנְאֶיךָ)이 강조하고자 하는 바는 이들이 하나님과의 관계를 단절했다는 점이다(cf. 말 1:2-5). 그들은 주님과 전혀 관계가 없는 자들인 것이다. 저자는 하나님을 대적하는 그들을 심히 미워할 뿐만 아니라(22a절), 그들을 자기 원수들로 간주한다(22절). 악인들은 하나님과 기자에게 공통적인 원수들이다. 영적으로, 혹은 윤리적으로 중립은 존재하지 않는다(Davidson). 하나님의 편에 서든, 원수가 되든 둘 중 하나만이 가능하다. 우리는 항상 하나님과 같은 편에 서려고 노력해야 한다.

원수들을 벌하라고 기도했던 기자가 하나님께 자신은 선처해 달라고 기도한다(23절). 하나님은 그에 대한 모든 것을 아시는 분이다. 세상 모든 것을 아시고(1-6절), 모든 곳에 계시는(7-12절) 주님이 그를 직접 창조하셨기 때문이다(cf. 13-18절). 그러므로 그는 하나님이 그에 대해 알고 계시는 것에 근거하여 호소하고 있다.

기자는 이 노래를 시작했던 말("나를 살피시고… 나를 아시나이다")(1절)로 마무리한다(23절). 주님이 그를 살피셔서 그의 마음을 아시고(23b절), 그를 시험하셔서 그의 뜻을 확인하시면(23c절) 주님은 분명히 그가 선하다는 것을 인정하실 것이다. 기자는 원수들의 악행을 보면서 이 노래를 불렀기 때문에 그들과 강력한 대조를 이루는 그의 삶을 보아 달라며 이렇게 기도하고 있다(Davidson).

'살피다'(חקר)는 진실을 밝히기 위해 반대심문(cross-examination)을 하는 것을 의미한다(cf. HALOT, NIDOTTE). '시험하다'(בחן)는 금속을 녹인다는 뜻을 지녔다(HALOT). 기자는 하나님께 프리패스(free-pass)를 바라는 기도를 드리지 않는다. 그는 하나님이 그를 매우 자세히, 섬세하게 시험하시기를 원한다. '내 뜻'(שַׂרְעַפָּי)(23c절)은 '내 불안한 생각들'을 의미한다(HALOT). 그는 하나님이 그의 정한 생각뿐만 아니라, 불안해하는 생각까지 시험하여 인정하시기를 바란다(Tucker & Grant).

하나님이 그를 시험하시면 그에게는 어떠한 악한 행위도 없다는 것을 인정하실 것이다(24a절). 하나님이 의로움을 인정하시면, 그는 주님이 그를 영원한 길로 인도하실 것을 소망한다(24절). 이 말씀을 통해 '세상의 길'과 '하나님의 길'이 대조되고 있다(VanGemeren). 하나님이 인도하시면 그는 지금처럼 거룩하고 경건한 삶을 영원히 지속할 수 있다. 기자는 하나님이 영원히 그와 함께하실 것을 소망하고 있다. 우리도 이 같은 염원으로 하나님을 바라보며 주의 인도하심을 기대해야 한다.

제140편

다윗의 시, 인도자를 따라 부르는 노래

I. 장르/양식: 개인 탄식시(cf. 3편)

이 노래는 '다윗 모음집'(138-145편)의 세 번째 노래이며, 억울하게 모함을 당한 사람이 의로운 심판자이신 하나님께 자기 형편을 아뢰며 도움을 청하는 노래이다. 이 시편을 왕족시(Eaton) 혹은 기도시로 분류하는 이들도 있지만(Goldingay), 대부분 학자들은 전형적인 개인 탄식시로 간주한다(Brueggemann & Bellinger, deClaissé-Walford et al., McCann, Tucker & Grant, Ross, VanGemeren).

이 시편이 탄식시이기는 하지만, 기자가 원수들에게 당한 일에 대해 구체적으로 간구하는 내용은 없다. 그러므로 만일 이 노래가 다윗에 의해 저작되었다면, 그의 삶에서 구체적으로 언제, 어떤 상황에서 저작되고 불렸는가에 대하여는 예측이 불가능하다. 내용이 보편적이다 보니 아무나, 아무 때에나 힘들고 어려울 때 사용할 수 있는 장점을 지닌 시이다.

저작된 시기로는 매우 일찍 왕정 시대에 저작된 시라고 하는 이도 있고(Dahood, Eaton), 포로기 이후 정도로 늦게 보는 이들도 있다(Anderson, McCann, Oesterly, Terrien). 이 시편의 내용으로는 저작 시기를 논하는 것도 매우 어렵다.

II. 구조

일부 학자들은 이 시편에서 사용되는 단어들과 개념을 바탕으로 다음과 같은 부분적 교차대구법적 구조를 파악했다(Allen, McCann). 이 시편의 핵심은 하나님의 주권에 있다는 것이다.

A. 폭력적인 사람들(1-2절)
B. 입술(3절)
C. 악인, 음모(4-5절)
D. 하나님의 주권(6-7절)
C′. 악인, 음모(8절)
B′. 입술(9-10절)
A′. 폭력적인 사람들(11절)
D′. 주권적인 하나님의 행동(12-13절)

한 주석가는 이 시를 다섯 섹션으로 나누어 각 섹션을 구성하고 있는 단어 수가 매우 비슷하다고 한다(Clifford). 1-3절은 23개 히브리어 단어와 '셀라'로 구성되었고, 4-5절은 23개 단어와 '셀라'로, 6-8절은 24개 단어와 '셀라'로, 9-11절은 23개 단어로 구성되었다. 네 섹션을 구성하고 있는 히브리어 단어 수가 거의 동일한 것이다. 마지막 섹션인 12-13절을 구성하고 있는 히브리어 단어 수는 확연히 다르며, 기자의 마무리 확신을 강조하기 위하여 단어 수를 다르게 했다고 한다(Clifford).

클리포드에 의하면 1-3절과 4-5절이 서로 다른 문단이기는 하지만, 내용은 같다. 그러므로 이 두 섹션을 하나로 취급하는 것이 바람직해 보인다. 이 주석에서는 다음과 같은 구조를 바탕으로 본문을 주해해 나가고자 한다(cf. deClaissé-Walford et al., VanGemeren).

A. 구원을 위한 기도(140:1-5)

B. 구원에 대한 확신(140:6-7)

A´. 정의를 위한 기도(140:8-11)

B´. 구원에 대한 확신(140:12-13)

III. 주해

기자는 원수들이 그에게 어떻게 해를 입히려 하는가에 대해 구체적인 언급을 하지 않으면서 주님께 그들의 악한 입에서 구원해 달라고 기도한다. 내용이 매우 일반적이어서 언제든 사용될 만한 노래이다. 그는 하나님이 그의 기도를 들으셔서 꼭 구원하실 것이라는 확신으로 이 시편을 저작했다.

1. 구원을 위한 기도(140:1-5)

1 여호와여
악인에게서 나를 건지시며
포악한 자에게서 나를 보전하소서
2 그들이 마음속으로 악을 꾀하고
싸우기 위하여 매일 모이오며
3 뱀 같이 그 혀를 날카롭게 하니
그 입술 아래에는 독사의 독이 있나이다 (셀라)
4 여호와여
나를 지키사 악인의 손에 빠지지 않게 하시며
나를 보전하사 포악한 자에게서 벗어나게 하소서
그들은 나의 걸음을 밀치려 하나이다

[5] 교만한 자가 나를 해하려고 올무와 줄을 놓으며
길 곁에 그물을 치며 함정을 두었나이다 (셀라)

기자는 자신이 겪고 있는 어려움이 어떤 것인가에 대해 구체적으로 말하지는 않지만, 악인들에게 심한 공격을 당하고 있음을 시사한다. 또한 악인들을 묘사하면서 단수와 복수를 섞어 사용한다. 구체적인 상황보다는 전반적인 원리를 묘사할 때 사용하는 기법이다(Kidner, cf. Tucker & Grant). 그러므로 일부 학자들은 이 시편의 일반적인 성향을 근거로 이 노래가 지혜시 성향을 어느 정도는 띄고 있다고 생각한다(Hossfeld–Zenger).

저자는 하나님께 악인에게서 건지시고 보전해 달라고 기도한다(1절). '악인들'(אָדָם רָע)의 문자적 의미는 '가치가 없는 사람, 도움이 되지 않는 사람'을 뜻한다(HALOT). 세상 말로 '영양가 없는 저질들'을 의미한다. 이런 사람들과 대화는 불가능하다.

저자는 악인들을 '포악한 자들'(אִישׁ חֲמָסִים)이라고도 하는데, '폭력을 일삼는 자들'이라는 뜻이다(VanGemeren, cf. 삼하 22:49). 혹은 지나치게 폭력적인 사람을 뜻한다(Anderson). 그들은 질이 좋지 않으면서 폭력적이기까지 한 자들이기 때문에 하나님이 건져 주셔야 하며, 방패가 되어 그를 보전해 주셔야 한다. '건지다'(חלץ)는 처한 위험에서 빼내다는 뜻을 지녔고, '보전하다'(נצר)는 보호를 위해 감시하는 것을 뜻한다(cf. HALOT). 기자는 원수들 앞에서 한없이 나약함을 느낀다. 그러므로 하나님이 그를 원수들이 만든 위기에서 꺼내 주시고 보호해 주셔야 살 수 있다.

저자는 악인들이 그를 지속적으로 공격한다고 한다(2절). 그들의 공격은 결코 사고도, 혹은 하다 보니 빚어지는 일도 아니다. 그들은 악의적인 의도를 가지고 공격한다. 악인들은 교만한 자들이며(5절) 악한 계획을 세운다(2a절, cf. 시 21:11; 35:4). 어떤 계획인가? 구체적인 것은 알 수 없지만, 기자는 그들의 계획은 그를 잡기 위한 올무와 줄이며, 그물과 함정이라고 한다(5절). 마치 새나 짐승을 잡는 것처럼 그를 잡으려고 온갖 계획을 세운다(cf. Tucker & Grant). 악인들이 쳐놓은 그물과 파놓은 구덩이를 피하느라 기자의 삶은 마치 지뢰밭을 지나는 것과 같았을 것이다.

그들은 매일 모여 싸우기 위하여 공격해 온다(2b절). '싸움'(מִלְחָמָה)은 일상적으로 군사적인 갈등을 의미하는데(cf. NIDOTTE), 종종 악의적인 말을 뜻하기도 한다(Tucker & Grant, cf. 시 109, 120편). 악인들은 어떤 공격을 해오는가? 그들이 뱀 같이 혀를 날카롭게 한다는 것으로 보아(3절), 언어적 공격이 확실하다(cf. 9, 11절). 예레미야 9:8은 혀(말)를 '날카로운'(שׁנן) 화살로, 시편 52:2은 '날카로운'(שׁנן) 칼로 묘사한다(cf. 시 64:3). 그들의 말은 독사의 독처럼 살기가 등등하다(cf. 시 58:3-4). '독사'(עַכְשׁוּב)는 성경에서 이곳에 한 번 사용되는 단어로 의미가 정확하지는 않다. 그래서 한 주석가는 '독거미'로 해석할 것을 제안하는데(Goldingay), 그럴 필요는 없다. 이 단어는 뿔을 가진 독사를 뜻한다(HALOT). 저질스러운 자들의 포악한 말이니 파괴력은 가공할 만한 상황이다.

기자는 주님이 독사처럼 대드는 악인들에게서 그를 건져 주시기를 기도한다(4a절). '악인'(רָשָׁע)은 하나님을 두려워하지 않는 자를 뜻한다(Goldingay, Tucker & Grant). 종교적인 뉘앙스도 지닌 단어인 것이다. 또한 그들은 매우 포악한 자들이기 때문에 최대한 빨리 벗어나야 한다(4b절). 악인들은 그를 공격하기 위해 손과 마음과 혀와 입술을 동원하고 있다(Schaefer). 그들은 모든 열정을 쏟아 기자를 괴롭히고 있는 것이다(Goldingay). 이런 상황에서 공격자들이 하나님을 경외하지 않는 포악한 사람들이라면 멀리 하는 것이 최상책이다. 만일 신속하게 벗어나지 못하면 그들은 그를 넘어뜨릴 것이다(4c절). 그는 매우 다급하고 절박한 상황을 묘사하고 있다(cf. Hossfeld-Zenger). 하나님이 도와주셔야 그는 이 위기를 탈출할 수 있다.

2. 구원에 대한 확신(140:6–7)

[6] 내가 여호와께 말하기를
주는 나의 하나님이시니
여호와여
나의 간구하는 소리에 귀를 기울이소서 하였나이다
[7] 내 구원의 능력이신 주 여호와여
전쟁의 날에 주께서 내 머리를 가려 주셨나이다

이 섹션은 이 시편의 핵심 메시지를 담고 있다(Allen, McCann). 기자는 과거에 하나님이 그를 구원해 주신 날을 생각해 본다. 여호와는 전쟁의 날에 그의 머리를 가려 주심으로 그의 구원의 능력이 되셨다(7절). 하나님이 '능력 있는 구원자가 되셨다'가 더 정확한 번역이다(Anderson). 마치 투구가 병사의 머리를 보호하는 것처럼 하나님은 그의 머리를 보호해 주셨다. 하나님이 그가 죽지 않도록 원수들의 공격에서 그를 보존해 주셨다는 뜻이다. 또한 머리는 사람의 명예를 상징한다. 하나님은 악인들의 온갖 음해에서 기자의 존엄성을 지켜 주셨다. 그러므로 주님은 그에게 능력 있는 구원자가 되셨다.

그때 일을 회상하며 기자는 이번에도 하나님이 그의 기도에 귀를 기울이실 것을 확신한다(6절). 그가 의지하는 여호와는 바로 그의 하나님이시기 때문이다(6b절, cf. 출 6:7; 렘 11:4; 30:22; 겔 36:28). 시편은 우리가 위기에 처할 때면 여호와가 하나님이심을 고백하라고 한다(시 31:15; 63:1; cf. 사 44:17). 곤경에 처한 우리를 가장 확실하게 도우실 수 있는 분은 바로 우리와 특별한 관계를 맺으신 하나님이시며, 우리의 '주인'(אֲדוֹן)이신 여호와시기 때문이다.

과거에 경험했던 일이 어려움을 겪고 있는 기자에게 믿음과 확신의 근거가 되고 있다. 우리가 과거에 경험한 하나님의 구원과 은총은 현실의 어려움을 이겨낼 수 있는 믿음과 힘이 되는 것이다. 그가 이번에도 하나님이 그의 기도를 들으실 것을 확신하는 것은 그와 하나님의 특별한 관계 때문이다. 기자는 이 관계를 강조하기 위해 하나님과 자신의 관계를 지속적으로 '나—당신'(I-You)으로 묘사하고 있다.

3. 정의를 위한 기도(140:8-11)

8 여호와여
악인의 소원을 허락하지 마시며
그의 악한 꾀를 이루지 못하게 하소서
그들이 스스로 높일까 하나이다 (셀라)
9 나를 에워싸는 자들이 그들의 머리를 들 때에
그들의 입술의 재난이 그들을 덮게 하소서
10 뜨거운 숯불이 그들 위에 떨어지게 하시며
불 가운데와 깊은 웅덩이에 그들로 하여금 빠져
다시 일어나지 못하게 하소서
11 악담하는 자는 세상에서 굳게 서지 못하며
포악한 자는 재앙이 따라서 패망하게 하리이다

하나님께 자기의 기도에 귀를 기울여 달라고 호소했던 기자가 주님께 악인의 소원은 허락하시지 말 것을 기도한다(8b절). 그는 하나님이 잘못된 것을 바로 잡으실 것을 호소한다(McCann). 그는 악인들은 하나님을 두려워하지 않는 자들이라고 했다(cf. 4절 주해). 이제 그는 자신과 하나님을 한편에, 반대편에 악인들을 세워 중간에 선을 긋는다(Tucker & Grant). 하나님은 그의 편이시니 악인들을 절대 도우시면 안 된다는 논리이다.

그는 하나님이 악인들을 도우시면 안 되는 이유 두 가지를 제시한다. 첫째, 그들의 소원은 악한 꾀에 불과하다(8c절). 그러므로 그들이 희망하는 바가 이루어지면 선의의 피해자가 생겨날 것이다. 기자도 그들의 악한 계획의 희생자들 중 하나가 될 수 있다. 둘째, 그들이 더 교만해질 것이다(8d절). 기자는 이미 악인들은 교만한 자들이라고 했다(5절). 가뜩이나 의기양양한 자들이 소원한 바를 주님이 허락하시면, 그들은 당연히 더 교만해질 것이다. 그러므로 기자는 하나님이 그들의 악한 계획을 허락하시지 말 것을 기도한다. 하나님이 가장 미워하시는 죄가 교만이기 때문에 이 기도는 분명 들어 주실 것이다.

기자는 4-5절에서 원수들이 온갖 올무와 함정을 파놓고 그가 걸려들기를 기다리고 있다고 했다. 이제는 아예 악인들이 그를 에워싸고 있다고 한다(9절). 스스로 빠져나갈 수 없도록 사방으로 악인들에게 포위된 상황이다. 그러므로 그는 하나님이 원수들의 손에서 건져내 주시기를 기도했던 것이다(4절).

그동안 악인들에게서 구원해 달라며 소극적인 자세를 취했던 저자가 하나님께 원수들을 벌해 달라며 공격적인 자세를 취한다. 하나님이 그들을 벌하시기를 기도하고 있는 것이다. 그는 하나님이 그들의 머리를 그들의 입술의 재난으로 덮기를 원한다(9절). 머리는 사람이 생각하는 곳이다. 그들이 악한 생각을 품고 온갖 악한 계획을 세웠으니 그들의 머리가 벌을 받아야 한다. '입술의 재난'(עֲמַל שְׂפָתַיִם)은 그들의 말로 인해 생긴 모든 문제를 뜻한다. 그들이 말로 저지른 온갖 죄악이 부메랑이 되어 그들에게 임하기를 바라는 저주이다(cf. Goldingay). 또한 숯불이 떨어지는 몸뚱이는 삶을 상징한다. 악인들의 머리와 몸과 입술이 저주를 받고 있다. 악은 뿌리에서부터 제거되어야 하기 때문이다(Gerstenberger).

더 나아가 하나님이 그들의 죄에 대한 심판도 그들 위에 내려 주시기를 기도한다(10절). 하나님의 심판이 뜨거운 숯불이 되어 그들 위에 쏟아지고, 그들이 불구덩이나 수렁에 빠져서 다시는 일어나지 못하게 해 달라는 기도이다. 악인들은 기자를 잡기 위하여 함정을 팠는데(cf. 5절),

그는 악인들이 자신들이 판 함정에 떨어져 빠져나오지 못하도록 해 달라고 기도하고 있다. 다시는 그들이 사람들을 괴롭히지 못하도록 해 달라는 기도이다.

하나님이 이 악인들을 벌해야 하는 이유는 주님은 이 세상을 다스리시는 분이기 때문이다. 선하신 하나님이 다스리는 세상에서는 선한 사람이 강성해지고 악한 사람들이 망해야 한다. 그러므로 기자는 하나님이 다스리시는 세상에서 악담하는 사람들과 포악하게 행하는 자들이 발을 붙이지 못하도록 기도한다(11절): "혀를 놀려 남을 모함하는 사람은, 이 땅에서 버젓이 살지 못하게 해주십시오. 폭력을 놀이 삼는 자들에게는 큰 재앙이 늘 따라다니게 해주십시오"(새번역). 남을 모함하는 말과 포악은 항상 함께 간다(Tucker & Grant). 기자는 많은 것을 바라지 않는다. 하나님이 공평하게 악한 자들을 대해 주시기를 바랄 뿐이다.

4. 구원에 대한 확신(140:12-13)

12 내가 알거니와
여호와는 고난 당하는 자를 변호해 주시며
궁핍한 자에게 정의를 베푸시리이다
13 진실로 의인들이 주의 이름에 감사하며
정직한 자들이 주의 앞에서 살리이다

불안한 마음으로 구원을 구하는 말로 시작한 노래가(1절), '내가 안다'는 확신으로 마무리되고 있다. 악인들의 폭력적인 공격이 두렵지만, 기자는 마음을 가다듬고 다시 한 번 하나님에 대한 신뢰를 고백한다. 여호와는 고난 당하는 사람들을 변호해 주시는 분이다(12a절). '변호하다'(דִּין)는 법정에 관한 용어다. 주님은 억울한 사람들이 당한 억울함을 헤아리시는 분이며, 더 나아가 그들의 입장을 변호하시는 분이다. 그러므로 자신은 악인들에게 참으로 억울하게 당하고 있다고 생각하는 저자는 하나님이 그를 변호해 주실 것을 확신한다.

또한 하나님은 가난한 사람들에게 정의를 베푸시는 분이다(12절). '궁핍한 자들'(אֶבְיֹנִים)은 경제적으로 가난한 사람들을 의미한다(HALOT). 하나님은 억울한 일로 인해 경제적으로 손해를 보는 사람들이 합당한 대우를 받도록 하신다(cf. Kraus).

그러므로 의인들은 정의로 세상을 다스리시는 하나님께 감사하며 살 수 있다(13a절). 그들이 억울한 일을 당하더라도 주님이 꼭 그들을 변호하실 것이기 때문이다. 현대어 성경은 '의인들'(צַדִּיקִים)과 '정직한 자들'(יְשָׁרִים)을 모두 '바르게 살려 몸부림 치는 이들'로 번역했는데, 본문의 의미를 잘 살린 번역이다. 악인이 성행하는 세상에서 바르게 살려고 몸부림치는 것은 의미 있는 삶이다. 여호와께서 인정하시고 변호하시기 때문이다.

제141편
다윗의 시

I. 장르/양식: 개인 탄식시(cf. 3편)

제5권의 '다윗 모음집'(138-145편)의 네 번째 노래이다. 이 시편은 개인 탄식시이며(Booij, deClaissé-Walford et al., Ross, VanGemeren), 이러한 결론에 이의를 제기하는 학자들은 거의 없다. 내용을 분석해 보면 시편 기자가 하나님에 대한 그의 신뢰가 무너지기 시작하고, 악인들처럼 살고 싶은 유혹이 생길 때 부른 노래로 보인다(Kidner, Kirkpatrick, Kraus, McCann, cf. Allen). 그래서 한 학자는 이 시편에 주기도문의 일부인 '우리를 시험에 들게 하지 마시옵고'(Lead us not into temptation)라는 제목을 주었다(Schaefer). 저자는 하나님이 흔들리는 그의 마음을 붙잡아 주시기를 기도하고 있다.

대부분 학자들은 이 시편이 저작된 시기에 대해 침묵하거나, 저자와 저작 시기를 논하기에는 증거가 불충분하다고 한다(Goldingay). 그럼에도 불구하고 다윗이 그의 시대에 지은 노래라는 이(Ross)가 있고, 바빌론 포로시대가 끝나고 성전이 재건되기 전에 저작된 것이라는 이(Terrien)도 있다. 저작 시기를 논하는 사람들은 포로기 이후 시대를 지목한다(McCann, Tucker & Grant).

이 시편이 어떤 정황에서 사용되었는가에 대하여도 알려진 바가 없다. 저녁 제물을 언급하는 2절을 근거로 성전에서 저녁 제물을 드릴 때 사용된 노래라는 추측이 있을 뿐이다(VanGemeren, cf. Ross).

II. 구조

학자들은 대체적으로 이 시편을 세 섹션으로 나눈다(cf. deClaissé-Walford et al., Tucker & Grant). 이 주석에서도 다음과 같이 세 파트로 구분하여 본문을 주해해 나갈 것이다.

A. 귀 기울여 달라는 간구(141:1-2)
B. 보호를 위한 기도(141:3-6)
C. 구원을 위한 기도(141:7-10)

III. 주해

기자는 하나님만 의지하고 살다가 세상에서 성공하는 악인들을 보고 그들처럼 살고 싶은 충동을 느낀다. 이러한 상황에서 그는 하나님께 그의 삶과 약한 의지를 이러한 유혹에서 지켜 달라고 기도한다. 이 시편은 오늘날 성도들이 느낄 수 있는 상황을 반영하고 있는 것이다.

1. 귀기울여 달라는 간구(141:1-2)

1 여호와여
내가 주를 불렀사오니 속히 내게 오시옵소서
내가 주께 부르짖을 때에 내 음성에 귀를 기울이소서
2 나의 기도가 주의 앞에 분향함과 같이 되며
나의 손 드는 것이 저녁 제사 같이 되게 하소서

기자는 1절에서 '부르다(קרא)… 오다(חוש)…부르짖다(קרא)… 귀를 기울이다(אזן)'를 사용하여 자신의 절박함과 긴급함을 호소한다. 그는 주님을 뵙기를 간절히 바라고 있다. 당장 주님께 아뢰고 도움을 청하지 않으면 안될 것 같은 절박한 감정에 사로잡혀 있다. 기자에게 하나님은 그의 삶에서 참으로 멀리 떨어져 있으신 분으로 느껴진다. 그러므로 그는 초월하신 하나님(the transcendent God)께 임재하신 하나님(God of presence)이 되어 달라고 기도하고 있다(Hossfeld-Zenger).

그러므로 그는 그가 드리는 기도가 분향과 저녁 제사같이 되어 주님께 반드시 열납되기를 간절히 바란다(2절). '분향'(קְטֹרֶת)은 매일 드리는 제물이었으며(출 30:7-8), 번제와 함께 드렸다(레 2:1-2). 분향은 저녁에 드리는 제물과도 연관이 있지만(Delitzsch, cf. 출 29:38-42), 제단에서 드리는 모든 제물을 상징할 수도 있다(Goldingay, cf. HALOT). '저녁 제사'(מִנְחַת־עָרֶב)의 문자적 의미는 '저녁에 드리는 화제(곡물)'이지만 이 또한 짐승을 제물로 드리는 제사를 의미할 수 있다(Goldingay, Tucker & Grant).

일부 학자들은 이 시편이 분향과 제사를 기도가 대체하고 있다고 하지만(Kraus), 지나친 해석이다(Mays, McCann, cf. 스 9:5). 기도가 제물을 대신할 수 있는 유일한 때는 제물을 드리는 일이 불가능할 때이다(Briggs). 저자는 그가 드리는 기도가 성전에서 드리는 예물이 주님께 열납되는 것처럼 반드시 열납되기를 간절히 바랄 뿐이다. 구약에서 제물과 기도는 항상 같이 가기 때문이다. '손을 드는 것'은 하늘을 향해 손을 들고 기도하는 모습이다(cf. 시 28:2; 63:4).

2. 보호를 위한 기도(141:3-6)

3 여호와여
내 입에 파수꾼을 세우시고
내 입술의 문을 지키소서

[4] 내 마음이 악한 일에 기울어
죄악을 행하는 자들과 함께 악을 행하지 말게 하시며
그들의 진수성찬을 먹지 말게 하소서
[5] 의인이 나를 칠지라도 은혜로 여기며
책망할지라도 머리의 기름 같이 여겨서
내 머리가 이를 거절하지 아니할지라
그들의 재난 중에도 내가 항상 기도하리로다
[6] 그들의 재판관들이 바위 곁에 내려 던져졌도다
내 말이 달므로 무리가 들으리로다

기자는 무엇 때문에 다급하게 주님께 기도하는가? 그는 3-4절을 통해 악인들처럼 살고 싶은 충동에 시달리고 있음을 고백한다.

첫째, 그는 악인들처럼 말하고 싶은 유혹을 당하고 있다(3절). 사람은 입으로 가장 많은 죄를 짓는다. 더욱이 악인들은 입으로 진실을 왜곡하고, 남을 음해하고, 심지어는 살인까지 저지른다. 저자도 이렇게 함부로 말하며 살고 싶은 충동을 느끼고 있다. 그러므로 그는 주님께 그가 악인들처럼 말하지 않도록 그의 입을 단속해 달라고 기도한다. 파수꾼을 세워 문을 지키는 것은 철두철미한 감시를 뜻한다. 기자는 스스로 말을 절제할 수 있는 능력을 지니지 않았다며 하나님께 자신의 무기력함을 고백한다. 그는 '침묵하는 은혜'(grace of slience)를 위해 기도하고 있다(Deitzsch).

둘째, 기자의 마음이 악한 일에 기울어져 있다(4a절). 마음은 행동으로 옮기기 전에 일을 계획하는 곳이다. 그러므로 선과 악은 항상 마음에서 싸운다. 그는 하나님의 말씀에 따라 선하게 살고 싶지만, 그의 마음은 악인들처럼 자꾸 악한 일과 하나님이 싫어하시는 일을 계획한다.

셋째, 그는 악인들처럼 살고 싶은 유혹을 당하고 있다(4b절). 그는 악인들과 먹고 마시며, 그들과 함께 죄악을 행하며 사는 것이 두렵다.

'진수성찬'(מַנְעַמִּים)은 온갖 귀한 음식으로 잘 차려진 밥상이다. 기자가 경험하고 있는 유혹이 얼마나 크고 강한가를 암시한다. 만일 하나님이 그를 돕지 않으시면, 그의 마음은 악한 일에 기울 것이 거의 확실하고, 그는 원하지는 않지만 악인들과 함께 악행을 저지르며 그들과 함께 호의호식할 것 같은 느낌이 든다. 이런 그를 유혹에서 건져낼 수 있는 분은 오직 하나님이시다.

말(3절)과 마음(생각)(4a절)과 행동(4b절)은 우리가 죄를 지을 수 있는 모든 영역을 요약하고 있다(VanGemeren). 또한 이 세 영역은 우리가 주님의 자녀로 살아가기 위해서는 반드시 다스려야 하는 영역들이다(cf. Goldingay). 의인과 악인의 차이는 바로 이 세 영역에서 일어나는 일로 구분된다.

이 시편 중 1-5c절과 8-10절은 별 어려움 없이 해석할 수 있지만, 5c-7절은 번역과 해석이 쉽지 않다. 마소라 사본이 많이 부패되었고, 사용되는 단어들도 쉽지 않기 때문이다. 상황이 얼마나 좋지 않은 지 한 주석가는 이 구절들의 번역과 해석은 불가능하다며 번역과 해석을 거부했다(Weiser). 다음은 각 번역본들이 5d-7절을 번역해 놓은 것이다. 모두 다 추측에 불과하기에 어느 번역본을 따르는 가는 그다지 중요하지 않다. 우리는 개역개정의 번역을 따르고자 한다.

개역개정	그들의 재난 중에도 내가 항상 기도하리로다. 그들의 재판관들이 바위 곁에 내려 던져졌도다 내 말이 달므로 무리가 들으리로다 사람이 밭 갈아 흙을 부스러뜨림같이 우리의 해골이 스올 입구에 흩어졌도다
칠십인역	악인들이 내 머리에 기름을 붓지 못하게 해주십시오 그들의 위대한 자들은 바위 곁에서 삼켜졌습니다. 그들은 나의 달달한 말을 들을 것입니다. 흙덩어리가 땅에서 깨어지듯, 우리 뼈들이 무덤의 입구에서 흩어졌습니다.
새번역	나는 언제나 그들의 악행을 고발하는 기도를 드리겠습니다. 그들의 통치자들이 돌부리에 걸려서 넘어지면, 그제서야 백성은 내 말이 옳았음을 알고서, 내게 귀를 기울일 것입니다. 맷돌이 땅에 부딪쳐서 깨지듯이 그들의 해골이 부서져서, 스올 어귀에 흩어질 것입니다.

아가페	나는 악을 행하는 자들을 위해 항상 기도하겠습니다. 그들을 다스리는 자들은 낭떠러지 밑으로 던져질 것입니다. 악한 자들은 내가 옳은 말을 했음을 알게 될 것입니다. 그들은 말할 것입니다, "사람이 밭을 갈고 땅을 파 일구는 것처럼, 우리의 뼈가 무덤의 입구에 흩어졌다."
현대인	그러나 나쁜 짓 하는 자들 겪을 불행 위하여 기도하리라. 그들의 지도자들이 바위틈으로 굴러 떨어질 때에야 사람들은 내가 한 말이 옳았다고 깨닫게 되리라. 밭갈때 흙덩이가 부스러지는 것처럼 그들의 뼈가 스올 문간 여기저기에 흩어져 있으리라.
공동번역	나는 언제나 그들의 악행을 반대하여 기도드립니다. 그들의 재판관들은 바위의 발톱에 잡혀 내 말이 옳았음을 깨닫게 될 것입니다. 맷돌이 땅에 부딪쳐 깨지듯이 우리의 뼈가 저승문 어귀에 흩어졌나이다.
NIV	나의 기도는 악인들의 악행을 반대합니다. 그들의 통치자들은 절벽에서 던져질 것이며, 악인들은 나의 말이 옳았다는 것을 깨닫게 될 것입니다. 그들은 말하기를 "쟁기질로 땅을 가는 것처럼 우리의 뼈들도 무덤 입구에서 흩어졌다"라고 합니다.
NAS	나의 기도는 그들의 악행을 반대합니다. 그들의 리더들이 절벽에서 던져져 그들이 나의 말을 좋게 듣게 되기를 바랍니다. 쟁기질이 땅을 파는 것처럼 우리의 뼈들도 스올의 입구에서 흩어졌습니다.
NRS	나의 지속적인 기도는 그들의 악행을 반대합니다. 그들이 그들을 정죄하는 자들에게 넘겨질 때, 그들은 비로소 제 말이 옳았다는 것을 깨닫게 될 것입니다. 사람이 바위를 쪼개 땅에 흩는 것처럼, 그들의 뼈들도 스올의 입구에서 흩어질 것입니다.
ESV	나의 기도는 그들의 악행을 반대합니다. 그들의 재판관들이 절벽에서 던져질 때, 그들은 비로소 나의 바른 말에 귀를 기울일 것입니다. 쟁기질이 땅을 파는 것처럼 우리의 뼈들도 스올의 입구에서 흩어졌습니다.
TNK	나의 기도는 아직도 그들의 악행을 반대합니다. 그들의 재판관들이 바위에서 미끌어지고, 나의 달달한 말이 들려지기를 원합니다. 땅이 열리고 쪼개지는 것처럼 우리의 뼈들도 스올의 입구에서 흩어집니다.

악인들이 사는 방식대로 살고 싶은 강한 충동을 느끼는 기자는 어떻게 해서든 그 유혹을 이겨내고 싶다. 그러므로 설령 하나님이 다른 사람들(의인들)을 통해 그를 징계하더라도 유혹을 이겨낼 수 있다면 달게 받겠다고 한다(5절, cf. McCann). 그는 하나님이 의인들을 사용하여 그를

치시더라도 은혜로 여길 것이다(5a절). 하나님이 그들을 통해 책망하실지라도 머리에 바르는 기름처럼 귀하게 여겨 거부하지 않을 것이다(5b-c절).

그가 혹시 악인들과 함께하게 되어 그들에게 내려지는 징계와 책망이 그에게도 임하게 되면, 그 징계와 책망을 받으면서 그는 하나님을 원망하기 보다는 오히려 기도할 것을 다짐한다(5d절). 하나님의 징계가 악인들에게 임하는 날, 그들의 재판관들(지도자들)은 심판을 받아 높은 바위에서 밑으로 던져질 것이다(6a절). 고대 사회에서 사형수들을 처형할 때 높은 바위에서 밀어 떨어져 죽게 한 풍습을 배경으로 한 말씀이다(Grogan). 그때에야 비로소 그들을 따르던 악인들은 악하게 행동하고 악하게 살면 안 된다는 기자의 말이 옳았다는 것을 깨닫게 될 것이다(6b절).

3. 구원을 위한 기도(141:7-10)

7 사람이 밭 갈아 흙을 부스러뜨림같이
우리의 해골이 스올 입구에 흩어졌도다
8 주 여호와여
내 눈이 주께 향하며 내가 주께 피하오니
내 영혼을 빈궁한 대로 버려 두지 마옵소서
9 나를 지키사 그들이 나를 잡으려고 놓은 올무와
악을 행하는 자들의 함정에서 벗어나게 하옵소서
10 악인은 자기 그물에 걸리게 하시고
나만은 온전히 면하게 하소서

기자는 만일 하나님이 도와주지 않으시면, 그도 다른 악인들처럼 비참한 종말을 맞을 것을 잘 알고 있다. 사람이 쟁기질을 통해 흙을 갈아

얹고 큰 흙덩어리들을 작게 부스는 것처럼, 하나님이 악인들의 해골(뼈들)을 스올(무덤) 앞에 흩으실 것을 알고 있다(7절). 하나님의 심판을 받아 죽음을 면하지 못할 것이며 제대로 된 장례도 받지 못할 것이라는 뜻이다(VanGemeren). 그러므로 기자는 어떻게 해서든 악인들과 한통속이 되고 싶지 않다.

저자는 하나님께 그를 버리시지 말라고 기도한다(8절). 그의 눈은 오직 주님을 바라보고 있으며, 그는 하나님의 품으로 피한다. 그렇지 않으면 죽을 것 같은 생각이 들기 때문이다. '내 영혼이 빈궁하다'(תְּעַר נַפְשִׁי)는 스스로 방어할 수 있는 능력이 없다는 뜻이다(cf. HALOT). 그는 악인들과 한통속이 되어 죽게 될 것을 두려워하고 있다(Goldingay, cf. 아가페, 공동, NIV, LXX).

기자가 하나님께 도피하여 자신이 처한 상황을 살펴보니 모든 것이 달라 보인다. 그동안 한없이 좋아 보였던 악인들의 말과 행실(cf. 3-4절)이 모두 그를 잡으려고 쳐 놓은 악인들의 올무와 함정으로 보인다(9절). 요즘 말에 비하자면 유혹을 당할 때는 로맨스로 보였던 것이 실제로는 간음이었던 것이다! 간절히 기도한 후에 드디어 왜곡되었던 상황의 실체를 보기 시작한 것이다.

그러므로 그는 하나님께 그를 지켜 주셔서 원수들의 올무와 함정에서 벗어나게 해 달라고 기도한다(9절). 기자는 하나님께 자신의 무능함과 무기력을 고백하고 있다. 악인들은 자신들이 쳐 놓은 그물에 걸리게 하셔서 그들이 부메랑 효과를 경험하도록 해 달라고 기도한다. 반면에 그는 그들의 그물에서 온전히 빠져나올 수 있도록 하나님께 도와 달라고 기도한다(10절).

제142편

다윗이 굴에 있을 때에 지은 마스길 곧 기도

I. 장르/양식: 개인 탄식시(cf. 3편)

이 시편은 '다윗 모음집'(138-145편)의 다섯 번째 노래이다. 이 노래가 왕족시라는 이도 있지만(Eaton), 대부분 학자들은 개인 탄식시로 분류한다(Brueggemann & Bellinger, Goldingay, Ross, VanGemeren). 이 시는 생명을 노리는 원수들에게 쫓기다가 지친 사람이 읊을 만하다(Tucker & Grant). 그러므로 한 주석가는 이 시편을 곤경에 처한 사람들이 어떻게 기도해야 하는가에 대한 교본이라고 한다(Broyles).

대부분 학자들은 표제가 시가 저작된 훗날 따로 첨부된 것이기 때문에 무시할 것을 제안하지만, 이 시편의 경우 표제의 내용과 시의 내용이 잘 어울리는 듯하다. 표제에 의하면 이 시편은 다윗이 사울에게 쫓길 때 부른 노래가 확실하다. 언제쯤일까? 다윗이 사울에게 쫓기다가 굴에 갇힌 경우가 두 번 있었다. 아둘람 광야에서(삼상 22:1, 4)와 엔게디에 머물 때이다(삼상 24:1-21). 그러므로 이 시편이 엔게디 경험을 회고하고 있다고 하는 이도 있고(Busch, Grogan, cf. Tucker & Grant), 더 절망적이었던 아둘람 상황을 배경으로 하고 있다고 하는 이도 있다(Ross).

시의 내용이 포로기 혹은 이후 시대와 잘 어울린다 하여 포로기 이후에 저작된 것이라는 견해가 있다(McCann). 반면에 이 시를 다윗의 경험과 연관 짓는다면, 저자는 당연히 다윗이다. 그러므로 이 시편이 왕정 시대에 저작된 것이라고 하는 이들이 있다(Eaton, Ross, Terrien). 아마도 다윗이 굴에 갇혀 있는 경험이 포로기에 타국에 갇혀 있는 이스라엘의 경험과 비슷하다고 해서 훗날 재활용되었던 것으로 생각된다. 그러므로 이 시는 언제든 영적—물리적 억압(갇힘)이 있을 때 사용할 만한 노래이다.

II. 구조

이 시편은 전형적인 탄식시 양식을 취하고 있다. 하나님께 귀를 기울여 달라는 호소(1–2절)와 절망감(3–5절)과 간구(6–7절)로 구성되어 있다. 또한 대부분 학자들은 3절을 반으로 나누어 서로 다른 섹션으로 구분한다. 이 주석에서는 다음과 같은 구조를 바탕으로 본문을 주해하고자 한다.

A. 호소와 신뢰(142:1–3b)
B. 탄식과 신뢰(142:3c–5)
C. 간구와 신뢰(142:6–7)

III. 주해

위험에 처한 기자는 하나님이 그의 기도를 들어 주시기를 간절히 기도한다. 그는 하나님께 호소하고, 탄식하며, 간절히 구한다. 인상적인 것은 기자가 이 과정에서 한 번도 하나님에 대한 신뢰의 끈을 놓지 않는다는 것이다. 그는 하나님이 그의 기도를 들으실 것을 확신하면서 이 노래를 읊조린다.

1. 호소와 신뢰(142:1-3b)

1 내가 소리 내어 여호와께 부르짖으며
소리 내어 여호와께 간구하는도다
2 내가 내 원통함을 그의 앞에 토로하며
내 우환을 그의 앞에 진술하는도다
3a 내 영이 내 속에서 상할 때에도
주께서 내 길을 아셨나이다

기자는 1-2절에서 네 동사를 사용하여 하나님이 그의 부르짖음에 귀를 기울이시기를 간절히 바란다: '부르짖다… 간구하다… 토로하다… 진술하다.' '부르짖다'(זעק)는 법정에서 원고가 자신의 억울함을 호소할 때 사용하는 단어이다(욥 35:9). '간구하다'(חנן)는 형편을 말하고 자비를 구할 때 사용된다(cf. HALOT). '토로하다'(שפך)는 쏟아 놓는다는 뜻이다(cf. NIDOTTE). 사람이 자기 속에 있는 것을 모두 말하는 것을 의미한다. '진술하다'(נגד)는 자신의 형편에 대해 설명한다는 뜻을 지녔다(cf. HALOT). 그러므로 이 네 동사들은 참으로 억울한 일을 당한 사람이 자기의 원통함을 항변하기 위해 사용하는 것들이다(cf. Broyles, Kirkpatrick).

저자는 자신의 원통함과 우환을 하나님께 모두 알리기를 원한다(2절). '원통함'(שִׂיחַ)은 슬픔을, '우환'(צָרָה)은 정신적 고통을 뜻한다(cf. NIDOTTE, HALOT). 그는 참으로 억울한 일로 인해 감당하기 힘든 고충을 호소하고 있다. 죄로 인해 벌을 받고 있다면 차라리 나을 것이다. 세상에서 가장 견디기 힘든 것이 억울한 고통이다.

그에게 있는 옵션은 하나님께 부르짖는 것 외에는 아무것도 없다. 사실은 오직 주님만이 그에게 위로가 되시고 힘이 되실 수 있다. 하나님은 우리의 영이 상할 때에도 우리의 길을 아시는 분이기 때문이다

(3a-b절). 더 이상 소망이 없다 싶어 우리 스스로 포기하려 하면 하나님은 우리가 가야 할 길을 알려 주신다는 뜻이다(cf. 현대인). 기자의 믿음과 신뢰의 고백이다(Gerstenberger, Kraus). 우리는 우리 자신을 포기해도, 하나님은 우리를 포기하지 않으신다.

2. 탄식과 신뢰(142:3c-5)

3c 내가 가는 길에 그들이 나를 잡으려고
올무를 숨겼나이다
4 오른쪽을 살펴 보소서
나를 아는 이도 없고
나의 피난처도 없고
내 영혼을 돌보는 이도 없나이다
5 여호와여
내가 주께 부르짖어 말하기를
주는 나의 피난처시요
살아 있는 사람들의 땅에서
나의 분깃이시라 하였나이다

원수들은 그를 잡으려고 그가 가는 길에 올무를 숨겨두었다(3c절). 그가 참으로 억울하다고 하는 것으로 보아 그들은 그를 이렇게 대할 만한 이유가 없다. 그는 남들에게 이런 대우를 받을 만한 일을 한적이 없다는 것이다.

그의 억울함에 절망을 더하는 것은 그를 변호해 줄 사람이 하나도 없다는 사실이다(4절). 오른쪽은 소송이나 재판에서 변호인이나 증인이 서는 자리이다(VanGemeren, cf. 시 16:8; 109:31; 110:5; 121:5). 그런데 그의 오른쪽이 텅 비어 있다. 아는 이도 없고, 피난처도 없고, 돌보는 이도 없다. 의지할 사람이나 피할 곳도 없는 기자는 홀로 이 억울한 상황을 헤쳐 나와야 한다. 그는 고독과 외로움을 토로하고 있다. 억울한 일을 당한 사람이 가장 힘든 것은 그의 곁에 아무도 없는 외로움이다.

그러므로 그는 여호와께 나의 피난처요 분깃이 되신다고 고백한다(5절). 과거의 경험을 바탕으로 생각해 볼 때 하나님이 그의 피난처가 되시고, 그의 분깃이 되셨기 때문이다. '피난처'(מַחְסֶה)는 그가 적들의 공격과 재앙에서 보호를 받을 수 있는 은신처이다. 하나님이 그의 '분깃'(חֵלֶק)이라는 것은 주님이 그가 이 땅에서 유일하게 자기 것이라 주장할 수 있는 소유라는 뜻이다(cf. NIDOTTE). 그는 이 땅에서 오직 하나님만 바라보고 의지하며 살아가고 있다는 것을 이렇게 표현하고 있다.

3. 간구와 신뢰(142:6-7)

6 나의 부르짖음을 들으소서
나는 심히 비천하니이다
나를 핍박하는 자들에게서 나를 건지소서
그들은 나보다 강하니이다
7 내 영혼을 옥에서 이끌어 내사
주의 이름을 감사하게 하소서
주께서 나에게 갚아 주시리니
의인들이 나를 두르리이다

이 세상에 자기 편은 오직 하나님 한 분이라고 고백한 기자가 주님께 도움을 청한다(6a절). 그는 겸손히 자기 자신을 낮추어 자신을 참으로 비천한 자라고 한다(6b절). '비천하다'(דלל)는 온갖 어려움으로 인해 매우 낮아졌다는 뜻이다(cf. NIDOTTE). 그는 자신을 더 이상 내려갈 곳이 없는 곳까지 내려간 인생이라고 한다.

반면에 기자를 괴롭히는 원수들은 그보다 훨씬 더 강하다(6d절). 그는 절대로 그들을 상대할 수 없다는 뜻이다. 그러므로 하나님이 그를 핍박하는 원수들에게서 건져 주셔야 그가 살 수 있다. 그는 한 번 더 간절히 주님의 구원을 바란다. 주님께서 그의 영혼을 감옥에서 이끌어 내 주시기를 기도한다(7a절). 일부 학자들은 '감옥'(מַסְגֵּר)이 실제 감옥인지, 은유인지에 대해 논란을 이어가고 있지만(Allen, cf. Goldingay, Tucker & Grant, VanGemeren), 기자는 원수들의 위협을 감옥에 갇힌 경험에 비교하고 있을 뿐이다. 하나님은 분명 그를 '감옥'에서 구원하실 것이다(7c절). 이 모든 억압과 위협에서 자유를 누릴 때, 그는 하나님께 감사할 것이다(7b절). 그는 외로움에 사무쳐 있는 자신을 많은 의인들(주님의 자녀들)이 둘러싸고 위로할 날을 꿈꾼다. 어려운 현실에서 그는 밝은 미래를 꿈꾸고 있다.

제143편
다윗의 시

I. 장르/양식: 개인 탄식시(cf. 3편)

이 시편은 7개의 참회시(penitential psalm) 중 마지막 것이다(cf. 6, 32, 38, 51, 102, 130편). 참회시는 일상적으로 죄 고백을 담고 있지만, 이 시에는 구체적인 죄 고백이 없다. 단지 "살아 있는 그 누구도 주님 앞에서는 의롭지 못하다"(2절)는 말에 간접적으로 암시되어 있을 뿐이다(cf. Anderson). 이 시편이 하나님의 은혜와 자비를 강조한다 하여 종교개혁자 루터(Luther)는 이 시를 '바울적인 시들'(Pauline Psalms) 중 하나로 불렀다(VanGemeren).

이 시는 개인 탄식시이며, 8절이 아침을 언급한다 하여 기자가 성전에서 밤을 새면서 드린 기도라고 하는 이들이 있다(cf. McCann). 이 시편은 결과가 사형이 될 수도 있는 부당한 법적 소송에 휘말린 사람의 억울함을 호소하는 기도라는 이들도 있다(Goulder, Kraus). 그러나 특정할 만한 상황없이 평범한 삶에서 경험한 애환과 핍박과 분노 등을 표현한 시라는 견해가 지배적이다(Gerstenberger, Hossfeld-Zenger, Ross). 그러므로 이 시편은 시간과 장소를 초월하여 반복적으로 사용될 수 있다(McCann, Tucker & Grant).

칠십인역(LXX)과 라틴어 버전(Vg.)은 표제의 '다윗의 시'라는 말에 "그의 아들이 그를 추격할 때"(ὅτε αὐτὸν ὁ υἱὸς καταδιώκει)라는 말을 더한다. 다윗이 압살롬에게 쫓길 때 부른 노래라는 것이다. 물론 그렇게 단정할 만한 증거는 없다.

만일 이 시가 다윗이 저작한 것이라면 당연히 왕정 시대에 유래한 것이다. 그러나 이 시편이 사용하는 언어가 다른 시편들을 상기시킨다 하여 포로기 이후에 저작된 것이라는 주장도 있다(Terrien). 대체적으로 학자들은 이 시편의 저작 시기에 대하여 어떠한 제안도 하지 않는다.

II. 구조

이 시편은 1-6절과 7-12절 크게 두 파트로 구분된다(cf. Allen, Tucker & Grant). 각 파트를 얼마나 세부적으로 문단화하는가는 학자들에 따라 천차만별이다(cf. Goldingay, McCann, VanGemeren). 이 주석에서는 다음과 같은 구조를 바탕으로 본문을 주해하고자 한다.

A. 의를 위한 기도(143:1-2)
　　B. 억울한 자의 탄식(143:3-6)
　　B′. 억울한 자의 간구(143:7-11)
A′. 의를 위한 기도(143:12)

III. 주해

참으로 원수들로 인해 생명의 위협을 느끼는 사람이 하나님께 도움을 청하는 기도이다. 기자는 의로우신 하나님이 정의를 행하셔서 그의 억울한 상황을 헤아리시기를 간절히 바란다. 그는 자신을 하나님의 종이라며, 주인이신 주님이 그의 호소를 들어주시기만 하면 모든 것이 해결될 것이라고 확신한다.

1. 의를 위한 기도(143:1-2)

[1] 여호와여
내 기도를 들으시며
내 간구에 귀를 기울이시고
주의 진실과 공의로 내게 응답하소서
[2] 주의 종에게 심판을 행하지 마소서
주의 눈 앞에는 의로운 인생이 하나도 없나이다

기자는 '들으소서(שׁמע)… 귀를 기울이소서(אזן)… 응답하소서(ענה)'라는 하나님의 경청을 구하는 세 동사로 노래를 시작한다(1절). 이러한 문장들은 시편 기자들이 자주 사용하는 정형화된 표현이며, 특히 애가에서 자주 사용되는 것들이다(cf. 시 4:1; 5:1-2; 17:1; 28:2, 6; 31:22; 55:1; 54:2; 61:1; 64:1; 86:6; 102:1; 116:1; 130:2; 140:6; 141:1). 억울한 일을 당한 사람의 하소연이 시작될 것을 암시한다. 그는 하나님이 그의 기도, 곧 간구를 들어주시기를 원한다. '간구'(תַּחֲנוּן)는 변론/호소를 의미한다(HALOT). 그는 참으로 부당한 일을 당했기 때문에 하나님이 그의 말을 들으시면 분명 진실과 공의로 응답하실 것을 확신한다(1d절). '진실'(אֱמוּנָה)은 성실함을, '공의'(צְדָקָה)는 올바른 판단을 뜻한다. 이 두 가지는 하나님의 가장 기본적인 속성이며 하나님과 이스라엘이 맺은 언약의 근간이다(VanGemeren). 그러므로 하나님과 언약관계에 있는 그는 하나님의 의로우심과 성실하심에 자기 자신을 맡기고 있다.

저자는 1절에서 하나님께 '행동하실 것'(action)을 호소했지만, 2절에서는 '행동하시지 말 것'(inaction)을 기도한다(Tucker & Grant). 그는 하나님이 그가 처한 상황을 헤아리기 전까지는 심판을 행하지 않으셔야 할 이유를 제시한다(2절). 그가 죄를 지어 벌을 받고 있다 할지라도 그가 당하고 있는 고통은 참으로 가혹하며 억울한 일이다. 모든 사람은 주님 앞에 의롭지 못하기 때문이다. 대체적으로 개인 탄식시 기자들은 자신들의 억울함과 무죄함을 강조하는데, 이 기자는 하나님 앞에 떳떳한 사람은 없다고 하는 것이 참으로 놀랍다(Kraus, McCann). 만일 하나님이 법대로 하신다면 그가 벌을 받는 것은 당연한 일이겠지만, 하나님의 심판을 받지 않을 사람은 세상에 한 사람도 없다는 논리이다. 시편 14:1-3과 53:1-3, 또한 로마서 3:10을 생각나게 하는 말씀이다. 또한 그는 자신이 하나님의 종이라며(2절, cf. 12절) 주인의 선처를 바라고 있다.

2. 억울한 자의 탄식(143:3-6)

3 원수가 내 영혼을 핍박하며
내 생명을 땅에 엎어서
나로 죽은 지 오랜 자 같이
나를 암흑 속에 두었나이다
4 그러므로 내 심령이 속에서 상하며
내 마음이 내 속에서 참담하니이다
5 내가 옛날을 기억하고
주의 모든 행하신 것을 읊조리며
주의 손이 행하는 일을 생각하고
6 주를 향하여 손을 펴고
내 영혼이 마른 땅 같이 주를 사모하나이다 (셀라)

기자는 그가 어떤 일로, 원수들에게 어떤 공격을 당하고 있는지에 대해 구체적인 언어가 아니라 보편적이고 일반적인 언어로 말한다. 그러므로 이 시편은 많은 사람들이 읽고 자기 자신들에게 적용할 수 있는 보편성을 지니고 있다(VanGemeren).

그는 원수들이 저지른 만행을 세 단계로 묘사한다(3절).

첫째, 그들은 그를 핍박했다(3a절). '핍박하다'(רדף)는 짐승을 사냥하듯 그를 쫓았다는 뜻이다(cf. TNK). 그러므로 사냥꾼들에게 쫓기는 짐승처럼 기자는 별 저항없이 죽음을 맞이할 수밖에 없다.

둘째, 원수들은 그의 생명을 땅에 엎었다(3b절). '엎다'(דכא)는 박살을 내다는 뜻이다(HALOT). 악인들은 사냥하듯 그를 쫓아 잡은 후에는 땅바닥에다 내동댕이치고 죽도록 짓밟았다는 뜻이다(cf. 아가페).

셋째, 그들은 기자를 죽은지 오래된 사람처럼 흑암 속에서 묻혀 살게 했다(3c–d절). 마치 죽은 사람처럼 숨소리도 내지 못하고 숨어 지내야 했다는 뜻이다.

이 세 단계는 '지상→지면→지하'의 움직임을 보이고 있다. 그는 원수들의 핍박으로 인해 살아 있는 사람이 누려야 하는 권리를 하나도 누리지 못하고 억압받는 삶을 살아왔음을 회고하고 있다.

저자는 원수들에게 이런 대접을 받을 만한 일을 한적이 없다. 그러므로 그의 심령은 상했고, 그의 마음은 참담하다(4절). '심령'(נֶפֶשׁ)은 생명을 뜻하며, '상하다'(עטף)는 기력이 쇠하여 아무것도 할 수 없는 상태를 의미한다(NIDOTTE, cf. 시 77:4; 142:3). '참담하다'(שׁמם)는 큰 충격을 받아 아무런 생각을 할 수 없는 상태, 곧 요즘 말로 '멍때린다'는 뜻이다(cf. Tucker & Grant, HALOT). 참으로 원통한 일을 당한 그는 완전히 무기력한 시간을 보내고 있다. 그는 심장이 멈춘 듯한 시간을 보내고 있다(VanGemeren).

다행인 것은 아무것도 할 수 없는 무기력한 상태에서 기자가 하나님께 기도하겠다는 의지를 발휘한 것이다. 그가 자신을 추스르고 하나님께 기도하게 된 가장 큰 이유는 하나님이 과거에 그를 대하시고, 그에게 어떤 은혜를 베푸셨는가를 떠올렸기 때문이다(5a절). 그는 하나님이 행하신 일들을 '기억하고(זכר)… 읊조리며(הגה)… 생각한다(שׂיח)'(5절). 모두 다 묵상과 연관된 동사들이다. 그는 주님과 행복했던 시간들을 떠올리며 절망스러운 현실을 이겨내고 있는 것이다.

지난날들을 묵상하며 용기를 얻은 기자가 주님을 향해 기도한다(6절). 그는 주님을 향해 손을 펴고 기도한다. 기도하는 자세들 중에서도 손을 펴는 것은 하나님께 전적으로 의지한다는 상징성을 지니고 있다. 이 시편에서는 하나님의 개입을 간절히 바란다는 뜻이다(Tucker & Grant). 마치 마른 땅이 단비를 사모하듯, 그는 주님을 간절히 바라본다. 오직 주님에게만 구원이 있기 때문이다.

3. 억울한 자의 간구(143:7–11)

7 여호와여
속히 내게 응답하소서
내 영이 피곤하니이다
주의 얼굴을 내게서 숨기지 마소서
내가 무덤에 내려가는 자 같을까 두려워하나이다
8 아침에 나로 하여금 주의 인자한 말씀을 듣게 하소서
내가 주를 의뢰함이니이다
내가 다닐 길을 알게 하소서
내가 내 영혼을 주께 드림이니이다
9 여호와여
나를 내 원수들에게서 건지소서
내가 주께 피하여 숨었나이다
10 주는 나의 하나님이시니
나를 가르쳐 주의 뜻을 행하게 하소서
주의 영은 선하시니
나를 공평한 땅에 인도하소서
11 여호와여

주의 이름을 위하여 나를 살리시고
주의 공의로 내 영혼을 환난에서 끌어내소서

앞 섹션(3-6절)에서 기자는 원수들의 혹독한 핍박으로 인해 죽을 것 같은 상황에서 과거에 하나님이 베풀어 주신 은혜를 생각하며 용기를 내어 주님께 도와 달라고 기도했다(3-6절). 이 섹션은 하나님이 도우실 것을 믿고 그 도움이 속히 와야 한다는 것에 초점이 맞춰져 있다. 그러므로 그는 매우 급하고 숨가쁜 모습으로 호소하고 있다(Allen). 그는 7-10절에서 동사 7개를 명령형(imperative)과 지시형(jussive)으로 사용하여 이러한 분위기를 조성한다.

그는 하나님이 속히 그에게 응답해 주시기를 호소한다(7절). 그는 매우 지쳐 있으므로 만일 하나님의 응답이 지연되면 견뎌낼 자신이 없다. 그러므로 그는 속히 주님의 얼굴을 뵙게 되기를 소망한다(7d절). 주님의 얼굴은 구원과 생명을 상징한다. 기자는 하나님의 은혜로 원수들의 손에서 벗어나 살고 싶다. 하나님의 응답이 지연되면 그가 죽은 사람처럼 무덤으로 내려가게 될까 봐 두렵다(7e절). '무덤'(בּוֹר)의 문자적 의미는 구덩이(cistern)이다. 구약에서는 사람이 죽으면 가는 곳이 '스올'인데, 이 단어가 지닌 부정적인 뉘앙스 때문에 개인 탄식시에서는 무덤과 구덩이로 대체된다(Gunkel). 그는 지치고 피곤하며 죽음이 임박했음을 직감하고 있지만 삶을 포기하지는 않았다. 그러므로 그는 자신을 사람이 한번 들어가면 나올 수 없는 스올이 아니라, 밖에서 누가 도와주면 빠져나올 수 있는 구덩이에 갇힌 사람으로 묘사하고 있다.

기자는 자신의 삶이 칠흑같이 어둡고 위험한 밤을 지나고 있다고 생각한다. 그러므로 그는 밤새 보초를 선 파수꾼이 아침을 사모하는 것처럼 그의 삶에도 속히 아침이 오기를 간절히 바란다. 하나님의 심판이 밤에, 하나님의 용서와 자비가 아침에 비교되고 있다(VanGemeren).

아침이 오면 그는 하나님의 인자하신 말씀을 듣게 될 것을 소망한다(8a절). 그는 하나님께 어떤 말씀을 듣기를 원하는가? 그가 다닐 길, 곧 그가 살아갈 길을 말씀해 주시기를 소망한다(8c절). 그는 자신은 전적으로 주님을 의지하고(8b절), 자기 영혼을 주님께 맡겼다며(8d절) 주님이 그를 가르쳐 주시기를 간절히 바란다. '길'(דֶּרֶךְ)과 '알다'(ידע)(8절)와 '가르치다'(למד)(10절)는 지혜문헌들과 연관된 단어들이다(Tucker & Grant). 기자는 하나님이 그에게 바르게 살아갈 지혜를 주시기를 기도하고 있다.

여호와는 그의 하나님이시니 그를 꼭 가르쳐 주님의 뜻대로 살게 하셔야 한다(10a–b절). 또한 하나님은 선하시니 부당하게 고통을 당하고 있는 그를 공평한 땅으로 인도하셔야 한다(10c–d절). '공평한 땅'(מִישׁוֹר אֶרֶץ)은 굴곡지지 않은 평평한 땅을 뜻한다(HALOT). 원수들로 인해 온갖 고통을 당하며 굴곡진 길을 걸어온 그는 이제 주님 안에서 평탄한 길을 가고 싶다.

저자는 자신이 가야 할 길에 대해 하나님이 깨우쳐 주시기를 간절히 바라지만, 그보다 먼저 하나님이 그를 위해 해야 할 일이 있으시다. 그를 원수들에게서 건져내시는 일이다(9b절). 그는 하나님의 도우심을 바라며 주님께 피해 숨은 상황이다(9c절). '피하다'(כסה)의 문자적 의미는 '덮다'이다(HALOT). 기자는 하나님이 그를 덮어 주셔야 살 수 있다고 고백하고 있다(Tucker & Grant).

그는 11절에서 다시 한번 주님의 이름(명예)과 공의를 위해서 그를 살리시고 환난에서 그를 꺼내 주시기를 기도한다. '환난'(צָרָה)은 비좁은 공간을 뜻하며, 구약에서는 하나님의 구원을 좁은 공간에 갇혀 있는 자를 넓은 공간으로 옮겨주시는 것으로 표현하기도 하는데, 본문이 이런 경우이다(Holst). 하나님이 그를 구원하시면 세상에서 주님의 명성이 드높아질 것이다(Brueggemann & Bellinger). 동시에 주님이 그를 돕지 않으시면, 그는 죽은 목숨이나 다름없다고 고백한다. 하나님은 누구든 주님께 피하는 자들을 도우시고 구원하신다. 그러므로 기자는 이러한 믿음을 근거로 주님의 구원을 간절히 바란다.

4. 의를 위한 기도(143:12)

12 주의 인자하심으로 나의 원수들을 끊으시고
내 영혼을 괴롭게 하는 자를 다 멸하소서
나는 주의 종이니이다

기자는 참으로 억울하게 고통을 당하고 있다. 그러므로 그는 정의로우신 하나님이 그를 원수들의 손에서 구원하셔서 모든 것을 바로잡아 주시기를 기도했다. 이 노래를 마무리하면서 그는 더 이상 자신의 억울함을 바탕으로 하나님의 도우심을 구하지 않는다. 이제 그는 주님의 '인자하심'(חֶסֶד), 곧 그와 하나님의 특별한 관계를 바탕으로 하나님이 그를 도우실 것을 호소한다. 그는 하나님이 그의 원수들을 모두 끊으시고, 그를 괴롭게 하는 자들을 모두 멸하시기를 기도한다. 그는 하나님의 종으로서 이렇게 기도할 자격이 있다고 생각한다(cf. 2절). 주인이신 하나님은 그의 종을 괴롭히는 자들을 응징하실 의무가 있다(cf. Goldingay).

제144편
다윗의 시

I. 장르/양식: 개인 탄식시(cf. 3편)

이 시편은 찬양, 축복, 간구, 탄식, 서원 등 다양한 장르로 구성되어 있다(Gerstenberger). 그렇다 보니 이 시편이 취하고 있는 양식에 대해 학자들은 다양한 시각을 내놓았다. 우리는 이 시편을 개인 탄식시로 구분하지만(cf. Gunkel, Ross), 개인이 아니라 공동체 탄식시라고 하는 이가 있다(Anderson). 탄식시가 아니라 선포적 찬양시라는 주장이 있는가 하면(Westeramnn), 전쟁으로 나가는 왕의 기도라며 왕족시라고 하는 이들도 있다(Kraus, Terrien).

이 시편은 포로기 이후 시대에 저작된 것이라는 견해가 지배적이다(deClaissé-Walford et al., Mays, McCann). 왕정 시대에 저작된 것이라는 견해가 있는가 하면(Terrien), 1-11절은 왕정 시대에, 그 뒷부분은 포로기나 그 이후 시대에 저작된 것이라는 주장도 있다(Allen, cf. Terrien). 저작 시기를 구체적으로 단정하기가 쉽지 않다는 주장도 있다(Gerstenberger).

칠십인역(LXX)은 표제에 '골리앗에 관한'(πρὸς τὸν Γολιαδ)이라는 말을 붙여 다윗이 골리앗과 싸우러 나갈 때, 혹은 승리하고 돌아와서 부른 노래로 간주했다(cf. 17장). 이때 다윗의 나이가 어린 소년이었던 점을 감안하면, 그가 그 나이에 이처럼 놀랍고 아름다운 노래를 부를 수 있었을까 의구심이 들 수도 있다. 한 가지 확실한 것은 이 시편과 다윗의 삶의 연관성이다. 이 시편은 시편 18편과 밀접한 연관성이 있는데(cf. 다음 도표 참조), 시편 18편은 사무엘하 22장에 기록된 다윗의 노래를 그대로 인용한 것이다. 그러므로 이 시편도 분명 다윗의 삶과 어느 정도는 연관되어 있음을 시사한다(deClaissé-Walford et al.).

이 시편은 여러 시편을 부분적으로 인용하고 있다. 다음 도표를 참조하라(cf. deClaissé-Walford et al., Goldingay, Kidner, McCann, Tucker & Grant). 이 시편은 특별히 18편과 깊은 연관성을 보인다. 아마도 포로기를 살아가던 기자가 왕족시인 18편을 변화시켜 다윗에게 내리셨던 축복을 자신에게도 내려 달라고 기도하고 있는 듯하다(Mays, cf. Allen).

시 144편	시 18편	나머지 시편
2절	1, 2, 3, 4, 46, 47절	
3절		8:4
4절	4절	39:5–6
5절	9절	
6절	14절	
7, 11절	16, 44, 45절	
9절		33:2–3
10절	표제	
15절		33:12

II. 구조

학자들은 이 시편의 구조에 대하여 다양한 견해를 내놓았다(cf. Allen, deClaissé-Walford et al., Hossfeld-Zenger, McCann, Ross, Terrien, VanGemeren). 이 주석에서는 다음과 같은 구조를 바탕으로 본문을 주해해 나가고자 한다(cf. 새번역).

A. 여호와 찬양(144:1-2)
B. 인간의 덧없음(144:3-4)
C. 기원(144:5-8)
D. 찬양과 기도(144:9-11)
E. 확신(144:12-14)
F. 축복(144:15)

III. 주해

기자는 옛적에 다윗 왕이 하나님께 고백했던 신앙을 자신의 신앙으로 고백하며 하나님의 은혜를 구한다. 주님이 다윗의 기도를 들으시고 그에게 내려 주셨던 축복을 그와 그가 속한 공동체에게도 내려 달라는 염원을 담아서 기도한다. 우리도 기자처럼 기도했으면 좋겠다.

1. 여호와 찬양(144:1-2)

1 나의 반석이신 여호와를 찬송하리로다
그가 내 손을 가르쳐 싸우게 하시며
손가락을 가르쳐 전쟁하게 하시는도다
2 여호와는 나의 사랑이시요
나의 요새이시요 나의 산성이시요
나를 건지시는 이시요 나의 방패이시니
내가 그에게 피하였고
그가 내 백성을 내게 복종하게 하셨나이다

기자는 하나님이 그를 전쟁에 능한 용사로 훈련시켜 주신 것을 찬양하며 노래를 시작한다(1절). 주님이 그의 손과 손가락이 전투에 능하도록 가르치셨다(1b−c절). 이러한 찬송은 전쟁으로 나가는 사람의 노래이다(cf. 7절). 그는 백성들과 함께 전쟁터로 떠나면서 꼭 승리하고 돌아오기를 염원하고 있다. 이러한 이유로 학자들은 이 노래를 왕족시라 하기도 하고(cf. 10절), 개인이 아니라 공동체의 노래라고(cf. 12−14절) 하기도 한다(Anderson, Kraus, Terrien).

저자는 즐겁고 흥분된 마음으로 하나님을 다섯 가지로 찬양한다(2절).

첫째, 하나님은 '그의 사랑'(חַסְדִּי)이시다(2a절). 기자가 자비와 인애로도 번역이 되며 주님과 백성의 관계를 강조하는 관계적인 언어를 제일 먼저 사용함으로써 그가 경험한 하나님의 은총은 모두 하나님과의 특별한 관계에 근거를 둔 것이며, 앞으로도 이 관계를 근거로 주님이 베푸신 자비를 즐기며 찬양할 것을 암시한다. 기자는 하나님과의 관계를 강조하기 위해 1인칭 대명사 '나, 내가'를 1−2절에서 8차례나 사용하고 있다(deClaissé−Walford et al., cf. Tucker & Grant). 전쟁으로 나가는 사람에게 가장 중요한 것이 바로 하나님과의 관계이다.

둘째, 여호와는 '그의 요새'(מְצוּדָה)이시다(2b절) 이미지는 적들의 어떠한 공격도 쉽게 막아 내실 수 있는 성이다. 하나님은 적들의 공격에서 그를 충분히 보호하시는 난공불락의 요새이시다. 하나님은 이 전쟁에서도 적들의 공격을 따돌리시고 기자를 보호하실 것이다.

셋째, 주님은 '그의 산성'(מִשְׂגַּבִּי)이시다(2b절). 험난한 산에서도 가장 높은 정상이어서 누구도 넘보지 못하는 곳이다. 하나님은 적들이 아예 공격할 꿈도 못 꾸는 곳에 그를 두실 것이다. 그러므로 하나님이 그의 산성이시라는 것은 가장 확실한 안전 보장이다.

넷째, 하나님은 '그를 건지시는 이'(מְפַלְטִי)이시다(2c절). 하나님은 곤경에서 스스로 헤어나지 못하는 사람을 밖에서 끌어내 그 위기에서 도피할 수 있도록 하시는 분이다. 기자는 전쟁 중에 적들에게 포위를 당해 곤경에 처할 수도 있다. 그럴 때마다 하나님은 적들의 포위에서 그를 빼내실 것이다. 때로는 우리도 하나님의 손에 이끌리어 강압적으로 위기를 탈출하는 경험을 한다.

다섯째, 여호와는 '그의 방패'(מָגִנִּי)이시다(2c절). 방패는 손에 들고 다니는 방어 무기다. 요새나 산성은 규모가 큰 은신처인 것에 반해, 방패는 군인이 항상 가지고 다니며 자신을 보호하는 도구이다. 하나님이 방패라는 것은 주님의 세심한 보호가 그를 상시 보호하실 것을 확신하는 고백이다.

하나님은 이처럼 자상하면서도 확실한 구원자이시다. 그러므로 기자는 과거에도 하나님께 피한 적이 여러 번 있다(2d절). 과거의 경험이 현재 상황에 대한 믿음을 준 것이다. '피하다'(חסה)는 숨었다는 뜻이다(HALOT). 그는 이때까지 전적으로 하나님을 의지해 전쟁을 해왔다. 그랬더니 하나님은 그에게 큰 승리를 안겨주셨다(2e절). 하나님이 그가 전쟁을 하던 백성들을 그에게 복종시키셨다. 마소라 사본은 '내 백성'(עַמִּי)을 복종하게 하셨다고 하는데, 흐름이 매끈하지가 않다(cf. Goldingay). 전쟁에 나가는 이유가 뭇 백성을 복종시키기 위해서이기 때문이다(cf. 7절). 그러므로 새번역, 공동번역, NIV, NRS, ESV, TNK 등은 '뭇 백성'으로 수정했다. '내 백성'을 그대로 유지하며 일종의 내란이 있었던 것으로 해석하는 이들도 있지만(Hossfeld-Zenger), 문맥과 맞지 않으며 설득력이 전혀 없는 추측이다.

2. 인간의 덧없음(144:3-4)

3 여호와여
사람이 무엇이기에 주께서 그를 알아 주시며
인생이 무엇이기에 그를 생각하시나이까
4 사람은 헛것 같고
그의 날은 지나가는 그림자 같으니이다

기자는 하나님이 얼마나 자상하고 확실하게 전쟁에서 그를 보호하시고 승리하게 하시는가를 생각해 보면 그저 감개가 무량할 뿐이다. 그는 하나님께 이런 대접을 받을 만한 자격이 없다는 사실을 잘 알고 있다(cf. 시 8:4; 욥 7:17). 그도 하나님이 창조하신 아름답고 놀라운 세상에서 별 볼 일 없는 비천한 인간에 불과하기 때문이다(3절). '사람'(אָדָם)은 흙으로 빚어진 인간의 연약함을(Brueggemann & Bellinger), '인생'(בֶּן־אֱנוֹשׁ)는 잠시 이 땅에서 살다가 순식간에 사라지는 허무한 존재라는 것을 뜻한다. 넓은 우주를 생각할 때 인간은 그 우주의 한 먼지와 같은 지구에 잠시 살다 사라지는 별 볼 일 없는 존재에 불과하다.

그런데도 하나님은 그들을 알아주시고, 생각해 주신다(3절). 본문에서 '알다'(ידע)는 부모가 자식을 알듯이 관계를 근거로 한 앎이다. '생각하다'(חשב)는 존귀하게 여긴다는 뜻이다(HALOT). 그러므로 이 두 동사는 하나님이 우리를 참으로 잘 아실 뿐만 아니라, 매우 소중하게 여기신다는 사실을 강조한다. 그러므로 기자는 그가 감당할 수 없는 하나님의 벅찬 은혜를 이렇게 밖에 표현할 수 없다: "인생이 무엇이기에!"

기자는 하나님의 관심과 사랑이 과분하다며 다시 한번 자신과 같은 인간이 지닌 한계를 겸손히 고백한다(4절). 사람은 헛것 같고 그의 수명은 지나가는 그림자 같다고 한다. '헛것'(הֶבֶל)의 원 의미는 '숨결'이며 허무함을 뜻한다(cf. 시 39:5, 11; 62:9; 전 1:2, 14; 2:11, 17; 3:19; 6:4, 11). '그림자'(צֵל)는 실체가 없다. 게다가 속히 '지나가는' 그림자는 참으로 허무하다(cf. 시 102:11; 109:23; 욥 8:9; 14:2; 17:7; 전 6:12). 사람의 한평생이라고 해도 참으로 덧없음을 강조한다. 이처럼 볼품없는 인간을 하나님이 사랑하시고 인도하시니 얼마나 감격스러운 일인가!

3. 기원(144:5-8)

5 여호와여
주의 하늘을 드리우고 강림하시며

산들에 접촉하사 연기를 내게 하소서
6 번개를 번쩍이사 원수들을 흩으시며
주의 화살을 쏘아 그들을 무찌르소서
7 위에서부터 주의 손을 펴사
나를 큰 물과 이방인의 손에서 구하여 건지소서
8 그들의 입은 거짓을 말하며
그의 오른손은 거짓의 오른손이니이다

기자는 1-2절에서 하나님을 무한한 능력을 지니신 구원자로 찬양했다. 이 섹션에서는 하나님이 이 땅에 강림하셔서 그를 원수들의 손에서 구원하시기를 기도한다. 그는 하나님이 하늘을 드리우셔서 그가 사는 이 땅에 강림하시기를 소망한다(5b절). '드리우다'(נטה)는 활을 늘어뜨릴 때 사용하는 단어이다(HALOT). 하늘에 계시는 주님이 활을 늘어뜨리듯이 하늘을 늘어뜨려 땅에 닫게 하심으로 이 땅에 강림하시기를 바라는 기도이다. 이렇게 되면 하나님은 하늘에서 누리시는 모든 권세와 영광을 하나도 포기할 필요 없이 이 땅에 임하실 수 있다.

저자는 하나님이 이 땅에 강림하셔서 산들을 접촉하여 연기를 내게 하시라고 한다(5c절). '접촉하다'(נגע)는 '만지다/치다'라는 뜻이며 '연기를 내게 하다'(עשן)는 연기로 감싸거나 연기가 흘러나오게 하는 것을 의미한다(HALOT). 연기로 가득한 산은 시내 산을 연상케 한다(cf. 출 19장). 그는 하나님께 시내 산에 임하셨을 때 지니셨던 영광과 위엄으로 이번에도 임하시기를 기도하고 있다.

기자는 영광과 위엄으로 임하신 하나님께 원수들을 공격해 달라고 기도한다(6절). 하나님이 우레와 천둥으로 그들을 흩으시기를 바란다(6a절). 우레와 천둥을 다스리는 것은 오직 하나님만이 하실 수 있는 일이다. 그는 하나님의 현현이 극대화되기를 기대한다. 또한 하나님이 화살을 쏘아 그들을 무찔러 주시기를 기도한다(6b절). 활은 천둥과 번개를 뜻할 수도 있지만(VanGemeren), 문자 그대로 화살을 의미할 수도 있다. 기자는 하나님이 천재지변과 전쟁 무기를 동원하여 적들을 치시기를 바란다. 5절에서 하나님이 저자에게 오시기 위해 드리우신 활이 그의 원수들을 향해서는 살상무기가 되기를 염원하고 있다.

하나님을 전적으로 의지하는 기자는 하나님이 원수들을 공격하여 물리치심으로 그를 구원하시기를 간절히 바란다(7절). 그가 바라는 구원은 하나님이 계시는 위(하늘)에서 주님이 손을 펴서 직접 이루시는 일이며 큰 물과 이방인들의 손에서 구하여 건져내시는 것이다. 하나님의 손은 주님의 창조 사역을 상징한다(Hossfeld-Zenger, cf. 시 8:6; 143:5). 특별히 혼란 속에서 질서를 세우시는 일을 의미한다(Tucker & Grant). 기자는 창조주께서 직접 오셔서 원수들로 인해 혼란에 빠져 있는 그의 삶에 질서와 평화를 세우시기를 간절히 바라고 있다.

'구하다'(פצה)는 억압에서 '해방시키다'는 뜻을 지녔고, '건지다'(נצל)는 빼앗다는 의미를 지녔다(cf. HALOT). 기자는 자신이 스스로는 절대 빠져나올 수 없는 상황을 상상하고 있다. 하나님의 손이 그를 빼내실 때만 원수들의 손에서 벗어날 수 있는 상황이다. 하나님의 '손'(יָד)은 구원하시는 손이며, 이방인들의 '손'(יָד)은 죽이는 손이라는 대조가 인상적이다. '큰 물'(מַיִם רַבִּים)은 고대 근동 신화에서 바다 신인 얌(Yam)을 의미할 수 있다(cf. VanGemeren). 그러나 본문에서는 단순히 '여러 갈래의 물'을 뜻한다. 기자는 그를 괴롭히는 원수들이 여럿이라는 것을 암시한다.

기자가 하나님께 도움을 청하는 것은 주님이 그와 특별한 관계를 맺고 있으시기 때문만은 아니다. 그가 상대해야 할 적들은 하나님이 싫어하시는 짓들을 하는 자들이기 때문이기도 하다. 그들은 온통 거짓을 행하는 자들이다(8절). 그들은 거짓을 말하며, 그들의 오른손은 거짓의 오른손이다. 그들이 하는 '거짓말'(דִּבֶּר־שָׁוְא)은 생각해 보거나 들어줄 만한 가치가 전혀 없는 쓸데없는(worthless) 말이다. 오른손은 행동과 실천의 상징이다(cf. VanGemeren). 그러므로 '거짓의 오른손'(יְמִין שָׁקֶר)은 그들이 행하는 일들 중 진실된 것은 없다는 뜻이다. 그들은 죄와 거짓을 일삼는 삶을 살고 있다. 그러므로 하나님은 이런 자들을 심판하셔야 한다는 것이 기자의 논리이다.

4. 찬양과 기도(144:9–11)

9 하나님이여
내가 주께 새 노래로 노래하며
열 줄 비파로 주를 찬양하리이다
10 주는 왕들에게 구원을 베푸시는 자시요
그의 종 다윗을 그 해하려는 칼에서 구하시는 자시니이다
11 이방인의 손에서 나를 구하여 건지소서
그들의 입은 거짓을 말하며
그 오른손은 거짓의 오른손이니이다

이 전쟁에서 주님이 그와 함께하실 것이라는 확신으로 가득 찬 기자는 하나님을 새 노래로 찬송하고자 한다(9절). '새 노래'(שִׁיר חָדָשׁ)(cf. 사 42:10; 시 33:3; 40:3; 96:1; 98:1; 144:9; 149:1)가 반드시 새로 지은 노래를 의미하는 것은 아니다(cf. Tucker & Grant). 새로운 마음과 태도로 부르는 노래를 뜻하기도 한다. 그는 마치 하나님을 처음 찬양하는 것처럼 감동에 찬 마음으로 악기(열 줄 비파)를 동원하여 열렬히 주님을 찬양하고자 한다.

기자가 하나님을 새 노래로 찬양하고자 하는 이유는 주님이 주의 백성의 왕으로 세우신 이들에게 구원을 베푸시는 분이기 때문이다(10a절). 기자가 이렇게 말하는 것은 아마도 그도 왕이기 때문일 것이다. 혹은 옛적에 이스라엘의 왕들을 구원하셨던 것처럼 자기도 구원해 달라는 염원을 반영한다.

그는 한 가지 예로 하나님이 다윗을 원수들의 칼에서 어떻게 구원하셨는가를 회고한다(10b절). 다윗은 하나님을 의지하고 살며 위기 때마다 주님의 구원을 간절히 바라는 사람의 상징이 되었기 때문이다(Tucker). 이 시편이 인용하고 있는 시편 18편에서 다윗은 용장으로 묘사되었지만, 이 시편에서 그는 오로지 하나님의 구원을 바라는 연약한 사람으로 묘사된다(Tucker & Grant). 하나님은 다윗과 평생 함께하시면서 위기 때마다 그를 구원하셨다. 이러한 구원이 그에게도 임하기를 기원한다. 전쟁터로 나가고 있는 기자는 11절에서 7b-8절을 후렴처럼 반복하면서 주님이 이방인 원수들의 손에서 그를 구원하실 것을 한 번 더 호소한다(cf. 7b-8절 주해).

5. 확신(144:12-14)

[12] 우리 아들들은 어리다가 장성한 나무들과 같으며
우리 딸들은 궁전의 양식대로 아름답게 다듬은 모퉁잇돌들과 같으며
[13] 우리의 곳간에는 백곡이 가득하며
우리의 양은 들에서 천천과 만만으로 번성하며
[14] 우리 수소는 무겁게 실었으며
또 우리를 침노하는 일이나
우리가 나아가 막는 일이 없으며
우리 거리에는 슬피 부르짖음이 없을진대

전쟁터를 향해 떠나는 왕은 하나님이 반드시 그의 원수들을 물리치실 것을 확신한다. 그러므로 이 섹션에서는 그가 전쟁에서 승리하고 돌아와 목격하게 될 주의 백성의 삶을 상상해 본다. 한마디로 말해 참 평안과 평화가 깃든 '샬롬 사회'이다. 그러므로 이 섹션의 관점은 종말론적이다(McCann).

노래가 이 섹션에서 갑자기 1인칭 복수로 바뀐다 하여 이 부분이 훗날 추가된 것이라고 하는 이들이 있다(cf. McCann, Tucker & Grant). 포로기 후에 살았던 기자가 옛 노래를 상당 부분 인용하여 이 노래를 저작했다면 충분히 가능한 일이다. 만일 이 노래가 예루살렘으로 돌아온 귀향민 공동체가 부른 노래라면 그들이 이겨내야 했던 참혹한 현실을 배경으로 읽으면 더 의미가 있다(cf. 느헤미야서; 학 1:6-11). 그들은 이 섹션이 노래하는 유토피아를 꿈꾸며 현실을 견디어 냈기 때문이다.

기자가 구하는 축복에는 분명 흐름이 있다. 처음에는 가족에 대한 축복을 구하고 농작물에 대한 복을 구한다(12-13절). 이어 국가적인, 군사적인 축복을 구한다(14절). 마지막으로 온 백성에게 복을 빈다(15절). 점차적으로 바라는 축복의 범위가 넓어지고 있는 것이다(Broyles).

첫째, 그는 자녀들이 왕성하고 아름답게 자란 세상을 꿈꾼다(12절). 아들들은 건장하게 자라 장성한 나무들 같을 것이며(12a절), 딸들은 왕궁을 장식하는 아름다운 모퉁잇돌들과 같을 것이다(12b절). 한마디로 말해 선남선녀(善男善女)로 가득한 세상을 상상하고 있다.

둘째, 그는 온 공동체가 곳간에는 온갖 곡식이 넘쳐나고, 가축들의 숫자는 셀 수 없을 정도로 풍족한 삶을 누리게 되기를 꿈꾼다. 하루하루 끼니를 잇기가 쉽지 않았던 사회에서 왕은 백성들의 삶을 염려하며 참으로 큰 꿈을 꾸고 있다. 지도자는 이러해야 한다.

셋째, 그는 사람과 짐승이 실패하는 일이 없는 사회를 꿈꾼다(14절). 14a절을 번역하는 일이 쉽지 않다. "우리 수소는 무겁게 실었다"는 마소라 사본을 문자적으로 번역한 것이며, 의미가 확실하지가 않다. 아마도 살이 쪄서, 혹은 임신을 해서 몸이 무겁게 되었다는 뜻일 것이다(cf. 새번역 각주). 대부분 번역본들은 각자 고유의 의미를 살리려고 노력했지만, ESV가 문맥에 가장 잘 어울리는 듯하다: "우리의 소들은 임신하여 몸이 무거워지고, 유산되거나 잘못되는 일이 없도록 되기를 바랍니다"(may our cattle be heavy with young, suffering no mishap or failure in bearing). 이 구절이 14절의 나머지 내용보다는 13절과 더 잘 어울린다 하여 NAS는 이 구절을 13절에 포함시켰다.

짐승들이 실패하는 일이 없을 것이라고 한 기자가 14b-d절에서는 사람들도 실패하는 일이 없을 것이라고 한다. 이 구절도 해석이 어렵다(cf. 새번역, 아가페, 현대인, 공동). 영어 번역본들도 다양하게 해석했다. 이 구절은 "성벽이 무너지는 일도 없고, 포로로 끌려가는 일도 없고, 거리에는 울부짖는 일도 없기를 바랍니다"라는 의미를 지녔다(cf. 아가페). 패배한 전쟁 상황을 묘사하고 있다. 그는 주의 백성이 다시는 전쟁할 일도, 적들의 침략을 받을 일도, 패할 일도 없게 되기를 염원하고 있다.

6. 축복(144:15)

15 이러한 백성은 복이 있나니
여호와를 자기 하나님으로 삼는 백성은 복이 있도다

기자는 앞 섹션(12-14절)에서 자신이 꿈꾸는 '샬롬 사회'를 묘사한 다음 자기와 함께 이런 사회를 꿈꾸고 이루려는 백성은 복이 있다며 노래를 마무리한다. 당연하다. 이 땅에서 이러한 평안과 평화를 누리며 사는 것은 결코 쉽지 않기 때문이다. 그러나 모든 사람이 여호와를 의지하고, 하나님이 꿈꾸시는 사회를 실현하려고 노력하면 가능하다. 그러므로 그는 여호와를 자기 하나님으로 삼은 백성은 참으로 복되다고 한다. 주님이 도우시면 우리는 이러한 사회를 이룰 수 있기 때문이다.

제145편

다윗의 찬송시

I. 장르/양식: 회중 찬양시(cf. 29편)

이 노래는 알파벳 시로 저작되어 있는 시편들 중 마지막 것이다(cf. 25, 34, 37, 111, 112, 119편). 특이한 것은 히브리어 알파벳 22개 중 눈(נ)이 누락되어 있다는 사실이다. 한국어와 영어 번역본들은 고대 번역본들인 칠십인역(LXX)과 시리아역(Syr.)과 라틴어역(Vg.)과 마소라 사본 중 하나(Kennicott manuscript 142)가 눈(נ)으로 시작하는 문장을 포함하고 있다는 사실을 근거로 13절과 14절 사이에 누락된 문장을 삽입한다(cf. Kimelman). 필사가의 실수로 이 구절이 누락되었다고 보기 때문이다. 그러나 구약과 시편의 여러 알파벳 시가 완벽한 형태가 아닌 상태로 발견되기 때문에 이 시에 눈(נ) 문장을 추가하지 않아야 한다는 주장도 있다(Goldingay, Hossfeld-Zenger). 원본에도 눈(נ) 문장이 없었을 것이라는 추측이다.

알파벳 시가 강조하고자 하는 바는 총체성과 포괄성이다. 이 시편은 여호와의 속성과 사역을 찬양하는 일에 초점을 맞추고 있다. 그러므로 모든 단어의 조합이 되는 알파벳이 총동원되어 여호와를 송축하는 것은 완벽하신 여호와를 온전히 경배하기 위해서이다(cf. Berlin). 또한 하나님의 통치의 완벽함이 '모두'(כֹּל)의 지속적인 사용(총 17차례)으로 더욱 더 강조된다(Tucker & Grant, cf. Goldingay). 한 주석가는 이 시편과 8, 33, 104편이 하나님이 창조하신 세상의 완벽함을 노래한다 해서 이 시편들을 '창조 노래'(songs of Creation)라고 부른다(Brueggemann). 그는 이 시편들 중 145편이 단연 으뜸이라고 한다.

이 시는 표제가 다윗과 연관된 시편으로는 마지막 노래이다. 또한 150편의 시편들 중에 '찬송시'(תְּהִלָּה)로 불리는 유일한 노래이기도 하다. 제5권의 '다윗 모음집'(138-145편)을 마무리 하는 시로써 적절한 타이틀로 생각된다. 이 시편은 제5권의 절정으로서 마지막 '찬양(hallel) 모음집'(146-150편)이 21절에서 추진력을 받기 때문이다(Wilson). 일부 학자들은 원래 시편 모음집이 145편에서 끝났을 가능성을 제시하기도 한다(McCann).

학자들은 이 시의 저작 시기는 포로기 이후 시대라고 한다(Anderson). 이유는 알파벳 시가 포로기 이후에 활성화되었다고 생각하기 때문이다. 그러나 그렇게 단정할 만한 증거는 없다. 이 시편은 언제든 주님을 찬양할 때면 사용할 수 있는 보편성을 지녔다. 유태인들은 오늘날도 아침과 저녁 기도에서 이 시편을 사용한다(Ross). 탈무드는 이 시편을 세 차례 이상 반복하여 읽으면 다가오는 세상(내세)을 누리게 될 것이라고 한다(b. Ber. 4b. cf. Ross).

II. 구조

이 시에서는 '송축하다/축복하다'(ברך)가 1절, 10절, 21절에서 사용되면서 '서주(prelude)—간주(interlude)—후주(postlude)'를 형성한다(Kimelman). 이러한 구조는 여호와에 대한 송축이 개인적 찬양(1-2절)—신실한 사람들의 찬양(10절)—모든 피조물의 찬양(21절)으로 이어지고 있음을 암시한다.

이 노래는 '송축하다/축복하다'(ברך)가 사용되는 1절과 10절과 21절을 기준으로 1–3절, 4–9절, 10–13a절, 13b–21절 네 섹션으로 나뉜다(McCann, VanGemeren). 각 섹션은 찬양으로 시작하여(1–2절, 4–7절, 10–12절) 주님의 속성을 묵상하는 것으로 이어진다(3절, 8–9절, 13a절). 마지막 섹션에서는 찬양과 묵상 순서가 바뀌어 13b–20절이 먼저 하나님의 속성을 선포하고, 21절이 찬양으로 시 전체를 마무리한다. 1–2절과 21절이 일종의 괄호를 형성하며 시 전체를 감싸게 하기 위해 마지막 섹션에서 찬양—묵상 순서가 바뀌고 있는 것이다(Lindars). 1–2절과 21절이 '축복하다(ברך), 찬송(תְּהִלָּה), 영원히(לְעוֹלָם וָעֶד)'를 공유하는 것도 이러한 구조를 반영하고 있다. 이러한 상황을 반영하여 이 주석에서는 다음과 같은 구조를 바탕으로 본문을 주해해 나가고자 한다(cf. Goldingay).

A. 개인적 찬양(145:1–2)
　B. 여호와의 위대하심 찬양(145:3–6)
　　C. 여호와의 선하심 찬양(145:7–9)
A′. 공동체적 찬양(145:10)
　B′. 여호와의 위대하심 찬양(145:11–13)
　　C′. 여호와의 선하심 찬양(145:14–20)
A″. 모든 피조물의 찬양(145:21)

III. 주해

이 시편은 처음부터 끝까지 왕이신 하나님을 찬양한다. 여호와는 참으로 위대하시고 선하신 분이므로 각개인 뿐만 아니라 온 세상의 찬양을 받기에 합당하신 분이다. 그러므로 세상 모든 피조물은 여호와가 창조주—왕이심을 찬양해야 한다. 이 시편은 주기도문을 마무리하는 "나라와 권세와 영광이 아버지께 영원히 있사옵나이다"를 확대하여 노래한다(Kirkpatrick).

1. 개인적 찬양(145:1-2)

[1] 왕이신 나의 하나님이여
내가 주를 높이고
영원히 주의 이름을 송축하리이다
[2] 내가 날마다 주를 송축하며
영원히 주의 이름을 송축하리이다

기자는 여호와를 왕으로 찬양하면서 노래를 시작한다(1절). 시편은 하나님의 왕 되심을 지속적으로 찬양한다. 그러나 왕에 정관사를 붙이는 경우(אֱלוֹהַי הַמֶּלֶךְ)는 본문과 시편 98:6이 유일하다. 이 정관사를 호격형(vocative)으로 해석하여 '나의 하나님과 왕'(My God and King)으로 번역하는 이들이 있다(NRS, NAS, ESV, TNK). 그러나 이 문구는 '나의 하나님이 그 왕이시다'(My God [is] the King)라는 의미로 해석되어야 한다(Hossfeld-Zenger, cf. NIV). 세상에 여호와 외에는 참 왕이 없다는 뜻이다(Tucker & Grant).

그는 주님을 '높이고'(רום)(1b절) 주님의 이름을 '송축하고'(ברך)(1c절), 날마다 주를 '송축하며'(ברך)(2a절), 주의 이름을 '송축할 것'(הלל)(2b절)이라며 네 차례나 주님을 찬양하겠다는 다짐을 한다. 이는 이 시편이 주님을 찬양하기 위해 저작된 노래라는 것을 암시한다. 여호와는 그의 찬양을 받기에 합당하신 분이므로 그는 주님을 '날마다/모든 날에'(בְּכָל־יוֹם) 찬양할 것(2a절)과 두 차례나 '영원히'(לְעוֹלָם וָעֶד) 찬양할 것을 다짐한다(1c, 2b절). 사람이 하나님을 영원히 찬양한다는 것은 묵상적 과장법(devotional hyperbole)이며 살아 있는 동안 주님을 예배한다는 뜻이다(Goulder). 유태인들은 이 시편을 아침 예배에서 두 차례, 저녁 예배에서 한 차례씩 매일 되뇌었다(VanGemeren).

저자는 '주의 이름'(שִׁמְךָ)을 찬양할 것을 두 차례나 언급하는데(1c, 2b절), 하나님이 그와 맺으신 언약을 신실하게 지키심을 찬양하겠다는 뜻이다(VanGemeren). 또한 그는 주님을 높이겠다고 하는데, 우리는 어떻게 이미 높으신 하나님을 더 높일 수 있는가? 기자는 경배와 찬양을 통해서라고 한다. 그러므로 그는 세 차례나 주님을 송축할 것을 다짐한다.

2. 여호와의 위대하심 찬양(145:3-6)

3 여호와는 위대하시니 크게 찬양할 것이라
그의 위대하심을 측량하지 못하리로다
4 대대로 주께서 행하시는 일을 크게 찬양하며
주의 능한 일을 선포하리로다
5 주의 존귀하고 영광스러운 위엄과 주의 기이한 일들을
나는 작은 소리로 읊조리리이다
6 사람들은 주의 두려운 일의 권능을 말할 것이요
나도 주의 위대하심을 선포하리이다

기자는 구체적인 사례를 말하지 않으면서 하나님의 위대하심을 묵상하고 찬양한다. 고대 근동에서 '위대함'은 왕권과 연관되어 있는 개념이다(Tucker & Grant, cf. 시 95:3). 기자는 하나님을 왕으로 찬양하는 일을 이어가고 있는 것이다. 여호와는 얼마나 놀라운 분인지 주님의 '위대하심'(גְּדוּלָּה)을 가늠할 길이 없다(3b절, cf. 시 48:1; 96:4; 147:5). '측량하지 못한다'(אֵין חֵקֶר)는 살펴 헤아릴 방법이 없다는 뜻이다(Anderson, cf. 시 5:9; 9:10; 36:26; 사 40:28). 그러므로 기자는 그저 하나님의 '위대하심'(גָּדוֹל)을 높이 찬양할 뿐이다(3a절). 그는 3절에서 하나님의 위대하심을 두 차례 강조하여 주님은 참으로 대단하신 분임을 고백한다. 하나님의 위대하심은 인간의 초라함과 보잘것없음을 가장 확실하게 드러낸다.

하나님이 '하시는 일'(מַעֲשֶׂה)과 주님의 '능력'(גְּבוּרָה)은 참으로 놀랍기 때문에 대대로(영원히) 큰소리로 찬양하기에 합당하다(4절). 또한 하나님의 존귀하고 영광스러운 위엄과 기이한 일들은 참으로 섬세하고 자상하기 때문에 개인적으로 묵상하기에도 적합하다(5절). '존귀하고 영광스러운 위엄'(הֲדַר כְּבוֹד הוֹדֶךָ)은 비슷한 낱말인 세 단어를 연속적으로 묶어 놓은 것이다(cf. 시 96:6-7). 하나님은 말로 형언하기가 어렵도록 존귀하신 분이라는 뜻이다. '기이한 일들'(נִפְלְאוֹת)은 주님이 행하시는 기적들을 뜻한다. '작은 소리로 읊조리다'(שִׂיחַ)는 감사와 찬양을 곁들여 묵상하는 것을 의미한다(HALOT, cf. 시 77:13; 19:48). 하나님의 위엄과 기적들은 세상을 떠들썩하게 하는 참으로 위대한 것들이지만, 동시에 우리에게 무한한 묵상거리가 되기도 한다.

여호와 하나님의 위대하심을 보고 사람들은 하나님이 하시는 놀랍고 신기한 일들에 대해 말할 것이다(cf. 아가페). 반면에 기자는 주님의 위대하심을 선포할 것이다. 사람들은 자신들이 목격한 하나님의 권능에 대해 증언할 것이지만, 기자는 주님이 어떤 분이신가를 온 세상에 알릴 것이다.

3. 여호와의 선하심 찬양(145:7-9)

7 그들이 주의 크신 은혜를 기념하여 말하며
주의 공의를 노래하리이다
8 여호와는 은혜로우시며
긍휼이 많으시며
노하기를 더디 하시며
인자하심이 크시도다

9 여호와께서는 모든 것을 선대하시며
그 지으신 모든 것에 긍휼을 베푸시는도다

사람들은 여호와의 크신 은혜와 공의를 기념하고 노래할 것이다(7절). '주의 은혜'(טוּבְךָ)는 여호와께서 주시는 축복과 건강을 뜻한다(HALOT). '주의 공의'(צִדְקָתְךָ)는 주님이 세상을 의롭게 다스리시고 판결하시는 것을 의미한다. 그들이 목격한 하나님의 두려운 일들(cf. 6절)은 창조주께서 세상에 내려 주시는 축복이자 다스리는 방식이라는 뜻이다. 이런 일을 경험한 그들은 8절에서 여호와의 속성을 4가지로 찬양한다. 이 말씀은 출애굽기 34:6-7을 부분적으로 인용한 것이며(cf. 시 86:15; 103:8), 하나님이 피조물을 대하실 때 드러나는 관계적인 속성들이다.

첫째, 하나님은 은혜로우시다(חַנּוּן)(8a절). 아무런 전제 조건 없이, 심지어는 받을 자격이 전혀 없는 사람들에게까지 베푸는 일방적인 배려를 뜻한다(cf. 출 33:12, 16-17). 하나님은 사랑할 만한 사람들만 사랑하시는 것이 아니라, 사랑할 가치가 없는 사람도 긍휼히 여기신다.

둘째, 하나님은 긍휼이 많으시다(רַחוּם)(8b절). 이 단어는 어머니의 자궁(womb)과 연관된 단어이다. 그러므로 이 단어는 어머니의 아이를 향한 모성적인 사랑과 관심을 의미한다. 하나님은 부모가 자식을 사랑하듯 자기 백성을 사랑하신다.

셋째, 하나님은 노하기를 더디 하시는 분이다(אֶרֶךְ אַפַּיִם)(8c절). 이 문구를 문자적으로 해석하면 '긴 코를 가지다'라는 뜻이다. 히브리 사람들은 사람이 화가 나면 코에서 열이 나는 것으로 이해했다. 그러므로 코가 길면 그만큼 열을 식힐 수 있는 공간이 많아서 화를 더디 낸다고 생각했던 것이다(Brueggemann).

넷째, 하나님은 인자하심이 크시다(גְּדָל־חָסֶד)(8d절). 본문이 인용하고 있는 출애굽기 텍스트는 '양이 많다'는 의미의 단어(רב)를 사용하는데,

기자는 양보다는 규모를 강조하는 단어(גָּדוֹל)를 사용하고 있다. 인자(חֶסֶד)는 근본적으로 언약/계약을 충실하게 이행한다는 뜻을 바탕으로 하고 있다(Sakenfeld). 그러므로 하나님이 인자가 크신 분이라는 것은 이스라엘과의 언약을 충실하게 지키며 이행하실 것을 암시한다. 뿐만 아니라 필요에 따라서 이스라엘의 많은 과오도 용서하시고 용납하셔서 언약관계를 유지하실 것이라는 표현이다.

이처럼 자비로우시고 따뜻하신 여호와께서 자신이 지으신 모든 피조물을 선대하시며, 긍휼을 베푸신다(9절). 창조주께서 모든 피조물을 '선하게'(טוֹב) 대하신다는 것은 주님이 하시는 일이 모두 피조물들에게 참 좋은 일이 된다는 뜻이다. '긍휼'(רַחֲמִים)은 부모의 마음처럼 따뜻함을 강조한다. 그러므로 이 말씀은 하나님이 부모의 마음으로 피조물들을 선처하신다는 뜻이다.

4. 공동체적 찬양(145:10)

10 여호와여
주께서 지으신 모든 것들이 주께 감사하며
주의 성도들이 주를 송축하리이다

하나님이 어떤 분이신가를 묵상하고 나니(4-9절) 저절로 찬양과 경배가 다시 시작된다. 창조주의 형언할 수 없는 사랑과 보살핌을 받는 피조물들이 가만히 있으면 죄가 될 것이다. 그러므로 주께서 지으신 모든 것들이 주님께 감사하며, 주의 성도들이 모두 주를 송축한다. '성도들'(חֲסִידִים)은 신실하고 경건한 사람들로 하나님을 전적으로 의지하는 사람들을 의미한다. 그들은 먼저 그들을 사랑하신 여호와를 찬양한다. 찬양은 은혜를 입은 사람의 가장 자연스러운 반응이다.

5. 여호와의 위대하심 찬양(145:11–13)

11 그들이 주의 나라의 영광을 말하며
주의 업적을 일러서
12 주의 업적과 주의 나라의 위엄 있는 영광을
인생들에게 알게 하리이다
13 주의 나라는 영원한 나라이니
주의 통치는 대대에 이르리이다

이 섹션은 이 시편의 한 중앙에 위치할 뿐만 아니라, 가장 핵심적인 메시지이다(Lindars). 또한 이 구절들은 각각 히브리어 알파벳 카프(כ)—라멕(ל)—멤(מ) 순서로 시작하는데, 이 세 글자의 순서를 뒤집으면 히브리어 단어 '왕'(מֶלֶךְ)과 '왕국'(מַלְכוּת)을 형성하는 글자들이 된다(Watson). 이 시편이 알파벳 시이기 때문에 이러한 현상이 우연일 수도 있지만(Hossfeld–Zenger), 이 시편이 처음부터 끝까지 하나님의 왕권과 왕국을 노래하고 있다는 점을 생각하면 어느 정도 상징적인 의미가 있는 듯하다(cf. Kraus).

하나님께 경배하고 주님을 찬양하는 성도들은(cf. 10절) 하나님에 대해 온 세상에 선포한다. 그들은 주의 나라의 영광과 주님의 통치 업적을 사람들에게 알린다. 주님의 나라는 영원하며 주님의 통치는 대대에 이를 것이기 때문이다. 사람이 믿든, 믿지 않든 상관없이 하나님의 나라와 통치는 앞으로도 영원할 것이다.

그러므로 이러한 사실을 믿으며 사는 사람은 이미 하나님의 축복을 누리며 살고 있다. 우리가 살아서 하나님의 나라와 영광을 말하고 주님의 역사를 볼 수 있는 것은 하나님이 은총을 내려 주셔야 가능하기 때문이다. 그러므로 한 학자는 위대하신 하나님이 인간에게 은총을 내리시는 것을 구약의 '케노시스'(κενοσις)(그리스도께서 모든 권세와 특권을 '비우시고' 이 땅에 임하신 것을 뜻하는 신약의 전문적인 용어)라고 한다(von Rad).

개역개정은 지나치고 있지만, 대부분 번역본들은 고대 번역본들인 칠십인역(LXX)과 시리아역(Syr.)과 라틴어역(Vg.)과 마소라 사본 중 하나(Kennicott manuscript 142)가 눈(נ)으로 시작하는 문장을 13절과 14절 사이에 포함하고 있는 것을 근거로 13절 후반부에 누락된 문장을 삽입한다(Kimelman, cf. 새번역, 아가페, NIV, ESV, NAS, NRS, RSV). 필사가의 실수로 이 구절이 누락되었다고 보기 때문이다. 누락된 눈(נ) 문장은 이러하다: "주님이 하시는 말씀은 모두 다 진실하고 그 모든 업적에는 사랑이 담겨있다"(새번역).

그러나 구약과 시편의 여러 알파벳 시가 완벽한 형태가 아닌 상태로 발견되기 때문에 이 시에 눈(נ) 문장을 추가하지 않아야 한다는 주장도 있다(Goldingay, Hossfeld-Zenger). 원본에도 눈(נ) 문장이 없었을 것이라는 추측이다.

6. 여호와의 선하심 찬양(145:14-20)

14 여호와께서는 모든 넘어지는 자들을 붙드시며
비굴한 자들을 일으키시는도다
15 모든 사람의 눈이 주를 앙망하오니
주는 때를 따라 그들에게 먹을 것을 주시며
16 손을 펴사 모든 생물의 소원을 만족하게 하시나이다
17 여호와께서는 그 모든 행위에 의로우시며
그 모든 일에 은혜로우시도다
18 여호와께서는 자기에게 간구하는 모든 자
곧 진실하게 간구하는 모든 자에게 가까이 하시는도다
19 그는 자기를 경외하는 자들의 소원을 이루시며
또 그들의 부르짖음을 들으사 구원하시리로다

**20 여호와께서 자기를 사랑하는 자들은 다 보호하시고
악인들은 다 멸하시리로다**

기자는 하나님은 창조된 세상을 선하게 대하시고 모든 사람에게 은총을 베푸신다고 했는데(9절), 이 섹션은 하나님이 어떻게 선하고 은혜롭게 세상을 대하시는가에 대해 설명한다. 창조주의 범우주적 섭리에서 하나님이 어떻게 자기 백성의 필요를 채우시는가로 주제가 변하고 있는 것이다(Davidson, cf. Allen).

첫째, 하나님은 넘어지는 사람은 누구든 붙드시며, 비굴한 자들을 일으키신다(14절). '비굴한 자들'(כְּפוּפִים)은 문자적으로 엎드린 사람들을 뜻하며, 개역개정이 번역한 것처럼 어떠한 부정적인 뉘앙스를 지닌 단어가 아니다. 단순히 남들의 억압에 의해 낮아진/짓눌린 자들을 의미한다(Tucker & Grant, cf. 새번역, 아가페). 하나님은 누구든 남에게 억압을 받거나 홀로 설 수 없을 정도로 연약한 자들을 도와 스스로 설 수 있도록 하시는 분이다.

둘째, 하나님은 모든 생명에게 때에 따라 먹을 것을 주신다(15–16절). 개역개정이 '모든 사람의 눈'이라고 번역해 놓은 히브리어 문구(עֵינֵי־כֹל)는 '만물의 눈'이 더 정확한 번역이다. 사람과 상관없이 창조된 세상에서 창조주께서 먹을 것을 주실 것이라는 기대에 찬 눈으로 주님을 바라보는 모든 피조물을 의미하기 때문이다(cf. 새번역, 현대인). 주님은 그들을 실망시키지 않으시고 먹을 것을 주셔서 만족하게 하신다(cf. 마 6:25–34).

셋째, 하나님은 항상 의로우시며 항상 은혜로우시다(17절). 개역개정이 '모든 행위'로 번역한 문구(בְּכָל־דְּרָכָיו)의 문자적 의미는 '모든 길'(in all his ways)이다. 이 문구는 하나님이 삶에서 추구하시고 지향하시는 모든 것이 항상 옳으시다는 뜻이다. '은혜롭다'(חָסִיד)는 '자비/긍휼'(חֶסֶד)과 연관된 단어이다. 하나님은 일을 하실 때 항상 자비로운 마음으로 하신

다는 뜻이다. 그러므로 이처럼 의롭고 은혜로운 창조주의 보살핌을 받는 우리는 얼마나 복된 사람들인가!

넷째, 하나님은 주를 의지하는 자들을 가까이하시며 그들의 소원을 이루신다(18-19절). 기자는 하나님이 가까이하시는 이들을 세 가지로 묘사한다: '주님께 진실하게 간구하는 자'(18절), '주님을 경외하는 자'(19a절), '주께 부르짖는 자'(19b절). '간구하다'(קרא)는 부르다는 뜻이며 '진실하게'(אֱמֶת)는 '성실하게/꾸준히'로 번역하는 것이 더 정확하다(cf. HALOT). 하나님은 지속적으로 주님을 찾는 이를 귀하게 여기신다. '경외'(יָרֵא)는 경건한 두려움을 뜻한다. 하나님을 참으로 존경하고 가까이하지만, 동시에 항상 하나님에 대한 두려움이 마음 한 구석에 도사리고 있는 상황을 묘사한다. '부르짖음'(שַׁוְעָה)은 도와 달라며 울부짖는 것을 의미한다(HALOT). 하나님은 한두 차례가 아니라, 항상 주님을 의지하고 오직 주님만 바라보며 사는 사람들을 가까이하시며 그들의 바라는 바를 모두 이루어 주신다.

다섯째, 하나님은 의인과 악인을 차별하신다(20절). 주님이 선처하는 의인은 어떤 사람인가? 바로 18-19절이 묘사했던 사람들, 곧 오직 성실하게 하나님을 의지하며 사는 사람들이다. 기자는 이런 사람들을 '주를 사랑하는 자들'이라고 하신다(20a절). '사랑하다'(אהב)는 구약에서 자주 사용되며 감정을 묘사하는 단어이다. 그러나 인간이 하나님을 사랑한다고 하는 말은 그다지 흔치 않다. 기자는 하나님이 마음속 깊은 곳에서부터 주님을 사랑하는 사람들을 보호하시고, 악인들은 모두 멸망시키신다고 한다. 그들이 이 땅에 발을 붙이지 못하도록 '끝장을 내신다'(שׁמר)는 뜻이다.

7. 모든 피조물의 찬양(145:21)

[21] 내 입이 여호와의 영예를 말하며

모든 육체가 그의 거룩하신 이름을 영원히 송축할지로다

기자는 자신의 입으로 여호와의 영예를 말하겠다고 하는데, '영예'(תְּהִלָּה)는 이 시편의 표제에 등장한 단어로 '찬송시'라는 의미를 지녔다. 이미 언급한 것처럼 표제에 이 단어가 사용되는 시편은 이 시가 유일하다. 기자는 자기 입술로 여호와를 영원히 찬양할 것을 다짐하고 있다. 또한 세상 모든 피조물도 그렇게 하기를 기원한다.

제146편

I. 장르/양식: 개인 찬양시(cf. 11편)

시편 146-150편은 '최종 찬양시'(Final Hallel) 모음집을 형성한다. 다른 찬양 모음집은 출애굽 사건을 기념하는 '이집트 찬양'(Egyptian Hallel, 113-118편)과 '위대한 찬양'(Great Hallel, 120-136편)이다. 이 시편은 개인 감사시(hymn of thanksgiving)로도 분류된다(deClaissé-Walford et al.). 감사시와 찬양시는 별 차이가 없기 때문이다.

이 모음집에 속한 다섯 편의 시는 각각 서술적 찬양시 성격을 띠며 '할렐루야'(הַלְלוּ־יָהּ)로 시작하여 할렐루야로 마무리된다. 그러므로 이 시편들의 시작과 마무리에 사용된 할렐루야는 총 10개에 달하며, 숫자 10은 완벽함을 상징하는 숫자이다. 이 섹션은 절대적이고 완벽한 찬양으로 총 150편에 달하는 시편 모음집을 마무리하고 있는 것이다(Hossfeld-Zenger). 또한 마지막 시편인 150편에서도 할렐루야가 10차례 등장하는 것도 이러한 해석에 설득력을 더한다.

칠십인역(LXX)과 라틴어 번역본(Vg.)은 표제에 이 시편이 학개와 스가랴에 의해 저작되었다는 말을 더한다. 시편에 사용된 일부 히브리어 표현은 포로기 이후 시대에 유래한 것으로(cf. McCann, Tucker & Grant),

저작 시기가 포로기 이후 시대임을 암시한다(VanGemeren). 더 구체적으로는 제2성전이 완성된 다음에 저작된 것이라는 추측이 있다(Terrien). 비록 저작 시기가 포로기 이후 시대라 할지라도 그보다 훨씬 더 오래된 전승을 배경으로 집필된 것이라는 주석가도 있다(Anderson).

II. 구조

여러 학자들이 교차대구법적 구조를 제시하지만, 서로 상이하게 다르다(Alden, Kselman, VanGemeren). 이 주석에서는 다음과 같은 구조를 바탕으로 본문을 주해해 나가고자 한다.

A. 시작하는 찬양(146:1–2)
B. 인생을 의지하지 말라(146:3–4)
C. 창조주—구속자 하나님(146:5–8b)
B′. 하나님을 의지하라(146:8c–9)
A′. 마무리하는 찬양(146:10)

III. 주해

이 시편은 오직 여호와만이 세상을 다스리시는 왕이요, 구원하시는 구세주이며, 창조주임을 노래한다. 또한 주님은 신실하시고, 공의로 세상을 영원히 다스리시는 분이다. 이러한 가르침은 시편 마지막을 장식하고 있는 최종 찬양시에 등장하는 모든 노래들의 주제이다(Scaioloa). 기자의 선언은 구약에서 매우 오래된 전통적인 가르침이지만, 그는 포로기 이후를 살아가는 새로운 청중에게 선언하고 있다(Kselman). 옛 교훈들이 새로운 의미와 시사성을 지니고 선포되고 있는 것이다.

1. 시작하는 찬양(146:1-2)

[1] 할렐루야
내 영혼아 여호와를 찬양하라
[2] 나의 생전에 여호와를 찬양하며
나의 평생에 내 하나님을 찬송하리로다

기자는 이 섹션에서 '찬양하다'(הלל)를 세 차례 사용하고 '찬송하다'(זמר)를 한 차례 사용하는 등 찬양과 연관된 동사를 네 차례 사용하여 오직 여호와만을 찬양할 것을 다짐한다. 그는 '내 영혼'(נַפְשִׁי)이라는 말을 통해 온전히 온 생명을 다해 여호와를 찬양할 것을 선언한다. 또한 '내 생전'(חַיַּי)과 '내 평생'(עוֹדִי)을 사용해 주님을 향한 그의 찬양이 한두 번으로 끝나는 것이 아니라, 생명이 다할 때까지 평생 찬양할 것임을 다짐한다. 하나님의 큰 은혜를 입은 사람만이 이러한 각오를 할 수 있다(cf. Kidner).

2. 인생을 의지하지 말라(146:3-4)

[3] 귀인들을 의지하지 말며
도울 힘이 없는 인생도 의지하지 말지니
[4] 그의 호흡이 끊어지면 흙으로 돌아가서
그 날에 그의 생각이 소멸하리로다

앞 섹션에서 평생 여호와만을 찬양하고 주님만을 바라보며 살겠다고 다짐한 기자가 이 섹션에서는 그가 왜 그렇게 다짐했는지 그 이유를 말한다. 사람은 살면서 인간을 의지할 것인가(자신을 의지하는 것도 포함), 혹은 하나님을 의지할 것인가, 이 둘 중 하나를 선택해야 한다. 이 두 옵션 중 인간을 선택하는 것은 참으로 어리석은 일이라는 것이 저자의 주장이다(cf. 시 118:8-9; 렘 17:5-7). 일상적으로 찬양시들은 하나님을 의지할 것을 암시적으로 권면하는데, 이 시편은 인간을 의지하는 것은 참으로 어리석은 일이라며 하나님을 의지할 것을 노골적으로 권한다(McCann). 인간은 삶에 도대체 도움이 되지 않는 존재이기 때문이다.

기자는 세상의 귀인들을 의지하지 말라고 하는데(3a절), '귀인들'(נְדִיבִים)은 권력이나 재력으로 남을 도울 수 있는 귀족들을 뜻한다(HALOT). 우리는 왜 귀인들을 의지할 수 없는가? 그들은 공의와 정의로 이 세상을 다스리는 일에 관심이 없다. 오로지 자기 이익을 추구할 뿐 남들에게 선을 베풀지 않는다. 오죽하면 권력은 썩고, 절대적인 권력은 절대적으로 썩는다는 말이 생겼겠는가!

저자는 인생도 의지하지 말라고 한다(3b절). '인생'(בֶּן־אָדָם)은 문자적으로 '사람의 아들'이란 의미를 지녔으며 이렇다할 능력도 없이 오늘 있다가 내일 사라지는 보잘것없는 인간의 삶을 강조한다. 그러므로 '귀인들(높은 자들)과 인생(낮은 자들)'은 한쌍을 이루며, 사람은 능력이 있는 자들이나 무능한 자들이나 할 것 없이 의지할 만한 존재들이 못된다는 사실을 강조한다. 더욱이 도울 힘이 없는 인생을 의지하는 것은 헛수고에 불과하다. 그러므로 이사야 선지자도 "너희는 인생을 의지하지 말라. 그의 호흡은 코에 있나니 셈할 가치가 어디 있느냐?"라고 권면한다(사 2:22, cf. 창 6:3; 시 104:30).

또한 사람은 죽어서 흙으로 돌아간다(4a절, cf. 창 3:19; 시 104:29). 흙으로 돌아가는 순간 그 사람이 지녔던 모든 생각과 계획도 그와 함께 사라진다. 인생의 덧없음을 생각하게 하는 말씀이다. 그러므로 이렇게 연약하고 순식간에 사라지는 인간을 의지하는 것은 참으로 어리석은 일이다. 우리는 오직 영원하시고 능력이 충만하신 하나님을 의지하고 주님만 찬양해야 한다.

3. 창조주—구속자 하나님(146:5-8b)

[5] 야곱의 하나님을 자기의 도움으로 삼으며
여호와 자기 하나님에게 자기의 소망을 두는 자는 복이 있도다
[6] 여호와는 천지와 바다와 그 중의 만물을 지으시며
영원히 진실함을 지키시며
[7] 억눌린 사람들을 위해 정의로 심판하시며
주린 자들에게 먹을 것을 주시는 이시로다
여호와께서는 갇힌 자들에게 자유를 주시는도다
[8] 여호와께서 맹인들의 눈을 여시며
여호와께서 비굴한 자들을 일으키시며

바로 앞 섹션에서 기자는 신분의 높고 낮음에 상관없이 사람을 의지하는 것이 얼마나 허무하고 어리석은 일인가를 설명했다. 이 섹션에서는 세상을 창조하시고 그 세상을 공의와 정의로 다스리시는 여호와를 의지하며 사는 사람은 참으로 복이 있다고 선언한다. 그들의 믿음이 결코 헛되지 않을 것이기 때문이다.

시편 1편을 시작했던 '복있는 사람'(אַשְׁרֵי)이 이 섹션을 시작한다(cf. 시 1:1; 33:12; 144:15). 이 말씀은 사람이 이 땅에서 행복을 누리며 살 수 있는 비결을 말하고 있는 것이다. 기자는 하나님을 도움으로 삼고 주님께 소망을 두는 자는 복이 있다고 한다(5절). '도움/돕는자'(עֵזֶר)는 창세기 2:18에서 서로 의지하고 돕는 부부관계를 묘사하며 사용되었다. 이와 함께 기자는 '자기'(וֹ)라는 접미사를 연거푸 사용하며 하나님과 복있는 사람의 관계를 강조한다. 마치 부부가 서로를 의지하듯 하나님을 의지하며 오직 창조주 하나님을 소망으로 삼는 사람은 참으로 복이 있으며 행복할 것이다. 창조주를 소망하는 것이 다소 이상하다고 생각될 수 있지만(Calvin), 시편에서 종종 등장하는 가르침이다(cf. 시 8:5-8;

69:35; 96:11).

여호와 하나님을 의지하고 소망하는 사람은 왜 복이 있는가? 여호와는 참으로 위대하고 자상하신 창조주이자 통치자이시기 때문이다. 저자는 하나님이 하시는 일을 11가지로 묘사한다. 그러므로 한 주석가는 이 섹션을 '여호와 찬송'(Yahweh hymn)이라고 부른다(Kraus). 이 11가지 중 본 섹션에서는 일곱 가지를 제시한다.

첫째, 야곱의 하나님 여호와는 천지를 창조하셨다(6a절, cf. 시 115:15; 121:2; 124:8; 134:3). 이곳에서 '야곱의 하나님'은 친근감을 유발하는 애칭으로 사용되고 있다(Briggs). 주님은 하늘과 땅과 바다를 지으시고 온갖 좋은 것들로 가득 채우신 창조주이시다. 그러므로 주님이 피조물인 우리를 보호하고 도우시는 것은 당연한 일이기 때문에 주님의 도움을 소망으로 삼아도 좋다.

둘째, 하나님은 영원히 진실함을 지키신다(6b절). '진실함'(אֱמֶת)은 성실함/꾸준함을 뜻하는 단어이다. 그러므로 이 말씀은 여호와께서는 신의를 지키시는 분임으로 세상을 창조하신 후 스스로 돌아가게 방치하시는 것이 아니라, 세상이 끝날 때까지 지속적으로 돌보시고 관리하신다는 뜻이다(cf. 새번역, 아가페, 공동, NIV). 하나님은 태초때부터 영원에 이르기까지 절대 변하지 않으시는 분이다(Anderson). 창조주로서 필요하면 끊임없는 새 창조를 통해서 세상을 채우시며 아름답게 하신다.

셋째, 하나님은 억눌린 사람들을 위해 정의로 심판하신다(7a절, cf. 시 89:14; 96:13; 97:2; 98:9; 99:4). 이 말씀이 여호와에 대한 여러 선언들 중 절정에 해당한다(Brueggemann). '억울린 사람들'(עֲשׁוּקִים)은 착취를 당하거나 억압을 당하는 사람들을 뜻한다(HALOT). 주님은 이들을 위해 '정의'(מִשְׁפָּט)를 행하시는 분이다. 그들이 억울하게 당하는 것을 지켜보지 않으실 것이며, 분명 개입하셔서 그들의 억울함을 해소하는 하나님이시다.

넷째, 하나님은 주린 자들에게 먹을 것을 주시는 분이다(7b절). 하나님은 세상 모든 생명을 창조하셨기 때문에 그들의 의식주에도 관여하신다. 그러므로 주님은 사람들뿐만 아니라 짐승들까지 먹이신다. 짐승들까지 보살피시는 하나님이 하물며 주님의 모양과 형상대로 빚으신 사람들은 얼마나 더 확실하게 보살피시겠는가!

다섯째, 하나님은 갇힌 자들에게 자유를 주신다(7c절). '갇힌 자들'(אֲסוּרִים)은 감옥 등 비좁은 공간에 억류된 사람을 뜻하지만, 어떤 것에든 얽매이는 것을 뜻하기도 한다. 그러므로 이 말씀은 육체적으로 갇힌 사람들뿐만 아니라, 영적인 얽매임에 갇힌 사람들도 의미한다. 주님은 사람들을 모든 얽매임에서 자유케 하시는 분이다. 모든 영혼이 자유를 누리며 살도록 창조하셨기 때문이다.

여섯째, 하나님은 맹인들의 눈을 여신다(8a절, cf. 사 35:5; 42:7, 17; 43:8). 이 말씀은 맹인들이 보게 하신다는 뜻으로 해석될 수 있지만, 어두운 곳에 갇혀 볼 수 없는 사람들을 해방시켜 다시 빛을 보게 하신다는 의미로 해석될 수도 있다(Goldingay). 바로 앞에서(5번째)는 육체가 갇힌 자들에게 자유를 주신다고 했는데, 이 말씀은 '시야가 갇힌 자들'을 자유롭게 하신다는 뜻이다. 하나님은 모든 사람이 주님이 창조하신 아름다운 세상을 보고 즐기기를 원하신다.

일곱째, 하나님은 비굴한 자들을 일으키신다(8b절). 시편 145:14에서 언급한 것처럼 '비굴한 자들'(פּוּפִים)은 짓누름과 억압으로 인해 비참하도록 낮아진 자들이다. 스스로 비굴한 자세를 취하는 자들이 아니다. 하나님은 세상에 밟히고 권력에 짓눌린 사람들을 일으켜 세우실 것이다. 필요하다면 그들을 짓누르는 자들을 벌하실 것을 암시한다. 공의로우신 하나님이 누구도 억울하게 억압당하지 못하게 하실 것이다.

4. 하나님을 의지하라(146:8c-9)

8c 여호와께서 의인들을 사랑하시며

[9] 여호와께서 나그네들을 보호하시며
고아와 과부를 붙드시고
악인들의 길은 굽게 하시는도다

기자가 5-10절에서 묘사하는 하나님의 사역 12가지 중 세 가지를 묘사하는 섹션이다. '의인(8c절)—사회적 약자들(9a-b절)—악인들(9c절)'의 구조가 의인들과 악인들의 차이는 그들 사이에 있는 사회적 약자들을 돌보는가(의인들) 혹은 억압하고 착취하는가(악인들)에 의해 결정된다는 메시지를 준다.

첫째, 하나님은 의인들을 사랑하신다(8c절). '의인들'(צַדִּיקִים)은 의로우신 하나님을 의지하여 주님의 의로우신 가치관과 기준에 따라 살려고 노력하는 사람들이다. 시편에서 의인들은 흔히 권력자들과 악인들의 핍박과 억압의 대상이 되기도 한다(McCann). 주님은 온 세상 사람들을 사랑하시지만, 이들을 특별히 더 사랑하신다. 당연하다. 주님을 닮아가려고 노력하는 이들이 얼마나 대견하고 자랑스러우시겠는가! 주님이 그들을 사랑하신다는 것은 그들의 모든 필요를 채우시고 보호하신다는 것을 전제한다.

둘째, 하나님은 약자들을 보호하시고 붙드신다(9a-b절). '나그네들'(גֵּרִים)은 이스라엘에 정착한 이방인들을 뜻한다. 차별과 불공평한 대우를 받는 이들의 상징이다. 이스라엘 사람들뿐만 아니라 이방인들에게도 시온은 절대적이고 영원한 성지라는 점을 암시한다(Grogan). 시온에 계시는 하나님이 그들을 보호하실 것이기 때문이다.

고아와 과부는 경제적으로 가장 어려운 계층의 상징이다. 경제적으로 어려운 계층이다 보니 법정에서도 정당한 권리를 행사하지 못하는 부류이다. 하나님은 사회에서 따돌림을 받거나 소외될 수 있는 사람들이 억울한 일을 당하지 않도록 보호하시며, 붙드신다. '붙들다'(עוד)는 '도와 세우다'라는 뜻이다(HALOT). 하나님은 넘어진 약자들을 도와 다시 서게 하시는 분이다. 필요하다고 생각되면 하나님은 이 약자들의 권리를 보호하기 위해 그들에게 불의를 행하는 자들을 벌하실 것이다.

셋째, 하나님은 악인들의 길을 굽게 하신다(9c절). 그들이 계획대로 하지 못하게 하신다는 뜻이다. 만일 악인들이 계획한 일들을 모두 이루면 세상은 온갖 죄와 혼란으로 가득할 수밖에 없다. 그러므로 세상을 아름답게 창조하신 하나님은 세상의 질서와 정의를 확립하기 위해서라도 악인들이 계획한 바를 굽게 하셔야 한다. 하나님이 의인들은 사랑하시고 악인들의 길은 굽게 하신다는 것이 지혜 사상의 일부로 해석되기도 한다(cf. Kselman).

5. 마무리하는 찬양(146:10)

10 시온아 여호와는 영원히 다스리시고
네 하나님은 대대로 통치하시리로다
할렐루야

기자는 이 때까지 10가지로 하나님이 하시는 일을 묵상하며 감사했다. 이 섹션에서는 마지막 한 가지를 더 추가하며 찬양을 마무리한다. 바로 하나님은 영원한 통치자라는 사실이다. 주님은 자신이 창조하신 세상을 영원히 다스리신다(10a절). 또한 주님은 대대로 통치하시는 분이다(10b절). 인간은 오늘 있다가 내일 사라질 연약한 존재들이지만(cf. 4절), 하나님은 우리가 죽은 후에도 영원히 통치하시며 자기 백성을 돌보신다.

하나님의 통치가 영원하다는 것은 악인들에게는 큰 경고이며, 의인들에게는 큰 위로가 된다. 악인들은 그들이 하는 악한 일들은 오래 가지 못할 것이며, 의로우신 하나님이 분명 그들의 만행을 바로잡으실 것을 깨달아야 한다. 의인들은 하나님이 반드시 그들의 억울함을 헤아려 주실 것이며 악인들의 억압과 착취에서 해방시키실 것이라는 사실을 믿고 기다려야 한다. 하나님의 나라와 통치는 영원할 것이다.

기자는 최종 찬양시 모음집의 첫 번째 노래를 '할렐루야'로 시작하여(1a절) '할렐루야'로 마무리한다(10c절). 이 단어는 들을 때마다 우리의 가슴을 뛰게 하는 단어인데(Cassiodorus), 너무나도 많은 성도들이 별 감동 없이, 습관적으로 사용하여 하나님의 이름을 망령되이 부르는 죄를 범하는 것이 안타깝다(Spurgeon, cf. Goldingay).

제147편

I. 장르/양식: 공동체 찬양시(cf. 11편)

이 시는 시편 전체에 대한 '축도' 역할을 하는 '최종 찬양시'(Final Hallel) 모음집(146-150편)의 두 번째 노래이며, 모음집에 속한 다른 시편들처럼 할렐루야로 시작하여 할렐루야로 마무리된다. 이 노래는 이사야 40-66장과 욥기 37-39장을 배경으로 저작되었으며(cf. McCann), 때로는 기자가 이사야 40장에 기록된 질문들과 하나님이 욥에게 하신 질문들을 찬양으로 바꾼 듯한 느낌을 준다고 하는 이가 있다(Kidner).

이 시는 공동체 찬양시이다(Brueggemann & Bellinger, aissé-Walford et al., Tucker & Grant). 칠십인역(LXX)과 라틴어역(Vg.)은 표제에 '학개와 스가랴의 시'라는 말을 더해 포로기 이후에 저작된 것으로 간주했다. 또한 이 고대 번역본들은 이 노래를 1-11절과 12-20절로 나누어 두 개의 독립적인 시편으로 취급한다. 오늘날도 이 시편에는 두 개의 독립적인 시가 있다고 간주하는 이들이 있지만(Hossfeld-Zenger, Tucker & Grant), 구조적인 요소들과 반복되는 단어들과 평행법이 이 시편을 하나의 통일성을 지닌 노래로 취급하기에 충분한 증거들이 된다(Allen, cf. Ross).

이 시가 비와 다음 추수와 율법을 언급한다고 해서 장막절에 사용된 것이라고 하는 이가 있다(Anderson). 예루살렘 재건을 기념하는 시라는 주장도 있다(Kirkpatrick). 그러나 이 노래는 여호와가 하신 특별한 일이 아니라, 보편적으로 온 세상을 유지하시는 사역을 기념한다. 그러므로 예배나 절기에서 사용된 것은 맞지만, 구체적으로 어떤 예배였는지는 알 수 없다(Goldingay).

포로기를 암시하는 것(2, 13절)은 이 시가 그때 저작되었음을 뜻한다(VanGemeren). 더 구체적으로 느헤미야가 예루살렘 성을 재건한 시대를 저작 시기로 보는 이들이 주류를 이룬다(Kraus, Ross, Terrien, Tucker & Grant, cf. 느 12:27).

II. 구조

이 시편은 1–6절, 7–11절, 12–20절 세 섹션으로 나뉜다. 각 섹션마다 하나님을 찬양하라는 권면(1, 7, 12절)으로 시작하며, 주님을 찬양할 이유를 나열하는 것(2–6, 8–11, 13–20절)으로 이어진다. 이 주석에서는 다음과 같은 구조를 바탕으로 본문을 주해해 나가고자 한다.

A. 하나님께 찬양을 드리라(147:1–6)

B. 노래와 악기로 하나님을 찬양하라(147:7–11)

C. 하나님께 영광을 돌리라(147:12–20)

III. 주해

기자는 재건된 예루살렘 성에 거주하는 사람들에게 여호와를 찬양할 것을 권면한다. 여호와는 온 세상을 창조하신 창조주이며, 세상을 보존하시는 분이다. 또한 자기 백성을 회복하시고, 자신의 의지와 뜻을 자기 백성에게 보여 주시는 하나님이다.

1. 하나님께 찬양을 드리라(147:1-6)

1 할렐루야
우리 하나님을 찬양하는 일이 선함이여
찬송하는 일이 아름답고 마땅하도다
2 여호와께서 예루살렘을 세우시며
이스라엘의 흩어진 자들을 모으시며
3 상심한 자들을 고치시며
그들의 상처를 싸매시는도다
4 그가 별들의 수효를 세시고
그것들을 다 이름대로 부르시는도다
5 우리 주는 위대하시며 능력이 많으시며
그의 지혜가 무궁하시도다
6 여호와께서 겸손한 자들은 붙드시고
악인들은 땅에 엎드러뜨리시는도다

앞 시편(146편)처럼 이 노래도 '할렐루야'로 시작하고 마무리한다. 기자는 하나님을 찬양하는 것은 선하고 아름다운 일이며, 우리가 해야 할 마땅한 일이라 한다(1절). '선하다'(טוֹב)는 좋은 것이라는 뜻이고, '아름답다'(נָאוָה)는 사랑스럽고 상쾌한 일이라는 의미이며, '마땅하다'(נָאוָה)는 적합하여 잘 어울린다는 의미를 지녔다(HALOT, NIDOTTE). 주의 백성이 주님을 찬양하는 것은 참으로 좋은 일이며, 하나님이 어떤 분이신가를 알게 되면 '찬양'(תְּהִלָּה)은 주님에게 참 잘 어울리는 아름다운 옷이라는 생각을 하게 된다.

그렇다면 하나님은 어떤 분이시기에 우리가 마음을 다해 찬양할 만한가?

첫째, 하나님은 예루살렘을 세우시고 그곳으로 이스라엘의 흩어진 자들을 모으시는 분이다(2절). 하나님이 성을 짓는 건축가와 흩어진 양들을 모으시는 목자로 묘사되고 있다(Tucker & Grant). 학자들이 이 시편이 포로기 이후에 저작된 것이라고 결론짓는 데는 이 구절의 주님이 예루살렘을 세우시고(재건하시고) 그곳으로 흩어진 자들 모으셨다고 하는 것이 큰 증거가 된다. '흩어진 자들'(נִדְחֵי)은 추방 등을 통해 쫓겨난 사람들을 의미한다(HALOT, cf. 겔 34:12-13). 선한 목자이신 하나님이 온 세상에 흩어진 자기 양들을 예루살렘으로 모으신다(cf. 겔 34:12-13).

그러므로 본문은 하나님이 폐허가 된 예루살렘을 재건하시고 바빌론에서 돌아온 귀향민들을 그곳에서 살게 하신 일을 묘사하고 있다. 이 일은 포로기 이후에 느헤미야가 성벽공사를 통해 예루살렘을 재건하고 귀향민들이 그곳에 살게 한 일로 해석될 수 있는 것이다(Kraus, VanGemeren, Ross, Terrien, cf. 느 6:15-7:3; 12:27-43). 하나님은 죄를 지어 내치신 백성들과 파괴된 도성을 내버려두지 않으셨다. 성을 재건하시고 성문들의 빗장도 견고하게 하셔서(cf. 13절) 그들이 다시 그곳에서 살 수 있도록 하셨다. 그러므로 그들을 회복하신 주님은 찬양 받기에 합당하신 분이다.

둘째, 하나님은 상심한자들을 고치시고 그들의 상처를 싸매시는 분이다(3절). '상하다'(שָׁבַר)는 깨어지거나 망가져서 제구실을 못하는 상황을 의미한다. 마치 벽이 갈라지고 망가져 제 역할을 못하는 물탱크처럼 말이다(렘 2:13). 그러므로 '상심한자들'(שְׁבוּרֵי לֵב)은 마음의 병으로 인해 제대로 생각하거나 살아갈 용기를 낼 수 없는 사람들이다. 주님은 이런 사람들을 고치신다(רפא). 그들의 마음을 치료하셔서 다시 살 수 있도록 하신다(cf. 겔 34:16; 사 61:2). 이 일을 위해 하나님은 그들이 삶에서 받은 온갖 상처들을 싸매신다. 하나님은 우리의 마음과 육체적 상처들을 치료하셔서 다시 건강하게 하시는 분이니 우리가 주님을 찬양하는 것은 당연한 일이다.

셋째, 하나님은 참으로 세심하게 세상을 보살피시는 자상한 창조주이시다(4절). 하나님은 피조물 중 생명을 가진 것들뿐만 아니라, 생명이 없는 별들의 숫자도 알고 계신다(cf. 사 40:26). 별들을 신들로 숭배했던 고대 근동에서 별들을 여호와의 피조물이라고 하는 것은 매우 과감하고 단호한 선언이다. 또한 하나님은 모든 별들의 이름을 다 아시고 별들의 이름을 하나하나 부르신다. 각 별에게 이름을 주어 부르시는 것은 하나님의 주권과 다스리심을 확인하는 일이기도 하다(Schaefer). 이처럼 모든 피조물을 인격적이고 자상하게 대하시니 어찌 주님을 찬양하지 않겠는가!

넷째, 하나님은 위대하시며 능력이 많으시며 지혜가 무궁하시다(5절). '위대하심'(גָּדוֹל)은 주님의 왕 되심과 연관이 있다(cf. 시 48:1; 95:3; 96:4; 99:2). 주님은 참으로 위대하신 왕이라는 의미이다. '능력'(כֹּחַ)은 힘을 뜻하고(cf. 출 9:16; 시 29:4; 렘 10:10-12), '지혜'(תְּבוּנָה)는 기술(skill)을 의미한다(Dahood). 하나님은 능력만 크신 것이 아니라 세상을 이해하고 다스리시는 기술도 견줄 자가 없다. 주님은 힘을 함부로 쓰시는 분이 아니라, 가장 지혜롭게 사용하시는 분이다. 그러므로 우리가 이처럼 지혜로우신 능력자를 찬양하는 것은 당연한 일이다.

다섯째, 하나님은 겸손한 자들과 악인들을 차별하신다(6a절). '겸손한 자들'(עֲנָוִים)은 악인들의 억압 등으로 인해 낮아진 자들이며 성경은 의인들을 이렇게 묘사한다. 주님은 이런 사람들을 붙드신다. '붙들다'(עוד)는 '도와 세운다'는 뜻이다(Tucker & Grant, cf. HALOT). 하나님은 세상에서 정치적—경제적—사회적 이유로 쓰러진 자들을 세워 다시 서게 하신다(Hossfeld & Zenger). 그러므로 억울한 일을 당해본 사람이라면 모두 주님을 찬양할 것이다.

반면에 악인들은 땅에 엎드러뜨리신다(6b절, cf. 시 1:6; 145:20; 146:9). '엎드러뜨리다'(שׁפל)는 수면 밑으로 집어넣는다는 뜻을 지녔다(사 2:9). 하나님은 악인들이 세상을 활보하지 못하도록 그들을 밟으시는 분이다. 때로는 하나님이 다스리시는 세상에서 악인들이 성행하는 것 같지만, 오래가지 못한다. 하나님이 그들을 벌하실 것이기 때문이다. 그들에게 핍박 받는 의인들을 위해서라도 그들을 엎드러뜨리실 것이다. 의인과 악인의 대조가 인상적이다. 악인들이 쓰러뜨린 의인들은 다시 서지만, 서 있는 악인들은 하나님이 쓰러뜨리신다. 그러므로 우리가 이런 하나님을 찬양하는 것은 당연한 일이다.

2. 노래와 악기로 하나님을 찬양하라(147:7–11)

7 감사함으로 여호와께 노래하며
수금으로 하나님께 찬양할지어다
8 그가 구름으로 하늘을 덮으시며
땅을 위하여 비를 준비하시며
산에 풀이 자라게 하시며
9 들짐승과 우는 까마귀 새끼에게
먹을 것을 주시는도다
10 여호와는 말의 힘이 세다 하여 기뻐하지 아니하시며
사람의 다리가 억세다 하여 기뻐하지 아니하시고
11 여호와는 자기를 경외하는 자들과
그의 인자하심을 바라는 자들을 기뻐하시는도다

앞 섹션(1–6절)을 시작하면서 우리가 여호와를 찬양하는 것은 선하고 당연한 일이라고 한 기자가 이 섹션을 시작하면서는 감사함(תּוֹדָה)으로, 또한 악기를 동원하여 주님께 찬양할 것을 주문한다(1절). 우리의 하나님을 향한 자세는 항상 감사한 마음이어야 한다는 뜻이다. 또한 하나님은 참으로 존귀하신 분이니 목소리로 찬양할 뿐만 아니라, 할 수 있으면 악기들도 동원하여 찬양하라고 한다. 우리가 드리는 경배와 찬양이 주님께 아름다운 소리가 되어 열납되기를 바라는 마음의 표현이다.

이어 저자는 우리가 왜 감사한 마음으로 하나님을 찬양하는 것이 좋은 일인가를 설명한다.

첫째, 하나님은 세상 만물에게 먹을 것을 주시는 분이다(8-9절). 하나님은 하늘을 덮는 구름이 비가 되어 땅을 적시게 하신다. 그리고 비를 받은 산에는 풀과 과일들이 자라게 하신다. 하나님은 이것들을 들짐승과 까마귀 새끼들에게 먹이신다. 어떻게 하나님이 날씨를 다스리셔서 사람과 짐승들에게 먹을 것을 주시는가를 설명하고 있다.

'들짐승'(בְּהֵמָה)은 야생에서 사는 짐승을 뜻할 수도 있고 사람들이 키우는 가축(소)을 의미할 수도 있다. 본문에서 '들짐승'이 까마귀 새끼와 쌍을 이루고 있는 것으로 보아 대조를 위한 것이라면 가축으로 해석하는 것이 바람직하다(cf. 아가페, NIV, LXX). 가축은 사람이 키우는 짐승이고, 까마귀는 야생에서 스스로 사는 짐승이기 때문이다. 그러므로 이 대조는 하나님이 사람들의 보호를 받는 가축뿐만 아니라, 야생에서 자생하는 까마귀 새끼까지 먹이를 주신다는 사실을 선언한다. 수많은 들짐승 중 까마귀를 언급하는 것이 특이하다. 까마귀는 부정하며 하찮은 짐승이기 때문이다(레 11:15; 신 14:14). 본문에서 하나님이 다 자란 까마귀도 아니고 '까마귀 새끼들'(בְּנֵי עֹרֵב)을 먹이시는 것은 중요한 상징성을 지닌 듯하다. 하나님의 먹이시고 입히시는 은총은 부정하고 하잘것없는 새끼 까마귀에게까지 임한다. 주님의 자비로운 보호에는 끝이 없음을 선언하고 있는 것이다(Hossfeld & Zenger). 하나님이 온 세상 생명을 먹이시니, 우리가 어찌 감사한 마음으로 주님을 찬양하지 않겠는가!

둘째, 하나님은 능력보다는 주님에 대한 경외를 더 기뻐하신다(10-11절). 주님은 말이 힘이 세다 해서, 혹은 사람('용사', 공동, 현대인, NIV, NRS)의 다리가 억세다 해서 기뻐하지 않으신다. 말과 용사는 전쟁과 연관된 언어이다. 그러므로 이 둘은 전쟁을 가장 잘 할 수 있는 능력을 상징한다(Tucker & Grant).

또한 개인적인 차원에서도 의미가 있는 말씀이다. 창조주께서 말은 힘이 세게 만드셨고, 사람의 다리는 억세게 만드셨기 때문에 이 피조물들이 능력을 지닌 것이 특별한 일은 아니다. 그러므로 그들에게 이러한 능력을 주신 하나님이 이들이 지닌 능력을 기뻐하실 이유는 없다.

반면에 주님은 하나님을 경외하는 자들과 주님의 인자하심을 바라는 이들을 기뻐하신다. '하나님을 경외하는 자들'(יְרֵאָיו)은 주님에 대한 건전한 두려움이 있는 사람들이다. 그들은 모든 능력이 주님 안에 있다는 것을 알기 때문에, 자신들이 지닌 능력은 별 의미가 없다는 사실을 고백하는 사람들이다. '인자하심'(חֶסֶד)은 주님이 맺으신 언약에 성실하게 임하시는 것을 의미한다. 그러므로 인자하심을 바라는 이들은 하나님이 그들에게 하신 약속에 따라 자비를 베푸실 것을 간절히 소망하는 사람들이다. 하나님은 오로지 주님을 의지하는 자들을 기뻐하신다는 뜻이다. 그러므로 하나님과 특별한 관계를 맺은 사람들은 주님을 감사함으로 찬양해야 한다.

3. 하나님께 영광을 돌리라(147:12-20)

12 예루살렘아 여호와를 찬송할지어다
시온아 네 하나님을 찬양할지어다
13 그가 네 문빗장을 견고히 하시고
네 가운데에 있는 너의 자녀들에게 복을 주셨으며
14 네 경내를 평안하게 하시고
아름다운 밀로 너를 배불리시며
15 그의 명령을 땅에 보내시니
그의 말씀이 속히 달리는도다
16 눈을 양털 같이 내리시며
서리를 재 같이 흩으시며
17 우박을 떡 부스러기 같이 뿌리시나니

누가 능히 그의 추위를 감당하리요
18 그의 말씀을 보내사 그것들을 녹이시고
바람을 불게 하신즉 물이 흐르는도다
19 그가 그의 말씀을 야곱에게 보이시며
그의 율례와 규례를 이스라엘에게 보이시는도다
20 그는 어느 민족에게도 이와 같이 행하지 아니하셨나니
그들은 그의 법도를 알지 못하였도다
할렐루야

예루살렘을 세우신 하나님을 찬양하라 했던(1절) 기자가 이제는 예루살렘과 시온에게 여호와를 찬양하라고 한다(12절). 주님의 은혜를 입은 도성이 여호와를 찬송하는 것은 당연한 일이다. 그는 13-20절에서 예루살렘과 시온이 여호와를 찬양할 여러 가지 이유를 제시한다.

첫째, 하나님은 예루살렘을 보호하시고 그 안에 사는 사람들에게 복을 주신다(13절). 예루살렘은 적들의 공격에도 끄떡없을 것이다. 주님이 도성의 문들을 견고하게 하셨기 때문이다(cf. 느 3:3, 6, 13-15). 시온은 하나님이 거하시는 곳이라는 사실을 감안할 때 하나님이 자신의 거처인 예루살렘을 보호하시는 것은 당연하다. 뿐만 아니라 주님은 그 안에 있는 '너(예루살렘)의 자녀들'(בָּנַיִךְ)에게 복을 주신다는데, 성 주민들을 축복하신다는 뜻이다. 복을 받은 사람들은 주님을 찬양해야 한다.

둘째, 하나님은 예루살렘의 경내를 평안하게 하시고 도성을 배불리 먹이신다(14절). 경내(גְּבוּל)는 국경/경계선을 뜻한다. 하나님은 예루살렘 도성뿐만 아니라 접경지역에까지 평안(שָׁלוֹם)을 주신다. 예루살렘이 전쟁이나 갈등에 시달리지 않도록 하시겠다는 뜻이다. 또한 '아름다운 밀'(חֵלֶב חִטִּים)로 배불리 먹이시겠다고 하는데, 문자적으로 '기름진 밀', 곧 최고로 질이 좋은 밀로 그들을 먹이실 것이다(cf. 신 32:14). 예루살렘이 번영하여 풍요로운 곳이 될 것을 상징한다. '배불리다'(שָׂבַע)는 만족할 때까지 먹이신다는 뜻이다. 사람들이 배고픔으로 허덕이는 일이 다시는 없을 것이다. 그러므로 배불리 먹은 사람들은 주님을 찬양한다.

셋째, 하나님은 예루살렘에서 자기 명령을 온 세상에 보내신다(15절). 예루살렘은 하나님의 처소인 성전이 있는 곳이다. 주님이 성전에서 하시는 말씀은 곧 온 세상을 향해 달려나간다. 성전에 계시는 주님이 말씀으로 세상을 다스리시고 질서를 유지하시는 모습이다. 하나님은 참으로 창조적으로 구원하고 사역하신다(Kraus). 주님의 말씀은 세상을 향해 '속히 달린다'(מְהֵרָה יָרוּץ). 지체하지 않고 신속하게 퍼져 나간다는 뜻이다. 우리는 온 세상을 말씀으로 다스리시는 하나님을 찬양한다.

넷째, 하나님은 날씨를 다스리신다(16-18절). 주님은 눈을 양털 다루듯이 하시고(16a절), 서리를 재 흩듯이 흩으신다(16b절). 우박을 빵 부스러기처럼 세상에 뿌리신다(17a절). 눈과 서리와 우박은 모두 물이 고체화되는 추위와 연관된 것들이다. 그러므로 기자는 아무도 주님이 보내시는 추위를 이겨낼 사람은 없다고 한다(17b절). 하나님은 추위에 떠는 사람들을 보시고 때로는 말씀을 보내셔서 모두 녹이신다(18a절). 추위를 해결하기 위하여 '말씀'(דָּבָר)을 보내신다는 것이 특이하기는 하지만, 아마도 하나님이 날씨에게 따뜻해지기를 명령하시는 것을 의미하는 것으로 생각된다. 하나님이 얼어붙은 땅에 바람을 불게 하시니 그것들이 녹아 물이 흐른다(18b절). 하나님이 세상의 날씨를 주관하심으로 날씨로 인해 고생을 하는 사람들은 하나님을 찬양해야 한다.

다섯째, 하나님은 이스라엘에게만 율법을 주셨다(19-20절). 주님은 야곱에게 말씀을 보이셨고, 율례와 규례를 이스라엘에게 보이셨다(19절). 이곳에서 '말씀'(דָּבָר)과 '율례'(חֹק)와 '규례'(מִשְׁפָּט)는 모두 율법을 상징하는 비슷한 말로 쓰이고 있다(Tucker & Grant, cf. 시 119:5-9). 이스라엘에게 율법을 주셨다는 뜻이며 율법은 하나님과 특별한 관계를 맺은 것을 상징한다. 그러므로 이스라엘이 율법을 받은 것은 하나님의 특별한 축복을 누린다는 뜻이다.

반면에 세상 어디에도 이스라엘처럼 하나님께 율법을 받은 민족은 없다(20절). 그러므로 열방은 주님의 법도를 알지 못한다. 하나님과 특별한 관계를 맺지 못했다는 뜻이다. 그들은 율법과 연관된 주님의 특별한 축복을 누리지 못한다. 이스라엘은 그들과 특별한 관계를 맺으시고 율법을 주신 하나님을 찬양해야 한다. 율법은 하나님이 그들에게 특별히 주신 선물이며 은총이기 때문이다.

제148편

I. 장르/양식: 회중 찬양시(cf. 29편)

이 시는 시편 전체에 대한 '축도' 역할을 하는 '최종 찬양시'(Final Hallel) 모음집(146-150편)의 세 번째 노래이며, 모음집에 속한 다른 시편들처럼 할렐루야로 시작하여 할렐루야로 마무리된다. 칠십인역(LXX)은 이 시편의 표제에도 '학개와 스가랴의 노래'라는 말을 더한다. 성전 재건과 연관된 시점에 저작된 노래임을 암시하기 위해서이다.

노래를 시작하고 맺는 '할렐루야'를 제외하고도 동사 '찬양하다'(הלל)가 10차례 사용되며 이 시가 여호와를 찬양하기 위해 저작된 것임을 암시한다. 더 인상적인 것은 이 시편에서 우주를 구성하고 있는 것들 30가지가 주님을 찬양하도록 명령을 받는다(Tucker & Grant). 이 시편처럼 이스라엘의 숨막히는(놀라운) 믿음을 포괄적으로 증거하는 것은 없다(Davidson). 여호와를 찬양함은 주님께 지음 받은 모두가 해야 할 일이라는 것이다.

이 시에서 30가지가 여호와를 찬양하도록 명령을 받은 것처럼, 시작하고 끝맺음을 하는 '할렐루야'를 제외하면 30행으로 구성되어 있다. 매우 확실한 짜임새를 보이는 것이다. 기자는 이러한 구조와 짜임새를 통해 온 세상은 창조주에 의해 면밀히 계획되고 유지되고 있음을 강조한다(Hossfeld & Zenger). 모든 만물이 여호와를 찬양하도록 권면하는 이 시는 창조시(creation psalm)이다(deClaissé-Walford et al., cf. 8, 19, 65, 104편). 포로기 이후에 예루살렘이 재건된 이후 저작된 노래로 보인다(McCann, Kirkpatrick, Terrien).

II. 구조

이 시편은 1-6절과 7-14절로 나뉜다. 1-6절은 하늘에서 시작된 찬양을 묘사하고 있으며, 7-14절은 땅에서 시작되는 찬양에 관한 것이다. 사람뿐만 아니라 우주 모든 것이 창조주 여호와를 찬양하도록 지으심을 받았다는 사실이다(Anderson). 시편의 흐름은 '하늘—세상—인류—이스라엘' 더 구체적으로는 하늘(1절)→천사(2절)→천체(3-6절)→땅(7절)→세상(8-10절)→백성과 이스라엘(11-14절)의 찬양 순서로 이어진다(Kidner). 이 주석에서는 다음과 같은 구분을 바탕으로 본문을 주해해 나가고자 한다.

A. 하늘을 향한 찬양 권면(148:1-6)
B. 땅을 향한 찬양 권면(148:7-14)

III. 주해

이 시편은 세상을 구성하고 있는 30(=10x3)가지에게 하나님을 찬양하라고 한다. 또한 이 노래는 30행으로 구성되어 완전수인 3과 10의 조합으로 이루어져 있다. 피조물들이 창조주 여호와의 완벽함을 찬양하라고 지시를 받고 있는 것이다. 또한 하늘에서 시작된 찬양은 땅에서도 이어진다. 이 땅에서 주의 백성이 드리는 찬양은 하늘에서 메아리친다(VanGemeren).

1. 하늘을 향한 찬양 권면(148:1-6)

[1] 할렐루야
하늘에서 여호와를 찬양하며
높은 데서 그를 찬양할지어다
[2] 그의 모든 천사여 찬양하며
모든 군대여 그를 찬양할지어다
[3] 해와 달아 그를 찬양하며
밝은 별들아 다 그를 찬양할지어다
[4] 하늘의 하늘도 그를 찬양하며
하늘 위에 있는 물들도 그를 찬양할지어다
[5] 그것들이 여호와의 이름을 찬양함은
그가 명령하시므로 지음을 받았음이로다
[6] 그가 또 그것들을 영원히 세우시고
폐하지 못할 명령을 정하셨도다

이 시편은 한 마디로 '찬양, 찬양, 찬양'이다. 기자는 창조주 하나님 여호와께 지음을 받은 모든 피조물은 여호와를 찬양할 것을 주문한다. 완벽하신 하나님이 세상을 완벽하게 만드셨기 때문이다. 또한 세상은 하나님을 찬양하도록 창조되었기 때문이다. 이 섹션에서는 하늘에 있는 모든 것들에게 여호와를 찬양하라고 한다. 하늘(또는 하늘의 하늘, 4절)은 하나님의 처소이며(시 115:3; 136:26), 하나님은 이곳에서 세상을 다스리신다(시 123:1). 하늘에서 시작된 찬양은 땅에서 화답을 받는다(Kirkpatrick).

일상적으로 찬양시들은 누가 여호와를 찬양할 것인가에 초점을 맞추는데, 이 노래는 어디서(장소) 찬양할 것인가에 초점을 맞춘다(Goldingay). 저자는 세상을 구성하고 있는 가장 높은 곳에서 여호와의 찬양이 시작되는 것을 꿈꾼다(1절). 그러므로 그는 세상의 가장 높은 곳인 하늘에서 찬양이 시작될 것을 주문하며 1절에서 '찬양하라'(הַלְלוּ)는 명령문을 세 차례 사용한다. '하늘'(שָׁמַיִם)과 '높은 데'(מְרוֹמִים)는 우리가 사는 세상의 가장 높은 곳이다. 여호와는 세상의 가장 높은 곳에서 찬양을 받기에 합당하신 분이다.

세상 가장 높은 곳에는 무엇(누가)이 있는가? 곧 누가 하늘에서 여호와를 찬양할 수 있는가? 기자는 세 가지로 정리한다.

첫째, 천군 천사들이 여호와를 찬양해야 한다(2절, cf. 시 103:20-21). 이들은 하늘에서 살도록 창조된 자들이며 종종 하나님의 명령을 받아 이 땅에 내려오기도 한다. 하늘에는 수많은 천사들이 있으며, 그들이 때로는 군대로 동원된다. 그러므로 하나님이 때로는 천군 천사를 호령하시는 '만군의 여호와'(יְהוָה צְבָאוֹת)라고 불린다. 하나님이 곁에 두시려고 창조하신 천사들, 때로는 주님의 군대를 형성하는 천사들이 그들을 창조하신 여호와를 찬양하는 것은 당연하다.

둘째, 해와 달과 별들이 여호와를 찬양해야 한다(3절, cf. 창 1:14-19). 천군 천사들은 생명을 지닌 존재들이다. 반면에 해와 달과 별들은 생명을 지니지 않은 것들이다. 그러므로 기자는 2-3절을 통해 하늘에 있으면서 생명을 지닌 자들과 생명을 지니지 않은 모든 것들이 하나님을 찬양할 것을 주문한다. 고대 근동 사람들은 해와 달과 별들을 신들로 숭배하기 일쑤였다. 기자는 이것들에게 여호와를 찬양할 것을 주문하면서 그것들은 신들이 아니라 여호와께서 창조하신 피조물들에 불과하다는 사실을 단호히 선포한다. 설령 신들이라고 믿고 싶더라도 이 천체들은 그들의 창조주 여호와를 예배해야 하는 삼류 신들이다. 창조주를 예배할 수 있는데, 이런 사이비 신들을 누가 믿고 따르겠는가!

셋째, 잠시 하늘에 머무는 물들(구름)이 여호와를 찬양해야 한다(4절, cf. 창 1:7). '하늘에 떠있는 물들'은 구름을 의미한다. 구름은 잠시 생겨났다가 비가 되어 땅을 적시고 사라지는 것이다. 하늘을 수놓고 있는 영원한 것들(해와 달과 별들)뿐만 아니라, 잠시 하늘에 머물다가 사라지는 것까지 모두 여호와를 찬양하라는 권면이다.

'하늘의 하늘'(שְׁמֵי הַשָּׁמָיִם)은 하늘 중 가장 높은 곳('지극히 높은 곳')을 뜻한다. 기자는 1절에서 하늘에게 여호와를 찬양하라고 했는데, 이 말씀을 통해 다시 원점으로 돌아와 하나님을 찬양할 것을 주문하고 있는 것이다(VanGemeren, cf. McCann). 하늘에는 살아 있는 천사들이 있고, 생명은 없지만 영원히 존재하는 해와 달과 별들이 있으며, 잠시 머물다가 사라지는 구름이 있다. 저자는 이 모든 것들이 하나님을 찬양하는 것이 당연하다고 한다.

왜 하늘에 있는 모든 것들이 여호와를 찬양해야 하는가? 하나님이 그들을 지으셨기 때문이다(5절). 피조물들이 창조주를 찬양하는 것은 당연한 일이다. 또한 하늘의 모든 것들은 주님을 경배하고 찬양하기 위해 창조되었음을 암시한다. 하나님은 이것들을 말씀(명령)으로 창조하셨다(cf. 창 1장; 시 33:9; 147:15).

하나님은 이것들이 영원히 하늘을 수놓으며 제기능을 하도록 명령하셨다(6절). '명령을 정하셨다'(חָק־נָתַן)는 법칙/규칙을 주셨다는 의미이다. 하나님은 이것들을 창조하시고 준수해야 할 규칙도 정해 주셨다. 천체들이 일정한 규칙에 따라 스스로 운영되도록 자연의 이치를 제정해 주셨다는 뜻이다. 물론 하나님은 필요하시면 언제든지 자연의 이치를 거스르실 수 있다. 우리는 이것들을 기적이라 한다.

세상 끝날까지 이것들은 영원히 하늘을 지킬 것이며 하나님이 정해 주신 자연의 이치에 따라 각자 역할을 해 나갈 것이다. 그러므로 이런 일을 하도록 지음을 받은 것들도 찬양해야 한다. 또한 이들이 제 역할을 다할 때, 땅에 사는 우리가 가장 큰 수혜자들이라는 점을 감안하면, 우리도 천군 천사들과 해와 달과 별들과 구름을 생각하며 감사함으로 하나님을 찬양해야 한다.

2. 땅을 향한 찬양 권면(148:7-14)

7 너희 용들과 바다여
땅에서 여호와를 찬양하라
8 불과 우박과 눈과 안개와
그의 말씀을 따르는 광풍이며
9 산들과 모든 작은 산과
과수와 모든 백향목이며
10 짐승과 모든 가축과
기는 것과 나는 새며
11 세상의 왕들과 모든 백성들과
고관들과 땅의 모든 재판관들이며
12 총각과 처녀와
노인과 아이들아
13 여호와의 이름을 찬양할지어다
그의 이름이 홀로 높으시며
그의 영광이 땅과 하늘 위에 뛰어나심이로다
14 그가 그의 백성의 뿔을 높이셨으니
그는 모든 성도 곧 그를 가까이 하는 백성
이스라엘 자손의 찬양 받을 이시로다
할렐루야

하늘의 모든 것들에게 창조주이신 여호와를 찬양하라고 한 기자가 초점을 이 땅으로 돌리고 있다. 먼저 그는 바다와 바다에 사는 것들에게 여호와를 찬양할 것을 주문한다(7절). '바다'(תְּהוֹם)는 깊은 바다를 뜻하며 '용들'(תַּנִּינִם)은 바다에 사는 리워야단 등 몸집이 큰 괴물들(악어, 고래 등)을 의미한다(cf. 창 1:2, 21; 시 104:26). 고대 근동 신화에서 이것들은 세상의 질서를 위협하는 것들로서 기자가 가장 위협적인 것들도 여호와를 찬양할 것을 주문하면서 이 섹션을 시작하는 것이 인상적이다(Westermann). 이 땅의 가장 두려운 것들까지도 하나님을 찬양하는 우리에게는 위협적인 요소들이 될 수 없음을 강조하기 위해서다.

또한 사람들에게 위협적인 이 짐승들도 분명 창조주께서 만드신 피조물이다. 그러므로 그들도 하나님을 찬양하는 것이 합당하다. '땅에서 여호와를 찬양하라'는 이들이 육지에 올라와서 여호와를 찬양하라는 것이 아니라, 하늘과 대조되는 이 땅(바다를 포함하는 지구)에서 주님을 찬양하라는 명령이다.

이어 기자는 이 땅에서 살거나 영향을 미치는 모든 것들에게 여호와를 찬양하라고 한다(8-14절). 순서를 보면 범세계적인 것들에서 주의 백성에 이르기까지 범위가 점차적으로 좁혀져 가고 있다.

첫째, 이 땅의 날씨를 주관하는 것들은 여호와를 찬양해야 한다(8절, cf. 시 147:15-18). '불(천둥, 시 18:12)과 우박과 눈과 안개와 광풍'의 날씨에 영향을 미치는 다섯 가지가 언급되고 있다. 비는 빠져있다. 앞에서 비가 되는 구름(4절)을 언급했기 때문이다. 때로는 천재지변을 일으키는 이것들은 모두 하나님의 말씀에 따라 움직인다(8b절). 이 땅 사람들이 가장 두려워하는 것들도 모두 주님의 통제 아래에 있다.

둘째, 자연을 구성하고 있는 모든 것들은 여호와를 찬양해야 한다(9-10절). 날씨를 주관하는 것들(불과 우박과 눈과 안개와 광풍) 다음으로 산들과 작은 산들(언덕들)과 이것들에 자라는 과수와 백향목이 찬양하라는 명령을 받고 있다(9절). 땅과 그곳에서 자라는 모든 식물들이 날씨의 영향을 가장 많이 받기 때문이다.

과수와 백향목이 좋은 날씨로 인해 잘 자라면 사람과 짐승과 모든 가축과 기는 것과 나는 새들이 그것들을 먹고 산다(10절). '짐승'(חַיָּה)과 '가축'(בְּהֵמָה)과 '기는 것'(רֶמֶשׂ)과 '나는 새들'"(צִפּוֹר כָּנָף)은 홍수 때 노아와 함께 방주를 타 보존된 생명들이다(창 7:14). 하나님은 죽음에서 구원하신 것들을 영원히 보호하시는 분이다. 또한 잘 자란 나무들은 사람들이 집을 짓는 일에 사용된다. 그러므로 기자는 이 네 가지 짐승에게 하나님을 찬양하라고 한다. 하나님이 먹고 사는 것들을 통해 그들을 축복하고 보호하시기 때문이다.

셋째, 세상 만민들은 여호와를 찬양해야 한다(11–13절). 하나님이 천지를 창조하셨을 때처럼 사람이 가장 마지막으로 언급되고 있다(cf. 창 1:28). 특이한 것은 창세기 1장에서처럼 인간은 하나님의 모양과 형상대로 만들어졌고 세상을 다스리는 소명을 받았다는 등 사람이 집중적인 조명을 받지는 못한다는 사실이다(Goldingay). 아마도 기자는 인간은 창조된 세상의 일부이기 때문에 다른 피조물들처럼 하나님을 찬양해야지, 하나님이 창조하신 세상을 파괴하는 일은 삼가해야 한다는 메시지를 주는 듯하다(Kässmann). 기자는 먼저 신분의 높낮이에 상관없이 모든 사람이 주님을 찬양할 것을 주문한다(11절). 왕들과 백성들은 다스리는 자들과 다스림을 받은 자들이다. 또한 왕들 밑에서 백성을 다스리는 고관들과 재판관들도 주님을 찬양해야 한다. 각계각층의 모든 사람들이 여호와를 찬양하라는 뜻이다.

이어 기자는 나이와 세대에 상관없이 여호와를 찬양하라고 한다(12절). 총각과 처녀들은 사회의 가장 중심이 되는 젊은 사람들이다. 노인과 아이들은 늙은 사람들과 어린 사람들을 의미한다. 우리 말로 남녀노소 가릴 것 없이 모두 여호와를 찬양하라는 명령이다. 그들은 모두 주님께 지음을 받았고, 주님의 보살핌 속에 살고 있기 때문이다. 그러므로 그들은 홀로 높으시고, 하늘과 땅에서 뛰어나신 여호와를 찬양해야 한다(13절). '홀로 높다'(שׂגב)는 인간이 도저히 범접할 수 없이 높다는 것을 의미하며(NIDOTTE), 하나님의 왕권과 연관되어 사용되는 단어이다(McCann, cf. 사 33:5). 하나님은 누구와 견줄 수 있는 분이 아니다. 홀로 영광을 받기에 합당하신 분이다.

넷째, 주의 백성은 그들의 하나님 여호와를 찬양해야 한다(14절). 세상 만민에게 신분과 나이에 상관없이 주님을 찬양하라고 했던 기자가 주님의 특별한 사랑을 받는 이들에게 주님을 찬양하라고 명령한다. 여호와께서 그들의 뿔을 높이셨으므로 그들의 찬양을 받기에 합당하시기 때문이다. 그들의 뿔을 높이신 것은 그들을 온 세상에서 가장 존귀한 자들로 삼으셨을 뿐만 아니라 그들이 세상을 살 수 있는 능력과 용기를 주셨다는 뜻이다(Anderson). 그러므로 그들이 감사한 마음으로 하나님의 특별한 선택과 사랑에 대하여 주님을 경배하고 찬양하는 것은 당연한 일이다.

사람은 하나님이 창조하신 피조물들 중 으뜸이고, 주의 백성은 그들 중에서도 으뜸이다. 그렇다면 주의 백성이 창조주를 찬양할 때마다, 모든 피조물은 그들의 찬양에 동참해야 한다(Kirkpatrick). 피조물들 중 으뜸이 주님을 찬양하면 나머지도 함께 찬양하는 것이 당연하기 때문이다. 우리가 찬양하면, 온 세상 만물이 우리와 함께 주님을 경배한다는 뜻이다. 노래를 시작했던 '할렐루야'가 다시 노래를 마무리하며 이 시편이 어떤 목적으로 저작되었는지를 암시한다. 온전히 여호와를 찬양하기 위해 만들어진 노래이다.

현대인들은 찬양이 창조주 하나님께 지음을 받은 피조물들이 주님께 반응하는 것이라고 생각하지만, 이 시편은 찬양은 하나님이 창조하신 세상의 구조의 일부라고 한다(Crawford). 마치 잘 만들어진 작품이 그 작품을 만드신 이를 찬양하며 모든 영광을 그분에게 돌리는 것처럼 말이다(Allen). 또한 세상 만물이 창조주 하나님을 찬양하는 것은 그들이 하나님께 지음을 받았기 때문만은 아니다. 그들이 창조될 때에는 분명 감당해야 할 역할이 있었는데 그 역할을 잘 할 수 있도록 하셨기 때문이기도 하다. 천군 천사는 하나님의 명령에 따라 세상의 일에 관여하는 것을 감사해야 한다. 하늘에 떠 있는 천체들은 낮과 밤과 절기들을 알리는 역할을 한다. 구름은 비가 되어 땅을 적시는 일을, 산들은 열매와 채소 등을 생산하는 역할을 할 수 있는 것을 감사하며 찬양해야 한다. 우리도 어떤 역할을 감당하도록 창조되었고, 그 역할을 감당하고 있다면 더욱더 하나님을 찬양해야 한다. 주님이 각자에게 주신 사명을 이루도록 하셨기 때문이다.

제149편

I. 장르/양식: 회중 찬양시(cf. 29편)

이 시편은 '최종 찬양시'(Final Hallel) 모음집(146–150편)의 네 번째 노래이며 이 모음집의 다른 시들처럼 '할렐루야'로 시작하고 '할렐루야'로 마친다. 양식은 '회중 찬양시'(Tucker & Grant)이며 내용이 소망과 저주적인 언어를 함께 사용한다 하여 '종말에 관한 시'(eschatological psalm, cf. 93, 96–99편)로 분류되기도 한다(Allen, Kidner, Mays, McCann, Terrien, VanGemeren, cf. Gunkel). 이사야 40–66장과 시편 96–98편을 배경으로 삼아 여호와의 왕권과 열방의 최종적인 패망을 노래하기 때문이다(Allen, cf. McCann). 말일에 오실 하나님을 노래하는 것이다(Kidner).

이 노래는 예식이나 예배 중에 사용되도록 저작된 것으로 보이지만, 정확히 어떤 절기나 예식인지는 알 수가 없다(Tucker & Grant). 어떤 이들은 주의 백성이 원수 국가들을 상대로 전쟁을 앞둔 전야에 사용하기 위해 저작된 노래라고 한다(Dahood, Kraus). 6절을 근거로 전쟁과 연관된 '칼 춤'(sword dance)에 사용하기 위해 만들어진 것이라는 견해도 있다(Goulder, cf. McCann).

열방의 침략과 어느 정도 연관된 노래인 것은 확실하며 제2편과 깊은 연관성을 지니고 있다(Wittman). 대부분 학자들은 주의 백성이 앞으로 할 전쟁에 관한 노래라고 하지만, 이미 얻은 승리를 기념하는 노래로 해석하는 이들도 있다(Westermann, Ceresko). 이스라엘이 자신들의 구속사(salvation history)를 묵상하며 여호와의 왕 되심을 기념하기 위한 예배에서 사용한 노래로 보는 이들도 있다(Weiser, cf. Anderson).

대부분 학자들은 이 시편의 저작 시기로 칠십인역(LXX) 표제가 암시하는 것처럼 포로기 이후를 지목한다. 더 구체적으로는 느헤미야 시대를 지목하는 이들이 있다(Perowne, cf. Ross).

II. 구조

여러 학자들이 이 시편을 1-3절, 4-6절, 7-9절 세 파트로 구분한다(cf. Allen). 그러나 대부분 학자들은 1-4절과 5-9절, 혹은 1-5절과 6-9절 두 파트로 구분한다(deClaissé-Walford et al., Goldingay, McCann, Ross, Tucker & Grant). 본문을 어떻게 나누든 간에 중앙에 있는 5절이 분기점이 되며 1-4절은 출애굽(cf. 6-7절과 출 15:34; 3절과 출 15:20)을, 6-9절은 땅을 차지한 일(cf. 출 15-20장)을 배경으로 구성되어 있다(Ceresko). 이 주석에서는 다음과 같은 구분에 따라 본문을 주해해 나가고자 한다.

A. 왕의 보호(149:1-4)
B. 왕의 통치(149:5-9)

III. 주해

이 노래는 크게 두 가지로 하나님을 찬양한다. 첫째, 주님은 우리를 창조하시고 보호하시며 우리를 기뻐하신다. 둘째, 하나님은 자기 백성을 괴롭힌 뭇 나라들에게 복수하시며 그들의 왕들과 귀족들을 벌하실 것이다. 그러므로 이러한 사실을 깨닫는 백성들은 주님을 찬양해야 한다.

1. 왕의 보호(149:1-4)

[1] 할렐루야
새 노래로 여호와께 노래하며
성도의 모임 가운데에서 찬양할지어다
[2] 이스라엘은 자기를 지으신 이로 말미암아 즐거워하며
시온의 주민은 그들의 왕으로 말미암아 즐거워할지어다
[3] 춤추며 그의 이름을 찬양하며
소고와 수금으로 그를 찬양할지어다
[4] 여호와께서는 자기 백성을 기뻐하시며
겸손한 자를 구원으로 아름답게 하심이로다

기자는 '새 노래'(שִׁיר חָדָשׁ)로 여호와를 찬양할 것을 명령하는데(1b절), 새 노래는 새로 작곡한 것이 아니라, 새로운 마음 자세로 신적(divine) 전사이신 여호와를 찬양하라는 의미를 지녔다(Tucker & Grant, cf. 사 42:10; 시 33:3; 96:1; 98:1; 144:9). 또한 이 시점에서 새 노래를 부르라는 것은 곧 새롭고 정의로운 세상이 열릴 것을 암시한다(Gerstenberger).

이 섹션의 분위기는 즐거움과 기쁨이다. 기자는 1-4절에서 수차례 기뻐하며 즐거워하라고 한다. 반복되고 있는 찬양 권면도 기쁨을 전제한다. 주의 백성이 꿈꾸는 새로운 세상, 곧 정의로운 세상이 임박했는데 어찌 흥분되지 않겠는가!

기자는 백성들이 어디서 찬양할 것인가도 정해준다. '성도의 모임 가운데에서'(בִּקְהַל חֲסִידִים) 찬양하라 한다(1c절). 성경에서 '모임'(קָהָל)은 이스라엘 사람들의 모임(레 4:14; 신 23:1-3), 예배를 위한 모임(욜 2:16; 시 22:22), 혹은 군인들의 모임(삿 20:2; 겔 17:17; 23:24; 렘 50:9) 등을 의미하는데, 잠시 후 주의 성도들이 전쟁에 참여하는 것을 감안하면(cf. 6-9절), 이곳에서는 군인들의 모임을 뜻한다(Hossfeld & Zenger).

주의 성도들이 찬양할 분은 바로 그들을 지으신 분이다(2a절). 여호와는 온 세상을 창조하셨을 뿐만 아니라(cf. 시 115:15; 121:2; 124:8; 134:3), 이스라엘도 지으셨다. 그러므로 지음을 받은 주의 백성이 창조주를 기뻐하고 즐거워하는 것은 당연한 일이다. 또한 여호와는 이스라엘의 왕이시다(2b절). 그러므로 왕의 은혜로운 다스림을 받는 백성이 그들의 위대하신 왕을 즐거워하고 찬양하는 일 또한 당연하다.

주의 백성들은 목소리로만 그들의 하나님을 찬양할 것이 아니라, 춤을 추며 소고와 수금 등 악기를 동원해서 주님을 찬양해야 한다(3절). 아름다운 소리를 동반하고 온 몸으로 춤을 추며 주님을 찬양하는 이유는 몸과 악기들도 주님이 주신 선물이기 때문이다. 또한 악기로 찬양하고 춤을 추는 것은 여호와의 우주적 통치가 임할 때 일어나는 현상이기도 하다(Hossfeld & Zenger, cf. 시 96, 98편). 많은 교회에서 드려지는 밋밋한 경배와 찬양과는 매우 강력한 대조를 이룬다.

주의 백성이 하나님을 기뻐해야 할 가장 큰 이유는 하나님이 그들을 기뻐하시기 때문이다(4a절). 하나님은 우리를 매우 자랑스럽게 여기셔서 매우 특별하게 대하신다. 또한 겸손한 자들을 구원하셔서 아름답게 하신다(4b절). '겸손한 자들'(עֲנָוִים)은 세상에서 억압받고 착취당하는 자들이다. 주님의 구원이 필요한 자들을 의미하며 주의 백성을 두고 하는 말이다. '아름답게 하신다'(יְפָאֵר)는 구원하신 자들에게 면류관을 씌워 참으로 영화롭게 하신다는 뜻이다(Tucker & Grant). 그러므로 곤경에서 주님의 구원을 받아 승자의 영화를 누리는 백성들이 하나님을 찬양하는 것은 지극히 당연한 일이다. 이 일은 이미 완성된 것이 아니라 앞으로 될 일이다(Goldingay).

2. 왕의 통치(149:5-9)

5 성도들은 영광 중에 즐거워하며

그들의 침상에서 기쁨으로 노래할지어다
6 그들의 입에는 하나님에 대한 찬양이 있고
그들의 손에는 두 날 가진 칼이 있도다
7 이것으로 뭇 나라에 보수하며
민족들을 벌하며
8 그들의 왕들은 사슬로,
그들의 귀인은 철고랑으로 결박하고
9 기록한 판결대로 그들에게 시행할지로다
이런 영광은 그의 모든 성도에게 있도다
할렐루야

기자는 하나님의 놀라운 구원을 입은 성도들이 즐거워하며 기쁨으로 노래하게 되기를 바란다(5절). 5-6절은 그렇게 되기를 바라는 지시형(jussive)이다. 5절은 이 노래의 가장 중앙에 위치할 뿐만 아니라 노래의 핵심 메시지이다(Ceresko). 성도들이 영광 중에 즐거워할 것을 바라는데, 하나님이 놀라운 은혜를 베풀어 그들을 구원하신 일을 참으로 기뻐해야 한다(cf. 공동, 새번역, 아가페). 그들은 침상에서도 구원을 기뻐해야 한다. '침상들'(מִשְׁכְּבוֹתָם)에서도 찬양하라는 것은 잠자리에 들어서도 감사와 찬양이 멈추지 않도록 하라는 권면이 될 수 있지만, 가장 사적인 장소에서도 하나님을 찬양하라는 권면으로 해석될 수도 있다(Prinsloo, Tucker & Grant).

여호와는 구원을 기뻐하는 백성들을 사용하여 열방을 응징하실 것이다. 이 일을 위해 성도들의 입에는 하나님에 대한 찬양이 있으며, 그들의 손은 양날 칼을 쥐고 있다(6절). '입'으로 번역된 단어(גָּרוֹן)는 목구멍을 뜻한다(HALOT). 목구멍과 입의 차이는 성경에서 목구멍이 훨씬 더 큰 소리를 상징한다는 것이다(Perowne). 입에 찬양이 있는 사람이, 손에 양날 칼을 쥐고 있는 상황은 이해하기가 쉽지 않다. 그러므로 일부 학자들은 1행과 2행을 연결하는 접속사(ו)를 대조(comparison)하는, 혹은 설명(explication)하는 기능으로 이해하여 "그들의 입에 있는 하나님에 대한 찬양이 손에 쥔 양날 칼처럼 되도록 하소서"라는 해석을 제안한다(Hossfeld & Zenger, Tournay).

어렵기는 하지만 6절을 그대로 해석하는 것이 바람직하다(Goldingay, Tucker & Grant). 기자가 꿈꾸는 성도들은 열심히 찬양하고, 열심히 전쟁하는 이들이다(Prinsloo). 이러한 이미지를 배경으로 '믿는 사람들은 주의 군사니'(찬송가 351장)라는 찬송이 나오지 않았을까?

하나님은 찬양하며 칼을 든 백성을 사용하여 열방을 응징하신다(7a절). 복수는 원래 하나님께 속한 것이다(신 32:35; 시 94:1). 이번에는 예외다. 주님은 성도들을 통해 민족들과 그들의 왕들과 귀인들을 벌하시고 결박하신다(7절). 앞에서는 이 권세자들에게 짓밟히고 억압을 당한 '겸손한 자들'(4절)이 세상을 호령하던 권세자들을 결박하는 것이 참으로 강력한 대조를 이룬다. 그들의 하나님 여호와가 세상을 다스리시는 왕이기 때문에 가능한 일이다.

하나님은 결박된 자들을 이미 내리신 선고에 따라 처형하도록 하신다(9a절, cf. 공동). 이미 내린 선고가 무엇인지 규명하는 것이 쉽지 않다. 이미 신명기에서 선언하신 대로 언젠가는 번뜩이는 칼로 열방에 보복하시겠다는 말씀(신 32:39-43)을 의미하는 것일 수도 있다(Alter, Tucker & Grant). 하나님을 대적하고 주의 백성을 핍박했던 자들이 처형을 당하는 것을 보는 영광이 모든 성도에게 임한다(9b절). 그들은 하나님과 함께 이 영광을 누릴 것이다(Hossfeld & Zenger). 세상의 높은 자들과 낮은 자들의 위치가 완전히 바뀌었다.

제150편

I. 장르/양식: 회중 찬양시(cf. 29편)

이 노래는 '최종 찬양시'(Final Hallel) 모음집(146-150편)의 마지막 노래이며 이 모음집의 다른 노래들처럼 '할렐루야'로 시작하여 '할렐루야'로 마무리된다. 이 시편은 찬양시(praise psalm)이지만 일반 찬양시와 상당히 다르다. 일상적으로 찬양시들은 찬양하라는 권면으로 시작한 후 주님을 찬양할 이유(주님이 하신 일, 베푸신 은총, 속성 등)를 제시한다. 이와는 대조적으로 이 시는 찬양을 권면하는 것으로 시작한 다음 2절에서 이유를 간단하게 말하더니 다시 찬양하라는 권면을 지속한다. 시편을 구성하고 있는 6절 중 2절을 제외한 나머지는 모두 '찬양 권면/초청'인 것이다(Goldingay, Mowinckel, cf. McCann, Tucker & Grant).

또한 이 시를 구성하고 있는 모든 행(line)에는 동사 '찬양하다'(הלל)의 명령형이 사용되고 있으며, 마지막 행만 지시형(jussive)을 사용한다. 동사와 명사의 순서가 바뀌었기 때문이다(McCann). 이 짧은 노래에서 동사 '찬양하다'(הלל)가 총 13차례 사용되는데, 시편 전체를 마무리하는 노래로써 적절한 형식을 취하고 있다고 할 수 있다. 시편은 성도들이 여호와를 찬양하도록 권면하는 책이며, 이 시는 책이 이때까지 선포한 메시지를 마무리하는 최종 축도(final doxology) 역할을 하고 있기 때문이다(VanGemeren, cf. 시 41:13; 72:19; 89:52; 106:48).

이 시편은 성전에서 예식이나 예배에 사용하기 위하여 저작한 것으로 보인다(Weiser). 학자들은 대부분 저작 시기를 '최종 찬양시' 모음집에 속한 다른 노래들처럼 포로기 이후로 간주한다. 제2성전 시대에 저작된 것이라 하고(Clifford), 에스라—느헤미야 시대 이후에 저작된 것이라 하기도 한다(Terrien).

그러나 왕정 시대에 저작된 것이라는 이들도 있다. 포로기 이후 시대에 저작된 역대기는 금속으로 만든 '나팔'(חֲצֹצְרָה)을 지속적으로 언급하는데, 이 시편은 양의 뿔로 만든 더 오래된 '나팔'(שׁוֹפָר)을 언급하기 때문이다(3절). 또한 '제금'(צֶלְצְלִים)은 성경에서 5절과 사무엘하 6:5에만 등장하는 악기라는 사실도 이 노래가 왕정 시대에 저작된 것임을 암시하는 증거로 제시된다(Goldingay). 그렇다면 이처럼 오래된 노래가 왜 포로기 이후 시대 노래를 모아 놓은 '최종 찬양시' 모음집에 속하게 된 것일까? 이 시편의 내용 전체가 여호와를 찬양하라고 권면하는 노래로써 150편으로 구성된 시편 모음집 전체의 적절한 결론이자 마무리이기 때문이다(Allen, Goldingay). 그러므로 일부 학자들은 시편 149편이 시편 모음집의 마지막 노래이고, 150편은 책 전체에 대한 결론적 찬양이라 한다(VanGemeren).

II. 구조

이 시편의 흐름은 간단하다. 1절은 누구를 찬양할 것인가를, 2절은 하나님을 찬양할 이유를 말한다. 이어 3-5절은 어떻게 하나님을 찬양할 것인가를, 6절은 누가 찬양할 것인가를 언급하며 노래를 마무리한다(cf. Kidner, Mays). 이 주석에서는 다음과 같은 구조를 바탕으로 본문을 주해해 나가고자 한다(VanGemeren).

A. 하늘의 하나님 찬양(150:1)
B. 위대하신 하나님 찬양(150:2)
B′. 온전히 하나님 찬양(150:3–5)
A′. 이 땅의 하나님 찬양(150:6)

III. 주해

율법대로 살아야 한다는 시편 1편이 편집자들의 의도적인 서론인 것처럼 이 노래는 율법대로 살면 여호와를 찬양하며 흠모할 것이라는 적절한 결론이다(Brueggemann). 기자는 처음부터 끝까지 여호와를 찬양할 것을 명령한다. 창조주이자 통치자이신 하나님에 대한 우리의 당연한 반응이기 때문이다.

1. 하늘의 하나님 찬양(150:1)

1 할렐루야
그의 성소에서 하나님의 찬양하며
그의 권능의 궁창에서 그를 찬양할지어다

기자는 성소에서 하나님을 찬양하라며 노래를 시작한다. '성소'(קֹדֶשׁ)는 예루살렘 성전을 의미한다(시 74:3; 134:2). 성전은 하늘과 땅이 만나는 곳이기도 하다(Kraus). 성전에서 시작된 찬양은 '권능의 궁창'에서도 이어져야 한다. '주님의 권능의 궁창'(רְקִיעַ עֻזּוֹ)은 하늘과 땅 사이에 있는 대기권을 의미하며, 하늘에 있는 물(구름)을 담고 있는 곳이다(cf. 창 1장). 본문에서는 하나님이 계시는 하늘을 의미한다(Tucker & Grant, cf. 겔 1:25; 시 19:1). 기자는 하늘과 땅으로 구성된 온 세상이 주님을 찬양할 것을 명령하고 있다(Eaton, Mathys). 여호와께서 하늘과 땅을 모두 다스리시기 때문이다.

2. 위대하신 하나님 찬양(150:2)

[2] 그의 능하신 행동을 찬양하며
그의 지극히 위대하심을 따라 찬양할지어다

일상적으로 찬양시는 여호와를 찬양하라는 명령(cf. 1절) 이후 하나님을 찬양할 이유를 나열하는데, 6절로 구성된 이 시편에서는 2절 말씀이 유일한 이유로 제시된다. 나머지 구절들은 모두 찬양하라는 권면으로 구성되어 있다.

기자는 우리가 여호와 하나님을 찬양할 이유로 두 가지를 제시한다. 첫째, 주님의 능하신 행동으로 인해 주님을 찬양하라고 한다. '능하신 행동들'(גְבוּרוֹת)은 하나님이 하시는 놀라운 일들을 전반적으로 묘사하는 포괄적인 개념이며 하나님의 온 세상에 대한 왕권과 통치권을 상징한다(시 24:8; 65:6; 66:7; 106:2, 8; 145:4, 11, 12). 둘째, 주님의 위대하심으로 인해 주님을 찬양하라고 한다. '위대하심'(גֹּדֶל)은 왕이신 하나님의 통치권과 연관이 되어 있는 개념이다(Hossfeld & Zenger, McCann, cf. 시 48:1; 95:3; 96:4; 99:2). 그러므로 기자는 하나님이 행하시는 모든 일과 주님이 왕이심을 찬양하라고 한다.

3. 온전히 하나님 찬양(150:3-5)

[3] 나팔 소리로 찬양하며
비파와 수금으로 찬양할지어다
[4] 소고 치며 춤추어 찬양하며
현악과 통소로 찬양할지어다

[5] 큰 소리 나는 제금으로 찬양하며
높은 소리 나는 제금으로 찬양할 지어다

기자는 우리가 목소리로만 여호와를 찬양할 것이 아니라 춤으로 찬양하고, 온갖 악기들을 동원하여 찬양할 것을 주문한다. 하나님의 왕되심을 고백하는 그의 백성이 해야 할 당연한 일이다(Hossfeld & Zenger). 기자는 온 몸과 도구들을 찬양에 동원하라고 한다. 그는 구체적으로 일곱 가지 악기들을 언급한다: 나팔, 비파, 수금, 소고, 현악, 퉁소, 제금. 이 악기들이 구체적으로 어떻게 생겼고 어떤 차이를 지녔는가를 규명하기는 쉽지 않다(cf. Allen, Hossfeld & Zenger, VanGemeren).

그러나 완전수인 '7'을 사용하여 모든 악기를 사용하라고 권면한다. 우리가 하나님을 찬양하는 데 사용할 수 있는 악기들 중에는 고음을 내는 것도 있고, 저음을 내는 것도 있을 것이다. 날카로운 소리를 내는 것도 있고, 부드러운 소리를 내는 것도 있을 것이다. 현악기도 있고 관악기도 있을 것이다. 기자는 온갖 악기들을 동원하여 찬양하라고 한다. 악기들은 모두 하나님이 우리에게 주님을 찬양하라고 주신 선물이기 때문이다.

또한 온 몸으로 찬양하라고 한다. 우리의 찬양은 입으로 하는 것으로 제한되지 않고 온갖 몸짓을 동원한 찬양이 되어야 한다. 더욱이 마음을 동원해 찬양하는 것은 말할 필요도 없다.

4. 이 땅의 하나님 찬양(150:6)

[6] 호흡이 있는 자마다
여호와를 찬양할지어다
할렐루야

기자는 찬양의 범위를 극대화한다. 호흡이 있는 자마다 여호와를 찬양하라고 명령한다. 살아 있는 모든 생물체에게 주님을 찬양할 것을 주문하고 있다. '호흡이 있는 것'(נְשָׁמָה)은 사람을 의미한다. 하나님은 인간을 창조하시고 그에게 자신의 '호흡'을 나누어 주셨다(창 2:7). 본문은 하나님이 인간에게 나누어주신 호흡은 곧 주님을 찬양하기 위한 것임을 알려 준다(Clifford). 또한 호흡은 창조된 모든 생물을 의미하기도 한다(창 7:22). 그러므로 생명이 있는 모든 생명체들은 주님을 찬양해야 한다(cf. Allen). 여호와는 그들의 경배를 받기에 합당하신 분이기 때문이다. 그들이 여호와를 믿든, 믿지 않든 상관없이 주께서 모든 사람을 창조하셨기 때문이다. 그러므로 창조주이신 하나님은 모든 피조물들의 찬양을 받으셔야 한다.

이 말씀은 또한 종말론적인 비전을 표현하고 있다. 온 세상 만물들이 여호와를 찬양할 날이 오고 있다. 그때까지 성도들은 이 땅에서 열심히, 성실하게 하나님을 의지하여 주님을 섬기고 찬양하며 살아가야 한다. 할렐루야!